99% SOBER

99% Sober

Published by Regal Books in the United Kingdom 2024

Paperback ISBN: 978-1-7385456-0-5
eBook ISBN: 978-1-7385456-1-2

Publishing partnership with The Writing House, www.thewritinghouse.co.uk
Cover design by Kieron Lewis, KieronLewis.com
Typesetting by The Book Typesetters, thebooktypesetters.com

The content of this book is for informational and educational purposes. Readers acknowledge that the author is not engaging in the rendering of medical or professional advice. This book is not is not intended to diagnose, treat, cure, or prevent any condition or disease. The author is not a medical practitioner or counsellor and this book is not intended as a substitute for consultation with a medical practitioner. Professional advice should be sought before embarking on any of the suggestions or recommendations in this book or any health-related programmes. The author and publishers cannot be held responsible for any errors, omissions or inaccuracies that may be found in the text, or any actions that may be taken by the reader as a result of any reliance on the information contained therein which are taken entirely at the reader's own risk.

Content Warning

99% Sober includes content that may not be suitable for some readers.
It contains memories of heavy alcohol use and references to suicidal thoughts.

99% SOBER

Improve Your Health, Wealth and Happiness by Taking Control of Your Drinking

PATRICK RUDDY

For my mum, dad and big sister, who protected me from the worst consequences of my drinking for the first ten years.

For my wife, who picked up the baton and ran with it for the next ten.

Thank you.

I've got it from here.

Contents

Introduction

I know what it's like to open a book searching for answers. The sense of urgency. Your patience while I gush about how thrilled I am to have you 'join me on this journey' is likely to be thin. I get it. Let's cut to the chase and set out what this book is all about, and how it could help you. Then we can take a breath, and I can get all gushy with you later, once we know each other a bit better.

This is not a book telling you that abstinence is the only way. Or a memoir dedicated to sharing the horrors of drinking and my struggle with it. It's more than that. While I will share the lows, I will go on to share the practical things that worked for me when it came to digging myself out of that hole.

I want to show you that if you're curious about cutting back, or stopping altogether, it can be an overwhelmingly positive experience.

I know you're sceptical. I was too. But don't worry. After twenty years of being a booze hound, I've been 99% sober now for two years, and I'm going to give you the low down on what your life could look like without – or with significantly less – booze. I promise you will still have fun without it. So let's get the basics covered.

What is 99% sober?

99% sober, or dry by default, is a label for those of us who are fed up with drinking on autopilot and want to control our relationship with alcohol, but who aren't ready to shut the door on it completely.

It's part of the wider trend of mindful drinking and being sober curious. People going 99% sober or dry by default are those who rarely drink but make the odd exception. It can make sense for those of us who don't want to put pressure on ourselves with a 'drinker' or 'non-drinker' label and it removes the angst of counting days.

How does 99% sober work?

I'm pro-choice recovery. I don't believe in a one-size-fits-all approach. So the below, and in fact the entire book, comes with the caveat that I'm sharing with you what worked for me. If you are someone who has already stopped drinking completely and this works for you, then I am in no way suggesting you should start again to try the 99% sober approach. The wise counsel from the 1970s sitcom *Different Strokes* should be kept in mind at all times:

> *Now, the world don't move to the beat of just*
> *one drum, what might be right for you, may not*
> *be right for some…*

Or if you want to get all highbrow, as the German philosopher Friedrich Wilhelm Nietzsche quipped back in the 1800s:

You have your way. I have my way. As for the right way, the correct way, and the only way, it does not exist.

There is nothing prescriptive about the 99% sober approach, so I use the term 'how it works' loosely, but a key benefit is that it alleviates the feelings of deprivation that typically come with 'giving up' by offering you the option to drink in the future, but only when it will enhance your experience or benefit you. We will dive into what we mean by this and the methodology behind it later in the book, so you don't start telling yourself that booze will enhance the experience of loading the dishwasher on a Wednesday afternoon.

For me, going 99% sober took the power away from alcohol. I wasn't 'giving up'. I was choosing not to. And, in the same way, I would also choose when I did want to. I would decide when and if it was worth it. Will it serve me? Does it enhance my experience? Rather than just running out of will power at a random event six months down the line.

It might sound trivial, but that 1% wiggle room, just keeping the door slightly ajar and giving myself the option, meant I no longer felt like I was depriving myself of anything. I wasn't poor abstinent Paddy with his non-drinking cross to bear. I had made a choice, and continued to make the choice, not to drink. It works for me. It might be worth a shot for you.

How can the book help you?

I tied myself in knots thinking of a way that could have got you to the 99% sober stage without going through three to six months of 100% sobriety first. It would have been a much more popular message to put out. It would have saved you a lot of the initial hard yards. But whichever way I cut it, I couldn't make it work. I would have been selling you a lie. The first three to six months of sobriety are the key ingredient. I can't give you a shortcut for this, but what I can do is help guide you through these months and hold your hand each step of the way. I have plenty to share, so to help bring some order to proceedings I've divided the book into three parts.

Part 1 covers life before sobriety. How alcohol starts as the slightly mischievous mate who helps you loosen up and have a good time, before becoming the wildly destructive 'he's not with me' type of mate who might possibly get you locked up or killed. Part 2 covers my six first months of sobriety and the tools I used, with the science behind why they work. My toolbox is filled with things you can do by yourself, from the safety of behind your computer screen. With the hardest yards behind us, Part 3 covers the new life that awaits you, and your options in terms of sticking with 100% sobriety or flexing to the 99% sober approach.

Toolboxes and hard yards? At this point you might be wondering if it will all be worth it. I promise you, it is.

If you haven't seen the film *Limitless*, watch it. Firstly, because it's a really good film, and secondly, because it is the best way I can think of to show you how much easier and better your life can be when you're not drinking by default.

In the film, Bradley Cooper plays a struggling author. He can't get his book finished, lives like a slob, sleeps late and has little motivation or ambition. After letting his girlfriend down with a series of broken promises, he is left alone when she breaks up with him.

Feeling like he has nothing to lose, he tries an experimental drug which unlocks the untapped potential in his brain. He acquires perfect recall and is able to analyse minute details and information at incredible speed. His focus and drive increase exponentially (cue a montage of him cleaning up his apartment and finishing his book). His professional life takes off, his relationships improve, and he wins back his girlfriend. I won't spoil the whole film, but you get the idea.

That's what I feel like now, around two years in. My mind is so much sharper. I have so much more energy, drive and focus. I've always loved reading, but when I was drinking I struggled to concentrate on a book and get through it. Even my favourites would take a month or two at a plodding pace. I felt too tired during the week after scraping through the day at work, and at the weekend, well, I was smashed.

Now, sober me inhales books. I get three or four out from the library in one go and alternate between them. I get through a book every week. As well as starting to pull together my journals and write this book, I've been inspired by the thrillers I've been reading and developed the plot for one of my own. I have two screens on the go when I'm writing, and I alternate between them as ideas pop into my head for each project. I still work long hours in finance and have two young kids, so this is all done in my spare time.

If you had told me this back in December 2021, when I was wiping the vomit from my face before jumping on a work call, I would have thought you were insane. Spare time wasn't something I had. I was too busy. I was too tired. I was too overwhelmed. I was just trying to survive.

Limitless was released in 2011. I was twenty-four and well on my way to becoming a world-class bevy merchant. I remember watching it and thinking if that drug were real, I would definitely take it. But it turns out I didn't need to take a wonder drug – I just had to stop taking alcohol.

You might think the whole 'limitless' thing sounds a bit farfetched. I promise I'm not exaggerating, or over egging it. Bradley Cooper is himself sober, having quit at twenty-nine. It turns out that he based his 'before' character in *Limitless* on his twentysomething drinking self, while the 'after' character was based on his thirtysomething sober self. That's probably why the film resonates so much.

If you are the cynical type of booze lover that I was, you will have definitely rolled your eyes a couple of times during those last few paragraphs. I get it. I was exactly the same. When you're trying to get sober the last thing you want is to listen to some Little Miss Sunshine character telling you how good it is. Understood. I just want to share what it's like on the other side, and that even if it's tough now, there is light at the end of the tunnel. But for now, let's dial the sunshine down several notches and get cracking with Part 1.

PART 1

Life Before Sobriety

22nd December 2021

I wake up face down on the pillow. Bright sunlight breaks through the curtains, which is strange because it's winter and usually still pitch black when I get up for work.

Wait, what time is it? I try to find my phone but move too quickly and feel the bile rise in my stomach. My head is pounding. I am fully clothed and have no recollection of how I got here. At least I am in my own house.

This set of circumstances is not unusual. I black out frequently, and I have woken up in situations that are a lot worse. This feels different, though, as it wasn't a special occasion. For a problem drinker, it's amazingly easy for the most mundane of events to merit 'special occasion' status and act as a perfectly valid reason to get blackout drunk. But this wasn't even one of those. I hadn't planned to drink at all. It was a Monday night. I was alone in the house. Wait, it's coming back to me. I decided to have 'a glass of red' while wrapping the last of the kids' Christmas presents. I remember wrapping the presents. Then nothing. What happened?

I can fill in the blanks later. For now, I need to firefight as I am clearly late for work. Time to kick into crisis management mode.

I find my phone in my jeans pocket. No missed calls or unread messages. Result. It's 10am. Workwise – that's salvageable. Thanks to the pandemic I am working from home. All I need to do is make it to the laptop, log on and send some messages about why I'm late clocking in.

I run through the usual lies. When you have a drink problem, lying to cover it up becomes as easy as lifting the glass, like muscle memory. I have only been in this job for two weeks, so while it's not great to be calling in late already, it also means I haven't exhausted the more plausible excuses in my back catalogue.

Waiting for the laptop to fire up, I settle on 'the nursery drop-off being bedlam' as the reason for my tardiness. I can embellish that later if anyone asks, but it's a good start. I have no idea if I'm supposed to be on a call or not, so while the system is logging on, I quickly vomit then splash water on my face and put on a fresh shirt. I actually look fine. Maybe I had a bad reaction to something I ate and then just genuinely overslept?

It turns out I'm not supposed to be in any meetings. No one has been looking for me. So I fire off a few emails to show my presence then make my way downstairs to find some clues as to what happened last night.

I feel anxious about what state the place will be in as I make my way down. I expect to find the usual trail of destruction that follows a one-man party. Empty bottles, music channel still blaring, broken glass, maybe some burnt food. When I open the living room door, I'm surprised to find the place looks immaculate. The Christmas presents have indeed been wrapped and are neatly stacked under the tree. The Christmas tree lights have even been turned off. It looks like a show home.

I go through to check the kitchen. It is also pristine, save for one empty wine glass, drying neatly on the draining board.

Nothing is coming back to me at all, but I surmise that I blitzed all the housework, and then celebrated with a well-earned glass or three of red wine before calling it a night. No harm in that. I start to feel a wave of relief. Drinking a bottle of red wine is nothing for me. The wine glass is ridiculously oversized, and so drinking two or three glasses would get me through the bottle with ease while still letting me tell myself I was only having a few. You know, like a responsible adult. Hey, it's Christmas, and I've smashed all the housework and wrapping – I've earned it.

I decide to grab a can of juice from the utility room. My heart sinks when I open the door. Neatly lined up are two empty bottles of red, and one bottle of white. Fucking hell. That's a heavy night, even for me. I've not been that bad for a while. I am disgusted with myself, but at the same time, nothing bad has happened. A blackout and a killer hangover don't even register as 'bad' for me now; usually after that amount of booze I would have some sort of mess to clean up. That's why waking up and shifting into crisis management mode is so easy for me. It's a well-trodden path.

I start to feel relief again. I almost have a spring in my step as I go back upstairs to work. Clearly it's a sorry state of affairs to plan to have one glass of wine and end up drinking three bottles, but it happens to everyone now and again (I assume) and I seem to have gotten away with it.

I just haven't found the right way to drink moderately. 'He drinks for oblivion' is one of the more poetic phrases used to describe my drinking and it is fairly apt. Once I start, I can't stop. I describe it as not having a handbrake. I've spent twenty years trying to find one, but I'm still looking.

Sitting at the laptop I try to get down to work but struggle to concentrate. My head feels a bit fuzzy, which alcohol poisoning will tend to do

Picking up my phone I get the sinking feeling again. Although I didn't have any missed calls, did I make any? The answer is a resounding yes. Eight outgoing calls to my wife, all after midnight. Hopefully she didn't pick up. I reckon I must have started drinking at 6pm and would have been a mess by then. Christ. Some of the calls are ten minutes long. Oh, and there's a FaceTime in there as well. Great. I'm fucked.

When I open WhatsApp, I see a lot of messages from my wife. They have all come in following the FaceTime and calls. I won't repeat them verbatim, but the messages are all too familiar given this isn't the first time I've fallen off the 'moderate drinking' wagon in spectacular fashion.

Disbelief, disappointment, concern, anger. Some of the language seems harsh and hits a nerve. The truth hurts and, for a problem drinker like me, is not always welcome. I immediately start to feel defensive. I couldn't have been that bad, I ticked off everything on the to-do list before getting smashed, and she and the kids weren't even here. What's the big deal? I scroll through the messages and notice I've sent a video. I click play.

I honestly don't recognise the person in the video. It is me, but I am totally out of it. The muscles in my face have relaxed to the point it has a drooping appearance, like I have suffered a stroke. My eyes are heavily glazed. I start to speak and I am saying something along the lines of, 'See, I'm not that bad, I've just had a few glasses of wine.' But this is a best guess as my speech is so heavily slurred my voice doesn't sound like my own.

For the last twenty years I have convinced myself that I don't have a drinking problem. That I sometimes just get carried away and take it a bit too far. I've justified it to myself. Given I only drink a few times a week, or can go weeks without a drink at all, I've decided I have it under control. I've convinced myself that I just need to find the right way to crack the 'drinking in moderation' nut to still get all the *essential* benefits of alcohol without the downside that my 'drinking for oblivion' brings. But the video has shattered my belief that I have any control over my drinking, or that it does me any good.

And so you find me at the start of a new chapter. I have decided that the quest for moderation must end here. Patrick Ruddy, at the age of thirty-five, after a distinguished twenty-year-long drinking career, will end it, here and now.

I've been here before, but I *really* mean it this time. This time I'm going to come up with a plan and throw myself into sobriety, rather than giving up for a few weeks to 'reset' then going back to the cycle of moderation and blowout. It all changes today.

But first, I really need a nap.

I send a few more emails, go to the bathroom and vomit again, then head back to bed.

After making it through work I spend that night researching how to quit for good. I am past the stage of googling 'Do I have a drinking problem?' 'Am I an alcoholic?' 'Why can't I stop after a few drinks?' 'Ways to cut back,' etc. I now accept I simply can't moderate. I find lists of quit lit and order them all.

Coming to this realisation is such a relief. I talk it through with my wife on the phone. She has been worried about my drinking for years and has heard me make these types of promises before. It might feel different for me, but I can tell she is sceptical. She describes having to keep me on the phone, begging me not to open another bottle of wine and go to bed, and then having to guide me up the stairs as I was so disoriented. She essentially has another kid when I am drinking. Previously she has been supportive of me trying to moderate my drinking, but I can tell this last failed attempt has pushed things to the limit. It feels like a choice between continuing with alcohol or being a decent husband and father. I can see that if I keep drinking, I'm on a path to not seeing my wife again except when I pick up the kids outside her new family house every second weekend. I don't want that.

Despite all the physical and mental harm alcohol has caused me and everyone around me, and the negative impact on my family life and relationships, I have devoted huge amounts of energy and time to finding ways to keep it in my life. Coming to the realisation that alcohol actually isn't doing me any favours, and I shouldn't have it in my life at all, feels liberating.

And yet, I am still anxious, apprehensive, nervous, even scared about giving up. If I don't drink, how will I be able to socialise? What will I tell people? What will people think when I ask for a diet coke at the bar? I'm used to being the life and soul of the party, the loud guy who chats to everyone, cracks jokes, gets the party going … I *need* to drink to be that guy.

Without drink, I'm destined to become the wedding guest whose name you search for on the seating plan and pray isn't at your table. It's bad enough I'm an accountant, but a *sober* accountant? That's a tough sell. I can already see people glancing over my shoulder and suddenly needing to be somewhere else when I introduce myself. Can I even go to these things sober? What would be the point? Nervously walking around clutching a warm glass of orange juice while everyone else gets on it. What is the warm orange juice all about anyway? Do they do that on purpose? 'Hey Stevie, make sure you store the cartons of radioactive orange juice next to the heater, we need it to be warm for the sober people arriving. Oh, and make sure the glasses are sticky.'

I can hear my mates giving me grief for it down the pub. The jukebox cutting off suddenly when I ask for a diet coke instead of a pint like everyone else. I can hear the questions. 'Why are you not having a drink, Paddy? What's wrong with you?'

What *is* wrong with me? Why can't I have a few drinks and enjoy it like everyone else? Why have I taken it so far and ruined it for myself?

These are the same questions that I ask myself after each mega blowout that eventually follows when I start drinking again. I tend to give up for a few weeks, maybe even a month, and then I convince myself that I have reset and can now make an attempt to drink moderately and be a 'normal' drinker.

I might have a few successful months of moderation using whatever method I'm trying. Depending on how many times you've tried, you might recognise some of these:

- Having a glass of water in between each drink.
- Not drinking spirits. (*It was the vodka's fault.*)
- Not drinking wine. (*Actually, it was wine, it was definitely wine's fault.*)
- Only drinking beer. (*Actually, let's stick to beer, it takes pints and pints of that to get you drunk – beer must be safe.* It's not.)
- Only drinking champagne. (*It'll be too expensive to drink lots.* It wasn't, and I was just skint that month.)
- Setting alarms on my phone to remind me to stop drinking at a certain point on a night out.
- Only drinking with a meal.
- Only drinking one night a week.
- Drinking every night of the week, but only having one drink each night.
- Not joining a round.
- Joining a round, but with someone who drinks slowly.

Some of these worked better than others, and for longer. For example, the drinking water in between each drink helped me pace it a bit, but eventually I just ended up staying out for longer to make up for the drinking time I had missed by being in the toilet so much. Joining a round with someone who drinks slowly seems like it would be fool proof, but we drinkers are a crafty bunch and I instantly corrupted my drinking partner and got them smashed at my pace.

Regardless of the method, the outcome was the same. Weeks depriving myself of any drink at all (to prove that I could take it or leave it) followed by slowly slipping back into heavy drinking by smashing through the self-imposed limits I had set.

So many times, I would promise myself that tonight would be the night where I would only have one or two drinks, go home early, and be fresh for the next day. But I could never quite crack it. I would always end up out until closing time and wake up rough the next day with no idea what happened.

Chasing moderation

Moderating alcohol is the elusive goal of all of us who love to drink. Even those who wouldn't class themselves as problem drinkers can struggle to stop once they've started. Why is it so hard? We will dive into the science behind the addictive qualities of alcohol later (in a friendly, accessible manner – I've sourced explanations in plain English from leading professors and medical experts), but in a nutshell – alcohol is an amazingly efficient drug. It alters your brain in myriad ways, but the big two are:

1. Reward system

As soon as we take those first few sips, alcohol causes our brain to release dopamine, which is known as the 'feel-good hormone'. Dopamine provides us with the initial high we get when we start drinking, and as we continue to drink, our brain produces more and more of it, leading to ever increasing feelings of pleasure.

Our brain's reward system creates a link that says, 'Drinking feels good. If you want to keep feeling like this, you need to keep drinking.' The thing is, our reward system doesn't know when to stop. It wants to keep chasing those feelings of pleasure at all costs. Drinking can cause our brain to pay too much attention to the reward system – the little kid jumping up and down who won't stop at one sweet and wants the whole bag. It's easy to go from 'just one drink' to 'just one more'.

2. *Rational decision-making and self-control*

Simultaneously, drinking lowers our inhibitions and impairs our decision-making abilities, which isn't the best combination. But why does alcohol do this? Alicia Gilber from sober-ish.co explains, "It's all to do with a critical part of our brain called the prefrontal cortex. Located directly behind your forehead, it's responsible for making executive decisions, handling complex thoughts, and managing our behaviour."[1] Alicia describes the prefrontal cortex as being 'like the CEO of your brain' – which is how I like to think of it. "One of its main duties is to keep our impulses in check and help us make rational, well-thought-out choices." Basically, all things we struggle with when drinking.

When alcohol enters your brain, it interferes with the prefrontal cortex – the CEO. It distracts the CEO and encourages them to start thinking about knocking off for the weekend. By the second or third drink, it has locked the CEO in the stationary cupboard and stolen their phone.

Your reward system, the little kid with the sweets, has

come alive and is shouting, 'This is awesome! More drink! More drink!' This is the very moment you need the CEO to spring into action and say, 'Ah, but wait. That's not a wise decision. You have work tomorrow, and we already decided two drinks would be the sensible amount. Time to go.' But the poor old CEO is helplessly trapped in the stationary cupboard; the little kid takes over.

Our brain is too busy focussing on short-term pleasure to give much thought to any long-term consequences.

From a teenager until the age of twenty-five, I didn't see any downside to getting blackout drunk every weekend, despite some glaringly obvious evidence to the contrary. I loved booze telling my CEO to take the day off. I embraced it.

My CEO was painfully dull and risk averse, but in fairness he had done a good job. Despite my increasing levels of self-sabotage and regular blowouts, the old boy (I imagine my CEO as a stern-faced, grey-haired chap in a well-cut suit) had steered the ship well. He'd got me to where I thought I wanted to be in spite of myself, from humble beginnings to living what I thought was the good life. I realise 'humble beginnings' and 'the good life' mean wildly different things to everyone, so let me quickly give you some context.

My family wasn't poor by any stretch of the imagination. My dad was a welder and my mum had a managerial position with social services. They worked hard to give me a comfortable and secure upbringing. I was and am loved. I didn't go hungry and never had to go without anything, but I was always aware that the money we had was hard earned, and that we had to be careful how we spent it.

While I didn't have first-hand experience of it, I knew there were other people who didn't worry about money. I was growing up in the 80s and 90s during the rise of the yuppie, when Michael Douglas was giving it the 'greed is good' chat in *Wall Street*. I loved all that. I wanted to be like those guys. They wore nice suits, drove flash cars, splashed the cash and drank champagne like it was water. I wanted that lifestyle. That was my idea of the good life

My CEO had taken this vague, materialistic aspiration and run with it. I was academically very strong, so he decided a career in finance would be the best course of action for us and guided us from those humble beginnings in Glasgow to living the good life in a tax efficient jurisdiction (or tax haven to you and me) in the Channel Islands.

With the firm's wealthy clients only nominally based there for tax purposes, I was packed off to meet them wherever they actually spent their time. The clients were covering the expenses and, for them, money wasn't an object. They would treat me as they liked to be treated. They put me up in hotels I could only dream of affording in places like Zurich, Geneva and London. They took me out for dinner to their favourite restaurants. I might have used the wrong fork a couple of times to begin with, but I eventually got the hang of it. As long as someone else was picking up the tab, I took to the good life like a duck to water.

I had a favourite champagne when I was with clients. 'Bollinger, if you've got it, please.' I liked a Malbec with my steak and a Hendricks at lunch. For someone who grew up thinking that adding lemonade to a pint tipped it into cock-tail territory, I quickly developed expensive tastes.

On the surface, I had achieved my goal. This was it. This was the good life. This was what I had always wanted. This was what everyone wanted, no? Certainly, if you looked on my social media, you'd think I had it all.

But inside, my anxiety was growing. I was constantly feeling like I would be caught out and exposed as a fraud, as someone who shouldn't be in the same room as all these people from money. As my anxiety grew, I drank more to drown it out. I lived in a perpetual state of alert. As the drinking increased, the lies I had to tell to cover for my drinking also got bigger. The hangovers got harder to shake, and the gaps between drinking sessions were getting shorter.

By my late twenties I had started to realise that my drinking was getting way out of hand. The damage it was causing was growing exponentially. I needed to rein it in to have any semblance of a normal life. And so I spent the best part of a decade in a constant loop: the big blowout, giving up drinking, deciding I'm not an alcoholic and that I should moderate, followed by another big blowout.

The big blowout

I would drink heavily every single weekend, all weekend, but every few months a big blowout would occur. A night out or an event where the wheels would come off in spectacular fashion and there was a consequence to my drinking other than a hangover. Apologies would have to be made to my colleagues, clients or even my boss. Criminal charges might be narrowly avoided. Trips to the hospital explained away.

Giving up drinking
A valiant effort using sheer willpower to deprive myself and give up my essential crutch would ensue. This usually lasted two to four weeks, depending on how big the blowout had been.

Deciding I'm not an alcoholic, and that I should moderate
As the willpower faded, I would start to google 'Am I an alcoholic?' 'Do I have a drinking problem?' I would read about the most extreme examples of what an alcoholic looked like and convince myself that they didn't apply to me because I could take or leave it. I would painstakingly research new methods to help me moderate.

Moderating
I would try out the new method of moderation. It would work for the first few times. I would feel like I had it under control. But as the weeks went on, I would slowly increase my drinking, eventually going back to regularly drinking heavily to until a blackout.

Another big blowout
Cue self-loathing, asking myself what was wrong with me, why I couldn't drink like a normal person, and returning to step two.

Repeat on loop for ten years.

This latest blowout, which started as 'a glass of red' while wrapping the last of the kids' Christmas presents, feels different. I'm not sure if it's the video, and having a graphic reminder of what my drinking actually does to me, or my endless reading of quit lit, but I have started to change how I view alcohol. Now I can see it for what it is. Alcohol is an addictive poison that doesn't do me any favours. By not having it in my life, my life will be better. This seems simple, but while it's how I see it now, it's not how I have always viewed it.

Until this point I have viewed alcohol as an essential ingredient of a happy and successful life. This view is shared by most people, and understandably so. The drinks industry spends billions on advertising and marketing to create the illusion that drinking is essential to a fun, exciting lifestyle.

Alcohol is so ingrained and normalised in our society that despite it being an addictive drug, we actively encourage each other to take it. We even challenge our friends and family when they don't join us for a drink. Imagine having to pretend you're on antibiotics to avoid smoking at a work event? Or taking the car to a family gathering so you have a good excuse for not taking a few lines of coke? We can see that would be ridiculous. But with alcohol, it's normal. 'Go on, you can at least have one? Leave the car here, get a taxi home and pick it up tomorrow.'

We don't apply this peer pressure to alcoholics. No, when people have become so addicted to the substance that they have been forced to stop taking it altogether, we can then stop trying to get them to take it. We can support them in their struggle. We can get them a diet coke and pity them. Poor them. They've taken it too far. Not like me. I can take it or leave it.

There is no medical definition of an alcoholic. There isn't

a threshold of units that determine when you cross the line from moderate drinker to heavy drinker to alcoholic. It's a self-diagnosed label. Only you can determine if you are an alcoholic. Only you can determine if you suffer from the disease of alcoholism. I don't understand why.

I started to question the usefulness of the concept of alcoholism as a disease, or medical condition that only affects alcoholics. People who regularly take cocaine don't suffer from 'cocainism'. People who smoke regularly aren't 'smokaholics'. They don't suffer from a disease. They have simply taken an addictive substance, cocaine or nicotine, become addicted and now use it regularly, even though it has a negative impact on their health and wellbeing.

I started to question why we view drinking differently. With alcohol, why do we view the person as the problem, rather than the addictive substance?

Looking back, I think the fear of being labelled an alcoholic was one of the things that spurred me on in my quest for moderation. What will people think when I say I can't drink? Will they think I'm an alcoholic? The fear of being labelled an alcoholic was another reason to keep on drinking. The irony is not lost on me.

This critical thinking, while challenging my long-held belief that alcohol was great, and that those who became addicted to it were defective, lesser, or somehow different from the rest of us, was a pivotal step on my journey to sobriety.

Rather than the black and white definition of Alcoholic, or Normal. I started to view dependence on drink as a scale, which we can move up or down, from zero to ten. My scale is in no way scientific, but it did change my approach to alcohol. There is a much more comprehensive 'Alcohol Dependence Scale', which is used by medical professionals and counsellors to assess the severity of someone's dependence on alcohol. That measure contains twenty-nine questions, which provide a score. Higher scores indicate more severe dependence. You've probably done a version of this online at some point. They ask questions like 'In the past twelve months, have you passed out as a result of drinking?' or 'Have you tried to cut down on your drinking and failed?' The resulting score tells you if you have a low level, intermediate level, substantial level or severe level of alcohol dependence.

The 'Paddy Scale of Dependence' is based purely on anecdotal and personal experience, but it is hopefully easier to relate to. At zero you have the never-touch-a-drop non-drinkers. As you move up to the twos and threes, you get to the people who have a couple of drinks every now and then, those who can stop with ease. These people fascinated me – I was in awe of them. Why didn't they lock their CEO in the stationary cupboard?

Then as you get to the fours and fives, it's the people who *have* to drink at least every week, but who don't think it is doing them any harm. The sixes and sevens are the people who know it is causing them issues; they have tried to cut back but couldn't. These people can still paper over the cracks and mask the issues it causes them. As you move up to the nines and tens, you get closer to the (often wildly inaccurate) cardboard-cut-out version of an alcoholic, who is showing outward signs of dependence that can no longer be hidden.

Viewing it like this sparked a mindset shift for me. I saw

alcohol for what it was and the role it played in my life. I had moved too far along the scale. I was up at seven or eight. Alcohol was an addictive substance that was having an increasingly negative impact on my health and wellbeing the further along the scale I moved.

My life had been narrowed by drinking. It was a life where I made it through work, got to the end of the week exhausted and reached for a drink. A lot of drinks. I started the next week sluggish from the weekend, limped through it and then repeated the cycle.

It was time to break the cycle.

Rock Bottom

I wish I could say the 'a glass of red while wrapping the kids' Christmas presents' blowout was rock bottom, but it wasn't. When people ask me about rock bottom, they expect me to give them the details of one big dramatic event like in the movies. A single moment where, after crashing the car while driving home after a heavy night on the sauce, or turning up to work drunk and being sent home, I finally decided enough was enough and got sober.

While I've done each of those things, and worse, they didn't trigger rock bottom. At the time they happened I would only have put myself as a four or five on my addicted scale. I was incredibly lucky to walk away from the car crash unharmed. I was in my early twenties and thought I was invincible. The car was a write-off. I dusted myself down and was back drinking within the week. I shrugged off the work incident. I got myself another job and went on a three-day bender to celebrate my new career.

In *The Unexpected Joy of Being Sober*,[2] Catherine Gray describes her rock bottom not as one event, but more as a series of tiny rock bottoms, where she realised her drinking had caused her actions to become unaligned with her values and the type of person she wanted to be. She, and many people in recovery, refer to these tiny rock bottoms as 'convincers'. For them rock bottom is just the point where they decide to stop digging, hurl their shovel down and start climbing out of their self-made pit.

That's what it was like for me. The day I described at the start of the book, when I looked at that video of myself after drinking three bottles of wine, wasn't particularly dramatic. I looked a mess and was a bit late for work. I have definitely had darker days, and most people would consider a car crash or being drunk at work as more serious, but, crucially, it came at a point in my life when the penny was beginning to drop. It was the last in a series of convincers that had been slowly building since I reached my thirties. You might have your own versions, and some will resonate more than others, but these are the ones that impacted me most and edged me further towards sobriety.

April 2016 – Drinking to blackout alone
Right from the beginning, if there was no one to stop me, I would regularly drink until I passed out. Even if everyone else was going home, I would continue to go in search of the next party. If I was in the house, I would watch music channels and text or call anyone I thought would still be up. I told myself I was a night owl, that I came alive at night. Rather than the truth, which was I just couldn't stop drinking once I had started.

Back when we lived in Guernsey, my then girlfriend, now wife, was off island for the weekend. I had the house to myself and, obviously, planned to spend it drinking. I had a big day out with the lads from the office. We met up for a whisky tasting session in the afternoon, went bar hopping for most of the day and ended up at the island's main club until closing. I had been out all day and night and when I got back to the flat, smashed, since there was no one to tell me to go to bed, I thought I would stay up to 'watch the sunrise' with some beers. I quickly drank the beers, and the sun wasn't up yet so I went hunting for booze in the flat. By this stage my girl-friend knew I had a problem and had started hiding any spare booze from me. I found a bottle of vodka at the back of the wardrobe.

I told myself I would just have one. That I could nurse it while waiting for the sun to come up. We didn't have anything in the house I could use as a mixer anyway, other than a mini-ature can of tonic, so it's not like I had much of an option. I poured a generous measure of vodka, finished the can of tonic, and then put the vodka back in the wardrobe. The sunrise passed me by as I was too busy thinking about ways to drink more vodka without a mixer.

Eventually I found a tin of plum tomatoes in the cup-board. I mashed them up, then proceeded to drink the rest of the bottle of vodka mixed with the tomato juice. I told myself it was a Bloody Mary. I sat drinking 'Bloody Marys' alone until six in the morning, despite having been out since early afternoon the day before.

I woke up on the couch later that afternoon. I looked around at the remnants of the Bloody Marys and empty vodka bottle and was disgusted with myself. What was wrong with me? I vowed to give up the booze. I lasted a week.

January 2018 – Drinking in secret

By January 2018 my wife and I had moved back to Glasgow and bought a family home in the suburbs. At thirty-two, when everyone else was tailing off their drinking, I was still regularly staying out after work on a Friday night, or staying up drinking alone watching music channels until I passed out. My wife, who loved and cared for me, started to get really worried about how much I was drinking, and why I could never stop once I started. She never forced me to stop, but she would help me monitor my intake, and support me on my attempts at moderation.

When I was sober, I was grateful for this support. But when I really wanted a drink, I resented it. It felt controlling. I rationalised that I should be allowed to drink as much as I wanted. That I worked hard and had earned the right to blow off steam at the weekend. And I did. Even on the Friday nights when I had promised to come straight home from work, I would have a few pints at the train station, then down cans of gin and tonic on the train. Despite it being only a twenty-minute journey, I could easily squeeze in three cans plus the pints before I reached our front door. The 'agreed limit' of booze for the night would then start. I would invariably either talk my way out of that limit and start upon a second bottle of wine, or sneak a few extra cans of beer to get my fill.

I kept this up for years, telling myself I had it under control and that my wife's idea of normal drinking was just not realistic. Then during Covid, around January 2021, despite having no intention to do so, I found myself picking up two cans of gin and tonic on the way to get my first immunisation jab. I swore to myself that I would only have one drink on the way there, and one on the way back. Both were drunk before I got to the centre, so I bought another two on the way back and drank them before I got home. I told no one, but I got a real fright. What type of person downs cans of gins and tonic on their way to a vaccination clinic? Again I vowed to give up the booze. This led to a run that, to be fair, lasted a few months, but then slipped back into moderation attempts, and the usual cycle.

September 2018 – I consider suicide
Things in my career were going well, and I landed a job at a new firm in a senior management position with real prospects for directorship or making partner. My wife had given birth to our first son and we were overflowing with love and happiness.

But this was also one of the most challenging periods of my life. Having no idea of the upheaval and amount of stress a baby would bring (a lot), I had two weeks of paternity leave, but then I expected (and my firm definitely expected) that I would go back to putting in big chargeable hours at work.

I tried to be both a supportive husband and father, while still trying to climb the ladder at my firm. What this looked like in practice was:

- Up at 5.30am to make it into the office for 7.30am.
- Working flat-out to cram as much chargeable work in as possible, then leaving at 5.30pm. (Sneaking out the office to try and avoid the unapproving glances and mutterings of 'part-timer'.)

- Getting back home just in time to help out with dinner, bath and bedtime.
- Logging back in on my laptop from 9pm and working while settling the baby if he woke or needed to be changed/fed until 1am.
- At 1am my wife taking over to let me get some sleep from 1am to 5.30am.
- Repeat

A rational person would look at that schedule and think, well, if there isn't even room for enough sleep, surely there isn't enough room for drinking? And they would be right. But I wasn't a rational person.

Rather than get to the weekend and think, 'Okay, I don't have work for two days, how can I recover and catch up on sleep? Or what can I do to support my family more? Can I give my wife a break from watching the baby?' I would come at it from the mindset of, 'I am exhausted. I have been working flat-out at work all week, and then working flat-out at home. I need to let off some steam. I've gone without a drink all week. I've earned it.' Looking back this seems incredibly selfish and self-centred, but at the time it seemed completely valid.

My wife would take a different view and we would bicker about it. She would argue that the weekend should be a time for us to rest and recover as a family without the pressure of my work and we couldn't do that if I was sitting up late at night drinking. After much back and forth, I would negotiate hard and we would eventually agree that I could have one night for a blowout at the weekend.

Despite promising otherwise, I would cram as much drinking as I could into the Friday night, deploying the tactic of drinking on the train before I got home, and sneaking extra booze to top myself up. I would invariably sit up until one or two in the morning, drinking myself into oblivion under the guise of blowing off steam and unwinding from a tough week.

I would be hungover for the rest of the weekend, feeling guilty about not doing more to support my family, and anxious about another intense week of work ahead. It was a vicious circle. The more under pressure I felt at work, the more I drank to let off steam. The more I drank, the more anxious I got and the less sleep I got. I would feel under more and more pressure, requiring bigger and bigger blowouts.

I've kept going on this loop for six months or so when the wheels come off. I am working on a particularly challenging engagement with a banking client which requires me to travel down to London and deliver a presentation in person.

As this is a major client, and a potentially tricky meeting where our substantial fees will be discussed, the partner asks me to travel down the day before. He wants me to get there early and do a dry run of our presentation with him well in advance of the client arriving.

Having been getting by on less than four hours' sleep a night for the last six months, I am eager to make the most of the time away. There is a chance of sleeping for ten hours undisturbed. I pack a book to catch up on reading, and my gym stuff to burn off any excess energy in the morning after a full night's sleep.

I have no intention of drinking. The client meeting is too important, and I am too exhausted. It does not cross my mind.

Then, on the flight down, the air hostess comes by with the complimentary drinks and snacks.

With years of experience, I am a dab hand at wangling extra drinks in situations like this and I am on autopilot when she asks me what I will have. 'Hmm I'm not sure. I'm torn between a beer, or a gin and tonic,' I say, as I stare up at her with puppy dog eyes. 'Here, sir, have both.'

Without making a conscious decision to, I've got a double gin and tonic and a cold beer on the tray in front of me, begging to be drunk. Well, I reason to myself, it will help me relax. I will just have these, then nothing more once I get to London. I down the drinks, then ask the same hostess for another beer from the trolley on my way back from the toilet. She smiles and passes me two. She must get this all the time, functioning-alcoholic businessmen shuttling back and forth from London. Anyway, I rationalise that I told myself I wouldn't drink in London, and I'm probably 30,000 feet over Manchester at this point, so I'm technically okay. I just won't have any more drinks once I get off the plane.

Predictably, though, the floodgates have been opened. Even though I booked a hotel that has a spa and gym, with plans to visit both when I get there and just grab room service later on, I am suddenly eager to go out and have dinner some-where I can 'have one glass of wine' and look out over the Thames. I can hear this nonsense in my head – I am lying to myself and telling myself that what I am doing is okay. I find a restaurant that does indeed look out over the Thames and order my dinner, and, more importantly, my 'one glass of wine'.

I get a large one, which is a third of a bottle. I tell myself I will make it last. I end up drinking four of these. I tell myself it's still early. I order a large gin and tonic instead of dessert. Then another for the road.

Your average bear would be pretty drunk by this point. Three double gins, three beers, over a bottle of wine. I don't feel like it's having much effect. It's only 10pm. Granted, I won't make it to the gym or spa in the morning, but I can still get back to the hotel and be tucked up in bed by 11pm and get eight hours of undisturbed sleep and feel like a new man in the morning.

I am ready to smash this presentation. I have been working on this client for months, know the topic inside out and feel confident that when we do the dry run with the partner in the morning, he will be happy to take a back seat and let me lead when closing out with the client. I will be on the fast track to becoming a director.

I make it back to the hotel, where the concierge asks if everything is going well with my stay and if I like the hotel. I say I've only been in to drop my bags off and have not seen much of it. He says I must stop off at the rooftop bar as there is a magnificent view of St Paul's Cathedral, which has been lit up beautifully. Well, I wouldn't want to miss that.

I have another double gin and tonic while 'enjoying the view'. Then another as a nightcap. Then another at last orders. Now I feel drunk. I also feel annoyed at myself, disappointed. All the usual self-loathing that comes with realising I have no will power. However, all is not lost. I will still be in bed by 12.30. It might not be eight hours, but I will still get six or seven good hours of rest, which is more than I have been getting.

I get back to my room, pick out my clothes for tomorrow, iron my shirt and make sure I am good to go. I am almost ready for bed when I grab a bottle of water from the fridge. It turns out to be a mini bar, which is well stocked. Despite having no intention to, and knowing it is madness, I find myself working my way through the mini bar.

I sit up watching back-to-back reruns of *The Sopranos* that happen to be on the Freeview channel. The mini bar has one miniature of each of the main spirits. Bacardi, Jack Daniels, Gordons gin, Smirnoff vodka. I polish them off, telling myself that each one will be the last, but one by one I keep going. There is a mini bottle of prosecco that I pop. A bottle of Peroni goes down no problem.

By three in the morning the only thing left in the mini bar is the bottle of water. I finally make it to that, but pass out before opening it.

By some miracle, I don't sleep through the alarm. I get up, vomit twice, have a cold shower, drink some coffee and make it to the office on time to have a dry run with the partner. I feel fucking horrendous. Rather than being fresh from eight hours' sleep, and confidently walking him through my presentation, I am anxious, sweaty and paranoid that I reek of booze and might still be drunk.

I pretend to have the flu. My tongue is thick in my mouth as I try to talk through the work. At the end, the partner gently lets me know that while my work is good, and the content of my presentation is spot on, he feels it would be better if he were to talk the client through it, especially since I have such a bad case of the flu. We are meeting the client later in the afternoon, so he suggests I have plenty of time to grab something to eat and get some fresh air before we meet them.

I see this for what it is. I've blown it. I make it through the client meeting, but my role is basically hitting next on the presentation deck and answering the odd technical question. I fly back that night. I get home at 10pm, exhausted. I take the night shift until 2am as I'm feeling guilty and lie, saying, 'I'm so well rested after a night off.' I get up at 5.30am to go back to the office. I check my emails on the way in and can see the client has given us the green light for our fees and sent more work our way. I now have even more chargeable hours to get through.

It's only Tuesday and I don't know if I can make it through the week. I feel constantly anxious. Anxious I'm not doing enough at home, anxious I'm not doing enough at work. I get out of the train station and wait to cross the road. The city centre is busy and buses are flying past at speed, inches from where I wait to cross.

As I wait, I think about what would happen if I just put my hand out and let it get hit by a bus. I don't think I want to die, but what if I could break a few bones in my hand, enough that I would have to go to hospital and wouldn't be able to work?

The green man sounds. I don't cross. I wait and stay standing by the road.

What about sticking a leg out? If I broke my leg badly and had to be in hospital for a few weeks, I would get some proper time away from it all. I worry that I might get dragged under the bus and do more damage than intended. I think about that for a minute.

The green man sounds again. Again I wait.

If I were to fully step out in front of one of these buses,

would it kill me instantly? I think about not being here and what would happen. Would it be classed as an accident? My life insurance would mean a pay-out of 350 grand. My work would pay out another 300 grand for death in service. My family would get 650 grand. I feel like such a fuckup that when weighing it up, I genuinely think they might be better off.

I think of my wife and son, I couldn't do it to them. I think of my parents and sister. They would be devastated. I put it to the back of my mind. The green man sounds again and this time I cross with the others. I never tell anyone about this. It is never processed or addressed. It's a shameful secret. Another emotion to be numbed and obliterated during the next blowout.

Looking back, it's crazy to think I kept on drinking for another three years. Why did it take so long to finally give up? Well, firstly, it's hard. Secondly, from the age of fifteen, drinking had become part of my identity. I used it as a way to gain the instant confidence needed to be the 'real me'. Party Paddy. The big-time extrovert. Quick with a joke and first on the dancefloor, the man you could rely on to get the party started and with the stamina to keep it going. I was worried I would be awkward, shy and socially stunted without it. Even though I could see the damage it was doing, I was too scared to be without it. I was still clutching on and striving for moderation.

While each of the convincers was horrible at the time, they stayed with me and served a purpose. They made me realise I had to stop, and that I couldn't be the type of person I wanted to be while drinking.

The False Friend

I should probably bring you some balance. There were loads of times over the years when I thought booze had served me well. For years I had told myself that without it, I would never have been as successful in my professional or personal life. We often do this with alcohol; we give it credit where it isn't due. And we can trace this back to our first interactions with it.

At school, I spent a lot of time in my head, worried about saying the wrong thing, or what people thought about me. I was anxious and painfully shy, probably like many teenagers. But at the time I thought this meant there was something wrong with me. With a few drinks, I felt like I could be myself, like the drink was bringing out the real me. I didn't feel awkward or think about what I was saying. I just said it. And people liked it. It felt good.

When I went off to the University of Glasgow, I used booze to help me shed my imposter syndrome and make friends. It was one of the UK's ancient universities, close to home and, as I wanted to learn about and get access to money, it seemed like the best place to do it. Initially, it felt like the perfect choice, with the cloisters and turrets, but after the first few classes and group tutorials, I felt seriously out of place.

The people in my class were going sailing and riding horses at the weekend. I spent my Saturdays serving meatballs in Ikea. They spoke in polished accents and had gone to private or top state schools. I was coming from a below average school where my results were an outlier, and my attendance here, especially on this course, was not expected. I felt like I shouldn't be there.

I was back to being anxious and shy. I didn't speak up in class or in group conversations, even when I was certain of the answer, as I was so filled with self-doubt. I quietly envied the others in my class, who would confidently discuss answers with ease. Even if the answer was bollocks, they would shrug it off and go on to answer the next one with the same confidence and authority. I would be so crippled with anxiety that during spaces between lectures I would ride the subway and go round in a loop until the next class rather than mix with anyone.

But rather than work through this, and give myself the chance to grow in confidence naturally, I turned to booze. I would get to student social events early and neck some double vodkas to take the edge off, then drink at a much faster rate than anyone else. Then the 'real me' would be out again. A world away from the quiet guy from lectures, I was loud and outgoing; people were engaged and eager to hear what I had to say. I made friends easily. All I had to do was drink.

Drinking started to become part of my identity. Hard-drinking Paddy who could drink you under the table, be the life and soul of the party, then still get up for his shift at the weekend, make it to his lectures during the week, and smash his exams. What a guy.

Even though my grades were good, there were plenty of warning signs that booze was doing me harm. I was now drinking to blackout every single time I socialised, and during a blackout I would have no idea what I had done. Three or four hours could easily be lost from the evening.

Twice I woke up in hospital with my head split open after a fall. I would wake up on the other side of the city with people I didn't know, with no idea how I got there. It was scary at times, but at that point I didn't think it was a problem. The embarrassing or dangerous things I did while drunk were quickly brushed off as hilariously funny stories to share down the pub. They were added to the hard-drinking Paddy persona.

I got the odd comment from my family or even friends' parents about maybe taking it easy for a while, but never anything serious. Like me, they probably thought I was just making the most of being a student, sometimes taking it too far but not really doing any harm.

And that was what it looked like. Despite my increasingly dangerous levels of drinking, I still managed to get a 2.1 Honours Degree in Accountancy and Finance and secure a graduate position at one of the 'Big 4' consultancy firms. Professionally I was on track, and I loved being out on the town, drinking hard and enjoying myself. I told myself I would knuckle down and cut back on the booze once I started my real job in finance. Little did I know.

Finance – 2008

If you are a heavy drinker and want to work in an industry where your heavy drinking won't be frowned upon, finance is for you. They might have tried to change it a bit now, but in the 2000s, the ability to get shitfaced with clients and still make it in for work the next morning was a prerequisite for success and career advancement.

My graduate induction was a two-week-long residential event at a five-star hotel up in the north of Scotland. Every single night there was a free bar. Drinking games and getting smashed were actively encouraged. I could not believe my luck. I fucking loved it.

I thought our luck might run out when the training wheels were taken off and we were sent out to clients as chargeable fee earners. I feared they might turn the booze tap off and expect us to be clear minded from now on in, but if anything the booze levels ramped up. Now we were earning the fees to pay for it, the alcohol flowed even more freely.

The hours were long. Overtime was expected. Starting at 8am and finishing at midnight wasn't uncommon. But after a long week, you were rewarded. On a Friday afternoon a trolley would come round the office laden with drinks. Beers were drunk at the desk while the last bits of work were finished up. Laptops were promptly closed at 5pm and everyone would pile into one of the posher bars for 'Partners Drinks'.

When I was first told we were going for Partners Drinks, I thought it might be where the firm invited the partners of all the staff out for a drink to thank them for taking up so much of their wives' and husbands' time. For making them work late and sending them home stressed out and exhausted. I thought that sounded like a nice thing to do. I said this to one of the managers and he laughed in my face. 'So naive, young Paddy. Get your coat.'

Partners Drinks involved one of the Partners of the firm putting their card behind the bar, and the staff getting smashed in a private area that had been reserved for us so we could properly let our hair down after the gruelling week, without causing any embarrassment to the firm.

Some of the behaviour was wild. Many office romances began and were abruptly ended at Partners Drinks. People threw up in the bathrooms, and said and did things they would be mortified about come Monday morning. On one occasion an ambulance had to be called for one of the young associates who had fallen down the stairs, paralytic. I wasn't shocked, just relieved it wasn't me for once. It was all just accepted as normal, and a perk of the job, and I flung myself into it with gusto.

My first few weeks with the firm were like the first few weeks at university, in that despite having earned the right to be there through my honours degree from an ancient university, and passing three rounds of interviews and multiple psychometric tests, I still felt like an imposter. I lived in fear of being found out when the Partners, colleagues and clients realised I wasn't one of them. I didn't come from money. I hadn't gone to the right schools. My accent wasn't right. I might have told them I read *The Times* and *FT* during the interviews, but in my house we read the tabloids and the local paper.

I suspect much of this 'outsider feeling' was in my head, but there were so many unwritten rules and practices that everyone else just seemed to know, but I didn't. On my first day in the office, I rocked up in a light silver-grey suit with thick gold pinstripes, matching gold tie and pocket square a la Gordon Gecko in *Wall Street*. In my mind this was how people in finance dressed. I thought I looked awesome. When I looked around at the navy and black suits, black shoes and sombre tones everyone else had on, I wanted the ground to swallow me up. I had just about gotten comfortable at university, but here I was back to feeling anxious, awkward and out of place. I couldn't just jump on the subway and hide again, but I knew I could rely on booze to help me out. More and more I relied on the Party Paddy persona to help me over come my imposter syndrome, and, again, people seemed to like it.

Guernsey – 2012
By my mid-twenties the quest for the good life took me to Guernsey, a tiny island in the English Channel near the French coast with a population of about sixty-five thousand.

When a recruitment agent suggested I take a job there, I looked it up online. I was taken in by the gorgeous scenery, quaint little cobbled streets and stunning sea views. You could drive around the entire coast in an hour. It looked like a great place to visit for a long weekend. It certainly didn't scream 'financial services hub'.

The recruitment agent assured me there was a huge demand for finance professionals on the island. She was confident she could get me a position there with a better salary and have them cover my relocation and living expenses. Having been taken in by the package and lifestyle being offered, I quickly said yes and asked her to set up an interview. Staying off the booze for the next few weeks to practise my interview technique, I learned all I could about Guernsey and made up reasons why I wanted to move there.

It didn't take long to figure out why there was such a demand for finance professionals. Guernsey has a basic rate of corporation tax of 0%. There are no capital gains, inheritance or sales taxes. £120 billion flows through companies domiciled in Guernsey every year,[3] and that's just what is declared. If I was looking for the good life, this was the next step.

The booze culture there made Glasgow look tame. The Friday drinks trolley came round at 4pm in Glasgow; in Guernsey it was wheeled round the desks from lunchtime onwards. And it was a much bigger trolley. The Partners would cut off the free bar tab at 9pm in Glasgow, while in Guernsey it would stay open until the last man standing had enough. With the firm being staffed by expats, everyone was living away from home, spending a few years working abroad to make their tax-free money. They often didn't have families to go home to. There was no reason to leave; everyone stayed out until closing.

They didn't just have events on a Friday either. 'Work Socials' spanned the weekend, with island hopping, booze cruises, pub golf, summer balls, winter balls, Christmas balls, St Patrick's Day balls. You name it the firm was having a ball for it, with champagne on arrival and a free bar once you were settled in.

Now this was what I'd had in mind when I pictured the good life. Lots of money floating around and free booze on tap. But I was keen to make a good impression. I had a three-month probation period and chartered accountancy exams to pass, and while I didn't think I had a drinking problem as such, I didn't want to risk doing anything to jeopardise my new career. I didn't trust myself not to go off the rails at a work event.

I had a little planning book in which I had written down my career goals. They were relatively simple. 'Stay off the booze, pass my exams, keep my head down, get promoted, get cash.' I would constantly revisit these goals. I used them as a mantra that I would repeat in my head whenever I was considering drinking.

And for the first three months, through sheer willpower and gritted teeth, I did it. I stayed off the booze. I kept my head down. I passed exams and got chartered. After my probation period was over, and I had an interview with my career coach, I was expecting to be praised for my exam passes. For keeping my head down. For racking up the chargeable hours. I thought I was smashing it and about to be promoted. I was in for a shock.

My career coach was a genuinely nice guy, and he tried to break it to me gently, but he made it crystal clear that passing exams and hitting chargeable hours targets were the minimum they expected here. Although there was talk of extending my probation period, he had fought my corner and the firm had decided to keep me on. However, if I wanted to be promoted and make this my career, I was going to need to be more of 'a presence'. I was too quiet in the office and at the social events. The Partners and senior staff barely knew I existed. I was a wallflower who hadn't made any impression on the clients.

I couldn't believe it. Thanking him for the heads-up, I promised to make more of an impact. This gave me all the excuse I needed to get back on the booze. Of course I was quiet – I was sober. If I felt out of place amongst the middle class in Glasgow, it was tenfold so in Guernsey. Several of my year group had been to Oxford and Cambridge. One of the guys was some sort of aristocrat whose family owned large chunks of Scotland. The chat at lunch was about where you went on your ski holidays as a child. I went to Benidorm every year until I was eighteen. Even if I could have contributed to the conversation, I was painfully aware that they couldn't really understand my Glaswegian accent.

Here was proof that I needed to drink if I wanted to be successful. It's all very well staying sober and passing exams, but if you are too shy to build networks you'll never get any-where. Plus, look at everything I was missing out on. I was sitting on booze cruises nursing a diet coke, stoically saying no while everyone else was having a great time. Passing up free champagne at a ball every other weekend while everyone else was wolfing it down. I convinced myself if I wanted to be successful, I needed booze. If I wanted to fit in, I would have to drink again. And so that's what I did.

My career coach chat was the week before the Christmas ball. Too quiet, eh? I'd fucking show them. I went to that Christmas ball and more than made up for my three months sober. I said yes to every drink. I was outgoing, I was confid-ent. I was back.

The next day I was the talk of the office. I was getting pats on the back all round. 'You've finally settled in then!' 'Some man!' 'What an entrance!'

This cemented it. To succeed, the 'real Paddy', with booze, was needed.

I devised a new system. When I had an exam or important deadline coming up, I stayed completely sober for the time required to study or complete it. Then I would get back on the booze and let the 'real Paddy' come out. The 'real Paddy' could help me navigate social situations and make the required impact with clients and colleagues.

The system seemed to work. With a few drinks under my belt, rather than feel self-conscious or inferior around my ridiculously posh clients and colleagues, I could play up to the differences.

'Where's your favourite place to go skiing, Paddy?'

'I've never been, old chap, but I do enjoy getting piste! Ha ha ha, more wine please!'

'You mean you've never been to America, Paddy?'

'I'm afraid not, squire, but I have been in some states! Another round of shots!'

I thought I had it sussed. I was using booze like a tool, to enhance my life when needed, then putting it down when a sober head was more beneficial.

Workwise I was knocking it out the park. Clients wanted me on the invite list when socials were being organised, and Partners wanted me booked to their jobs. My salary quickly increased, and the bonuses got bigger. I was earning more than I'd ever imagined. The good life was here!

Growing up I had a black and white picture of George Best on my bedroom wall with the quote, 'I spent a lot of money on booze, birds and fast cars. The rest I just squandered.' I thought this was such a cool attitude, and it was something I wanted to emulate now that I had the cash to do it. As soon as I got my first bonus, I went car shopping. I lived a two-minute walk from the office, and there was an island-wide speed limit of 30mph. A bicycle or a small city car would have been a sensible choice, but I couldn't picture George Best in one of those. I went straight to the Mercedes dealership and got myself a sports car. I had arrived. The old CEO in my head had delivered us to the good life, and we could switch between Party Paddy, and sensible Paddy at will. All we needed was a few drinks.

The Lies We Tell Ourselves

Despite all the 'rock bottom convincers' and suicidal thoughts that had been piling up by 2018, on paper you wouldn't have known that I had any issue with alcohol. I had a successful job in finance, a loving wife, two kids, and a nice big house in the suburbs. The whole checklist was ticked off.

This was part of the problem. My life didn't look like my idea of the life of someone with a drinking problem. I wasn't homeless, drinking cider on a park bench. I didn't wake up wanting a drink or pour vodka on my cornflakes. But I did love drinking, and most of the time it felt like the benefits outweighed the downsides. I felt that without drinking, I wouldn't have been as successful in my career. That people wouldn't like me as much. That my wife wouldn't want to stay with me. That I'd never have a good time again.

There were serious events that I look back on now and realise were major warning signs, but at the time they were brushed off and put to the back of my mind. I was so desperate to be able to drink that I would rather have given up anything other than booze. I had it on a pedestal. I thought that I needed alcohol to succeed and enjoy life.

Many of us do, and it's no wonder. Society tells us that alcohol is the solution when things go wrong, and the way to celebrate when things go right. Just got some bad news? Take a drink to take the edge off. Just got some good news? Pop the champagne. Baby just born? Let's wet their head. Someone just died? Let's raise a glass to them.

I thought that I needed alcohol. From those first drinks as a teenager to making friends at university through to working in finance, I used it as a way to give me the instant confidence needed to be the 'real me'.

Whenever I was considering giving up drinking, or whenever I was challenged on my drinking, the reasons I would give for 'choosing' to stick with it were:

1. I need it to socialise and it gives me confidence.
2. It helps relieve stress.
3. It makes me happy – I enjoy it.

As long as I held these beliefs, it was going to be impossible for me to stop drinking for any sustained period of time. Multiple studies have shown that willpower is a finite resource.[4] For a behavioural change to happen, it requires a change of perspective.

In her book *This Naked Mind*, Annie Grace explores the thinking behind each of my reasons, plus a whole load more in a very scientific and methodological way. So if you have other reasons for drinking (e.g., I like the taste, it's just a habit, it helps me have better sex) and want to explore these reasons further, I'd highly recommend it. When it comes to my main three reasons, I can talk about them with some authority. See if any of it resonates:

1. I need it to socialise and it gives me confidence
I have read a lot of books on sobriety. When I read them at the point I was just starting to think about giving up, I felt they were reluctant to acknowledge that there are some benefits to booze, even if they are superficial and fleeting. It always felt like they dived straight into the downside, which, when I was drinking, put me off engaging. I will, therefore, try not to make the same mistake. Even as a non-drinker, I can still see that booze is the ultimate social lubricant. In our society it is part of practically every social occasion, and I can genuinely see why.

A great example for me is being an all-day guest at a wedding. You've made it through the ceremony and are assigned a table for dinner, and many of the people don't know each other. If there hasn't been much booze provided up to this point, there might be some polite small talk as you get seated about how you know the groom and bride, how lovely the bride looks and how they were lucky with the weather. Yawn. It's all quite formulaic and stilted. There are often gaps in the conversation and awkward pauses as everyone gets to know each other and how they fit in the group dynamic.

I would find these gaps in conversation and awkward pauses excruciating and would either take charge of going to the bar and procuring drinks for the table, or eagerly start pouring generous glasses for everyone, if the drinks had already been provided. I would guzzle down my glass, pour myself another, and keep everyone topped up in the process.

And just like magic, after those first few glasses, the initial

52

insecurities that made the group a bit shy or reserved would melt away. The conversation would begin to flow, as we all became more and more extroverted. By the time the speeches were over, we were all best mates, cracking jokes and over-sharing without a care.

Say what you want about booze, but it is pretty efficient in this regard. There is science behind its effectiveness. Right from the first few sips, the booze reduces your ability to process your surroundings. This curbs your awareness of any potential social risk, like awkwardness or rejection. In turn, it can lead to you feeling friendlier and more outgoing towards others. Beyond that, it activates your brain's reward system and boosts dopamine (the neurotransmitter we discussed earlier associated with motivation and pleasure). All of these feel-good emotions can add to an elevated confidence. This can all make you feel more at ease when talking to others.[5]

What's not to love? Well, if you can stop after one or two drinks, nothing really.

In an interview with CNN Health, University of Missouri psychology professor Kenneth Sher, who runs the university's Alcohol, Behaviour and Health laboratory, tells us that at the 'slight buzz' level, alcohol is a social lubricant which often improves mood. You start to let go of a few worries, pay attention to the moment with friends. 'It's telling that, outside of people with alcohol dependence, most people drink in a social situation,' says Sher. 'The overall enjoyment is more pleasurable, because it's enhancing that social experience. Drinking in groups creates cohesion, enhances group bonding and formation, and that's a clear social benefit.'[6]

However, the very fact that alcohol makes us disinhibited,

and makes us behave more impulsively, also makes it very hard for a lot of us to stop after one or two. Before I sat at the table, I would have told myself that I was only going to have a couple to get that 'slight buzz'. But after the first drink, the resolve would lessen, and after the second, it would be gone completely. Once we go past the 'slight buzz' level of one or two units, the sociable benefits have been achieved, but in my case, I would carry on.

The NHS provides a nice guide' on the short-term effects of alcohol at each stage of consumption, based on the assumption that you have a normal tolerance for alcohol. I didn't have anything like a normal tolerance, so the units required to hit each level would have been much higher, but the markers are useful. Let's stick with the wedding example to follow it through.

1 to 2 units (a 125ml glass of wine or 330ml bottle of beer)
After drinking 1 to 2 units of alcohol, your heart rate speeds up and your blood vessels expand, giving you the warm, sociable and talkative feeling associated with moderate drinking.

This is the nice bit of the wedding I mentioned above. The rough edges have been smoothed out. I'm a bit more outgoing and chatty and feel nice and relaxed. Very sociable. If I could stop here, perfect.

4 to 6 units (two pints of lager)
Your brain and nervous system start to be affected. It begins to affect the part of your brain associated with judgement and decision-making, causing you to be more reckless and uninhibited. The alcohol also impairs the cells in your nervous system, making

you feel lightheaded and adversely affecting your reaction time and coordination.

For me, this stage is likely to be the point in the wedding when I am first up on the dance floor, dragging others up with me and generally 'getting the party going'. Ironically, despite my newfound desire to dance, I don't have any natural ability to do so. I am terrible when sober, significantly worse when alcohol has 'adversely affected my reaction time and coordination'. But generally no harm would be done here, just some mild embarrassment that can easily be brushed off as over-enthusiasm and having a good time. Still sociable.

8 to 9 units (eight 25ml measures of vodka)
After drinking 8 to 9 units of alcohol, your reaction times will be much slower, your speech will begin to slur. Your vision may begin to lose focus. Your liver, which filters alcohol out of your body, will be unable to remove all of the alcohol overnight, so it's likely you'll wake with a hangover.

At this stage, although not an offensive or aggressive drunk, I may have made an inappropriate joke or insensitive comment to someone. I'm definitely getting loud and rowdy. Maybe I'll start singing. My wife starts to get embarrassed. Significantly less sociable.

10 to 12 units (six pints of lager)
After drinking 10 to 12 units of alcohol, your coordination will be highly impaired, placing you at serious risk of having an accident. The high level of alcohol has a depressant effect on both your mind and body, which makes you drowsy. This amount of alcohol will begin to reach toxic (poisonous) levels. Your body attempts to

quickly pass out the alcohol in your urine. This will leave you feeling badly dehydrated in the morning, which may cause a severe headache. The excess amount of alcohol in your system can also upset your digestion, leading to symptoms of nausea, vomiting, diarrhoea and indigestion.

By now, I am legless. I am banging into people on the dancefloor, bouncing off tables on the way to the bar, and generally being a nuisance. If I am sitting at a table, it's likely I will be repeating myself and not making sense. On the plus side, I usually always make it to the toilet if I need to be sick. Doesn't sound very sociable now, does it?

More than 12 units (a big session)
If you drink more than 12 units of alcohol, you're at considerable risk of developing alcohol poisoning, particularly if you're drinking many units over a short period of time. Alcohol poisoning occurs when excessive amounts of alcohol start to interfere with the body's automatic functions, such as:

- *breathing*
- *heart rate*
- *gag reflex, which prevents you choking*

Alcohol poisoning can cause a person to fall into a coma and could lead to their death.

Granted I wouldn't generally fall into a coma, or die, but it would be down to my wife to get me home safely from the wedding. She would get help from someone and ask them to pour me into a taxi. Provided we could get a taxi to take us. She would then struggle to get me to walk the short distance from the taxi to our front door. Eventually, she would get me into the spare room, and put me in the recovery position with a basin and some water. She would stay awake and listen out for me in case I choked on my vomit. Twice she has had to shake me and force sick out of my throat. Even when my denial was at its peak, I would struggle to swing that as a 'sociable' outcome. So if you're like me, and can't stop after one or two, it's unlikely that alcohol is helping you to socialise. It might briefly, but the wheels quickly come off.

Seems pretty clear cut that the downsides of those latter stages are not worth the initial gains. Why would I keep going? Well, for each of the stages, I would only remember, if I remembered at all, my drink-warped perspective on it. In my head I was getting the party started by getting up to dance; in my head my dancing was awesome. When I was banging into people, they were out of time, not me. When people didn't react well to my jokes, or join in with my singing – well, they needed to loosen up a bit. I was being fun. They were being a stick in the mud.

I definitely wouldn't remember being poured into a taxi, or my wife having to force vomit out of my throat. I would only accurately remember those initial stages, when the booze was working in my favour. My distorted memory of my drinking experience would be the sociable and talkative feeling associated with moderate drinking.

Very few people in my life would challenge or properly hold me to account for my behaviour in the later stages, either because they were also pretty far gone or because it's so socially accepted. 'Was I bad last night?' I would nervously text people the next morning. And the reassuring responses would come flooding in. 'You were fine, X was much worse.' 'Ah you weren't that bad.' 'We've all been there.'

The thing is, I really was that bad, and it was always me who was there. I just couldn't see it at the time and was happy to lie to myself. I'm in my thirties, so I've just missed the era of filming and sharing every part of a night out on social media; I would only have my own distorted, rose-tinted memory of the evening, and other people's reassuring words in the morning. Even when my wife started to challenge me on it, she was up against twenty years of denial, and it took a long time for her perspective to sink in.

Okay, so maybe we agree it's not quite the flawless social lubricant we thought it was. What about confidence? Surely it's hard to argue that alcohol doesn't give us confidence?

Again, it's all a bit of a con because we have been conditioned to think that alcohol gives us confidence, makes us braver or gives us courage. How many times have we seen the hero in a film ask for a stiff drink to steady the nerves before undertaking some pivotal task? How many times is it offered to someone if they are feeling anxious or afraid? Fear of flying? Have a few drinks before you board, and you'll be fine. People are quick to cite the English sailors and soldiers being given shots of rum or gin to help them face the battle ahead.

We understand that this isn't genuine confidence. We knowingly refer to it as liquid or Dutch courage. We know that all the drink is doing is temporarily removing our inhibitions or fear to let us act with confidence and self-assurance while we're under the influence. The effects are fleeting. If everyone goes into it with their eyes open and knows it's just a temporary fix, what's the issue?

For me, the issue was that I was relying on the temporary fix on a permanent basis. I lacked confidence in a group or social setting and would feel awkward or uneasy, but I knew that a few drinks would be able to sort me out. I relied on it as an instant cheat sheet to socialise with ease. This meant that rather than giving me confidence, alcohol was stealing it from me, by making me more and more reliant on it.

It might have helped me in the moment, but it was false and short-lived. Real confidence is an inner self-assuredness that sticks around when the drink has left. I've now realised that it doesn't come naturally to everyone, and that is okay. It's okay not to be the life and soul of the party, or to be introverted and shy. If you want to be more outgoing, confidence is a skill you can learn. But like most skills, it's difficult to master if you're half cut. It takes allowing yourself to work through it and practising for a bit, without booze. I would never have believed it, but two years on from quitting, I now feel more confident without booze than I ever did with it. Though I'm still a terrible dancer.

2. *It helps me to relieve stress*

This was another reason I clung to and put out as a defence whenever I was challenged on my drinking, or whenever I considered quitting. I told myself that because I worked long hours and had a very stressful job, I needed a drink to let off some steam. That I was drinking because it helped me unwind and de-stress. That after a tough week (or as my consumption increased, a tough day), I had earned it. We've been brainwashed into accepting this as some sort of universal truth.

Social media churns out memes about 'mummy juice' being needed after the kids have gone to bed. Our screens are awash with professionals pouring themselves a large glass of wine or a whisky on the rocks at the end of a gruelling day. We are so accustomed to this that we don't question it. A drink at the end of a hard day relieves stress. A pint at the airport helps you relax and ease into the holiday. It just makes sense. Well, does it? Again, it's a bit of a con.

Denise Graham, a counsellor in Cleveland Clinic's Alcohol and Drug Recovery Centre, points out that while drinking that glass of wine or whisky on the rocks can, indeed, 'provide you with a bit of relaxation, it is only a short-term fix that can lead to long-term problems. If you rely on alcohol for numbing the stress, then that can actually cause significant problems down the road,'[8] Graham notes. 'You're not learning how to cope with things as they are right now. You're not learning to cope in healthy ways. Instead, if someone increases their dependence on alcohol to deal with stress, that leads to the exacerbation of depression and anxiety.'

As well as the mental aspect, it has physical impacts that make it more difficult to deal with stress. 'It's quite disruptive to your sleep cycle and can cause you to be more fatigued,' says liver specialist Dr Christina Lindenmeyer, MD, also from Cleveland Clinic. That's because alcohol reduces the amount of time you spend in the REM (rapid eye movement) stage of sleep. 'You may fall asleep faster and you may sleep more deeply for the first few hours, but you're not reaching the truly restorative stage of the sleep cycle – the REM stage. As a result, the next day you are likely to be drowsier and feel less rested.'

Now that I no longer drink, I can see that drinking was doing the opposite of helping me to relieve my stress and anxiety. I was just using it to numb my mind and black out my problems. With every Friday night blowout, I was pouring more and more stress and anxiety into my life.

Whatever problems or stress I was facing at work, they were, unsurprisingly, not cured by the eight or nine pints I would throw down my neck on a Friday night. Instead, when the booze wore off, those problems would still be there, and I would have added to them. Maybe a lost wallet or phone. An unwise comment to the boss. An argument with my wife as I bounced in late with some half-arsed excuse. Whatever it was, I would wake up with more problems than I began with, and I would have to face them knackered because I hadn't slept properly, with the feeling of impending doom and dread brought on from a hangover.

3. *It makes me happy – I enjoy it.*

I would regularly tell myself and others that I drank because it made me happy. And I think that, perhaps in the very early days, and before it got too out of hand, this might have been true. But when it got to the stage of being on a cycle of failed moderation attempts, even at the peak of my denial I knew this had stopped being fun. The link between depression and alcohol consumption is undisputed. Alcohol is a depressant; it alters the delicate balance of chemicals in your brain. Drinking heavily and regularly is associated with depression.[9]

So why was I so sure it was making me happy? Yet again, it's the insidious nature of alcohol that cons us into feeling like this. If you are feeling low, alcohol can *temporarily* lift your mood by giving you an initial dopamine kick. The first few drinks make our body produce extra dopamine, which travels to the parts of the brain known as reward centres – the bits that make us feel good and make us want to do more of whatever we're doing.

So, our first couple of drinks are likely to make us feel good. They're also likely to make us want to drink more. Then, the dopamine high will eventually be pushed aside by the less pleasant effects of alcohol: confusion, clumsiness, nausea and being more likely to put ourselves at risk of harm. Even in the very short term, alcohol can make us feel depressed – the hangover after a heavy drinking session can be a thoroughly miserable experience.

In the longer term, the body becomes used to the short-term dopamine boosts it's getting from alcohol and makes less dopamine naturally to compensate. When we get to this stage, it means that without alcohol, we feel depressed. Then when we have a drink, the dopamine kick it gives us brings us back to normal levels. You will start to feel (because, chemically at least, it is true) that you need alcohol to feel happy. But it was alcohol that caused the issue to start with.

The longer this cycle continues, the more dopamine-deficient we become and the lower our mood becomes on a more consistent basis. For some, this leads to clinical depression, and it can be a trigger for suicidal thoughts. There is a strong association between regular heavy drinking and suicidal attempts and thoughts (such as calculating the insurance pay-out your family would get if you stepped out in front of a bus) and death from suicide.[10]

The good news is that reducing or stopping drinking can improve your mood and mental health. In fact, people who are depressed often find that cutting out alcohol entirely for just four weeks makes a clear difference in how they feel. The Royal College of Psychiatrists recommends that, for people who need help with both their drinking and depression, it's usually best to tackle the alcohol first and then deal with the depression afterwards if it hasn't lifted after a few weeks.

This was certainly my experience. I never thought of myself as being depressed at the time, but now that I no longer drink, I can see that drinking was doing the opposite of making me happy. It's difficult to describe without sounding like a tosser, but there is a lightness to how I feel now. A sunniness to my disposition. There is definitely less anxiety and no more feelings of impending doom of the kind that seemed to haunt me in my drinking days.

So the 'rock bottom convincers' had done their convincing, and I had debunked all my old excuses and reasons to drink. I was now thoroughly on board with the idea that drinking was not doing me any favours. Smashing. Let's stop – why didn't I think of that already?

Well, like I said, I had tried to stop countless times in the past, but with limited success. I even managed to do dry Jan a couple of times. I would tell anyone who would listen about this in great detail, and regularly cite it as evidence of my not having a drinking problem. But I did this through sheer will-power, and by the end I was always mentally exhausted, gasping for a drink, and ready to continue in my quest for moderation.

What was so different this time? What was the secret? Let's move on over to Part 2, where I share the tools I used to get me through the first six months, and the science behind why they work.

PART 2

Going Sober

15 Tools for the First 6 Months

Remember at the start of the book, 22nd December 2021, when I was giving you the big chat: *And so you find me at the start of a new chapter. I have decided that the quest for moderation must end here. Patrick Ruddy, at the age of thirty-five, after a distinguished twenty-year-long drinking career, will end it, here and now.*

Well, it was easy to feel like that the morning after a blowout when it was painfully clear that drinking was making me physically sick, and I was neck deep in the consequences. But typically, after a few days, when the immediate hangover had subsided, a little drinking voice in my head would start planting seeds of doubt, saying, 'It wasn't all that bad' or 'Granted, you shouldn't have drunk three bottles, but if you had stopped at one it would have been okay. Lesson learned, and you won't do that again.'

With a fresh batch of fully charged willpower, and my body still feeling battered by the latest assault, the old CEO in my head would tell the drinking voice to be quiet. He could bat the drinking voice away with ease, and even put it on mute for a while. Side note – I realise that referring to the voice of the CEO and the drinking voice in the third person might seem odd. But this is genuinely what it was like for me when I was giving up. The drinking voice was alcohol's biggest fan and top sales rep. The voice of my CEO would provide reason and logic; he had my best interests at heart, like the little angel on your shoulder in a cartoon. Then there was me, in the middle, wrestling between the two and deciding whom to listen to. I would never have admitted to anyone at the time that I had these multiple voices in my head, and I thought this was unique to me, but I would go on to discover that it is not unusual for people with a form of addiction.

By the middle of the week, when I was starting to feel 'fine' (I now realise that what I thought was fine was actually just 'slightly less ill') and the battery on my willpower was starting to fade, the drinking voice would start getting louder.

'That was a rough start to the week, but you've almost made it through. A nice glass of wine with dinner tonight to celebrate getting over the hump would take the edge off.' It would be harder to ignore, but the CEO could still just about shout over it with some logic and reason.

By Friday lunchtime the drinking voice would be throwing his weight about, having found his rhythm. Now impossible to drown out, he would start making more and more sense. 'Okay, Paddy, you've made it through the week without a drink. Good for you. You've proved your point. But it's been a tough one. You've worked hard. A cold pint of lager on the way home would be nice. Just one. You've earned it.' The CEO would be staring down at his feet, sheepishly muttering that maybe he had a point.

By 4pm on a Friday the CEO would have knocked off

early for the weekend, and the drinking voice would have found himself a megaphone and a marching band. 'A PINT WOULD BE NICE. A PINT WOULD BE NICE. A PINT WOULD BE NICE. A PINT WOULD BE NICE.'

When it got to 5pm and a colleague asked if anyone wanted to go for a quick pint after work, I wouldn't even need to think. There would only be one voice to listen to. I would repeat what I had been hearing in my head for the past hour. 'Yeah, actually, now you mention it, a pint would be nice.' And so that attempt at sobriety would come to an end, one week in.

The run at sobriety which started on the 22nd December could just as easily have ended up like all the others. While I can't put it all down to one thing, I found that a key difference came from shifting my approach to focusing on what I was gaining, rather than what I was giving up.

What do I mean by that? Well, the old me would have thought, 'A pint would be nice, but I can't go; I've given up drinking. Poor me, missing out on a Friday night out when everyone else is getting on it.'

This time I would think about the things I was gaining by not going for a drink. 'I want to get home in time to see my family rather than letting them down by getting home late, drunk.' Or, 'I want to get up early tomorrow and go to the gym, rather than be hungover and spend the morning in bed feeling anxious and depressed.'

The immediate action was the same – I wasn't going for a pint – but the subtle shift in the story I told myself made it seem like the easy choice rather than a difficult one requiring restraint and willpower.

For the first couple of weeks, not letting my family down and making it to the gym at the weekend were my go-to positives. I would think of those as my reasons for choosing not to drink. The longer I stayed sober, the more I realised that the list of positives was growing. I will use Part 3 of the book to share more of these positives and how much better my life is without booze, but for now you should try and think of your equivalent. What are your go-to positives? Maybe it's the money you normally spend on a night out being used for something else? Maybe it's not the gym but meeting your friend for a coffee the next morning? Or going for a walk? Maybe it's not making it home to see your family that night, but finally getting round to reading that book?

While the mindset shift is key, it may not be enough on its own. So below are fifteen of the more hands-on practical things that I used in the first six months. We're all different, so perhaps not all of them will work for you, but some may, and the ones that do could make the difference:

1. *I read all the quit lit*

This was a game changer for me. Previously I might have read the odd memoir by someone with a drinking problem, but this was often an attempt to make myself feel like I had less of a problem in comparison. Or I might have skimmed some articles on addiction after wandering down a rabbit hole during a guilt-induced 'Am I an alcoholic?' Google session. This time I decided to treat my sobriety like I was planning a project and give it the attention it deserved. I knew I would give myself the best chance of success by being armed with the insights of others who had gone before me.

It turns out there is an entire genre of books dedicated to this and I had a huge appetite for them all. It is often referred to as 'quit lit', which made it sound a bit girly to me, but I found the books to be gender neutral. When we're battling addiction, the problems we face are remarkably consistent (booze is definitely an equal-pay type of boss that spreads the misery consistently and evenly, regardless of gender). When I was getting close to finishing one, I would order the next. Every night for the first two to three months I had my head in one of these books. I didn't have the confidence and was too ashamed to speak to someone about what I was going through, but I felt like by reading about someone else who was going through it, I wasn't doing it alone.

Below are my top picks:

- *The Unexpected Joy of Being Sober* by Catherine Gray
- *This Naked Mind* by Annie Grace
- *The Sober Diaries* by Claire Pooley
- *The Easy Way to Control Alcohol* by Allen Carr
- *Dry* by Augusten Burroughs
- *Sober Curious* by Ruby Warrington
- *Glorious Rock Bottom* by Bryony Gordon
- *We Are the Luckiest* by Laura McKowen

I fully connected with *The Unexpected Joy of Being Sober*. At times I felt like the author was writing about me. I found the science and psychology of *This Naked Mind* fascinating. I regularly re-read both of these books when I feel like I'm questioning my decision to stop drinking or feel like I'm having a wobble.

2. I started to keep a journal

I used to violently cringe when adults said they did this. How self-indulgent. Keep a journal? Who do you think you are, Adrian Mole? Grow up. But as I worked my way through the quit lit, I found that the writers I most related to all suggested it was a key part of them getting and staying sober.

It might not be for everyone, but having done it, I found that there was something about having to write down my thoughts that helped me to understand them more clearly. Some people like to talk about their problems, and if that's you, there are so many groups that will help. But at the start I wasn't ready to talk about what I was going through. I was just getting comfortable being honest with myself, and so writing it in a journal, a la Adrian Mole, was a way for me to 'share' without embarrassment or fear of judgement.

There are numerous studies extolling the benefits of journaling on mental health, especially when it comes to managing anxiety, reducing stress and coping with depression.[11] There are even studies which show it can reduce your blood pressure and boost your immune system,[12] so it's worth giving it a go. I felt like a bit of a wanker when I first started writing, but I stuck with it and after the first couple of pages, it all came pouring out. For someone who would rather die than talk about 'my feelings', this was a way for me to get them out, rather than drown them in booze.

At first it was a very stilted and factual account of my day. Here is my first day giving up the booze. This is what I did. This is how I feel. Then it started to become a compare and contrast exercise: here is my day now, versus what my day would have been like if I was still drinking (I've shared some of these entries in Part 3, in the Split Screening chapter). Then it turned into my thoughts on how much better my life was now that I wasn't drinking, which snowballed into this book.

3. I used *Addictive Voice Recognition*

I first learned about Addictive Voice Recognition in Catherine Gray's book *The Unexpected Joy of Being Sober*. The technique involves separating out the voice in your head that is suggesting you drink, and assigning it a separate identity. You can then observe and critique that voice in a passive manner, rather than having to act upon its suggestion. So instead of hearing, 'I want a drink,' you can reframe it as 'I don't want to drink – it (the drinking voice) wants to drink.' Once you've realised that you can dismiss and ignore the drinking voice, and that a thought can't make you drink, maintaining sobriety can become much easier.

Having lived with the CEO voice and the drinking voice battling for attention in my head, it felt like I had found a soul mate when I read that Catherine had a 'disembodied voice in her head, constantly chat-chat-chatting about why it would be a great idea to have a drink right now'.

The idea of using the voices to our advantage is an approach that has been around since the 80s. Jack Trimpey,[13] a recovered alcoholic who works in the field of treatment of alcoholism and other drug addictions, pioneered the Addictive Voice Recognition Technique. If you are keen to understand the science behind it, the full book is referenced in the end notes.

People who use this technique will often give their drinking voice a name. For example, The Beast, The Wolf, The Wine Witch, etc. Catherine started out calling her drinking voice Gollum, before eventually landing on Voldemort. I toyed with the idea of giving mine an equally villainous name, but this didn't really fit the way my own drinking voice operated.

He – it was definitely a he – wasn't such an obvious villain. He was suave, silver tongued and a master of marketing. He could pull together a convincing pitch for boozing in almost any situation, and at a moment's notice. I realised he was Roger Sterling – Don Draper's old boss in *Mad Men*. Roger looked immaculate in his tailored suits, downing endless glasses of straight vodka like it was water while never getting visibly drunk and flawlessly delivering lines like, 'We drink because it's good. Because it feels better than unbuttoning your collar. Because we deserve it. We drink because it's what men do.' I would often remind myself that Roger is a fictional character, and that even in a series which seriously glamorises drinking, he had two heart attacks in the same year as a result of his lifestyle choices.

During the first few weeks of any sober run, Roger was loud. He would go toe to toe with my CEO, and in my previous runs at sobriety would often win by the first Friday night. But by the time I got to the three-month mark, Roger's powers were seriously waning. By listening to him less and less, his voice got smaller and less influential. He could still have his moments and muster up some serious volume to deliver a good sales pitch, but these were usually when a specific situation brought me back to a rose-tinted drinking memory. Now I had the power to realise he was just a voice.

A voice couldn't make me drink and didn't hold any power over me. I could choose to listen to the CEO, and choose not to drink.

4. I cut myself some slack

When you stop drinking, you stop applying a numbing agent to your mind. You will inevitably feel things more, and have more emotions. Moreover, when you are not dealing with a monumental hangover, or firefighting the chaos caused by a two-day bender, you tend to have a bit more headspace and time to think.

Sometimes that headspace is good, and it gives you time to appreciate all the positives in your new booze-free life, but sometimes it creates space for long-banished memories of things you've said or done in the past to come bubbling to the surface.

For the first month I tended to flip flop between the two. On the good days I would feel amazingly proud for staying off the booze, and bask in the glow of the better person I thought I had become as a result. The next day I would be hit by the realisation that this meant for a large chunk of my life, I hadn't been that better person.

On previous runs at sobriety, I would have let this get me down. I would have revisited the past and dug around in it, feeling guilty and ashamed about the times I let people down or caused pain. This would have led to a pity party, which would have involved a well-stocked bar. This time, I cut myself some slack. My advice is to do the same. You don't need to deal with everything as it comes up. Right now, all you need to do is not drink. For the first 30, 60, 90, even 180 days, that's enough. You can fix deeper issues later on.

5. *I hit the gym a lot*

I had always wanted to be someone who went to the gym regularly, but when I drank I could never get it to stick. I used to log on to my gym app on a Monday night, after a heavy weekend on the booze, and optimistically book classes for the upcoming Saturday that started at half six in the morning. The theory being that if I knew I had to be up at 5.45am to put myself through a class called 'Mega Intense HIIT' or 'Medieval Torture Masquerading as Body Pump', there was no way I would even think about boozing on Friday. This never worked.

I thought a bonus benefit of going sober would be that my planned gym sessions wouldn't be derailed. While this was true, I found going to the gym and exercising was one of the best things to help me deal with the overwhelming emotions and initial cravings of the first few weeks. When I dug into it further, there were so many studies and articles detailing how exercising can help you deal with the first few rough weeks of withdrawal, and then getting sobriety to stick.

Again, if you are interested in the science, I've detailed studies in the end notes,[14] but you probably don't need to read scientific studies to get this. At a core level, we all know exercising is good for us, and alcohol is bad. No shit. But having read this and then pushed myself through the first few gym sessions and first sober weeks, I began to link going to the gym with feeling good and strong, and I realised that alcohol had been making me feel bad and weak.

I wanted to keep feeling good and strong. Whenever I felt

like I wanted to drink, I would go for a walk or a run, or hit the gym.

6. *I developed a seriously sweet tooth*
And so, with regular gym sessions and exercise, my sober physique took shape, and my body began to look like one chiselled from marble, perfectly sculpted and toned. Hmm … not so much. While my appetite for exercise went through the roof, this was matched in almost linear fashion by my appetite for cheesecake, chocolate and anything with sugar.

Initially, I worried I was replacing one addiction with another, but after I read up on it, I learned that this is pretty common, with one study[15] suggesting that 40% of people who stop drinking will up their sugar intake in the days and weeks after quitting. It turns out that long-term alcohol use disrupts your body's ability to regulate your blood sugar, with many drinkers having low blood sugar. This can become especially apparent when alcohol, which has loads of sugar, gets removed from the equation.

Plus, here is what happens to your brain when you give it a sugar hit:[16]

- It activates reward pathways.
- It releases dopamine, which promotes desire for more.
- It rewires your brain to encourage greater consumption.
- It gradually desensitises you to the effects, requiring you consume more to get the same 'feel-good' response.

Sound familiar? It turns out that your brain on sugar isn't so different to your brain on alcohol, or any other addictive substance. It triggers dopamine receptors, and over time you can become desensitised, while experiencing strong cravings. For me, this sorted itself out and the sugar cravings passed as I picked up more and more healthy habits through not drinking. If it doesn't pass for you in the first six months, don't stress. We can fix it later. Eat what you want right now. Just don't drink.

7. *I got the basics right*
Eat. Sleep. Regular breaks.

When I was drinking, I would regularly skip meals. I would go out for drinks straight after work, miss dinner and get my calories from booze instead. I would stay up late, chasing the next bar or party, and get little sleep. I would rely on coffee and diet coke to get through the next day, and I rarely drank water. I would miss or put off medical appointments as I was too hungover to deal with them.

In short, I wasn't getting the basics right. There are fundamental things humans need if we want to be okay. We understand this when it comes to how we treat babies and children. Regular feeds, health visits, fresh air and exercise during the day, keeping a routine with a consistent bath and bedtime, cuddles and soothing when required. As we get older, life gets busy and things get in the way. We push through, prioritise other things, and stop getting the basics right.

For most people, not getting the basics right might result in them getting a bit cranky or tired. 'Oh, I snapped at Bob there for no reason. I think I'm a bit hangry; best grab a snack and go say sorry.' For people giving up drinking, who are already pretty fragile, not getting the basics right can result in making us more likely to reach for a drink. 'Oh, I snapped at Bob there for no reason. I feel awful about it. These cravings are making me so short-tempered. I don't know if I can keep this up; maybe I'm better off drinking.'

Eat

The 'empty feeling' and cravings when first giving up are often just hunger for food or thirst for water. To avoid getting the cravings mixed up, I avoided letting myself get to the point of being overly hungry or thirsty. I ate three meals a day, with regular snacks (admittedly cheesecakes and chocolate for the first few months, but eventually I moved on to cashew nuts and healthier alternatives), and I kept a water bottle by my side and made sure I drank from it throughout the day. I know this seems simple, but it really did make a massive difference.

Sleep

This also plays a massive role in recovery. When we don't get enough sleep at night, we don't give our bodies a chance to recover properly. It also has a knock-on effect on how the next day will go. You might drag yourself out of bed, bleary-eyed, and just about make it through the day, but you're more likely to rely on sugary foods or caffeinated drinks to get there. It's unlikely you are feeling good about yourself, and you'll be exhausted and vulnerable.

Get a good night's sleep, on the other hand, and you are more likely to wake up feeling bright eyed and bushy tailed, ready to handle what the day throws at you, without feeling you need a drink to help you through it. There's an interesting article[17] I've referenced which goes into this in detail, but, much like exercise, you probably don't need to read scientific studies to get this. At a core level, we all know getting enough sleep and eating well is good for us.

Just like a baby, the key for me to get a good night's sleep was following a routine. You'll find what works for you, but I followed (and still follow) this method below and it worked wonders:

- I went for a really hot bath one hour before bed.
- I stopped looking at my phone a few hours before bed.
- I made 3.30pm the cut-off point for coffee.
- I went to bed at the same time every night.
- I set my alarm to wake up at the same time every morning.

Again, I know this seems simple, but it worked. The routine is so ingrained now that I naturally wake up just before the alarm. (I would have wanted to punch someone who said this back when I was quitting. Sorry, but it's true. And remember I'm trying to help!)

Regular breaks

Similar to eating before I got too hungry or having a drink of water before I got to the spitting feathers stage, I found that giving myself regular short breaks throughout the day, rather than pushing through to the point of exhaustion, made a big difference in helping me stick with not drinking.

Previously I would spend my working week in back-to-back meetings, working longer and longer hours in a bid to meet multiple, often self-imposed deadlines. 'I want to get this done by the end of the day.' 'I need to get this cleared by the end of the week.' By the end of the working day I would be wired, and feel like I *needed* a drink to unwind. By the end of the working week I would be exhausted and burnt out, and I'd feel like I *needed* a drink to blow off some steam.

This time, when I started to feel like I was getting overwhelmed, or needed a break, I took one. I broke up my day by going for a walk in the morning before I started work and again at lunchtime. I stopped skipping lunch or eating it at my desk. If I was panicky or stressed during the day, I stepped away from my desk and took some deep breaths (flick to the Practical Self-help chapter for some more details on breathing). I felt better and less like I needed a drink at the end of the day.

If you read this and think, 'Yeah, that's fine for him, but I'm too busy, I can't take a break in my job, there's too much to do,' then you are just like I was. It is so easy to convince yourself you do not have the time to take breaks, but there are multiple studies[18] that show this is counterproductive. A few minutes away from your desk and a decent lunchtime have been shown to have a positive relationship with wellbeing and productivity. By taking regular breaks you can boost your performance and get more done. Plus, you're less likely to want to dive into a sea of booze at the end of the week. Win-win.

8. *I prioritised my sobriety*

I tried to find another way to say 'I prioritised my sobriety' without sounding pretentious, but couldn't. I toyed with 'put sober first' but that sounded like a political slogan from a right-wing campaign hat. So here we are, with me sounding like a wellness guru instead, forgive me.

In the early days, the most important thing was just not to drink. We can master everything else later, but right now, in the first 30, 60, 90 days, you are mastering a new skill: choosing not to drink.

You've probably had decades of practice mastering the old skill of choosing to drink, so much so that drinking feels natural and muscle memory kicks in when you are in certain places or social situations. In these situations, you automatically say yes to a round or reach for a glass. For me, the best thing I did was just avoid those situations initially. Previously, I would have gone to the after-work drinks and tried to drink diet coke, but then crumbled when gently pressed on why I wasn't having a pint.

This time, rather than put myself in that situation and test my resolve, I simply avoided it. If you don't feel confident yet about telling people you are giving up booze (like me) and don't feel comfortable going to the pub (like me), just lie (like I did). A lot of the time I would just say, 'Sorry I can't make it. I've got plans.' If I felt they warranted a bigger explanation, I would add something about picking up kids or other family commitments. I knew that my 'choosing not to drink' muscle was still developing, and until it was bigger, I didn't want to put it up against my well-oiled Ivan Drago in *Rocky 4* 'choose to drink' muscle. Especially not on its home turf.

There's an old saying popular in recovery circles: 'If you hang out at the barbers long enough, sooner or later you're going to get a haircut.' Meaning that if you hang around a pub long enough, you're going to take a drink. So, in the early days, while we're still building up our new 'choosing not to drink' muscle, take away the temptation. I'm not saying become a hermit and close yourself off from the world – that the last thing you should do – but just give the pub a miss for a bit.

It wasn't until I got to the three-month mark that I truly felt comfortable putting myself in the after-work drinks situation again, but by then my perception of fun had changed, and I realised that even though I could easily be in the pub after work, it was actually pretty rubbish. If something seems fun only when you are a bit drunk, it's probably worth thinking through how fun it is at all.

9. I got rid of the booze

I've had multiple runs at sobriety come crashing down because of readily available booze I kept in the house. Looking back, I think this was unconscious self-sabotage. I did the same thing when I gave up smoking the first few times. I would keep a 'forgotten about' twenty deck in an old suit jacket. Said suit jacket would get urgently pulled out of the wardrobe after a few drinks when the willpower crumpled. When it came to drinking, I would follow the same pattern of behaviour. I would be loath to throw out perfectly good booze, and instead keep bottles of spirits and wine at the back of the cupboard (you know, in case I wanted to give them as gifts or had guests). When I hit the difficult second or third week, knowing it was there made it impossible to resist.

Professor Simone Pettigrew, an academic who focuses her research on how to encourage people to adopt healthy lifestyle behaviours, such as quitting smoking and drinking less alcohol, sums it up nicely.[19] 'Not keeping alcohol in the house is an obvious and effective method to kerb drinking behaviour.' Instead of keeping a supply of booze nearby, make your house a booze-free zone. If you have to go to the shops to get some, the effort required means you'll be less likely to act on an impulse. As Pettigrew says, 'We're a very reactive species so if something is in front of us, we will consume it.'

10. I treated myself

Research from Alcohol Change UK[20] shows the *average* drinker in the UK spends around £62,899 on alcohol over the course of a lifetime.

When I read this I felt sick. Sixty-plus grand on what? And I definitely wasn't an average drinker by any stretch. Also, that sixty grand only counts the amount spent on the actual booze itself. It doesn't factor in all the unplanned cash that gets flung about on a night out. The taxis needed after staying at the pub and missing my train. The maximum withdrawals at the casino. Cigarettes that became essential after the third pint. Then you've got the next day and money spent helping deal with the hangover. The bacon rolls, painkillers, coffee. Then there's the collateral damage from a big night out. Replacing a wallet, phone or jacket, or getting a new set of keys cut. Mind-blowing.

As Dr Richard Piper, Chief Executive of Alcohol Change UK, asks, 'The average UK adult spends a huge amount of money on alcohol in a lifetime. But what do we really get back from all that expenditure?'

Some rough math told me I could easily be 100 grand up if I managed to stay sober. Thinking of it like this made splashing some cash on treats to reward myself for keeping it going seem more like an investment, rather than being frivolous. If you can afford it, you should do the same, especially during the first few months when the going is particularly tough. Celebrate the wins and reward yourself. Whatever a reward feels like for you, you've earned it. And in the long run, it's paying for itself.

11. I bought nice stuff

Closely linked to treating myself – and I realise this makes me sound very shallow and materialistic – buying nice stuff genuinely made me feel good, and it helped. When I say buying nice stuff, I mean buying things on the basis I would keep and look after them. When I was drinking, I had to treat almost everything I had as disposable.

Wallets, watches, sunglasses, clothes. I bought them cheap so I wouldn't be upset when they inevitably got lost or damaged as a result of my reckless behaviour. The screen on my iPhone was constantly smashed, but it made no sense replacing it when I knew that, like me, it would just end up getting smashed again next week.

Now I knew I was going to be sober and could trust myself to take care of my possessions, I invested in quality. I got a new phone with a functioning screen. A decent wallet. I bought clothes that were well made and I felt confident in. I don't have any science to prove this works; I can just tell you it worked for me. Having nice things that I was able to look after went hand in hand with looking after myself.

12. *I took loads of baths*

In the first few weeks of sobriety, I would sometimes feel achy and heavy at the end of the day, and I found that a nice long bath helped soothe those aches away. Plus, the bathroom can be one of the few places where no one will bother you, so you can have some time to think. The steam inhalation helps open your lungs, increasing oxygen levels, which can help calm and relax you. I went heavy on the muscle soak and came out smelling lovely and feeling much better. Plus, it set me up for a good night's sleep.

13. *I got right into gardening and DIY*

I felt I was most vulnerable to thinking about drinking when I was sitting around not doing anything, particularly in the first thirty days, but there were only so many times I could realistically go for a run or go to the gym in one day (no wonder I was feeling achy, actually). I had to find something else to keep me moving. Gardening and DIY were it for me. Some people swear by cleaning, others try knitting; go for whatever keeps you busy and your mind focused on something else.

14. *I used replacements*

I would have struggled to get through the first few months on diet coke and coffee alone, so I found myself some non-alcoholic drinks that felt grownup and a bit of a treat to enjoy. If you have certain rituals that revolve around alcohol, switch them out. If you usually stay in with a bottle of wine on a Friday night, stay in with a takeaway instead. If you usually listen to music with a beer, keep the music but try it with a non-alcoholic drink instead.

Some people swear by non-alcoholic versions of beer and wine, but others find them too close to the real thing. There's no right or wrong answer, just whatever works for you. When I was at home, I would have tonic in a big fish-bowl glass with lots of ice and cucumber and a Clean G (alcohol-free gin). It tasted good and was easy to put together, but still felt like something different and a bit of a reward. When I was out, I really enjoyed Guinness Zero. A lot of places started putting that on draught, so it was nice to have a pint and fit in, even though it didn't have alcohol. Failing that, an Erdinger AF or Lucky Saint were my go-to for a bottle of beer.

15. I took off the rose-tinted drinking glasses

Whenever I was in a situation where I felt I was missing out by not drinking, I forced myself to follow through beyond the memory of the first drink. For example, a few weeks in I was at a work event I couldn't get out of, and there was complimentary champagne on arrival. I had a severe case of envy at everyone else wolfing it down. I thought, 'I wish I could have just one of those to take the edge off.'

I forced myself to say, 'Okay, let's follow that through.' I can't moderate, so one of those leads to another, which leads to pints, then gin and tonics, and then me sat at dinner smashed, making an arse of myself in front of my boss. It then leads to me waking up my wife and kids when I fall through the front door at two in the morning. It carries on into the next day and leads to me sleeping in and coming in late to work, with the fear. Struggling through the day avoiding eye contact with everyone, dreading the 'enjoy yourself last night' wink-wink nudge-nudge, or, even worse, the 'I've got a bone to pick with you' chats. The day would finish with me getting home, rushing through bedtime with the kids, then collapsing on the sofa, exhausted and depressed and using the last hour before bed to deal with the fallout with my wife.

Or:

I don't drink the champagne. I ride out the feeling of being left out for a few minutes. It passes. I watch as someone else makes an arse of themselves at dinner. I roll in to work on time, head held high, hangover free. I make it to the gym at lunchtime. I go home to a happy house, fully engage with the kids, spend quality time with them and enjoy the evening with my wife.

By putting it like that, and following through beyond the first drink, it made it easy for me to pass on the champagne.

The bonus silver bullet

There isn't one. And be wary of anyone preaching otherwise. The fifteen tools above are the things that worked for me and got me through, but we are all different. Some of these things will work for you, and others won't. The key thing is to find what does work for you and do it regularly, before the urge to drink gets out of hand.

If baths are your thing, don't wait until you're gasping for a wine before deciding to run one. If exercise works for you, do it regularly, not just when your cravings kick in. It's like putting petrol in your car; better to keep on top of it and fill up before you set off, rather than desperately searching for a station when the warning light is flashing and you're running on fumes.

Socialising Sober

While you may be coming round to the benefits of cutting back or ditching the booze, most of the time this will put you in a minority. As humans, we like to run with the pack, follow the crowd. Weddings, funerals, work events, birthday parties, dinners, nights out, most social events, especially in the UK – they will almost always centre on 'having a few drinks'.

Deep down everyone might know that booze isn't doing them any good, but as a society we still view it as the gateway to a good time, so we cajole and prod each other into it. 'You're not drinking, don't be boring!' 'Ah come on, loosen up, you can have one.' Sound familiar? For someone who was used to being one of the party people, who was the self-appointed life and soul, I found this particularly challenging. Indeed, so many of my runs at sobriety ended because someone called me boring for not drinking, or jokingly said I was lightweight or couldn't handle it. Childish, I know, but true.

Claire Dooley sums it up nicely in *The Sober Diaries*,[21] when she speaks about navigating her first sober Christmas party season:

'It's the party season. And parties are often the trickiest thing about getting sober. I think it's especially hard for us because we, my friends, used to be the party people! That's what got many of us into this mess in the first place, isn't it? We were the dancers, the raconteurs, the life and soul of the party, the last to leave.

'But we didn't do it alone, did we? We always had our friend – the booze – with us. Until our best buddy turned on us and made our lives hell. Believe me, parties can and will be fun again. However, it's probably the area that takes the longest to deal with'

Claire provides a 'Party Season Survival Guide' in her book, which I found invaluable for navigating parties in the first six months. Here is mine.

First Sober Party Season Survival Guide

1. You don't have to stay too long

Almost every night out I went on turned into a marathon drinking session. A few drinks would easily turn into eight hours bar hopping. A work event would lead to a nightclub or an after party. Even a diner party or gathering at someone's house would run to six hours. I could do that because I was hyped up / blacked out on booze. The alcohol numbed my brain to the point that spending long spells in the same company repeating ourselves loudly seemed fun. Sober, it won't. So don't feel like you need to stay.

Master the Irish Exit (leaving without announcing it or saying goodbye). No one will notice; they will all be drunk and you will save yourself the hassle of all the 'Ah just stay for a bit longer – have another drink' drama. Just slip out and give yourself a high five. Also, remember the hassle of getting home after a night out? Squinting at your phone with one eye to see the train times? Trying to find a taxi that would take you? Not anymore my friend. Now you can just hop in the car and cruise on home.

2. You don't even have to go

If you are seriously worried about an event, or think there is a good chance you will go and struggle to stay sober … just don't go. Sorry to refer back to the pretentious 'prioritise your sobriety' chat, but, seriously, put sobriety first. What are you going to miss, really? Another rubber chicken dinner at a work do? Another session down the pub with your mates? The first round of social events sober is the hardest part, and there will be plenty more when you are feeling stronger and more able to handle them. You don't even have to make a big deal about it. Just tell a white lie. 'Sorry, I've already got something on that night.' (A gym session and then a hot bath.) Think about all the parties you've been to where someone wasn't there. 'Where's John?' 'Oh, he's not coming.' What was your reaction? It wasn't a big deal. You shrugged and tore back into the booze. That's what everyone else will do.

3. Break it up

Even if you want to go and stay at a party until the wee small hours, it doesn't mean you need to be 'on' the whole time. Without booze, even the best parties may require you to take a break. Most other events that run for more than a couple of hours factor in breaks. Presentations, seminars, training, even entertaining things like the theatre all have intervals factored in, as they know that, after an hour or so, we switch off or need to stretch our legs and move around. Put social events into the same bucket. Give yourself a break whenever you feel like it. If it's a big venue, explore a section that isn't part of your function. Go outside for a bit of fresh air or a quick walk. Chill out in reception for five minutes. At first, I was self-conscious about doing this and used to pretend to be taking a call. Or that I was going to the bathroom. But eventually you realize no one cares if you disappear for a break now and again, and you stop making excuses.

4. *Fake it till you make it*

I can go to parties now and say I don't drink and it's no big deal. I don't feel awkward or apologetic about it. I say no thanks to the alcoholic drink offered and ask for something else. The same way a vegetarian might say no thanks to the beef and order the pasta. For the first few parties (actually, for the first eight months), this was definitely not the case. It is a big change, and you might feel under pressure to drink. You might feel awkward about not drinking and feel the need to explain. We will go on to cover telling people later, but for the first few parties the last thing you need is having to talk about it unnecessarily. Why put yourself through it? Just hang on to something that looks like it could be an alcoholic drink (most people assume anything in a tall glass is a vodka or gin mix) and it means that when you're asked if you want a drink, you can just say, 'I'm good for now, thanks.' No drama. No one will notice. They will all be fixated on their own drink, and whether they have enough.

5. Channel your inner David Attenborough

Once it gets to the later stages of the evening, the more enthusiastic drinkers will be on another level to you. It's never kind to be smug, especially as it's likely we've done something worse, but taking time just to observe these people can remind you of what you want to avoid. The inner David Attenborough monologue style is optional, but it always makes me laugh.

'And here we see Simon from Accounts. Normally a rather timid creature in the office, occasionally spotted popping his head up from his monitor in a meerkat-like fashion, it is extremely rare to see him strut around a venue with such bravado and confidence. Notice how he invades the personal space of the others in the group as he sways on his feet, and sprays his saliva far and wide as he makes inappropriate jokes in a booming voice.

'And as we move towards the bar area, we see signs of aggression and frustration from Colin, who has chosen this moment, eight pints deep and sweating profusely, to share his dissatisfaction at the size of this year's bonus pot with the chief executive. As he makes his case for increased remuneration and promotion, one can only assume the tie wrapped around his head karate-kid-style is doing him no favours.'

6. Forgive and forget

When you are at a drink-centred social event (all of them), and especially if you make it to the later stages, there's a chance you will be reminded of your previous drunken behaviour. There were many times I was observing others and would be struck by a flashback from when I was in a similar state, or worse. I would physically cringe as I remembered these occasions. I would feel guilty/ashamed/mortified depending on the memory. When this happens, cut yourself some slack. Reflect on that memory of being 'the drinking you'. Forgive yourself, move on and focus on how much better you feel as the non-drinking you.

7. Choose which voice you listen to

If the drinking voice we talked about earlier resonated with you, then the first party season is when your Roger Sterling equivalent will be out in force. A few of the classic lines that were delivered with panache by my old pal Roger included:

'Look how much fun everyone is having. Literally every single person here is drinking. Even Simon from Accounts is on it! You should have one, just to fit in. You could make it last for ages. One of those welcome drinks wouldn't even count, really.'

'You haven't told anyone you've got a problem, or that you've quit. No one knows. You could easily just have a few drinks, enjoy yourself, and then go back to be being good again starting from tomorrow.'

'This is so boring. And it's hard work. Are you just going to stay here watching everyone else get drunk and have a good time? How much easier would this be if you could join them?'

'Actually, maybe it's you. Maybe you are the one that's boring and hard work without a drink. Everyone is probably thinking that. Look at big boring Paddy over there not drinking. You're fooling no one with the tonic water in a tall glass. Everyone knows. Everyone is looking at you and thinks you're a weirdo. Big boring weirdo Paddy drinking tonic water.

What a loser.'

'Come on, Paddy, it's a party. You can have just one drink. Just one to be sociable. What harm will one do?'

While Rodger would be at full volume in a social setting, especially upon arrival when I was feeling anxious and would typically rely on the booze as a crutch, I now had the tools to realise he was just a voice. Remember what we talked about earlier – a voice can't make you drink. It doesn't hold any power over you. You can choose to listen to your good voice, and choose not to drink.

When your Roger equivalent is romanticising the good old times when you could tuck into the booze, remember to follow through beyond the memory of the first drink. To take off the rose-tinted drinking glasses. If you could just have one or two, you wouldn't be reading this.

If you find yourself listening to your inner Roger too much, think about taking a break (point 3) or just making an Irish Exit (point 1). You won't regret it.

8. *Focus on the next morning*

If I really want to stay at a social event and am finding it tough not to drink, I visualise the next morning. There's a saying I heard somewhere that resonated with me: 'When we drink, we just steal happiness from the next day.'

Think about how bad your hangover used to be after a party. About the wasted day in bed with a sore head and the feelings of anxiety and despair. All the regrets as you piece together your night.

Now picture the mornings you have when you don't drink. When you wake up feeling great. While everyone else here is still in bed groaning, you will have been to the gym and had a steam and sauna. Or been out at the park or done something productive or that you enjoy. That's your payback – that's your reward.

Telling people

There is no right or wrong approach to when, or if, you tell people you're giving up or cutting back on booze. It's completely personal. One school of thought is that the sooner and the more people you tell, the better, as this means you have people who will hold you accountable, who will know you are not drinking. If you've already told people you don't drink and why, then you don't have to go through multiple explanations or rotate through excuses about being on antibiotics or training for a marathon to explain that you don't want to get shit-faced.

While this makes complete sense to me, and in hindsight might have saved some of my earlier runs at sobriety from failing, I couldn't approach it like this. I had to go through several stages before I felt comfortable just being upfront and saying, 'No thanks, I don't drink.' It took about eight months to get there.

Why did it take me so long? Well, in a social setting, especially in the UK where socialising is drink-centred, saying no to drink inevitably leads to the question, 'Why not?' And answering that truthfully, especially when you're just figuring out the answer yourself, is hard.

It's much easier to say yes, go along with the crowd and avoid the question. It's why so many people make up excuses about driving, antibiotics and marathon training when they are trying to cut back.

I didn't think I'd be referencing Bradley Cooper (ironically of *Hangover* fame) so much in this book. It wasn't intentional and I promise I'm not some mega fan; it's just he talks a lot of sense on this topic. 'I was so concerned about what you thought of me, how I was coming across,' he said. 'I always felt like an outsider. I just lived in my head.'

That really resonated with me, and I think it resonates with a lot of people when they are giving up drinking. What will other people think if I say I don't drink? What will they say? This was of huge importance to me in the first six months. I think that because my own self-esteem and sense of worth were so low (and can be for a lot of us when we are in a place of beating ourselves up for 'failing' to moderate, 'failing' to drink normally, 'failing' to be sober), I placed an undue importance on the opinion of others.

I spent a lot of time working through why I placed such importance on this, and I share some of the research and tips that helped me get over it in a later chapter (Practical Self-help Condensed), but I now realise that our fears about what other people think of us are overblown and rarely worth getting worked up about.

Marcus Aurelius clocked on to it almost 2,000 years ago when he piped up with: 'It never ceases to amaze me: we all love ourselves more than other people but care more about their opinion than our own.'[22]

The way I think of it now is that everyone goes through life assuming they are the lead character of the film. That the scenes that play out each day are pivotal moments and plot twists that are keeping the audience glued to their screens, and that we are all watching the same movie.

In truth, we are all too busy watching our own movie to bother noticing what's going on in anyone else's. While you might be getting hours of screen time in yours, and playing the role Brad Pitt or Julia Roberts would take on, most of the time you will be playing the role of 'man walking dog in background' or 'woman hailing cab' in everyone else's.

Like I said, it took me about eight months to get to the stage of not being so hung up on what others thought about my not drinking. Here are the stages I went through to get there:

First two months
During this stage, drinking was still ingrained in my sense of self. When I was at social events, I still felt that 'the people' would expect to see Party Paddy, the leading man in the film. I felt under pressure to drink, and I dreaded facing the 'Why are you not drinking?' question. I was still ashamed, like I had failed at something, and I definitely wasn't ready to talk about it. During this stage I adopted the 'fake it till you make it' approach from point 4 above.

While this was effective, and it got me through the hardest weeks of giving up, I knew it wasn't a long-term solution. All the research and reading I had done had told me that keeping it secret wasn't the way to go, and that being open and honest would make me feel better about myself, and more likely to stay sober.

Plus, there was always someone buying a round who, with the best intentions, would ignore me saying, 'I'm good for now thanks, got one here', and get me a very real pint of

Guinness or vodka tonic. I was then left with the problem of ditching it, or switching it out with a fake. I knew one day it wouldn't take much for me to go, 'Actually, that looks rather good, and it's right in front me. One won't hurt …'

Months two to four

To avoid having drinks put in front of me, and to be marginally more honest, I started to use the excuses loads of people use when they want to go to a social event but not drink. Read that sentence back. It's the reality, but it's crazy we need to make up excuses not to drink. I said I was driving. Or that I was on antibiotics. But even these caused me issues. Sometimes I didn't actually have the car when I said I was driving, and people would ask me for a lift home. 'Err, I'm not going that way.' Or people would ask me what type of antibiotics I was on and I had to throw out a random one, only to be met with 'Amoxicillin? Ah, I've been on that. I asked the doctor about it and he said it was no problem to drink on them. Didn't do me any harm. You'll be alright, Paddy. Here, have a pint.'

Months four to eight

I then progressed to the much closer version of the truth and said I was taking a break from drinking. But I was never honest about the reason. It was always dressed up as being for health or fitness.

It didn't feel natural or good telling people this. I felt like a knob. 'My body is a temple. You fill yours up with nasty booze all you like, but not for me thanks,' was the vibe I felt I was giving off. And it just wasn't me. Plus, when you put yourself up on a pedestal and say you are not drinking as some sort of virtue, the booze hounds will inevitably make it their job to knock you off and get you back on the sauce with them.

More importantly, 'the people' didn't like the 'health and fitness' vibe. The masses watching my film didn't respond well. In my mind, I had lost the crowd. They dismissed me as a health nut. This says more about me than what anyone actually thought. When I was boozing and I met people in this boat, I would instantly switch off. Oh Christ, this one wants to talk about his marathon times. Yawn. Next.

Month eight

What did work better for me, and what got a much better reaction from 'the People', was honesty. It's easier to listen to someone saying, 'I don't drink because once I start, I don't tend to stop,' or, 'I was a liability when I was drinking and I'm trying not to be now,' than someone preaching about their health reasons for not drinking. People respond better to someone being genuine and self-deprecating. Showing vulnerability is endearing. People can get on board with that. I also tried to inject a bit of humour into it, so it wasn't a total conversation killer and people didn't feel like I was taking myself too seriously. Here's a few of the lines I used:

'There were times when I would go for a quiet pint after work on Friday in Glasgow, then wake up on Sunday afternoon in Newcastle with no idea how I got there.'

'See that bloke there, dancing on the bar with his tie around his head? Drinking me would have make him look like the sensible one.'

'I wouldn't say I had a drinking problem. I was great at

drinking. It's the stopping part I could never quite master. I had a stopping problem.'

Lines like this help show that I'm not ashamed about it and it's no big deal. People pick up on this, so they don't treat it like one either. A lot of the time they will go on to share some of the things they feel vulnerable about, and you can have a decent chat.

There will be the odd person who just doesn't let it go, who will try and make you feel small for not drinking. I've had these in response to a 'No thanks, I don't drink':

'What's the point in coming the pub if you're not drinking?'

'Oh Christ, look at Saint Paddy on the soft drinks.'

'Ah! You don't drink anymore because you can't handle it, eh? Too much of a lightweight, are we?'

'I don't trust people that don't drink.'

Each of these was delivered by someone who was, in one way or another, a complete knob. When people hit you with this chat, realise it says more about them than you. In all likelihood, they feel threatened by you not drinking, as it holds a mirror up to their own relationship with booze. It's their issue to deal with, not yours. Leave them to it.

What will people say?

So apart from the odd knob, how do most people react when you tell them you've quit drinking? Well, it varies, but for me they tended to fall into the buckets below:

They say, 'Really, what happened?'
A lot of the time people expect there to be some dramatic,

one-off explosive incident that signalled the end of your drinking days. The stereotypical 'rock bottom' moment they have seen in countless films. If that has happened to you, and you feel like sharing, great. Tell them all about the time you drove your car through a wall after pouring too much vodka on your cornflakes and had to be whisked off to rehab for the twenty-eight days that transformed your life.

If it wasn't like that for you, how much you tell them is up to you. If we were close and I wanted to share with them, I might explain about the lots of little mini rock bottoms that added up until I felt like I couldn't go on drinking if I wanted to be happy. Most of the time I will just explain that it wasn't a big one-off event, just that I gradually realised drinking was doing me more harm than good and leave it there.

They say, 'I didn't think you were that bad.'

This was the most common response among my circle of close friends. Granted, most of them were pretty heavyweight drinkers (up until I went sober myself, being able to join me on a binge was a prerequisite for being one of my close friends) and so the bar of 'that bad' was high. Even so, I think they said this partly to be reassuring and in an attempt to make me feel better, and also because I didn't fit in with their cardboard-cut-out version of what an alcoholic looks like. I was skilled at hiding the extent of my drinking and the impact it had on me from most people in my life. Over time I would share some of this with them, and the 'I didn't think you were that bad' comments would fade as they realised that, actually, I was.

They say, 'That must be tough. I'm sorry.'
Depending on how it's delivered, and who it comes from, I took this in one of two ways. From some people it was sincere, i.e., it must have been tough to give up drinking and I'm sorry you had to go through that. Or I'm sorry things got so difficult you had to give up something you enjoy.

With these people, I engaged and kept the conversation going if the setting and relationship was appropriate. I might share with them that, yeah, the first six weeks were very tough, but it got easier and easier, and by the third month not drinking was second nature. I might go on to share how much better my life is without drinking, but again this depends on the setting. If you're out with your mates and they want to get shitfaced, banging on about how much better it is not drinking is a hiding to nothing.

When some people delivered this line, it didn't feel sincere at all. It felt like it was being said in a patronising 'that must be tough, poor you, spoiling it for yourself' way. Again, it's all about the setting and your relationship in terms of how much effort you put into it. The response typically came from strangers, and while it grated on me a bit, I was so far into the 'not caring about what other people think' stage that I would just smile and move on.

There was the odd time I would say something along the lines of, 'Nah, don't feel sorry for me. My life is a lot better, and I'm happier without it,' but this tended to get their back up, and I suspect that if I kept going, it would have led to them unveiling themselves as one of the knob types from above, so I started just leaving it.

They say, 'Now you're happy again, can you start drinking again but just have a few?'
What a good idea, just to have a couple, why haven't I thought of that? I tried to not be overly sarcastic, and I would often just keep it light and wheel out a few of the one-liners from earlier. 'I woke up in Newcastle after going for one drink in Glasgow,' etc. Or if the person was genuinely interested, I might go into some of the background as to why asking someone who can't moderate to have just one drink is akin to asking a heavy gambler to stick just one pound in the fruit machine and then walk away. Plus, the very reason I'm happy again is *because* I'm not drinking, and why would I want to give that up?

They say, 'What do you do now instead of drinking? Do you still go out?'
This just reflects how heavily ingrained drinking is in our culture in the UK. People think it's not possible to socialise without drinking. Or if I somehow make it to the pub, it will be a massive struggle to stop myself vaulting over the bar and hoovering up lager straight from the taps. I gently explain I'm good, and that they can enjoy their pint without fear of me downing it while they aren't looking.

They say, 'Well, I've never had a drinking problem.'
Good for you, mate, though I didn't say you did.
    This response was pretty common among the heavier drinkers, and it's the response I would have had when I was at the peak of my drinking. This response is about the person rather than you. They are probably feeling defensive as deep

down they might be worried about their own drinking. Telling you about how they only drink on the weekends, or could easily stop if they wanted, is for their self-protection. Another one for the smile and nod approach.

They say … absolutely nothing.
Some of my closest friends and family studiously avoid talking about it. They don't really acknowledge that I'm not drinking. I'm completely fine with this. I'm not sure if they avoid talking about it as it makes them uncomfortable, or if they think it will make me uncomfortable. Either way, as I don't like a big deal being made about it, this suits me. For some people, though, giving up drinking will be an achievement and something they want to share. If it is, there are loads of sober groups that will totally get it. Share it with them and they will absolutely celebrate your sober accomplishments.

They say, 'Fair play, mate, well done. What do you want instead?'
This is my favourite reaction. It acknowledges it and I get a brief buzz from the well done. They then quickly follow it up with another question so it doesn't need to be the topic of the conversation. We can move on with our night. Magic.

Genuine connections

Socialising and feeling connected to others is important for your mental and physical health. Dr. Craig Sawchuk, a Mayo Clinic psychologist, tells us that being around people is key to good health. 'We are social animals by nature, so we tend to function better when we're in a community and being around others. People who spend too much time alone may have an increased risk of depression and lower quality of life. Just being able to shoot the breeze can be a very, very positive type of thing.' Dr. Sawchuk says socialising not only staves off loneliness, but also helps sharpen memory and cognitive skills, increases happiness and wellbeing, and may even help you live longer.[23]

When I was drinking, I thought I was the most sociable person on the planet. I could talk to anyone, about anything. I joked that you could have sat me next to Saddam Husain at a party and by the end of the night we would have been downing shots and doing karaoke together. It was never put to the test, but you get the idea. I felt like this because of the booze. Like I covered earlier, alcohol is the ultimate social lubricant; it increases our confidence to the point where everyone is chatty and there is no space for awkward silence. It dulls our brains to the point that we never notice jokes falling flat or embarrassing behaviour.

While using booze gives you an instant cheat sheet to socialising, it's difficult to make genuine connections with people when you are in a chemically altered state. The next time you are out, watch a group of people chatting as they progress from the two or three drink stage. They will get louder, and there will definitely be more talking, but when people talk when they are drinking, they are talking (or shouting over each other depending on the stage of the night) with the intention of being heard. There's never much listening going on.

Looking back, I realise when I caught up with friends, I was the same. After a few drinks I was always a broadcaster, rather than a receiver. I spent so much time in my head thinking about what I would say next. What funny anecdote should I share to keep 'the People' interested or entertained? Or even when I wasn't talking and trying to listen, there was always a background chatter about drink going on in my mind.

'Am I drinking too fast here? I suppose it's technically a work event, maybe I should slow down. But wait, it's only a free bar until nine; surely people want to make the most of that?'

'I'm in a round with x, y and z, but they are taking too long to finish their drink. Should I just go to the bar and get myself one to keep myself topped up now? Will that look like I've got a problem? If I do that, do I need to offer to get one for this guy I'm talking to? Then I will be in two rounds. But wait, maybe that's a good thing?'

Even when I did cut through the internal noise, and managed to listen enough to realise we were on the same wavelength, or they were interesting or a good person who was worth getting to know, I would get to know them while on a drinking session. While this definitely accelerates the getting-to-know-you process, as a big boozing session can be like five years of real-life bonding (you can go from introductions at the start of the night to 'I feel like I've known you forever' after pint eight), like all the other 'benefits' of alcohol, it is superficial and temporary.

What do I mean? Well, have you ever become best mates with someone on a night out? You click, share loads with each other, and have lots in common. So much so that you're planning to go to events in the future, or even on holiday if it's a big session. You end up swapping numbers at the end of the night, giving it big hugs and promising to stay in touch forever. Then you wake up the next day and see the number on your phone or your newly added friend on Facebook and think, 'What was that all about?' Or worse, you bump into them in real life sober the next day or week and are forced to have a bum-clenchingly awkward encounter. 'Some party last week, eh? Probably shared a few things that I shouldn't have. Oh yeah, ha ha, our holiday, ha ha ha, yeah no, no, me neither.'

That's what I mean. Bonding on the sauce is cheap and temporary. When you bond with someone sober, it might take more time (you need to naturally shift through the gears; you can't just pour eight pints on the relationship and go from first gear to sixth), but it is a genuine bond. Now I am sober, I find that when I catch up with friends or meet new ones, I can actively listen to them. I understand them more and it's a more meaningful, genuine connection – a solid base upon which to build a friendship.

Day time over night time

While it is possible to have fun socialising at booze-centred events, and after a while you will be able to do it without much effort, you might find that you don't want to. That other non-drinking activities you had previously written off start becoming more appealing.

When I was drinking, I was always the last man standing. I was determined to keep the party going. Pubs closing? Let's go to a nightclub. Nightclubs closing? Let's go to the casino. I told myself it was because I loved the buzz of nightlife, of hitting the dance floor or the roll of the dice at the casino. But in reality, I just liked staying out and going to these places because I could keep drinking. The night time, in pubs, clubs and casinos, was my natural habitat. I was happiest in these places because I could get my fill of drink there without feeling out of place.

Non-drinking activities were a waste of time for me. I remember going out for brunch once and being shocked that the waitress wouldn't put vodka in my Bloody Mary as it was before 11am on a Sunday. It's not brunch then, is it? What's the point in me being here if I can't have a Bloody Mary? Activities that normal people enjoy, such as walks in the park, road trips, visits to the beach, whatever it was, if I couldn't drink, it was just an unwelcome prelude to the all-important drinking.

Now that I don't drink, the thought of stomping around a sticky dance floor bouncing into sweaty strangers fills me with dread. The idea of rocking up at a casino out of my skull, taking £300 from the cash machine and basically handing it over to the croupier seems madness. Spending eight hours traipsing from pub to pub seems a lot of wasted effort. My weekends used to be: go out for a drink, drink to blackout, sleep, deal with the hangover, repeat. My weekends would fly by in a booze-filled haze, and Monday morning would arrive with me feeling wrecked and depressed, wondering where the weekend had gone.

When booze isn't the activity each weekend, you free up time to do loads of other more fulfilling activities. We're all different, and what I class as a 'fulfilling activity' might be your idea of hell, but you get the idea. Weekends become longer, with more time spent being present during daylight hours, rather than out of it at night.

For me, this meant more time outdoors, actually making it to the gym, reading a good book or writing one. Things I could never seem to get around to back when I was drinking.

Practical Self-help Condensed

When I was drinking, and quitting, I was incredibly sceptical of self-help and anything that was remotely linked to 'wellness'. The way therapy speak is flung around in everyday conversation still grates. 'I had to take some time out to focus on myself, to re-centre, you know?' Erm, you spent two weeks at an all-inclusive in Tenerife, Stevie, let's dial it down on the Gwyneth Paltrow chat, mate.

I can, though, acknowledge that some of the things I picked up from the self-help world helped me get and stay sober. Much like the way I hoovered up all the quit literature and flung myself into research, I followed the same approach with self-help books. To avoid peppering the book with references to it and risk having you cringe or roll your eyes the way I would, I've filtered and condensed everything I found useful from the self-help world into one section for you to ignore, or flick through and try.

There might be a tiny bit of wellness-style, slightly pretentious chat here, but it's just for this one chapter, promise!

Gratitude

Setting aside the 'should I throw myself in front of a bus / depths of the despair' stage of dependent drinking, I was generally quite an upbeat and happy person. But while I had a lot of material possessions, and at times earned a lot of money, it was never enough. I was always chasing more. There was an emptiness I was trying to fill by drinking and partying or buying more things. I'd get a bigger bonus than I ever expected, only to ponder how much the people above me must have got. I got myself a Tag Heuer watch after longing after one for years. After a few weeks, I still thought it was nice but had noticed the partners at work all had Rolexes. I was motivated by money. I would constantly compare myself to others and want what they had. Then I read a book called *Think Like a Monk* by Jay Shetty,[24] which helped change my perspective. I read it cover to cover and couldn't put it down.

In the book Jay distils the wisdom he learned from his time as a monk into practical steps anyone can take to live a less anxious, more meaningful life. It provides a wide range of useful guidance on subjects from how to overcome negativity and stop overthinking through to why kindness is crucial to success and how to find your purpose. The chapter that had the biggest impact on me was the one on Gratitude,[25] so I've summarised some of it here, but I would recommend reading the full book.

In *Think Like a Monk*, Jay explores the importance of amplifying gratitude to the health of our minds and bodies. Jay notes that gratitude has been linked to better mental health, self-awareness, better relationships and fulfilment:

'UCLA neuroscientist Alex Korb found that we cannot

focus on positive and negative feelings at the same time. Gratitude also benefits the physical body. Since, as Korb discovered, when we live in gratitude, we are blocking the toxic emotions and their harmful effects on our bodies.'

Jay cites the research of Robert A. Emmons, a leading scientific expert on the science of gratitude who lists lower blood pressure, improved immune function and better sleep as positive side effects of gratitude. Emmons's studies also showed that gratitude can lessen depression, anxiety and substance abuse disorders, and it can also help prevent suicide:

'When we are caught in the mind of poverty, we focus on what we are lacking; we feel we don't deserve love; and we ignore all that we have been given … practising conscious gratitude allows us to be open to the possibility that the reality we have seen doesn't have to be where we stay.'

I started to practise gratitude every day. When you put your mind to it, you start to see that the world is full of things to be grateful for. This helped me overcome negative thought patterns and reframe the 'giving up' mentality that previously used to get in my way. I would get up, turn on the shower and think, 'This is amazing. I just turn this tap, and boom; I have instant hot water.' I would start the day like that, and it would build. Where once being woken early in the morning would have annoyed me, I would now think, 'Great, I'm up now and can get a bit of writing done before I start work.' I started to see opportunities where once I would see obstacles. By purposefully looking for and acknowledging what I was grateful for, it transformed my life. (I saw that eye roll. I told you, just one chapter. Let me have it!)

Mindfulness

A lot of workplaces offer access to mindfulness apps to show they care about their employees' mental health and wellbeing (here is your free subscription to Headspace, but we still expect you to bill seventy hours this week), which is how I came across it. Unable to talk to anyone about my suicidal thoughts, and realising that drinking wasn't drowning them out anymore, I downloaded the Headspace app and gave it a go.

There is a lot of jargon around mindfulness. While the technique has roots in Buddhism and meditation, you don't have to be spiritual, or have any particular beliefs, to try it. In a nutshell, the theory behind mindfulness is that by using various techniques (I've linked to some from Mind.org in the end notes)[26] to bring your attention to the present, you can:[27]

- Notice how thoughts come and go in your mind. Learn that they don't have to define who you are, or your experience of the world, and that you can let go of them.
- Notice what your body is telling you. For example, you might feel tension or anxiety in your body, such as a fast heartbeat, tense muscles or shallow breathing.
- Create space between you and your thoughts. With this space, you can reflect on the situation and react more calmly.

Studies show that practising mindfulness can help manage common mental health problems like depression, anxiety and stress. I found it really useful in reducing the underlying anxiety I would previously have used drink to temporarily alleviate. For more information on how mindfulness works, the Oxford Mindfulness Centre website is a good port of call; they also provide free online mindfulness sessions. If you can afford it, or your work gives you a free subscription, then the Calm and Headspace apps are handy to have on your phone.

Breathing

My wife, an avid reader of self-help books, raved about one by Stuart Sandeman. Stuart is a breathing expert (I know, I didn't know such a thing existed either) who helps people improve their life, simply by changing the way they breathe. I was, of course, terribly cynical, but eventually relented and decided to give it a skim. The cover of the book is simply the title *Breathe In, Breathe Out*,[28] and I thought, 'This guy can't be serious.' Breathe in, breathe out? He's not even trying. How has he stretched that out into a book? The old adage about judging books by their covers is true. By the second chapter I was hooked. It turned out I had been breathing all wrong for most of my adult life.

I was a 'chest breather' – someone who engages the small muscles between the ribs instead of the diaphragm, which results in them having a shallower flow of breath. Chest breathing can be perfectly natural for short bursts, but it should not be the default setting. It tends to occur in times of stress or when startled. If you constantly chest breathe like I did, it may be due to habitual stress or long-term anxiety. Working at a desk all day, or holding your stomach in to look slimmer (guilty), can also contribute.

I know this sounds farfetched, but by simply working through the exercises in the book and addressing the bad breathing habits I had picked up over the years, I was able to use my breathing to help me stay calm, and improve my physical and mental wellbeing in a wide range of situations. I added it to Gratitude and Mindfulness as one of my potential tools. I found the breathing exercises around reducing anxiety particularly useful just prior to a social event, as I could take a few minutes to myself, and use my breathing to feel calm, rather than relying on drink to alleviate my social anxiety.

Not caring what other people think

'How to Build a Life' is a weekly column by Arthur Brooks tackling questions of meaning and happiness, which is run in *The Atlantic.*[29] I'm not sure how I came across it, but I read one titled 'No One Cares!' that explained why our fears about what other people think of us are overblown and rarely worth fretting over.

The link to the full article is in the end notes, and it is a quick read. The first half covers why it's natural for us to worry about what others think of us, but it's the second half of the article, which offers practical steps to help us care less about it, which I found most useful in getting over my 'what will the people think when I say I'm not drinking' panic. I've pulled out my two key takeaways below:

> 1. Remind yourself that no one cares
> *The ironic thing about feeling bad about ourselves because of what people might think of us is that others actually have much fewer opinions about*

us – positive or negative – than we imagine. Studies show that we consistently overestimate how much people think about us and our failings, leading us to undue inhibition and worse quality of life. Next time you feel self-conscious, notice that you are thinking about yourself. You can safely assume that everyone around you is doing more or less the same.

2. Stop judging others

To judge others is to acknowledge a belief that people can, in fact, legitimately judge one another; thus, it is an implicit acceptance of others' judgement of you. The way to free yourself from this belief is to stop judging others, and, when you accidentally do so, to remind yourself that you might well be wrong.

Disregard what others think and the prison door will swing open. If you are stuck in the prison of shame and judgement, remember that you hold the key to your own freedom.

Power Pause

Last but by no means least, a book by my wife. The avid self-help reader, who decided to write one of her own. In *Power Pause*, Alison provides a science-based yet practical framework to help you understand your purpose and master the small yet powerful changes required to achieve your goals. I was a guinea pig for a lot of the techniques in the book, and her coaching was a massive driver in taking me from someone who journaled to help stay sober to someone who had the belief and discipline to write a book. This one!

PART 3

The New Life That Awaits

Journey to Limitless

The 'limitless' point I described at the start of the book was when I was around two years sober, but it wasn't a sudden change. It was more that there were many tiny little improvements, that had been slowly piling up on top of each other since going sober, that snowballed and made my life better and better. It just happened to be that when I was pulling together this book, I looked around and noticed how dramatic the change was. I'm not saying that giving up drinking was the *only* reason for this better life. There were lots of other good habits I picked up when I was sober that led to this. But these good habits were ones I could never get to stick while I was drinking.

When I was drinking, taking on good habits was an uphill struggle, but picking up more bad habits was a piece of cake. It made sense. I was already drinking myself to oblivion, what difference was a few crafty fags going to make? And the next day? You drank your bodyweight in lager last night, Paddy, a bacon roll this morning isn't going to hurt.

Think about how candy floss is made (bear with me here). The flossy threads of cotton candy spin round and round the drum. They stay there, until you pay the man your money (three quid in Glasgow, twenty in London) and he puts the stick into the drum. He twirls the stick for a bit, effortlessly picking up the flossy threads and gathering them into your big stick of candy floss.

My bad habits were the flossy threads of candy. Drinking was the stick. The anchor of my bad habits. Without drinking, the bad habits would have had nothing to cling to. They would have kept spinning harmlessly around the drum.

The same analogy applies for my sobriety – it was the anchor of my good habits. It was a different stick, and I was putting it into a drum filled with good habits. My sobriety gave them something to cling to. As my ability to stick with good habits improved, so did my self-respect, health, relation-ships, work, finances; you name it, it got better without booze. I'm not exaggerating when I say that every aspect of my life has improved. I know this sounds farfetched, but here are some examples (and no more candy floss analogies):

Improved sleep
There's a strong link between increased alcohol consumption and poor-quality sleep. Multiple studies[30] show you're more likely to suffer insomnia and other sleep disorders when you are drinking.

Even when I drank to blackout, I didn't wake up rested. I might have got to sleep quickly because I had literally drunk myself to the point of being unconscious, and stayed asleep until late in the afternoon the next day, but I woke tired and hungover. Then, during the week, even when I wasn't actually drinking, I would dive into bed exhausted, having limped through the day, desperate to get a good night's sleep and recover. Again, I would get to sleep quickly, but I would often wake up in the middle of night, my anxious brain replaying all the problems that plagued 'drinking me', overthinking small issues and catastrophising them until they became insurmountable. My fitful and broken night's sleep would leave me struggling to recover from the weekend session, and I was barely feeling more human again before it was almost Thursday or Friday and time to do it all over again.

Nowadays, I sleep like a baby. I follow the same routine I used to help me when I was quitting (pop back to the Going Sober chapter and the 'I got the basics right' section if you want a refresh), and I fall asleep quickly and stay asleep. I get a solid seven or eight hours depending on the season (in summer the sunlight or birds tweeting wake me up a bit earlier, like the princess in a Disney film – I kid you not), and I wake up well rested and energised.

I'm up before the rest of the house, and I take time to write (I'm writing this chapter at half five in the morning, in the hour before the kids get up and we need to be ready for school and work), or I have a coffee and read in peace. I was inspired by Claire Pooley, who did the research for and wrote her first book during the same morning slots. The improvement in sleep she felt was one of her big sober wins:

'I am sleeping for a solid nine hours of deep, uninterrupted sleep. No more psychedelic dreams, no more getting up to wee again and again, no more getting up for water, no more turning molehills into mountains … I wake up and after 15 minutes I'm bouncing around like the Duracell bunny on speed … God, I love sleep. It's making me think going sober might actually be a really good thing.[31]

Like eating nutritious food, drinking water and exercising regularly, getting quality sleep is an important component of overall health. Scientists and health care professionals agree there are numerous benefits to consistently getting a full night's rest, with most adults recommended to get between seven and nine hours of sleep each night. Jay Summer from the Sleep Foundation[32] says that while sleeping, we perform a number of repairing and maintaining processes that affect nearly every part of the body. As a result, a good night's sleep, or a lack of sleep, can impact the body mentally and physically. I have referenced the full article in the end notes if you are keen to understand more of the science behind this, but I have noted the main benefits Jay outlines here:

- **Improved mood** – A consistent sleep routine can often resolve anxiety, depression and irritability.
- **Healthy heart** – Quality sleep promotes cardiac health, while a lack of sleep causes blood pressure to remain high for an extended period of time, increasing the risk of heart disease, heart attack and heart failure.
- **Regulated blood sugar** – Sleep impacts the body's relationship with the hormone insulin, which helps blood sugar, or glucose, enter the body's cells. Without enough sleep, the body's resistance to insulin increases because cells are not able to use insulin appropriately, which leads to too much sugar in the bloodstream.
- **Improved mental function** – Sleep is believed to help with memory and cognitive thinking; a good

night's sleep can lead to better problem-solving and decision-making skills. Sleep-deprived people perform poorly in activities that require quick responses and attention to multiple tasks, such as driving.

- **Stress relief** – Getting appropriate sleep each night can help manage stress. When people wake up refreshed, they avoid the stressors that come with functioning while sleep-deprived, such as poor performance, difficulty thinking clearly and lack of energy.

- **Maintaining healthy weight** – Quality sleep is an important part of maintaining a healthy weight. During sleep, the body naturally produces more of an appetite suppressor, called leptin, while reducing production of the appetite stimulant ghrelin.

These benefits are impressive, and they would be life changing for most people. I now had them because I was getting the right amount and quality of sleep. But I was also taking away booze. I was removing a negative as well as adding a positive, causing a multiplier effect. It was like I was compounding the interest. Sleep was restoring my body and mind, so I had loads more energy and felt more positive. I was using this energy to do activities like going to the gym, spending more time outdoors or reading and writing. Those activities, in turn, also improved my body and mind, and gave me more energy and made me feel more positive.

After a big gym session, I found I needed an extra hour of sleep. I started getting even more high-quality sleep, which improved my body even more, which meant I woke up feeling even more energised and positive. It was the opposite of the boozing, beating myself up and trying to recover cycle I had been stuck in. This was a much more positive cycle I was happy to be in; it was making my life so much better.

Improved finances

By simply not spending so much money on booze, your finances will improve. I touched upon the average £60k (which I reckon was closer to £100k for me) in the previous chapter as a justification for why you should treat yourself. But it's not just the cost of booze and the direct expenses (taxis, takeaways, replacing lost wallets and phones, etc., after a night out) that were negatively impacting my financial situation.

When I was drinking, I had little motivation or ability to be bothered about what I would call 'life admin'. At the weekend I was smashed, and during the week I was just trying to make it through the day at work. Anything more than that seemed like a struggle.

I would put off opening letters that looked official for days, sometimes weeks. When I eventually did open them and they required some sort of action, I would put off said action until the deadline, or often miss it. Stuff them in a drawer and forget about it. Hope it went away.

Of course, none of these things ever do go away. And while you are waiting for them to go away, they still sit at the back of your mind, increasing your anxiety and feelings of despair. You just make the problem worse and it snowballs. The first letter, which was a friendly payment reminder for your upcoming credit card bill that could have been dealt with instantly, has now become several, much less friendly letters notifying you of late payment charges on top of the gazillion percent monthly interest.

You know those letters that they are required to send you to give you a chance to get a better deal on your car or home insurance before they auto-renew you and almost double your premium? I would read them in outrage and say, 'That is terrible – there's absolutely no way I'm putting up with that.' But I would never actually get around to doing anything about it. I might make a brief attempt at calling to haggle, or go on a comparison website, but after a few minutes on hold, or having to type in too many details online, I would think, 'Ah fuck it, it's too much hassle,' and just let them auto-renew me.

Sober me is an absolute wizard when it comes to life admin. I signed up for those Martin Lewis 'Money Saving Expert' weekly emails and I am all over it. You can switch current accounts for a £200 welcome bonus? Great – I'm on my fifth provider since going sober. Coming to the end of an introductory offer? I've already got a reminder on my phone and I'm cancelling two days before the end. Dare to increase my broadband or TV subscription? I will be straight on the blower threatening to leave, and working my way through the multiple layers of the retention team like I'm playing an old school video game trying to get to the boss at the end. The one who can actually give me the good deal they are advertising to new customers.

As I got further into my sobriety, I went on to tackle bigger things such as increasing my pension contributions and re-organising my investments to avoid unnecessary fees. I always knew how to do these things, but I just couldn't be arsed when drinking. Again, you get the multiplier effect. You have more money because you spend less drinking. You compound the interest by dealing with the life admin you put off when you were drinking. I am amazed how quickly, and drastically, my financial situation has improved since going sober.

Improved career progression

In my twenties, first starting out in my career in finance, I was joining a workplace culture where my drinking was positively encouraged. Being able to handle your drink and 'work hard, play hard' was admired. Wild nights out requiring you to come straight to the office with little sleep were seen as a rite of passage. As I moved into my thirties, these attitudes started to shift. There was an expectation that as your level of responsibility increased, you would calm down on the partying and start behaving like an adult. Leave the playing hard to the more junior staff and focus more on the working part.

Because my drinking was steadily increasing rather than decreasing, this proved to be a challenge for me. As the impact of a decade of hard drinking took its toll, the days where I was going through the motions or had to get colleagues to cover for me started to pile up. I thought I was getting away with it, but when it comes to promotion time at a senior level, the Partners remember who was skipping out the door first on a Friday and who was sneaking in late on a Monday morning looking like a corpse in a suit.

My career stalled and I was stuck at the same level for years, as others around me moved up. Since cutting out the booze, I've been promoted twice in two years. I didn't have to put in more hours or do anything particularly dramatic to get these promotions. Purely taking away the impact of booze was enough. When you turn up fresh and fully engaged on a Monday, and not stale and distracted from a weekend of boozing, people notice. Your performance and consistency speak for themselves, and they put you closer to the front of the queue when it comes to promotion time.

Improved relationships

My drinking had a negative impact on my closest relationships. I was in denial about it at the time, but in hindsight it is blindingly obvious. I was defensive, or often lied, about my drinking. 'I've only had a couple of pints,' I would slur, as I stumbled through the door. This understandably caused trust issues. 'Sorry, I'm not going to make it today, feeling rough, think it must have been something I ate.' I was liable to cancel plans or back out of commitments at the last minute as I was too hungover. It made me unreliable and less present in my life.

Now I had removed the obstacle of drinking and so many aspects of my life were improving, I had the time and energy to fix up the relationships I had with those around me, in particular:

I'm a better husband

Drinking caused the most damage to my relationship with my wife. I could hide the worst of the impacts of my drinking from almost everyone else, but she could see through it, and was the one who was most impacted by it. Like I touched on before, when I was out drinking and my wife was with me, it was like she was looking after a child. She took responsibility for keeping me out of trouble and getting us home. When we went on to have kids, it was my wife who got up early with them the next day while I recovered from my hangover. This caused tension and resentment.

The next day after one of my blowouts, I would feel awful about my drinking. I would be apologetic and full of despair and self-pity that I had failed to moderate yet again and had let her and myself down. I would try to make it up to her. This often included keeping a low profile and avoiding disagreements. Because I had fucked up the weekend with my drinking, and was living in fear of anxiety and just trying to make it through the week, I never voiced my feelings or disagreed with anything. I let my wife make the decisions, and just went along with whatever she felt was the right course of action to have a quiet life. I now see that this wasn't actually helping my wife at all. It was just pushing more responsibility on to her, as I checked out more and more and became a passenger in our life.

Now that I'm not drinking, there is much more balance to our relationship. We are a partnership. When we have disagreements, we voice them, work through them and move on. There are no simmering resentments about my drinking.

I'm a better dad
'When I was drinking, I thought I was the greatest dad in the world but looking back … you're selfish without realising it when you're drinking a lot.' (Damien Hirst)[33]

This quote summed me up. I couldn't see it at the time, and would have strongly challenged any suggestion of it, but drinking was stopping me from being the dad I wanted to be. I had the red line of 'I never drink in front of the kids', which was great. But it just meant I waited until they were in bed to get smashed. It didn't do anything to stop me rushing through their bedtime. I was going through the motions reading *The Three Little Pigs*, but all I could think about were the three massive gins going straight down my neck as soon as I got downstairs.

On the rare occasions I would take a turn getting up early with them, I would struggle through with a hangover. Plopping the oldest in front of the TV, while I fed the youngest with one hand and scrolled through my phone with the other. When I took them to the park or a soft play, I was physically there, ticking the box of things good dads do with the kids at the weekend, but mentally I wasn't. I was either recovering from a hangover or thinking about when it would next be acceptable to drink.

I am eternally grateful I quit drinking when I did. My eldest son was three, and my youngest just a baby. They are amazing, wonderful little humans that light up our lives and bring us so much joy. And now I get to be there, present, in the moment with them while they do. Plus, dealing with a tantrum is much less hassle when you're not absolutely hanging.

I'm a better son, brother and friend
I'm a better son and brother for similar reasons to those responsible for my being a better husband and father. Less time drinking and recovering from drinking has resulted in more time to spend with my mum, dad and sister.

With friendships, it's less straightforward. Since stopping drinking, there are some friendships which haven't made it. It isn't due to anything dramatic or malicious; it's just that when you stripped the booze out, we didn't really have much else left in common. Sometimes that happens, and I think it's okay. I feel much closer to the old friends that remain, and sobriety has brought me some brilliant new ones.

Increased confidence

As I took control of my drinking and my mood, finances, relationships and ability to deal with life in general all improved, so did my confidence. Don't get me wrong, when I was eight pints deep I was the most confident man on the planet. I would have no qualms about dancing on a table, putting on impromptu concerts or bearing my soul to strangers. Anything. But without a drink, I was increasingly anxious, stuck in my head, and I would struggle to look people in the eye. When I wasn't actually drunk, I wanted to be invisible. While I thought booze was giving me confidence, it was stealing it from me as I became more and more reliant on it.

If I was meeting you in a bar, I would wait outside until you got there, then go in with you. If we had to book a taxi somewhere, I wanted you to phone for it as I was too shy to speak on the phone. If the kitchen in work was busy, I would wait until it was empty rather than go in and chat to people. I would sneak past people and hope not to be noticed. I was making myself as small as possible. I wanted to be invisible. Now I had taken away my crutch, and realised I could not only cope but thrive without it, I built up real confidence. That inner self-assuredness that sticks around when the drink has left. I would never have believed it, but I now feel more confident without booze than I ever did with it. I can even phone my own taxis!

Increased self-respect

After self-confidence joined the merry band of improvements, self-respect wasn't far behind. When I was drinking, and especially when I was stuck on the failed moderation loop, I had a very low opinion of myself. My lack of self-respect meant I was heavily reliant on what others thought about me. I needed external validation. If I met you, I would be in my head wondering what you thought about me. I would jump through hoops seeking your validation. I used to quip that after a few drinks I could spend time with and get on with even the most dull / annoying / bad people. Why did I want to?

Now when I meet people, I ask myself some pretty basic questions, which I imagine normal people run through as a given. Do I think this is a good person? How do they make me feel? Are they interesting? Nice? Is it someone I want to spend my time with?

I held up the same lens to the places I went to and the activities I took part in. Old me went to anything I could drink at. A guy from the office I've never spoken to is having a leaving party? Don't want to miss that. Drinks in a dingy pub with no windows as it's the closest place that serves booze? Sign me up for eight hours getting shitfaced in the darkness.

Now I'm much more discerning about who, what and where I spend my time on. How will this make me feel? Is it worth it? Having the self-respect to ask these basic questions means I avoid being at events, or with people, where I need to drink to make them interesting or bearable. I have the self-respect to take responsibility for my own happiness, rather than relying on others or copious amounts of booze to make me feel good.

Quickfire Wins

Improved sleep, finances, relationships, confidence and self-respect – those were the heavyweight wins. The foundations of my new sober life, the big hitters. But there were loads of other bonus wins. At around the four-week mark, other people started to comment on the physical improvements they had noticed since I stopped drinking. This was a bit of a confidence boost and it helped spur me on during the tougher times or when I was having a wobble or questioning my decision. It led to my listing them all down in my journal and referring back to them when I needed a pick-me-up. Let's fire through some:

Wins I could see

Despite the nice packaging and marketing that does a great job convincing us otherwise, booze is literally a toxic chemical that our body needs to work hard to eliminate and recover from. I don't want this book to be preachy, so I won't get on the soap box for long, but it's easy to forget that alcohol is a poison that is terrible for our body.

Although the liver does the bulk of the work in eliminating toxins, alcohol use impacts all the other major organs as well. In fact, it contributes to a whole host of health problems, including heart disease, cancer and strokes[34] – it's not an exhaustive list but you get the idea. When we put alcohol into our body, it's like filling up our car with diesel instead of petrol. It's going to break it. When we stop doing that, it works a lot better. Here some of the ways I could physically *see* my body improving, from head to toe, as I dried out:

1. Hair
This was unexpected, but since quitting my hair has improved drastically. I always had thick hair, but since my early twenties it had become dry and brittle and had the texture and appearance of a Brillo pad. I tried all sorts on it, but eventually just got into a routine of loading it up with gel to hide it. I could never leave the house without putting something in it. Now, I have a thick strong mop that, while it's still a bit wild, actually resembles human hair, rather than something that should be used for cleaning the oven.

I looked into it and it turns out that alcohol and hair do not get along. Over time, alcohol use can cause dry, brittle, breaking hair, and even excessive hair loss. The combination of dehydration and malnutrition makes it hard for your body to rebuild your hair and function at its best.[35]

2. Eyes
After a big session my eyes would be bloodshot, but even in day-to-day life they were dry and irritated. I blamed this on wearing contact lenses, or the air conditioning in the office (literally anything other than booze), but when you look into

it, booze does not do our eyes any favours. At the extreme end of the scale you can do long-term damage but, fortunately, most short-term impacts on the eyes should improve as the body rebounds from alcohol exposure.[36]

3. Skin

Around the age of fifteen I started to get terrible, cyst-like acne. The type that was deep under the skin and painful to have, never mind painful to look at. It was terrible for my self-esteem. Given my age, the various doctors and dermatologists I went to were always of the opinion that it was due to teenage hormones and that I would grow out of it. I never did.

I was eventually put on a drug called isotretinoin in my mid-twenties, which is powerful but has multiple side effects and is not suitable for long-term use. So, while I would have bursts of clear skin when I was on those drugs, the acne would come roaring back during my off cycles. Since I stopped drinking, I no longer need to use it. My skin has miraculously cleared itself up of its own accord. I now get compliments on my glowing complexion.

Coincidence? The research would say not. While there is no direct link between alcohol and acne – no proof, for example, that one pint of lager equals one cyst in the morning – the multiple harmful health effects of alcohol on the immune system, liver function, inflammation and hormone balance reduce overall skin health, and can indirectly cause acne or make it worse.[37]

Clarins[38] (a big make-up company for the men not in the know) commissioned a team of experts to weigh in on the question of the impacts of alcohol on your skin. They went well beyond acne. Dry skin, enlarged pores, puffiness and rosacea were all added to the mix. The key takeaway was that there is no level of alcohol intake that's good for your skin. If you want to ensure your skin is in top condition, avoid alcohol and stay well hydrated. Oh, and stick on sunscreen while you're at it.

4. Face

I've not got any science to back this one up, so this is just my own personal experience. As I reached my thirties, I noticed that my face was puffier and more bloated in pictures. I just attributed this to being something that happens as we get older. But since I quit, my jawline has returned, and my cheekbones are back. (Quietly strikes *Zoolander* Blue Steel pose.)

5. Beer belly – gone!

A beer belly was another thing I figured you just needed to accept as you got older. By my mid-twenties I had a bit of paunch, which slowly grew year on year. By my early thirties I had a well-defined beer belly. I got a personal trainer and tried multiple diets (intermittent fasting, the 5:2, tracking calories), but I could never shift it. Eight months after quitting, admittedly once I stopped replacing booze with cheesecake, it just sort of left of its own accord.

This isn't all that surprising when you take into account how calorie laden booze is. A pint of lager contains roughly the same calories as a bar of Dairy Milk.[39] I was consuming the equivalent of nine chocolate bars on a Friday night, then topping it off with a kebab or some chips and cheese on the way home. Waking up the next day, I would crave something stodgy to take the edge off the hangover, before doing it all again on the Saturday. It's no wonder I was piling on the pounds. A study for *The Times* reported that the average wine drinker puts on half a stone of fat a year.[40]

Again, similar to finances, there is a bit of a multiplier effect here. It's not just that I was taking away the calories from booze; I was also replacing the unhealthy food I craved when I was drinking with healthier alternatives. It's not like I've got a six pack, but I no longer have to suck in my belly and hope no one looks at me as I dash from the lockers to the pool when I take the kids swimming.

6. *Goodbye unexplained bruises*

When I was boozing, I had what seemed like permanent bruises on my shins, legs and thighs from banging into things. Some days I would wake up with hand marks on my arms from, I can only assume, being manhandled out the way in my more inebriated states. I told myself that I 'bruise like a peach'. I don't. Nowadays I rarely get bruises, because nowadays I walk into tables a lot less.

Wins I could feel

As well as the outward signs of improvement, there were lots of internal wins that happened as I backed away from the booze. Now that I wasn't applying a numbing agent, I was far more aware of what was going on internally:

1.   More energy

The difference between my energy levels pre and post drinking is huge. When I was drinking, I was always struggling through the day mid-week. When I got in from work, I had no energy. I wanted to flop onto the sofa, switch off my brain and watch Netflix until bedtime. Even really basic stuff like hanging up the washing, emptying the dishwasher, cleaning the bathroom – these all seemed huge, insurmountable challenges. I had to mentally summon the gumption to get these things done.

Now I have so much energy, I don't want to sit still when I get in from work. I'm looking for things to do. Tasks like emptying the dishwasher get done without thinking about it. They are routine, no sweat. Plus, just doing them when they need to be done, at the time, saves all the mental anguish of putting them off, or having a debate with my wife about whose turn it is to do them.

2.   Increased productivity

Linked to this, and another multiplier effect, was increased productivity. Along with the increased energy, I also had an increased focus and attention span to apply to them. You don't need me to quote scientific studies to know that after a few drinks, you become distracted and don't want to get much work done. (There's a link to one at the back of the book though, if you do.)[41] There was nothing that derailed my productivity quite like booze. Even when I wasn't directly under the influence, it still sapped my attention and made it difficult to focus. Tasks took longer than expected, or didn't get started at all. Lots of them got flung into the 'maybe next week' column of the to-do list. When you go sober, your focus and attention span will improve, allowing you to do more.

3. Sunnier disposition

Before going sober, minor things could often have a disproportionate impact on my mood, or cause an overreaction. I only realised this when I was in the showers at the gym, about a year sober. The first shower I tried was cold. Not cold as in 'oh, it's not quite as hot as I like it,' but cold as in 'mother of god, are you trying to give me a heart attack?'

I tried a few more showers but they were all the same. Eventually I thought, 'Sod it, let's give it a go.' Once I got my head and shoulders under, it wasn't that bad. I put my hair and shower gel on just out of range of the ice blast, then went under and rinsed it off quickly. Granted, it was intense, but I was clean and certainly fresh.

As I was coming out of the shower, another guy asked me if the one I left was cold as well. I said, 'Yeah, I think they're all the same.' He went on a rant about the amount he was paying for his membership, about how much of a disgrace it was. He was furious.

I found myself trying to calm him down, telling him about an interesting article I had read about the health benefits of cold showers, especially after exercise. Reduced muscle fatigue, improved immunity, it can even boost your mood.[42] 'I've just had one there, mate, and surprisingly, I feel pretty good – it's worth a try.'

He looked at me like I was insane and said, 'Fuck that, I'm going to speak to the manager.' Off he went, marching on out to reception in his flip flops. I remember having a similar reaction to a cold shower the morning I woke up in a hotel with a murderous hangover. I was hoping that a hot shower would miraculously wash away some of the pain. Just like Mr Angry Flip Flops, I was furious when the water ran cold and vented said fury on the hotel manager. It didn't get me anywhere. The water was out for the entire block; there was nothing the manager could do. I didn't feel good about how I had spoken to him later on, and I still had the immediate choice of the cold shower or not having one at all.

Now I'm sober, I'm much more able to handle minor setbacks, or changes of plan, without making a drama of it. And it makes life easier. I was changed and walking out of the gym by the time Mr Angry Flip Flops had finished having a go at the receptionist. 'There's nothing she can do about it,' he informed me. 'It won't be fixed until Monday at the earliest, mate.' I didn't care. I was showered already and headed out into the sunshine.

I made up the last bit for effect. It was Glasgow in October, so I walked out into gale-force winds and rain, but at least I was clean and able to get on with the rest of my day.

4. Unearthing the real me

For close to twenty years, I thought that booze brought out the real me. The Party Paddy who loved being out in big groups, being the centre of attention and going from one noisy venue to the next. I thought I was a huge extrovert. I now realise that's not me at all. I would much rather spend time with people one on one or in a small group, and I don't like being the centre of attention all the time (though I still have my moments). My perfect weekend is much more likely to involve reading a good book, trips to the park, a bit of writing and going to someone's house for lunch. Staying out at a noisy club or burning through cash in the casino until 3am is now my idea of hell.

What happened? Why the change? A huge eureka moment for me was realising that booze wasn't bringing out the real me at all. It was just that I was anxious and nervous in a group setting, and I learned that I could use booze as an instant cheat sheet to socialise with ease. I could go from struggling to look you in the eye when you introduced your-self to dragging you up for a dance in the space of a few drinks. I spent twenty years thinking that this altered state was who I was supposed to be. I chased the chances to feel like that. I never wanted to spend time alone. I wanted to be out, in big groups, partying. Boozing.

Once I had stopped drinking, the real 'real me', who had been drowning under a sea of booze for the last twenty years, was getting a chance to come back out. And it turned out he was a lot like the teenager who had started drinking. He hadn't really changed; he was still anxious and quiet in a group setting, but he was also a lot kinder and thoughtful and less self-centred than Party Paddy.

Now that I wasn't striving to be an over-confident, exag-gerated version of myself, I had the chance to get to know him, and get comfortable in my own skin. I was able to work through a lot of hang-ups and insecurities that belonged to teenage Paddy, and put some effort into learning what I genuinely liked and didn't – what made me feel good, what made me feel bad. Basic things that I'm sure most people just pick up gradually as they go from teen to adult, without being smashed for most of it.

7. Food tastes better

I appreciate that 'unearthing the real me' is quite heavy, soul-searching stuff, so let's lighten things up with something practical. You know all that chat about red wine making meat taste better, and making sure to pair white wine with fish? It's all bollocks. Deep down you knew it was bollocks. (Mmm … I'm definitely getting a hint of oak from this Chablis … chomped down on many oak trees, have you?) Drinking alcohol, be it fancy red wine or pints of super-strength cider, impairs your sense of taste.[43] When you're next out for dinner in a big group, look around at the people adding loads of salt and pepper to their food, or asking for chilli flakes. I bet it's the faster drinkers.

When I was drinking, I viewed going out for dinner as a waste of time; eating was a chore, an unnecessary expense that was distracting from the all-important drinking time. Now I can properly taste it, and have not suppressed my appetite with eight pints, I appreciate and enjoy good food.

6. Fewer missed appointments

I was forever phoning to cancel appointments, or just not showing up, because I couldn't face them due to a hangover or because there was an unexpected drinking session to attend. I now make (and keep) way more appointments, for things drinking me considered optional, but which are actually essential. I go to the GP whenever an ailment comes up that I'm worried about, rather than just hoping it goes away on its own and adding it to the list of things to catastrophise about late at night. I regularly attend the dentist, hygienist and physiotherapist – my smile and back have never been happier!

7. *I wake up where I'm supposed to be*

Funny thing, I never wake up on the couch of a random flat with no idea how I got there after going for one or two tonics after work. No more awkward chats, no more piecing together the night by joining snippets of memories, analysing bank statements or voicemails. Now, I wake up where I'm supposed to. Every single time. It never gets old.

8. *My conscience is clearer*

I was plagued by 'the fear'. I dreaded the Monday morning, or the next day. 'Oh, here he is. Enjoy yourself last night, big man?' or 'You better hope the boss left before you (insert hilarious anecdote of me making an arse of myself)' style chats.

Piecing together how bad I was and what fires I needed to put out after a blackout drinking session was a normal part of my life. When I spoke to people the next day, I would be analysing their behaviour to pick up signs that I had offended them the night before. I was a paranoid mess. All that is gone. I know what I did last night, and every other night. I was there, present, with my faculties and all-important inhibitions intact. Sooo much easier.

9. Stepping off the 'should I drink tonight?' roundabout

I wasted so much mental energy on this. If there was an event coming up, I would run through the pros and cons of drinking at it. Should I drink at this one? It's a work event and I made an arse of myself last time; maybe I shouldn't drink and keep a low profile. But everyone else will be drinking. It will look weird if you don't, especially after the last one, like you've got a problem or something. Maybe you could go but just have a couple … but you struggle with having a couple. Maybe you shouldn't drink at all. Maybe you should just not go, maybe that would be easier.

This internal back and forth would rage for weeks in the build-up to said event and it was pointless. I went. I drank. I got shitfaced. Every. Single. Time.

I no longer need to put myself through this. My default setting is that I don't drink. It's that easy.

The longer you stay sober, and as the quickfire wins pile up and get added to the heavy-hitting ones, the easier it becomes to see the positives of sobriety. The balance tips and it becomes obvious you are gaining so much more than you are missing out on by not drinking. It becomes a no brainer of a choice.

Up until relatively recently, especially in booze-soaked Britain, you would have felt like an unheard minority thinking like this. You would have had to work pretty hard to find other people who shared your view. Not anymore. Online searches for 'sober curious' and 'mindful drinking' (which encourages people to take a more conscious and intentional approach to alcohol consumption) have increased 96% and 41% respectively[44] in the past five years. The times, my friend, are a-changin.

The Times They Are A-Changin

My friends and family struggled to reconcile the shift from 'unless someone has died, *do not* phone me before noon on a weekend' to 'anyone up for going on a hill walk on Saturday morning? If we leave at 7am we could have the place to ourselves, and build up an appetite for a big breakfast when the cafe opens at 9am.'

When I put up suggestions for early morning activities on the group chat, my mates would send back laughing emojis. They assumed I was taking the piss or being ironic. To be fair, this is understandable. For twenty years Sean Kingston's catchy little 'We like to sleep all day, and party all night, this is how we like to live our life' number was basically my theme tune. Drinking and partying was how I socialised. I'm sure the story of a shy teen who used booze as a shortcut to easing social anxiety and became more and more dependent as they got older is incredibly common. There's a generation of us who suspect that if it wasn't for alcohol, we wouldn't have made any friends at all. It's a sweeping statement, but for millennials in the UK, underage drinking was a rite of passage. Getting smashed together was how we socialised. Helping each other through the hangover and piecing together the night before were the foundations of most of our friendships; it gave us a sense of belonging.

When we grew up and went off to university, or started new jobs, or moved to new places, we kept it going. We knew how to make instant friendships – just add booze.

Generation Z

The next generation (Gen Z refers to those born between 1997 and 2012) aren't going down the same path we did, or at least not with as much vigour. In June 2023 *Forbes Magazine* published an article which noted that 'Gen-Z drink on average 20% less than millennials, who themselves drink less than the previous generation, mainly because of an increased awareness of the dangers and effects of alcohol and the rise of health-consciousness as a lifestyle'.[45]

There are loads more stats and evidence that support this view, but rather than fire them all off, I think a good way to illustrate the point is through music. Back in the 2000s and early 2010s, when we millennials were reaching our late teens and getting on it every weekend, the drunk anthem was at its peak. We were all 'in the club gettin tipsy'. Nowadays – not so much. I'm painfully aware that no one wants the views of a middle-aged accountant on what's hip or not (do they still even say that?). My first ever concert was Jimmy Nail, and my most recent was Marti Pellow. Both were amazing, but I can't claim to have my finger on the pulse of what's popular, so I will let the infinitely cooler Daisy Jones, writer, author and social commentator, who worked with GQ on this very topic, give her take on it:[46]

'According to a study released in 2013, among 720 songs in Billboard's most popular songs lists in 2009, 2010 and 2011, 23.2 percent mentioned alcohol. To add, the context in which booze was mentioned was nearly always positive (has any one song sounded more furiously 2010 than Flo Rider's "Club Can't Handle Me" featuring David Guetta?)

'Fast forward 10 years, though, and the fun drunk anthem has all but dried up. There are a couple in the charts, including Taylor Swift's "Cruel Summer" and "Dial Drunk" by Noah Kahan with Post Malone, but these aren't exactly vibey adverts for getting on it. In "Dial Drunk", Kahan sings "For the shame of being young, drunk, and alone" meanwhile Swift is "drunk in the back of the car" and crying "like a baby coming home from the bar." When it comes to big party anthems, none of them mention alcohol positively. Dua Lipa's "Dance the Night" doesn't mention drinking, and, in "Paint the Town Red" Doja Cat even raps: "I am so much fun without Hennessey / They just want my love and my energy."'

It's not a big leap to say that the musical shift is reflective of the cultural shift in attitudes to alcohol. In an article for Foodnavigator.com (a news and analysis site for the food and drinks industry) Oliver Morrison noted that 'the hashtag

#mindfuldrinking has over 24 million views on TikTok and #sobercurious has over 711 million. There's even been a 12% decline in those looking for "cocktail recipes" online over the past year, compared to a 19% increase in "mocktail recipes". People are becoming more mindful of what they consume, both literally and culturally. Young people especially seem to be adopting a more mindful approach to drinking.'[47]

The rest of us

That's great for the kids, you may say, but what about the rest of us – the Millennials (1981–1996), Gen Xs (1965–1980) and Boomers (1946–1964)?

If you're in one of these groups, even though not drinking can make your life immeasurably better, it can still feel like you're swimming against the tide when you don't drink, especially in Britain. But even for the older age groups, that tide is starting to turn.

For every person who challenges me on not drinking, or dishes out some 'banter' about me being a lightweight, there is another who quietly catches me alone and asks what it is like to be sober because they are worried about their own drinking and want to try it.

Among all ages, there has been a rise of 'positive sobriety' or 'mindful drinking' movements, particularly in the form of online communities, and initiatives like Dry January and Sober October. But why is this happening? Kasia Delgado, Chief Features Writer for *The i Paper*, sat down with Professor David Nutt, professor of neuropsychopharmacology (try saying that after a few pints) at Imperial College London, to find out more.[48]

As an aside, Professor Nutt was the UK government's drugs adviser but was sacked in 2009 by the then Home Secretary after he, along with a team of top British scientists, worked on a study which pointed out that alcohol is actually more dangerous than crack or heroin.

The study,[49] carried out on behalf of the Independent Scientific Committee on Drugs and published in *The Lancet*, ranked twenty drugs based on the harms a drug produces in the individual and the harms to others to assign a harm score from 0–100. Overall, alcohol was the most harmful drug (harm score 72), with heroin (55) and crack cocaine (54) in second and third places. Tobacco (26) was a distant sixth.

Why was the guy who was tasked with advising the government on drugs sacked for sharing his findings from a scientific study about drugs? Well, the findings run contrary to the government's long-established drug classification system. The one that gives a big thumbs up to alcohol. The paper's authors argue that their system – based on the consensus of experts, rather than politicians – provides a more accurate assessment of harm for policy makers.

'Our findings lend support to previous work in the UK and the Netherlands, confirming that the present drug classification systems have little relation to the evidence of harm,' the paper says. 'They also accord with the conclusions of previous expert reports that aggressively targeting alcohol harms is a valid and necessary public health strategy.'

The findings did not go down well, and the government asked Professor Nutt to resign the day after it was made public. The report was first published a decade ago and as time has passed, an increasing number of people are now willing to listen to his message. Kasia asked him why we are seeing such a shift in attitudes.

'The sea-change is down to a combination of things, but it seems absolutely clear now, that while alcohol is a great drug for socialising, it's also harmful. Science has demolished the idea that there are health benefits, so the alcohol industry can no longer hide behind that pretence. People are generally more health conscious,' he says, 'and for many people the target is health, not hedonism. Health used to be seen as boring but now it's become a goal in itself. People are starting to see that there's one simple thing you can do to improve your health, and that's to reduce your drinking.'

That's not to say that the entire country is embracing sobriety – far from it – but fewer people are drinking. 'In the last seven years, there's been a change in the attitude of both young and old people towards alcohol,' says Nutt, 'and there are people who are deciding to drink less because it's harmful, it affects sleep, it affects relationships, careers, mental health, and the body. This "low and no" movement is one of the biggest changes in attitudes for 100 years, since the temperance movement (a social movement that campaigned against the recreational use and sale of alcohol).'

I genuinely feel like we are at the tipping point of a societal shift in our relationship with alcohol. We'll look back one day at old footage from city centres where people were getting arrested at night and getting into fights. Or read about the domestic violence and family trauma, of people dying of lifestyle cancers and liver damage caused by drinking, and we'll think … What the hell was that all about? What were we thinking? Why did we let people do that?

Why was that even legal?

It might take decades, but I think my grandkids will find it mindblowing that people used to choose to drink, and that we did it everywhere.

The new smoking

It wasn't that long ago smoking was as ingrained in our society as alcohol.[50] The ability to smoke was designed into all modes of transport. Car manufacturers made sure you had a cigarette lighter built into the dashboard so you could spark up on the road, and tiny little ashtrays were built into the seat rests of trains and planes, so there was somewhere for you to flick the ash and stub out when you were done.

If you went out for dinner, the ashtray on your table was as expected as the salt and pepper shakers. No pub would be complete without a cigarette machine next to its jukebox. Smoking was advertised as glamorous and cool. My grandparents' generation thought nothing of smoking everywhere.

My parents' generation saw it decline. In the 70s and 80s you could ask to be seated in the non-smoking section in cinemas and restaurants. Restrictions started to be placed on where it could be advertised. By the 90s it was banned on trains and planes.

My own generation saw the UK go 'smoke free' and ban smoking in all enclosed public spaces, including pubs and restaurants. That was in 2007. I'm old enough to remember before it happened. It was normal that after every night out, you would come home stinking of cigarettes. And then it wasn't. Smoke free became the new normal. It now seems unbelievable that smoking was a thing. If you sparked up in a restaurant now, someone would put you out with a fire extinguisher.

In 1974, 46% of adults in the UK smoked, by 2022 it was down to 13%.[51] It took us decades, but as a society we eventually saw through the advertising and realised smoking was causing us harm, and we did something about it. The first medical reports linking smoking to lung cancer appeared as early as the 1920s. By the 1950s and 1960s the link was undeniable, and it was proven that tobacco caused a range of serious diseases.[52] Why did it take so long for us to act?

When those medical reports linking smoking to lung cancer started circulating in the 1920s, Big Tobacco got prepared. It was only a link to lung cancer; there was no definitive evidence. By the 1930s, tobacco companies had an army of doctors ready to debunk you as a crank for even suggesting something as benign as a tiny little cigarette could give you cancer. In fact, in the 1940s, they started using doctors to promote smoking, pitching their cigarettes as healthy, even to pregnant women and young people.

There is a treasure trove of bogus old ads, still viewable online, featuring claims by tobacco companies that cigarettes pose no health risks, or even that they're beneficial to your health.[53]

Tobacco companies set up Medical Relations departments that advertised in medical journals. They paid for research and cited it in ads. In 1946, Reynolds (the makers of Camels) launched an ad campaign with the slogan 'More doctors smoke Camels than any other cigarette.' They'd solicited this 'finding' by giving doctors a free carton of Camel cigarettes, and then asking what brand they smoked.

As the independent scientific research which proved that smoking was killing people mounted up, the tobacco industry's response was to fund studies of their own to 'prove' that tobacco smoking was safe. This disingenuous marketing, fake research and political lobbying helped to mislead the public for decades.

There is an excellent timeline produced by the Action on Smoking and Health (ASH).[54] ASH is an independent public health charity set up by the Royal College of Physicians to end the harm caused by tobacco. The timeline walks though the key dates in tobacco regulation from 1962 to 2020. It is unbelievable how slow governments around the world were to protect their citizens from the harms of smoking.

The level of influence that the tobacco industry had, and the ability it was given to either self-police or heavily influence government policy, even after the harm of its products was proven and well known is terrifying. I've linked the article in the end notes and would recommend reading it. The key takeaway is that, every step of the way, Big Tobacco has done everything possible to block any attempt to reduce the use of cigarettes, regardless of the known impact on people.

In recent years Big Tobacco has turned its attention to vaping or e-cigarettes with a similar approach towards advertising. In 2021, the Bureau for Investigative Journalism, in partnership with *The Observer*,[55] produced a great piece noting that British American Tobacco have pursued non-smokers and a new generation of customers with its highly addictive nicotine and tobacco products in the quest for more growth and increased profits.

These tactics include:

- Presenting nicotine products as cool and aspirational in glossy youth-focused advertising campaigns;
- Paying social media influencers to promote e-cigarettes, nicotine pouches and tobacco on Instagram;
- Sponsoring music and sporting events, including an F1 e-sports tournament that was streamed live on YouTube and watched by children,
- Offering free samples of nicotine pouches and e-cigarettes, which appears to have attracted underage people and non-smokers.

Why the detour into Big Tobacco? Well, there is another industry that sells an addictive, harmful product, and it's following a similar playbook.

Big Alcohol

I ummed and ahhed about going down this path. I was worried if I started to discuss how the suits from Big Alcohol are colluding with governments to ignore the medical and scientific evidence and keep us drinking, it would sound a bit farfetched. I was worried I would 'lose the reader'. I flung myself into the research here and I was worried you might think I had gone down a rabbit hole with it. 'Don't listen to the government, don't trust the media. The truth is out there.' Err, alrighty then, Agent Mulder … (closes book and sighs).

I decided to keep this section in, because a) you've made it this far, so there's a chance some of this is resonating, and b) on the off chance this book is read by more than my immediate family, it would be a missed opportunity to at least contribute to the discussion and potentially help someone.

Just like with tobacco in the 40s and 50s, we have reached the tipping point where the scientific and medical communities are concluding that, healthwise, there is no safe level of drinking. The message is often lost in the sea of other propaganda and marketing, but in January 2023 the World Health Organization (WHO) attempted to cut through this with a pretty punchy press release:[56]

> *No level of alcohol consumption is safe for our health.*
> The risks and harms associated with drinking alcohol have been systematically evaluated over the years and are well documented. The World Health Organization has now published a statement in *The Lancet Public Health*: when it comes to alcohol consumption, there is no safe amount that does not affect health.
>
> Alcohol is a toxic, psychoactive and dependence-producing substance and it was classified as a Group 1 carcinogen by the International Agency for Research on Cancer decades ago – this is the highest risk group, which also includes asbestos, radiation and tobacco.
>
> Alcohol causes at least seven types of cancer, including the most common cancer types, such as bowel cancer and female breast cancer. Ethanol (alcohol) causes cancer

through biological mechanisms as the compound breaks down in the body, which means that any beverage containing alcohol, regardless of its price and quality, poses a risk of causing cancer.

The risk of developing cancer increases substantially the more alcohol is consumed. However, the latest available data indicates that half of all alcohol-attributable cancers in the WHO European Region are caused by 'light' and 'moderate' alcohol consumption – less than 1.5 litres of wine or less than 3.5 litres of beer or less than 450 millilitres of spirits per week. This drinking pattern is responsible for the majority of alcohol-attributable breast cancers in women, with the highest burden observed in countries of the European Union (EU). In the EU, cancer is the leading cause of death – with a steadily increasing incidence rate – and the majority of all alcohol-attributable deaths are due to different types of cancers.

It's not a new message. The medical and scientific community have been banging the drum for decades.[57] I found an article from 1970 where the World Health Organization first recommended member states develop strategies to reduce the use of alcohol. In the UK, government research shows that alcohol is now the biggest killer of working-age adults, overtaking ten of the most dangerous forms of cancer.[58] If you know this, and go into it with your eyes open and make an informed choice, fair enough. The thing is, a lot of us don't.

A study by the British Medical Council found that public knowledge of the association between alcohol and cancer is low.[59] Unprompted (i.e., asked an open question about what causes cancer), only 13% of respondents identified cancer as a potential health outcome of alcohol consumption. Even when prompted (i.e., asked, 'what about alcohol?'), this only rose to 47%.

It's not surprising. We've been subject to decades, and billions of pounds worth, of advertising and marketing that have told us that drinking in moderation is okay, or even good for us. Unless you happen to be an avid reader of *The Lancet* or *The British Medical Journal*, you wouldn't know otherwise. What's been the response of Big Alcohol and the government to this blind spot we have with booze? Slapping cancer warnings on bottles of wine? Adverts telling kids not to start drinking and avoid getting hooked in the first place? Not so much. It's all just a little bit of history repeating. (Reading that last sentence in the style of Shirley Bassey is optional, but heavily encouraged.)

In America

The response from Big Alcohol in America has been alarmingly similar to that of Big Tobacco. Deflect, deny, discredit. Don't like the results of independent studies? Just pay for your own.

In 2018 *The New York Times*[60] blew the whistle on just how much control Big Alcohol has on the agenda in America. The investigative journalism shed light on the alarming ties between the alcohol industry and the National Institute of Health (NIH). The NIH is America's medical research agency, and part of the U.S. Department of Health and Human Services, similar to the NHS in the UK.

The New York Times published documents and interviews proving that in 2013, officials at this government agency tasked with studying the health effects of alcohol aggressively courted alcohol executives to fund a $100 million clinical trial on 'moderate drinking'.

The most shocking detail in the story is that the researchers behind the trial reportedly persuaded alcohol industry executives to fund them by arguing the trial 'represents a unique opportunity to show that moderate alcohol consumption is safe and lowers risk of common diseases' – before they had even enrolled their first patient.[61]

The study 'is not public health research – it's marketing,' Michael Siegel, a professor of community health sciences at Boston University School of Public Health, told *Times* reporter Roni Caryn Rabin. A task force was set up following *The New York Times* article to review the study; they determined that it should be terminated. 'The early and frequent engagement with industry representatives calls into question the impartiality of the process and thus, casts doubt that the scientific knowledge gained from the study would be actionable or believable,' the panel wrote.

If it wasn't for the dogged determination of a journalist to get to the bottom of who was bankrolling it, the study would have been presented to the American public as scientific, independent evidence from a government agency that moderate drinking is good for you. They would have had no idea it was bought and paid for by, amongst others, Heineken, Diageo and Carlsberg.

In the UK

Ah, but that's America. That would never be allowed to happen in the UK, would it?

Yes, dear reader, yes, it would. I found a study by the University of York that noted that since 2009, there has been a 56% increase in research funded by alcohol companies or affiliated organisations here in the UK.[62]

As the university's website notes, 'The research team from the University of York found just under 13,500 studies are directly or indirectly funded by the alcohol industry.' According to the researchers, 'The scale of alcohol industry sponsorship of scientific research raises concerns over the potential for bias, conflicts of interest and selective reporting of outcomes.'

A co-author of the study, Dr Su Golder from the Department of Health Sciences at the University of York, stated, 'Our study identified a worrying trend – While there has been a steep decline in the alcohol industry conducting its own research on health at the same time there has been an increase in the alcohol industry funding such research, by providing financial support to researchers or via alcohol related organisations. This allows alcohol companies to exploit a "transparency loophole" as many people assume these organisations are charities and don't realise the connection to the industry.'

The university quotes co-author of the study Professor Jim McCambridge:

'While researchers are meant to declare funders in peer reviewed research publications this often doesn't happen and we don't get the level of transparency we should have.

'It is well known that by sponsoring research pharmaceutical and tobacco companies successfully conspired to subvert the scientific evidence-base in order to influence policy for decades. While alcohol companies may claim they are carrying out a civic duty through their funding of research, these are studies that independent academics would be much better placed to conduct.'

The Drinkaware Scandal

At the end of an advert for booze on the radio or TV in the UK, there will be a bit where they say, as fast as humanly possible, 'Please drink responsibly. For the facts visit Drinkaware. co.uk.' If you look closely enough at the label on the back of a bottle, there will be a little circular logo with an image of a pregnant lady crossed out, and then: 'Know your limits. For the facts visit drinkaware.co.uk.'

Well, like most people, before Catherine Gray set me straight,[63] I assumed that Drinkaware was some sort of government website. Or maybe it was the NHS. Or at a push it might have been the World Health Organisation.

You could have given me a hundred guesses and I would never have gotten close to the reality. Drinkaware, the dispenser of 'the facts' about alcohol, is funded by the alcohol industry itself.

Yep, you read that correctly. The place we are directed to go for 'independent information' to 'help us make better choices about drinking' is bankrolled by the very people selling us the booze.[64]

Catherine is used to this reaction:

'When I tell people about this link, this buried bank-rolling, the health website masquerading, the reaction is always similar … How crooked is that? … That would be like a fizzy drink producer setting up a shell "charity" and calling it "sugaraware" and directing unsuspecting consumers to its website, rather than to an independent, unbiased health website. "Go to Sugaraware for the facts!" it would say on the drink cans. Yet we live in some parallel universe where the industries that cause untold mental – and physical – damage somehow get to provide "the facts" to the public.'

This isn't just Catherine going off on a rant. The view is shared by experts across the medical and scientific community. The British Medical Association said back in 2012, 'the involvement of the Drinkaware Trust in providing public health communications is a significant area of concern.'[65]

In 2014 a leading team of experts produced a paper titled 'Be Aware of Drinkaware'.[66] They noted, 'Drinkaware began as a website set up in 2004 by the Portman Group, an alcohol producer-funded organisation which has attempted to influence the evidential content of policy debates through a range of tactics, including attempts to pay academics to write anonymous critiques of World Health Organization evidenced based reviews. Both long-standing and more recent developments indicate very high levels of industry influence on British alcohol policy, and Drinkaware provides one

163

mechanism of influence. We suggest that working with, and for, industry bodies such as Drinkaware helps disguise fundamental conflicts of interest and serves only to legitimise corporate efforts to promote partnership as a means of averting evidence-based alcohol policies.'

Back in 1982 when Big Tobacco funded the 'Health Promotion Research Trust', I found a great quote from a prominent surgeon who responded with, 'It's like entrusting moral education about organised crime to the Mafia.' Thirty years later and we are letting it happen again.

In 2022 *The Guardian* ran a piece shining the light on UK pupils, as young as nine, being taught about alcohol with 'misleading and biased' information materials funded by the alcohol industry.[67] The article states:

> 'Teachers in thousands of UK schools employ lesson plans, factsheets and films produced by bodies with close ties to the drinks trade even though they "portray alcohol as a normal consumer product to impressionable young minds", the researchers found. The materials are intended to deter young people from underage drinking, but they are potentially harmful because they downplay the harms drink can cause and seek to "blame-shift" responsibility for problems from manufacturers on to young people, the researchers say. They conclude: "All programmes promoted familiarization and normalization of alcohol as a 'normal' adult consumer product, which

children must learn about and master how to
use responsibly when older."

What do we mean by promoting familiarization and nor-
malization of alcohol? The article highlighted a slide 'produced by Drinkaware for secondary schools containing the
words "drinking alcohol makes you happy" alongside an
image of young people drinking wine' as an example. The
drinks industry is telling our children that alcohol is normal,
and that it is peer pressure, or a lack of self-control that is the
cause of any problems, rather than the addictive nature of the
substance itself.

When *The Guardian* contacted Drinkaware for comment,
their response was 'Drinkaware has since removed the materials analysed by the researchers from its website. The materials
included in this research are out of date and don't reflect our
current guidance. They should have been removed from our
website and they now have been. We're sorry this didn't
happen sooner.'

Hmmmm. I'm going to take off my Agent Mulder hat
and leave it there, but I will wrap up this section with two
asks:

1. Please don't listen to back-of-the-fag-packet research
See what I did there? If your brain is directing you to the
myriad articles you've read over the years along the lines of 'a
glass of red wine a day is good for your heart', then let's put it
to bed. In a recent interview with *The Standard*,[68] Professor
Monika Arora, from the World Health Federation, said: 'The
portrayal of alcohol as necessary for a vibrant social life has

diverted attention from the harms of alcohol use, as have the frequent and widely publicised claims that moderate drinking, such as a glass of red wine a day, can offer protection against cardiovascular disease.

'These claims are at best misinformed and at worst an attempt by the alcohol industry to mislead the public about the danger of their product … The evidence is clear: any level of alcohol consumption can lead to loss of healthy life.

'Studies that claim otherwise are based on purely observational research, which fails to account for other factors, such as pre-existing conditions and a history of alcoholism in those considered to be "abstinent".

'To date, no reliable correlation has been found between moderate alcohol consumption and a lower risk of heart disease.'

2. *Please don't wait on the government to tell you it's bad*
You've seen some of the ways in which Big Alcohol has an undue influence over government policy. We've gone through the timeline on how long it took for the government to catch up with the science on smoking. I haven't even touched on the lobbying, political donations and other dealings that go on in the corridors of power. That would be a book in itself.

What I will do is quote a report from The House of Commons Public Accounts Committee which looked at the government's record on alcohol. It was issued in May 2023.[69] These committees are staffed by MPs and their purpose is to hold the government accountable. The lead MP noted:

'Today's report lays bare the lack of political will to address alcohol harm. The Government's record on alcohol harm is one of policies scrapped and promises broken. Alcohol harm is a deepening public health crisis that affects us all and it is wrong and unfair to believe that it is only alcohol dependent drinkers who are affected.

'Shamefully, it has been 11 years since the last Government UK Alcohol Strategy. The measures set out in the 2012 strategy were, and remain, effective evidence-led health policies that prevent death, improve public health and alleviate pressures on our public services. The abject failure to deliver on promised initiatives has certainly contributed to tragic yet preventable levels of alcohol harm felt across the UK.

'In recent years, there has been a concerted and somewhat successful effort from the Government to implement strategies aimed to tackle obesity, gambling, tobacco, and illicit drugs. Arguably the most harmful and legal drug, alcohol, remains unchallenged. During the Public Accounts Inquiry, the Department provided no credible justification as to why alcohol remains a conspicuous outlier.'

Think back to Covid. The bloke from Wetherspoons seemed to have as much influence on government policy as the health care professionals and scientists. It seems surreal now, but we really did class off-licences as 'essential' shops that must stay open during the peak of the pandemic. We really did prioritise getting the pubs open before libraries, schools or leisure centres.[70] Seriously, don't rely on the government to put your wellbeing first.

Growing options

Anyway, I've said my piece and shared what I found interesting on the 'Drinking is the New Smoking' angle. Rant over. Agent Mulder standing down. Like all my previous advice and insights, it's just my view. But if it does persuade you to give cutting back or completely ditching the booze a try, you will be part of a growing market, with more and more offerings being catered to it.

In June 2023, sales of low- and non-alcoholic beer at Tesco outstripped those in dry January by 25%.[71] Retailers are picking up on this and launching lines of low or no alcoholic drinks. In pubs, sales of low and no-alcohol beer have risen by 23% during the past year, and have more than doubled since 2019, according to the British Beer and Pub Association.[72]

Alcohol-free bars are popping up all over the country. There's also a growing number of alcohol-free social clubs who put on virtual and in-person events, creating spaces for non-drinkers and those who are interested in going alcohol free. Sobersocials.co.uk is a great site which collates the sober groups operating in the UK and Ireland by region; it's a good place to check what's in your area if you're interested. From sober raves and comedy clubs through to book clubs, there's sure to be something to float your sober boat. Alternatively, if you're ever near Glasgow and fancy going on a hill walk to build up an appetite for a big breakfast when the cafe opens at nine, look me up.

Split Screening

Early in my recovery, I read an interview with Veronica Valli in *The Guardian*.[73] Veronica is a recovery coach and author of *Soberful*.[74] She discussed the way it has been deeply ingrained in us by the media, culture and our peers that alcohol is the best way to have fun and, therefore, sobriety must be boring. At the time of the interview, she had been sober for twenty-three years, and she'd found the opposite to be true. She couldn't think of a single thing that isn't more fun without alcohol. She talked about us giving too much credit to alcohol. That we spoil things that are already fun by adding alcohol to them and making them just like any other day. The example she used was Christmas.

'I loved Christmas when I was a kid: sitting around with loved ones exchanging gifts, eating delicious food and watching movies is inherently fun. You really don't need to embellish a day like that with alcohol. In my drinking days, I cancelled out all the joy of Christmas by opening the champagne at breakfast and passing out by late afternoon with a glass of whisky in my hand. Only now do I realise that I was wasting one of the best days of the year; drinking made it just like any other day. Of course, Christmas might not be your thing, with or without alcohol. But spending time with people you love, in any context, is often more enjoyable when you're sober. Valentine's night, for instance, becomes a much more romantic occasion when you're not hammered on pink champagne. Certainly there is something about not needing to keep a bucket on standby beside the bed that reignites the magic in a relationship.'

When I first read this article, I was still in the first few weeks of recovery. It didn't resonate as I was still trying to shake the 'giving up' mindset. Then, around two months in, I went out for a steak with my wife sober and had a beautiful evening, sans the litres of red wine that would normally accompany it. That's when I had my big aha moment, and got what Veronica meant. It clicked.

The morning after, I journaled about what my evening would have been like if I was drinking, and did a compare and contrast. I found this 'split screening' useful for reminding me what I was gaining by not drinking. I've pulled out a few of my journals from the first twelve months to give you a flavour.

Out for dinner – February 2022 – Two months sober
I'm two months sober, which has coincided with restrictions from the pandemic loosening up. My wife and I have got a babysitter and have decided to go out for steak, which is always one of our favourite things to do. When my wife says, 'Shall we go out for steak?' my mind jumps straight to the large goblets of Malbec that go hand in hand with it.

Wine and steak are so interlinked in my mind I was worried I would really struggle to go back to a steak restaurant and enjoy it without drinking. The old routine for steak night was embedded in my mind.

To make the most of having a babysitter, I would want to have a couple of drinks in the house before we go out, you know, just to get the evening started so we could relax. It would begin well, with my wife nursing her way through a glass while she was getting ready, while I would be ready first and get down to the kitchen and make sure I finished off most of the bottle. I would make a show of topping up my wife's glass so I could convince myself that she had two glasses and it was a fairly even split.

We would then get a taxi or the train into town, depending on where the restaurant was. My wife would want to go straight to the restaurant, but I would be angling for us to pop into a nearby cocktail bar for some pre-dinner cocktails. This would be under the premise of us 'making the most of the evening' but really it was just another way for me to get more booze in. My wife would acquiesce and we would pop in to some overpriced cocktail bar. If I was brutally honest with myself, I would have been happy downing warm cans of gin and tonic on the train or taxi there, but I was still deluding myself that I was drinking socially, and so the cocktail bar added an element of sophistication and glamour to the booze, which also kept my wife on board.

While my wife was looking for cocktails that contained flavours that appealed to her, or that would look pretty, I would be running the numbers on the potential alcohol content of each, while simultaneously weighing this against the size of the glass it would be served in, and the likelihood of it being overly iced, which would dilute the booze and thus defeat the purpose.

We would order and the mixologist / cocktail curator or whatever name they were giving the barman would start putting on a show by mixing the drinks. This is why we were paying through the nose for the drinks and, along with the high-end surroundings, this was the very thing I was supposed to be savouring. My wife was. But by now it would have been a while since the last drink, and I would be getting agitated that it was taking so long for my drink to come. I would watch the mixologist / curator throwing a bottle of vodka over his head, or dramatically rolling the mixers across his shoulder, and picture myself grabbing him by the scruff of the neck and shouting at him to pour the drinks and stop fucking about.

But I would never do that – it would blow my cover. Instead, I would smile and nod, ooh and ahh with the rest of the normal people, while clenching my teeth and white-knuckling it until, eventually, after much unnecessary farting about and fanfare, the drinks would be presented to us.

My wife would be delighted with hers and take her time, savouring it. I would be quietly dying inside that my drink was too small and that it had taken so long to 'curate'. I would inhale mine instantly and make a comment about not being able to taste any alcohol in it. About it being mainly ice. I would immediately order a double gin and tonic to drink while my wife drank her cocktail.

When we got to the restaurant, I would get a large gin and tonic as soon as we sat down, then engage in some pretentious chit-chat with the waiter about which red would best complement our choice of steak. This was completely performative. By this point I would be half cut, and I could have been drinking pints of unleaded for all the notice I was paying to the taste. I wouldn't bother with starters as I no longer had much of an appetite. I would eat the steak, but it was competing for space with litres of booze. It was wasted on me. By this stage I would have been just as happy chomping down on a kebab.

My wife wouldn't be drinking at anywhere near the same pace as me. We would be on completely different levels. By the time the mains were finished, she would be gently reminding me I had already told her that story. Or I was being a bit loud and we might need to keep it down. What was supposed to be a treat for us both, a break from the kids, would end up with my wife babysitting me, persuading me we'd had enough, and that it was time to go home. When she got me home, depending on the state I was in, she would go through the exhausting process of negotiating how much more drink I was going to sit up and have, or put me in the spare room with a basin.

This time when my wife and I go out for dinner, I drive. We have skipped lunch and are starving by the time we get there. We order a mix of starters to share and work our way through them all. We savour the steak when it comes. We genuinely enjoy the food and appreciate it. We are both on the same level and use the time away from the kids to engage with each other, properly talk. It's lovely. When we eventually finish and ask for the bill, it's much less than normal. I think they have made a mistake. They haven't, it's just that we've had a couple of soft drinks and water with our meal, instead of expensive bottles of red and cocktails. It's a third of what it would normally be. I've paid so much less but gotten so much more out of the evening. I drive us home, and we chat and laugh all the way. When we get home, the basin stays in the kitchen, and I'm not in the spare room.

Work trip away – April 2022 – Four months sober
Work trips were always a great excuse to get on it. In finance there is a big 'work hard, play hard' culture, which knocks up a gear when you're on an away job. As the pandemic restrictions continue to lift and things get back to normal, there is an expectation I will be flying down to London more regularly. The upcoming trips will be a test of my resolve. A big reason I have managed to stay sober so far is because I've told my wife I will, and I don't want to let her down. I haven't told anyone at work I don't drink yet.

My April trip is for three days. Realistically I could get back on it, let the good times roll for the first couple of days and then dry out for the last one and be back home like nothing happened. My wife would be none the wiser. It crosses my mind.

I'm going to be travelling down with two lads who have the same all-or-nothing approach to boozing as I did. My last trip down to London with them was like a stag do. We had a few pints at the airport, and then took full advantage of the free drinks on the British Airways London City flight. We were pretty drunk when we got there, and the sensible thing would have been to grab dinner then call it a night and be up fresh for the morning.

Instead, we went out to the pub nearest the hotel, and used our dinner expenses on bar snacks and five or six pints before getting back to the hotel bar for a night cap. The next morning was a disaster. I had made it to bed but passed out before setting an alarm, so I woke late. I hadn't unpacked or ironed any of my clothes, so I had to do that while fighting back the urge to vomit. I arrive at the client site dishevelled, late, and feeling and looking like death.

I gave the client my apologies and referred to the food at my hotel being a bit ropey and suspecting some sort of food poisoning. They were understanding and re-worked some of my meeting slots to try and make up for the late start. I got through it, but this was far from my best work. I spent the day on the back foot, trying to make up the time while fighting the fear and anxiety that went along with the physical pain of a hangover.

I met my colleagues for the last flight back home from London City. They must have been in the same shape as me, but it was brave faces all round. We had a few tender sips of our pints in the departure lounge, had a laugh about the night before, and shared war stories of how we each made it through our days. I had a few Bloody Marys on the flight back in the hopes the 'hair of the dog' would take the edge off the hangover.

When I got home, I was exhausted, yet had a terrible sleep that night running through the things I forgot to say during the meetings, and thinking about what I would have done differently if I was more prepared. The next day I was knackered, summoning the resolve to pull myself together and limp through the week to make it to Friday.

This time, my trip is a world away from that.

As I'm still avoiding talking about my not drinking, I

duck the question of why I'm not having pints in the airport by booking a slightly earlier flight than my colleagues.

At the airport I chill and read a book with a coffee. When I arrive at my hotel, and for the first time ever, I make use of the gym. I hit it hard, then go for a swim, sauna and steam. I feel great, and I have worked up an appetite for dinner.

I would normally choose somewhere to eat based on their willingness to mask the bar tab as a dinner receipt (for it to make it through expenses and look like we actually used the dinner allowance for food); this time I decide based on the type of food I want like a normal person.

London is awash with choices, and a colleague recommends a great place to try. I go alone, with my book, and make my way through three courses. Drinking me would never have had the confidence to eat in a restaurant alone, but it's no biggie now. Again, by not boozing, my bill is much smaller than expected and is covered by my expenses policy, rather than me having to make up the difference.

After dinner I go for a walk, then head back to my hotel, iron my clothes and get everything ready for the morning. I get a solid eight hours of sleep and wake rested. I get to the office early and am well prepared for my meetings. It's a back-to-back day, but I am confident I can deliver, rather than on the back foot making excuses.

I'm out for dinner in a large group with the client on the second night. I use some of the tricks from the going sober chapter. I make sure to buy the first couple of rounds and get myself a Guinness Zero. When we are seated at the table, I let them pour a glass of red for me and have it in front of me but move on to fake 'gin and tonics' quickly. Later, one of the more enthusiastic drinkers clocks I haven't touched the red. I say I filled myself up on Guinness and had to move on to gin. They don't care; they just want to know if they can have it. I gladly say yes.

When some of them want to head to a pub after dinner, I use the change of location to make my excuses to the more senior clients, who are also leaving, and peel off and head back to the hotel. The second and third days are a repeat of the first, with me being well rested and well prepared.

When I'm heading back to the airport to fly home, I'm doing so with plenty of time. I don't feel harassed or like I'm chasing the clock. I board the flight and play back how I would normally feel returning from a work trip, versus how I feel now. I give myself a pat on the back. Although it's been a busy few days, I don't feel knackered. If anything, I am energised. I can now relax, read my book and chill. The trolley comes round with the complimentary drinks and I consider, for the briefest moment, if I can just have one. I knock the idea around in my head. I realise that as soon as I have one, I will try another, and another. I leave it and get myself a ginger ale.

Holiday – September 2022 – Eight months sober
For most Brits, holidays are entwined with drinking. We've grown up watching our dads have the ceremonial airport pint at departures, and we've helped mum with the trolley dash in duty free on the way home. Whether it's the first ice-cold beer of the day, or trying new cocktails and local wines at dinner, drinking is part of the routine of the British holiday.

Before I had kids, holidays were almost exclusively

centred on drinking. The destinations might have gotten more upmarket as I got older, as fish bowls on the strip gave way to cocktails on the terrace, but the premise of going away for two weeks to drink as much as possible was the same.

The outcome was also fairly consistent. In public, I would return uttering variations of, 'It was great, but I think I need a holiday to get over the holiday hahaha.' In secret, I would be embroiled in negotiations with my travel insurance provider about how much of the cost of my hospital visit (three times) and lost phone / passport / travel documentation (ten plus) they would cover. I would be more stressed, more overweight and more tired than when I'd gone away.

Even when we went on holiday with the kids, and the focus was on things we could do with them, I was still trying to shoehorn in some drinking. Get the kids to sleep so we can have a drink on the balcony. Sneak off for a walk and get a few quick pints in – it's my holiday, too, after all.

This month we are off to Center Parcs. A wholesome family-friendly destination – surely easy to stay off the booze on holiday there? You'd think, but this is my second visit, and I know otherwise. The suits at Center Parcs know how to make money, and making sure that an overpriced pint for dad or white wine for mum is never far from reach is profitable. Taking the kids to the arcade or visiting the soft play? Bar is just to the left. Enjoying a family swim in the subtropical splash centre? Recreate the beach vibe by having a frozen daiquiri or pint of ice-cold beer at the poolside while you're keeping an eye on the kids.

From last time, I know it wasn't acceptable to get 'I've lost my passport' smashed, but keeping a middle-class buzz throughout the holiday was encouraged. I might not need to claim on my insurance, but I would still come back heavier and exhausted.

This time, without the booze, I've come back well rested, and having fully taken part in loads of activities with the kids rather than sloping off to the bar while they were occupied. I feel fitter than before I went.

Christmas – December 2022 – Twelve months sober
Technically this will be my second sober Christmas. The first coming just three days after my last mini rock bottom. The hangover was still fresh and my 'never again' resolve was high. Despite this, it was still pretty tough to avoid drinking.

Christmas 2021
We are spending Christmas with my wife's family. She went ahead early with the kids (which is why I was alone in the house for my one-man-three-bottles Christmas present wrapping party) and I get there on Christmas Eve.

My wife's family know me as a big drinker. My mother-in-law is a nurse on a renal unit. She sees the effects of alcohol abuse daily as she helps people on and off dialysis machines for most of her shift. She has voiced concern about my drinking multiple times. But it's Christmas, and she is a good host, so she has a beer waiting for me on arrival. 'That's you finished work. The Christmas holidays have officially begun, and I've got you a beer.' My quick response is, 'Oh, I might just have a cup of tea and warm up first. Thanks, though.'

Later at diner I manage to dodge the wine with excuses about expecting the kids to be up super early to see what

Santa has brought them and wanting to be fresh. The next morning, as we are about to go out for a morning walk, my father-in-law hands me a Baileys with ice. It's 10am. Normally I would have been delighted, downed it and kicked off the day, but now I'm looking at it like it's poison. I chink glasses, pretend to drink, then set it down and misplace it.

The day continues like this. My wife's family are not big drinkers in the slightest, but at Christmas it is constant. I hadn't noticed when I was taking part, but now that I'm not I really see it. Smoked salmon and buck's fizz for breakfast. Try this mulled wine … Irish coffee anyone? Who wants white and who wants red, or will we open both? It feels like an endurance test. I am batting away offers with 'I'm good for now thanks, will get one later,' but it is hard work.

And then something awful happens. Our youngest child is taken seriously ill. We thought he just had a bad cough, but after dinner his temperature spikes and there is nothing we can do to get it down. We call NHS 24, and they tell us to take him to hospital immediately.

The rest of the house is in a panic as they debate who will be the least over the limit and best to drive. Apart from my wife, there is genuine shock when I say I've not been drinking and will be driving. No one else has noticed, and it was just assumed I was smashed as usual. I get my son and wife in the car and then to the hospital in no time. He has a severe case of bronchiolitis but is thankfully able to be treated right away. The doctors and nurses are amazing. Holding him in my arms and seeing him burning up, but not being able to do anything, is one of the scariest moments of my life. I will always be grateful to live in a country where we have access to life-saving treatment when we need it.

The next morning, I am the talk of breakfast. 'What would have happened if Paddy wasn't sober?' my mother-in-law says with a beaming smile. I'm not overly religious or spiritual, but I believe I was sober that day for a reason, and it spurred me on for the first few months.

Christmas 2004–2020

Life-saving hero and first sober Christmas aside, Christmas day from the age of sixteen onwards has seen me either topping myself up from Christmas Eve or, having saved myself for the big day, diving into an all-day drinking session with vigour.

My birthday is on the 15th December, so between that, the office Christmas party and every other excuse during the 'season to be jolly', I would spend the entire second half of December drunk or nursing a hangover. I absolutely loved this time of year. It was when everyone seemed to drink the way that I did, and I thought drinking was what made Christmas awesome.

But one year sober, I'm looking back without the rose-tinted glasses and coming round to Veronica Valli's assessment that by drinking I was 'cancelling out all the joy of Christmas by opening the champagne at breakfast'. There were so many years where my mum had spent days preparing a delicious Christmas dinner only for me to be too hungover to enjoy it or too smashed to appreciate it. (Sorry Mum.) Or where the day ended in an argument between family members over a drunken comment or misunderstanding. Veronica was right. Getting together with the people you love, eating nice food, swapping presents – that sort of thing is good in its own right. Adding booze is only likely to diminish that experience.

Christmas 2022

We are hosting my family this year. By now they all know I don't drink, so I don't need to spend the day pretending to lose drinks or repeating 'I'm good for now thanks, maybe later.' As we know that the kids will be up from 5am, we arrange a big Christmas breakfast, rather than the usual dinner.

Everyone arrives at 10am and we spend the day watching the kids open and play with their new gifts and exchanging our own. We eat awesome food, go for walks, watch films and even have a go at Articulate and Trivial Pursuit. Both are much easier sober, but I still find the questions on Trivial Pursuit infuriatingly difficult (seriously, how can anyone be expected to know who the official hair consultant to the 1984 Los Angeles Olympics was?). There are plenty of nodding heads when I suggest using the junior questions for the later rounds.

The day wraps up around 4pm, with the family leaving so we can get the kids bathed and try to let them wind down a bit before bed. If drinking were involved, this would never be the case. I would have wanted to put the kids to bed and keep the party going. When the kids are in bed, my wife and I chill for a while and watch a Christmas film and chat through our highlights of the day before heading to bed ourselves. It is bliss. Oh, and the answer was Vidal Sassoon, just in case you need it in the future.

Relapse: The Pivot to 99%

I hate all the negative connotations of the word relapse. It reeks of stigma and judgement, but that's what it seems to be known as and we should cover it, as it's pretty likely to happen at some point.

It's difficult to get stats on the people who try and go sober without seeking external help, but the rates of relapse for those who enter recovery from alcohol addiction are quite high. Multiple studies[75] reflect that about 40–60% of individuals relapse within thirty days of leaving an inpatient alcohol treatment centre, and up to 85% relapse within the first year.

If I was to follow the strict definition of time spent sober, and was actively counting days and following a more traditional approach to sobriety, then my current run should not have started on the 22nd December 2021. It would be about six months later, on the 31st July 2022, when I came back from a stag do, after my first and so far only 'relapse'. If I was following the more traditional methods, I would have had to reset the timer, and start counting the days all over again. I don't follow the more traditional methods because they don't work for me, but more on that, and the importance of being flexible and finding what works for you, in the next chapter.

Back to 'relapse': 'falling off the wagon'; 'slipping back into old ways'; whatever we want to call it. I wasn't sure if I should put it in, which probably gives us an insight into the stigma and shame around it. I wondered if it would make me less credible. Who is this guy to be giving us advice? He only lasted six months before he relapsed. I considered not sharing the 99% sober approach at all and making this a more traditional memoir about 100% sobriety. If I had started the book from 31st July 2022, it would have let you pick up the story from there, offering a nice little arc of recovery and then sailing off into the sunset. However, I would argue that my relapse was a big part of the process and laid the groundwork for the next full year of sobriety. It was the beginning of my 99% sober methodology. The relapse cemented my approach. Plus, you would have missed the first six months, where all the heavy lifting occurred. Here's how the decision to drink again snuck up on me.

July 2022

I had already signed up to go to this stag do prior to deciding to stop drinking. One of my closest friends from my time in Guernsey was getting married. It would be a great chance to see him and all my other close friends from my Guernsey days in one place. I knew what I was signing up for. A booze-filled weekend in Ireland where we got paralytic together and reminisced about the good old days. I was buzzing about it.

However, since deciding to stop drinking, the date was now loaded with fear and doubt. Would I be able to go and not drink? Should I tell people I had stopped drinking? Would that make it easier? Should I even go at all? As the date grew closer, however, I was more and more confident and comfortable in my sobriety. I had been getting on well using the tips from my Socialising Sober guide and I was cruising through nights out, drinking tonics or pints of Guinness Zero – 'faking it'. I was declining drinks with an easy, 'No thanks, I'm good for now, got one here,' like it was nothing.

Remember the advice I was dishing out in the Going Sober chapter about prioritising your sobriety through avoiding high-pressure situations until your 'choosing not to drink muscle' is more developed? Well, it's not that I ignored this advice; it's just that I got a bit complacent. I thought that my 'choosing not to drink' muscle was much bigger than it was. I completely underestimated how strong the Ivan Drago 'choose to drink' muscle would be when I was back among all my old Party Paddy mates. In Ireland. On a stag do.

After much deliberation, I decided to go on the stag do. The plan was to not drink, but also not tell anyone. I would just stick to Guineas Zero for the first few drinks, and if one of the nights got too much for me, I could take a breather, or go home early. No big deal. This approach had served me well so far, but with hindsight it was very naive to think it would work on a stag do, or perhaps subconsciously I knew this and just wanted to go and get paralytic anyway. The event itself was just too wrapped up in drinking. I couldn't properly take part; it would have been a much more diminished experience without my drinking.

I managed to stick to Guinness Zero for the first few rounds. But eventually some very real pints of Guinness started to pile up in front of me. 'Not like you to be off the pace, Paddy. Have you still not drunk that last one?' I wasn't ready to explain. I was in Ireland. I was back with all my mates from Guernsey. They were getting ridiculously drunk all around me, having a great time. So I crumbled, in the first pub of the first night. I drank. I fully joined in. I kept it going for the full weekend. I absolutely loved it.

As the first few drinks went down, I wondered if my drinking style had changed at all. Maybe my tolerance would be lower? Maybe I would be a more responsible drinker now that I had managed six months off? Maybe the hangover wouldn't be as bad? The answers were no, no and no.

I picked right back up where I left off, drinking in the old 'foot to the floor' manner and downing pints at an alarming rate. I remember noticing this in the second pub of the night and I had a eureka moment. I realised that even if I took years off from drinking, whenever I picked it up again it would always be like this. It's like if Stevie Wonder took a year off from performing. He wouldn't lose all his talents because of the time off. Stick him back in front of a piano and I'm sure he would still be able to bang out a tune.

The hangover after the first night was just like all the others, and the way to feel better was to get back on it, the same as it had always been. So that's what I did. Again, I loved it.

With a day of travel to get back home from Ireland, this provided a natural cut-off point and let me dry out by the time I got home.

Previously I would have returned from the stag do and been disappointed in myself and beat myself up. What was wrong with me? Why was I so weak willed I couldn't say no to a pint of Guinness? Was I a schoolboy who had to cave to peer pressure? Eventually I would have started to rationalise it. I would have thought, right, I've had six months off the booze with no problems. I've proved I'm not an alcoholic; I've reset. While I may have to be extra careful, and work hard at it, I don't want to go fully abstinent and never drink again and miss out on events like that. I will try to moderate and be one of the 'normal drinkers'. I would then have gone through the usual cycle of attempts at moderation, failing and then beating myself up. The old loop would continue.

But this time was different. It might have been a new perspective after six months off drinking, the longest I'd gone to date. It might have been the masses of addiction research and quit literature I had read. It might have been something in one of the self-help books I had been leaning on to get me through.

This time, while acknowledging I didn't plan to end my six months of sobriety on the stag do, rather than getting back home and diving into feeling like I had failed, or thinking, 'Well, its fucked now, may as well stay on it,' I was able to let my feelings sit for a while. I used the journaling technique from the Going Sober chapter and wrote them all down and tried to understand them more.

If I was being honest with myself, I knew even if I was able to go back in time and relive the stag do, 100 times out of 100 I would have ended up on the booze. Refreshingly for me, I didn't feel any shame or guilt about this. It was just true. The nature of who I am. I was able to say, 'Do you know what? I really enjoyed that, and all things being equal, I would do it again.' I was proud of my six months sober, but there hadn't really been any events during that period where drinking in the 'foot to the floor' way that I drink would have enhanced the experience.

I underlined that last bit when I went back to read it again the next day. Events *where drinking would enhance the experience.* There was something in that for me. Drinking in moderation does not work for me. It's all or nothing. If I feel like I am depriving myself, abstinence will only work for short periods, and eventually my will power will run out and I will end up drinking again.

What if, rather than setting myself up for a fall, bouncing between failed moderation and abstinence, I decided to drink only on occasions where *drinking would enhance the experience?*

What if I only drank when I would be able to look back the next day and feel like I did after the stag do, that it was worth it, and I would do it again?

If you're at the stage I was when I quit, you'll think that's a nonsense statement. Your mindset will be that drinking on *any* occasion can enhance your experience. I get it. I used to agree. But that's why I would say you need at least three to six months of sobriety to give yourself a chance. The longer the period you can spend sober, the more space you will have in your life for things other than drinking. And the more you experience things sober, the less likely you will feel that alcohol does enhance the experience, or that alcohol is making your life better overall.

And so I flexed my approach. It was undeniable that my life was a million times better without booze. I knew that my sleep, finances, relationships, confidence, self-respect and one-hundred-and-one other things had all skyrocketed since choosing to stop. I knew that, logically, the benefits of not drinking massively outweighed the exceptionally rare times it genuinely did enhance the experience. I knew all that. But, six months in, I also knew myself a whole lot better as well.

I knew that deep in the back of my mind, I would feel hard done by, or that I was depriving myself of something, if I was to rule out the possibility of ever joining in on a stag do. I also knew way more about alcohol. I had spent six months inhaling research on it and widening my understanding of alcohol and my relationship with it.

I previously worked on the basis that there were two distinct types of people: those who could drink 'normally' and then 'the alcoholics'. The alcoholics had ruined drinking for themselves and could never drink again. The alcoholics in my mind were caricatures. The type you would see in an ITV drama. They couldn't be in the same room when drink was consumed, such was the power it held over them. A single sniff would send them back to rock bottom and they'd be back on the park bench drinking cider or pouring vodka on their cornflakes.

I was desperate not to be one of the alcoholics. I couldn't face never drinking again, so I tried and tried and tried again to be one of the normal drinkers who could have a few to be sociable and then stop.

Now, I knew that it was much more nuanced than that, and I needed a more nuanced approach. With my improved confidence and self-esteem, I knew that I could come up with an approach that worked for me. Or give it a go, and if it didn't work, I could not beat myself up about it and have the confidence to try again until it did.

So I devised a '99% sober' approach. I thought this approach was going to be my revolutionary gift to the world, but it turned out the movement was already well up and running long before I flew back from Ireland with a hangover and a headful of ideas. It's part of the wider trend of mindful drinking and being sober curious. Those who rarely drink, but who make occasional exceptions. It makes sense for people who don't want to put pressure on themselves to give up completely.

I did more research. I've referenced articles from *The Guardian*[76] and *Men's Health*[77] if you are keen and want more detail, but in a nutshell, 99% sober – sometimes referred to as 'dry by default' – is a lifestyle in which you only drink on special occasions. Outside those occasions (i.e., 99% of the time), you are sober. I felt like this approach would work for me. Instead of restricting myself with the 'drinker' or 'non-drinker' labels, I was placing myself as somewhere in between. I was, however, a bit worried about the looseness of the concept of 'drinking on special occasions'.

I had tried drinking only on special occasions before, when I was at the peak of my drinking, but it just meant the bar for an occasion to be 'special' was dropped incredibly low. 'Oh, we've not had an Indian in ages; this is a bit of a treat, a special occasion. Let's get eight pints to wash it down.' For it to work for me, I was going to have to spend a bit of time locking down what this meant and giving myself strong parameters, but it felt like this approach was giving me control. I was going to decide when I would drink.

Rather than 'drinking on special occasions', my focus was going to be on drinking when it would enhance the experience. Consciously deciding when, all things considered, drinking is worth it. When will it serve me? When will I look back the next morning without regrets? When is the hangover worth it? Does it enhance my experience? Rather than just running out of will power at a random event a few months down the line. So, I sat down a few days after the stag do and pulled together my list of genuine special occasions. What were the events I was likely to attend *where drinking would enhance the experience*?

I ran through loads. Weddings? I've shared with you what a liability I was at them when I was drinking. I didn't want to go back to being the one being carried out and bundled into a taxi at the end of the night. I liked being able to take in and remember the day.

Christmas? Again, the sober version was much better. Same with birthdays, holidays, work events, dinners. When I held up the lens of 'is this an event *where drinking would enhance the experience*?' after six months of being sober, the answer was usually no. After much deliberation, I eventually arrived at the following scenarios, where I would willingly take off the sober hat and *choose* to drink:

- Another stag do. If one of my close friends were getting married again, I wouldn't want to not go to their stag do. And if it was anything like every other stag do I've been on, this would mean putting myself in a situation that revolved around drink. In this situation, I knew that drinking was the only way to fully participate. I accepted this, and I really enjoy a stag do. For the next stag, I'd give myself a pass.

- Vegas. I'd been to Las Vegas twice, and had a great time partying hard, gambling and boozing. I genuinely think Vegas was an experience that was enhanced by drinking. I couldn't imagine going and not having a drink. If I ever found myself back in Vegas, all bets were off.
- Ibiza. Along the same lines as Vegas. I'd been for a week and fully taken part in the hedonistic lifestyle. Pool parties by day, clubbing at night. It was all fuelled by copious amounts of alcohol. If I ever went again, I'd want the same experience.

And for me, that was it. Stag do, Vegas, Ibiza. Those were my three. The occasions that passed the test, when I thought that if I drank in the way I drink, it would enhance the experience and be worth it.

For twenty years my identity was wrapped up in my ability to consume alcohol, so this was a big shift. Looking at the list I had given myself, it was also likely that I would end up being 99.99% sober. Most of my close friends are married already. And at thirty-seven with two young kids, the opportunities to party hard in Vegas and Ibiza don't really come up that often. I also knew I would be cheating myself and the whole 99% sober ethos if I was to start creating them. 'I think the kids would get a lot out of a trip to Vegas this year, love. Centre Parcs is becoming a bit dull.'

Since the stag do in July 2022, there haven't been any others, and I've been sober ever since. I don't count days, and you could argue that my list is pointless. Even so, just allowing myself that 1% wiggle room, keeping the door slightly ajar and giving myself the option, meant that I no longer felt like I was depriving myself of anything. I wasn't poor abstinent Paddy with his non-drinking cross to bear. I had made a choice, and continued to make the choice, not to drink. It works for me.

Do What Works for You

While the 99% sober approach might be working for me, it may be a terrible idea for you. You may prefer the more binary choice of 'I don't drink at all', where you can take comfort from the certainty that brings. And that's okay. Throughout this book I've shared what works for me, and what may be worth a try, but we are all different. In *The Unexpected Joy of Being Sober*, Catherine Gray sums up the different approaches nicely:

> 'If there is one thing I've learned about being sober, it's that what works for me will not necessarily work for someone else. Hitting upon the right mix of tools is like chancing upon the correct combination that opens a safe door. *Cue a satisfying clunk.* The door swings open and beyond it, there is freedom from alcohol…
>
> 'I know successfully sober people who did ten-plus years of AA, decided it wasn't for them, and swapped it out for yoga and medit-

ation; I know people who switch up Smart Recovery and AA; people in Refuge Recovery; people who do straight AA five times a week and yet have never done the steps or gotten a sponsor; people who rely exclusively on CBT therapy; people who simply read a lot about recovery.'

What worked for me was reading the memoirs of people like Catherine, who got sober, carrying out a tonne of research (articles, studies, podcasts, wandering down rabbit holes on sober forums and blogs), keeping a journal, exercise and, even if initially grudgingly, embracing self-help – gratitude, breathwork and mindfulness.

I had to run through lots of attempts at moderation, and attempts at going 100% sober, before I found the combination that worked for me. Where I was going wrong for the decade or so before was that I wasn't learning from each failed attempt and then trying something different. All my attempts were a version of viewing it as 'giving something up' and then relying on sheer willpower, which would eventually run out.

As the saying goes, 'Insanity is doing the same thing over and over again, but expecting different results.' (Unknown.)

While I can't give you a magic fix, I can hopefully save you some time by offering this advice; don't doggedly keep trying something that worked for someone else, or that you think should work for you. If you try out something and it doesn't work, chalk it up as a learning experience and try something else. Don't view it as failure; it's just trial and error.

Your way

Twelve-steps-based treatment programmes, online and in-person therapeutic communities, residential-based rehabilitation, cognitive-behaviour-based therapy, contingency management, motivational enhancement, intervention-based recovery … I've not even scratched the surface.

Up until I properly flung myself into it in December 2021, my understanding of what going sober meant was based on what I had seen in films or on those ITV dramas I mentioned earlier. It was the alcoholic detective, grimly sitting through another 'meeting' in the basement of a church hall, sipping bad coffee from a paper cup. Even films centred on substance abuse were pretty restricted in their view of recovery. The alcoholic character would have their dramatic rock bottom, then get locked away for twenty-eight days in rehab to be fixed. They would emerge with a steely determination to spend their life 'working the programme, doing the steps'.

I have zero first-hand experience of Alcoholics Anonymous or any other group-based methods of recovery, but I didn't think AA was for me and couldn't get past the initial fear of sharing in a group. I also knew that a residential programme was out of the question. (I didn't have any spare money to pay for it, because, you know, booze, and I certainly didn't have the sick days to cover it, again, booze).

So, if I couldn't go to AA, and couldn't 'check in to rehab', by default this left me to my own devices, and another crack at sobriety using willpower, or a misguided attempt at moderation. But now, having dived head-first into the sober sphere, I know there is a world of options. As I prefer the ones that don't involve engaging with other people to directly talk about drinking (e.g., research, breathwork, meditation, exercise, journaling), I haven't touched on the others much in this book. But if talking about it helps you, then you really are spoiled for choice.

Your GP is a good first port of call as they can set you up with support in your area, including free one-to-one counselling sessions. There is also Drinkline, the national alcohol helpline operated by the NHS, which you can call free in complete confidence on 0300 123 1110.

Then you have Alcoholics Anonymous. Its twelve-step programme involves getting sober with the help of regular support groups. There is SMART recovery – SMART stands for 'self-management and recovery training' – which focuses on the latest scientific research. It is strongly influenced by cognitive behavioural therapy. There is Rational Recovery (this is where the Addictive Voice Recognition came from), and Women For Sobriety (which, as the name suggests, provides more female-focused support). There's lots more – One Year No Beer, Hello Sunday Morning, Club Soda and The Luckiest Club, to name a few. Learn a bit more about them all and see what you think will work for you.

Whatever one you choose to learn more about, I've found that, to paraphrase Kevin Costner in *Field Of Dreams* – if you Google it, the adverts will come. Each will promote their method as the most effective. I'm not knocking any one method over another; whatever works for whoever it works for, fair play. All I will say is that there is no consensus among the scientific or medical communities that one form of treatment is better than another. I've shared a link to evidence-based studies[78] in the back if you are keen, but the only thing they can all agree on is that doing something is better than nothing. Basically, it's up to you to find what works for you.

Your label

Although the terms alcoholic and alcoholism are used a lot when we talk about heavy drinking, the scientific and medical communities have been moving away from these for years.[79] The term 'alcoholic' carries cultural baggage and stigma. Historically, substance misuse has been treated as a moral failing rather than a serious mental health condition. Thinking about someone as an 'alcoholic' can be a limiting approach that downplays the fact that unhealthy alcohol use and alcohol use disorder is something that can be resolved.

The fear of being labelled an alcoholic was one factor that kept me searching for moderation. What will I tell people? What will they think when I say I don't drink? Will they think I'm an alcoholic? The fear of being branded an alcoholic was another reason to keep drinking. So, what words should you use?

The more clinically accepted term is unhealthy alcohol use, or a person with an alcohol use disorder, but again, I would say it's up to you to decide. There are those who own the alcoholic label and wear it with pride. There is a school of thought that says the more we own the label, and speak honestly about our experiences of recovery, the less stigma there will be.

I touched on this at the start of the book but, for me, in an ideal world we wouldn't have the term at all. I personally question how useful it is to approach alcoholism as a disease, a medical condition that only affects alcoholics. As I said before, people who regularly take cocaine don't suffer from 'cocainism'. People who smoke regularly aren't 'smokaholics'. They don't suffer from a disease. They have simply taken an addictive substance, cocaine or nicotine, and become addicted to it and now use it regularly, even though it has a negative impact on their health and wellbeing. I think the term alcoholic encourages people to view drinking differently. Alcoholic lends itself to viewing the person as the problem, rather than the addictive substance.

We don't live in an ideal world. The label is here. And for the people who want to own it, and feel comfortable, I am full of admiration. I think they are right. The more open and honest we are, and the more society sees a wider range of people who have alcohol problems or have recovered from them, the more the stigma is removed. The quicker we will be able to move away from the ITV drama alcoholic-detective caricature most of us start with and view it as a nuanced topic that affects a range of people.

For me, personally, at the time of writing (November 2023), I am not there. I still don't feel it fits me to say, 'I am an alcoholic.' I was addicted to alcohol, no doubt. I fell into the bucket of 'person with an alcohol use disorder', but I don't like being called an alcoholic. It just doesn't feel right. I feel much more comfortable saying I am 99% sober, or dry by default.

As an aside, I also don't like being called Pat; that doesn't feel right for me either. For me, there is only one Pat. Her second name is Butcher. All the other Pats are just playing for second prize. Paddy is great, Patrick if you want to be formal.

If I'm asked directly, 'Are you an alcoholic?' (which happens more frequently now that I'm more open about not drinking), rather than get into a debate about the term and feel like a buzzkill on a night out, I will say something like 'I don't know if I would call myself an alcoholic, but I know my life is much better without drinking,' and leave it there.

Alcoholic, recovering alcoholic, teetotal, friend of Bill's, non-drinker, cutting back, just taking a break, Pat, or no label at all. Whatever you go for, it's for you to decide. Find what fits and what is comfortable. Don't let others pick your label for you.

Your time

I know my main message in all this has been to find what suits you and make your own choices. One thing I would strongly recommend, though, if you genuinely want to give sobriety a go, is that you try and get past the three-month mark.

This is when it gets easy. It's when the good habits and quick wins pile up on top of each other and you notice the difference. When the graph of effort versus rewards inverse. The first thirty days are when you are navigating the stormiest waters. By sixty days there are no storms in sight. Maybe just the odd wave of a craving that approaches from nowhere, but generally pretty calm. By ninety days it's plain sailing. (You'll be relieved to know that's me all out of nautical metaphors.)

When people tell me they tried going sober and it wasn't for them, they have usually tried dry January, or going sober for October, which is awesome, and I'm not knocking it. Any break from booze you can manage will undoubtedly be a good thing. But I also feel sorry for them a bit. The first thirty days are the most hellish. I've done them loads of times. You've done the absolute hardest yards, then not stuck around to get the rewards.

Imagine there was a job advertised that was your absolute dream. You read the job spec and benefits package and know that if you got that job, you would earn loads more money, be under less stress and anxiety, have more free time and be way happier than in your current role. You used to like your current role, but you're stuck in a rut, and begun to suspect it's causing you mental health problems; plus, it's impacting your relationships with friends and family.

You speak to other people who work in your new job. They confirm, yes, it is as amazing as it sounds, but there is a tough interview process. CV screening, psychometric testing, multiple rounds of group and one-on-one interviews. The people offer to help you prepare for the interviews, give you hints and tips, share some of the questions, but ultimately, it's up to you to land the job.

You know the job sounds awesome, but that interview process does sound like a lot of work. Your current job is so demanding. By the time you finish work you are knackered. You don't even know if you would have the time and energy to get your CV into decent shape, never mind preparing for all those interviews. You can't face making up answers to the 'tell me about a time when you … what would you say is your biggest weakness?' type nonsense.

Nah, fuck that, you think. It's not for me. I probably couldn't get the new job anyway. Why go through all that just to find out I'm not right for it? Plus, the people in the new job must have been overegging it. They seemed to love it a bit too much; they must be on commission to recruit people or something. My old job isn't so bad. It pays the bills. I know what I'm doing here. It's less hassle to stay. Plus, we did that annual staff survey, and the results were terrible; they promised they were going to put an action plan in place to improve morale, there was talk of a wellness centre being built.

So, you stay, and you give your old job another chance, try and make adjustments to get your work life balance right.

A few months later you're back to dreaming about the new job. You're still terribly unhappy with the old job. The attempts at work life balance had no impact. The wellness centre turned out to be a bean bag flung into the stationary cupboard where they now play dolphin music. You summon the gumption to interview for the new job. You can do this!

You get back in touch with the people that work in your new job. They are delighted to see you and think you will love it. They are friendly and generous with their time. They help tailor your CV for you and talk you through the interview process. They are rooting for you.

The interview process is tough. But you are making progress. Much of the time, it's the nervousness and preparation in the build-up to each interview that is most challenging rather than the interview.

After a month of psychometric testing, smashing the 'where do you see yourself in five years?' questions, you finally make it to the last stage. It's billed as 'just a chat with the CEO', but you know that this is the last step.

You meet for a quick coffee. You get on famously. She is already talking about 'us' and 'we' like you're part of the team.

You think you've smashed it. This is actually happening!

By the time you get home they have emailed an offer and contract. Wow, the salary is even bigger than you expected. The perks are insane.

But then, instead of accepting the offer, you question yourself. Wait, if the interview process was that much effort, imagine what the job will be like? I don't know if I can do this. Plus, I can't leave all my old workmates behind.

You reply and reject the offer. After all the hard work, just when you were on the cusp of getting the reward, you don't take the final step. You're back at your old desk and by Friday you are back in the rut.

You don't need to rely on my sailing or new-job analogies; do your own research and check the articles linked in the references. It's widely accepted that the first thirty days are the toughest.[80] Everyone's timeline is different, but, in general, while you are over the worst of it by weeks three to four it takes until the three-month mark to get the overall 'improved energy and general sense of wellbeing'[81] that makes it all worthwhile.

Plus, by not drinking, you give yourself a chance to replace your old drinking habits with new positive ones. In a study[82] published in the *European Journal of Social Psychology*, a research team decided to figure out just how long it takes to form a habit. The study examined the habits of ninety-six people over a twelve-week period. Each person chose one new habit for the twelve weeks and reported each day on whether they did the behaviour and how automatic it felt. On average, it takes more than two months before a new behaviour becomes automatic – sixty-six days to be exact.

And how long it takes a new habit to form can vary depending on the behaviour, the person, and the circumstances. In the study, it took anywhere from 18 days to 254 days for people to form a new habit. In other words, if you want to set your expectations appropriately, the truth is that it will probably take you anywhere from two months to eight months to build your new non-drinking habit into your life – thirty days isn't going to cover it.

In terms of getting to the three-month mark, and how you break up that chunk of time, it's back to being up to you. Loads of people benefit from the 'one day at a time' approach heavily referenced in twelve-step recovery groups. I get this, and I have applied it to lots of other difficult situations in my life. One day at a time reminds you to focus on the present and what you need to do in the next twenty-four hours. If you can do this and not stress over the future or past, then it can be a great tool. When it came to drinking, though, personally, the idea of taking it one day at a time was off-putting. It was like I was having to think about it every day. I didn't want to think about it every day. I needed something more solid. I initially landed on 'forever'. That gave me the security I needed. Then at the six-month mark I pivoted to 'forever but only 99% of the time'. I don't track the time at all now.

There are lots of ways to cut up the time, days, weeks, months, and there are apps to support you if that's your thing. There are groups you can join which focus on a targeted time off the booze, like One Year No Beer or the 100 Day Sober Challenge, which give you a community of others to do it alongside. Again, try a few, keep going with the ones that work, and ditch and switch what doesn't.

Your choice to share

My approach to recovery in the first eight months was to talk openly about it as little as possible. I had no interest in discussing my drinking problems. I could read about other people's, or write about my own, for hours, but having a conversation, and saying it out loud, did not appeal. We covered the things that helped me avoid this, from the antibiotics and fake-drinks stage to the 'just taking a break' stage.

Despite this, when it comes to your not drinking, some people will feel like they have the right to know why, to discuss this with you and drill you for information. It's easier said than done, but if you don't want to, don't. So many times I felt backed into a corner, and talked about it when I didn't want to. It didn't make me feel good because I wasn't ready. It's your choice to tell people, and share it with them, if and when you want to.

While my not-sharing approach worked for me, I was conscious I was taking a lot from the sober sphere without giving anything back. I rummaged the comments sections and blogs looking for tips, but never left a comment. I read other people's articles and listened to their podcasts. I took a lot but never really contributed. In a small way, I hope this book is a way of putting some of that back out there.

Respecting others' choices

'Basically, I'm for anything that gets you through the night – be it prayer, tranquillisers or a bottle of Jack Daniels.' (Frank Sinatra). This was another quote that used to be up on my bedroom wall; it was emblazoned across a black and white image of Frank Sinatra stepping off a helicopter, drink in hand. It was pride of place next to the George Best one. (The writing was literally on the wall for me from a young age.)

It's an unusual quote for a recovery book, but I still love the sentiment. If you do choose to go sober, and get to experience all the amazing, positive experiences that go along with it, it's likely that at some point you will want to share it with everyone. You might be tempted to convince others to join you. While this is great, and well intentioned, be careful about how you go about it.

Just like we get to choose to be sober, and how we do it, others get to choose too. If someone asks for your help, or if someone else's drinking is severely impacting you or your loved ones, then yes you should seek help for them or do what you can to intervene and support. In many cases, though, while you might think someone drinks too much, they might be quite happy as they are. Just as it's not fair for someone to feel like you owe them an explanation for not drinking, the same goes the other way. If people are ready and want to talk about it with you, they will, but don't force it. Choose to let others choose.

Last Orders

I dreaded hearing the bell ring for last orders. As soon as it went off, I would get a big round in to make sure I could use up every minute of drinking time. Inevitably I would drink that round faster than expected, and panic that I didn't have enough to last until chucking-out time. I would then find myself back up at the bar, trying to squeeze in an order for more drinks after the final bell had been rung. I would offer the barmaid ridiculously generous tips, sing, cajole and beg to be served just one more drink for the road. I hated the night (or more accurately, the drinking) ending.

Now I have dropped the drinking and picked up writing, I worry I've swapped one compulsion for another. I hit my word limit well before we reached this chapter, but I feel like I have so much more to get down and share with you. I will keep writing on sobriety via my blog 99percentsober.com, and I am halfway through mapping out the plot for my second book, which is going to be a thriller. I am considering making the detective in it someone with a drinking problem, but I worry it's a cliché. What is it about the stereotypical alcoholic that makes them such great detectives? I reckon it's all the blackout sleuthing required to piece together the night before. I digress. Best to finish this book before starting on the next.

Before you hopefully head on over to my blog and we continue there, there are some things to take with you after turning the last page. Whether you're already convinced and want to try the 99% sober life, are still pondering it or it's already a hard no, these are the three things that I wish someone had told me years ago.

Booze takes way too much credit
Finishing up work early on a Friday, going to watch live music, chilling by the pool on holiday, catching up with old friends over dinner.

We have been brainwashed into thinking that we need to add booze to make these things fun, but those things are fun in their own right. Just because alcohol has pushed itself to the front and centre, doesn't mean it's earned the right to be there. As a society, we even do the marketing for it. You have a great time catching up with friends over dinner because they are good company, but when the pictures are taken it will be one of everyone holding their wine glasses aloft, like it was the magical wine that did it.

You could have been happily chilling by the pool with a good book all morning, but when it comes to sticking a picture on Instagram, you will wait until you order a fancy cocktail for the 'wish you were here' post. Why do we do that? Alcohol is the player who was an unused substitute for the cup final, but who insists on hogging the limelight during the victory lap and getting his picture taken with the trophy.

I promise, all the fun things will still be fun without booze. And like I said earlier, if something only seems fun when you are a bit drunk, it's probably worth thinking through how fun it is at all.

Nobody regrets going sober

Literally no one. In all the memoirs, research articles, blogs and interviews, I've yet to come across a single person who says, 'I went sober, and I really regret it. Worst decision I've made. I wish I could get those three months back. What a waste.'

If you give it a go, and don't think it's for you, fair enough. But what have you got to lose? How many years of your life have you spent on autopilot, drinking by default? What harm would it do to try a few months of something else?

And like we covered, you don't need to be an 'alcoholic' to cut back. You don't even need to be a 5 or 6 on the sliding scale. While the 7s or 8s might notice a more dramatic change than the 3s or 4s, you won't know how much it will impact you until you give it go.

Don't tie yourself in knots asking, 'Am I an alcoholic?' 'Do I have a drinking problem?' Flip it on its head. Ask yourself, 'Would my life be better with less alcohol?' If the answer is yes, or even maybe, it's worth a shot.

Shit still happens

'Accept certain inalienable truths, prices will rise, politicians will philander, you too will get old, and when you do you'll fantasise that when you were young prices were reasonable, politicians were noble and children respected their elders.' (Mary Schmich)

As amazing as your new sober life may be, I can't promise you that quitting or cutting back on alcohol will be a cure for everything. Shit will, inevitably, still happen.

What I can promise is that by taking control of your drinking, you can improve your finances, health and energy. You can have better sleep, a deeper sense of wellbeing and improved relationships. And I can promise you that these improvements will leave you feeling more equipped to handle whatever life throws your way.

I'll level with you, back in December 2021 when I made the decision to stop, I wasn't looking forward to it. I wasn't skipping towards sobriety with a spring in my step. I was scared and felt hard done by.

Sobriety was something I dragged myself towards because the alternative was a life separated from my wife and kids, moving further up the 'Paddy Scale of Dependence', drinking myself closer to oblivion with every blowout. Sobriety was the lesser of two evils. I felt resigned to my fate. That's it for me. The sober accountant no one wants to sit next to at the wedding. Oh well, I've made my bed.

Time for poor abstinent Paddy to collect his non-drinking cross and bear it stoically. But as I trudged further along, and the sober weeks and quick wins piled up, I realised I had got it all wrong. Sobriety wasn't a cross to bear, or a punishment to be endured; it was a superpower.

I traded in a life filled with hangovers, anxiety and regrets for one filled with energy, happiness and fulfilment. A life beyond my biggest dreams. The reason I've written this book, and shared so much with you, is because I want *you* to get the chance to make that trade. I've done my best to describe how much better life is being 99% sober and shared the tools I used to help me get there. Now it's over to you. The dream job is there, you've been asked to apply and it's yours if you want it. Now go and dust off that CV.

Note From The Author

Thank you so much for reading. If you have enjoyed it, I would be incredibly grateful if you could leave a brief review using the QR codes below, even if it's just a few sentences. If you haven't enjoyed it, keep it to yourself!

Want to read more?

Send an email to patrick@99percentsober.com and I will let you know you when my next book is being released, along with the chance to order at a discounted price.

Visit 99percentsober.com

Follow me @99percentsober on Instagram.

Scan the QR code to leave your one click review:

United States   UK   Canada   Australia

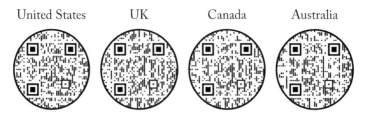

If your country isn't listed, please leave a review using your local Amazon website. Thank you.

Acknowledgements

The sober community is packed with people who share their story and act as a guide and inspiration for others. Throughout the book, I've referenced and recommended those who have had the biggest conscious impact on me, but there are many more who have added to the feed of information that helped me question my relationship with alcohol and inform this book. Thank you.

Writing a book isn't something I could have done without a lot of support. Few people knew I was writing one, so there are friends and family that provided support without question, or ever knowing why I needed it. Thank you.

My coach and mentor, Amy Warren from The Writing House, has read, edited, and improved multiple versions of this book. She helped make what could have been a painful process, pretty fun. For your expertise, patience and guidance, thank you.

My sons, Roderick and Roman. Amazing little people who bring us so much laughter and love. Wanting to be the best version of myself and set a good example to you provided me with the extra impetuous I needed. Thank you.

Finally, my wife, Alison. Without you, this book would never have been written. You provided the tools and frameworks that helped me go from someone who thought they could write a book one day, to someone who gets one written. When added to the love, support and encouragement you provide every day, I couldn't help but finish it. Thank you.

End notes

[1] Gilbert, Alicia. 'Why Can't I Stop Drinking Once I Start? 4 Major Reasons.' *Soberish*, 30 April 2023, https://www.soberish.co/why-cant-i-stop-drinking-once-i-start/. Accessed 1 September 2023.

[2] Gray, Catherine. *The Unexpected Joy of Being Sober: Discovering a Happy, Healthy, Wealthy Alcohol-free Life*. Octopus Books, 2017. Accessed 27 October 2023.

[3] Guernsey Investment & Funds Association. 'Guernsey chosen as the domicile for new fund administration business – Guernsey Investment & Funds Association.' *Guernsey Investment & Funds Association*, https://gifa.gg/guernsey-chosen-as-the-domicile-for-new-fund-administration-business/. Accessed 27 October 2023.

[4] Atre, Dr. Sandeep. 'Will power is a finite resource.' *Socialigence*, 16 March 2019, https://www.socialigence.net/blog/will-power-is-a-finite-resource/. Accessed 28 October 2023.

[5] Schultz, Alicia. 'The Truth About Liquid Courage: Finding Confidence Without Alcohol.' *Ria Health*, 21 February 2023, https://riahealth.com/blog/liquid-courage/. Accessed 1 September 2023.

[6] Barnett, Bob. 'Does drinking reduce my stress?' *CNN*, 24 September 2013, https://edition.cnn.com/2013/09/24/health/drinking-reduces-stress-upwave/index.html. Accessed 1 September 2023.

[7] NHS. 'Alcohol misuse – Risks.' 04 October 2022, https://www.nhs.uk/conditions/alcohol-misuse/risks/. Accessed 1 September 2023.

[8] Cleveland Clinic. 'Why You Shouldn't Rely on Alcohol During Times of Stress.' *Cleveland Clinic Health Essentials*, 16 April 2020, https://health.clevelandclinic.org/alcohol-during-times-of-stress/. Accessed 9 September 2023.

[9] Boden, J. M., and D. M. Fergusson. 'Alcohol and depression.' *PubMed*, 7 March 2011, https://pubmed.ncbi.nlm.nih.gov/21382111/. Accessed 17 September 2023.

[10] Edwards, et al. 'Alcohol Use Disorder and Risk of Suicide in a Swedish Population-Based Cohort.' *PubMed*, 1 July 2020, https://pubmed.ncbi.nlm.nih.gov/32160767/. Accessed 17 September 2023.

[11] University of Rochester Medical Centre. 'Journaling for Emotional Wellness – Health Encyclopedia – University of Rochester Medical Center.' *URMC*, https://www.urmc.rochester.edu/encyclopedia/content.aspx?ContentID=4552&ContentTypeID=1. Accessed 22 September 2023.

[12] Reflection. 'Top Evidence-Based Benefits of Journaling for Mental Health.' *Reflection.app*, 27 December 2022, https://www.reflection.app/blog/benefits-of-journaling#benefit-2-journal-writing-can-help-boost-immune-function. Accessed 22 September 2023.

[13] Trimpey, Jack. *Rational Recovery: The New Cure for Substance Addiction*. Gallery Books, 1996.

[14] Prior, Flip. 'Replacing alcohol with exercise and making it a lasting habit.' *ABC*, 20 May 2019, https://www.abc.net.au/everyday/replacing-alcohol-with-exercise-and-making-it-a-lasting-habit/11095384. Accessed 22 September 2023.

[15] Alarcon, Regis. 'Sugar intake and craving during alcohol withdrawal in alcohol use disorder inpatients.' *Wiley Online Library*, 2 October 2022, https://onlinelibrary.wiley.com/doi/abs/10.1111/adb.12907. Accessed 22 September 2023.

[16] Hatanaka, Miho. 'Is Sugar an Addictive Drug?' *Healthline*, https://www.healthline.com/health/food-nutrition/experts-is-sugar-addictive-drug#What-is-an-addiction? Accessed 28 October 2023.

[17] Journey Pure. 'Sleep Is Very Important in Recovering from Drug Addiction.' *JourneyPure Lexington*, 16 August 2019, https://journeypurelexington.com/the-importance-of-sleep-in-recovery/. Accessed 22 September 2023.

[18] Hughes, Gareth, and Ann Kirkman. 'The Importance of Taking Breaks.' *The Wellbeing Thesis*, https://thewellbeingthesis.org.uk/foundations-for-success/importance-of-taking-breaks-and-having-other-interests/. Accessed 22 September 2023.

[19] Mitchell, Thomas. 'How to curb drinking as data shows West Aussies drink 141 bottles of wine a year.' *WAtoday*, 3 May 2017, https://www.watoday.com.au/national/western-australia/curb-your-booze-binge-as-data-shows-west-aussies-drink-141-bottles-of-wine-a-year-20170503-gvxy8y.html. Accessed 22 September 2023.

[20] Alcohol Change UK. 'Press release: The average drinker spends an estimated £62,899 on alcohol over the course of a…' *Alcohol Change UK*, 3 July 2023, https://alcoholchange.org.uk/blog/2023/press-

release-the-average-drinker-spends-an-estimated-62-899-on-alcohol-over-the-course-of-a-lifetime. Accessed 22 September 2023.

[21] Pooley, Clare. *The Sober Diaries: How One Woman Stopped Drinking and Started Living*. Hodder, 2019.

[22] Aurelius, Marcus. 'Quote by Marcus Aurelius: "It never ceases to amaze me: we all love oursel…"' *Goodreads*, https://www.goodreads.com/quotes/815113-it-never-ceases-to-amaze-me-we-all-love-ourselves. Accessed 29 September 2023.

[23] Williams, Vivien. 'Mayo Clinic Minute: The benefits of being socially connected.' *Mayo Clinic News Network*, 19 April 2019, https://newsnetwork.mayoclinic.org/discussion/mayo-clinic-minute-the-benefits-of-being-socially-connected/. Accessed 1 October 2023.

[24] Shetty, Jay. *Think Like a Monk: Train Your Mind for Peace and Purpose Every Day*. Simon & Schuster, 2020. Accessed 29 October 2023.

[25] Shetty, Jay. 'Jay Shetty On Expanding Your Attitude Of Gratitude And How It Transforms Your Mind And Body.' *Think Like a Monk*, https://thinklikeamonkbook.com/Gratitude/. Accessed 24 October 2023.

[26] Mind.Org. 'Mindfulness exercises and tips.' *Mind*, https://www.mind.org.uk/information-support/drugs-and-treatments/mindfulness/mindfulness-exercises-tips/. Accessed 24 October 2023.

[27] Mind.Org. 'What is mindfulness?' *Mind*, https://www.mind.org.uk/information-support/drugs-and-treatments/mindfulness/about-mindfulness/. Accessed 24 October 2023.

[28] Sandeman, Stuart. *Breathe In, Breathe Out: Restore Your Health, Reset Your Mind and Find Happiness Through Breathwork*. Hanover Square Press, 2022. Accessed 24 October 2023.

[29] Brooks, Arthur C. 'How to Stop Caring What Other People Think of You.' *The Atlantic*, 11 November 2021, https://www.theatlantic.com/family/archive/2021/11/how-stop-caring-what-other-people-think-you/620670/. Accessed 23 October 2023.

[30] Volkow, Dr. Nora. 'Connections between Sleep and Substance Use Disorders.' *National Institute on Drug Abuse*, 9 March 2019, https://archives.nida.nih.gov/news-events/noras-blog/2020/03/connections-between-sleep-substance-use-disorders. Accessed 28 October 2023.

[31] Pooley, Clare. *The Sober Diaries: How One Woman Stopped Drinking and Started Living*. Hodder, 2019.

[32] Summer, Jay. '8 Health Benefits of Sleep.' *Sleep Foundation*, 27 June

2023, https://www.sleepfoundation.org/how-sleep-works/benefits-of-sleep. Accessed 3 October 2023.

[33] Clinton, Jane. 'My days of booze and burglary by art bad boy Damian Hirst.' *Daily Express*, 12 May 2013, https://www.express.co.uk/news/uk/398893/My-days-of-booze-and-burglary-by-art-bad-boy-Damian-Hirst. Accessed 28 October 2023.

[34] Vincent, Robert M. 'Cancer Prevention and Heart Health — What Role Does Alcohol Play?' *The Substance Abuse and Mental Health Services Administration*, 1 February 2023, https://www.samhsa.gov/blog/cancer-prevention-heart-health. Accessed 28 October 2023.

[35] Fuller, Tiffany. 'Alcohol And Hair Loss: Are They Connected?' *The Hope House*, 1 November 2022, https://www.thehopehouse.com/alcohol-abuse/related/alcohol-and-hair-loss/. Accessed 7 October 2023.

[36] Mile, Heroes. 'Alcoholic Eyes: Drinking Alcohol & Your Eyesight.' *Heroes' Mile*, https://www.heroesmile.com/alcoholic-eyes-drinking-alcohol-your-eyesight/. Accessed 7 October 2023.

[37] Yellayi, Sirisha. 'Does alcohol cause acne? Effects on the skin.' *Medical News Today*, 24 June 2020, https://www.medicalnewstoday.com/articles/does-alcohol-cause-acne#does-it-improve-acne. Accessed 7 October 2023.

[38] CLARINS. 'What are the Effects of Alcohol on Your Skin? The Experts Weigh In.' *Beauty Daily | by CLARINS*, https://beautydaily.clarins.co.uk/wellness/health/alcohol-skin-ageing/. Accessed 7 October 2023.

[39] Nutracheck. 'Calories in Chocolate.' *Nutracheck*, https://www.nutracheck.co.uk/calories/calories_in_snacks_and_confectionary/calories_in_chocolate#url. Accessed 7 October 2023.

[40] Smith, Rebecca, et al. 'Average wine drinker puts on half a stone of fat a year, says campaign group.' *The Telegraph*, 18 April 2009, https://www.telegraph.co.uk/news/health/news/5171660/Average-wine-drinker-puts-on-half-a-stone-of-fat-a-year-says-campaign-group.html. Accessed 7 October 2023.

[41] Hørrisen, Mikkel Magnus T. 'Association between alcohol consumption and impaired work performance (presenteeism): a systematic review.' *NCBI*, 16 July 2019, https://www.ncbi.nlm.nih.gov/pmc/articles/PMC6661906/. Accessed 8 October 2023.

[42] Hame, Sharon. '6 cold shower benefits to consider.' *UCLA Health*,

25 January 2023, https://www.uclahealth.org/news/6-cold-shower-benefits-consider. Accessed 8 October 2023.

[43] Graff, Steve, and Abbey Anderson. 'Effects of Smoking and Alcohol on Smell and Taste (It's Not What You Think).' *Penn Medicine*, 10 April 2017, https://www.pennmedicine.org/news/news-blog/2017/april/effects-of-smoking-and-alcohol-on-smell-and-taste. Accessed 9 October 2023.

[44] Morrison, Oliver. '"The times they are a-changin": Alcohol has gone out of style and out of the music charts, research reveals.' Food Navigator, 1 November 2023, https://www.foodnavigator.com/Article/2023/11/01/alcohol-has-gone-out-of-style-and-out-of-the-music-charts-research-reveals. Accessed 20 December 2023.

[45] Ludmir, Clara. 'Why GenZ Is Drinking Less And What This Means For The Alcohol Industry.' *Forbes Magazine*, 22 September 2021, https://www.forbes.com/sites/claraludmir/2023/06/27/why-genz-is-drinking-less-and-what-this-means-for-the-alcohol-industry/?sh=5c4d9e3848d1. Accessed 11 November 2023.

[46] Jones, Daisy. 'How the drunk party anthem sobered up.' *British GQ*, 22 August 2023, https://www.gq-magazine.co.uk/article/party-anthem-music-drinking-lyrics. Accessed 29 October 2023.

[47] Morrison, Oliver. '"The times they are a-changin": Alcohol has gone out of style and out of the music charts, research reveals.' Food Navigator, 1 November 2023, https://www.foodnavigator.com/Article/2023/11/01/alcohol-has-gone-out-of-style-and-out-of-the-music-charts-research-reveals. Accessed 20 December 2023.

[48] Delgado, Kasia. 'I spent the night at a new alcohol-free pub and saw how the UK is slowly embracing sobriety.' *iNews*, 28 August 2023, https://inews.co.uk/inews-lifestyle/new-alcohol-free-pub-uk-sobriety-2569330. Accessed 14 October 2023.

[49] Nutt, David. 'Drug harms in the UK: a multicriteria decision analysis.' *The Lancet*. https://www.thelancet.com/journals/lancet/article/PIIS0140-6736(10)61462-6/fulltext.

[50] Jacobson, Bobbie. 'Key dates in tobacco regulation.' *Action on Smoking and Health*, https://ash.org.uk/uploads/Key-Dates.pdf. Accessed 15 October 2023.

[51] Ibid.

[52] Cancer Council. 'A brief history of smoking.' *Cancer Council NSW*, https://www.cancercouncil.com.au/news/a-brief-history-of-smoking/.

Accessed 15 October 2023.

[53] Lorgat, Imran. 'Smoking: a 100-Year Story That Doesn't End Here.' *RGA*, https://www.rgare.com/knowledge-center/article/smoking-a-100-year-story-that-doesn-t-end-here. Accessed 15 October 2023.

[54] Jacobson, Bobbie. 'Key dates in tobacco regulation.' *Action on Smoking and Health*, https://ash.org.uk/uploads/Key-Dates.pdf. Accessed 15 October 2023.

[55] Chapman, Matthew. 'New products, old tricks? Concerns Big Tobacco is targeting youngsters.' *Bureau of Investigative Journalism*, 21 February 2021, https://www.thebureauinvestigates.com/stories/2021-02-21/new-products-old-tricks-concerns-big-tobacco-is-targeting-youngsters. Accessed 22 October 2023.

[56] World Health Organization. 'No level of alcohol consumption is safe for our health.' *World Health Organization (WHO)*, 4 January 2023, https://www.who.int/europe/news/item/04-01-2023-no-level-of-alcohol-consumption-is-safe-for-our-health. Accessed 29 October 2023.

[57] Coltart, Cordelia. 'The need for a global alcohol strategy: "upscaling the issue in a downstreaming environment."' *RCP Journals*, https://www.rcpjournals.org/content/clinmedicine/12/1/29. Accessed 22 October 2023.

[58] MacKey, Boris. 'Alcohol Misuse: The Biggest Cause Of Working Age Mortality In England.' *Rehab 4 Addiction*, 21 February 2022, https://www.rehab4addiction.co.uk/blog/alcohol-misuse-biggest-cause-working-age-mortality-england. Accessed 22 October 2023.

[59] BMC Public Health. 'Public awareness of the link between alcohol and cancer in England in 2015: a population-based survey'. *BMC Public Health*, 30 November 2016, https://bmcpublichealth.biomedcentral.com/articles/10.1186/s12889-016-3855-6. Accessed 22 October 2023.

[60] Rabin, Roni Caryn. 'Federal Agency Courted Alcohol Industry to Fund Study on Benefits of Moderate Drinking (Published 2018).' *The New York Times*, 17 March 2018, https://www.nytimes.com/2018/03/17/health/nih-alcohol-study-liquor-industry.html. Accessed 29 October 2023.

[61] Almendrala, Anna. 'Alcohol Companies Are Funding Research To Convince You Drinking Is Healthy.' *HuffPost*, 14 April 2018, https://www.huffpost.com/entry/alcohol-companies-want-you-to-drink-

more-and-theyre-funding-research-to-make-it-happen_n_
5ad123bce4b077c89ce8a835/amp. Accessed 22 October 2023.
[62] Golder, Su. 'Increase in alcohol-industry funded research is a cause
for concern, study suggests.' *University of York*, 17 September 2020,
https://www.york.ac.uk/news-and-events/news/2020/research/
alcohol-research-funding/. Accessed 22 October 2023.
[63] Gray, Catherine. *Sunshine Warm Sober: Unexpected Sober Joy That
Lasts*. Octopus Publishing Group, 2021. Accessed 29 October 2023.
[64] Drinkaware. 'About Drinkaware.' *Drinkaware*, https://www.
drinkaware.co.uk/about-us. Accessed 29 October 2023.
[65] Institute of Alcohol Studies. 'Government's Alcohol Strategy.'
Institute of Alcohol Studies, 19 June 2012, https://www.ias.org.uk/
uploads/pdf/News%20stories/hcr-alcohol-strategy.pdf. Accessed 29
October 2023.
[66] McCambridge J. 'Be aware of Drinkaware – PMC.' *NCBI*, 2013,
https://www.ncbi.nlm.nih.gov/pmc/articles/PMC3992896/. Accessed
29 October 2023.
[67] Campbell, Denis. 'UK pupils taught about alcohol with "misleading"
industry-funded resources.' *The Guardian*, 20 January 2022, https://
amp.theguardian.com/society/2022/jan/20/uk-pupils-taught-about-
alcohol-with-misleading-industry-funded-resources. Accessed 23
October 2023.
[68] Blake, Elly. 'Healthy' glass of wine is a myth, experts say.' *Evening
Standard*, 21 January 2022, https://www.standard.co.uk/news/health/
daily-glass-of-wine-healthy-myth-world-heart-federation-b977985.
html. Accessed 23 October 2023.
[69] UK Parliament Committees. 'Government not taking "appalling"
harms from alcohol seriously enough.' *UK Parliament Committees*, 24
May 2023, https://committees.parliament.uk/work/7257/alcohol-
treatment-services/news/195391/government-not-taking-appalling-
harms-from-alcohol-seriously-enough/. Accessed 29 October 2023.
[70] Miller, Sarah, et al. 'The fact that pubs are reopening, but schools
aren't, is a national disaster.' *The Telegraph*, 9 June 2020, https://www.
telegraph.co.uk/family/schooling/fact-pubs-parks-open-schools-
arent-nationaldisaster/. Accessed 29 October 2023.
[71] Tesco. 'Brits creating record all year-round demand for no and low
alcohol beer.' *Tesco PLC*, 3 July 2023, https://www.tescoplc.com/brits-
creating-record-all-year-round-demand-for-no-and-low-alcohol-

beer/. Accessed 11 November 2023.

[72] Delgado, Kasia. 'I spent the night at a new alcohol-free pub and saw how the UK is slowly embracing sobriety.' *iNews*, 28 August 2023, https://inews.co.uk/inews-lifestyle/new-alcohol-free-pub-uk-sobriety-2569330. Accessed 14 October 2023.

[73] Delaney, Sam. 'I gave up booze and am having more fun than ever. These seven tips could help you do the same.' *The Guardian*, 10 February 2023, https://www.theguardian.com/society/2023/feb/10/i-gave-up-booze-and-am-having-more-fun-than-ever-these-seven-tips-could-help-you-do-the-same. Accessed 17 October 2023.

[74] Valli, Veronica. *Soberful. Uncover a Sustainable, Fulfilling Life Free of Alcohol*. Sounds True, 2022. Accessed 29 October 2023.

[75] Sternlicht, Lin, and Aaron Sternlicht. '10 Most Common Reasons For Addiction Relapse.' *Family Addiction Specialist*, https://www.familyaddictionspecialist.com/blog/10-most-common-reasons-for-addiction-relapse. Accessed 10 October 2023.

[76] Saner, Emine. 'The 99% sober movement: should we keep dry January going all year?' *The Guardian*, 19 January 2023, https://amp.theguardian.com/society/2023/jan/19/the-99-sober-movement-should-we-keep-dry-january-going-all-year. Accessed 10 October 2023.

[77] Metcalfe, Charlie. '99% Sober Is the Sobriety Strategy for Men Who Want to Quit Alcohol… Just Not Completely.' *Men's Health*, 12 January 2023, https://www.menshealth.com/uk/health/a42395173/mindful-drinking/. Accessed 10 October 2023.

[78] Jhanjee, Sonali. 'Evidence Based Psychosocial Interventions in Substance Use.' *NCBI*, 2014, https://www.ncbi.nlm.nih.gov/pmc/articles/PMC4031575/. Accessed 11 October 2023.

[79] SMART Recovery. 'Moving Away from the Terms "Alcoholic" and "Alcoholism."' *SMART Recovery*, 10 April 2019, https://www.smartrecovery.org/moving-away-from-the-terms-alcoholic-and-alcoholism/. Accessed 11 October 2023.

[80] Hayes Clinic. 'The First 30 Days of Recovery.' *The Haynes Clinic*, https://thehaynesclinic.com/blog/the-first-30-days-of-recovery/. Accessed 13 October 2023.

[81] Molyneux, Alex. 'Timeline of what happens when you quit drinking.' *Delamere Health*, 17 February 2020, https://delamere.com/blog/a-timeline-of-what-happens-when-you-quit-drinking-for-good. Accessed 13 October 2023.

[82] Lally, Phillippa et al. 'How are habits formed: Modeling habit formation in the real world.' *ResearchGate*, 2010, https://www.researchgate.net/publication/32898894_How_are_habits_formed_Modeling_habit_formation_in_the_real_world. Accessed 13 October 2023.

Printed in Great Britain
by Amazon

Counseling and Psychotherapy

An Integrated, Individual Psychology Approach

Third Editon

Don Dinkmeyer, Jr., Ph.D.
Western Kentucky University

Len Sperry, M.D., Ph.D.
Medical College of Wisconsin

Merrill,
an imprint of Prentice Hall
Upper Saddle River, New Jersey   Columbus, Ohio

Library of Congress Cataloging-in-Publication Data

Dinkmeyer, Don C., 1952–
    Counseling and psychotherapy: an integrated, individual
psychology approach/Don Dinkmeyer, Jr., Len Sperry.—3rd ed.
        p.   cm.
    ISBN 0-02-329671-2
    1. Psychotherapy.   2. Adlerian psychology.   3. Counseling.
I. Sperry, Len. II. Title.
RC480.5.D56   2000
616.89'14—dc21

99-16927
CIP

Cover photo: © Super Stock
Editor: Kevin M. Davis
Editorial Assistant: Holly Jennings
Production Editor: Linda Hillis Bayma
Copy Editor: Key Metts
Production Coordination and Text Design: Carlisle Publishers Services
Design Coordinator: Diane C. Lorenzo
Cover Design: Janoski Advertising
Production Manager: Laura Messerly
Director of Marketing: Kevin Flanagan
Marketing Manager: Meghan Shepherd
Marketing Coordinator: Krista Groshong

This book was set in Garamond by Carlisle Communications, Ltd. and was printed
and bound by R.R. Donnelley & Sons Company. The cover was printed by
Phoenix Color Corp.

© 2000 by Prentice-Hall, Inc.
Pearson Education
Upper Saddle River, New Jersey 07458

Earlier editions, entitled *Adlerian Counseling and Psychotherapy,* © 1987 by Merrill Publishing Company and © 1979 by Wadsworth Publishing Company, Inc.

Printed in the United States of America

10 9 8 7 6 5 4 3 2 1

ISBN: 0-02-329671-2

Prentice-Hall International (UK) Limited, *London*
Prentice-Hall of Australia Pty. Limited, *Sydney*
Prentice-Hall of Canada, Inc., *Toronto*
Prentice-Hall Hispanoamericana, S. A., *Mexico*
Prentice-Hall of India Private Limited, *New Delhi*
Prentice-Hall of Japan, Inc., *Tokyo*
Prentice-Hall (Singapore) Pte. Ltd., *Singapore*
Editora Prentice-Hall do Brasil, Ltda., *Rio de Janeiro*

Dedicated to Don Dinkmeyer, Sr.: father, colleague, teacher, and friend to all in the counseling professions

Discover the Companion Website Accompanying This Book

The Prentice Hall Companion Website: A Virtual Learning Environment

Technology is a constantly growing and changing aspect of our field that is creating a need for content and resources. To address this emerging need, Prentice Hall has developed an online learning environment for students and professors alike.—Companion Websites—to support our textbooks.

In creating a Companion Website, our goal is to build on and enhance what the textbook already offers. For this reason, the content for each user-friendly website is organized by topic and provides the professor and student with a variety of meaningful resources. Common features of a Companion Website include:

For the Professor—

Every Companion Website integrates Syllabus Manager™, an online syllabus creation and management utility.

▼ Syllabus Manager™ provides you, the instructor, with an easy, step-by-step process to create and revise syllabi, with direct links into Companion Website and other online content without having to learn HTML.

▼ Students may logon to your syllabus during any study session. All they need to know is the web address for the Companion Website and the password you've assigned to your syllabus.

▼ After you have created a syllabus using Syllabus Manager™, students may enter the syllabus for their course section from any point in the Companion Website.

▼ Class dates are highlighted in white and assigned due dates appear in blue. Clicking on a date, the student is shown the list of activities for the assignment. The activities for each assignment are linked directly to actual content, saving time for students.

▼ Adding assignments consists of clicking on the desired due date, then filling in the details of the assignment— name of the assignment, instructions, and whether or not it is a one-time or repeating assignment.

▼ In addition, links to the activities can be created easily. If the activity is online, a URL can be entered in the space provided, and it will be linked automatically in the final syllabus.

▼ Your completed syllabus is hosted on our servers, allowing convenient updates from any computer on the Internet. Changes you make to your syllabus are immediately available to your students at their next logon.

For the Student—

▼ Topic Overviews—outline key concepts in topic areas

▼ Electronic Blue Book—send homework or essays directly to your instructor's email with this paperless form

▼ Message Board—serves as a virtual bulletin board to post—or respond to—questions or comments to/from a national audience

▼ Web Destinations—links to www sites that relate to each topic area

▼ Professional Organizations—links to organizations that relate to topic areas

▼ Additional Resources—access to topic-specific content that enhances material found in the text

To take advantage of these and other resources,
please visit the *Counseling and Psychotherapy: An Integrated, Individual Psychology Approach,* Third Edition, Companion Website at www.prenhall.com/dinkmeyer.

Preface

Individual Psychology continues to dramatically influence the fields of psychology, psychotherapy, counseling, social work, and brief therapy. As we embrace a new century, the helping professions continue to seek better methods of understanding each individual's potential for change.

The third edition of *Counseling and Psychotherapy: An Integrated, Individual Psychology Approach* reflects the growing interest in and acceptance of Adlerian concepts. The first two editions were titled *Adlerian Counseling and Psychotherapy*. In this edition, we detail the threads of Individual Psychology that are increasingly woven into other contemporary psychological theories and practice, and the new title reflects this integration.

The three major sections of this text are (1) Theory, (2) Skills and Strategies, and (3) Applications. In the first section, we present a new chapter, which demonstrates the integrative themes drawn from Individual Psychology into other therapy systems. Separate chapters on personality development and psychopathology complete this section.

In the second section, we detail techniques of analysis and assessment. The lifestyle assessment, an Adlerian contribution to psychology, is presented. Our approach to treatment planning, a contemporary necessity, is also detailed. The section also contains chapters on psychotherapeutic and psychoeducational interventions.

The third section details applications of Individual Psychology to specific populations. Children, adolescents, and the elderly are discussed. Health counseling, group therapy, and time-limited therapy are presented. The text concludes with specific chapters on family and marital therapy.

This book is a major revision of our prior work with two distinguished Adlerians. W. L. Pew was a co-author in the first edition, published in 1979. Don Dinkmeyer, Sr. was the first author on the first edition as well as the second edition, published in 1986.

This text reflects our intensive involvements with Individual Psychology. We have been profoundly influenced by Rudolf Dreikurs' pioneering work. Don Dinkmeyer, Jr. served two terms as President of the North American Society of Adlerian Psychology. Len Sperry has served as a faculty member of the Adler School of Professional Psychology.

It is impossible to list all of the inspiring colleagues and teachers who have contributed to the book. We are grateful for your influence. We particularly wish to thank the reviewers of this edition: John C. Dagley, University of Georgia; Ed Jacobs, West Virginia University; Charles H. Morgan Jr., Morehead State University; Keith A. Pierce, University of Nevada, Reno; and Edward Watkins, University of North Texas. We also wish to thank the reviewers of the previous edition: Dr. Michael Nystul, New Mexico State University; Dr. Roy Kern, Georgia State University; and Bernard Shulman, Stone Medical Center, Chicago. Special thanks to Deborah Kaye Dinkmeyer and Patti Sperry for their support and encouragement during this process.

We fervently hope the reader will find the content comprehensive and easy to understand. You will see ways to use Individual Psychology with your populations. Adlerians have a saying, "Trust only movement." In this book you will find many keys to your movement as a healer and teacher.

Don Dinkmeyer, Jr.
Len Sperry

Brief Contents

Contents

Theory

Adlerian Counseling and Psychotherapy: An Overview

A lfred Adler's Individual Psychology is one of the oldest and most useful schools of psychological thought. It emerged during Adler's 9-year association with Sigmund Freud as both developed their ideas about human nature. Adler's approach, with its practical applications to psychotherapy and counseling, has continued to experience steady growth after a long period in which Freudian (psychoanalytic) ideas occupied center stage. Today, Individual Psychology is acknowledged as the precursor to many current systems of thought and approaches to counseling and therapy. Its effect can be detected in countless arenas—among them, child rearing, marriage and family therapy, mental health services, and school counseling.

A BRIEF BIOGRAPHY

Alfred Adler was born on February 7, 1870, in Penzing, a suburb of Vienna. He was the second of six children. His father was a middle-class Jewish merchant, his mother a homemaker. In his early childhood, Adler suffered from poor health, but this stimulated his interest in becoming a doctor. He received a medical degree at the prestigious University of Vienna in 1895.

Adler became a practicing physician in Vienna. In the fall of 1902, Freud invited him to join discussion groups. The groups developed into the Vienna Psychoanalytic Society, of which Adler became president in 1910. Adler resigned from the society one year later, partly because of Freud's insistence on uniformity and strict allegiance to his theory. In this decade of discussion are the roots of modern psychology. Contrary to popular notion, Adler was not a "disciple" of Freud. He was never psychoanalyzed by him. In fact, Adler's ideas were often in conflict with Freud's.

After he severed his ties with Freud's psychoanalytic approach, Adler devoted himself to developing his own psychology. In 1912, the Society for Individual Psychology was born with many members from the group who had belonged to Freud's Psychoanalytic Society. After serving in World War I as a medical officer, Adler created many child-guidance clinics in the Vienna public schools. They served as training vehicles for teachers, social workers, physicians, and other professionals. Adler demonstrated his techniques in front of groups of professionals—an institutional idea that had never been used. Despite their revolutionary nature, the guidance clinics grew rapidly in Vienna and throughout Europe. At one point nearly 50 clinics thrived throughout Europe. However, political obstacles soon began to interfere with the growth of Adler's psychology in Europe. The Nazi movement would soon threaten Adler and his colleagues.

In 1926, Adler made his first lecture tour in the United States. His visits became more and more frequent. In 1935, he left Europe and settled in the United States, where he taught and lectured extensively. He died in 1937 in Aberdeen, Scotland, while on lecture tour. A recent and useful biography of Alfred Adler is the *Drive for Self* (Hoffman, 1994).

ADLER'S LEGACY

Adler published more than 300 books and articles. Countless lectures and public demonstrations in the United States and abroad attest to the popularity and usefulness of Adler's ideas for professionals and the general public. Adler's practice of public demonstration, parent and family-education centers, and the dissemination of useful, practical information continues by Adlerians throughout the world.

After Adler's death, interest in his work declined. The Nazi regime and World War II were primarily responsible, forcing many Adlerians to scatter across the European continent, and North and South America. Many came to the United States, where they found extreme resistance to Adler's work. It was seen as the antithesis of Freudian psychology. This erroneous perception of Adler's ideas in America, the destruction of Adler's accomplishments in Europe, and the preeminence of the Freudian approach were the main causes of the temporary decline in the recognition of Adler's contributions and in the number of practitioners of Individual Psychology.

Rudolf Dreikurs

Rudolf Dreikurs, a prolific writer and founder of the Alfred Adler Institute of Chicago, nurtured the growth of Adlerian psychology in the United States during the period of heavy psychoanalytic dominance. Dreikurs emigrated to the United States in 1937. His dream was to establish Adlerian child-guidance centers throughout the world. Dreikurs made significant contributions to Individual Psychology before his death in 1972. The most important were his understanding of children and his unique insights into the counseling process.

Inspired by the basic Adlerian principle that all behavior has a purpose, Dreikurs formulated the four goals of misbehavior in children—attention, power, revenge seeking, and display of inadequacy. He saw in those goals the explanation for all children's disruptive behavior. Dreikurs' four goals offered parents and teachers an invaluable tool for dealing more effectively with children's misbehavior.

Dreikurs also made contributions to counseling. He stressed that initial interviews with clients are valuable opportunities for counselors to show their imperfections. Insights were considered not indisputable truths but rather tentative hypotheses. In Dreikurs' opinion, the counselor should look at each interview "as if" it might be the last. If the client left the interview without having learned something, the counselor failed. Dreikurs would begin each session by asking the client, "What do you remember from last time?" This stressed the client's responsibility for change and the continuity from session to session. Dreikurs is also credited with introducing the multiple-therapist procedure to psychotherapy as a teaching method for both therapist and client.

Rudolf Dreikurs was a colorful, courageous theorist and practitioner. His insights continue to reach thousands through his writings and the ongoing work of those he encouraged during his lifetime. A highly readable biography, *The Courage to be Imperfect* (Terner & Pew, 1978), profiles a fascinating man who battled massive professional odds with tremendous personal strength.

ADLER, A MAN AHEAD OF HIS TIME

Adler left a wealth of ideas and techniques that still serve the counseling professions. His son, Kurt, a practitioner in New York City, gathered what he considered the most significant examples of his father's pioneering contributions to psychotherapy and counseling (Adler, n.d.).

Alfred Adler was the first to work publicly with clients. He practiced group and family therapy in front of large audiences of doctors, teachers, and parents. These demonstrations helped professionals to learn by observing the counseling relationship at work. No other practitioner had ever risked or shared as much as Adler did through these public demonstrations. In addition, of course, the client was helped.

Adler explained neurotic symptoms as "safeguards" against threats to one's self-image and against the challenges of the outside world. Freud, instead, saw neurotic symptoms as defense mechanisms against the repression of internal, instinctual drives. Freud's interpretation of neurotic symptoms was later amended by his daughter, Anna, who recognized the existence of defenses against external, and not only internal, demands. The existence of such defenses was first recognized in children and later expanded to include the safeguarding devices employed by teens and adults.

Adler suggested that a child's bedwetting problem has a psychological, as well as a physiological, component. Contemporary research confirms that in many instances, the physiological element is nonexistent or insufficient to explain the problem. Adler's understanding of the interaction between psychic and physiological factors is still useful today.

In the 1920s, Adler predicted that two more generations would pass before women would achieve true equality. Women's struggle for equality attests to the accuracy of this prediction. Adler didn't see much difference between domination by males and domination by political regimes that oppressed Europe before and during his lifetime. A contemporary misconception in Adler's times saw women as inferior. Adler, however, stressed that inequality makes loving relationships and mutual cooperation impossible. His commitment to the equality of all people is reflected in Danish sculptor Tyra Boldsen's plans for a monument commemorating the enfranchisement of women. Boldsen, an early "liberationist," planned a sculpture that would have many women but only one man, Alfred Adler.

FROM AUTOCRACY TO DEMOCRACY

The revitalization of counseling through Adler's ideas has paralleled the democratic revolution in our cultures. Adler's strategies for changing behavior, beliefs, and feelings work. A therapist-dominated approach, like Freud's, was appropriate in an autocratic era. It was fitting under such circumstances that the therapist would authoritatively prescribe and the client would passively accept the therapist's wisdom. The client's passive position on the therapist's couch symbolizes the nature of the relationship. In an age of democracy, however, when people demand to be treated as equals, Adler's approach to counseling offers a model that views the client as a full and equal participant in the change process.

The shift from autocratic to democratic procedures also has brought about a revolution in counseling and psychotherapy. In the past, the training of psychiatrists, psychologists, and social workers was often heavily influenced by the psychoanalytic school of thought. Emphasis was on cause and effect, instinctual drives, and a mechanistic explanation of behavior. While the psychanalytic theory still has a following, there is an increasing acceptance of other approaches. Examples include Rational–Emotive Behavior Therapy, Behavior Modification, Reality Therapy, and Client-Centered Therapy (Corsini, 1979). These approaches view people as decision-making beings, responsible for their own behavior, and capable of changing it.

Walter O'Connell (1976), a past president of the North American Society of Adlerian Psychology (NASAP), referred to the attitude of many contemporary practitioners and theorists as a "yes, but" acceptance of Adlerian principles. He pointed out that none of them (he specifically mentioned Viktor Frankl, Colin Wilson, Ernest Becker, Ira Progoff, and Rollo May) call themselves Adlerians, yet their belief in human development parallels Adler's. All these "friends" acknowledge many of Adler's ideas in their own contributions to psychology, yet they qualify their similarities.

CURRENT STATUS

NASAP is Individual Psychology's central organization in the United States and Canada. The society was founded in 1952, largely through Dreikurs' efforts. Dreikurs edited the *Journal of Individual Psychology* after Adler's death and disseminated Adlerian concepts across the North American continent, as well as abroad. Through his efforts and those of his colleagues, numerous local societies and organizations have emerged.

Adlerian training institutes can be found across North America. The Adlerian movement experiences steady growth in an era where eclectic practitioners do not restrict themselves to a single school of psychological theory.

NASAP continues to publish a quarterly journal and monthly newsletter. It has established six interest sections: (1) Clinicians, (2) Adlerian Counseling and Therapy, (3) Family Education, (4) Theory and Research, (5) Education, and (6) Business and Organizations. NASAP has an annual convention. Annual conferences are conducted in diverse locations such as Myrtle Beach, South Carolina; Eugene, Oregon; and Vancouver, British Columbia. NASAP is a member of the International Association of Individual Psychology (IAIP). Once every three years, IAIP meets to bring together people who are interested in Individual Psychology. Adlerian Psychology continues to grow across the globe.

REFERENCES

Adler, K. (n.d.). *Alfred Adler, a man ahead of his time.* Unpublished paper.

Corsini, R. J. (Ed.). (1979). *Current psychotherapies* (2nd ed.). Itasca, IL: Peacock.

Hoffman, E. (1994). The drive for self: Alfred Adler and the founding of individual psychology. New York: Addison-Wesley.

O'Connell, W. E. (1976). The "friends of Adler" phenomenon. *Journal of Individual Psychology, 32*(1), 5–17.

Terner, J., & Pew, W. L. (1978). *The courage to be imperfect: The life and work of Rudolf Dreikurs.* New York: Hawthorn.

CHAPTER 2

Adlerian Psychotherapy and Other Psychotherapy Systems: Integrative Themes

Psychotherapy textbooks tend to accurately reflect the status and changing trends in the theory and practice of counseling and psychotherapy. Accordingly, when clinicians thought in terms of clearly delineated "schools" or "systems" of psychotherapy as recently as 10 years ago, textbooks described the major systems of psychotherapy. The textbooks emphasized the ideological differences among and uniqueness of these systems. In the past few years these ideological differences seem to become less important theoretically and practically.

In fact, today there is increasing interest in emphasizing the commonalties and converging themes among psychotherapy systems. Several laudatory efforts to clarify theoretical, methodological, and language issues have been reported (Goldfried & Castonguary, 1992; Beitman, Goldfried, & Norcross, 1989). *Psychotherapy integration* is clearly the current shibboleth among many psychotherapy theorists, researchers, and practitioners. One indication of such interest is that at least three journals with psychotherapy integration themes have recently begun publication. But is this focus and quest for integration new? From an Adlerian perspective the answer would be "no."

Actually, Adlerian psychotherapy can be viewed as an integrative perspective. In his history of psychodynamic therapies, Ellenberger (1970) suggests that the concepts and methods of many psychotherapy systems overlap considerably with Adlerian psychotherapy. However, the assertion that the Adlerian approach is an integrative perspective had not been empirically established. In 1987, Sherman and Dinkmeyer published a landmark study in which they offered empirical verification that one component of Adlerian psychotherapy, Adlerian Family Therapy, was an integrative approach. Sherman and Dinkmeyer (1987) compared the independent rating of 66 family therapy concepts by experts in six family therapy systems and noted a 92.4 percent general agreement of the Adlerian approach with the majority of the five other family therapy approaches studied. Essentially, the study established the convergence of the various family therapy systems with the Adlerian approach. This research effort may represent one of the most important publications in the psychotherapy literature in the 20th century. It is important not only because it evidenced the centrality of Adlerian influence on other theories, but also because its significance was recognized by non-Adlerians

One of the most important tasks for Adlerian psychology is to extend the Sherman and Dinkmeyer research to all the psychotherapy perspectives and systems, both individual as well as family systems in relation to the Adlerian perspective. This chapter is an initial effort in this monumental undertaking. Clarkin, Frances, and Perry (1985) believe that the multitude of psychosocial treatment approaches can be categorized in terms of four basic orientations or perspectives:

1. *psychodynamic*—including classical, object relations, and self-psychology
2. *cognitive–behavioral*—including behavior therapy, cognitive therapy, and rational emotive behavior therapy
3. *experiential*—including Rogerian, Gestalt, existential, and some aspects of self-psychology
4. *systems*—including structural family therapy, strategic therapy, and solution-focused therapy

Tables 2–1 through 2–4 provide overviews of the different approaches in these four perspectives.

Table 2–5 summarizes these four perspectives in comparison with the integrative Adlerian perspective. These comparisons are the focus of the remainder of this chapter.

This chapter describes the convergent and integrative nature of the three basic constructs in Adlerian psychotherapy as they relate to these four psychotherapy perspectives. Figure 2–1 suggests the integrative relationship among these psychotherapy perspectives and Adlerian psychotherapy. It will be shown that considerable commonality exists among each of these perspectives and the Adlerian approach. The three basic constructs in Adlerian psychotherapy are (1) therapeutic focus, or the centrality of the lifestyle and lifestyle convictions as the focus of psychotherapy; (2) therapeutic relationship, or the cooperative and collaborative nature of the client–therapist relationship; and, (3) therapeutic change, or the process of reeducation and reorientation.

TABLE 2–1 *Psychodynamic Approaches*

Theory	Main Proponents	Key Concepts	Psychotherapeutic Process	Interventions
Classical Psychoanalysis	Freud	Psychic conflicts; instincts; id, ego, and superego; defense mechanisms; unconscious processes.	Resolution of intrapsychic conflicts and restructuring the personality as necessary. Importance of insight in effecting change.	Dream analysis and free association to explore unconscious processes; confrontation; clarification; interpretation; working through.
Object Relations	Klein, Fairburn, Kernberg, Mahler, Winnicott	Transitional object; object-seeking; good enough mothering; projective identification; separation–individuation.	The goal of therapy is the release of bad objects from the unconscious and the development of a healthy true self.	Interpretation of resistances and transferences; squiggle technique.
Self-Psychology	Kohut, Goldberg	Self-object; mirroring and idealizing transferencies; self-cohesion; narcissistic injury; empathic deficits; grandiose self.	Reducing narcissistic vulnerability and empathic deficits through the therapist's empathy and acceptance.	Mirroring; free association; dream work; transmuting interpretations.

TABLE 2-2 *Cognitive–Behavioral Approaches*

Theory	Main Proponents	Key Concepts	Psychotherapeutic Process	Interventions
Behavior Therapy	Skinner, Wolpe	Focuses on overt, observable behavior; psychopathology results from maladaptive learning; relapse prevention.	Reduce and replace maladaptive behavior, strengthening desired behavior and relapse prevention.	Assertive training; exposure; systematic desensitization, skill training; self-management training; behavioral rehearsal; reinforcement; modelling.
Cognitive Therapy	Beck	Dichotomous thinking; cognitive distortions; core schemas; cognitive triad; collaborative empiricism.	Recognize and challenge dysfunctional cognitions in favor of more functional beliefs.	Cognitive restructuring; cognitive rehearsals; behavioral rehearsal; exposure.
Rational–Emotive Behavior Therapy	Ellis	Emotional disturbance results from illogical or irrational thought processes; catastrophizing.	Assist the client to learn to dispute irrational or illogical thoughts.	Cognitive disputations, shame-attacking exercises; bibliotherapy; behavioral techniques; and psychoeducation.

TABLE 2-3 *Experiential Approaches*

Theory	Main Proponent	Key Concepts	Psychotherapeutic Process	Interventions
Person-Centered	Rogers	Inherent self-actualizing tendencies; the role of the self and the client's internal frame of reference (schema); fully functioning person	When the therapist provides the core conditions, i.e., empathic understanding, the client will move toward a more self-actualizing state.	Requires the use of listening skills to communicate empathic understanding and establish other core conditions.
Gestalt	Perls	Movement from dependence to independence; being integrated and centered in the here-and-now	A dialogue between the therapist and client whereby the client becomes aware of what is occurring in the here-and-now.	The therapist models authenticity and facilitates the client in becoming aware and centered in the present. Use of empty-chair technique; guided fantasy.
Existential Therapy	Frankl, May, Bugental	Uniqueness of the individual; authentic awareness; freedom of responsibility; and being and nonbeing	Emphasizes the therapeutic relationship over techniques. Goals include searching for personal meaning and becoming aware of choices.	Paradoxical intention; dereflection; existential encounter; "staying with" the client; "phenomenological reduction."

TABLE 2-4 *Systems Approaches*

Theory	Main Proponents	Key Concepts	Psychotherapeutic Process	Interventions
Structural Family Therapy	Minuchin	Systemic concepts such as boundaries; power; sub-systemic schemas, triangulation, hierarchy, and enmeshment.	Therapist joins the family to alter structure of the interaction between family members.	Joining, clarify and restructure boundaries; increase flexibility of family interactions; tracking; reframing; enactment.
Strategic Therapy	Haley, Madanes, Erickson	Communication patterns and power struggles determine the nature of the relationships between family members.	Attempts to directly resolve presenting problems with little attempt to provide insight from past events.	Define relationship between family members; reframing paradoxical injunctions; directives, "prescribing the symptom."
Solution-Focused Therapy	de Shazer, Wiener-Davis, O'Hanlon	Focus on solutions, not problems; dysfunction arises from faulty attempts at problem solving and the family system becomes "stuck."	Therapist aids family members in discovering their own creative solutions for becoming "unstuck."	Formula tasks; emphasize strengths; "miracle question"; "exception question."

TABLE 2-5 *A Comparison of Four Perspectives and the Integrative Perspective*

Perspective	Psychopathology	Psychotherapeutic Process	Interventions
Psychodynamic	Result of defensive reactions to anxiety, and/or scheme/object representations related to childhood experiences.	Understanding and resolution of conflict areas and defense mechanisms used; reworking personality structures related to childhood conflicts/self-object/schemas.	Clarification; confrontation; interpretation; mirroring; working through/ desensitization.
Cognitive–Behavioral	Result of dysfunctional cognitions/schemas and/or maladaptive patterns behavior.	Recognize and modify dysfunctional cognitions/schemas and behavior pattern to be more functional.	Cognitive restructuring. Desensitization strategies: ▪ Systematic desensitization ▪ Exposure ▪ Cognitive & behavioral rehearsal Skill training Modeling and reinforcement
Experiential	Result of discrepancy between real and ideal self (schemas), and/or disturbance in boundary between self and others so that one is not centered in the here-and-now.	Increase authentic awareness of self, courageously face existential fears thereby facilitate becoming a more fully functioning and centered person.	Empathic listening and responding. Desensitization strategies: ▪ "phenomenological reduction" ▪ "staying with" ▪ "empty-chair technique" ▪ guided fantasy ▪ enactment
Systems	Result of dysfunctional patterns of family boundaries, schemas, power, intimacy, and skill deficits.	Reestablish more functional system boundaries, schemas, power and skills in problem-solving strategies/ solutions.	Joining Skill training (e.g., parenting skills); boundary restructuring. Desensitization strategies: ▪ paradox ▪ reframing ▪ enactment
Integrative/ Adlerian	Result of intrapersonal, interpersonal and system dynamics arising from family structure, constellation and basic schemas/lifestyle convictions.	Increase awareness and functioning (personally, occupational, social, and intimacy) and social interest.	Tailored integration of above interventions.

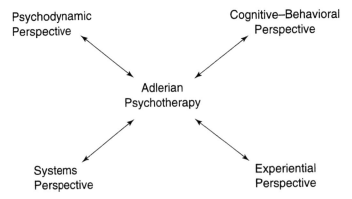

Figure 2–1 The Integrative Relationship of Adlerian Psychotherapy to Four Other Major Psychotherapy Perspectives

THERAPEUTIC FOCUS

An individual's lifestyle convictions is the main therapeutic focus of Adlerian psychotherapy. Lifestyle convictions make up the cognitive organization of the individual and can be described in terms of convictions about self, the world, the self-ideal, and ethical convictions (Mosak, 1989). Adler first used the term *schema of apperception* to refer to the individual's view of self and the world in his book *Science of Living* in 1929. For Adler, psychopathology reflected the individual's "neurotic schema" (Adler, 1956, p. 333). Recently, the use of the terms *schema* and *schema theory* has emerged as central in the various subdisciplines of cognitive science, as well as by various psychotherapy schools (Stein, 1992; Stein & Young, 1992). Essentially, schemas reflect lifestyle convictions.

In this chapter, the terms *schema* and *lifestyle convictions* are used synonymously. This section describes the pervasiveness of constructs similar to the Adlerian focus of treatment across the four major psychotherapeutic perspectives.

Psychodynamic Perspectives

While classical psychoanalysts focused on libidinal drives, modern analysts have focused instead on relational themes—emphasizing the self, the object, and the interaction of the two, while a number of ego psychology and object relations theorists have emphasized schema theory. Inderbitzin and James (1994) view object relations theory as centered on "inner mental schemas that conceptualize other persons . . . as object relations" (p. 111). Strupp and Binder (1984) emphasize the importance of understanding the patient's self-representation and world-view. Eagle (1986) and Wachtel (1982) also have devised schema theories.

Slap and Slap-Shelton (1981) describe a schema of a model of psychoanalysis, which they contrast with the structural model devised by Freud and refined by the ego psychologists. These authors contend that Freud's structural model—the tripartite model of id, ego, and superego—is a theoretical and clinical cul de sac. They contend that the schema model is a parsimonious model of mental functioning and psychopathology that better fits the clinical data of psychoanalysis than the structural model.

The schema model they propose is a bipartite model consisting of the ego and sequestered schema. The ego consists of many schemas, which are loosely linked and integrated with one another and relatively accessible to consciousness. These schemas are based on past experience but are modified by new experience and form the basis of adaptive behavior. Sequestered schemas are organized around traumatic events and situations in childhood that were not mastered or integrated by the immature psyche of the child. These schemas remain latent and repressed. To the extent these sequestered or pathological schemas are active, current relationships are cognitively processed according to these schemas rather than being treated objectively by the more adaptive schemas of the ego. Essentially, current situations cannot be perceived and processed in accord with the reality of the current event but rather as replications of unmastered childhood conflict.

Treatment consists of helping the client to describe, clarify, and work through these sequestered, pathological schema. These schemas are exposed to the client's mature, adaptive ego to achieve integration. Clients are helped to recognize how they create and recreate scenarios that reopen their pathologic schemas. The repeated demonstration and working through of the traumatic events that gave rise to the pathological schemas engenders a greater degree of self-observation, understanding, and emotional growth.

Another variation of ego psychology is the approach described by Weiss (1993). Weiss contends that in his later writings Freud espoused the "higher mental functioning hypothesis" in which psychopathology is a function of pathogenic beliefs. For Weiss, psychotherapy is a process in which the client is helped by the psychotherapist to change these beliefs. These pathogenic beliefs involve self-view, world-view, and the moral and ethical assumptions of others. These beliefs, which are unconscious to varying degrees, organize the individual's personality and psychopathology. One's personality reflects one's attempts at mastery and adaptation. These beliefs warn the individual about the dangerous consequences of pursuing certain goals or experiencing certain wishes, affects, or ideas. Clients who enter psychotherapy with a plan or "strategy" for solving problems and disconfirming pathogenic beliefs. The client's strategy has both conscious and unconscious elements for failing to affirm pathogenic beliefs. It may involve both discussion and exploration as well as testing beliefs within the relationship with the therapist. In testing a pathogenic belief, such as that the therapist will be angry if the client is late for a session, the client carries out a trial action to see if the therapist can comfortably tolerate this behavior. When the therapist fails to affirm the client's pathogenic expectations by showing no anger, the "test is passed" and therapy can proceed.

Weiss states that his approach is basically consistent with Cognitive Therapy. However, he notes that, unlike Cognitive Therapy, pathologic beliefs are oriented to be repressed and unconscious. Similar to Cognitive Therapy, psychotherapy for

Weiss is a process in which the therapist helps the client change these beliefs. However, Weiss's approach differs in that the therapist's task is to help the client become conscious of the beliefs and to change them through both interpretation and "passing the patient's tests." But if the therapist confirms the client's pathogenic expectation (e.g., shows anger that the client was late), the test is "failed" and the client is likely to show signs of discouragement and lack of progress.

Horowitz (1988) offers another view of schemas within psychoanalytic perspective. He proposes that everyone has a repertoire of schemas of self and other. Self-schemas include ways to gain pleasure or avoid displeasure—called *innovational schemas;* relating to other people and the world—called *role schemas;* and ways of helping an individual decide which of two motives to choose—called *value schemas.* Finally, there are *superordinate schemas,* which articulate the self to the other schemas.

Self-schemas develop from the interaction of genetic and environmental factors. Role relationship models develop in the context of interpersonal behavioral patterns. In psychotherapy, the client's schemas become manifest in the role-relationship modes between therapist and client. The therapeutic relationship allows the client to develop insight into these schemas. During the process of working through, the client is assisted in gradually replacing or modifying these schemas.

Cognitive–Behavioral Perspectives

There was little room in classical behaviorism for any discussion of structure of the mind. However, Beck and his co-workers have pioneered schema theory within the cognitive–behavioral perspective. Beck (1964) introduced the schema concept with reference to depression and more recently (Beck & Freeman, 1990) to the treatment of personality disorders. Early developments in cognitive therapy focused on cognitive distortion and dysfunctional beliefs as they related to depressive and anxiety disorders. But cognitive therapists began pursuing a third level of analysis, schemas, to aid in the understanding and treatment of personality disorders that proved to be impervious to the treatment methods based on the first two levels of analysis. Thirty years ago, Beck first described the cognitive triad of depression as negative views of the self, the world, and the future. More recently he has proposed other schemas and sub-schemas in a manner similar to lifestyle convictions. He has described various types of schemas: cognitive, affective, motivational, instrumental and control schemas. Most well developed, however, are the cognitive schemas regarding self-evaluation and world-view or evaluation of others. Some cognitive therapists (Young, 1990) have described early maladaptive schemas and triggering schemas that are strikingly similar to Adlerian formulations of various personality disorders. Finally, Bandura, (1978), a social learning theorist described "self systems," and Kelly (1955), whom many regard as a crypto-Adlerian, described "personal constructs" in a manner reminiscent of lifestyle convictions.

Systems Perspectives

Psychoanalytically oriented family therapists—particularly the object–relations approaches—and cognitive behaviorally oriented family therapy systems that reflect the schema-based perspective with individual patients also use schema formulations with couples and families. This is particularly evident in Beck's (1988) book on marital therapy, and Wachtel and Wachtel's (1986) book on combining individual and family therapy.

Experiential Perspectives

Carl Rogers person-centered psychotherapy (Raskin & Rogers, 1989) describes the "self-concept," the "self-ideal," and the "self-structure" as the perception of the relationship of the "I" or "me" to others and to various aspects of life (p. 169). Furthermore, Kohut's self-psychology articulates the "self" and its differentiation from the "self-object" (Kohut, 1977). Self is also differentiated from the "object" in Gestalt Schools (May & Yalom, 1989) and also emphasizes "I-Thou relations" (Yontef & Simkin, 1989, p. 339; Rogers, 1986). Although not formally labelled as lifestyle convictions or schemas, the experiential perspective clearly "allows" for this therapeutic focus.

THERAPEUTIC RELATIONSHIP

Focus on collaboration and mutuality between therapist and client is a relatively recent development in most psychotherapy systems. Previously, the therapist's role was understood as that of being superior, being both expert and healer, while the client's role was that of inferior, being the learner and one in need of healing. Now these roles are described more in terms of equality, wherein client and therapist are fellow travelers on life's journey. However, some 60 years ago Adler stated that psychotherapy was essentially an exercise of cooperation. He noted that treatment failure always involved a lack of cooperation between client and therapist. "Therefore, cooperation between patient and consultant, as the first, serious scientifically conducted attempt to raise social interest, is of paramount importance, and from the start, all measures should be taken to promote the cooperation of the patient with the consultant" (Adler, 1956, pp. 340–341). Mosak (1989) states that for the Adlerian, "a good therapeutic relationship is a friendly one, between equals" (p. 84). This section describes the pervasiveness of constructs similar to the Adlerian view of the client–therapist relationship across the four major psychotherapeutic perspectives.

Psychodynamic Perspectives

Among classical psychoanalytic writers the terms *therapeutic alliance* and *working alliance* had strong overtones of therapist's role of expert and healer (Horowitz, Marmat, & Krupnick, 1984). More recently, proponents of ego psychology and object relations viewpoints are more likely to endorse a more collaborative and co-operative relationship. Strupp and Binder (1984) describe it this way: "The therapeutic stance should be that of a reasonable, mature. and trustworthy adult who fosters a symmetrical relationship between equals" (p. 46). Luborsky (1984) likewise uses the designation *helping alliance* to reflect this more respecting, cooperative stance.

In Weiss's (1993) approach, the therapist and client have the same purpose: the altering of pathogenic beliefs. When clients perceive their therapist to be sympathetic to their plans, they typically react by feeling less anxious, more secure, and more confident in their therapist. Accordingly, therapists should not be neutral, like the traditional psychoanalyst and psychoanalytically oriented therapist, but rather should become their clients' ally in their efforts to change pathogenic beliefs and pursue more adaptive goals. Therapists' interventions are most helpful to clients when they are compatible with the client's plan or strategy. This contrasts with the traditional psychoanalytic view that the therapist's task was to help the client make the unconscious conscious particularly by interpreting the client's resistances. For Weiss, interpretation is not the basic therapeutic technique. In fact, Weiss trusts that clients may be helped to change these pathogenic beliefs and pursue more healthful goals primarily by their experiences with their therapists. After this is accomplished they may feel safe enough to develop insight on their own without the benefit of interpretation. As with self-psychology, Weiss recognized the curative role of therapist warmth and empathy as opposed to the stance of neutrality.

In self-psychology, the therapist's role is clearly not neutral. Rather, the therapist becomes a participant observer in therapeutic process. In this process, empathy is essentially strengthening the self-structure. Kohut (1984) considered empathy to be a form of "vicarious introspection" and saw it as having two functions: understanding and interpretation. While understanding is an immediate apprehension of the client's subjective world, interpretation is used to help clients see that their current reactions are based on empathic failure of significant others in childhood. Thus, empathy serves to validate and help clients organize their subjective world. Eventually, this results in a cohesive sense of self.

This view of empathy is somewhat different than the traditional psychoanalytic view in which empathy is used primarily to develop insight or understanding into the client's unconscious dynamics. This understanding is used by the analyst to construct a model of client dynamic which is fed back in the form of interpretation and other insight-provoking efforts.

Cognitive–Behavioral Perspectives

Perhaps the most outspoken proponent of collaboration is Cognitive therapist Aaron Beck. He uses the term *collaborative empiricism* to refer to a therapeutic relationship that is "collaborative and requires jointly determining the goals for treatment . . . and where the therapist and patient become co-investigators" (Beck

& Weishaar, 1989, p. 301). Beck also believes that the therapist's role is that of a guide and catalyst who promotes corrective experiences in addition to using warmth, accurate empathy, and genuineness to appreciate the patient's personal world-view.

Several other Behavioral and Cognitive therapists endorse the collaborative perspective (Schwartz, 1988; Woolford, 1988; Fishman, 1988). Meichenbaum (Turk & Meichenbaum, 1983) accentuates the clinical value of a collaborative relationship when he advocates the importance of "entering the patient's perspective." In so doing, "the patient and therapist can work together to establish a similar understanding and common expectations (of treatment)" (p. 7).

Systems Perspectives

As noted in Sherman and Dinkmeyer's (1987) comparative analysis of family therapy systems, the communications approach of Satir, the strategic approach, the structural approach, and the MRI interactional approach all place a premium on collaboration between therapist and the client couple or family, particularly with regard to cooperation and realigning roles and relationships. In addition, Bowen's (1978) family systems approach is quite compatible with the Adlerian approach, and thus endorses a collaborative relationship, wherein the therapist's role is largely that of a coach. Foley (1989) concludes that in the object relations family system (Bowen), and structural and strategic perspectives, the therapist's role is that of teacher and a role model of positive healthy behavior, rather than that of expert.

Experiential Perspectives

Carl Rogers (1951) who developed person (client)-centered therapy emphasized the importance of the therapist's use of warmth, accurate empathy, and genuineness to appreciate the client's inner world, as well as to effect change. Existentialist psychotherapists believe that a collaborative relationship of equals is fundamental to good therapeutic work (May & Yalom, 1989). Kohutian self-psychology clearly emphasizes the importance of collaboration, with its focus on the therapist's empathic mirroring to connect with the patient's inner world from the vantage point of the experiencing insider (Kohut, 1977, 1984).

THERAPEUTIC CHANGE

While therapeutic focus answers the "what" question, and therapeutic relationship answers the "who" question, therapeutic process answers the "how" question. More specifically, *therapeutic change* refers to the mechanisms of change that underlie the psychotherapeutic process. Adler taught that neurotic symptoms served the purpose of safeguarding the client's self-esteem (Adler, 1956). Freud originally conceived of ego defense mechanisms as "protection of the ego against instinctual demands"

(Freud, 1936, p. 157). As the term *ego defense mechanism* is used today, it refers to the safeguarding of the self from outside threats. Adler believed that uncovering this neurotic safeguarding was the most important component of psychotherapy. He noted that this uncovering process takes place in a step-by-step, incremental fashion through encouragement, re-education, and reorientation. Beitman and Mooney (1991) argue that desensitization is the common mechanism for change in psychotherapy. Desensitization is a process of extinguishing an emotional response, such as anxiety, dysphoria, guilt, and so on, to a stimuli that formerly induced it. This section describes the phenomenon of desensitization across the four major psychotherapeutic perspectives.

Psychodynamic Perspective

In traditional psychoanalysis, neurosis develop when defense mechanisms protect the ego from instinctual drives and the remittent anxiety. The change procedure in traditional psychoanalysis consists of four distinct procedures: (1) confrontation, (2) clarification, (3) interpretation, and (4) working through (Greenson, 1967). During confrontation, the issue or concern, such as resistance, is made evident and explicit. In clarification, the concern is brought into sharper focus by pointing to several instances that exemplify it. In interpretation, the unconscious meaning or cause is made conscious. Finally, working through refers to the repetitive and incremental process of exploring resistances that prevent insight from lending to change. The theory is that the unconscious keeps forbidden and terrifying fantasies, impulses, thought, and feeling from consciousness. Psychoanalytic therapy attempts to minimize and desensitize anxiety by moving in small increments toward the feared object, as Adlerian therapy uncovers and removes the neurotic safeguard in an incremental fashion.

Cognitive–Behavioral Perspective

Wolpe (1983) and Marks (1987) describe systematic desensitization as a step-by-step procedure for replacing anxiety with relaxation while gradually increasing the client's exposure to an anxiety-producing situation or object. Thus, exposure, in varying degrees, leads to or produces desensitization. These various exposure treatments ranging from desensitization in fantasy to desensitization invito, from implosion or flooding in fantasy to real-life flooding, modeling, operant conditioning, and cognitive rehearsal. In the process, desensitization and extinction clients must redeploy their attention away from negative self-evaluations and toward either the feared object itself or helpful environmental aspects. As a result, they learn a greater degree of self-control or mastery (Beitman & Mooney, 1991). Similarly, more cognitively oriented therapy approaches such as Cognitive Therapy and Rational–Emotive Behavior Therapy target cognition to be desensitized through cognitive restructuring or disputation.

Experiential Perspective

Yalom (1980) contends that existential psychodynamics are similar to the psychoanalytic view of neurosis and desensitization. While the psychoanalytic formula has instinctual drives arousing anxiety which is then contained by defense mechanisms, the existential formula has awareness of ultimate concerns arousing anxiety which is contained by defense mechanism. Ultimate existential concerns are, of course death, meaninglessness, isolation, and freedom. The therapeutic strategy used in the experiential and existential approaches involves helping the client face the feared awareness of each ultimate concerns. Common to these various therapeutic approaches is helping clients gradually face their fears and stay with them. For example, Havens (1974) proposes that direct human-emotional contact by the therapist desensitizes isolation. Exposure via human contact can extinguish the fear that led the individual to become isolated from others. Havens describes that in the process of facing their fears the phenomena of "phenomenological reduction" occurs. This means that attitudes are reframed or reconfigured based on more totally experiencing the other persons. In "staying with," the therapist remains in the phenomenological world of the other to expose the client to an ultimate human connection. Beitman and Mooney (1991) suggest that other experiential approaches such as the Gestalt therapies, and by extension Client-Centered Therapies, effect change through the same mechanism of desensitization.

Systemic Perspective

Trust as *phenomenological reduction* is a curative dimension in the experiential perspective, *reframing* is a classic curative mechanism in systemic and family therapeutic approaches, reframing of the client's reality changes the conceptual or emotional context of the problem so that its meaning can be reconstrued in a more manageable and acceptable way. While the concrete facts remain unchanged, the client's perception of the facts is changed. Reframing is often used early in the course of strategic therapy and structured family therapy to enable the client to take some initial steps toward the therapeutic perspectives, the mechanism of exposure and desensitization occurs in an incremental fashion (Watzlawick, Weakland, & Fisch, 1974).

CONCLUDING COMMENTS

It has been argued that Adlerian psychotherapy is clearly an integrative perspective, at least with regard to therapeutic focus and the client–therapist relationship, and the Adlerian view in these three areas were clearly incorporated in the four major psychotherapeutic perspectives. This is signified by the direction of the arrows from the Adlerian approach to the four perspectives. However, it is important to recognize that each of the major orientations have also made important contributions that have been likewise incorporated by Adlerian psychotherapists. This is signified in Figure 2–1 by the arrows from the four perspectives to the Adlerian approach. This sharing might be called *reciprocal gifting*. Probably the most obvious examples of reciprocal gifting involves developments in the cognitive therapies. Both Ellis (REBT) and Beck (Cognitive Therapy) have incorporated the Adlerian notion of maladaptive beliefs or convictions into their therapeutic systems. Yet both have refined strategies and techniques for challenging and disputing dysfunctional beliefs that have since become incorporated and commonplace in Adlerian psychotherapeutic practice.

REFERENCES

Adler, A. (1956). The Individual Psychology of Alfred Adler In H. Ansbacher & R. Ansbacher (Eds.), New York: Harper and Row.

Bandura, A. (1978). The self-system in reciprocal determinism. *American Psychologist, 33,* 343–358.

Beck, A. (1964). Thinking and depression, II: Theory and therapy. *Archives of General Psychiatry, 10,* 561–571.

Beck, A. (1988). *Love is never enough.* New York: Harper and Row.

Beck, A., & Freeman, A. (1990). *Cognitive therapy of personality disorders.* New York: Guilford.

Beck, A., & Weishaar, M. (1989). Cognitive therapy. In R. Corsini & D. Wedding (Eds.), *Current psychotherapies* (pp. 285–322). Itasca, IL: F. E. Peacock.

Beitman, B., Goldfried, M., & Norcross, J. (1989). The movement toward integrating the psychotherapies. *American Journal of Psychiatry, 146,* 138–147.

Beitman, B., & Mooney, J. (1991). Exposure and desensitization as Common Change processes in pharmacotherapy and psychotherapy. In Beitman, B. & Klerman, G. (Eds.) *Integrating pharmacotherapy and psychotherapy.* Washington, DC: American Psychiatric Press.

Bowen, M. (1978). *Family therapy in clinical practice.* New York: Jason Aronson.

Clarkin, J., Frances, A., & Perry, S. (1985). The psychosocial treatments. In R. Michaels, A. Cooper, S. Gunze, et al. (Eds.), *Psychiatry* (pp. 293–324). Philadelphia: J. B. Lippincott.

Eagle, M. (1986). The psychoanalytic and the cognitive unconscious. In R. Stern (Ed.), *Theories of the unconscious* (pp. 155–190). Hillsdale, NJ: Analytic Press.

Ellenberger, H. (1970). *The discovery of the unconscious: The history and evolution of dynamic psychiatry.* New York: Harper and Row.

Fishman, D. (1988). Paradigmatic decisions in behavior therapy: A provisional road map. In D. Fishman, C. Franks, & E. Rotgers (Eds.), *Paradigms in behavior therapy: Present and promise.* New York: Springer.

Foley, V. (1989). Family therapy. In R. Corsini & D. Wedding (Eds.), *Current psychotherapies* (pp. 455–502). Itasca, IL: F. E. Peacock.

Freud, S. (1936). *Inhibitions, symptoms and anxiety.* London: Hogarth Press.

Goldfried, M., & Castonguary, L. (1992). The future of psychotherapy integration. *Psychotherapy: Theory, Research, Practice, Training, 29,* 4–10.

Greenson, R. (1967). *The technique and practice of psychoanalysis, Vol. 1.* New York: International Universities Press.

Havens, L. (1974). The existential use of the self. American Journal of Psychiatry, *131:1,* 1–10.

Horowitz, M. (1988). *Introduction to psychodynamics: A new synthesis.* New York: Basic Books.

Horowitz, M., Marmat, C., Krupnick, J. et al. (1984). *Personality styles and brief psychotherapy.* New York: Basic Books.

Inderbitzin, L., & James, M. (1994). Psychoanalytic psychology. In Stoudemire, A. (Ed.), *Human Behavior: An introduction for medical students* (2nd ed., pp. 107–142). Philadelphia: Lippincott.

Kelly, G. (1955). *The psychology of personal constructs.* New York: Norton.

Kohut, H. (1977). *The restoration of the self.* New York: International Universities Press.

Kohut, H. (1984). *How does analysis cure?* Chicago: University of Chicago Press.

Luborsky, L. (1984). *Principles of psychoanalytic psychotherapy: A manual for supportive–expressive treatment.* New York: Basic Books.

Marks, I. (1987). *Fears, phobias and rituals.* New York: Oxford University Press.

May, R., & Yalom, I. (1989). Existential psychotherapy. In R. Corsini & D. Wedding (Eds.), *Current psychotherapies* (pp. 363–404). Itasca, IL: F. E. Peacock.

Mosak, H. (1989). Adlerian psychotherapy. In R. Corsini & D. Wedding (Eds.), *Current psychotherapies* (4th ed., pp. 65–118). Itasca, IL: F. E. Peacock.

Raskin, N., & Rogers, C. (1989). Person-centered therapy. In R. Corsini & D. Wedding (Eds.), *Current psychotherapies* (pp. 155–196). Itasca, IL: F. E. Peacock.

Rogers, C. (1951). *Client-centered therapy.* Boston: Houghton Mifflin.

Rogers, C. (1986). Rogers, Kohurt and Erickson. *Person-Centered Review, 1,* 125–140.

Schwartz, G. (1988). Cognitive behavioral therapy and health psychology. In D. Fishman, C. Franks, & E. Rotgers (Eds.), *Paradigms in behavior therapy: Present and promise* (pp. 197–231). New York: Springer.

Sherman, R., & Dinkmeyer, D. (1987). *Systems of family therapy: An Adlerian integration.* New York: Brunner/Mazel.

Slap, J., & Slap-Shelton, L. (1991). *The schema in clinical psychoanalysis.* Hillsdale, NJ: The Analytic Press.

Stein, D. (1992). Schemas in the cognitive and clinical sciences: An integrative construct. *Journal of Psychotherapy Integration, 2,* 45–63.

Stein, D., & Young, J. (1992). Schema approach to personality disorders. In D. Stein, & J. Young (Eds.), *Cognitive science and clinical disorders* (pp. 272–288). San Diego: Academic Press.

Strupp, H., & Binder, J. (1984). *Psychotherapy in a new key: A guide to time-limited dynamic psychotherapy.* New York: Basic Books.

Turk, I., & Meichenbaum, D. (1983). *Pain and behavioral medicine: A cognitive-behavioral approach.* New York: Guilford.

Wachtel, P. (1982). *Resistance: Psychodynamics and behavioral approaches.* New York: Plenum.

Wachtel, P., & Wachtel, E. (1986). *Family dynamics in individual psychotherapy.* New York: Guilford.

Watzlawick, P., Weakland, J., & Fisch, R. (1974). *Change: Principles of problem formation and problem resolution*. New York: Norton.

Weiss, J. (1993). *How psychotherapy works: Process and technique*. New York: Guilford.

Wolpe, J. (1983). *The practice of behavior therapy* (3rd ed.), New York: Pergamon.

Woolford, R. (1988). The self in cognitive behavior therapy. In D. Fishman, C. Franks, & E. Rotgers (Eds.), *Paradigms in behavior therapy: Present and promise*. New York: Springer.

Yalom, I. (1980). *Existential psychotherapy*. New York: Basic Books.

Yontef, G., & Simkin, J. (1989). Gestalt therapy. In R. Corsini & D. Wedding (Eds.), *Current psychotherapies* (pp. 323–362). Itasca, IL: F. E. Peacock.

Young, J. (1990). *Cognitive therapy for personality disorders: A schema-focused approach*. Sarasota, FL: Professional Resource Exchange.

CHAPTER 3

Personality Development

T his chapter addresses the Individual Psychology view of personality development. What makes a human being unique? Why do identical twins display distinctly different personalities? When are personality traits first visible in human development? Adlerians have unique and helpful perspectives for counselors, therapists, and educators.

Infants enter the world with certain immovable genetic endowments in an environmental context with other human beings. For most infants, this context is a family with certain values, brothers and sisters, and parental roles. Infants immediately react to external stimuli and play an active role in responding to and influencing their environment. Through what appears at first to be almost trial and error, children "learn" what works and what doesn't work. Whatever seems to work, they persist in; whatever fails to influence the significant people around them (their social field), they discard. Each new situation is met with an ever-increasing storehouse of experiences. These experiences are influenced by *subjective interpretation* of reality.

Children are more than a bundle of disorganized drives and instincts. The tremendous creative power of infants and small children is often overlooked. Even at birth a human being has the capacity to make important contributions to another human being. By nursing at the mother's breast, the baby facilitates the third stage of labor, reduces maternal hemorrhage, and relieves great congestion. Yet this unique ability is often overlooked, even denied, and a subtle and important cooperative relationship is missed. The drive to *belong* is an important part of each child's development.

The infant's ability to perceive and make choices is illustrated in a baby with deaf-mute parents. The infant soon learns that sound is ineffective, so he screws up his face, gets red, flails his arms and legs, and "cries" without sound. Later the child may learn to have a temper tantrum by stomping on the floor so that his parents can feel the vibrations.

Children actively create their personalities. Although they may be good observers, they are often poor interpreters. A child's *subjective perception,* the unique interpretation of events, is always a factor. They come to conclusions about themselves and life that are based on imperfect assumptions. As they create their guidelines and establish their blueprints for the future, children tend to operate with an "only if" absurdity. For example, a child may conclude "Only if I am pleasing (or in control, or comfortable, or good, or competent, or right), can I really belong." This kind of thinking is based on the faulty assumption, "I don't really belong." Yet most of us spend a great deal of time and energy looking for a place we have merely by virtue of our existence.

The "only if" premise is based on avoiding what we fear most. If we choose to belong by pleasing, our greatest fear is of rejection. If control is our priority, humiliation is what we hope to avoid. If comfort has precedence, the worst thing is stress. And if moral superiority is what we value most, the feeling of meaninglessness is what we must avoid at all costs. The Adlerian view is that the infants establish this "Number One" priority very early, perhaps within the first year. It is along this guiding line that they begin to construct their personalities, which will include a complex of prejudices, biased perceptions, conclusions, and convictions. Certainly by the sixth year of life, personal assumptions about how to belong in the human community are firmly in place. These assumptions are a unique and distinct personality.

Because this process begins preverbally, as older children or adults we are only dimly aware of our own style of living. The child doesn't have to start from scratch with each new experience, but this process is absolutely essential for survival.

INFLUENCES ON THE DEVELOPING PERSONALITY

Genetic Factors

The evidence to support genetic influences on the development of personality is growing. However, it must be reconciled with observations of individuals such as fraternal and identical twins. In identical (one egg) twins, who have exactly the same genetic makeup, we often see strikingly different personalities. One explanation for this difference appears frequently when we interview adult identical twins. After relating the same early recollection, the twins usually reach opposite conclusions about the incident. This is a way of saying what we are born with or what we are born into is usually less of an influence than our perceptions and decisions about life.

Constitutional Factors

We are unable to measure the effects of the various body systems, such as the endocrine system or the central nervous system, on personality development, except in cases of obvious physical or mental defect. But we know that intelligence, although static, is still something of a factor in influencing lifestyle, because intelligence is a necessary tool for coping behavior. A healthy, attractive boy or girl will experience certain environmental reactions and find certain opportunities that are different from those that some of their friends will meet. Similarly, intelligent children see alternatives that other children may miss. But it is not the constitutional trait itself that is causative; what is important is how the youngster perceives the trait.

If a child is born with a physical defect, she may be discouraged and operate as if she had a deficiency, or she may overcompensate and, for example, become an outstanding athlete despite her deficiency. All children make their own decisions as to how they perceive their genetic endowment and the environmental situation they find themselves in.

Cultural Factors

Culture provides a child with a particular way of looking at the world, thus emphasizing some tendencies in the development of the lifestyle. For example, in Greece and in some Latin American countries, the culture is still quite autocratic and male dominated. It is not surprising that, in these countries, both girls and boys tend to grow up with exaggerated ideas about the importance of males. In North America, the culture can be characterized as competitive. Competition seeps into all our relationships, including family relationships, providing a cultural influence that leads many children to be very competitive. As we become a multi-cultural society, culture becomes an even greater factor. Each child now has more decisions about which cultural ideas are accepted, or rejected.

Prenatal and Perinatal Factors

Methods of studying the developing fetus are becoming more sophisticated. The fetus processes stimuli and decides in some sense what to make of the stimuli. Legend has George Gershwin developing his gift for syncopated rhythm as a result of the paroxysmal tachycardia that his mother had during pregnancy; that is, he was subjected for nine months to an irregular heartbeat, which perhaps predisposed him toward syncopated rhythm.

The perinatal period is the time just before, during, and immediately following birth. Studies already show that this is a critical time of life. For example, if a mother holds her unclothed newborn baby immediately after delivery, she is significantly more likely to talk with the child as a 2-year-old than the mother who has been denied that experience.

FAMILY INFLUENCE

All children are born into certain social milieus, and their interpretation of their roles in those casts of characters is crucial.

Birth Order   Many studies have been published concerning birth order, but the sum total of the studies is inconclusive. They don't consider the child's attitude and movement, the formation of alliances and opposing groups within the family, and the unique ways children approach the social situation in their search for a place for themselves. The studies don't take into consideration children's perception of their birth order. For example, if a *firstborn* child is severely handicapped, the second child may take over and function as the firstborn. Another child, preceded by a stillborn, might be treated as a more special "firstborn" than usual.

Birth order, then, must be explained dynamically by considering how much the child influences the other members of the family and how they influence the child. A child's striving is directed toward satisfying a feeling of belonging. No two children are ever born into the same family situation. With the birth of each child, the situation and therefore the environment changes because (1) the parents are older, more experienced, and either more encouraged or discouraged about raising a family; (2) the parents' economic circumstances may be different; (3) the parents may have moved to another geographic location; and (4) because of divorce or death, there may be a stepparent.

The following birth order typologies are offered as constructive guidelines:

Only children have a potentially difficult start in life, because they spend their early childhood among adults. But this is not necessarily a disadvantage. It is true that only children may be pampered and, as a consequence, may expect to be the center of interest. But it is also true that they have the opportunity to be the only beneficiary of the adults' roles as models and educators and therefore may become a more competent and cooperative participant in the life of the family.

The *firstborn* position often puts oldest children in a favored spot, but this may be only temporary, because all first children undergo the experience of being dethroned. First children, then, must choose whether to try to maintain the number one position, hold their competitor back in the number two position, or become discouraged and let themselves be overrun by the second child. Naturally, innumerable variations exist among these alternatives.

Second children may feel that they are in a constant race and often develop personalities that are the opposite of their older sibling's personality, particularly if the children are close in age and of the same sex. If a third child arrives, second children also become "squeezed" children. As such, they have one of two tendencies— to let themselves be pushed down by the older and younger siblings or to elevate themselves at their expense.

Youngest children tend to either try to overtake all the others or to remain the baby, expecting help, service, and consideration. In large families, the children usually divide into subgroups. A family of five, for example, may be seen by the youngest as made up of three older children, and two younger children. This means that, when we look for subgrouping in a family, we must do so from the point of view of the person whose lifestyle we are trying to understand and keep in mind that this point of view is not the same for all the children in the family.

Shulman (1973) emphasizes that the ordinal positions are *psychological* more than *chronological,* citing the instance in which a firstborn may be dethroned and play the role of the middle child and the second born, by overrunning the first, actually plays the role of the firstborn.

Family Constellation   This term describes the sociopsychological configuration of a family group. The personality characteristics of each family member; emotional bonds among family members; birth order; the dominance or submission of the various members and their age differences; sex of the siblings; and size of the family are all factors in the family constellation. A child's position in the family constellation exerts a strong influence on the development of the child's personality. It is essential that the therapist or counselor take birth order and family constellation positions into consideration to understand the client's dynamics.

Children try to find their place in their family. It makes a difference how close or distant the family members are; who was born when; how the siblings perceived their position in the birth order; and who is the boss, or at least who is seen as boss (if there is one). The family constellation does not directly describe a particular child. Rather, it offers a dynamic way of understanding, for example, the fact that first and second children are often quite different in personality, particularly if they are close in age and of the same sex. Another example illustrates the role of gender. An only boy among girls, or an only girl among boys, may experience the family constellation in a special way, particularly if that family favors either boys or girls.

The much larger family presents, of course, many more possibilities. There may be, for example, subgroupings within the sibling group, so that a child who is the "eldest" of the younger group may share some of the characteristics of the firstborn child. In stepfamilies, the blending of birth orders may seem confusing. However, it is clarified when we understand what each child or teen decides to do with this new opportunity.

Family Atmosphere   There are a number of typical family atmospheres to which the growing child reacts. These reactions can develop in the direction of accepting the attitudes and values shared by the family, in the direction of rejecting them, or in a direction somewhere between these two.

The attributes that children in a particular family share—such as love of reading, musical aptitude, or athletic ability—are a reflection of the family atmosphere. They express shared family values. In a family that values athletics, it is quite likely that all children will, to some degree, be athletically inclined. The attributes that are not shared by the children are, to some extent, a product of the atmosphere of competition within the family, which grows out to the competition between the parents. For example, if one parent is neat and the other is messy, some of the children are likely to be neat and some messy.

As another example of how children respond to the family atmosphere, all five children in a family may exhibit an unusual interest in music (shared family value because both parents are musical). However, each child chooses a different instrument, and one child finds a unique place by being "tone deaf" and making a musical contribution through percussion. The musical talent, then, represents the family atmosphere of shared family values. The difference in the way the talent is manifested is the result of the competition among the siblings. In this family, if one parent had been musical and the other had not, we might have expected two or three children to be musical and the others to be relatively uninterested in music.

Here are some of the family atmospheres and their characteristics. A family often has more than one of these factors at work in their dynamics:

- The *rejective* atmosphere is exemplified by parents who fail to separate the deed from the doer and who constantly criticize and reject their children.
- The *authoritarian* atmosphere is rigid, stresses obedience, and is likely to produce either extreme conformity or rebellious children.
- In an atmosphere of *martyrdom,* suffering nobly is greatly valued. The spouse of an alcoholic, who by his or her "heroic" behavior ends up encouraging the partner's drinking, is a classic example of this situation.
- In the *inconsistent* atmosphere, the children don't know what to expect of others or what is expected of them. However, Dreikurs often observed that most of the time in such atmosphere it is the adults, rather than the children, who are confused and that it is usually the parents who need to learn to become a match for their children.
- The *suppressive* atmosphere limits the freedom to express thoughts and feelings and sometimes stimulates excessive daydreaming or produces children who are good at "putting up a front." Example of this kind of family are a family made up of humorless people or a group of narrowly religious people, who talk little among themselves and are not demonstrative.
- The *hopeless* atmosphere can be described as one filled with discouragement.
- The *overprotective* atmosphere denies children the opportunity to learn to be responsible for their own behavior.
- The *pitying* atmosphere often stimulates the development of "victims," who become so creative and flexible in their capacity to suffer that they can suffer about anything.
- The *high-standards* atmosphere leads the children to feel that they are never good enough.
- The *materialistic* atmosphere underplays the significance of human relationships and often produces life failures both among those who want to be "the best" and among those who, despairing at being the best, may work at being "the worst."
- The *disparaging* atmosphere is characterized by frequent criticism. The parents operate as if anybody who is not a member of the family is an outsider, thus teaching their children the basic skills of prejudice.
- In the *inharmonious* atmosphere, the children grow up feeling that they are in an enemy camp.
- In deeply troubled families, one of two opposite atmospheres may prevail—a very *disorderly* atmosphere or a very *orderly* atmosphere. An example of a disorderly family is a family in which bickering and fighting go on almost constantly, from the time the first family member gets up in the morning to the time the last one goes to bed at night. An example of an overorderly

atmosphere is a family in which the new stepmother—long single and highly efficient as a nurse—tries to operate the family like a hospital ward and fails to establish any kind of rapport with her stepchildren, who refuse to accept her disciplinary attitude and avoid her company as much as they can.

Early Experiences

Early experiences, no matter how dramatic or potentially traumatic, do not cause personality traits. Children determine for themselves the significance of the experiences. The power of the subjective interpretation of reality is apparent, for example, if one interviews adult identical twins about a shared incident that occurred early in their lives. It is clear from their recollections that the twins do remember the same incident; but when they are asked to pinpoint the most vivid moment in the incident and how they felt at that moment, their answers are likely to indicate that they experienced the incident totally differently.

Impasses

We call *impasse* what children decide they must avoid at all costs. If we are correct in assuming that the number one priority is chosen very early, we can speculate that the impasse has something to do with the family situation and the methods of training. People with a number one priority of control probably have perceived themselves in their childhood as being overpowered and overcontrolled. People with a number one priority of superiority have often grown up in a family where good and bad, right and wrong, success and failure were emphasized and shaming was a common method of child training. These people seem to have felt doubtful about their belonging as very young children and have probably concluded that meaninglessness or nothingness is the most difficult thing to imagine. People with a number one priority of comfort have probably experienced much stress or pain and decided to organize their life so as to avoid repetition of that discomfort. People with a number one priority of pleasing often have been literally rejected in some way and have experienced one or more kinds of behavior on the part of their parents that betrayed significant lack of respect for the dignity of the child.

THE LIFESTYLE[1]

In Adlerian psychology, the term *lifestyle* refers to a person's basic orientation toward life. Ansbacher and Ansbacher (1956) observed the term denotes a dynamic state rather than a rigid and static entity. From this point of view, it is more or less equivalent to terms such as *personality, psyche, character,* and *ego.*

Because a person's lifestyle is based on one's private logic, develops out of one's life plan, and is powered by the fictional goal one established for oneself, we can begin our discussion of lifestyle by analyzing these three basic concepts.

---

[1]The Adlerian term for personality has been expressed as life-style, life style, or lifestyle. The terms are synonymous, and we use the term lifestyle in this text.

The Private Logic

The general knowledge of what is right and wrong—of what one should do and not do—can be looked at as a kind of common sense (Dreikurs, 1969). When people don't do what a situation calls for, they are often operating on the basis of their *private logic,* which may differ widely from the logic of the human community. Behind every action are plans, goals, expectations, and decisions that cause the behavior but of which we are only vaguely aware. Most of our actions are the consequences of thinking processes that we don't recognize and often prefer not to know but that, nevertheless, have a definite influence on our actions. All of these thinking processes, which never reach the threshold of consciousness, can be considered part of the private logic.

Whenever we act contrary to our conscience, we are acting with the sense of our "private" logic. This does not occur only when we want to evade the requirements of the situation. In daily life we do not deal with actual realities but operate with a subjective impression of the world, which is not always in accordance with reality. We call this subjective evaluation of events the *phenomenological field,* within which each human being is moving, and which is valid for that person alone. We never can conceive of "facts" as such. We have only a more or less accurate impression in our imagination of the "facts," but these impressions are used in determining our actions, our attitudes and our goals (Dreikurs, 1969, pp. 70–71; quotation translated by Pew).

Cognitive processes that take place below the threshold of consciousness and yet determine our actions are a significant influence on our lifestyle. First, there are the far-reaching basic goals of the lifestyle. These are the fictions according to which we act and of which we are not conscious. Different factors contribute to this process. Second, these attitudes form when we are so young that we are hardly able to understand consciously what is happening within or around us. But more significantly, the reason we are unable to know these fictious goals lies in the very necessity of subjectivity. Each of us has to act "as if" our judgment were the only possible and absolutely correct one.

Although long-term goals provide the substance of the lifestyle, we have the power to take different attitudes toward current events. In other words, our own self-created limitations within the lifestyle still do not limit our individual creative power—that is, the ability to make decisions about immediate situations. Because we are never rigidly forced to assume an attitude, make a decision, or establish a goal, we must also recognize the short-range goals that we set for ourselves in the immediate experiences of our lives.

In addition to long-range and short-range goals, private logic also includes a form of thinking that Dreikurs called *hidden reason.* Most of us not only don't know why we do something, but we are also unaware of the mental process results in that reason. The hidden reason therefore appears to be an unconscious justification and force behind the movement toward the goals in a given situation.

To be aware of the process, we would have to imagine that we could examine our own minds whenever we said or did something. Nevertheless, when a counselor (or someone else) accurately guesses the hidden reason, the feeling of being understood is often so overpowering that even psychotics and juvenile delinquents are unable to hold themselves back from admitting the reason for their behavior.

The Life Plan

Small children are not prepared to deal with the demands of life. To cope, they must learn the rules of the game in the human community—a community experienced almost exclusively through the family, which seems to represent "life" and the "human condition." All difficulties children encounter are experienced personally and interpreted as difficulties that everyone encounters, just as all successes are incorporated and interpreted as examples of successful living. Children go through a trial-and-error process in which they accumulate behaviors and assumptions that, in their opinion, work for them. This process can be summarized in the phrase, "*No one ever throws away a behavior that works.*"

Children develop safeguarding mechanisms and fictional solutions to problems. We operate under the assumption that we can feel safe only under some circumstances and that we can be worthwhile only if we act in certain ways. Children constantly create and operate in terms of dichotomies—good or bad, on top or at the bottom, masculine or feminine, for example. What makes up the character of a human being is none other than the manifestation of a certain plan the person laid down as a child in preparation for living. The life plan grows out to the constant repetition of attempts to cope with real or imagined difficulties. Out of this plan develops the lifestyle, which, like a characteristic musical theme, accompanies the individual throughout life.

The Fictional Goal

We all develop in early childhood a fictional image of what we need to be like to be safe, to be superior, to belong. The actualization of this functional image becomes the central goal of the lifestyle and, as a consequence, limits to some extent the range of the individual's actions.

The life plan and its fictional goal are the outcomes of children's assessment of their experiences. This assessment is often inaccurate because, although children are excellent observers and have extraordinarily sharp perception, they lack the experience and maturity necessary to evaluate their observations adequately. Children's perceptiveness is perhaps due in part to their lacking a set style of life. Without a set style, one is open to all possible perceptions instead of limited by a style of life that almost completely prevents the experience of "pure" perception. Guided by the fictional goal, children do the best they can to find for themselves a style of life that gives them an immediate feeling of belonging and promises a greater sense of belonging for the future. The style of life they seek is also one that gives them a sense of superiority as they define it for themselves. Once set, the style of life tends to become self-perpetuating.

Because the lifestyle and the guiding fictional goal are so intimately related, the guiding fiction tends to approximate the lifestyle. One's guiding fiction is a certain image of the world and of oneself; therefore, a person's lifestyle is likely to be such that the observer can rather accurately infer the individual's guiding fiction.

The concept of lifestyle refers to our manner of handling ourselves with respect to our self-chosen guiding fictional goal. This means that, since our creativity is practically limitless (especially when it comes to the manner of staging our own lives), there is nothing in any given guiding fiction that forcibly entails a set style of life. Thus, even after having formulated our guiding fictional goal and, to that extent, limited the range of our actions, we still have a tremendous amount of freedom in the choices we constantly make with regard to our style of living.

Development of the Lifestyle

The style of living is created in the course of an ongoing drama that takes place in the theater of the family, with parents and siblings all playing a part—a drama in which children function as their own director and whose last act they have already sketched out. The family *is* society to small children, and their efforts to find a place in this society influence how they create their lifestyle. In identifying an individual's lifestyle, the counselor tries to get some idea of what it was like to be in that childhood drama, what roles were played by the different actors, and how the "director" interpreted the drama—that is, what role the child played and what conclusions he drew about himself and about life.

The drama analogy helps us see the role of another element in the construction of the lifestyle. This element is the order of appearance of each actor on stage—the birth order. We must keep in mind, however, that the importance assigned to this element is always the doing of the "director"; it is a value judgment on the part of the individual whose personality we are trying to understand. We can make some guesses about the individual's personality if we know her ordinal position. These guesses, however, will be based on *nomothetic laws,* such as, "Oldest children are . . . ," "Middle children tend to be . . . ," and so on. But the actual case can be quite different, depending on how the individual sees the situation and what she does about it—*idiographic laws.* Nomothetic laws concerning the family constellation help reveal the individual's idiographic laws—that is, the individual's lifestyle.

Understanding the role the family constellation plays in the creation of one's lifestyle always involves trying to reconstruct the drama from the individual's point of view. Drawing a diagram of the family constellation helps the counselor perceive patterns. This family-constellation diagram is from the oldest child's (Mary) point of view. Her sister Susan is two years younger (11) than her, and her brother Bobby is eight.

Helen	George	
33	35	
Mary	Susan	Bobby
13	−2 years	−5 years

The diagram often reveals the existence of more than two "parents." Aunts, uncles, grandparents, and much older siblings can all be "parents" from the viewpoint of the child if they were an intimate part of the family drama during the years (up to age 6 or 7) in which the child was creating a style of living. For the diagram to be complete, it should also include brothers and sisters who have died.

Earlier in the chapter, we discussed the various factors that influence personality development. One's style of living is the result of the individual's subjective interpretation to these factors. The weight of each is creatively determined by the individual. We have mentioned, for example, genetic endowment and environmental influences; both are important, but the individual determines the degree of importance.

Children create their lifestyle from raw materials, which also include the method of training by the parents, the cultural influences in the immediate and larger community, as well as illnesses, injuries, and hospitalizations—all grist for the mill. During those first few years, children will have created their own idiosyncratic answers to: Who am I? What must I do? What is good? What is bad? Children create their own private logic, which, to some extent, will make each of them different from any other human being. Dreikurs (1969) points out that we don't know how many typical life plans exist, but probably no two human beings share the same ideas and goals. Still, we find considerable similarities in styles of living. Perhaps it is the poverty of our language that forces us to use the same words for different observations and experiences. Communication in any form, then, will always be an approximation both as it is sent and as it is received. It is also conceivable that each culture has a dominant perceptual mode and that its members share similar ideals and values.

Some styles of living are relatively broad, providing a basis for the solution of almost all life problems, while others have such a narrow basis that they run the risk of failing. Despite the inherent cognitive defects in lifestyle, any individual can get along quite reasonably until the lifestyle is challenged by the realities of life. Remember, the style of living is self-created and is also self-consistent. After the first years of life, each new experience merely confirms convictions. An individual will report the same early recollections with the same basic themes year after year, with little influence from outside reality. In other words, the individual has created her own convictions (or fictions) about what she must become and what she can expect of life, of the outside, and of other people.

Mosak divides these convictions into four groups: (1) the self-concept—the convictions I have about who I am; (2) the self-ideal (Adler's term)—the convictions concerning what I should be or am obliged to be in order to have a place in the world; (3) The Weltbild (picture of the world)—what the world demands of me; and (4) ethical convictions—the personal "right/wrong" code (Mosak & Dreikurs, 1973).

LIFESTYLE AND COUNSELING

The concept of lifestyle is extremely useful in counseling as both a tool and an attitude. Adlerian counselors believe that lifestyle is self-created; therefore, they are likely to approach their clients with a positive attitude—the attitude that as long as there is life, people can grow and change. If we instead view personality as the result of inevitable internal or external forces, one has reason to be less optimistic, for genetic influences are relatively unchanging, and the childhood environment cannot be relived.

Children tend to move in line with the expectations of the adults around them. Even gathering the data necessary to understand a client's style of living, without any interpretation on the part of the counselor, is useful. Hearing clients describe their childhood family atmosphere and constellation and some of their interpretations about their position in the family often provides counselors with extremely useful information.

When clients tell about their childhood family constellation and atmosphere, in a sense they are reliving the situation and the vivid moments and emotional experiences connected with it. By sharing their clients' emotional experiences, counselors can achieve deeper understanding and be in a better position to help clients discover more alternatives in their lives. With the help of the counselor, clients come to see themselves and all their biases, guidelines, and convictions more vividly. It is as if a mirror were being held up in front of them, and they were able to then decide which basic convictions they want to keep and which basic mistakes they choose to alter.

A change in the lifestyle is not necessarily the goal in counseling, because within a given style of living rests a wide range of behavioral alternatives. For example, one person's lifestyle may include the conviction "I must fight to belong." If this conviction is challenged, the person might react with "What do you expect me to be—a doormat?" Many other alternatives lie between being a fighter and being a doormat.

Some warnings are in order. Elucidating lifestyle is *not* for the purpose of predicting behavior, but rather for the purpose of understanding and helping another human being. Also, people often use their style of living as an excuse: "What can you expect of me? It's my lifestyle." Finally, we need to distinguish between lifestyle as we use the term here, and lifestyle as a broader term meaning an individual's modus operandi, such as a suburban life style versus an urban lifestyle. The style of living is what makes individuals unique, what distinguishes them from every other human being.

REFERENCES

Ansbacher, H. L., & Ansbacher, R. R. (Eds.). (1956). *The individual psychology of Alfred Adler*. New York: Harper & Row.

Dreikurs, R. (1969). *Grundbegriffe der individualpsychologie*. Stuttgart: Ernst Klett Verlag.

Mosak, H. H., & Dreikurs, R. (1973). Adlerian psychotherapy. In R. J. Corsini (Ed.), *Current psychotherapies*. Itasca, IL: F. E. Peacock.

Shulman, B. H. (1973). *Contributions to individual psychology*. Chicago: Alfred Adler Institute.

CHAPTER 4

Psychopathology

T his chapter has three purposes: First, it describes Adler's basic view of normality and psychopathology along with some observations which extend and clarify it. Second, it compares the Adlerian view with the nosological or classification system of the *Diagnostic and Statistical Manual of Mental Disorders, Fourth Edition* (DSM-IV). Finally, it describes the common patterns of psychopathology in terms of early life experiences, mistaken convictions, and symptom formation.

ADLERIAN VIEWS OF PSYCHOPATHOLOGY

The Basic Theory

According to Adlerian theory, healthy, nonpathological people typically move through life meeting various tasks with courage and common sense. This is the meaning of social interest, but it does not suggest that the individual is perfect. Occasionally, healthy people use private logic, experience some discouragement and a sense of inferiority for which they compensate in ways that are outside the reaches of social interest. Most people believe that imperfections and failures are part of the human condition. On the other hand, pathological people believe that they must be perfect and then justify their thinking and actions as the only way to achieve perfection. For Adler, all personality dysfunction was the outcome of erroneous conceptions of how to achieve personal superiority. For the most part, he believed that these faulty conceptions were formed early in one's life (Adler, 1956).

A *neurotic disposition,* Adler's term for the predisposing conditions which can result in psychopathology, stems from childhood experiences characterized either by overprotection or neglect, or by a confusing mixture of both. From these experiences, the young child develops a set of psychological convictions—about self, the world, and life goal, which become the lifestyle—about the child's inability to master or cope with the tasks of life. This conviction is confounded and reinforced by the child's perception of a frankly hostile, punishing, or depriving environment at home or school, or one that is subtly demanding or frustrating. Rather than providing encouragement to engage in other efforts involving mastery and achievement, these experiences leave the youngster feeling discouraged and fearful. Rather than experiencing trusting and loving relationships the young child grows to become distrustful and manipulative. To compensate for these exaggerated feelings of insecurity and anxiety, the child becomes self-centered and uncooperative.

The dysfunctional lifestyle is an inflexible lifestyle. Problem-solving is based on a self-protective "private sense" rather than a more task-oriented and socially useful "common sense." Once this set of faulty psychological convictions has coalesced and self-protective patterns of coping are established, it comes very difficult for the individual to see or respond to life in any other way. The result is that dysfunctional individuals cannot productively cope with the tasks of life nor really enjoy the rewards of their labors, much less their relationships with others. In contrast, a set of psychological convictions and coping patterns that are shaped positively by the child's healthy experiences of mastery, creativity, and loving and pleasurable relationships will result in a flexible lifestyle.

Adler presented a unitary theory of psychopathology wherein individuals arrange their symptoms uniquely to serve as excuses for not meeting the tasks of life or to safeguard their self-esteem either by aggression or distancing themselves from others. Adler discriminated dysfunctional behavior along the dimensions of social interest and degree of activity. For instance, neurotics have more social interest than psychotics. Neurotics respond to life tasks with: "Yes, but." With the "yes" they acknowledge their social responsibilities, and with the "but" they present their symptoms that excuse their responsibilities. Mosak (1984) describes two types of "yes, but" responses: "Yes, but I'm sick," which is the classic response of the psychoneurotic, and, "Yes, but I defy it," the acting-out response of the character neurosis or personality disorder. Psychotics respond to life tasks with, "No," and cut themselves off from the common world. As to activity level, Adler noted a low degree is found in neurotic conditions such as depression and obsessive-compulsion, with a higher degree in anxiety neurosis, schizophrenia, and alcoholism. The highest levels were in manics and criminals, particularly murderers (Adler, 1964a).

Developments in the Theory

Adler believed that there were three main components common to all psychopathology: (1) discouragement, (2) faulty conceptions, and (3) lifestyle beliefs. Furthermore, he posited that an undeveloped social interest and personality dysfunction was basically the outcome of an erroneous way of living. This represents Adler's views on normality versus abnormality at the time of his death. It should be noted that at the outset of his career, Adler believed that psychopathology stemmed from various organ inferiorities. This was a rather biological and reductionistic position. Later, his view changed to a more intrapsychic one in which dysfunctional behavior was seen as a conflict between inferiority and superiority feelings. He described the neurotic disposition as the predisposing factor in the development of neurosis. The term *pampered lifestyle* eventually replaced this term. Still later, Adler developed a more sociopsychological view in which psychopathology represented movement toward self-importance at the expense of the common good. In many respects, the last version of Adler's theory represented one of the first attempts at developing a holistic view of psychopathology (Adler, 1964b). Although it encompassed features from the biological (organ inferiority and organ dialect) and the social realms, it was primarily a theory of emotional development and dysfunction which integrated all processes through the prism of the lifestyle:

> This is notably the case with the lungs, the heart, the stomach, the organs of excretion and the sexual organs. The disturbance of these functions expresses the direction which an individual is taking to attain his goal. I have called these disturbances the organ dialect, or organ jargon, since the organs are revealing in their own most expressive language the intention of the individual totality. (Adler, 1964b)

The eminent Adlerian clinician Irvin Neufield (1954) distinguished the psychosomatic approaches from the biopsychosocial or holistic approaches like Individual Psychology. Most psychosomatic theories failed to fully appreciate the multifaceted dynamics and interdependence of all the biological, the psychological and the social dimensions of human existence. Failure to appreciate all of these multifaceted dimensions leads to the same narrow reductionism Neufield criticized in many psychosomatic theories.

There has been a tendency among those espousing a holistic theory to play down some of these dynamics, particularly the biochemical and neuropharmacological ones. This is particularly true in the treatment of depressive disorders. Awareness is increasing that depression is not a single entity but rather a spectrum disorder. As such, depression is currently viewed by many as a group of discrete illnesses that span a biopsychosocial continuum in which symptom patterns appear to be more influenced by biochemical factors at one end of the continuum and more by psychological factors at the other end.

To illustrate the holistic or biopsychosocial perspective, it might be helpful to speculate about how a depressive disorder develops. We can only speculate because no empirically validated theory or model of depression exists. So, based on recent research we can hypothesize that a person who experiences a major depression, such that brain pathways and circuits dealing with emotions like pleasure are fragile and poorly buffered from external influences. Add to this some early life traumas such as the loss of or separation from a significant other—such as a parent—that undermines self-confidence and esteem and for which the individual responds with safeguarding patterns. Subjecting the individual to a severe psychological stressor at a later point in life in some way echoes the early experience of loss or separation. When existing social support systems and personal coping strategies of safeguarding methods are not sufficient to neutralize this stressor, the already compromised brain biochemistry is overtaxed, resulting in the familiar biological symptoms of depression such as sleep and appetite disturbance, psychomotor retardation, reduced energy, inability to experience pleasure, and somatic symptoms such as constipation and headache. This reduced physiological functioning further reinforces the individual's lifestyle beliefs about self, the world, and the future. Pancner (1985a) suggests a similar hypothesis.

On the other hand, a dysthymic disorder, or neurotic depression as it used to be called, which has probably more psychosocial loading and less genetic and biological loading, most often presents with fewer biological symptoms and more dysfunctional lifestyle beliefs and coping skills. Thus it is not surprising that dysthymic disorders respond well primarily to psychologically oriented therapies, while major depressive disorders usually respond to biochemical therapies such as antidepressant medications, often in conjunction with psychotherapy. Psychotherapy will be a necessary adjunctive treatment assuming that a pampered lifestyle or neurotic disposition interferes with functioning in the life tasks. But when there is little or no life task dysfunction, as is sometimes the situation, then psychotherapy is probably not warranted. In an address titled "Biochemical Theory and Adlerian Psychology," Ronald Pancner (1985b), a past president of the North American Society of Adlerian Psychology, proposed this same idea. Responding to the reluctance of some to minimize or deny the biological aspects in their theory and practice, he added:

> We need to be open to the multiplicity of factors involved in mental illness; none of us have all the answers. . . . But to become dogmatic and say "this is the only way" or "that is the only way," I think is closed. To really understand a person we have to look at them holistically, and keep all these things in mind" (Pancner, 1985a).

CLASSIFICATION SYSTEMS: ADLERIAN AND DSM-IV

Quite unlike other psychological systems that are based on a disease model, Adlerian theory is based on a growth model. It tends to view the dysfunctional individual as discouraged rather than as mentally ill (Mosak, 1984). There are two major types of classificatory systems of psychopathology: (1) descriptive and (2) psychodynamic. The descriptive approaches emphasize observable or reportable symptomatology. A diagnosis is made by comparing the individual's symptoms with specified criteria that represent specific diagnoses. The more formal systems include inclusion as well as exclusion criteria for each diagnosis, which are designed to insure both the reliability and validity of the diagnosis. Thus the descriptive approaches lend themselves to statistical data collection and analysis, and the comparison of the incidence and prevalence of diagnoses across groups and cultures. The psychodynamic approaches to psychopathology emphasize the psychological reasons or mechanisms that are considered to be the bases for explaining disordered behavior and symptoms. Rudolf Dreikurs wrote elegantly on the psychodynamic approach to psychopathology (Dreikurs, 1967a) and wrote many articles promoting the Adlerian approach to assessing psychopathology. *Psychodynamics, Psychotherapy, and Counseling,* published in 1967, is a collection of Dreikurs' most important papers on this topic.

In the Adlerian approach, observations about an individual's movement and descriptions about the uniqueness of the individual are considered more valuable than diagnostic categories and classification. However, for didactic purposes, Adler did characterize four personality types: the ruling, the getting, the avoiding, and the healthy, socially useful person. The first three types are discouraged and low in social interest and so would be considered dysfunctional. Mosak (1959, 1971, 1973, 1985) has briefly described several other personality types and has provided in-depth analyses of the getting and controlling types.

Adler considered the obsessive-compulsive neurosis to be the prototype for Freudian theory. Indecisiveness and doubt, depreciation of others, godlike strivings, and focus on minutiae were the safeguarding methods that Adler routinely noted were used by his compulsive neurotic patients in seeking their goal of personal superiority. He noted that various neurotic and psychotic individuals might use different safeguarding methods, but their movement was nevertheless the same: avoidance or rejection of the life tasks.

The standard diagnostic classification adopted by many clinicians and insurance carriers in the United States is the *Diagnostic and Statistical Manual of Mental Disorders, Fourth Edition* (American Psychiatric Association, 1994), usually referred to as DSM-IV. Unlike the Adlerian approach with its unitary theory of psychopathology, DSM-IV describes 17 major classifications and diagnostic criteria for more than 200 mental disorders. Each disorder has a unique set of descriptive—rather than dynamic—diagnostic criteria. A DSM-IV diagnosis can be made when a match exists between the facts from a particular individual's history and clinical presentation and the diagnostic criteria for a particular mental disorder. In short, the DSM system is based on the medical model and a psychology of possession, while the Adlerian approach is based on a growth model and a psychology of use. Consequently, Adlerian therapists might not be as concerned about making a DSM-IV type of descriptive diagnosis as they would be in understanding the individual's dynamics—that is, movement and lifestyle themes (Sperry & Maniacci, 1992).

Similar to the Adlerian emphasis on life task functioning, DSM-IV views pathology as clinically significant behavioral or psychological syndromes or patterns associated with maladaptive functioning in one or more of three areas: social relations, occupation, and leisure. As the Adlerian approach strives toward a holistic—biopsychosocial understanding of the individual, DSM-IV allows for a multiaxial classification so that interrelated biopsychosocial or systems facets of a person's life may be considered. Five axes are used:

Axis I: Clinical Disorder (e.g., dysthymic disorder)
Axis II: Personality Disorder or Mental Retardation (e.g., borderline personality disorder)
Axis III: General Medical Conditions (e.g., angina)
Axis IV: Psychosocial and Environmental Problems (e.g., threat of job loss)
Axis V: Global Assessment of Functioning (GAF)(e.g., GAF-53)

In Adlerian terms, the Axis I diagnoses would be the presenting problems. These would be determined by examining, in part, what Dreikurs referred to as the "subjective condition" (Dreikurs, 1967b). Axis II diagnoses provide a glimpse of the lifestyle. Given a certain set of beliefs, clients will present with a particular style. For Adlerians, Axis III would provide information about organ inferiorities, medical conditions, organ dialects, or other potential handicapping conditions that individuals might subjectively perceive as overburdening situations (Adler, 1956). Regarding Axis IV, Individual Psychology has long emphasized understanding people in their social field. Adler (1956) referred to understanding the "exogenous factor" (p. 296). In fact, he listed 10 "typical occasions for the onset of a neurosis or psychosis," which are similar to those listed in the DSM-IV (Adler, 1956, pp. 296–297). In terms of Axis IV, the corresponding component in Adlerian psychology for the GAF Scale would be an assessment of the life tasks. Whereas Axis I examined the subjective condition, this axis would be an assessment of what Dreikurs (1967b) referred to as the "objective situation."

Understanding Axis V has another benefit—assisting clinicians in minimizing resistance. Adler (1956), Dreikurs (1967b), and other Adlerians have defined a cardinal characteristic of resistance as being a misalignment of goals between the therapist and client. The GAF Scale offers two scores, the current level of functioning and the highest level of functioning, or baseline, in the past year. A discrepancy between the current level and highest level in the past year usually indicates an acute condition with a good prognosis. The prognosis for an individual with a major depressive episode with a current GAF score of 40 and a baseline of 70 would have a much less guarded prognosis and recovery than someone with a baseline of 45. The wise clinician will consider GAF scores in setting treatment goals, choosing interventions, and establishing duration and pacing. For example, a woman whose current and highest in the past year GAF score is 41 may not have the same goals in therapy as a woman whose scores are 55 currently and 85 in the past year. Clinicians who determine treatment goals without examining GAF scores and gaining collaboration from clients may experience undue resistance.

Integrating the Five Axis System into an Adlerian Case Formulation

Putting the above into a unified case formulation involves practice and supervision, but once learned, it can prove to be quite beneficial. Briefly summarized, it would be something like this: A client with this particular lifestyle (Axis II) has encountered a situation for which she is not adequately prepared (Axis IV). To safeguard, the client uses a particular group or cluster of symptoms to sidestep the demands and create distance (Axis I). The "chosen" symptoms may be due to an organ inferiority or an overburdening situation such as a disability (Axis III). The adequacy for which the client meets the tasks of life can be assessed. Similarly, the degree of involvement she expects to return to can also be assessed to gain a quick barometer of the amount of social interest present, as well as to help align treatment goals (Axis V). In such a formulation, the principles of Individual Psychology are not violated, and Adlerians can become integrated in contemporary clinical practice, thus allowing their ideas and conceptualizations to be heard in a common language of their peers. An investigation of the lifestyle using traditional methods would only add to the formulation.

Many holistically oriented therapists, including Adlerian, would argue for the inclusion of a sixth axis: a holistic–biopsychosocial formulation. The mere listing of biopsychosocial information in the various axes does not in and of itself constitute a holistic formulation.

Practically speaking, can DSM diagnostic categories be integrated with Adlerian theory? Mosak (1968), in what many consider to be a classic in the psychopathology literature, has helped a generation of clinicians to interrelate central themes or basic lifestyle convictions with DSM diagnostic categories. These central themes are determined from clinical observation, psychological testing, and particularly through early recollections. Mosak lists the eleven most common themes: (1) getter; (2) controller; (3) driver; (4) to be good; (5) perfect; (6) right; (7) martyrs; (8) victims; (9) "aginners"; (10) feeling avoiders; and (11) excitement seekers; and combinations of these themes with 19 diagnostic categories. For example, the lifestyle of a person who would traditionally be diagnosed as a depressive neurosis would likely be a composite, in varying degrees, of the getter, the controller and the person needing to be right (Mosak, 1979). For the antisocial personality the themes would likely be those of the getter, the aginner, and the excitement seeker. Consult Mosak (1968, 1979) for a fuller description of this unique integration of diagnostic categories and lifestyle themes.

Sperry and Carlson (1993, 1996) have described the classification DSM disorder in terms of Adlerian psychodynamics. The following DSM-IV disorders are discussed and illustrated: schizophrenia; delusional disorders; delirium, dementia, amnesia and other cognitive disorders; substance-related disorders; mood disorders; anxiety disorders; somatoform disorders; dissociative disorders; sexual and gender identity disorders; eating disorders; personality disorders; adjustment disorders; and selected childhood and adolescent disorders.

COMMON MANIFESTATIONS OF PSYCHOPATHOLOGY

The results of the monumental NIMH Epidemiological Catchment Area (ECA) Study (Regier et al., 1984) lists the most prevalent psychiatric disorders, which incapacitate to some degree 19 percent of the U.S. population. Several Adlerian writers have published on these disorders (Sperry, 1987; Sperry, 1990; Slavik, Carlson, & Sperry, 1992a; Slavik, Sperry, & Carlson, 1992b, to name a few.) Following is a discussion of six of these ECA disorders: bipolar disorder; schizophrenia; depressive disorders; antisocial personality disorder; anxiety disorders; and addictive disorders. Also included is a discussion of the borderline personality disorder, and a brief Adlerian interpretation of suicide. Each discussion will include a descriptive definition of the disorder followed by an Adlerian interpretation focusing on childhood experiences, inferiority feelings, compensation, approach to the life tasks, and resulting symptom formation.

Anxiety Disorders

Anxiety disorders were classified in DSM-I and II as neuroses or neurotic disorders. The term *neurosis* was largely subsumed under Anxiety Disorders in subsequent DSMs. The subclasses of Anxiety Disorders are Phobic, Obsessive Compulsive, Panic, Generalized Anxiety, Post-Traumatic Stress, and Atypical Anxiety. In this group of disorders, overwhelming anxiety is either the predominant disturbance as it is manifested in Panic and Generalized Anxiety Disorders, or the anxiety is experienced as the person attempts to master the symptoms, as when confronting the dreaded object or situation in a Phobic Disorder. When the anxiety is manifested when resisting an obsession or compulsion, obsessive-compulsive disorder is the diagnosis. The basic feature of phobic disorders is persistent avoidance behavior related to irrational fears of a specific object, activity, or situation. Agoraphobia is one type of phobic disorder. The essential feature of panic disorder is recurrent anxiety attacks and nervousness. These attacks are characterized by a sudden onset of intense apprehension or terror, and are often associated with feelings of impending death. Basic to a diagnosis of generalized anxiety disorder is at least six months of generalized and persistent anxiety without the specific symptoms of phobic, panic, or obsessive-compulsive disorders. Recurrent and persistent ideas, impulses of images that are not voluntarily produced, or recurrent and compelling stereotyped actions that are attempts to relieve obsessions or fears are the essential features of obsessive-compulsive disorders.

The following case example illustrates an increasingly common anxiety disorder:

> Mrs. G. is a 47-year-old wife of the mayor of a suburban community who sought psychotherapy because she had a fear of being in church. As the story unfolded it became clear that she really feared leaving home. Before she developed a fear of going to church, she would become uneasy while shopping and driving her children to school. The onset of this agoraphobic behavior was related to her husband's heart attack 18 months earlier. Because he was 62 years old, she was fearful that he might have another heart attack, this time fatal, and leave her as the sole support of her children. The thought of this was unbearable, and although she was quite dependent on her husband, she could not understand her developing fear of leaving the home.

Adler taught that anxiety is used to create distance between the individual and the life task so as to safeguard self-esteem when the person fears defeat. Neurotics are considered ambitious people who have lost their courage, and so live in constant dread of their weaknesses being discovered. Adler would say that neurotics have a "hesitating attitude" or a "yes, but" response to life. These individuals postpone decisions and try to keep a safe distance from others and difficult tasks.

> Agoraphobia, anxiety neurosis, and all the forms of phobias may originate at this point (the individual's unwillingness to admit his fear of defeat), but, whichever it may be, it fulfills its purpose of blocking the way to further activity. Thus, what was desired is attained—namely, the ordeal is evaded without disclosing, even to its owner, the hated feeling of inferiority. All the other symptoms, such as compulsion ideas, fits, fatigue, sleeplessness, functional disturbances such as neurotic heart, headaches, migraines and so on, develop out of the severe tension of this very difficult concealment. (Adler, 1964b, p. 11)

These neurotic patterns are laid down in early childhood. Because pampered children are ill prepared to perform the tasks of life, they find their courage taxed when another child is born; school life begins; or a major change occurs in their environment, such as a move to another neighborhood or the death of a parent. The first nervous symptoms often take the form of organ dysfunction such as abdominal pains, respiratory symptoms, enuresis, or temper tantrums. The purpose of the symptoms is to compel the parents to give in to these children and relieve them of certain responsibilities. These symptoms are among the first weapons children use to get their own way (Dreikurs, 1950).

Bipolar Disorder (Manic-Depression)

The core feature of this syndrome is a disordered mood with both manic and depressive phases. In the beginning of its course mania may resemble normal euphoria but gradually becomes uncontrolled and psychotic, with 20 percent of manics experiencing delusions and hallucinations. The depressive phase is usually profound. The attacks are usually separated by months or even years, but the person may occasionally cycle from one to the other over days or actually present contrasting symptoms simultaneously. The first episode is often manic and begins before age 30, resolving in a few months. If untreated, most go on to the depressive phase. The following is a classic example of a bipolar disorder:

> Mr. C. is a 32-year-old attorney who was admitted to the psychiatric unit of the community hospital in an acute manic episode. He was extremely hyperactive, distractible, irritable, and demanding. He exhibited pressured speech, flight of ideas, and marked hostility to his wife for what he described as infidelity. Five years earlier, he was treated for a depressive episode following hysterectomy surgery on his wife. Since that time he had developed manic symptoms in the early spring and depressive symptoms in the late fall. Prior to the onset of his depression he was described as an outgoing perfectionistic and a firstborn. Between episodes, he was rather successful as a trial attorney and showed no evidence of personality deterioration.

According to Peven and Shulman (1983), Adler had relatively little to say about the dynamics of bipolar disorders. They summarize Adler's statements on this condition as (1) an underlying cyclothymic personality disorder is present; (2) the moods range from feelings of exaltation and grandiosity to those of powerlessness; (3) these individuals lack faith in their own competence; and (4) mania is viewed as a maneuver to deceive self and others. In their review of the literature these authors found that no dynamic theory adequately accounted for this disorder, including Adler's formulation, which underplays the disturbance of mood. They suggest that the neurovegetative signs of mania and depression are probably best understood as physiological rather than as primarily psychological in etiology.

In their own research evaluating extensive psychological profiles of 17 patients who met DSM-III criteria for the bipolar disorder, Peven and Shulman found eight factors common to those so diagnosed: Bipolars had unrealistically high goals regarding the achievement of prominence and prestige. They typically try to impress others with side goals if they cannot achieve their goals directly. Their self-image does not assure them that their goals are within reach, but they blame this on their own ineptness rather than on the unachieveability of their goals. They carry within themselves an inner protest against the burdens of these goals, yet they are not free to discard these goals because of their cognitive style, which is characterized as being impulsive, internally controlled, and antithetical. In other words, they are either/or people who think in the concrete extremes of right/wrong, black/white. They tend to be feelers rather than thinkers, as such they are excitement seekers, and they are extremist in what they think, feel, and do. Finally, they tend to be first-borns.

For Peven and Shulman (1983), the manic phase of the illness is viewed as a heightened attempt by bipolars to achieve impressive feats, while the depressive phase represents an exhausted refusal and intensified protest to participate in life when it denies them their achievements but nevertheless demands the burden of achieving. Based on their research findings, Peven and Shulman are not in total agreement with Adler's notion that bipolars have a premorbid cyclothymic personality or that mania is "a frantic attempt to force a success in the service of his goal of superiority" (Adler, 1961). Given the biological predisposition and the characteristic ways manic-depressives behave, the authors conclude that "mania can result from being aroused by a success or by pleasant excitement and not knowing when to stop or how to moderate the arousal. Bipolars, in fact, court the arousal since that is the way they feel most comfortable" (p. 14).

Schizophrenia

Schizophrenia represents a large group of psychotic disorders that show characteristic disturbances of language and communication, thought, perception, affect, and behavior that last at least six months. The characteristic disturbance of thought is marked by alterations in concept formation that can lead to misinterpretation of reality and misperceptions, as well as hallucinations and delusions. There are genetic, biochemical, and sociocultural theories for this group of disorders as well as several psychological theories. Following is an example of schizophrenia of the paranoid type:

Mrs. H. was admitted to a psychiatric hospital the day after her 33rd birthday. For the past nine months her family had noted strange behavior characterized by withdrawal, inappropriate mood, preoccupation with religious ideas, and the delusion that her husband and other elders in her church were "trying to do away with her like they did with Christ." She was convinced that she "would be put to death" on her 33rd birthday and accordingly had barricaded herself in her bedroom for the three days before her birthday, claiming that only if she fasted for 40 days and nights would she be able to foil the plot. In the hospital she was markedly suspicious of the entire staff, accusing them of trying to poison her food, or "crucify" her in group therapy sessions, and so on. Much of the time she was withdrawn, claiming God could not communicate directly to her if she was in the company of "heathens." Her affect was flattened and times she talked readily but inappropriately.

According to Adler, schizophrenics have a very low sense of self-esteem which is compensated by an overly idealized and inflated goal of superiority. Because of extreme deprivation, ambivalent mothering, organic factors, prolonged illness, or separation from parents, or any combination of these reasons, as children, they develop a magnified sense of inferiority. This experience leads to the view that they are utterly special and great and that others are enemies who frustrate their desires. Thus, they not only withdraw and are uncooperative but also exploit others. People around them are used for the personification of their difficulties and are accused of keeping them from achieving their grandiose designs. Paranoid projection and other delusions, as well as hallucinations are safeguards that protect them while freeing them from responsibility for the consensually validated tasks of life (Adler, 1958, 1979).

Shulman (1968, 1980) has systematically articulated an Adlerian interpretation of the psychotic process, particularly as it relates to schizophrenia. Sperry (1991) has integrated brain-mind research with Shulman's interpretation. This integration provides further validation of Shulman's clinically-based observations and theory.

Gazzaniga (1988) has developed a cognitive theory of central nervous system vulnerability or organ inferiority based on research findings from the neurosciences. He suggests that individuals generate a series of internally consistent schemas or beliefs about themselves and life that allow daily living to be predictable and meaningful. He refers to these cognitive schemas as the "brain interpreter," which is remarkably similar to lifestyle convictions. The interpreter does not always have correct data but must interpret it anyway it can. Gazzaniga further postulates an urge to create order in the information being processed, which is an effort to compensate for central nervous system dysfunctioning.

The psychoses are thus conceptualized as disorders in which the brain's interpreter—typically the verbal, left hemisphere—attempts to create order out of what is most likely endogenous, or inner-generated, brain chaos. This chaos is spurious neural actions precipitated by faulty biochemical brain states, such as sharp rises or decreases in neurotransmitters that adversely affect the typically symbolic, image-generating right hemisphere. The interpreter makes decisions about what meaning to assign to chaotic events. As the right hemisphere continues to generate odd, unexplainable images and impressions, the left hemisphere desperately attempts to "interpret" and integrate these aberrations according to some consistent, logical, rule-governing system.

Endogenous brain changes, particularly changes in the level of neurotransmitters such as dopamine, create new circumstances to which the brain's interpreter must continually react. That reaction in turn produces perceptions that can become powerful guides for the mental outlook of the patient. Such a change in neurotransmitter activity in the limbic system, also called the reward-generating system, alters brain circuits so that pleasant associations and rewards are no longer produced. Thus it is easy to imagine how bizarre thoughts fill this void. Without input of thoughts from the normal reward system, schizophrenics are in a chronic information vacuum. They search for information from their current environment, but because of their increasing social isolation, there is little to be found. As consensual validation decreases, their interpreter creates an alternative reality which accounts for hallucinations and delusions.

Intrusive thoughts may begin to flood this chronic informational vacuum. As schizophrenics cope with these unwanted intrusions into thought, thought itself becomes unusually disordered, which is often followed by social withdrawal. However, rather than helping, social isolation compounds the problem. At first, the brain's interpreter had to deal with imagined sounds and voices, but it now has to comprehend them without the steadying influence provided by contact with friends and family. The same can be said about delusions. At times, all persons experience some paranoid thinking. Episodes of overwhelming vulnerability that arise in the absence of a threatening stimulus is usually due to some transitory biochemical balance in neurocircuitry which the brain's interpreter easily dismisses as unsubstantiated. But when the condition moves beyond the episodic to a chronic condition, the brain's interpreter can create prominent delusions in its attempts to "explain" its neurochemical dysfunction.

Depressive Disorders

Depression is a spectrum disorder ranging from symptoms of sadness, grief reactions, nonpsychotic depression or dysthymic disorders and finally, major or psychotic depression. The essential feature of the dysthymic disorder is a chronic disturbance of mood involving either depressed mood or loss of interest or pleasure in all, or most, usual daily activities, and associated symptoms. These symptoms must be present for at least two years, but are not of sufficient severity to qualify as a major depression. In an earlier section, we described the biopsychosocial dimensions of major depression. A major depression can be so profound that the individual may lose contact with reality, developing delusions and often becoming a serious suicide risk. A diurnal variation is common with the most severe symptoms noted early in the day. The individual awakens early in the morning with disturbed appetite, somatic symptoms, self-deprecatory thoughts, and guilt feelings. Whereas psychotherapy is the treatment of choice for the dysthymic disorders, medication and sometimes electroconvulsive therapy (ECT) are necessary adjuncts to psychotherapy for the major depressions. Here is an example of a major depressive disorder.

Mrs. J. is a 41-year-old homemaker who was evaluated at a community mental health center after complaining of nausea, spontaneous crying, and depressed mood. Her symptoms had begun four months earlier following her discovery that her husband was having an affair with another woman. She noted disturbances of appetite and concentration, early morning awakening and somatic symptoms such as nausea, menstrual pain, and headaches, in addition to guilty feelings dysphoric mood. No obvious psychomotor retardation was noted. She had no previous history of mood swings, but noted that her mother had been taking antidepressant medication for the past 10 years.

Much of the Adlerian theory of depression was directed toward the depressive neurosis, although it has some bearing on the major depressions as well. Adler believed that depressed individuals inflate the hazards of everyday life as they strive for unreachable fictional goals, and then blame others or life circumstances for the failure to achieve those goals. Depressives display both their anger at not getting their own way and their contempt for others. They have learned to exploit their weakness and complain in order to force others to give them their way and thus avoid life's responsibilities. They are willing to go to any length to prove to others how sick and disabled they are, and in the process can escape social responsibilities. Depressives were often discouraged children who might have used tears to tyrannize others, and were probably excessively dependent on others. They may have had difficulty recovering from illnesses and other stresses and perhaps found it was easier to exhort sympathy and active help from others rather than attempt to develop some self-sufficiency.

Kurt Adler (1961) pointed out depressives' obvious disdain for others during their healthy interludes. During these times their excessive ambition takes over and they reveal their ruthlessness and unwillingness to exert effort to achieve results. When they fail, depressives regularly blame others, their upbringing, ill fortune, or even their very depression.

Suicide is often considered a feature of depression. In 1910, Adler proposed that suicide has a social intention. He considered adolescent suicide an act of revenge, in which one's death is designed partly to cause sorrow to one's relatives, partly to force them to appreciate what they have lost in the one whom they have always slighted (Adler, 1956). In later life, a beloved person, an institution, or even the world at large is chosen as the object of this act of revenge. Adler also believed that the potential suicide reflects low social interest and a pampered lifestyle, and that the threat of suicide is a way of controlling others. Kurt Adler (1961) proposed that the suicidal person holds three myths about suicide: that it is a heroic act, that it will hurt other people, and that it requires courage to go through with it.

Antisocial Personality Disorder

Previously called psychopathic or sociopathic behavior, the essential features of this disorder are a history of continuous and chronic behavior in which the rights of others are violated. The onset of this disorder must begin before age 15 and antisocial behavior must persist into adult life. Poor occupational performance shown by frequent job changes; absenteeism or unemployment; and a history of arrests, marital problems, impulsivity, hedonism, promiscuity, unreliability, and drug and alcohol abuse are common features. Following is an example of an antisocial personality disorder.

B. H. is the 18-year-old son of well-to-do parents who was ordered by the court to undergo psychiatric evaluation. Some three weeks before, B. H. and two younger juveniles
had trespassed into a cemetery after closing time, tipped over several gravestones, and
attempted to break into an above-ground mausoleum. Damages were estimated at $4,000.
All three were found to have blood alcohol levels which showed them to be legally in-
toxicated. His parents noted problems in school as early as age 9. At age 12 he was arrested for shoplifting a small portable radio. From the age of 13 through 17 he was frequently involved in minor delinquencies but he usually managed to escape punishment
because of his family's position in the community, and because his father was willing and
able to make restitution. B. H. was 10 years older than his twin sisters and he reported
that he was never really close to anyone, including his parents. He felt no remorse for
his antisocial behavior and indicated that though his parents verbally disapproved of this
behavior, they encouraged it in subtle ways. At the age of 8 he was put on anticonvul-
sant medication after he experienced seizures following a bicycle accident. He refused to
continue taking it after three weeks, even though he was told he remained at risk for repeat seizure activity.

Perhaps more than any other great pioneer in psychiatry, Adler not only had personal experience consulting with criminals but wrote extensively on the lifestyle and
treatment of the criminal. At the root of criminality, as in the neurotic, Adler found
a lack of social interest. But unlike neurotics, criminals do not content themselves
with receiving help and being a burden to others. Rather they act as if the whole
world were against them. Adler contended that as children, criminals develop a
"cheap superiority complex" and are recognized because they get their own way by
hurting others. He distinguished three types of criminals: those who were pampered
children who were trained to receive and never give and kept this pattern as adults;
those who were neglected as children and directly experienced the hostile world;
and those who were so-called ugly children who rebelled because of their perceived
defect. But whatever their original situation, all three types showed the same intense
striving for superiority, even though they were essentially cowards. Adler found that
that criminals never fight fairly; they commit offenses only when in a position of advantage. Because they often commit several crimes before being arrested, criminals'
feeling of superiority was strengthened. They could cooperate, but only with their
own kind (Sperry, 1990a, 1990b). Adler (1956) found the criminal to be totally irre-
sponsible, "always looking for...reasons that 'force' him to be a criminal" (p. 413).

Addictive Disorder: Alcohol, Drugs, and Sex

A common understanding of alcoholism or drug dependency is that of an individual
having a pathological relationship with a mood-altering substance. For example, the
alcohol or drug addict's relationship with the substance becomes more important
than work, friends, and even family. As this relationship progresses, addicts need the
substance to feel normal. Ironically, feeling "normal" for addicts also means being
isolated and lonely because the primary relationship upon which they depend is a
substance rather than a person. There is growing awareness among professionals
about the commonalties among the various addictive behaviors. Thus, obesity,
smoking, workaholism, and uncontrollable sexual behavior are being considered ad-

dictions. The pathological relationship usually involves a substance, but it could be situations, such as excessive work or uncontrolled sexual behavior. In each case, the addict's relationship with the mood-altering "experience" becomes central in her life (Carnes, 1983). The following is a case example of alcoholism or alcohol dependence with withdrawal in DSM-IV terms.

> Mr. D. is a 42-year-old single newspaper columnist with a 20-year history of heavy alcohol use. One Thursday night after finishing his column, he started drinking with friends and continued to drink until the bar closed at 4 a.m. He returned to his apartment and slept for a few hours. Upon awakening, he had no appetite for food but downed several scotch and waters. Later he went to a lounge that newspeople frequent and drank wine until late that night. This pattern of all-day drinking persisted for four days. On Monday morning, he went to his office and began to shake so violently while attempting to drink a cup of coffee that he spilled the hot liquid over his shirt and trousers. A few sips of brandy calmed his nerves enough to begin work on his column. When his editor asked about his whereabouts on Friday, Mr. D. could not recall and fabricated a story about being ill. Later that morning, he left his office and went to see his family doctor because of "internal" tremulousness and marked tremors of the hands. When his physician questioned him about his drinking, D. reported that he had experienced about five other weekend binges over the past eight months, in which he had missed a total of 10 days and for which he had used up all of his sick days. He had been told by friends that he had a drinking problem, but believed that he could handle his liquor and had refused to attend an AA meeting at the invitation of a friend. He also noted that his fiancee threatened to leave him if he didn't get some help for his drinking.

Adler (1956) observed that the beginning of an addiction is based on an acute feeling of inferiority marked by shyness, a desire for isolation, oversensitivity, irritability, and impatience as well as by neurotic symptoms such as anxiety, depression, and sexual insufficiency. Sometimes, the craving for the mood-altering experience begins with a superiority complex in the form of boastfulness or longing for power. Adler further noted that "in all cases of addiction, we are dealing with people who are seeking alleviation in a certain situation" (p. 423).

Lombardi (1973) studied the lifestyles of drug addicts in comparison with matched controlled subjects. Themes in the early recollections revealed that the addicts saw themselves as leaning—dependent people who lacked direction in life. They had undeveloped social interest and saw the world as a hostile and dangerous place. Thus, the addicts would not attempt to compete or excel in life, but responded to life with childishness, impulsivity, isolation, oversensitivity, irritability, impatience, and neurotic symptoms such as anxiety, depression, and sexual difficulties. The addicts could only feel competent when they were high on drugs, giving them "a feeling of omnipotence." The early life training of these individuals showed that they were neither overprotected nor neglected and rejected. They were not prepared by role models or by their own experiences to live life as an adult in a socially responsible manner. The addicts willingly admitted to socially undesirable traits in themselves and to their difficulties in forming warm and lasting interpersonal relationships.

Although focusing primarily on the sexual addictions, Carnes (1983) believes that his analysis of the core beliefs of sexual addicts are the bases for all addictive behaviors. The faulty core beliefs are (1) I am basically a bad, unworthy person, and no one would love me as I am (self-view); (2) My needs are never going to be met if I have to depend on others (world-view); and (3) The addictive, mood-altering experience is the most important thing in my life (fictional goal). Addicts do not trust people, and use strategies and safeguards such as rage, secretiveness, and manipulativeness to achieve their goals.

Borderline Personality Disorder

The borderline personality disorder is characterized by a complex presentation including diverse combinations of anger, anxiety, intense and labile affect, brief disturbances in consciousness including dissociation and depersonalization, identity confusion, volatile interpersonal relations, and impulsive behavior including self-injury. Stress can precipitate transient psychosis. Following is a case example of a borderline personality disorder.

> G. W. is a 24-year-old unemployed male who was referred to the hospital emergency room by his therapist at a community mental health center after two days of sustained suicidal ideation. G. W. had cut his wrists on previous occasions and had been hospitalized twice because of this suicidal gesture. He appeared to function adequately until his senior year in high school when he became preoccupied with transcendental meditation. He had considerable difficulty concentrating during his first semester of college and seemed to focus most of his energies on finding a spiritual guru. At times massive anxiety and a feeling of emptiness swept over him and he found it would suddenly vanish if he would lightly cut his wrist enough to draw blood. He had been in treatment with his current therapist for 18 months and increasingly became hostile and demanding as a patient, whereas earlier he was quite captivated with his therapist's empathy and intuitive sense. Lately, G. W.'s wife seemed to center on his twice weekly therapy sessions. The most recent suicidal thoughts followed the therapist's disclosure that he was moving to another clinic on the West Coast.

From an Adlerian perspective, the borderline personality would have its origins in a family situation where the child felt unfavored and incompetent to face the demands of life. Feelings of self-pity, helplessness, and disadvantage lead borderlines to claim special privilege in coping with the world. Their cognitive style is inflexible, with rigid abstractions that easily lead to grandiose, idealized perceptions of people, who are not seen as real people but as personifications of all good or bad individuals. Borderlines reason by analogy from past experiences and do not easily learn from new relationships. Because of their external locus of control, they will usually blame others when things go wrong. If they blamed their own incompetence, they would feel even more powerless about the possibility of changing the situation. Accordingly, their emotions fluctuate between hope and despair because of external circumstances beyond their control. Not surprisingly, their interpersonal relationships will be stormy and characterized by dependency, rebellion, and manipulativeness because they have never learned to respond to constancy in a relationship. Their self-esteem is very fragile because it fluctuates constantly with emotions. For borderlines, there is no commitment, no feeling of belonging, and little sense of obligation (Shulman, 1982).

Adler described a clinically relevant theory of normal and pathological behavior, although he would not have been satisfied with such terminology. He preferred, instead, to speak of socially useful or useless behavior, emphasizing the social interest dimension. Adler's view of movement is consistent with today's clinical emphasis on functioning and impairment. Adler's theory is not inconsistent with DSM-IV. Whereas DSM-IV is essentially an atheoretical model. Adler's approach is theoretical embodying dynamic, cognitive, and systemic dynamics. Hence, Adlerian psychology offers a fuller approach to the understanding and treatment of psychological disorders.

REFERENCES

Adler, A. (1956). In H. H. Ansbacher & R. R. Ansbacher (Eds.), *The individual psychology of Alfred Adler*. New York: Harper & Row.

Adler, A. (1964a). *Superiority and social interest*. In H. H. Ansbacher & R. R. Ansbacher (Eds.). Evanston, IL: Northwestern University Press.

Adler, A. (1964b). *Problems of neurosis*. In P. Mairet (Ed.). New York: Harper and Row.

Adler, K. (1958). Lifestyle in schizophrenia. *Journal of Individual Psychology, 14*(1), 68–72.

Adler, K. (1961). Depression in the light of individual psychology. *Journal of Individual Psychology, 17*(1), 56–67.

Adler, K. (1979). An Adlerian view of the development and treatment of schizophrenia. *Journal of Individual Psychology, 35*(23), 147–61.

American Psychiatric Association. (1994). *Diagnostic and statistical manual of mental disorders*. (4th. ed.). Washington, DC: Author.

Carnes, P. (1983). *The sexual addiction*. Minneapolis: CompCare Publications.

Dreikurs, R. (1950). *Fundamentals of Adlerian psychology*. New York: Greenburg Publishers.

Dreikurs, R. (1967a). Psychodynamic diagnosis in psychiatry. In R. Dreikurs (Ed.), *Psychodynamics, psychotherapy, and counseling: Collected Papers of Rudolf Dreikurs*. Chicago: Alfred Adler Institute, 95–102.

Dreikurs, R. (1967b). The psychological interview in medicine. In R. Dreikurs (Ed.), *Psychodynamics, psychotherapy, and counseling: Collected Papers of Rudolf Dreikurs*. Chicago: Alfred Adler Institute, 125–152.

Gazzaniga, M. (1988). *Mind matters: How mind and body interact to create our conscious lives*. Boston: Houghton-Mifflin.

Lombardi, D. (1973). The psychology of addiction. In H. H. Mosak (Ed.), *Alfred Adler: His influence on psychology today*. Park Ridge, NJ: Noyes Press, 71–75.

Mosak, H. (1959). The getting type: A parsimonious social interpretation of the oral character. *Journal of Individual Psychology, 15*(2), 193–198.

Mosak, H. (1968). The interrelatedness of the neuroses through central themes. *Journal of Individual Psychology, 24*(1), 67–70.

Mosak, H. (1971). Lifestyle. In A. Nikelly (Ed.), *Techniques for behavior changes: Applications of Adlerian theory*. Springfield, IL: Charles C. Thomas, 77–81.

Mosak, H. (1973). The controller: A social interpretation of the anal character. In H. H. Mosak (Ed.), *Alfred Adler: His influence on psychology today*. Park Ridge, NJ: Noyes Press, 43–52.

Mosak, H. (1979). Mosak's typology: An update. *Journal of Individual Psychology, 35*(2), 92–95.

Mosak, H. (1984). Adlerian psychology. In R. Corsini & B. Ozaki (Eds.), *Encyclopedia of Psychology.* New York: Wiley–Interscience, 232–238.

Mosak, H. (1985, May). *Mosak's typology: Behaviors, psychopathology and psychotherapy.* Paper presented at North American Society of Adlerian Psychology, Atlanta.

Neufield, I. (1954). Holistic medicine versus psychosomatic medicine. *American Journal of Individual Psychology, 10*(3, 4), 140–168.

Pancner, R. (1985a, July). Biochemical theory and Adlerian psychotherapy. Audiotape. *International Association of Individual Psychology.* Montreal.

Pancner, R. (1985b). Impact of current depression research on Adlerian theory and practice. *Individual Psychology: The Journal of Adlerian Theory, Research & Practice, 41*(3), 289–301.

Peven, D., & Shulman, B. (1983). The psychodynamics of bipolar affective disorders. Some empirical findings and their implication for cognitive therapy. *Journal of Individual Psychology, 39*(1), 2–16.

Regier, D., Myers, J., Kramer, M., Robins, L., et al. (1984). The NIMH Epidemiological Catchment Area (ECA) Program: Historical context, major objectives, and study population characteristics. *Archives of General Psychiatry, 41,* 934–941.

Shulman, B. (1968). *Essays in schizophrenia.* Baltimore: Williams and Wilkins.

Shulman, B. (1980). *Essays in schizophrenia* (2nd ed.). Chicago: Alfred Adler Institute.

Shulman, B. (1982). An Adlerian interpretation of the borderline personality. *Modern Psychoanalysis, 7*(2), 137–153.

Slavik, S., Carlson, J., & Sperry, L. (1992a). Adlerian marital therapy with the passive–aggressive partner. *American Journal of Family Therapy, 20*(1), 25–35.

Slavik, S., Sperry, L., & Carlson, J. (1992b). The schizoid personality disorder: A review and an Adlerian view and treatment. *Individual Psychology, 48*(2), 137–154.

Sperry, L. (1987). Common psychiatric presentations in clinical practice: DSM-III and dynamic formulations. *Individual Psychology, 43*(2), 131–143.

Sperry, L. (1990a). Dissociation multiple personality, and the phenomenon of evil. *Journal of Pastoral Counseling, 25*(1), 90–100.

Sperry, L. (1990b). Personality disorders: Biopsychosocial descriptions and dynamics. *Individual Psychology, 48*(2), 193–202.

Sperry, L. (1991). The psychotic disorders: An update. *N.A.S.A.P. Newsletter, 24*(4), 5–6.

Sperry, L., & Carlson, J. (1993). *Psychopathology and psychotherapy: From diagnosis to treatment.* Muncie, IN: Accelerated Development.

Sperry, L., & Carlson, J. (1996). *Psychopathology and psychotherapy: From diagnosis to treatment of DSM-IV disorders.* (2nd ed.). Philadelphia: Taylor and Francis/Accelerated Development.

Sperry, L., & Maniacci, M. (1992). An integration of DSM-III-R diagnosis and Adlerian case formulations. *Individual Psychology, 48*(2), 175–181.

PART Two

Skills and Strategies

CHAPTER 5

Analysis and Assessment

T he theory of Individual Psychology is socioteleological. It understands people as social, creative, active, decision-making beings moving toward unique goals and influenced by unique beliefs and perceptions.

The phrase *trust only movement* is helpful when understanding clients. It gives considerable direction to the counseling process. Let us first clarify, however, that our discussion focuses on both counseling and therapy. Counseling is primarily concerned with enabling someone to modify self-defeating behaviors, make effective decisions, and solve problems more effectively. Psychotherapy is primarily concerned with influencing the lifestyle; changing faulty, mistaken, and self-defeating perceptions; and influencing the individual's beliefs and goals. The same theory and techniques apply to both counseling and therapy.

PRINCIPLES OF ADLERIAN COUNSELING

Socioteleological Orientation

Seeing the purposive nature of all behavior. Adlerian psychology is unique in its focus on purpose. This orientation, in contrast to a historical–causal approach, has significance for the transactions between counselor and client. The emphasis is not only on removal of symptoms and changing behavioral patterns, but on the clients' understanding that they are not powerless victims of circumstances and that they act of their own accord (Dreikurs, 1953).

All the client's discouragements are understood in terms of their purpose. Behavior patterns, such as failure to get along with people, are seen not as static problems but as valuable indicators of the pattern of psychological movement. What happens as a result of this "ineptness"? For example, by displaying ineptness, children may get their parents to do their homework or house chores for them. By not handling certain situations themselves, adults may get someone else to "fix" situations on their behalf. In the same way, the inability to face other challenges of living may enable individuals to be treated as special or may afford them control or power over relationships. This power includes being excused from an expectation or commitment. The counselor's goal is to help clients see these motives and, consequently, accept the notion that all their behavior makes sense in terms of their premises about life. Clients act in a certain way because it serves some purpose for them. In other words, clients do not "throw away" behavior that meets their needs.

For example, if a man complains that he is unable to find satisfaction in his relationships with women, the counselor tries to understand the purpose of this behavior—that is, how ineffectiveness with women pays off. Perhaps that ineffectiveness enables the client to feel excused from functioning in that arena and to put all his efforts into his work—an area of life in which he feels competent. Or maybe the man's ineptness worries his friends, and they double their efforts to "find him the right woman." He may have a large number of people concerned and involved in establishing contacts for him. Once the counselor sees the payoff of the client's behavior—the often unconscious motives of the behavior—the counselor can help the client become aware of these motives and how they affect his lifestyle.

Stimulating Social Interest   Adlerian psychology sees people as social beings who cooperate with others to realize their goals and function fully. Thus, Adlerians believe that mental health can be measured in terms of one's social interest, the willingness to participate in the give and take of life and to cooperate with others. A typical Adlerian suggestion for people who are discouraged is to become involved in helping others; to look outward instead of inward. Social interest and concern for others are contrasted with self-interest and concern only for one's own good, or currently discouraged position.

People Are Creative, Decision-Making Beings

People don't merely react to the stimuli around them. We have an active influence on the course of our lives. A simple counseling lead that helps clients see this and assume responsibility for the events in their lives is the question, "How do you keep yourself from _____ or from being involved with _____?" If a client says, "I can't cooperate more with my (husband, teacher, boss)," the counselor asks the client to rephrase the statements as "I will not cooperate. . . ." thereby taking full responsibility for the relationship. The counselor makes it clear that the client can always decide to change, but that, for some reason, it apparently suits the client's purpose not to change. The client then examines the payoff, which may involve being treated as special, getting service, being in control of a relationship, getting even, or whatever else is rewarding to the individual.

THE GOALS OF ADLERIAN COUNSELING

Adlerian counseling has four main objectives, which correspond to four stages in the counseling process:

- Establishing an empathic relationship between counselor and client, in which the client feels understood and accepted by the counselor.
- Helping clients understand their beliefs and feelings, as well as their motives and goals that determine their lifestyle.
- Helping clients develop insight into mistaken goals and self-defeating behaviors.
- Helping clients consider alternatives to the problem behavior or situation and make a commitment to change.

Establishing an Empathic Relationship

The relationship is one between equals, a collaborative effort in which counselor and client are active partners working toward mutually agreed goals.

The counselor is responsible for providing the necessary conditions for an effective helping relationship. The client is not a passive recipient "being counseled" but an active party in a collaborative, cooperative relationship. The relationship can be spelled out in a contract. The contract specifies the goals of the counseling process and the responsibilities that each equal partner in the process must undertake. This emphasis on equality and responsibility is counter to the popular notion that one goes to counseling to be "cured." In Adlerian counseling, clients recognize that they are responsible for their behavior. The contemporary issue of "informed consent" is consistent with this Adlerian concept of client involvement.

The goals of the relationship are explicit. Both counselor and clients can evaluate progress. Mutual goal alignment expresses respect for the clients' capacity to direct their lives. It also clarifies the counselor's commitment to help the client's movement.

Throughout the counseling process, the counselor helps clients become aware of, accept, and use their assets. Counseling does not focus on analysis of deficits and liabilities. The counselor's most powerful tool is encouragement. Encouraged clients are aware of their strengths and the personal power to change beliefs, feelings, goals, and behaviors.

This positive approach stresses assets rather than liabilities. Clients begin to perceive barriers and obstacles in less threatening terms. A poor relationship at work or in the home, a mistake, or a failure is understood as an opportunity to learn and grow. Mistakes become learning experiences.

Confidentiality and privacy are essential. The relationship is usually more effective when the client is voluntarily engaged in the process. Individuals who are assigned to counselor custody or probation may agree to cooperate only to avoid more onerous consequences. Until the client chooses to cooperate, even in those circumstances, counseling usually does not progress smoothly.

However, mandated counseling has become more commonplace. Such counseling benefits from simple Adlerian concepts: maintain mutual respect, establish clear and simple goals for the relationship, and understand the client as both discouraged and goal-directed. The first step is to create a therapeutic alliance between counselor and mandated client.

Understanding Beliefs and Feelings, Motives and Goals

Lifestyle is a fundamental concept in Adlerian counseling. The lifestyle is a personal construct, a structure built on beliefs, perceptions, and feelings about oneself and others. The counselor listens closely, identifying the person's beliefs, perceptions, and feelings. It is a unique form of reflective listening—an active attempt to understand all the verbal and nonverbal components of communication. The counselor also observes movement to identify beliefs and goals. A holistic synthesis takes place. All material is understood in terms of how it fits the lifestyle and how it can be used to increase understanding of one's dynamics so as to become more effective in life (Dreikurs, 1967).

The counselor is not interested in fragmentary analysis of elements; IQ scores, personality tests, and past history are only elements that must be understood in relation to the *pattern*. The counselor looks at the meaning of the total psychological movement.

Each statement is considered in relation to the preceding and ensuing statements—that is, in terms of its relationship to the client's pattern. When a client says "I do my best, but others are often not satisfied: I really keep trying to make them happy," the counselor deals not only with the feeling of discouragement but with the belief about the importance and purpose of pleasing. Is the client attempting to be a victim or a martyr through pleasing? By "doing it only for you," perhaps the goal is to make others feel indebted. It is appropriate to ask, "Is it that you can't or that you won't please?"

Once the counselor, by actively listening and applying the principles of holistic synthesis, has reached an understanding of the client's lifestyle, the counselor is in a position to help the client reach the same understanding by seeing basic beliefs and perceptions influence lifestyle. The very act of communicating to the client that the lifestyle makes sense—and showing explicitly how this is so—has a therapeutic effect and a profound influence on the counseling relationship. True understanding of someone's lifestyle is the highest form of empathy. When clients feel understood and accepted, they can confront their problematic behaviors and faulty premises and begin to change them.

What beliefs are revealed in the counseling process? Here are a few. "Life is unfair," "People are no good," "I must be right," "I must please," "I'm something only if I'm first," and "Winning is everything." Even such a short list of beliefs clearly reveals people's different approaches to the challenges of living. Here the counselor identifies the underlying belief:

Michele: *I do everything I can to please the boss, but he's never satisfied. I can't figure him out.*

Counselor: *Perhaps what you're feeling is that, if you can't please, there's no sense in trying.*

Beliefs create feelings. By empathizing with the client—listening closely and reflecting back feelings—the counselor helps the client identify feelings, the beliefs behind them, and the purpose the feelings achieve. Here the counselor identifies the underlying feeling:

Michele: *I do everything I can to please the boss, but he's never satisfied. I can't figure him out.*

Counselor: *You're confused, perhaps disappointed?*

This response by the counselor leads the conversation into a discussion of feelings and enables counselor and client to explore the feelings more intensively. But until Michele becomes aware that her basic belief is "I must please or I won't be successful," just exploring the feelings will not enable her to become aware that her belief is influencing her feelings. It is the Adlerian position that beliefs influence feelings. Your belief about being shy creates your feelings of awkwardness, not the other way around.

While Adlerian counselors explore feelings to understand motives, develop empathy, and improve the relationship, they always go beyond the feelings to discuss the beliefs behind them. It is through confronting faulty beliefs that clients become aware that they are not at the mercy of their feelings but can be in control of them, and begin to change them. Here the counselor moves the relationship forward by offering a tentative hypothesis:

Michele: *I do everything I can to please the boss, but he's never satisfied. I can't figure him out.*

Counselor: *Is it possible that you believe that, if you can't please, there is no point in trying? Your boss's failure to recognize your efforts justifies your becoming less cooperative or even quitting.*

The counselor would make this response only after having heard the client's feelings and getting in touch with her beliefs. We have repeated the client's statement in the preceding three examples to show the variety of possible counselor responses. This third response is designed to go beyond empathy and understanding and to stimulate action. Note that the communication is tentative ("Is it possible . . . ?"), so Michele can decide for herself. At the same time, the counselor's response moves the transaction toward a consideration of purpose. Until Michele is in touch with her goals and intentions, she is not going to be motivated to make significant moves toward change. Awareness of purpose is accompanied by the awareness that Michele has chosen her purpose and has the power to change it.

The next example illustrates the need for the counselor to go beyond empathy and deal with the purpose of the client's feelings, rather than merely reflect them:

> Jim, a first-year teacher, explains how things go for him with his students: "I spend hours preparing for class. I even use my personal funds to purchase materials. Despite my best efforts, the students don't appreciate my concern. They are disorderly in class, don't get involved with the class, and seldom do the assignments. I give up. Why try? It's useless!"

Jim is deeply discouraged about his progress as a teacher. The purpose of his complaints is to give himself the justification to stop working so hard. He believes that, if he shares his despair, the counselor will be sympathetic and excuse him from the responsibility of constructively facing his students. If the counselor focuses only on understanding and empathizing with feelings, without trying to get at the purpose of these feelings, the dialogue between Jim and the counselor might go like this:

Jim:	*Wow! I've tried everything with these students, but nothing works.*
Counselor:	*It seems pretty hopeless.*
Jim:	*Nobody could do anything with students like these.*
Counselor:	*Sounds as if there's no way you can be successful. You're feeling discouraged.*
Jim:	*That's not all. At home . . .*

The example illustrates that mere empathy tends to stimulate more feelings of inadequacy in the client. A more appropriate approach is to hear and share the feelings first and then move beyond the feelings into cognition, beliefs, attitudes, and purposes, so that Jim can become more aware and motivated to change:

Jim:	*Wow! I've tried everything with these students, but nothing works.*
Counselor:	*I get the idea that you have the belief, "I can't be successful."*
Jim:	*I sure don't feel successful.*
Counselor:	*I have a hunch that the students sense that and deal with you on the basis of your belief.*
Jim:	*Well, I'm discouraged; nothing works!*
Counselor:	*Could it be that your belief that the students are impossible justifies your lack of success? By openly declaring your inadequacy, you become the victim.*
Jim:	*Perhaps. But what can I do?*

By acquainting Jim with his beliefs and the purpose of his feelings, the counselor makes it possible for Jim to consider other alternatives.

Developing Insight into Mistaken Goals and Self-Defeating Behaviors

Perception is primary in organizing motives and the ensuing movement. We act on the basis of how we see things, not on the basis of others' perceptions.

> Individual psychology holds that behavior is always a movement toward a goal. The goals are motivators; they act as a final cause for behavior; they are the end point of intentions. Goals themselves are often unconscious or at best dimly understood. Counseling helps clients understand and change their goals (Shulman, 1985).

Most people come to counseling believing they are doing something wrong. The counselor understands this as a lack of effectiveness in their approach to the tasks of life. Counseling helps individuals recognize their mistaken ideas about the tasks and understand why they act the way they do. In other words, the goal is to have clients understand the purpose of their behavior and how that behavior helps them achieve their goals, which are often unconscious.

The counselor is empathic and accepting, but also confronting. Insight about hidden purposes and goals occurs through confrontation and encouragement, as well as through interpretation and other techniques designed to facilitate self-awareness and awareness of how we interact with others. This insight into what keeps one from functioning more effectively helps clients resolve apparent contradictions. Clients begin to give up their mistaken goals to achieve functional behavior.

Seeing Alternatives and Making New Choices

In the final stage of the counseling process, we move toward reorientation. This is the action-oriented phase of counseling—putting insight into action—in which a variety of active techniques are used to promote movement. The beliefs are understood, the goals and purposes perceived, and the feelings accepted, clarified, and explained in light of the accompanying beliefs and goals. Attention is directed toward seeing alternatives and making new choices.

Michele: *I do everything I can to please the boss, but he's never satisfied. I can't figure him out.*

Counselor: *You're discouraged and believe that, unless you please, you're a failure. This is an idea you have decided to accept for yourself. You could believe, instead, "I will do my best, and if he's not pleased, that's his problem." What do you think about that?*

The counselor hears the feelings, clarifies the belief and purpose, but does not reinforce it. This is often the point at which the inexperienced counselor gets bogged down—for example, by echoing the client's ideas. The experienced counselor instead offers alternative ideas or beliefs for consideration.

Certain elements contribute to the success of the reorientation phase. Encouragement is the prime element in stimulating change in the client. Encouragement generates self-confidence and self-esteem that enables people to act on their concerns. As we have indicated, discouragement is one of the basic factors in failure to function. Encouragement increases confidence and courage and thus promotes change. When courage is stimulated, there is a tendency to move in more positive directions and to be open to encouragement and support from others. In turn, when clients learn to encourage others, they are encouraged themselves. This becomes a reinforcing cycle in which behaving courageously stimulates greater self-confidence.

Another element that promotes change is clear goals, including the purposes of the counseling process. Clearly stating specific goals and purposes fosters the client's involvement and commitment to change.

A study of what produces change in the client revealed that insight is the factor most frequently mentioned as instrumental to therapeutic change. It also found that change occurs through interpretation of goals and purposes (Kal, 1972). However, the clinicians surveyed in the study also stressed the importance of action outside therapy; that is, putting insights into practice by experimenting with alternative ways of behaving. Thus, insight should be considered a powerful adjunct to behavioral change but not a prerequisite, since people can make profound behavioral changes without developing insight.

GETTING STARTED

It is important that clients understand the nature of the counseling relationship from the beginning. Many individuals who come to a counselor have had no exposure to this type of relationship. Lack of experience and inaccurate impressions derived from the media may lead clients to have a number of faulty expectations. They may anticipate that the counselor will simply listen, or perhaps supply answers to questions.

It is therefore essential that, at the first session, counselors spell out their role. Counselors must also clarify that they can help clients consider alternatives, but that the decisions are up to the client.

The relationship is collaborative, without superiors or inferiors. No movement can occur until the goals for counseling are spelled out and mutually agreed on. In the first session, clients should begin to formulate a plan or contract concerning what they want, how they plan to get there, what is keeping them from successful pursuit of their goals. The plan includes how they can modify their nonproductive behavior, and how they can use their assets and strengths to achieve their purposes.

Beth: *I understand that you can help people like me.*

Counselor: *Tell me something about yourself and why you are here.*

Beth: *I've been told I have good ability, but I get poor grades in school. I can't seem to get interested. My reading is weak. Do you tutor in reading?*

Counselor:	*I'm not a reading tutor, but I can help you find one. You seem to feel you're not living up to your expectations.*
Beth:	*It's not just my expectations. My parents are very disappointed. I'm afraid I may be flunking.*
Counselor:	*There is pressure from home also.*
Beth:	*Yeah. Dad is really mad. He says I'll never grow up and be responsible. I'm so confused I don't know what to do.*
Counselor:	*There's a lot of pressure from home, and you also sound discouraged about yourself. What would you like to get from our counseling sessions?*
Beth:	*I'd like to understand why I'm not motivated, and I'd like to learn how to get my parents off my back.*
Counselor:	*What should we talk about first?*
Beth:	*Why I'm not motivated.*
Counselor:	*Our purpose, then, will be to understand your motives as they relate to school and to determine what keeps you from succeeding.*

During the initial stage, the counselor listens closely and moves consistently toward helping Beth establish why she is there and what she hopes to accomplish. The session is not open-ended, but focuses on clarifying what is being sought. Beth may later change her goals, but the focus and purpose for the original contract have been established.

It is essential that clients understand what the counselor offers and how they are expected to participate in the relationship. The counselor must have a clear conceptualization of the process and be able to articulate it to the person seeking help.

THE EFFECTIVE HELPING RELATIONSHIP

Motives and Expectations

People often have faulty expectations about counseling. Because some of their expertise is in the area of motivation, counselors are well equipped to discern an individual's motives for seeking help. Mosak and Gushurst (1971) clarify some ways to determine the purpose and meaning of a clients' statements about their motives. For example, a person may say, "I'm confused and immobilized, I feel as if I'm pulled in two directions, and I can't decide." As soon as the counselor attempts to help the person attack the dilemma, the client responds with, "Yes, but . . .," indicating that the counselor has a good point but must certainly weigh the considerations on the other side of the issue. People who go through life with a "yes, but" approach will surely save face, but they will not go far. Neurosis is face saving, and the stance of the neurotic is a "yes, but" stance. As Mosak and Gushurst (1971) observe:

His statement, in other words, contains the hidden intention "I'm not going to go anywhere" and the "conflict" is his method of immobilizing himself. The reasons for such immobilization vary from patient to patient, but they tend to fall into one or the other of two major categories: protection from a loss or retention of a gain. (p. 428)

By not taking a stand or choosing a direction, individuals don't run the risk of losing something and can reap the subtle benefits while protecting their good intentions. In other words, by being undecided, one can maintain more than one position. For example, a student complains, "If I quit my job and put full effort into my studies, I can't afford school; but if I keep my job, I don't have the time to do well in my studies." As a result, this student can continue to put less than full effort into academic work. The counselor helps the client see alternatives to the two extremes of work and school efforts.

Another statement heard frequently is, "I guess you'd say I'm a dependent person." As Mosak and Gushurst (1971) indicate:

From an Adlerian perspective, however, dependency is a life movement in which the individual places others in his service. Convinced of his own inadequacy and consequent exemption from responsibility, the dependent person concentrates on evoking and maintaining the assistance of others whom he sees as stronger and therefore obligated to help him. Another way of declaring impotence is contained in the statement "I can't seem to let go of myself" and here the patient is generally referring to his feelings and his inability to live spontaneously. In reality, the manner of stating the problem conceals the patient's investment in keeping himself "held in," keeping himself safe, in control, free of blunders and exposure. This kind of statement is frequent among controllers and perfectionists, people who want to keep their best profile forward. (p. 429)

Clients can be aware from the start that the counselor understands their motives, even motives that may be hidden from their consciousness. When the counselor responds not only to the feeling or belief but also to the purpose, the client's awareness expands and the possibilities for change increase. Furthermore, recognition by the counselor that one's statement makes sense—the counselor accepts the person's private logic—is a way to establish instant rapport. The ensuing task for the counselor is to move the client from faulty private logic to acceptance of the common logic.

Real and Hidden Meanings   As the client speaks, it is important that the counselor catch the meaning of words and their purpose. Let's consider two ways of leading.

Christopher: *I can't seem to let go of myself.*

Counselor: *It's very discouraging, and you feel defeated.*

Christopher: *Yes. I'd like to relax like other people, but it doesn't seem right.*

Counselor: *You're really tied up.*

In this dialogue, the counselor focuses on feelings and alludes to beliefs. The following dialogue moves on to possible purpose:

Christopher: *I can't seem to let go of myself.*

Counselor: *You're afraid to relax?*

Christopher: *Yes. If I relaxed, I could make a mistake and look foolish.*

Counselor: *For you, it is dangerous to make mistakes. Is it possible that you feel comfortable only if you are in control and can predict what will happen?*

In this dialogue, the counselor is empathic, but quickly begins to talk about beliefs and the purpose of Christopher's movement. This counselor influences the client to become more actively involved in looking at his life and the choices he makes.

Often the Client's Stated Problem Is Not the Real Problem   The concerns clients express in the first session may be a way of testing whether the counselor is really listening and how perceptive the counselor is. If the counselor appears to be naive or overly accepting, clients may not share their true concerns. Early involvement with real and hidden meanings increases clients' faith in the counselor's ability and increases the possibility of earlier entry into the change process.

Particularly with children and spouses, clients may indicate that they are there because someone referred them or "made me come here." In these instances, it is important to openly discuss how the clients feel about being sent by someone else. They may be angry, feel inadequate, or think they have been treated unfairly, which can be discussed. It is also important to clarify the counseling relationship and to build a bridge toward goal alignment by helping the clients choose what they want to work on. For example, a parent may send a child to the counselor to help her become more motivated about school, whereas the child's major problem may be with a sibling or a peer. It is more productive to begin with the child's goals than to attempt to force her to discuss what she was sent to discuss.

For clients who go into therapy to appease a spouse, the counselor should help them determine their true concerns, which may be different from those of the spouse. Clients are encouraged to discuss their feelings about counseling, and the counselor makes it clear that they will work with the clients' perception of the marital relationship.

Negative and Unrealistic Expectations   People come to counseling for a variety of reasons and with different expectations. Some who are pessimistic may believe "I can't change," "Nobody can help me," "Life is unfair," or "People are no good." They expect little to happen, and their negative expectations often become self-fulfilling prophecies; their discouraged outlook and faulty self-defeating beliefs about life actually interfere with their involvement in counseling. It is important to get a clear contract with those who have negative expectations, otherwise they may decide to stay in counseling just to prove that nothing can be accomplished. The purpose of negative expectations (to keep from moving) or resisting counseling (to prove that nothing can happen) can be confronted. When clients see how their mistaken perceptions influence their experiences, they can change.

Other clients may have unrealistically high expectations of the counseling process. They may also be dependent and attempt to transfer responsibility for their progress to the counselor. They may believe, "Life owes me everything," "Others must protect me," "I can do no wrong," "Others are at fault," or "My problems are simple. If you are competent, you should be able to help me in a short time." Clients with the latter belief are quick to blame the counselor or situation if they do not see rapid changes in their life tasks.

In the first session, the counselor clarifies the opportunity. Careful listening, empathy, understanding, identification of client beliefs, and insight into client purposes and behavior help stimulate action and change. Clients are expected to be honest, open, congruent, involved, and committed to considering alternatives and making choices. The counselor can help, but for movement to occur, clients must put their understanding to work and be committed to specific change.

The expectations in the preceding paragraph are not limited to a mythical or ideal "YAVIS" client (young, affluent, verbal, intelligent, sophisticated). All clients are treated "as if" they can be helped. Clients benefit from these beliefs, including the idea that clients *can* change.

Clients begin to recognize that counseling is work. In part, this occurs when the counselor anticipates their full involvement and cooperation. The client must not only talk, but decide and act as well. The counselor helps the client take insight from the session into actions throughout the client's world.

Ingredients

Training of counselors and psychotherapists was once less systematic than it is today. It was believed that counseling skills could be developed just by reading the theories of established leaders in the field, almost by osmosis. Professionals had some supervision during training, but the training was not systematic, and specific programs focusing on skill development were not available.

The research of Rogers, Gendlin, Kiesler, and Truax (1967) and Truax and Carkhuff (1967) presented the first evidence that professional counseling and psychotherapy may be "for better or for worse." The evidence was based on research showing that the results of professional counseling were difficult to predict. All counselors were not equally effective and therapeutic, even if they have had the same training.

These findings led to studies of the ingredients of effective helping. In these studies, the counselor's ability to function in specific emotional and interpersonal dimensions had a significant influence on the counselor's "for better or for worse" effectiveness.

The interpersonal dimensions determined to be essential ingredients of the helping relationship were identified by Rogers et al. (1967) as empathy, unconditional positive regard, and congruence; and by Truax and Carkhuff (1967) as accurate empathy, nonpossessive warmth, and genuineness.

Carkhuff (1972) reported:

> Perhaps the most important extension within helping has been to expand the helper dimensions from responsive to initiative dimensions. Thus the original formulations emphasizing helper empathy, unconditional regard, and congruence were complemented by the more action-oriented dimensions of helper concreteness (Truax & Carkhuff, 1967), confrontation and interpretations of immediacy. (Carkhuff, 1972, p. 71)

The Helper's Perceptual Organization

Counselors need more than one theory, or a book which reviews the major theorists. They need a clear understanding of the dynamics of behavior change and the specific skills necessary to implement this change. Effective counselors also need a perceptual organization (that is, a system of beliefs and perceptions) conducive to a helping relationship with their clients.

Combs, Soper, Gooding, Benton, Dickman, and Usher (1969) researched the perceptual organization of workers in the helping professions—for example, counselors and clergy—and found a high degree of similarity in the perceptual organization among effective workers in the helping professions. These researchers identified the beliefs that effective helpers share, including:

Beliefs about What People Are Like   Effective helpers perceive others as having the capacity to deal with and find solutions to their problems. They have confidence in people's ability to handle themselves and their lives. They see others as friendly and essentially well intentioned. They recognize and respect the worth and dignity of others.

Effective helpers see others as essentially developing and unfolding from within, not as the products of external events. They believe that behavior is predictable and understandable.

Beliefs about Self   Effective helpers feel fundamentally adequate. This creates the ability to attend to the needs of others and identify with them. Effective helpers see themselves as dependable and able to cope with life's challenges.

Beliefs about the Counselor's Purpose   Effective helpers see their purpose as one of freeing, rather than controlling, people—assisting, releasing, and facilitating, rather than controlling, manipulating, and coercing.

Effective helpers tend to be more concerned with large rather than with small issues. They are more likely to be self-revealing than self-concealing. Their purposes are altruistic rather than narcissistic.

Beliefs about the Approach to the Counseling Task   The effective helper is concerned with people rather than with things which affect people such as objects, events, rules, or regulations. Effective helpers are likely to approach others subjectively, since they are more concerned with people's perceptual experience.

Combs et al. (1969) directed attention to the importance of the helper's perceptual organization. They have also provided the counseling field with valuable guidelines as to what beliefs make a helper effective. These concepts developed through research are consistent with Adlerian theory about the helping relationship.

It should be clear that any opposing beliefs can interfere with a successful counseling process. It is important that counselors be exposed to intensive training experiences in interpersonal communication. These experiences will help identify beliefs and the ways these beliefs can help or hinder the counseling process. Experienced counselors continue to participate in experiences which create feedback about their beliefs and their effect on their clients. The contemporary need to maintain professional proficiency through Continuing Education Units (CEUs) should focus, in part, on an effort to be continuously aware of self.

THE ADLERIAN COUNSELOR

Characteristics

The counselor's portrait that emerges from the studies we have discussed is similar to the portrait of the good Adlerian counselor. Throughout this chapter, we have stressed the elements that constitute the essence of the Adlerian counselor's role. In light of the preceding discussion, some of these elements are worth summarizing.

Counselors may choose a theory of counseling that fits their personality as well as their values. Adlerians are no exception. We, too, have models that influence the way we approach the counseling process. First, we are active participants. We collaborate with the client, and, at the same time, we recognize and accept responsibility for the process. We bring this active dimension to the counseling process through concern with the purpose of behavior and the unique laws of psychological movement. As we listen, we are more than empathic and reflective. We also attend to how the client's message reveals beliefs and goals and how we might intervene most productively to help the client see how beliefs and goals influence feelings and approaches to life tasks.

Through chosen responses, we direct the discussion toward consideration of all these elements. We are aware that moving from empathic reflection to tentative confrontation accelerates the process. We do not wait for some magic moment in which clients, having processed all of this information, develop a sudden awareness of why they are functioning in a certain manner and how they might change. Our commitment is to active procedures, such as confrontation, interpretation, and disclosure. These procedures not only challenge clients' beliefs and goals, but influence them to translate insight into specific actions and behaviors that reflect the changes that have occurred in their beliefs, self-concepts, and goals.

Our personalities are useful in the helping process. While it is important to have a theory of personality and to be acquainted with a variety of counseling techniques, this knowledge must be integrated into the personality of the helper. The counseling process necessitates creative and spontaneous response to the changing interpersonal demands of the helping relationship. Regardless of our theoretical orientation, we are behavior models for our clients. They are influenced by our views, values, goals, and feelings, and we must keep this in mind all the time. An "eclectic" counselor has not yet integrated these concepts.

Here are some of the most important characteristics of the good Adlerian counselor.

Awareness of One's Beliefs   Counselors must be able to answer clearly the questions "Who am I?" "What do I believe?" and, most important, "How do my beliefs affect my counseling?" Good counselors are aware that they, too (not just the clients), can have mistaken beliefs about counseling and the counselor's role. Thus they explore their reasons for being in a helping profession and know the motives, goals, attitudes, and feelings that can create blind spots.

Awareness of One's Feelings   Counselors are trained to listen to others' feelings and to pick up nonverbal indicators of feelings. But they must also be aware of their own feelings, particularly as they affect the counseling process. Involvement with their clients can inspire enthusiasm about progress or discouragement about setbacks or lack of movement. When this occurs, counselors become aware of these fluctuations.

If the client grows, that growth is a result not only of the counselor's good work but also of the client's understanding and initiative. In the same fashion, failure to make progress is often a result of the client's unwillingness to apply what has been learned. Although failure to progress may result from faulty diagnosis or the counselor's inability to help the individual move from insight to outsight, counselors should not assume that there is an automatic relationship between counselor behavior and client progress. A skilled consultant can be helpful to a counselor who is experiencing difficulties in a counseling relationship. This consultant can be a peer, a supervisor, or teacher. The consultant can help clarify whether lack of progress is due to faulty diagnosis, ineffective communication by the counselor, or lack of motivation on the part of the client. The essential point the counselor must keep in mind is that no progress can occur without the client's cooperation.

Awareness of the Counselor's Modeling Role   Whether or not they intend to, counselors serve as models to their clients. Clients are sensitive to the counseling relationship and expect counselors to handle their own personal relationships effectively, so they don't interfere with their professional lives. A counselor with a confused and stormy personal life is less believable as a professional resource. If a counselor's own children, marriage, or friendships are not satisfying, that counselor's ability to help others may be affected. This does not suggest that counselors must be free of problems, but that they must be aware of the powerful effect their own lifestyles have on their clients. They must have the ability to resolve these challenges.

To effectively influence the counseling process, counselors must understand how their clients perceive them and what type of model they communicate. Our clients often learn from what we do and how we approach our own challenges in living.

High Ethical Standards   Counselors must be trustworthy and concerned about their clients' welfare. They must not reveal confidential information. Although ultimate allegiance is to society, the counselor's primary responsibility is to the client. Whatever is discussed in the private session can be shared with others only with the client's consent and only when there is clear danger to the client or others. Counselors must be dependable and responsible, that is, they must have a strong commitment to a set of ethical behaviors.

Awareness of the Conditions That Are Essential to the Client's Development   If counselors are to help clients lead a more satisfying life and achieve the purpose for which they come to counseling, certain conditions are essential:

Empathy Seeing the world the way the client perceives it. This comes by accurately perceiving the individual's feelings and being able to communicate this perception to the client. It involves understanding the individual's private logic and beliefs as well as emotions.

Caring and concern These are demonstrated by verbal and nonverbal attending and by showing deep and genuine concern about the welfare of the client.

Genuineness and openness Both are greatly facilitated by the counselor's self-disclosure. Self-revelation is part of a constructive relationship, because counselors' words are congruent with their actions.

Positive regard and respect The counselor shows these attitudes for the client's individuality and worth as a person.

Understanding and clarification of the meaning and purpose of the individual's behavior Through the counselor's tentative hypotheses and disclosure, clients develop insight into the motivations that direct their lives.

Action-oriented techniques The use of these techniques, such as confrontation and encouragement, enables the client to change.

REFERENCES

Carkhuff, R. R. (1972). New directions in training for the helping professions. Part 1: The development of systematic human resource development models. *The Counseling Psychologist, 3*(3), 4–11, 12–30.

Combs, A. W., Soper, D. W., Gooding, C. T., Benton, J. A. Jr., Dickman, J. G., & Usher, R. H. (1969). *Florida studies in the helping professions* (University of Florida Monographs, Social Sciences No. 37). Gainesville: University of Florida Press.

Dreikurs, R. (1953). *Fundamentals of Adlerian psychology*. Chicago: Alfred Adler Institute.

Dreikurs, R. (1967). *Psychodynamics, psychotherapy, and counseling*. Chicago: Alfred Adler Institute.

Kal, E. (1972). Survey of contemporary Adlerian clinical practice. *Journal of Individual Psychology, 28*(2), 261–266.

Mosak, H. H., & Gushurst, R. S. (1971). What patients say and what they mean. *American Journal of Psychotherapy, 25*(3), 428–436.

Rogers, C., Gendlin, E. T., Kiesler, D. J., & Truax, C. B. (1967). *The therapeutic relationship and its impact*. Madison, WI: University of Wisconsin Press.

Shulman, B. (1985). Cognitive therapy and the individual psychology of Alfred Adler. In M. J. Mahoney & A. Freeman (Eds.), *Cognition and psychotherapy*. New York: Plenum.

Truax, C. B., & Carkhuff, R. R. (1967). *Toward effective counseling and psychotherapy: Training and practice*. Chicago: Aldine.

CHAPTER 6

Psychotherapeutic Interventions

The Adlerian counseling process consists of four phases: (1) establishment of the relationship, (2) analysis and assessment, (3) insight, and (4) reorientation. All leading theorists have stressed the importance of the counseling relationship, and its necessary conditions. This chapter elaborates the phases and techniques of the counseling process and presents the Adlerian view of the relationship between counselor and client. Therapeutic interventions occur in the context of the relationship and its stages of development.

THE RELATIONSHIP

Dreikurs (1967b) states the nature of the relationship:

> The proper therapeutic relationship, as we understand it, does not require transference but a relationship of mutual trust and respect. This is more than mere establishment of contact and rapport. Therapeutic cooperation requires an alignment of goals. When the goals and interests of the patient and therapist clash, no satisfactory relationship can be established. Winning the patient's cooperation for the common task is a prerequisite for

any therapy; maintaining it requires constant vigilance. What appears as "resistance" constitutes a discrepancy between the goals of the therapist and those of the patient. (p. 65)

Mutual Trust and Respect

Mutual trust and respect are essential elements of the Adlerian helping relationship—an egalitarian relationship in which there are no superiors and inferiors. By working in the context of a collaborative effort directed at creating psychological movement, clients feel responsible for their own lives.

To facilitate change, Adlerian counselors use a variety of procedures. Although the techniques may be used in any facet of the session, we will discuss them in the phase of the counseling process in which they are most likely to occur. To help you identify with the procedures, we will address you, the reader, as if you were the counselor.

Attending Behavior and Attentive Listening

The effective therapeutic relationship begins with your focusing on the concerns as presented by your client. That focus is facilitated if you initiate and maintain good eye contact. This visual contact is not a fixed stare. Your posture should be relaxed. It conveys interest and involvement through a slightly forward body position, indicating that contact is being maintained. Your comments follow directly from what your client says and reinforces the client's free expression, without adding new data. This helps clients express themselves spontaneously.

An effective counseling relationship requires you to be responsive to the client's communication and to clearly communicate your attentiveness. In most everyday situations, we rarely encounter people who really listen and who hear not just the words but the content, the feelings, and the intentions. Thus, coming in contact with someone who does listen is a powerful encouragement to keep talking.

Emilio: *I feel bad about not being able to work up to my parents' expectations. I don't think I'll ever be able to meet their standards.*

Counselor: *You feel it's pretty futile to try.*

Emilio: *I've tried, but no matter what I do, it's not enough. This feeling I have all the time that I'm not making it really makes me very angry. For example. . . .*

You hear the message, follow the content and the feelings, and seek verification about what you believe you heard. Especially during the first few minutes, it is useful to reflect what you have heard and observed. This encourages Emilio to spontaneously tell more about how he feels. It is important never to let anything pass that you have not fully understood.

Appropriate attending and listening behaviors are essential to developing mutual trust and respect in the counseling relationship. This atmosphere increases the potential for the counselor's underlying assumption about change and movement to be clearly understood and accepted by the client.

Clients are made aware of the counselor's belief that they have the power to change. *This belief is demonstrated by helping clients see how "can't" often really means "won't."* When a clients says, "I can't stop from supervising my son's homework," the client may be asked to reword the statement so it is more accurate and say instead, "I won't stop supervising my son's homework."

This simple technique often helps clients recognize they are choosing to behave in a way that keeps them in trouble. At some point, they may feel uncomfortable even when they say "I won't," because these words clearly imply that they are acting by choice. Thus full responsibility is placed on clients for their behavior. The counselor conveys this sense of responsibility in a respectful way. This indicates the belief that, once clients are aware of the decisions they are making, they will decide for their own good.

Goal Alignment

Counseling is conversation with a purpose. Adlerians emphasize the alignment of the client and counselor's goals. The session has the purpose of developing awareness, generating insight, and stimulating movement. Cooperation and focus on a common therapeutic task are essential for change to occur. Small talk is kept to a minimum, and attention is devoted to the beliefs and mistaken perceptions that interfere with one's progress in meeting the challenges of life.

An important aspect of the helping relationship is to establish a contract that clearly states why clients are seeking help and what they expect from counseling. Dreikurs' statement provides clear guidelines for recognizing when lack of movement or resistance arise from a discrepancy between the goals of the counselor and those of the client. For example, the counselor may have decided that it is important for Shonda to recognize that her poor schoolwork is a symptom of a power struggle with her parents. The counselor sees Shonda's behavior as an attempt to prove that no one can make her study and an indication that she enjoys the power of defeating her parents' efforts. Shonda, on the other hand, seems more concerned with getting her parents off her back and with developing her own social skills. The counseling process can be effective only if it deals with what the client recognizes as important and wants to discuss and change. Eventually, by working with her concerns as she perceives them, Shonda may become motivated to develop a new approach to schoolwork.

In a counseling session, you will occasionally become aware that the client is not working on the problem, is avoiding a topic, or is not following up on a comment you have made. It is your role to reestablish the focus by commenting on what is happening in the here-and-now conversation. Refocusing on the task enables clients to better understand how they avoid certain issues. It also helps to reestablish the purpose of the contact and the implicit contract—to work on the concerns that keep clients from effectively meeting the challenges of life.

To align goals, you may ask, "Is this the person you want to be? Can you think of a different way to act? What do you imagine will happen if you continue in this pattern?"

Claudia:	*I'm very mad about the way Paul treats me, and I don't intend to stand for it.*
Counselor:	*You are angry and feel that you have to do something.*
Claudia:	*I get mad, but I get over it. Did you see that TV movie last night? It was really good.*
Counselor:	*I notice that, when we get to the point of discussing your anger and what to do, you usually talk about something else, as you are now. I'm wondering whether you have noticed that, too. How do you feel we can deal most effectively with this problem?*

You refuse to be sidetracked and talk about how the client hinders the process.

Reflection of Feelings and Empathic Understanding

The effects of counseling are related to the counselor's level of functioning on emotional and interpersonal dimensions, such as empathic understanding. For our purposes, empathy is best defined as the communication of understanding. We see the client's world through their eyes, mind, and heart. The counselor therefore understands the client's feelings, beliefs, and intentions.

Empathic understanding involves capturing the essence of someone's feelings and communicating the understanding. Once this understanding is established, a firm foundation for counseling and change has been created.

Empathy involves both the feelings expressed by the client and the feelings elicited in the counselor listening to the message. Reflection of feelings helps clients become aware of and express the feelings they are experiencing. Responding to cognitive content deals with the literal meaning of a person's communication; it is like listening to the words of a song without the music. The process of understanding both feelings and content is crucial to the counseling relationship. It increases the client's awareness and self-understanding, and makes it possible for the counselor to develop the necessary conditions to facilitating change.

Nina:	*I'm tired of being controlled by the group and forced to compromise. I can't function this way.*
Counselor:	*You are angry about the group's control and want to be free to make your own decisions.*
Nina:	*I know I can be happier without them, because then I'll be able to decide for myself.*

Productive Use of Silence

It is not always easy to appreciate the meaning and value of silence. Too often the counselor feels compelled to say something to break the silence. In some instances this is done with a "closed question"—a question that requires only a yes or no on the part of the client—which only compounds the problem.

Silence can be used productively. Letting the client assume responsibility for the continuation of a topic is one way of doing so. By accepting silence without becoming anxious, clients begin to recognize their responsibility for initiating topics and sharing their concerns. After accepting the silence for a time, you might ask, "What do you think is going on right now?" Another approach is to explore with the client the hidden reason for the silence—for example, "Could it be . . . ?" and allude to a possible purpose. Possible reasons for a client being silent include to control, get special service, retaliate, or perhaps show that nothing can be done about the situation.

Silence might also indicate that the counselor and the client have not developed mutually acceptable goals. Goal alignment may not have been achieved, or there may be some false assumptions on the part of the client. An example is the belief that counselors dispense advice and take full responsibility for the interview. In this situation, a reformulation of goals is necessary.

Silence may also mean avoidance. Observation of body movement may produce a clue as to the purpose of the silence. For example, if the client's eyes appear to be fixed on something, but not focused, it is probable that the person is engaged in a productive silence. If, instead, the client is tense and nervous and avoids eye contact, it is possible that the person is avoiding the topic. By being in touch with your own feelings during the silence, you may also be able to understand the client's purpose. Anger may indicate that the client has a desire to control; confusion, instead, may indicate that the client believes you can do nothing about the situation.

Silence can also be productive. Client-initiated silence might mean that the individual is considering an idea, engaging in self-examination, attempting to fully understand a new insight or awareness, or evaluating new directions. These are all good reasons for silence, and you need not intervene.

Silence can also be used to slow the pace of the interview so that individuals can absorb understanding of their feelings and purposes. Letting clients know that you are willing to wait without demanding that your needs be satisfied can be a very positive and reassuring way to communicate understanding and acceptance.

Nonverbal Communication

While most communication in counseling is verbal, its nonverbal components—facial expressions, body position, voice tone, and breathing tempo—are also very important. Every time a person talks, all of the person talks. If you fail to comprehend this, you may miss the real message. The voice may say one thing and the body indicates something else.

Be aware of voice tone and eye contact. Posture, muscle tonus, facial expressions, and gestures all emit continuous nonverbal signals. Various possibilities to note include relaxed or stiff posture with hands clenched or relaxed. A client may sit in a posture that conveys defiance, distance, and self-control, or her facial expression may reveal anger, confusion, or recognition. The *recognition reflex* is that characteristic grin that communicates instantly that your client understands a tentative hypothesis regardless of what words are said. At all times, the client communicates nonverbally.

If you observe a pattern in the client's nonverbal communication, it is often productive to interpret the message in the form of a tentative hypothesis. You might say, "It seems this is very difficult for you to talk about. . . . Could it be that the thought of it makes you angry? . . . Is it possible you believe no one could understand?" This may improve the relationship, create insight, and facilitate change. You must also be aware of your own nonverbal behavior and how such behavior encourages or discourages a line of exploration. Your nonverbals may convey approval or disapproval of the client.

One important aspect of communication involves tears and crying. Counseling requires total involvement, which can easily mean tears. It is handy to keep a box of tissues within reach. When clients show signs that they are about to cry, give them the tissues or say, "It's okay to cry." If a client is fighting back tears, you can discuss what this means, for example, if he believes that crying is a sign of weakness.

Tentative Hypotheses and Encouragement

In Adlerian counseling, a great deal of effort is put into providing tentative hypotheses about the purpose of clients' behavior. Hypotheses are offered and discussed even in the early stages of counseling. It is important that counselors help clients understand the purpose of their behavior. The counselor's recognition that one's behavior makes sense from one's own point of view extends to recognition of the meaning behind the behavior. For example:

Kali: *I've been trying to listen to my husband's opinions; but I find they don't make sense, so I follow my own ideas.*

Counselor: *You're disappointed you can't count on him.*

Here the counselor only empathizes with the client, and this could lead to a lengthy exploration of feelings. An alternative course would be to formulate a tentative hypothesis about the relationship between husband and wife.

Kali: *I've been trying to listen to my husband's opinions but I find they don't make sense, so I follow my own ideas.*

Counselor: *Is it possible that you have to be in control? You seem to believe that you must be right, and this justifies negating your husband's views.*

Here the counselor focuses on beliefs and meanings and conveys the message that the behavior makes sense from Kali's point of view. At the same time, by dealing with the movement instead of simply identifying the feelings, the counselor makes it more likely that the goals and beliefs influencing the feelings and the behavior will be modified.

The counseling relationship is enhanced by discussing tentative hypotheses. By sharing a view about the hidden motives and goals of behavior and dealing with them through interpretation, the Adlerian counselor conveys a form of empathy that makes the relationship more effective.

Encouragement is also part of the relationship from the beginning. The whole process of attending closely to verbal and nonverbal messages, focusing on the client's concerns, and being sensitive to both verbalized and implied feelings is encouraging. For some people, it may be the first caring, congruent, close human relationship they have ever experienced.

Disturbances That May Interfere with the Relationship

Certain psychological disturbances may interfere with the client's cooperation. For some, the counseling relationship is an implicit threat to self-esteem and to the habitual mode of dealing with people and meeting the challenges of living (Shulman, 1973). Shulman identified some of the disturbances that interfere with the counseling relationship:

Fear of Being Defective   Coming for counseling is an admission of weakness, because one should be able to handle one's problems alone.

> Abe, a self-made man who has fought his way to the top in his profession, has nothing against his wife and adolescent daughter going for counseling. However, he feels very strongly that, if he should have some problems of his own, he should be able to work them out by himself.

Fear of Being Exposed   Sharing one's thoughts and feelings will destroy the image one wants to project.

> Kayla, a 38-year-old single woman, is very concerned with not making mistakes. A successful teacher, she has learned to project the image of a well-organized, self-controlled person who never makes such errors. She is in a relationship but isn't sure this is the right one; in her own words, "I don't want to make a mistake." She is unable to express her feelings about the relationship.

Fear of Disapproval   Revealing oneself will produce disapproval even on the part of the counselor.

> Carla has been trained to believe that she can belong only when she is pleasing. Therefore, she finds it very dangerous to reveal the anger, even rage, that underlies her incapacitating depressions.

Clients may also use certain defenses to save their self-esteem or to defeat the counselor. Shulman (1964) categorizes those defenses:

1. *Externalization* ("The fault lies outside of me"). Externalization is employed to preserve self-esteem and shun responsibility for one's own behavior. By externalizing, people blame others and consider themselves the victim of circumstances. The varieties of externalization include the following:

Cynicism ("Life is at fault"). These individuals escape responsibility for their own behavior by blaming those in charge, the "system," and so forth. They see people as getters, concerned only with meeting their own needs.

Cory, 33, has won and lost a fortune. He is understandably distressed but blames others for what happened. He concentrates on their behavior rather than on his own and overlooks his own greed and poor judgment, which led him to financial disaster.

Inadequacy ("I'm just an innocent victim"). The person demonstrates incapacity and inability to function.

At age 32, Lynn has a long history of running away from responsibility. She never completes a program or task she sets for herself and spends months at a time incapacitated. A victim of incest as a child, she still detects injustice everywhere she turns, and, whenever demands become too pressing, she "takes a vacation."

Rebellion ("I can't afford to submit to life"). These individuals challenge all the ordinary rules of life. They battle with life not just to win but to defeat the commonly accepted rules of society.

Hugh, 25, has pushed his crusade against the current "rules of life." In his attempt to create his own rules, he is hardly able to eat a meal for fear that the food has some noxious additive or lacks the appropriate nutrients.

Protection ("It's all their fault"). The person suspiciously blames others and shuns all responsibility for what has happened.

In a large business, several of the department managers are doing poorly. The president blames them for the company's slow progress instead of recognizing a share of responsibility for not supplying them with the information and resources they need to do well.

2. *Blind spots* ("If I don't look at it, it will go away"). By refusing to face a problem, the person pretends the problem is not there.

Despite the fact that three of her five children have had serious psychiatric incidents, Mary consistently avoids counseling for her family, vigorously insisting that hers is a completely normal, healthy family.

3. *Excessive self-control* ("I won't let anything upset me"). Self-control is so powerful that all emotions, pleasant or unpleasant, are strongly suppressed and the person is protected from both joy and sorrow.

Although Luis' 16-year-old daughter is failing in school, has no friends, and is obese, Luis is always smiling when he tells others that everything he tries as a father fails.

4. *Arbitrary rightness* ("My mind is made up; don't confuse me with the facts"). The person makes arbitrary decisions and allows no doubts.

Stephanie is a highly successful attorney. Her steel-trap mind is all advantage in her profession, but her arbitrary rightness is intolerable to her husband and children.

5. *Elusiveness and confusion* ("Don't pin me down"). These individuals attempt to conceal themselves from others by lying, pretending ignorance, or changing the subject.

Kay is often confused, and this gives her a convenient excuse to avoid responsibility or decision making.

6. *Contrition and self-disparagement* ("I'm always wrong"). These individuals express feelings of guilt. These feelings permit them to continue the behavior while affirming good purposes that they have no intention of carrying out. Ben is an intelligent, verbal adolescent who tyrannizes the household with temper tantrums and then wallows in guilt feelings.

7. *Suffering as manipulation* ("I suffer to control others"). These persons get what they want by protesting how much they will suffer if they don't get it. They may even put on the martyr act to glorify themselves in the eyes of others.

Things are always going wrong for Jill, and she is quick to let her family know how much she suffers. Through family counseling, the members of Jill's family are finally beginning to understand why she is always so successful at getting things her own way.

ANALYSIS AND ASSESSMENT

The phase of analysis and assessment has two purposes: understanding the lifestyle and seeing how the lifestyle affects the individual's functioning in the life tasks (Mosak & Dreikurs, 1973). The counselor begins by exploring the current situation and how the client approaches social relationships, work responsibilities, and the sexual role, as well as his feelings about himself. Although this investigation may be carried out in an open-ended manner that allows data to surface, information regarding the lifestyle is generally gathered systematically. Here are some of the questions the counselor is likely to ask:

Social relationships: How are things going in your social life? Do you have a few close friends? Do you have many acquaintances, or do you feel isolated? Are you satisfied with the number of friends you have? Do you find satisfaction in your relationships with other people? Do you feel belonging and acceptance?

Work: How do things go for you in your work? Do you enjoy what you are doing? Are you successful? Are you a workaholic—overinvolved with and overcommitted to your work? What do your fellow workers (or students) think of you? How do you respond to authority? Is work a rewarding and fulfilling task, a chore, or an all-encompassing part of your life?

Sexuality: Are you glad you are a man (or a woman)? Do you see yourself as very masculine (or feminine)? How do things go for you in your relationships with others? Do you feel any special concerns in relating to women (or men)?

Feelings about self: How self-satisfied and self-accepting are you? What do you do for fun? How do you enjoy yourself? Do you pressure yourself? Do you feel good about yourself? Do you like yourself?

Sometimes the interviewer may also ask: What are your goals? What are the meaning and purpose of your life as you understand them?

The investigation may also involve asking clients to numerically rate their current feelings about success in the areas of social relationships, work, sexuality, self, spiritual life, leisure, and parenting. A scale of 1 to 5 or 1 to 10 allows quantification of the client's self-perception in these tasks.

Paraphrasing

Paraphrasing is the process of checking with clients to be certain you understand their ideas as they intended them. Paraphrasing requires paying selective attention to content. It gives back the essence of what the client said. The process involves your mirroring the client's thoughts to see whether you are hearing accurately, as well as communicating your understanding. Thus, the task is twofold: listening intensively and accurately and expressing what you have heard so the client knows that you understand.

Paraphrasing is not word swapping or parroting; it is communication of understanding. It is empathy in action. This may be achieved either by generalizing the client's message or by making it more specific.

Claudia:	*I don't know about him. At times he's very nice, but then, again, he can be very nasty.*
Counselor:	*You are not sure how he's going to act. He's hard to predict.*

Paraphrasing may also allude to the goal or purpose implied in the client's communication; for example, "It seems you want to get even" or "I get the impression you want to show they can't control you."

The relationship flounders if the counselor misses or misunderstands the client's content. While paraphrasing helps to establish the relationship, it also serves as a checkpoint in the counselor's analysis and assessment of the client's perceptions.

Priorities and Lifestyle Scale Themes

The client's priorities in making decisions are also investigated. Adlerians believe that determining a person's number one priority is a useful clinical method. It quickly identifies one aspect of the lifestyle. For teaching purposes, Adler presented four types of number one priorities: ruling, getting, avoiding, and the socially useful. Adler indicated that each type of priority, unless challenged, continues to characterize the individual, thereby determining the person's unity or lifestyle. The concept of priorities is not used to categorize people, because every individual is too complex to be classified on the basis of type. Priorities are used to understand short- and long-range goals and to get at core convictions.

The number one priority is determined on the basis of the person's answers to the questions, "What is most important in my quest for belonging?" and "What must I avoid at all costs?" There are many priority typologies. For example, Kefir (1972) defined four number one priorities: comfort, pleasing, control, and superiority. Tia might list the priorities in this order:

Important to my belonging	To be avoided at all costs
Comfort	Stress
Pleasing	Rejection
Control	Humiliation
Superiority	Meaninglessness

Thus, if Tia's number one priority is comfort, she will give precedence to comfort over pleasing, control, or superiority. Her priority is based on the mistaken conviction, "Only when I'm comfortable do I truly belong." The avoidance stance would be, "The worst thing for me is to be under stress. I must avoid it at all costs." These avoidance priorities have a crippling effect on our lives, because they severely limit our courage and social interest.

A second approach the counselor can employ during the analysis and investigation phase is a priorities interview. Kefir and Corsini (1974) propose that a quick assessment of a particular facet of a client's lifestyle and core convictions could be accomplished by a clinical intervention currently referred to as investigation of the client's number one priority. Extrapolating from the lifestyle typology information and from Adler's original work on types, Kefir developed an interview technique to assess four basic priorities—superiority, control, comfort, and pleasing.

Superiority   Possibly the most common number one priority is superiority in its various forms: being competent, being right, being useful, being a victim, and being a martyr. People whose number one priority is superiority will attempt always to move toward it regardless of circumstances or others' behavior. They will also consistently evoke certain feelings in those who encounter them, usually various degrees of inferiority or guilt.

The price for superiority is overinvolvement, overresponsibility, fatigue, stress, and uncertainty about one's relationships with others.

Control   Another common number one priority is control, which is usually one of two types. In one type, the emphasis is on control of others; in the other type, the emphasis is on control of self. People whose number one priority is control of others consistently achieve, or at least move toward, their goal, but they also evoke feelings of challenge and resistance in those around them. Methods of control vary widely, but the number one priority is the same. The price for this priority is distance from others.

A number one priority of self-control can lead to an "uptight" person. These people evoke feelings of frustration in others, which often lead to distancing oneself from the self-controller. Self-controllers can also pay an additional price of diminished spontaneity and creativity.

Comfort   Those whose number one priority is comfort or self-indulgence will not wait for gratification. They want their pleasure and satisfaction immediately. While getting what they are after, they annoy others in the process. The price they pay is diminished productivity, because they will not risk frustration and do not want responsibility.

Pleasing   Pleasers neither respect themselves nor expect respect from others. An immediate reaction to the pleaser is, "Here's a nice guy," but further acquaintance-ship often evokes negative responses from others, such as rejection, frustration, de-spair, and exasperation. The price the pleaser pays is stunted growth, alienation, and retribution.

We can expand these descriptors by viewing them on an active/passive contin-uum, as suggested by Wheeler, Kern, and Curlette (1986) and Langenfeld and Main (1983). An active person with a priority of superiority, for example, may lean toward martyrdom or righteousness, while a passive person may lean toward saintliness and victimization. Controllers of others may accomplish their priority actively by being tyrants, or passively by being artful dodgers. Self-controllers are likely to be more passive. Comfort seekers may pursue their goal actively by behaving at times like spoiled persons, or by sitting passively, expecting to be served.

Pleasers may be quite passive, always subordinating their desires to those of oth-ers, or they may be exceedingly active, continuously looking for someone to please. They evoke pity and, at first, elicit in others a desire to help them. That desire, how-ever, may soon be replaced by frustration and despair. Active pleasers are continu-ously looking for what they need to do to be rewarded or stroked by others. At first we may react to these individuals with pleasure, but our feelings may turn to frus-tration when we see that they lack opinions and decision-making skills of their own.

Pinpointing the Priority

Clients' number one priorities can be pinpointed by asking them to describe the de-tails of a typical day—what they do and how they feel when they do things. The counselor infers from these descriptions. A second technique for determining the pri-ority is to ask them directly to indicate which of the four priorities is most important. You can briefly describe each priority and then ask, "Which of these four statements best describes you? 'It's most important for me to be in control. . . .' 'It's most im-portant for me to please others. . . .'" and so forth through the four priorities.

As an alternative you might wish to create a scenario that addresses two ques-tions as to why a client adopts a certain priority in dealing with life situations. The two basic questions are "How do I use my number one priority to belong?" and "What must I avoid at all cost when using that chosen priority?" Kefir claims that com-fort seekers avoid stress, pleasers avoid rejection, controllers avoid being humiliated by situations or others, and superiority seekers avoid meaninglessness in life.

Thus clients for whom comfort is the number one priority will find ways to cre-ate comfortable situations in their environment. The client's priority of comfort might be based on the mistaken conviction that, "Only when I am comfortable do I truly belong or am accepted by others." The converse, or the avoidance stance operating within this particular client's conviction, might be, "The worst thing for me is stress, so I must avoid it at all costs." Because stress is a normal condition, one can see how a client's priority of "only if I am comfortable in life" could inhibit the courage to grow and demonstrate social interest toward others.

Another possible assessment technique is a brief, written survey. This is a 35-item self-report instrument that the client may complete during the session or at home. The Kern Lifestyle Scale (Kern, 1982, 1997) categorizes lifestyle into five factors: control, perfectionism, need to please, self-esteem, and expectations. Though Kefir's descriptions of the priorities are somewhat similar, the Kern Lifestyle Scale attempts to obtain a more expansive description of a client's lifestyle rather than a specific aspect of the private logic. Other advantages of the instrument are that it is quick to administer, yields a quantitative profile of lifestyle themes, and provides immediate data that may help the counselor understand the client. A further advantage is the scale's use as a research tool to further understand the lifestyle concept. It is discussed in Appendix C.

BASIS-A

Another extremely useful assessment tool has been developed by Kern and his colleagues (Kern, Wheeler, & Curlette, 1993). The BASIS-A Inventory (Basic Adlerian Scales for Interpersonal Success—Adult Form) measures five lifestyle themes: Belonging-Social Interest, Going Along, Taking Charge, Wanting Recognition, and Being Cautious. The BASIS-A Inventory also contains five HELPS scales to expand and facilitate interpretation of the five BASIS-A scales. These scales are Harshness (H), Entitlement (E), Liked by All (L), Perfectionism (P), and Softness (S). The Kern scale and BASIS-A are discussed in Appendix C.

Dealing Effectively with Priorities and Lifestyle Themes

After a number one priority or theme has been pinpointed and understood by counselor and client, alternative behaviors and attitudes can be considered. The counselor does not usually work toward changing the priority or theme; it is likely that if one is discarded, another will replace it and be just as troublesome. The goal is to help clients understand the feelings they evoke in others and to determine how much they are willing to pay to maintain the priority. The goal is to lead the client away from the absurd position of "only if" ("Only if I please, can I belong" or "Only if I am in power, can I find my place") into recognizing that he can belong and find his place without going to extremes; to make slight modifications.

> Jared was a 56-year-old stockbroker who apparently could not handle his recent demotion from office supervisor to account executive. When the therapist offered tentatively, "Could it be it's important for you to supervise others?" Jared denied this by saying, "No, I really helped more people when I managed all 15 account executives." Paraphrasing Jared's statement as, "So you had more control when you were office manager," counselor and client agreed that the number one priority was in fact control.

As stressed previously, however, Jared and the counselor could not have come to that insight if their relationship had not been one of cooperation in which the client felt safe and "understood." The understanding component of the relationship might well be expedited by the counselor's ability to pinpoint the number one priority or lifestyle theme generated from the Lifestyle Scale. When the counselor can make this connection, the discouraged client understands and believes there are alternatives to a particular problem.

Confrontation   Confrontation is a procedure by which counselors enable clients to become aware of discrepancies between their behaviors and their intentions, their feelings and their messages, their insights and their actions, and so forth.

Shulman (1973) indicates that confrontation is the combination of a challenge and a question designed to evoke the feeling that an immediate response is required. Thus, it stimulates therapeutic movement by mirroring a client's mistaken goals. Shulman suggests a number of techniques, depending on the intent of the confrontation.

Confronting with Subjective Views   Dreikurs (1967a) refers to this confrontation technique as "revealing the hidden reason." That is, counselors confront clients with the private justifications that clients give themselves to make their behavior acceptable in their own eyes. For example: "I'm acting this way just because I'm drunk," or "I had so little sleep that, even if I went to work, I couldn't get anything done," or "I'm too nervous" (Shulman, 1973).

Dreikurs suggests that counselors pursue the confrontation by asking, "What were you thinking of at the moment?" or "What did you say to yourself then?" He also suggests that, if counselors want to be understood and to make the confrontation effective, they must put the hidden reasons into their clients' words. Paraphrasing during confrontation allows clients to hear their own words from a respected individual.

Confronting with Mistaken Beliefs and Attitudes   The beliefs and attitudes to which this type of confrontation refer are clients' basic convictions about their own nature, the world, and the meaning and requirements of life. Shulman (1973) says, "These basic convictions fill in the following blanks: I am _____; life is _____; therefore _____" (p. 201). For example, people who complain that others pick on them might be confronted with, "You look, talk, and behave like a pushover, so you invite people to pick on you. Don't blame anyone but yourself, because you invite them."

Confronting with Private Goals   This confrontation may be used with clients who attempt to deny a feeling. The confrontation is brought about by offering a tentative hypothesis such as, "Could it be that you wanted to get them upset?" or "Is it possible you thought this would be an excuse?" These statements may produce a recognition reflex or an acknowledgment of acceptance of the confrontation.

Confronting with Destructive Behavior   This confrontation deals with the here-and-now, for example, "You just changed the subject. Were we getting too close to something?" or "I notice you are arguing about one word and ignoring the concept. How come?"

As Shulman (1973) states, "Confrontation techniques are intended to challenge the client to give an immediate response, make an immediate change or an immediate examination of some issue" (p. 205). Adlerian confrontation is intended to help clients become immediately aware of their goals, private logic, and behavior. It stimulates their courage and ability to change.

Interpretation

Interpretation deals with the reasons a person behaves a certain way—that is, with the purpose of the behavior, belief, or feeling. By shifting away from the client's internal frame of reference, interpretation provides a new perspective for understanding. In other words, you can use this technique to help clients consider and develop a new point of view, thus gaining access to a wider range of alternatives.

Interpretation is effective only if the client is receptive and can understand it and use it. To minimize resistance, interpretation is usually presented in a tentative format, such as, "Could it be . . . ?" or "Is it possible . . . ?" and at a time when you believe the client is ready to hear and seriously consider the interpretation.

Toban: *I'm confused about how well I can do my work. I can do some of it. But, if I do well, they expect more of me, and I can't live up to their other expectations.*

Counselor: *You are not sure of your ability. Could it be that you don't do too well so they will excuse you?*

You hear the feelings and allude tentatively to the purpose of displaying inadequacy.

"The Question"

This counseling technique, first developed by Adler, is used to determine whether a symptom has an organic or a functional basis. Brief therapy has a similar technique, the "miracle question." If the person complains of a physical symptom, such as headache or difficulty in breathing you ask, "What would be different if you were well?" If the basis of the condition is functional and therefore has a purpose, the person might say, "I could go back to work," or "I could study harder." This tells you what is being avoided by having the physical symptom. If no such purpose is indicated, the condition probably is organic and has a physical cause. While there may be a physical ailment without psychological etiology, the client may still use the ailment for a special purpose.

FORMULATION OF THE LIFESTYLE

The lifestyle denotes the basic premises and assumptions on which psychological movement through life is based. Lifestyle can be expressed in terms of the syllogism "I am _____; the world is _____; therefore,_____" (Allen, 1971b). We believe, feel, intend, and act upon these premises, and we move psychologically to justify our point of view. Our lifestyle is formulated from our pattern of beliefs, convictions, and attitudes.

Investigation of the lifestyle begins with the first psychological transaction between counselor and client. Body language, tone of voice, and expressed attitudes reveal a person's style of life. Therefore, counselors need to learn to understand the scripts and what the scripts really mean (Mosak & Gushurst, 1977). It is essential that, when the self-defeating or maladaptive patterns are discussed, the client not be made to feel accused. As Mosak and Dreikurs (1973) state, "the therapist will have to assist him in distinguishing between being assessed, i.e., understood, and being blamed, a distinction not easy to make or accept" (p. 55).

Analysis of the Family Constellation

The lifestyle is formulated by assessing the individual's family atmosphere through a family constellation questionnaire and early recollections. The family atmosphere is understood by asking questions that seek to determine the relationship between the client and his parents, as well as the family's values, attitudes, and disciplinary procedures. In asking these questions, the counselor is guided by a lifestyle form. Appendix A shows examples of these forms.

Adlerians believe that siblings often have as much, or more influence over each other as the parents. In many families, children influence parents as much as parents influence children. Parents, however, do set the tone for the family atmosphere, particularly in the early years.

The Family Constellation Questionnaire   The questionnaire provides insight into the individual's perception of self, the relationships among siblings, influential forces to which one reacted, and the experiences that affect the decisions one makes about life.

The questionnaire investigates factors that Adlerians believe to be influential, such as birth order, sibling characteristics and ratings, and transactions and interactions among siblings and between children and parents. Emphasis is not on birth order per se, but rather on the children's psychological position in the family—how they perceived their position and what they did with it.

Guided by the questionnaire, the counselor begins by asking why the client is seeking counseling and how satisfied the person is with the way things are going in the basic life tasks. Next, the counselor asks for a description of the client's parents, their names, ages, and occupations, and a brief list of their outstanding personality traits. After gathering this initial information, the counselor asks, "Who was your father's favorite? And your mother's? Did your parents have ambitions for their children? What was your father's relationship with the children? And your mother's? Who was the sibling most like your father? In what ways? Most like your mother? In what ways?" Then the counselor inquires about the client's relationship with the parents and, finally, about other parental figures in the family and the effect they may have had on the client's outlook on life (Eckstein, Baruth, & Mahrer, 1975).

After posing questions about the parents and their relationships with their children, the questionnaire asks for a description of the client's siblings. Each sibling is listed, beginning with the oldest and including the client, giving name, age, and a description of character and personality traits. Deceased siblings are noted in their respective positions and identified in some way—for example, with a broken circle around the name (Eckstein et al., 1975). The family constellation questionnaire then asks "Who among your siblings was most different from you? In what respect?" If the client is an only child, ask, "Who in your peer group was most different from you? In what ways?" The next question is, "Who was most like you? In what respect?" This gives the counselor an understanding of the client's self-appraisal and the traits with which the client identifies most and least. Other questions that can be asked are, "Which siblings fought and argued? Which played together? Who took care of whom?"

Now the focus shifts to the client. The counselor asks, "What kind of child were you? Did you have any unusual talents, achievements, or ambitions? What was your physical development like? Were there any physical or psychological handicaps?" The client is then asked to describe sexual development in terms of first relationships and experiences. If the client is a woman, she may be asked to describe her experience with her first menstrual period.

The next item in investigating the family constellation is rating the client in relation to the siblings in terms of a list of attributes. To do this, the counselor takes one of the 24 attributes listed in the questionnaire—for example, intelligence—and lists, in one column, the sibling who was most intelligent and, in another column, the sibling who was least intelligent. If the client is at neither extreme, the counselor indicates the client's position in relation to the siblings.

Attribute	Most	Least
Intelligence	Mary (Sam)	George

Hence, Sam, the client, is closer to Mary in his intelligence rating. He sees himself as intelligent but not the most intelligent in the family. This ranking procedure is done for all attributes the counselor believes will help portray the client's self-perceptions.

Family Dynamics An infinite number of personalities result from the family atmosphere, ordinal position, psychological position (the way individuals perceive and interpret their position in the family), and methods of training. The oldest child may adopt the patterns of the parent believed to have more power. For example, if father is demanding and gets his way, the child may tend to copy these traits. On the other hand, if mother controls by passive–destructive methods, such as withdrawing and using silence, the child may adopt these tactics. First children may attempt to emulate the parent's traits they consider most important or may give up because they cannot live up to those standards.

The second child is usually very perceptive of what is expected and needed to become important in the family. By noting the behavior of the first child and the behaviors valued by the parents, the second child often chooses to adopt parental traits the older child has overlooked. The second child also closely identifies areas in which the first child has not succeeded and, if this provides acceptance and belonging inside the family unit, quickly moves into those territories. As Shulman (1973) states, "divergence in behavior between siblings is partly due to competition between them for a place in the sun, the second avoids the territory of the first and goes elsewhere to seek his fortune" (p. 49).

According to Dreikurs, personality traits are the children's responses to the power politics within the family group. "Similarities and differences . . . indicate alliance and competition" (Dreikurs, 1957). The siblings who are most alike are the allies. Conversely, the siblings most different from each other are the main competitors, even though there may be no open rivalry. Dreikurs distinguishes between rivalry and competition, describing the first as an open contest, the second as having "a much deeper impact on each child, leading to the development of opposite character traits as each child seeks success where the other one fails" (Dreikurs, 1957). Competition develops mainly with the proximal sibling, the one who always had to be taken into account during the formative years (Shulman, 1973, p. 49).

It is clear that siblings have a significant influence on the emergence of one another's personality traits. The psychological position in the family is often as important as the parents' method of training.

In summary, the analysis of a family constellation requires four things: (1) a solid and comprehensive familiarity with the factors that Adlerian theory considers most influential in personality development, the implications that Adlerians find in certain types of phenomena, and the common lifestyles identified by Adlerians; (2) the ability to recognize, discover, and characterize patterns; (3) the ability to compare patterns for the presence of similarities and differences, and (4) the ability to make accurate inferences, either by extrapolation within an already identified coherence, or through an intuitive, empathic grasp of a particular phenomenal world (Gushurst, 1971, p. 32).

Interpretation of Early Recollections

Early recollections are another crucial type of information the Adlerian counselor collects in the course of formulating the lifestyle. Early recollections are specific incidents recalled from early childhood. Clients can remember clear details, almost as if they could see them, and include the feelings and thoughts at the time of their occurrence. They are not merely reports about a person's early life; they reveal beliefs, basic mistaken attitudes, self-defeating perceptions, and unique laws of psychological movement. Early recollections are valuable because, according to the Adlerian theory of personality, they are indices of current attitudes, beliefs, and motives (Mosak, 1958; Gushurst, 1971) and because Adlerians believe that people remember only those events from early childhood that are consistent with their current views of themselves and the world (Adler, 1958). As Gushurst (1971) indicates, early recollections "provide a brief picture of how an individual views himself, other people, and life in general, what he strives for in life, and what he anticipates as likely to occur in life" (p. 33).

[Early recollections] are first interpreted thematically and second with respect to specific details. . . . The characters incorporated in the recollection are not treated in interpretation as specific individuals but as prototypes. They represent people in general or authority figures rather than the specific individuals mentioned. While the content of the recollection is given primary consideration, a sequential analysis provides a more rounded picture of the individual. The characteristic outlook rather than the characteristic behavior is portrayed. (Mosak, 1958, pp. 107–108)

The main theme or pattern is to be interpreted in a manner similar with the TAT (Thematic Apperception Test) theme or projective figure drawings, and are not to be broken into separate fragments. Starting with hunches, individual themes are brought together and their unity and pattern spell out a message—the client's feelings and emotions provide the main interpretative clue. (Nikelly & Verger, 1971, pp. 57–58)

Individuals select only certain events from the vast number of experiences that occurred earlier in life; they emphasize certain aspects of each memory and play down or completely omit others. Memory is a product of selective and evaluative processes; hence, it can provide projective data from which we infer the basic elements of the current lifestyle (beliefs and goals). These elements influence and shape the recollection as it is articulated to the counselor.

Kopp and Dinkmeyer (1975) present a standardized procedure for use in the interview. Although appropriate for any age, they are referring to the collection of recollections from students:

Think back as far as you can to the first thing you can remember . . . something that happened when you were very young (it should be before you were seven or eight years old). It can be anything at all—good or bad, important or unimportant—but it should be something you can describe as a one-time incident (something that happened only once), and it should be something you can remember very clearly or picture in your mind, like a scene.

Now tell me about an incident or something that happened to you. Make sure it is something you can picture, something specific, and something where you can remember a single time it happened.

As the student begins to tell the memory, listen for the visual and specific part of the memory. Some background details may be appropriate. Do not, however, spend too much time setting the stage with facts leading up to or surrounding the incident itself. Instead, concentrate on what actually happened.

Phrases such as, "We were always . . . would always . . . used to. . . ." or "would happen" suggest incidents that occurred repeatedly. Ask the student to choose one specific time that stands out more clearly than the others and tell what happened that one time. If one particular incident does not stand out over others, eliminate this event and choose a different early memory which can be described as a single incident.

Before moving on to the next memory, ask the following questions and write down the student's response:

Do you remember how you felt at the time or what reaction you had to what was going on? (If so), please describe it. Why did you feel that way (or have that reaction)?

Which part of the memory stands out most clearly from the rest—like if you had a snapshot of the memory, it would be the very instant that is most vivid and clear in your mind? How did you feel (what was your reaction) at that instant?

Our experience indicates that, although we can begin to see a student's basic beliefs and motivations in the first memory, the accuracy of these interpretations increases when they are based on additional memories. The counselor's assessment thus should be based on at least three memories. Typically, from three to six memories are collected. (p. 24)

Counselors can make the directions less specific by stating, "I want to record a particular incident that you recall in the first seven or eight years of your life. Tell me what happened, what moment is most vivid, and how you felt at that moment." If the client follows the directions, the counselor then takes down the story verbatim. If the client doesn't follow the directions, the counselor may use other tactics. If the client is resistant or says, "I can't remember any specific incident," the counselor might ask the person to make one up or imagine one. Most people at that point remember an incident that actually occurred. Even if made up, it reveals the client's beliefs about self and others.

When that happens, the counselor is likely to suspect that the client is someone who tends to do the opposite of what is expected. Some people, on the other hand, are much more creative. They may intermittently invent and recall incidents; they may embellish a partially recalled incident; and, at times, they may claim they are unable to invent an incident. An invented incident is just as useful diagnostically as something that actually happened. Other creative variations are the attempt to offer recollections from a later age period and the attempt to give reports.

When people are unwilling to cooperate with the early-recollections process, the counselor can suggest that they probably are unconsciously unwilling to reveal much about themselves—which is their prerogative. This insight often prompts clients to bring in some early recollections at a later session.

Sweeney (1975) provides some additional guidelines about how to use the early recollections:

Is the individual active or passive?

Is he/she an observer or participant?

Is he/she giving or taking?

Does he/she go forth or withdraw?

What is his/her physical posture or position in relation to

What is around him/herself?

Is he/she alone or with others?

Is his/her concern with people, things, or ideas?

What relationship does he/she place him/herself into with others? Inferior? Superior?

What emotion does he/she use?

What feeling tone is attached to the event or outcome? Is detail and color mentioned?

Do stereotypes of authorities, subordinates, men, women, old, young, etc., reveal themselves?

Prepare a "headline" which captures the essence of the event; for example, in relation to the woman's recollection of the ice cream: Girl Gets Job Done!

Look for themes and an overall pattern.

Look for corroboration in the family constellation information. (p. 49)

Watkins summarizes the value of early recollections:

> Early recollections (ERs) can be a useful and effective assessment tool in the counseling process. They often provide the counselor with considerable insight into a client's dynamics. . . . It is important, however, to understand that the assumed usefulness of ERs as a projective technique is based largely on critical opinion. The clinical usefulness of ERs has not been validated statistically. (Watkins, 1985, p. 32)

Watkins's statement concerning the lack of statistical validity for the procedure and abundance of favorable clinical opinion reflects the Adlerian emphasis on practical clinical procedures.

Identification of the Basic Mistakes

The summary of the family constellation and the interpretation of early recollections enable the counselor to specify mistaken and self-defeating perceptions. These perceptions are often very different from the guidelines of Adlerian "social interest," which emphasize the give-and-take, cooperative, egalitarian, and responsible nature of human relationships. Early recollections and the investigation of the family constellation frequently indicate self-interest, concern with power, avoidance, and withdrawal—all of which are identified as mistaken perceptions.

Mosak and Dreikurs (1973) offer the following classification of the basic mistaken and self-defeating perceptions.

1. *Overgeneralizations.* "People are hostile." The "all" is often implicit. "Life is dangerous," with the "always" implicit.
2. *False or impossible goals of "security."* "One false step and you're dead" or "I have to please everybody."
3. *Misperceptions of life and life's demands.* In the extreme, one can observe these in the delusions and hallucinations. Typical convictions might be, "Life never gives me any breaks" and "Life is so hard."
4. *Minimization or denial of one's worth* (Adlerians accept the worthwhileness of every individual). "I'm stupid" and "I'm undeserving" or "I'm just a housewife."
5. *Faulty values.* "Be first even if you have to climb over others." (p. 57)

Integration and Summary

One of the counselor's major tasks is to integrate and summarize the information gathered from the investigation of the clients' family constellations, from the interpretation of early recollections, and from the identification of basic mistakes. The goal of this diagnostic task is to extract:

> a brief description of the individual's role within his family (either alone or in comparison with the roles played by the other members of the family), his major areas of success and failure, the major influences which seem to have affected his decision to adopt the role that they did, and perhaps also an inferential statement about his apparent major goals and/or conceptions of himself, others, life in general, or of some particular aspect of life, such as sexuality, physical handicaps, religion, and so forth. (Gushurst, 1971, p. 31)

This process of integration should result in a clear, concise summary that reveals the client's mistaken and self-defeating perceptions, as well as assets, so that the individual can easily recognize their interpersonal dynamics. The summary is presented to the client for consideration and can be refined by discussing specific points.

In summary, the Adlerian counselor proceeds by extracting the major features that appear in an individual's answers to the family-constellation questionnaire, thereby obtaining a brief picture of his nascent personality, the individual's current outlook on life is then obtained by interpreting his early recollections; and the mistaken elements in his approach to life are then specified by comparing his contemporary convictions with those which seem to be required by the "logic of social living." Most importantly, when these diagnostic procedures have been completed, the individual has before him some very specific problem areas on which to focus, should he decide to change his life. (Gushurst, 1971, p. 34)

Sometimes counselors present the summary of the lifestyle in the presence of the client. This procedure offers the opportunity to stop and discuss areas that raise questions. A client can even be invited to read the summary aloud at a second session. The counselor can learn by hearing the client read and by being alert to slips and to what emphasis the client gives the reading. Nonverbals are also rich resources in this process.

Although this procedure may appear deceptively simple, it requires a good grasp of Adlerian theory to be clinically useful. One can synthesize and integrate the lifestyle material only by understanding the basic concepts of Adlerian psychology.

Because of the basic unity and pattern of the personality, one can identify a number of common lifestyles. Mosak (1971) provides a set of guidelines that facilitate analysis of common syndromes. As he states, "The lifestyle forms a unifying principle, a gestalt to which behavior is bound in accordance with the individual 'law of movement' " (p. 77). Mosak illustrates some commonly observed lifestyles:

The "getters," who exploit and manipulate life and others.

The "drivers," overtly overambitious, overconscientious, and dedicated.

The "controllers," who keep spontaneity and feelings in check to control life and ensure that life will not control them.

People who need to be right and hence feel superior to those whom they perceive as being wrong,

People who need to feel superior. These individuals, when they cannot be the best, settle for being the worst.

People who want to please everyone and who are always dependent on the approval and evaluation of others for their own self-esteem and worth.

People who feel morally superior because of high standards that elevate them over others.

The "aginners," who oppose all expectations and demands of life and who rarely know what they are for but who always seem to know what they are against.

The "victims," who pursue disaster and elicit the sympathy and pity of others. Victims are very creative. They are willing to suffer for anything—not just for a cause, as martyrs do—and they reveal a great deal of flexibility and imagination.

The "martyrs," who suffer like the victims but die for a cause. Often referred to as the "injustice collectors," they either silently endure or make their suffering very visible.

The "babies," who find their place by exploiting others through their charm and cuteness.

The "inadequate" individuals, who behave as if they couldn't do anything correctly and, therefore, constantly needed the help of others.

The "rationalizers" and the "intellectualizers," who avoid feelings and spontaneity and who are comfortable only in situations in which intellectual talents are valued.

The "excitement seekers," who despise routine and repetitive activity and who create and stimulate excitement.

Additional research findings from the Department of Counseling and Psychological Services at Georgia State University indicate that there may be fewer categories than those proposed by Mosak (Wheeler, Kern, & Curlette, 1986). One must keep in mind, however, that these and similar typologies merely represent examples of various kinds of psychological movement. They are useful in that they give a concise word picture of behaviors and beliefs, but each lifestyle is unique and must be understood in terms of its unique pattern regardless of proposed "types."

These patterns are, of course, not the only lifestyles we observe. We must develop the capacity to see relationships among the various data and formulate new patterns. After certain patterns are identified, we compare them for similarities and differences. Differences between the client and the rest of the family may be areas of competition, while areas of similarity may reflect alliances among the siblings, role modeling, or acceptance of family values. If parents set a highly competitive atmosphere, they will stimulate differences in siblings' attributes.

The information from the lifestyle analysis is valuable not only because it helps us understand the perceptions of the client but, more importantly, because it helps the individual feel understood. This type of understanding transcends establishment of rapport and of a good working relationship; it creates faith in the counselor and stimulates hope that things can change. The counselor's reflection of feelings and empathy are important, but the kind of understanding we are describing has the power to stimulate movement.

There is a great difference between dealing with someone who simply recognizes that you are angry and receiving from someone the insight that your anger is dictated by the belief "I know what is best." This kind of understanding goes beyond empathy and confronts you with the fact that you are deciding to display a particular emotion (for example, anger) and, therefore, you can also choose to respond differently.

Analysis of the lifestyle helps counselor and client develop a plan for the counseling relationship and for the nature and direction of the counseling process. The lifestyle and the mistaken or self-defeating perceptions will reoccur in the course of counseling. The lifestyle, then, is not a static, one-time diagnostic formulation but a consistent theme that is continuously discussed in relation to the client's approach to the various challenges of living.

INSIGHT

Adlerians believe that behavior develops not from what we are, but from what we *believe* we are; that is, behavior is not the result of our experiences but of how we interpret them. Our behavior is based on our expectations and on the resultant self-fulfilling prophecies.

The insight phase of counseling is concerned with helping clients become aware of why they choose to function as they do. Although the counselor does not lecture or give advice, counseling is an educational process in which clients learn about themselves. Through constant emphasis on beliefs, goals, and intentions, the individual's private logic is explained and discussed.

All of us operate with varying degrees of common sense and private logic. People who exhibit dysfunctional behavior, however, don't see life in terms of common sense but only in terms of their private logic. They solve their problems in a self-centered way that shows a lack of normal social interest and willingness to cooperate with others.

Adlerians interpret the pattern of behavior holistically, in terms of its unity. Therefore, they don't accept a dualism of intellectual and emotional insight and don't believe that the client should defer dealing with a problem while seeking to develop insight. Intellectual insight may be only a ploy to keep the person involved in counseling instead of becoming involved in problem resolution.

Those who clearly indicate that they understand, yet make no attempt to change their beliefs or try on new behaviors, must be confronted with the purpose of such behaviors. By staying in counseling, clients publicly declare their good intentions to the counselor and to those close to them. By refusing to become involved or to make a commitment to change, however, these people defeat others' attempts to help them, while protesting their good intentions and well-meaning efforts. This is the situation that Adler called the "yes, but" game—"I know I should stop, but. . . ."—with all its concomitant excuses, which reveal the person's psychological movement.

Interpretation is concerned with creating awareness of (1) lifestyle; (2) current psychological movement and its direction; (3) goals, purposes, and intentions; and (4) private logic and how it works. Insight is created through constant reference to the basic premises of one's lifestyle and to how these mistaken, self-defeating premises keep the individual from leading a successful and satisfying life.

This information is derived from the person's here-and-now behavior and position in the family constellation. It also comes from hunches about the client's ordinal position and from an understanding of the individual's psychological position in the family constellation. Early recollections are used to clarify and sharpen the interpretation. Finally, inquiry about the various challenges of living (work, social contacts, sexual relationships, self-image, and spiritual concerns) provide insight into the motives and purposes of behavior.

Adlerian interpretation can be clearly differentiated from classical psychoanalytic interpretation. Adlerian interpretation is done in relation to the lifestyle, which is the central theme. The interpretation is not done statically—in terms of clients' current position—but is continuously related to their movement. It refers to the direction and course of their transactions with others. It also alludes to where they are going and to what they expect to get by their behavior—to be special, to be in control, or to obtain special service. Thus, interpretation enables clients to see the pattern of movement and its meaning.

Characteristically, interpretation deals with the purpose of behavior and its consequences. The focus is on here-and-now behavior and on expectations and anticipations that arise from clients' intentions. Interpretation is always done holistically, in terms of the meaning and scope of the pattern of movement. No attempt is made to analyze elements separate from the pattern.

Method of Presentation

The method of presenting an interpretation is crucial. Interpretation is generally made tentatively: "Could it be . . .?" "Is it possible . . .?" "I have an idea about you I'd like to share." The open-ended sharing of hunches and guesses is powerful, because it relieves counselors of the burden of being always right; one doesn't have to be perfect to offer a hunch or guess. It also provides a mirror through which counselors can look at their clients' behavior. Because the interpretation is offered tentatively, clients are not forced to defend themselves and are truly free to agree or disagree. And when the counselor is wrong, both parties are able to consider other alternatives.

The guessing method is a perfectly acceptable scientific process and is functional within the counseling relationship. If the counselor guesses correctly, the client feels understood. An incorrect guess gives the counselor an opportunity to demonstrate the courage to be imperfect and thereby contribute another valuable element to the relationship. There are times, however, when interpretation is presented confrontationally. This happens when there is a discrepancy between what clients say they intend and what they actually believe. Discussing the purpose of this behavior helps individuals recognize the basic beliefs and goals that motivate their transactions in life.

At times, clients are encouraged to interpret for themselves. Some believe that, if clients are able to interpret for themselves, the interpretation will be retained better. As clients become familiar with their own lifestyles, they can start to contemplate their alternatives. To elicit a client's own interpretation, the counselor may ask, "From what you understand about your lifestyle, how would you explain the current experience you have just been describing to me?"

Goals

Occasionally, counselors may offer a deliberately exaggerated interpretation, so that clients can see the ridiculous elements in their behavior. This type of interpretation has the same purpose as the paradoxical intention. Both can, by their very extremity, influence or even create movement.

Generally, interpretation should not take place before trust and rapport have been established. However, a meaningful interpretation may actually build and solidify the relationship.

Because interpretation is directed at the movement and purpose of behavior, it also helps clients begin to "catch themselves." An example of what we mean is someone who muddies up conversation with the phrase "you know." Each person has her own ideographic meaning for that phrase; for some, it means "You know, don't you?" For others, it means "You don't know" or "Could you possibly know?" or "No one has ever known." And for still others, it means "You ought to know." Most people are unaware of how frequently they interject the phrase "you know." If they are interested in making their communication clear, they will learn to catch themselves in the act of muddying what they are saying. Often we maintain a symptom by being constantly on guard against it. Instead of fighting the habit of using the phrase "you know," clients are advised to catch themselves when they say it and laughingly say, "There I am, up to my old mischief again."

This ability to intervene in one's self-defeating perceptions as they are about to occur or to become aware of the purpose of one's behavior as it is happening epitomizes the goal of insight. By catching oneself and interfering with the undesirable behavior, one is learning to stop self-defeating patterns. This opens up the opportunity to practice active–constructive behavior and to replace faulty goals with positive goals. Examples of new beliefs and new positive goals that may result are "I belong by contributing" (goal: involvement); "I can decide and be responsible for my behavior" (goals: autonomy and responsibility for one's own behavior); "I am interested in cooperating" (goals: justice and fairness) and "I can withdraw from conflict" (goal: acting maturely by avoiding power contests and by accepting and understanding others' openness).

How an individual reacts to the counselor's interpretation provides guidelines for the next steps in the counseling process. Remember that interpretations are always made tentatively ("Could it be . . .?" "Is it possible . . .?"), so there is no need for the counselor always to be right. Also, a tentative approach ensures that, if the counselor is wrong, clients will not be harmed; they will simply indicate it is not how they perceive things. If the counselor is not upset by a failure to guess correctly, the client may benefit from learning that counselors also make mistakes and survive them unharmed. The counselor is modeling the courage to be imperfect, which often teaches as much as an insightful interpretation. Clients begin to see that the world does not come apart just because someone makes a mistake.

Results

If the interpretation is accurate and helpful, several things may occur. At the time of the interpretation, the individual may give a recognition reflex—a grin or smile indicating that what the counselor said makes sense. In other words, the interpretation "rings a bell" and is personally applicable. Or the client may have a contemplative look, which generally indicates consideration of the counselor's ideas.

Interpretation from the Adlerian frame of reference is never nomothetic (dealing with generalities) but ideographic, that is, designed to fit the unique lifestyle of each individual. Interpretation involves communication about all kinds of interpersonal transactions, with emphasis on purpose rather than on cause and on movement rather than on description. In other words, Adlerian interpretation is dynamic rather than static.

By exposing the hidden intentions responsible for the client's self-defeating behavior and by clearly illustrating them, the counselor helps the client see these intentions as unpalatable. This is what Adler was talking about when he used the expression "spitting in the patient's soup," which means that, though one may still eat the soup, it will never taste quite the same. The person may still engage in a self-defeating behavior, but will not like it, or do so without awareness of the purpose.

REORIENTATION

In the reorientation phase, counselors and clients work together to consider alternative attitudes, beliefs, and actions. The approach is to reeducate and remotivate clients to become more effective in their approach to the challenges of living. But counselors must go beyond developing mere awareness of alternatives. The courage to risk and make changes must also be developed. This is often accomplished by focusing on the immediate interpersonal situation rather than on past experiences. By seeing how they can change within the counseling relationship, clients develop the motivation to experiment in other relationships.

Establishing Realistic Goals

A beginning step in reorientation is to clarify with clients what they want. The relationship phase focused on mutual goal alignment. Now, in reorientation, clients' goals are clearly established. The counselor attempts to determine whether clients' complaints are about the environment or about themselves. It is important to make it clear that, as people change themselves, they also change their environments. Changing a belief such as "I must win every conflict" to "I am willing to cooperate, listen to others, and give in when appropriate" can have a major effect on one's relationships. The change will stimulate totally different responses in others, and, as a consequence, one's feelings, goals, and actions will also change.

It is important to determine whether the client's goals for change are realistic. Unrealistic goals will only discourage; for example, someone who has not been able to relate to women may decide to become involved with a popular and attractive woman. If this relationship doesn't work, he can justify his lack of success by taking the self-defeating approach of "See? I tried, but I can't make any progress." Instead of letting this person "prove" his faulty assumption that he is not acceptable to women, the counselor encourages him to establish the intermediate goal of becoming better acquainted with women.

> To initiate behavior change after the client has recognized the basic life pattern, the therapist may suggest, "Is this the kind of person you want to be? Could you think of another better way to act? What do you suspect will eventually happen if you continue this pattern for a long time?" (Nikelly & Bostrom, 1971, p. 104)

A new orientation toward people and the life tasks, which is the goal of the reorientation phase, comes about as clients' beliefs, perceptions, feelings, and goals become more appropriate and more in line with common sense. This phase actually involves showing how one's behavior and relationships relate to one's intentions and beliefs. The counselor mirrors to clients how they and they alone choose their own goals and intentions and that they influence all their actions, feelings, and approaches to the tasks of living.

> The therapist must understand that the client behaves according to his interpretation of what is meaningful and significant to him. The client learns or forgets whatever serves his purposes; however, such selectiveness may hamper his sense of social relatedness and inhibit self-realization. (Nikelly & Bostrom, 1971, p. 105)

At this point in the process, the client is made aware that insight has little value by and of itself. It is only a prelude to action. Outsight—moving ideas into action—is the real aim of the process.

Problem Solving and Decision Making

Problem solving and decision making are basic skills in the action phase of the counseling process. They are employed to help the client explore and understand the problem adequately, so that the goal can be defined precisely. The next step involves considering alternative courses of action and helping the client examine and order values. Each course of action is considered in terms of how it helps the client realize goals and values.

Carkhuff (1973) schematizes this phase in terms of the following steps:

1. Define problem: Develop accurate grasp of situation
2. Define goal: Clearly determine task to be achieved
3. Develop alternative courses of action: Develop means to achieve goals
4. Develop client's value hierarchy: Describe things that matter to client
5. Choose course of action: Evaluate course in terms of value hierarchy
6. Implement course of action: Develop a way to act on a course of action

In the Adlerian counseling process, counselor and client align their goals, consider possible alternatives and consequences, evaluate how these alternatives will help the client meet goals, and then reorient by taking a course of action. The counselor helps the client consider how mistaken, self-defeating perceptions keep the client from making effective decisions.

Tasha: *I'd like to get a great job, but I'm not sure I would be hired. So maybe I'll just work as a temp.*

Counselor: *You are not sure of yourself. Your belief that you have to have it all or nothing seems to keep you from deciding to pursue that great job.*

Seeing New and More Functional Alternatives

The goal of Adlerian counseling is active–constructive behavior that enables individuals to become happier and more effective. Any failure to take forward steps should be interpreted in terms of its purpose. Clients are helped to see the purpose and the payoff of persisting in the self-defeating behavior. To that effect, it may be useful to get the client to ask "What is the worst thing that could happen if I changed?"

The client is then likely to recognize that the "worst thing" is not so bad after all and that, as a matter of fact, changing the behavior will probably result in positive situations—for example, relating better with others. Through this process, clients learn once again the effects of the choices they continually make about life. Even more importantly, they see the power they have to change their beliefs, perceptions, and goals, and hence their feelings and actions as well.

The Adlerian orientation is primarily a motivation-modification system, not a behavior-modification system—that is, the focus is on changing attitudes, beliefs, perceptions, and goals, so that behavior will also change. This does not prevent the Adlerian counselor from suggesting from time to time "Act as if . . . ," encouraging the client to assume a certain behavior so as to start experiencing the world differently.

It is important to show clients how they create and maintain their own ineffectual approaches to the challenges of life. By creating a goal that is unattainable or by adopting a belief that is dysfunctional, people set themselves up for failure.

Damon believes "I can do as I please; I make my own rules" and also "I'm not as much as others." His goal is to find excitement. When things don't go well for him in school, he drops out. Not having salable skills, he gets a menial job that is everything but exciting or rewarding. To find excitement, he becomes involved with drugs. His belief that "I can make my own rules and do as I please" leads him to believe that he will not be caught.

The counselor's task is to help Damon see how these self-defeating beliefs get him in deep trouble and that they provide a false base of security. Damon needs to be helped to see that there are active, constructive ways of finding excitement, which will be rewarding instead of destructive. By changing his beliefs about himself and life in general, Damon will be able to consider a new and more challenging type of work and to develop confidence in his capacity to relate successfully to people.

> Maria believes, "It is dangerous to express feelings," "People are no good and treat me unfairly," "I must please others no matter what," and "If I'm not on top, I'm nothing." Her goal is to stay ahead of others by being right and in control. Because she is unwilling to express her feelings, she has difficulty in her social and family relationships. Her hiding behind a facade of inconsequential talk creates and maintains a wall between her and others. Her children don't respect her and keep alluding to how inadequately she provides for the family. Maria uses the children's attitude to fortify her belief that people treat her unfairly. Instead of expressing anger at her family's lack of appreciation, she dejectedly accepts their criticism.

If Maria is to lead a more functional and satisfying life, she must start to express her real feelings and stop pleasing others at her own expense. The counselor helps to point out ways she does this and encourages her to find specific new ways to express her feelings and to feel okay about herself even if she is not on top.

Dreikurs (1967b) states:

> To motivate reorientation, I employ a mirror technique confronting the patient with his goals and intentions. Moreno also employs a "mirror technique" for similar purposes in psychodrama. Interpretation of goals is singularly effective in stimulating change. When the patient begins to recognize his goals, his own conscience becomes a motivating factor. Adler called this process "spitting in the patient's soup." However, insight into goals and intentions is not merely restrictive; it makes the patient aware also of his ability to make decisions, of his freedom to choose his own direction. (p. 70)

The focus on change involves helping clients clearly see their self-defeating mistaken beliefs, mistaken ideas about human relationships, mistaken ideas about life's demands, and mistaken purposes and goals. When they see the interrelationships among these factors, clients are in a position to change and move in a positive direction.

Specific Strategies

Among the variety of strategies that can be incorporated in the Adlerian counseling process are the following. Each will be discussed briefly.

immediacy

encouragement

paradoxical intention

spitting in the client's soup

acting as if

catching oneself

creating movement

task setting and commitment

terminating and summarizing the interview

Immediacy Immediacy means expressing how you are experiencing the client in the here and now. Because the immediacy dimension has the potential to upset as well as to advance the relationship, it is usually approached tentatively. If the client has progressed in self-awareness and self-understanding, the communication of immediacy can be more direct.

Immediacy is used to help clients become aware of what they are communicating both verbally and nonverbally. Healthy, mature people communicate congruently. They say what they intend to say. In the immediacy aspect of the relationship, you make explicit the relationship between you and the client.

Ling: *I want to do something to help me get started; but it's no use. They are all ahead of me.*

Counselor: *You say you want to get started, but I get the impression from your tone of voice that you have given up and are still concerned with how you compare with others.*

In this example, you share your impression that the client is defeating himself.

Encouragement Encouragement focuses on helping clients become aware of their worth. By encouraging them, you help your clients recognize and own their strengths and assets, so they become aware of the power they have to make decisions and choices (Dinkmeyer, 1972).

One's identity is a product of interpersonal relationships, because the feedback one receives is internalized and creates identity. If someone feels discouraged and inadequate, the lack of self-esteem produces dysfunctional behavior and failure to become involved in the tasks of life. Encouragement is the most powerful procedure available for changing the client's beliefs.

Encouragement focuses on beliefs and self-perceptions. It searches intensely for assets and processes feedback so the client will become aware of her strengths. In a mistake-centered culture like ours, this approach violates norms by ignoring deficits and stressing assets. The counselor is concerned with changing the client's negative self-concept and anticipations.

Encouragement can take many forms, depending on the phase of the counseling process. At the beginning, you let your clients know you value them by really listening to their feelings and intentions, and stimulate their confidence by accepting them as full and equal participants in the process. In the assessment phase of counseling, which is designed to illuminate strengths, you recognize and encourage the clients' growing awareness of their power to choose and their attempts to change. In the reorientation phase, you promote change by stimulating the individual's courage. Thus, encouragement is a vital element of every aspect of the counseling process.

Briana: *School grades have little meaning for me. I could do it, but my teachers demand too much and go too fast.*

Counselor: *You feel you could do the work at a different pace.*

You sense the discouragement and value Briana's belief in her own ability. If she accepts her ability, then procedures for modifying the pace can be considered. You demonstrate that Briana has resources.

Paradoxical Intention Adler called the paradoxical intention "prescribing the symptom," and Dreikurs called it "antisuggestion." It is a technique in which clients are encouraged to emphasize or develop their symptoms even more. For example, if the child doesn't do her arithmetic homework, you might suggest that this is a good way to resist authority and encourage her not to do any schoolwork. If an individual bites two fingernails, you encourage biting even more nails.

Usually it is best to make the paradoxical recommendations for a specific period of time and treat them as an experiment. This process of experimentation encourages clients to see what they learn from the experience.

The paradoxical intention makes people dramatically aware of the reality of their situation and that they must accept the consequences of their behavior. When you confront clients with your paradoxical refusal to fight their behavior, the behavior becomes less attractive in the clients' eyes. This procedure implicitly indicates confidence that, when the individual sees the problem in a magnified perspective, she will choose to change her behavior. Also, this technique can make the symptoms appear so ridiculous that the client finally gives them up.

Kirk: *Mr. Hughey is very unfair. He bugs me all the time, and, when I talk back, he sends me to the principal.*

Counselor: *You feel that Mr. Hughey is unfair. But why do you cooperate with him?*

Kirk: *Cooperate? Ridiculous! I never do.*

Counselor: *It seems to me that you play his game. You say he gets you in trouble; but you could really defeat him if you didn't go for the bait. Can you imagine how he'd look if you didn't respond?*

You suggest doing exactly the opposite and "winning" by failing to cooperate with the teacher. Both student and teacher "win" with this paradoxical intention.

Adler and Dreikurs taught that to maintain a symptom, one must fight against it. The paradox is often effective because, when the client comes for help, the counselor tells her to go back and do what she was doing. By no longer fighting it, the client may be free to choose.

Spitting in the Client's Soup	Adler's technique—which he also referred to as "besmirching a clean conscience"—comes from the boarding-school practice of getting someone's food by spitting on it. It is one application of the Adlerian strategy of modifying behavior by changing its meaning to the person who produces it. The counselor must determine the purpose and payoff of the behavior and spoil the game by reducing the behaviors pleasure or usefulness in the client's eyes.

Sef:	*You've said that I don't function unless I can be first or best. I suppose I should give that up.*

Counselor:	*You can continue.*

Sef:	*I'm confused.*

Counselor:	*All I'm saying is that you always have to be so careful about being first that you don't try a lot of things you'd enjoy. But you are entitled to miss them if you want to protect yourself.*

You point out that Sef has a right to insist on being first, but you also clearly show how that approach restricts him. The choice is still with the client, but it is now less palatable.

Acting as If	This is an action-oriented procedure used with clients who plead, "If only I could. . . ." It consists of suggesting that, for the next week, the client can "act as if"—behave how one wishes. The client will probably protest that it would only be an act, and not the real person. This is how Mosak and Dreikurs (1973) suggest you deal with such protestations: Show the client that acting isn't always a pretense. In fact, action comes only when one agrees to behave in that manner.

Drew:	*I just can't get acquainted with girls. If only I could be like Dirk and walk up to a group and talk about the game.*

Counselor:	*It's difficult for you to talk with girls. For this week, I'd like you to act as if you were Dirk and just begin by talking about the game.*

You suggest a limited task, such as acting as if Drew had the courage to talk to girls. The expectation is that the plan will work. If it doesn't, you explore what kept it from being a good experience.

Catching Oneself	Through confrontation and interpretation, clients become aware of their goals. Once they decide to change, the counselor suggests that they learn to "catch themselves" in any behavior they want to change. At first, they will catch themselves too late and recognize that they have again fallen into the trap of seeking attention or trying to prove their power, for example. With awareness and practice, clients learn to anticipate the situation—both their self-defeating perceptions and the behavior that ensues. As a result, they can learn to avoid the situation or to change their behavior when they are in a situation that tends to stimulate the behavior in question. This approach requires a sense of humor and the ability to laugh at one's ineffective behavior instead of becoming discouraged about it.

Kirsten: *I know I shouldn't, but I seem to keep getting trapped into power struggles with Jack.*

Counselor: *You recognize that he stimulates you to prove you are right.*

Kirsten: *Yes, we get into lots of quarrels, mainly over who's right.*

Counselor: *I suggest that, as you sense a struggle coming, you catch yourself—become aware that you're about to get involved in being right and more powerful—and just withdraw by refusing to get involved in the argument.*

Creating Movement   The counseling process reorients clients toward a new perspective by helping them understand the purpose of their behavior. Often this movement occurs by mutual consent and interaction. When it does not, you have alternatives by which you can create movement.

No tactic, strategy, or other counselor intervention can succeed unless the client wishes to succeed. Strategies and tactics that can effectively move the client depend on the quality of the counselor/client relationship. The counselor needs to enlist the cooperation of their clients, whatever their resistance to the reorientation process may be. Clients may lose faith in the therapist if they perceive any of the counseling techniques as threatening (Dreikurs, 1967b). Movement tactics, such as surprise, should be used judiciously. Indiscriminate use of movement tactics—that is, a use that fails to consider the appropriateness of the tactic to each setting—will result in failure.

When you surprise a client, the client is hearing and seeing unexpected counselor behaviors. The purpose of surprise is to create movement by drawing dramatic attention to a specific behavior of the client.

One form of surprise allows you to agree, for the moment, with the client's faulty belief.

Claudia: *Whenever I go out with boys, they always criticize me. I'll never date again!*

Counselor: *Yes, I agree. Don't ever date critical men again. They can't possibly have anything valid to say.*

You have adopted the client's point of view, advocating her despairing remark about dating. Because the client has dealt with the issue in absolute terms ("never"), you reflect her certainty ("Don't date critical men again"). By temporarily agreeing with the faulty belief, you have focused on the belief and diplomatically pointed to the problems inherent in that belief.

Task Setting and Commitment   Task setting and commitment are the steps clients take to do something specific about their problems. Thus, these steps take clients beyond simply considering alternatives and lead them to actual implementation of change. To be effective, the task should be specific and chosen by the client. You can, however, assist the client by creating awareness of the various alternatives.

It is essential that the task be for a limited period of time. Clients are more resistant if they think they are signing up for life. When clients are successful at a specific task and within a limited period of time, you have something concrete to encourage. As previously discussed, tasks can be considered "experiments."

The step of setting tasks and developing specific commitments helps clients translate new beliefs and feelings into action, generates energy for the process, and provides feedback for evaluating progress. When the task is not accomplished, you help the clients evaluate the effectiveness of the plan. If the plan is not effective or appropriate, revise it.

Task setting involves helping the client establish a specific task. The goals of the tasks should be realistic, attainable, and measurable, so that, at the next meeting, progress can be discussed in terms of specifics.

Terminating and Summarizing the Interview   Effectively closing an interview is often a problem for the inexperienced counselor. You should have some idea of the minimum and maximum time the interview should last. Generally, 30 minutes with children and 45 to 50 minutes with adolescents and adults are sufficient counseling periods. Clients should know when the interview begins and when it will be over. It is important to establish these limits not only for practical purposes (such as being available for the next client) but also because clients often postpone talking about their major concerns. If they are aware of time limitations, clients will tend to get to the important issues more quickly.

Termination deals with what has been discussed, not with new material. If the client brings up a new topic, you can suggest, "That might be a good place to begin next week." Asking the client to summarize the interview helps you have a clear picture of the client's perceptions and intentions. An effective technique is asking the client to complete the sentence, "I learned . . ."

In this chapter we have considered the basic elements of the helping relationship and the perceptual organization of effective helpers. Goals of counseling, a theory of change, and a number of counseling techniques have been described. The techniques must become a part of the counselor, not merely a professional procedure. They require a sensitive, empathic listener who uses active methods because he cares and because they are more likely to produce movement and change on the part of the client.

REFERENCES

Adler, A. (1958). *The practice and theory of individual psychology.* Patterson, NJ: Littlefield, Adams.

Allen, T. W. (1971a). Adlerian interview strategies for behavior change. The *Counseling Psychologist, 3*(1), 40–48.

Allen, T. W. (1971b). The individual psychology of Alfred Adler: An item of history and a promise of a revolution. *The Counseling Psychologist, 3*(1), 3–24.

Carkhuff, R. R. (1973). *The art of problem solving.* Amherst, MA: Human Resource Development Press.

Dinkmeyer, D. (1972). Use of the encouragement process in Adlerian counseling. *Personnel and Guidance Journal, 51*(3), 177–181.

Dreikurs, R. (1957). *Psychology in the classroom.* New York: Harper & Row.

Dreikurs, R. (1967a). A psychological interview in medicine. *Journal of Individual Psychology, 10,* 99–122.

Dreikurs, R. (1967b). *Psychodynamics, psychotherapy, and counseling.* Dubuque, IA: Kendall/Hunt.

Eckstein, D., Baruth, L., & Mahrer, D. (1975). *Lifestyle: What it is and how to do it.* Chicago: Alfred Adler Institute.

Gushurst, R. S. (1971). The technique, utility, and validity of lifestyle analysis. *The Counseling Psychologist, 3*(1), 30–40.

Kefir, N. (1972). *Priorities.* Unpublished manuscript.

Kefir, N., & Corsini, R. J. (1974). Dispositional sets: A contribution to typology. *Journal of Individual Psychology, 30,* 163–178.

Kern, R. M. (1982, 1997). *Lifestyle scale.* Coral Springs, FL: CMTI Press.

Kern, R. M., Wheeler, M. S., Curlette, W. L. (1993). *BASIS-A Inventory.* Highlands, NC: TRT Associates.

Kopp, R., & Dinkmeyer, D. (1975). Early recollections in lifestyle assessment and counseling. *The School Counselor, 23*(1), 22–27.

Langenfeld, S., & Main, F. (1983). Personality priorities: A factor analytic study. *Journal of Individual Psychology, 39,* 40–51.

Mosak, H. H. (1958). Early recollections as a projective technique. *Journal of Projective Techniques, 22,* 302–311.

Mosak, H. H. (1971). Lifestyle. In A. G. Nikelly (Ed.), *Techniques for behavior change.* Springfield, IL: Charles C Thomas.

Mosak, H. H., & Dreikurs, R. (1973). Adlerian psychotherapy. In R. Corsini (Ed.), *Current psychotherapies.* Itasca, IL: Peacock.

Mosak, H. H., & Gushurst, R. S. (1977). What patients say and what they mean. In H. H. Mosak (Ed.), *On purpose.* Chicago: Alfred Adler Institute.

Nikelly, A. G., & Bostrom, J. A. (1971). Psychotherapy as reorientation and readjustment. In A. G. Nikelly (Ed.), *Techniques for behavior change.* Springfield, IL: Charles C. Thomas.

Nikelly, A. G., & Verger, D. (1971). Early recollections. In A. G. Nikelly (Ed.), *Techniques for behavior change.* Springfield, IL: Charles C Thomas.

Shulman, B. H. (1962). The family constellation in personality diagnosis. *Journal of Individual Psychology, 18,* 35–47.

Shulman, B. H. (1973). Confrontation techniques in Adlerian psychotherapy. In B. H. Shulman (Ed.), *Contributions to individual psychology.* Chicago: Alfred Adler Institute.

Sweeney, T. J. (1975). *Adlerian counseling.* Boston: Houghton Mifflin.

Watkins, C. E. Jr. (1985). Early recollections as a projective technique in counseling: An Adlerian view. *American Mental Health Counselors Association Journal, 7,* 32–40.

Wheeler, M. S., Kern, R., & Curlette, W. (1986). Factor analytic scales designed to measure Adlerian lifestyle themes. *Journal of Individual Psychology, 42,* 1–16.

CHAPTER 7

Psychoeducation and Psychoeducational Interventions

A dlerian psychology has a long tradition of educational interventions. Parents, teachers, and counselors all benefit from this emphasis on education. This chapter emphasizes methods of psychoeducation intervention with parents, some possible problem areas, and usual challenges across the spectrum of psychoeducation opportunities.

The term *psychoeducation* (PE) has had connotations ranging from clinics offering remediation of learning disabilities, to patient education in medical settings, to school curriculums for the affective domain. PE has become synonymous with a variety of adjunctive treatment methods: homework (L'Abate, 1986; Last, 1985); bibliotherapy (Gambrill, 1985); enrichment (Guerney, 1977; Smith, Shoffuer, & Scott, 1978); and social skills training (Curran & Monti, 1983). Interest in PE is increasing among marital and family therapists, particularly in integrating PE with marital therapy (Guerney, Brock, & Coufol, 1986; Carlson & Dinkmeyer, 1986).

THE PSYCHOEDUCATIONAL MODEL

Adler can be considered the first educator from the psychology field. His public demonstrations were intended to inform and educate those in the audience. In addition to being helpful to the patient, those in attendance were able to learn about the process through Adler's demonstration of concepts and techniques.

Adlerians continue this process of public demonstrations in a variety of areas. Most commonly, education is presented to parents, teachers, and students.

What Is Psychoeducation?

Psychoeducation is not advice giving. A barrage of information avenues give advice—books, videos, audiotapes. If the information is not anchored in a strong therapeutic relationship, it is not psychoeducation. And while psychoeducation is not a substitute for a good counseling relationship, it can serve as a concrete avenue for the patient's ability to change during the time between sessions.

Advice giving is a lose–lose situation. If the therapist gives good advice, the client learns to come back to the therapist for the next answer. In effect, the client is being given fish instead of being taught how to fish. If the therapist's advice is no good, the client can say the therapist is ineffective, or, even more detrimental, may conclude that the therapist is incompetent, and become even more discouraged.

Twenty years ago, Guerney, Stollak, and Guerney (1970) strongly argued for the adoption of a psychoeducational mode. The PE model was clearly articulated by Authier, Gustafson, Guerney, and Kasdorf (1975). According to these authors, the uniqueness of the psychoeducational model was its opposition to the traditional medical model of psychopathology and psychotherapy. Advocates of the psychoeducational model framed their approach, not in terms of pathology–diagnosis–prescription–therapy–cured, but in terms of the teaching of personal and interpersonal attitudes and skills which the individual could apply to solve present and future psychological problems, as well as enhance life satisfaction.

The role of the therapist working within the psychoeducation model is basically analogous to that of the teacher. Clients in psychoeducational therapy are viewed and treated as students capable of learning and applying the skills taught, rather than as patients whose symptoms need to be removed by an expert healer. Of course, what sets therapists who use psychoeducational methods apart from typical classroom teachers is the affective–behavioral–interpersonal nature of what is being taught.

The origins of PE can be traced back to the traditions of humanistic psychology and behavioral psychotherapy. In the humanistic tradition, Carl Rogers can be credited for his role in liberating "therapists" from the pathology of the medical model. Rogers' insistence on referring to individuals in therapy as "clients" instead of "patients" clearly represented this new point of view. In addition, Rogers believed that clients have the capacity for self-direction and for dealing constructively with their problems.

Yet the therapist using PE differs from Rogers with regard to treatment. For Rogers, the most important function of the therapist was to provide an interpersonal environment in which clients could begin to experience their own sense of worth and significance. Within this environment, clients could begin to understand the nature of their problems through talking. Rogers believed that under these conditions the clients' own capacity for growth would be unblocked and they could begin to become their own therapist. For the therapist using PE, on the other hand, the best way to assist clients to grow and become their own counselors is to give them an understanding and competence in using specific, effective techniques and methods for changing their behavior. Carkhuff (1971), another proponent of the humanistic approach, recognized the value of combining understanding with competence by describing training as a mode of treatment.

The development of PE is also indebted to the behavioral orientation. Principles and techniques of the behavioral concepts of modeling and reinforcement are central to the practice of PE. Not only are modeling and reinforcement practiced by therapists in teaching PE, but they are also taught to clients to help them learn new skills, to change their own behavior, and then to help others change their behaviors. Another legacy of the behavioral approach has involved the development of modular units in PE programs. Several years ago, behavior therapists began to recognize that the teaching of a single social skill such as relaxation had limited use unless it was combined with a number of other related social or coping skills. Cautela (1967) proposed teaching clients five self-control skills: (1) relaxation, (2) desensitization, (3) thought stopping, (4) covert sensitization, and (5) assertiveness. Clinicians practicing PE have also found it necessary and useful to develop modular units to use with clients and couples.

WORKING WITH FAMILIES

Parents are responsible for the psychological environment in which a child is raised. This is a significant influence on the individual's development. The Adlerian term *family atmosphere* refers to parental decisions about values. As pointed out earlier, the child's position in the family constellation also influences growth, and interaction with siblings helps to develop certain beliefs about how to get along with others. When the family structure and atmosphere are troubled and unhealthy, a child's choices are necessarily affected.

Parents are the earliest and often the only models for a child. It is from parents that beliefs, attitudes, and techniques are chosen. The parent's agreement or disagreement create the atmosphere of the home, i.e., whether it is peaceful or warlike; cheerful or depressing; warm, close, and involved; or cold, distant, and detached.

It has long been apparent to Adlerians that education is necessary for mothers, fathers, and others in child-rearing roles. Our biological heredity does not guarantee the necessary skills. Past experiences are often the basis on which we raise children. If parents and other parental figures are unsuccessful in their own experience, their children may be discouraged or, at least, without a good model for dealing with the multiple challenges of parenting. Family of origin experiences, for better and worse, profoundly influence the next generation's family dynamics.

In our society, the "average parent" and the "typical home" are becoming increasingly rare. The nuclear family is only one of a growing number of family types. Grandparents and other relatives often assume parenting roles. It is almost impossible to draw a meaningful picture of the "average" home and parent. Less than 4 percent of the residences in the 1990 census contained a working father, caregiver mother (both on their first marriage) and two children. Marriage, remarriage and divorce rates seem to hover at the 50/50 success rate. The number of children in a family is decreasing. Clearly, the family is changing.

Traditional autocratic parenting roles are often not successful. Although many parents grew up in comparatively autocratic family atmospheres, this no longer reflects effective relationship beliefs. The basic shift toward equality in our society has not spared the family.

Women and children, once submissive minorities, have a status equal to that of the head of the household. The autocrat's approach of "Do as I say," which implies a superior/inferior relationship, is no longer appropriate or effective. Today's children are unwilling to be less than equal. When told to "jump," instead of asking "How high?" today's child asks "Why?" The child's statement reflects a belief in equality and entitlement.

Parents therefore need to learn techniques and approaches which are effective in this environment. The new skills help to create a more cooperative and democratic relationship with their children. The movement toward equality can be beneficial for both parent and child only if the parent develops the necessary skills of listening, communicating, motivating, encouraging, and helping the child assume responsibility.

Adler's Work with Families

Adler began to work with families by establishing the first child guidance clinic in Vienna. Although the first public demonstrations of ongoing cases were with problem children, the public nature of this counseling allowed many "normal" parents and teachers to learn preventive methods.

By 1930, there were 32 clinics conducted by schools and parent-teacher associations. Adler's assumption that educational approaches were the most effective treatments for emotional disturbances spurred Rudolf Dreikurs to continue the development of educational demonstrations and written materials. Dreikurs made significant contributions throughout North America, Israel and Europe in a lifetime devoted to psychoeducation.

Rationale for Parent Education

The goal of parent education is to improve the relationship between parent and child. This is accomplished by offering alternatives in discipline, motivation, and communication ideas for parents. Parent education brings an openness to new ideas and techniques. This is crucial in resolving current problems and reducing future ones.

Rather than criticize or disprove parents' ideas, the parent education process offers new ideas. Parents then decide which of the new ideas fit their needs, belief system, and goals for their children.

Most parent education is presented in groups. Parent education groups do not prescribe "cures" or perform therapy. Instead, they allow parents to use powerful and often ignored forces in traditional learning settings. It does not consist of lectures or advice. Parent education is essentially interaction among group members, facilitated by a leader. Counselors and other helping professionals are the usual leaders of parent education groups.

Traditionally, Adlerian family education centers have provided education groups. These settings now include churches, parishes, and synagogues; schools and alternative schools, including adult night education classes; outreach programs by residential adolescent psychiatric hospitals, mental health agencies and Employee Assistance Program (EAP) contracts. Parent education is also found in judicial systems as part of a mandated, remedial treatment approach for abusive or neglectful parents. It is found in the military family service centers and individual practitioner's offices. Parent education now reaches parents through diverse professions and institutions. Through education, parents influence the quality of their relationship with their children.

In parent education, the sphere of influence extends beyond the group, because the sessions also have an influence on the participants' spouses, children, and children's teachers. The number of people who are directly influenced by a parent study group that meets for an hour or two each week can easily reach 50 or more.

Basic Adlerian Theory for Parent Education

One of the goals of parent education is to teach, in simple and understandable terms, a theory of human behavior. A child's misbehavior is best understood by identifying its goal. Once we identify the purpose of the behavior parents can develop alternatives, which, in turn, will encourage alternative behaviors in the child.

It is important to discuss and understand this basic theory as soon as possible in the parent-education group. Often the first several sessions focus on the purpose of misbehavior. Topics in the next sessions include (1) emotions as a purposeful tool, (2) I-messages, (3) encouragement, and (4) alternatives to punishment. The objective of ensuing meetings is to focus on specific techniques and skills.

The most widely used educational programs are the *Systematic Training For Effective Parenting* (STEP) programs (Dinkmeyer et al., 1997). Three books from these programs address the needs of parents by age group: *Parenting Young Children* (ages 0–6), *The Parent's Handbook* (ages 6–12), *Parenting Teenagers* (age 13 and older).

The Four Goals of Misbehavior

The first step in parent education is to understand the four goals of children's misbehavior. Dreikurs (1991) classified all child misbehavior into four categories, each corresponding to the goal of the misbehavior: (1) attention, (2) power, (3) revenge, and (4) display of inadequacy.

The idea that a child's misbehavior has a goal is often new information for a parent. They find their children's actions confusing and annoying and, in extreme cases, a cause of much frustration and bewilderment. When parents don't understand the purposive nature of behavior in general and of misbehavior in particular, they may resort to extremely damaging measures, such as physical or psychological abuse.

Although parents may at first react to the four goals with confusion or even skepticism, they learn to identify the goals by using two techniques: their own response to the misbehavior and the child's response to the parent's chosen behavior. This approach allows parents to use themselves as accurate indicators of the child's behavior. The four goals are discussed in detail in the following section.

Attention Each of the four goals of misbehavior reflects a degree of discouragement in the child. The first goal, attention, has many positive aspects and is particularly appealing to children as they explore and discover the world around them. "Are you noticing me? Am I still here?" express the purpose of the child's attention-seeking behavior.

Chantel, a 3-year-old, adores her mother and follows her around the house whenever possible. At times she comes up to her mother and unties one of her shoelaces or tugs at her slacks. Although annoyed, the mother generally acknowledges Chantel's behavior with a friendly "Hey!" or a slightly less friendly "Stop it!" depending on how annoying the attention-getting behavior is. Chantel is pleased that her mother recognizes her efforts to attract her attention, and she stops her efforts whenever she realizes that her mother doesn't enjoy what she is doing.

In this example, the mother is *annoyed* by the child's behavior and probably confused by her daughter's seemingly pointless efforts to annoy her. Chantel's response to her mother's annoyance is to temporarily stop the behavior for the simple reason that she has achieved her goal: attention.

Once parents recognize their children's ability to make their own decisions based on their own subjective needs, misbehavior makes as much sense to parents as it does to the children. This is true even in the more "unacceptable" behaviors of power and revenge.

Power The second goal, power, is sought by children who exaggerate their need to be in control. The power-seeking child is guided by the faulty belief "I can count in this world only if I am in control of everybody else."

Parental reaction to this type of misbehavior is often anger and a feeling of "Who is in charge here, you or me?" The autocratic parent, a model many parents experienced as children, often becomes blinded by power-oriented misbehavior, since such behavior challenges the parent's autocratic rule and authority.

Parents who choose to struggle with the child to establish who is really more powerful may win the battle but lose the war. The child who loses a power struggle over bedtime, playtime, and other issues becomes convinced of the importance of power. Mother or father show, by struggling for power, that it is indeed important to be more powerful than the child, so in the eyes of the child, power becomes even more attractive.

Revenge The goal of revenge is the result of a child feeling hurt, betrayed, or otherwise unfairly treated. Children who seek revenge are trying to get even with the person responsible for the "injustice" they have suffered. Because it is unlikely that children are able to retaliate directly, they will try to get even in other ways.

Children are aware of what misbehaviors are particularly unacceptable to their parents and may choose to use one of them, such as abusive language, in revenge. The parent, unaware of the goal of the child's behavior, is likely to be confused by what appears as the child's senseless need to hurt and often returns the revenge in kind, thus perpetuating the cycle.

Display of Inadequacy   The four goals of misbehavior are expressions of a child's increasing discouragement about belonging in a positive way. The fourth goal expresses the most extreme discouragement. This goal is sometimes accurately called fear of failure or seeking to give up.

> Blake is the youngest of three brothers. On weekends, his father often takes the children to the basketball court, shooting and scrimmaging with the boys. Blake hasn't yet mastered the art of dribbling the ball. Whenever he gets the ball, he quickly passes it. Soon the weekend comes when Blake doesn't want to go to the court. "It's too hot out. Besides, I'm no good anyway." He has competed but, discouraged at his lack of progress, has decided to give up the pursuit altogether. A child at "goal 4" believes they are not able and therefore do not try. If the parent can be convinced that the lack of effort is also a lack of ability, no expectations from the parent will be made.

Children may seek any of the four goals, depending on how they interpret the opportunity. Misbehavior does not necessarily progress through all four goals, beginning with attention and ending with display of inadequacy. The idea *"nobody throws away a behavior that works"* helps to illustrate the concept of goal-directed misbehavior.

The child's misbehavior will stop when the parent chooses to respond to the situation in a different way. Blake's father, for example, must recognize his son's goal and extreme discouragement with his basketball abilities. While Blake may not necessarily be aware of his goal, he is aware of its consequences. If he succeeds in convincing his family that he is inadequate, he will be excused from the embarrassment of being the "worst" basketball player, when in fact he is only the youngest. The father's corrective strategy for his son's behavior would include encouraging positive efforts, modifying the games so that Blake can compete on an equal level, and other efforts that act "as if" the child is capable.

Books for Parent Groups

Parent education has many avenues, including book study groups. A typical format for a book study group session includes five basic topics: (1) discussion of the activity and homework from the previous session, (2) discussion of the current reading assignment, (3) a practice exercise, (4) summary, and (5) reading and other homework assignments for the following session. The leader may rely on prepared questions to allow discussion of the specific technique presented in the session—for example, natural and logical consequences.

Leadership also involves moving the group from discussion of theory into practical application of the theory to their own relationships. The practice exercise allows participants to work with a specific concept or skill, such as reflective listening.

Because the group implies a work commitment for each member, the leader must skillfully make sure each member has the opportunity to share new experiences. The leader may also develop a group expectation that reading and trying new skills are necessary activities and that involvement outside the group session is also part of the process.

Parent groups that use books have functioned successfully for many years. Their advantage lies in the availability of a single source for reading and referral. The drawback is that this type of group demands inherently motivated, literate participants.

Parent C-Groups

C-Groups Parent C-groups are an adaptation of teacher C-groups and have similar goals—going beyond the study of principles into the sharing of experiences (Dinkmeyer, Jr., et al., 1994). Awareness of how we function and how our attitudes, beliefs, and feelings affect our relationship with our children is an essential element of the C-group. The C stands for the many forces that occur in the group:

Consultation provided and received by all group members

Collaboration on the concerns of group members who work together as equals

Cooperation among members, so that they can offer and receive encouragement

Clarification of the concepts under discussion as well as of member's belief systems and feelings

Confrontation of the purpose, attitudes, beliefs, and feelings that interfere with successful modification of the parent/child relationship; if change is to occur, confrontation of old, useless beliefs must take place, and a norm of confrontation—not to prove who is right but to share discrepancies and observations—is established by the group leader at the beginning of the group

Confidentiality assures that members' concerns will be shared only by the group

Commitment to the task confronting each member, which go beyond reading the assignment and discussing it at the next meeting

Change the purpose of involvement in the group, assessed by each member in specific terms, from the point of view of both rate and targets

STEP Programs The Early Childhood STEP, STEP and STEP/Teen (Systematic Training for Effective Parenting) programs are the most widely used and researched Adlerian parent-education materials (Dinkmeyer, et al., 1997, 1997, 1998). They have reached more than 4 million parents: STEP has been translated in to Spanish, Japanese, German, and Greek. The publisher reports more than 50 research studies on the STEP program.

The group experience provided by STEP programs is based on sharing a parents' handbook, and videotaped examples and exercises. Discussion rules also structure the group experiences. A leader's resource guide covers the format for each of the seven sessions in each program. The guide also contains additional information on necessary leader skills such as dealing with problem members, optional handouts for parents, publicity materials, an assessment tool, videoscript, and session guidelines. The leader has the option of using the prepared session guidelines or using professional judgment to move the group in particular discussions.

Starting Groups

Organizers of group programs for parents may face the problem of having more prospective participants than can be accommodated in a single group. Groups should not exceed 12 participants, so that members can enjoy the advantages of the small group. It is important that participants have children of about the same age, so that the basis of their experiences and challenges is somewhat similar.

STEP programs provide an introductory 8-minute videotape that outlines the focus of the program and some of the topics. Parents get a sample of the program and find that their need for education is not a sign of weakness, but rather a sign of intelligent commitment to growth.

This point is especially important and deserves the leader's full attention. In the absence of past "explanations," parents must deal with the many possible reasons for becoming involved in an education program. Often a parent rationalizes that "It worked for my parents, so it'll work for me," yet realizes that a defensive posture does not work. In such cases, the leader must help the person appreciate the shift from autocracy to democracy that has left many parents without effective strategies for dealing with their children. It is not that parents lack ability, but that they lack skills and models. It is up to the leader to point out this essential difference and the implications to parents.

Group-Leadership Skills

Parent group leaders must use certain skills to make group experiences constructive. These skills are similar to those required in other group settings, but the focus is on learning and on the universalizing quality of being a parent.

Structuring Structuring allows the group to know exactly what will be expected of each member. Meeting times and places, length of sessions, and purposes and goals will all be used to structure the group. Structuring occurs during the group's first sessions. As the group progresses, the leader must be constantly aware of what is going on in the group, so that she can determine whether the current situation is in the best interest of the group's stated goals and purposes.

Universalizing Universalizing helps members become aware that their experiences are similar to others'. Groups provide many opportunities for group members to realize how much they have in common. It is up to the leader to tap this well of common experiences and bring the similarities to the surface for everybody's benefit. When a member shares a problem with the group, the leader can elicit reactions from the others by asking, "Has anyone had a similar difficulty?" or some other open-ended question that invites participants to share experiences. Often a parent reacts spontaneously in agreement, verbally or nonverbally, and the leader can then encourage additional response from that member.

Linking   Linking is the process of identifying common elements in the group members' comments. A leader often finds that an idea keeps coming up time and time again—a "theme" of the members' experiences. With parent groups, this may be "Bedtime is usually pretty difficult" or "Sometimes, spanking is really the only way to get the message across." It is important for the leader to use these themes in positive ways to link members during the early stages of the group. Linking and universalizing promote cohesiveness, a feeling of togetherness, and a sense of purpose. Once a theme is expressed and detected, the leader can articulate the common element with comments such as, "I sense that both Don and Deborah feel concerned about their middle child." The group can then briefly discuss the problems common to most middle children and possible new ways to deal with them.

Focusing on the Positive   It may be difficult for parents to see the positive side of their children while they are immersed in a power struggle or other conflict. Yet the parents' ability to focus on the positive and to encourage their child's skills and assets often helps to change the child's behavior. The leader can model encouraging behavior by looking for assets and efforts. Parents often don't see improvement until others in the group help them realize that changes have taken place.

Commitment   Leaders help stimulate commitment to the group. It is important that the person make a commitment to attend all sessions, participate in discussions, and apply the ideas in their family relationships. This homework is an essential part of the group process. A leader asks for specific commitments at the end of the session and, at the start of the next session, asks members to share their experiences.

Summarizing   The summary at the end of the session deals with feelings and ideas as they occurred at any time during the session. It may deal with the content of the meeting or with the commitment each member has made for the upcoming week. The leader can begin by asking each participant to complete the sentence "I learned. . . ." This procedure allows members to share what they have gained during the session and gives the leader an opportunity to correct or clarify confusions or doubts.

Encouragement   Encouragement is a skill that parents may find especially difficult. It is often mistaken for praise, a more widespread form of motivation in our culture. The essential difference between the two is that praise generally focuses on external results, while encouragement recognizes inherent abilities and positive expectations.

Group Stages

What happens in a parent education group? While groups reflect the unique mix of the leader and participants, we find they follow three predictable stages:

I. "Fix the Child"—Parents come to the group looking for ways to change some of their children's inappropriate behaviors. They expect the leader to tell them how to accomplish this task. The change in the relationship is expected to come from the child.

II. "You mean I have to change?!"—In the transition to this insight, the parents learn the most effective results occur when they are responsible for their own behaviors. To make changes in the relationship, parents must feel encouraged to begin to do something different. If a parent has little flexibility or courage to change, they will be most likely to drop out of the group at this point.

III. "We're working!"—The parents are encouraged. Life with the children and teens is improving as each finds some aspect of the new ideas to apply to their families. In this final stage of the group, it is often difficult to end the group because parents feel genuine support from the group.

Additional Psychoeducation Materials

The authors have developed a variety of psychoeducation materials for many other populations. Examples include marital education through Training in Marriage Enrichment (TIME) (Dinkmeyer & Carlson, 1984); for teachers in Systematic Training for Effective Teaching (STET) (Dinkmeyer, McKay, & Dinkmeyer, 1980); for adolescents in Preparing Responsible and Effective Parents (PREP) (Dinkmeyer et al., 1985); and elementary school children through Developing Understanding of Self and Others (DUSO) (Dinkmeyer & Dinkmeyer, 1980). The materials were all first-authored by Don Dinkmeyer Sr. His contribution to Individual Psychology through educational programs has been immense.

PSYCHOEDUCATION IN THE TREATMENT OF COUPLES

Levant (1986) heralded PE as a "new professional field" emerging within marital and family therapy. Actually, twenty years before that, Bach and Wyden (1968) advocated "fair fighting." David Mace began publishing about marriage enrichment in the early 1960s. Guerney's classic text on Relationship Enhancement (1977) was one of the first primers on skills training with couples. In addition, Marriage Encounter and a host of other PE and enrichment programs have been developed and well-received by both professionals and the public.

Guerney, Brock, and Coufol (1986) note that marital therapists who follow the PE model help couples focus on positive relationship goals instead of diagnosing the faults of the relationship. PE therapists help couples define the kind of relationship they would like to have and then teach them the skills to reach those goals. The ". . . marital therapist does not use the curative, subtractive model of traditional medicine, but strives to add knowledge, skills, and confidence in dealing with a loved one. The teaching, enrichment, wholistic goal becomes the major goal of the marital therapist. The appropriate professional model here is not the physician, but the teacher" (Guerney, Brock, & Coufol, 1986).

Guerney (1977) was the first marital therapist using PE to catalogue a number of relationship attitude and skill training modules relevant to working with couples. Guerney's work has been imitated, elaborated, and researched by many in the intervening years. Later in this chapter, several representative PE programs for couples will be highlighted.

THE RELATIONSHIP BETWEEN PE AND MARITAL THERAPY

PE overlaps with but is somewhat different from traditional conceptions of marital and family therapy. Doherty and Baird (1987) describe a five-level model that delineates the relationship between psychoeducational approach and marital and family therapy:

Level One   This level represents individual psychological intervention with little or no thought about the family.

Level Two   This refers to active involvement with couples or family around cognitive but not affective issues. A lecture or consultation session in which information is being provided to a couple would be an example of this.

Level Three   This level involves cognitive information plus an affective component where couples could be invited to share how they relate personally through the content of a lecture or a consultation.

Level Four   This level is the proper domain of PE. In PE the couple or family has committed themselves to a particular number of sessions focusing on specific topics with an educational as well as affective and expressive components. Information, attitude formation, and skills training are the main focus of PE sessions.

Level Five   This represents marital or family therapy proper. Therapy would be defined as a more intensive and intrusive work that potentially and if necessary can deal with anything in the couples' lives. It is apt to be longer and more open-ended than PE.

Doherty clearly articulates differences among these five levels of intervention. The Family Systems Training program used by Guerin, Fay, Borden, & Kautto (1987) illustrates the clear distinction between psychoeducation for couples and couples therapy. However, it is quite common to see a blurring between Doherty's levels four and five.

The Effectiveness of PE with Couples

Numerous psychoeducational programs have focused on marital and family enrichment. But are these programs effective? Giblin, Sprenkle, and Sheehan (1985), reported the results of the sophisticated meta-analysis of 23 programs. They noted a mean effect size 44, meaning that the "average" program participant changed for the better more than 67 percent of the persons who did not participate. Giblin's data also challenges the clinical lore that enrichment programs are not effective with "clinical" populations. Other data also suggest that education is strikingly effective with severely troubled couples, even more so than with nonclinical populations (Ross, Baker, & Guerney, 1985).

In fact, psychoeducational interventions have been shown to be so potent in the treatment of psychiatric disorders in couples and families that they have become the primary mode of treatment in some programs (Anderson, Reiss, & Hogarty, 1986).

CRITIQUES OF PE

PE approaches to marriage and family have been criticized as being unrealistically optimistic and too focused on the strengths of the couple or family. On the other hand, marital and family therapy have been criticized for their emphasis on pathological deficits. Doherty and Bowman (1989) note that those using PE need to become more aware of the dark side of couples and families while family therapists need to become more aware of the light side.

It may be helpful to note that there are certain factors working against the adoption of the PE approach. Authier, Gustafson, Guerney, and Kasdorf (1975) point out the difficulty that many therapists have in forsaking the familiar doctor–patient role associated with the medical model. These roles have and continue to accord the therapist with a considerable amount of prestige and power. Doherty and Bowman (1989) note that the more the therapist adheres to the medical model the more difficult it is for the therapist to be influenced by valuable aspects of the psychoeducational approach.

In addition to power and prestige issues, there is the matter of third-party reimbursement. Some insurance companies have refused to pay for psychotherapeutic services that appear to be educational in nature. The potential power of economics in maintaining support for the medical model cannot be underestimated. Perhaps this is why many therapists have chosen to use PE as an adjunct for couples or family therapy.

A final criticism of PE involves the clinical dangers of reductionism. Hunter, Hoffnung, and Ferholt (1988) describe some of the dangers inherent in an exclusive use of the psychoeducational approach, particularly with severely disturbed families. These authors note that it is possible that psychoeducation increases the use of denial regarding emotional pain and may actually engender pseudomutuality. In contrast, they proposed a nonreductionistic approach to couple and family treatment in which the psychoeducational and psychoanalytic approaches are used conjointly.

REFERENCES

Anderson, C., Reiss, D., & Hogarty, G. (1986). *Schizophrenia and the family: A practitioner's guide to psychoeducation and management*. New York: Guilford Press.

Authier, J., Gustafson, K., Guerney, B., & Kasdorf, J. (1975). The psychological practitioner as teacher: A theoretical historical and practical view. *The Counseling Psychologist, 5*(2), 31–50.

Bach, G. R., & Wyden, P. (1968). *The intimate enemy*. New York: William Morrow.

Carkhuff, R. (1971). Training as a mode of treatment. *Journal of Counseling Psychology, 18,* 123–131.

Carlson, J., & Dinkmeyer, D. (1986). TIME for a better marriage. *Journal of Psychotherapy and the Family, 2,* 19–28.

Cautela, J. (1967). Covert sensitization. *Psychological Record, 20,* 459–468.

Curran, J., & Monti, P. (Eds.). (1983). *Social skills training: A practical handbook for assessment and treatment*. New York: Guilford Press.

Dinkmeyer, D., & Dinkmeyer, D. Jr. (1980). *Developing understanding of self and others.* Circle Pines, MN: American Guidance Service.

Dinkmeyer, D., McKay, D., & Dinkmeyer, D. Jr. (1980). *Systematic training for effective teaching.* Circle Pines, MN: American Guidance Service.

Dinkmeyer, D., & Carlson, J. (1984). *Training in marriage enrichment.* Circle Pines, MN: American Guidance Service.

Dinkmeyer, D., et al. (1985). *Preparing responsible and effective parents.* Circle Pines, MN: American Guidance Service.

Dinkmeyer, D. Jr., Carlson, J., Dinkmeyer, D. (1994). *Consultation: School mental health professionals as consultants.* Muncie, IN: Accelerated Development.

Dinkmeyer, D., McKay, G., Dinkmeyer, D. Jr. (1997). *The Parent's Handbook* from Systematic training for effective parenting (STEP). Circle Pines, NM: American Guidance Service.

Dinkmeyer, D., McKay, G., Dinkmeyer, J., McKay, J. and Dinkmeyer, D. Jr. (1997). *Parenting Young Children* from Early childhood STEP. Circle Pines, NM: American Guidance Service.

Dinkmeyer, D., McKay, G., Dinkmeyer, D. Jr. (1998). *Parenting Teenagers* from Systematic training for effective parenting of teens (STEP/Teen). Circle Pines, NM: American Guidance Service.

Doherty, W., & Bowman, T. (1989, May/June). Therapy and enrichment: Enemies or allies? *Family Therapy News,* 6–7.

Doherty, W. J., & Baird, M. A. (Eds.). (1987). *Family-centered medical care: A clinical casebook.* New York: Guilford Press.

Dreikurs, R. and Soltz, V. (1991). Children: The challenge (reissue) New York: NAL/Dutton.

Gambrill, E. (1985). *Bibliotherapy.* In A. Bellack & M. Hersen (Eds.), *Dictionary of behavior therapy techniques.* New York: Pergamon Press.

Giblin, P., Sprenkle, D., & Sheehan, R. (1985). Enrichment outcome research: A meta-analysis of premarital, marital and family interventions. *Journal of Marital and Family Therapy, 1,* 257–271.

Guerin, P., Fay, L., Borden, S., & Kautto, J. (1987). *The evaluation and treatment of marital conflict: A four stage approach.* New York: Basic Books.

Guerney, B. (1977). *Relationship enhancement: Skill-training programs for therapy, problem prevention and enrichment.* San Francisco: Jossey-Bass.

Guerney, B., Brock, G., & Couful, J. (1986). Integrating marital therapy and enrichment: The relationship enhancement approach. In N. Jacobsen & A. Gurman, (Eds.), *Clinical handbook of marital therapy.* New York: Guilford Press.

Guerney, B., Stollak, G., & Guerney, L. (1970). A format for a new mode of psychological practice: Or how to escape a zombie. *The Counseling Psychologist, 2*(2), 97–104.

Hunter, D., Hoffnung, R., & Ferholt, J. (1988). Family therapy in trouble: Psychoeducation as solution and as problem. *Family Process, 27,* 327–337.

L'Abate, L. (1986). *Systematic family therapy.* New York: Brunner/Mazel.

Last, C. (1985). *Homework.* In A. Bellack & M. Hersen (Eds.), *Dictionary of behavior therapy techniques.* New York: Pergamon Press.

Levant, R. (1986). An overview of psychoeducational family programs. In R. Levant (Ed.), *Psychoeducational approaches to family therapy and counseling.* New York: Springer Publishing Co.

Ross, E., Baker, S., & Guerney, B. (1985). Effectiveness of relationship enhancement therapy versus therapist's preferred therapy. *American Journal of Marital and Family Therapy, 13,* 11–21.

Smith, R., Shoffuer, S., & Scott, J. (1978). Marriage and family enrichment: A new professional field. *The Family Coordinator, 28,* 87–93.

PART Three

Applications

CHAPTER 8

Children and Adolescents

Counseling children and adolescents differs enough to warrant treating the groups separately. With young children, most counseling involves the parents, teachers, or parent surrogates. As children become more verbal, they can be counseled individually and in groups. Adolescents (13 years of age and older) present unique challenges to the counselor. These challenges involve decisions about an emphasis in therapy: Do we stimulate autonomy for the adolescent, or work to improve the functioning within the system (school or family)? Counselors seek to maintain a balance between these two goals. Adolescent counseling usually involves increasing self-esteem and social interest.

Lifestyle assessment is another element that differentiates child counseling from adolescent counseling. In most child counseling, the use of Dreikurs' four goals of misbehavior and knowledge of the child's family constellation makes formal lifestyle assessment unnecessary. Misbehavior on the part of young children is for the most part directed toward adults. Adolescents, however, become more and more concerned with belonging with peers and less concerned with pleasing adults. Peer pressure, the desire for excitement and experimentation, and the profound physical and psychological changes that are taking place are some of the elements that make counseling adolescents qualitatively different from counseling children.

COUNSELING YOUNG CHILDREN

Young children may be categorized as babies, toddlers, and preschoolers. Many Adlerians believe that even preverbal toddlers can understand psychological interpretations. When the recognition reflex is elicited in a demonstration setting, toddlers clearly show that they understand the counselor's recommendations to their parents. These children realize the behavior in question is no longer going to "work," and they change their way of acting. The following case, not unusual in family education centers, illustrates the situation.

> Cynthia, 19 months, was described by her mother as a destructive terror. She was constantly into everything, emptying drawers, tearing things apart, and creating chaos. Her mother was at her wit's end. The eldest of six siblings, she had considered herself competent as a parent until she began to deal with Cynthia. The fact that she could elicit no cooperation from her daughter was particularly galling because her profession was that of a labor mediator. She was deeply hurt by Cynthia's behavior and said she even, at times, disliked her daughter.
>
> The counselor's tentative hypothesis about Cynthia's goal was revenge. The mother was asked if she would be willing for one week to go immediately to the bathroom, without any comment, each time Cynthia began tearing the house apart. In her desperation, the mother agreed, but predicted that she would be forced to retire to the bathroom at least ten times a day before Cynthia would believe her mother meant business. But she agreed to keep a chart.
>
> The mother was dismissed from the stage (this example is taken from a public demonstration) and Cynthia entered. She was a normal toddler who didn't say a word during the interview but listened attentively. She had a marked recognition reflex when the goal of revenge was presented. Apparently, she felt that in some way she had been mistreated, so her feelings were hurt and she wanted to get even. The counselor then told her about Mom's experiment. She would go to the bathroom each time Cynthia began destroying something. The counselor asked the toddler if she thought this arrangement was fair. Cynthia shook her head no. When the counselor asked Cynthia if she believed that her mother would actually carry out such a recommendation, the child looked uncertain.
>
> One week later, Cynthia's mother returned to the family education center. She reported that the relationship between herself and her daughter had undergone a dramatic change, that she enjoyed her daughter and was actually having fun with her. She also reported that on the first day she had retired to the bathroom six times, on the second day twice, and, except for one flurry the night before the return visit to the family education center, she hadn't found it necessary to use the "bathroom treatment" again.

The mother would have been fairly successful even without Cynthia's involvement in the counseling process. It is our impression, however, that Cynthia's new awareness of the goal of her misbehavior, coupled with the knowledge that her mother was going to deal with her differently, contributed significantly to the dramatic change.

In our experience, interviewing toddlers is useful primarily for diagnostic purposes. As children become more verbal, they can be drawn into the counseling process itself, their cooperation can be enlisted, and their involvement and participation can be stimulated. Furthermore, because Adlerians believe that every misbehaving child is a discouraged child, specific encouragement of the child by the counselor and, in the case of the family education centers, by members of the audience, is a significant part of the counseling process. In the centers, younger children are often interviewed separately from their parents. Many of them enjoy being in front of the audience, particularly when audience members are asked to give comments on what they sincerely appreciate about the children who have been interviewed. Young children profoundly influence those around them. Consequently, they play an important role in the family counseling process.

> Reba, 8 months, was the youngest of five children. The older four had all gone through periods of minor behavioral disturbances, and now the parents were concerned about Reba. When the entire family was interviewed together at the family education center, it became clear that this 8-month-old was tyrannizing the rest of the family merely by sucking on her lower lip. Throughout the entire session, Reba would periodically suck on her lip, and one of the parents or children would get up, walk across the room, and pull her lip out.

As children get older and more verbal, individual therapy is often the best way to deal with their problems.

> Marc, age 4, was badly bitten by a neighbor's dog. At the time of his referral, he had become enuretic, asthmatic, plagued with nightmares, and extremely fearful. Because litigation was involved, the child was interviewed by his attorney, who asked him to describe the incident. Marc did so by drawing pictures and writing "Bowser bit Marc." In Marc's case, although the parents needed help in understanding how to deal with the child, the therapists at the center elected to work directly with Marc in "talking therapy."

This case demonstrates that when we talk about feelings, beliefs, and purposes, young children understand. "Talking therapy" means just that—sitting down with the child and talking for part of the session, establishing a warm and trusting relationship, and, from time to time, gently challenging the child's mistaken views about self and the world. Another approach to working with children was pioneered by Michael Nystul (1980). This approach emphasizes the counselor's role as an encourager through verbal and nonverbal avenues.

Nursery-school, preschool, kindergarten, and primary-grade teachers report success in classroom group discussions. Children are encouraged to discuss classroom affairs as well as their personal feelings and concerns. These discussions can focus on the affective as well as cognitive issues for children.

Some adults are so prejudiced about what young children can and cannot do that they overlook children's capability to participate in the counseling process. Counselors who work with young children need to be familiar with the normal developmental process and its many variations. At the same time, counselors must not misuse developmental stages as a means of labeling children and failing to see and respect them as unique individuals.

The primary goal of counseling with *families* is to help the parents with their children. The primary goal of counseling with *children* is to win their cooperation and help them see that it is to their benefit to operate with, rather than against, their parents. If a child is seen separately from the parent, guardian, or stepparents, it is essential that the counselor inform the child as fully as possible of what is discussed with the parents.

COUNSELING OLDER CHILDREN

Children who are 6 or 7 (or older) can be counseled individually, in peer groups or in family groups. Counselors are expected to treat children with mutual respect, just as they would treat adult clients. It is not necessary to change vocabulary or tone of voice, nor is it necessary to "get down to the child's level." Young people are delightful with their creativity, imagination, intelligence, and spontaneity. Dance, music, psychodrama, movement, and art all represent nonverbal channels that many children find quite comfortable.

The Developing Understanding of Self and Others (DUSO) programs (Dinkmeyer & Dinkmeyer, 1982) are excellent resources for counseling with children. The 83 stories, primarily on picture flipcharts but with audiocassettes for those who prefer to not read the stories, are keyed to specific behavioral goals. Each story and accompanying activities has a consistent purpose. They help children learn to develop an understanding of self, of others, and choices. They provide the stimulus for discussion of purposive behavior. The format for discussions of each story includes the following:

1. review of the story facts
2. discussion of the feelings and behavior of the people or animal characters in the story
3. discussion of how the child might feel or act in a similar situation

The Communication Activities within DUSO are a unique contribution with considerable potential for child therapists (Dinkmeyer & Dinkmeyer, 1982). Skill development in the Communication Activities focuses on three areas: (1) communication, (2) encouragement, and (3) conflict management. These skills were chosen because they are the basis of social interaction and because they are areas in which people commonly experience difficulty. The activities are interdependent and carefully sequenced. Early lessons build the communication skills needed for the more complex conflict-management activities. As students proceed through the lessons, they learn to clarify their own feelings and to express these feelings to others.

Children have an opportunity to develop skill in attending, listening to feelings, expression of feelings, empathy, reflective listening, and sending I-messages. There are also skills in encouragement and conflict resolution. Instead of leaving development of skills to chance, they are presented in a systematic sequence. These materials can be a useful therapeutic tool which makes counseling with children more systematic and effective.

Establishing a Relationship with Children

Children aren't necessarily good interpreters, but they are good observers. They often have mistaken interpretations, but most seem able to change their views easily and quickly. It is easy to establish rapport with children almost instantly, as the following example illustrates. We have adapted an example by Pew (1969) which shows many of the elements of establishing the relationship with children:

> I am asked to see a 6-year-old for evaluation. I go to the waiting room and escort the child to my office. I close the door and sit down. The child remains standing, and I ask him, "Are you used to having people tell you what to do?" He may respond either verbally or nonverbally in the affirmative. Using the "goal-disclosure" method, I say, "Can I guess why you don't do what people ask you to do?" The child will usually give me some encouragement to continue. Then ask him, "Could it be that you don't do what you're asked to do so you keep people busy, thus letting them know that you're around?" (This question probes for the goal of attention.) I seldom get a response to this.
>
> However, I frequently get a response to the presentation of the second goal: "Could it be that you want to show people that you are big and strong and that they can't make you do what they want you to do?" The child may respond with what Dreikurs referred to as the "recognition reflex." Even though he shakes his head negatively, there is a twinkle in his eyes and a roguish smile on his face. He may blush, and he may even attempt to hide his face. When I obtain this type of response, I know I am on the right track. I then assure the child in a variety of ways that he is in fact stronger than me and that I have no intention whatsoever of attempting to overpower him or force him to do things that he doesn't want to do. The most common response at this point is for the child to very neatly sit down, and from that time on we are friends.

Rapport is, of course, easier to create with small children. When interview techniques are demonstrated publicly at family education centers, observers often remark that the counselors don't talk with children any differently than they talk with adults. Children respond quickly to any adult who treats them with respect and doesn't talk down to them. Also, small children respond well to an adult's fair, firm, and friendly attitude and to the early disclosure that their behavior makes sense.

Sometimes, the children's relief in discovering that an adult understands them is so great that it finds rather touching expression, even after relatively short interviews. For example, the child may shyly offer the counselor a piece of candy, shake her hand, or even give her a hug.

Whenever adults don't know what to do with children, they may call them names ("lazy," "fearful," or "aggressive") or use more sophisticated terms such as "attention deficit disorder" or "developmentally delayed." Adlerian counselors are not satisfied with dealing with the observed behavior alone. They understand the purpose of the child's fear or aggression or incapacity to read. If we can understand the goal of the child's mistaken behavior, we can plan with the child what approaches will be helpful to him.

The counselor who works with school-age children will try to bring about general agreement among parents, school, and the child concerning the best course of action. Frequently, the parents blame the school, the school blames the parents, and the child is unaffected. The counselor must avoid this situation. Because counselors can be misunderstood, a meeting of all parties concerned, including the child, is helpful to achieve common purposes and goals.

Counselors must recognize that most teachers are well qualified to teach children who want to learn or children who want to behave, but frequently have no idea what to do with children who don't want to learn or don't want to behave. Therefore, counselors must be willing and able to teach teachers and parents the basic principles of working and relating with children. Approaches to working with teachers are discussed later in this chapter, approaches with parents were discussed in Chapter 7.

CONFRONTATION IN COUNSELING CHILDREN

Adlerian confrontation is designed to put the challenge or problem directly before the child for the purpose of helping her understand why she behaves as she does.

Some counselors are cautious about using confrontation, believing that it lacks empathy and caring. We believe a counselor who really wants to motivate change must at times challenge a client to make movement. Avoidance of challenging techniques may indicate a counselor's lack of therapeutic involvement with the client.

Confrontation is obviously not a technique for the first moments of the relationship. But, it is based on the development of rapport and caring. The purpose of confrontation is to create insight and movement. It often stimulates emotions and thoughts that might not come to the surface under other situations. After confrontation, other techniques can help children understand their feelings—for example, "When I challenged you, you looked as if you felt very hurt. Tell me more about that."

Areas for confrontation include the following:

1. *Confronting subjective views.* The child is confronted with the private logic or hidden reason that makes the behavior acceptable. This type of confrontation makes the child aware of the purpose of behavior.

2. *Confronting mistaken beliefs and attitudes.* The child is confronted with mistaken beliefs and attitudes that work against positive, social development. The focus is on basic convictions about one's nature, the world in which one lives, and the nature of life and its meaning. These basic convictions fill the blanks developed by Shulman:

I am. . . . _____ , life is _____ , therefore _____ (Shulman, 1973).

3. *Confronting private goals.* This confrontation may be used when the child attempts to deny feelings the counselor believes are hidden. Confronting statements may actually produce the "recognition reflex," a nonverbal indicator such as a sudden shift in body position or of the eyes and facial muscles.

4. *Confronting destructive behavior.* The client may become self-destructive by avoiding an issue passively or aggressively or by acting out and becoming aggressive toward the counselor. In this situation the counselor confronts the child with the behavior at that moment in the therapeutic relationship. This type of confrontation brings the client to an awareness of the here and now, and how behavior affects others.

Confrontation is a powerful tool for the counselor, but it cannot be used effectively unless trust has been developed in the counseling relationship. After trust develops, the child can even be confronted effectively about passive or destructive behavior.

ADLERIAN TECHNIQUES ADAPTED TO CHILDREN

Paradoxical Intention

Paradoxical intention involves having children become aware of and even actually attempt to increase their own self-defeating behavior. Children are asked to practice, emphasize, enlarge, and develop the symptoms to an extreme or absurd degree. As children become aware of the unproductiveness of the symptom, they usually give up or change the behavior.

In using paradoxical intention with children, be certain you are not in a situation of power or personal revenge with them. If so, the children will work against you. Instead, the paradoxical intention can be treated as an experiment. Whatever it is that they are doing, have them do it in the extreme. For example, if the child is biting her fingernails, ask her to bite all her fingernails even more thoroughly. If she is trying to prove that she is independent, ask her to work without cooperating with anyone.

Acting as If

This technique is used when the child believes a situation is controlling his actions. Generally the child uses the ploy, "If only I could. . . ." to relieve himself of responsibility for the situation. By trying out a different role, the child often finds that he not only can act a part, but can become a different person in the process.

COUNSELING ADOLESCENTS

Adolescence is a recent invention, a product of Western, consumer-oriented, industrialized society. Adolescence as we talk about it is not recognized in many cultures. In some families and some communities, adolescence is now so prolonged that the term can include people into their 20s.

Another factor that contributes to the difficulty of counseling adolescents is the variety of views everyone has of the young person, including parents, teachers, peers, and the community at large. Often it is difficult for an adolescent to find useful ways to contribute to the community. Overcoming loneliness and achieving intimacy are major concerns for most adolescents. Many react by emphasizing the social aspects of their development, particularly with peers. This behavior leads many parents and teachers to see adolescents as members of a different culture. The tendency of young people to adopt fads in clothing, language, music, dance, and other culture variables contributes to the adolescents' isolation from the adult community.

Because useful avenues are frequently blocked, adolescents tend to find belonging in ways that many adults find objectionable. Today, adolescence is characterized by an ever-increasing disregard for adults' opinions and an ever-increasing concern for the recognition and acceptance of peers. Many adolescents view themselves as outside the mainstream of social and cultural expectations, banding together with other similarly isolated youths, seemingly at war with adult authority as represented by parents and school.

It is not difficult, however, to understand adolescents if we focus on these issues as values clarifications. For example, by age 16, some adolescents are buying into the values of the adult society and, within a year or so exhibit adult behaviors. Others resist adult values well into their own adulthood. Adolescence is a period of examination of values. Despite their apparent isolation from the adult community, the vast majority of adolescents really want to know what adults think, particularly the adults close to them and especially parents. This tremendously important fact is often overlooked by the parents and counselors.

Counselors always face a difficult dilemma. Should they put their efforts into helping adolescents accept what can be a faulty family system? Or should they concentrate instead on helping adolescents develop a constructively critical attitude that, if coupled with a sense of responsibility and leadership, can bring about much needed change in the system?

All the psychopathological conditions in adults are also found in adolescents; however, adolescents have the ability to change rapidly. Psychiatric disturbances that in adults often necessitate long-term therapy can change in adolescents within three or four counseling sessions. On the other hand, the counselor must be aware of the frequency and depth of depression in many adolescents and the serious potential for suicide. For the most troubled or troublesome adolescents, a counseling relationship can literally mean the difference between life and death.

Life Tasks

In working with adolescents, either individually or in groups, it is helpful to keep in mind the life-task areas of work, friendship, love, getting along with oneself, search for meaning, and leisure and recreation. Each of these areas may be an important source of information for the counselor. A simple self-rating process is useful in understanding how adolescents view themselves. The rating can be on a scale of 1 to 5, 1 to 10, or even a simple "thumbs up" or "thumbs down."

The self-rating can be expanded to take into consideration how the adolescents predict their parents will rate them and then, if the parents are involved in the counseling process, to see how parents do in fact rate their son or daughter. If extensive counseling is anticipated, a lifestyle assessment is appropriate for the adolescent.

After rapport and a mutually respectful relationship are established, many adolescents can be helped by a systematic interview. The interview helps the adolescent identify goals and strengths. The theme of this interview is "How Purposeful is Your Life?" Through specific questions and rating scales the adolescent explores significant themes. A series of incomplete sentences also examines motivating factors in the adolescent's life. Sentence stems can include "I am happiest when . . . My biggest fear is . . . My parents . . ." Their purpose is to explore the subjective world of the adolescent. These activities are an opportunity to identify the priorities that direct behavior.

Symptom Bearers and Identified Patients

Many adolescents referred to in counseling have been elected "symptom bearers" for their family. The term *identified patient* has been used, implying the family system's problems are due solely to a single person. This is illustrated in the following case:

> Jessica, age 15, a talented musician, superb athlete, and good student, kept running away from home. She told the counselor that she would even take drugs to get herself into a drug-treatment center, so that she wouldn't have to be at home with her family. Her parents, ostensibly solid citizens, turned out to have a very unfulfilling marriage. The father dealt with the marital conflict by getting drunk. But when his daughter saw him intoxicated, her mother denied the obvious by simply stating, "Father doesn't drink." The father also seemed unusually interested in seeing his daughter nude or partially clothed, although he never made overt sexual overtures. The more Jessica ran away, the more controlling her father became, insisting that she must stay within the family to "help get the family together."

As the family dynamics became clear, the counselor realized that Jessica was the best adjusted member of her family; the one who could see clearly what was going on—yet she didn't know what to do about it. Once a foster-home placement was arranged, Jessica made great personal strides.

Many young people deal with such situations by abusing drugs; engaging in juvenile delinquency, sexual misbehavior, academic failure; or even by attempting suicide. The moral of the stories symptom-bearers bring to us has a single theme—problems are interpersonal.

Drug Use

Adolescence is a time for experimentation. Many youths become involved to some degree with consciousness-altering drugs. In counseling, we see three types of drug involvement: (1) those who are merely experimenting, looking for excitement and peer approval; (2) those who are looking for a new personality; and (3) those whose discouragement is so profound that they are seeking oblivion. The drug scene is constantly changing and may be decidedly different from one school district to another. In the same community, students in one high school may use primarily marijuana, alcohol, and tobacco while only a few miles away, students at another high school may be experimenting with even stronger drugs. Drug availability seems inherent in the adolescent years of passage to adulthood.

An example is marijuana, an illegal drug in our society. One must question why a person would choose to get high several times a week, just as one would question why a person would choose to get drunk several times a week. What is missing in that person's life? What is being avoided?

Just as behavior can change profoundly with drug use, when drug use stops, behavior also shows profound changes. While using marijuana, many youths fail to function effectively in any of the life-task areas. When they stop using the drug, they often make great academic progress; become gainfully employed; and find a place in their family, with their friends, and in their community.

The use of drugs is so widespread among adolescents that any counseling should include exploration of this area. Counseling with anyone who is under the influence of any substance, regardless of age, is not likely to be effective. Heavy drug use may be an indication for residential-treatment approaches. We are seeing alcohol and other drug abuse even in grade schoolers, and alcoholism has certainly become a significant problem among adolescents. The use of tobacco in any form— smoked, chewed, or dipped—is a major health hazard.

What is the prognosis for adolescents who are deeply involved with drugs? As clinicians, we have seen many young people come through rather extreme and bizarre uses of chemicals and end up as fully constructive and unaffected young adults. We have also seen others—for example, those who have injected amphetamines intravenously—who have never returned to their prechemical state and have never really recovered. The three types of drug involvements may be helpful as part of an initial diagnosis of the purpose and prognosis for adolescent drug use.

Sexual Behaviors

Sexual experimentation results in a number of social problems. There is often a profound difference between the values of many adolescents and those of adult society. Our educational system, with few exceptions, does a poor job of dealing with the area of human sexuality, particularly as it relates to interpersonal relationships. Because counselors of adolescents can be almost certain that their clients will pose some questions or express concerns about sexuality, it is most important that the counselors think through their own values in this area. Although the willingness on the part of many adolescents to talk openly about sexuality is a positive element for the counseling process, such frankness may represent a problem for the counselor who is not prepared to deal with it.

School-Related Problems

Many adolescents express their rebellion against adult society and values by failing to conform to academic expectations. This is a complex area and we are reluctant to make sweeping statements. But one thing we can say with confidence: adolescents, like younger children, are not—for the most part—full-fledged partners in the educational system. Therefore, many of them feel justified in excluding themselves from the process. They fail to see a meaningful relationship between what goes on in school and what they see going on in society at large.

The frequent conflict between the demands of the school system and the requirements of the adolescent for healthy growth and development poses a serious problem for the counselor. Unfortunately many school workers have no idea how to deal with troubled or troublesome adolescents. Approaches to working with teachers, including high school teachers, are discussed later in this chapter.

The Adolescent's Parents

The adolescent's parents are often a great source of difficulty for the counselor. The more the adolescent displays autonomy, the more resentful some parents become, with their resentment often directed at the counselor. Counselors must be willing to maintain confidentiality with regard to their clients while, at the same time, walk a tightrope with the parents. The parents often demand to know what their teen is thinking, doing, or feeling. They frequently demand that information "because I pay for this treatment." When this occurs, family therapy may be indicated. The counselor can focus on whether the teen can return to the family system, or should be emancipated. Some adolescents are so close to their families that they reach adulthood without having made a successful separation from their families. In these cases, too, the most hopeful approach is family therapy. Here is an example of one such case:

> Trahn, 17 years old and a high school junior, had never had a date, preferring to spend his spare time at home tinkering with gadgets. His mother, a widow, greatly enjoyed Trahn's company. They were good friends and shared many common interests. Mother didn't date or engage in other activities outside the home. Toward the end of his junior year, Trahn began developing symptoms in the form of anxiety attacks with chest pains. Initially seen individually, he was then introduced to group therapy. In both individual and group therapy, he gained a lot of insight, but there was no change in his behavior or reduction in his symptoms.
>
> Only after a number of joint counseling sessions did Trahn and his mother begin to see how important it was that they develop their own lives, independent of each other. In the next several years, although Trahn continued to live at home, he completed his schooling, became a pilot, and used his interest in gadgetry to make several inventions on the job. His mother, a school teacher, became active in local organizations and in various activities in her church. The previously pathological symbiotic relationship between mother and son developed into a cooperative, interdependent relationship that allowed each party to move out and become a person in his or her own right.

We have found it helpful to supplement parent counseling with books based on Adlerian ideas. (These books are discussed in detail in Chapter 7.) Parents are given the book at their first session and told to read specific chapters. In ensuing sessions, parents have opportunities to raise questions and apply the ideas to their adolescent.

COUNSELING COLLEGE STUDENTS

Many college students are still adolescents by most definitions. It is estimated that two out of five college students will seek some kind of counseling service during the college years. Much of the college mental-health services are essentially adolescent counseling. The transition from high school to college has predictable developmental stages.

To be effective, however, a counselor must know something about the system in which the college student must operate. How are decisions made, who wields the power on the campus? High-achieving high school students seem particularly susceptible to some sort of transitional breakdown. If they were successful in high school but for the wrong reasons—perhaps to be better than others, or to gain parental approval—on the college campus they often show a dramatic reversal. Students who were the best at being "good" become the best at being "bad," and the reversal may appear as academic failure, sexual misbehavior, crime and delinquency, drug abuse, psychosis, or neurosis.

For most college students, group therapy is the treatment of choice. However, individual sessions may be necessary to build trust and allay fears before involving the student in a therapy group.

> Renata was a student in a community college, yet she had never learned to read properly. She had become skillful at gleaning information by taking extensive lecture notes, and participating in study groups. She achieved good grades despite having never completely read through an assignment. She had difficulties in her relationships with boys as well as with her elderly parents (she was an only child). Renata came to the clinic looking for help in these areas but was so embarrassed about her reading disability that she initially refused to consider remediation. A brief lifestyle assessment was completed. During this period, Renata developed a trusting relationship with her counselor, who was also the co-counselor of an ongoing open-ended group. The next quarter, she joined that group, had a positive experience, and became encouraged to seek help with her reading challenges.

Adolescence is fraught with difficulties. Successful counselors accept all adolescents as they are at the moment, are nonjudgmental and flexible, and approach and particpating in counseling as a learning experience. Because adolescents' difficulties are often in group interactions, working out their problems in groups is generally an effective form of therapy. Many of the problems that adolescents face are related to the way they are treated by society and at home. Therefore, to be effective, counselors must remain somewhat detached. If they become too involved as advocates for the adolescent against the family, school, or community, the effectiveness of the counseling is likely to be significantly reduced.

INFLUENCING CHILDREN AND ADOLESCENTS THROUGH TEACHERS

Adlerian psychology has specific ideas for teachers. Effective school counselors, working with all facets of the education process, are usually the most effective way to reach teachers. They have skills that allow them to work with individual teachers by request, but also permit them to initiate group education and problem-solving experiences for teachers. The latter is preferable, since groups can be more productive and successful than individual consultation. They are also more time efficient and give the counselor a wider sphere of influence within the school.

Whether in groups or individually, consultation with teachers has a theoretical framework for understanding human behavior. Teachers often have no instruction on understanding behavior. The following ideas illustrate common mistaken assumptions about human behavior.

Common Mistaken Assumptions about Human Behavior

Behavior Is a Product of Environmental Factors "Anya is a problem child because she comes from a difficult home." This example suggests that where you live determines how you behave. While environment influences behavior, it is not the sole determinant.

Behavior Is a Product of Heredity This view—expressed by the catch-all phrase "The genes did it!"—is more prevalent among parents than teachers. While recent research gives strong evidence of genetic influences on temperament and other personality characteristics, it is not the sole variable in student behaviors.

Behavior Is a Product of Age and Stage of Development Those who hold this view see behavior as a function of chronological age—the terrible twos, the troubled teens. Like the environmental view, the opinion ignores the wide variability among individuals—in this case, of individuals at the same age or stage. It does not explain the mature 12-year-old and the immature adult.

Behavior Is a Product of Gender Sex-role stereotyping is perhaps becoming less prevalent, but it accounts for differences in behavior by "blaming" the gender of the child. Although not many people today say that girls are made of "sugar and spice" and "boys will be boys," these stereotypes still subtly influence our perception of student behaviors.

These four minitheories of human behavior *explain away,* rather than understand, behavior. What can a counselor do when a teacher subscribes to one or more of these "theories"? Short of having children change home, genes, age, or sex, these beliefs leave the teacher powerless to make an effective intervention.

Applicable Adlerian Principles

A few simple yet profound concepts from Adlerian psychology can help the teacher understand student behaviors.

Behavior Must Be Seen Holistically   The student is a whole person, not small fragments, or certain confusing behaviors. Look for the overall pattern. If we focus exclusively on a student's high achievement test score, for example, it apparently contradicts the student's low grades. The two elements appear inconsistent until we recognize another factor—motivation. Through the broader picture of overall psychological movement we begin to understand the student's behaviors.

All Behavior Has a Purpose   When a student misbehaves, instead of asking "Why?" ask "What is the purpose of that behavior?" When we start from the premise that all behavior has a goal (whether we like the goal or not), student behaviors begin to makes sense.

All Behavior Has Social Meaning   All individuals, adults and children alike, seek to belong to groups. When students don't succeed in their quest for belonging, they experiment with other ways to fit into the classroom. Class clowns, for example, feel that to be noticed by others is so important they will risk being punished by the teacher. The price they pay to achieve a unique place in the classroom, to them, makes sense.

Each Student Operates on the Basis of Private Logic   Private logic plays an important role in classroom behavior. How does each child seek to be known? Their decisions reflect a private subjective logic. Until we understand the child's private logic, we are unable to effectively change the child's undesirable behavior. Why would a student want to be difficult? It makes immaculate sense to that individual. The phrase "nobody throws away a behavior that works" illustrates this concept of private logic.

Behavior Is Always Consistent with the Student's Self-Concept and Lifestyle   This principle enables us to distinguish one's patterns and themes—for example, "I count only when I'm being noticed; therefore, I must attract attention at all costs," "I must be in control; therefore, I won't hesitate to hurt or embarrass others," "I am incapable; therefore, I will not try." When we don't understand a student's behavior, we must seek to understand the private logic and self-concept that makes the behavior meaningful and reasonable from the person's point of view.

All Behavior Reflects One's Degree of Encouragement or Discouragement   When students tackle a new task, they have certain expectations about their probability of success. Encouraged or courageous students feel adequate and capable of coping with the task. Discouraged students believe they cannot succeed; therefore, they will not try. Overambition, inadequacy, and high standards are all affected by the level of encouragement or discouragement the child experiences.

Rules for Successful Teacher-Student Relationships

Four points are especially relevant when considering the role of teachers:

1. Teachers are more effective when they change their behaviors, not student behaviors. It is often assumed that the teacher must change the child; in fact, teachers must first change themselves.

2. Teachers must be more involved with encouraging the discouraged child than with praising the good or accomplished student. The counselor can facilitate teacher growth in this area by explaining the difference between praise and encouragement.

3. Teachers cannot always protect their students from failure, whether in the classroom or in other parts of the students' world. Teachers are not responsible for their students' behaviors; therefore, they should not feel compelled to shield children from unpleasant experiences.

4. Teachers should attempt to create greater balance between students' cognitive and affective needs. Our education system concentrates on the cognitive "three R's" and ignores another important set of R's: responsibility, resourcefulness, and respect. The counselor can concretely assist the teacher in this area by sharing resources for the teacher to use in the classroom.

There are two basic formats for implementing a successful teacher/counselor relationship: one-to-one consultation and small groups. Both formats seek to give teachers fresh perspectives on their classroom challenges.

CONSULTING WITH THE INDIVIDUAL TEACHER

The consulting relationship with a teacher can take many different forms, depending on the teacher's expectations. Some teachers expect expert advice from the counselor, an attitude that reflects unhealthy dependence on the counselor.

> Mrs. Hartz teaches a third-grade class. One of her students, Keela, doesn't like to do math. Keela spends most of math time daydreaming, doodling on the margins, and talking with other children. It is the talking with the others that really upsets Mrs. Hartz. On one particularly talkative day, Keela simply ignores the teacher's pleas, threats, and punishments. Mrs. Hartz, frustrated, decides to see the counselor.
>
> As she approaches the counselor's office, Mrs. Hartz has several thoughts about the problem and its possible solutions. These thoughts may get in the way of a successful resolution of the situation. "I can't do anything more about this," "The problem is with Keela," or "Our counselor will give me some good ideas on how to get Keela to be quiet." These beliefs are all likely but ineffective premises about the student-teacher relationship.

The counselor/teacher relationship is collaborative. If the counselor deals only with the crisis between Keela and Mrs. Hartz, it will be advice on how to improve this specific situation. Advice ensures one of two things: If the crisis is solved, the counselor becomes a "crisis fixer" and stimulates a mounting number of crises that need fixing. If the counselor's advice fails, Mrs. Hartz has no evidence the counselor can be helpful. Advice-giving is a lose–lose proposition for school counselors.

The collaborative nature of the counselor/teacher relationship asks the counselor to "give away your skills" so the teacher will be able to understand misbehavior and create alternatives. The counselor acts "as if" the teacher is capable of learning these new ideas. The teacher is a critical resource in the consultation procedure. Teachers often don't see themselves as part of the student behavior problem they take to the counselor. But the teacher is the client with whom the counselor must work; thus, the relationship between counselor and teacher is similar to the counseling relationship.

Counselors must avoid crisis intervention, and must understand when a crisis is being used to manipulate their time. It is imperative that the counselor spend the first weeks of the school year getting to know the teachers on a friendly and non-threatening basis. Spending time with the teachers in their own environment, whether the teachers' lounge or their classrooms after school, the counselor communicates accessibility and equality with teachers.

To increase the chances of teachers' self-referral, counselors create three conditions:

1. *Awareness of consultation opportunities.* Through presentations at faculty meetings, printed materials, and personal contact, teachers become aware of the services the counselor offers.
2. *Flexibility and accessibility.* The school counselor makes time for teachers and creates times where teachers can see the counselor.
3. *Administration support.* The school administration supports consultation with teachers as a valid counselor activity. If the principal does not support this role, it is unlikely that the school counselor will override this barrier.

The importance of goal alignment with the administration is critical. The principal may see counselors as disciplinarians or administrative clerks. Direct agreement between counselor and principal creates mutual goals and an atmosphere for successful teacher consultation.

Counselors' concerns with the school environment, with the image they project, and with the services they provide are best summed up in a single question: "If the counselor is missing from the building for one day, who notices and for what reasons?"

Systematic Procedure for Collecting Data

A systematic procedure for collecting information from a self-referred teacher helps structure the initial meeting and provides an opportunity for the counselor to listen to the teacher's problem (Dinkmeyer & Carlson, 1973). Figure 8–1 shows one consultant referral form used to collect the necessary data.

Anecdotes

A vital technique in data collection is the anecdote. The anecdote is the recollection of an interaction between the child and teacher that demonstrates the specific dynamics

Child's name _____ Grade _____ Age _____
Teacher _____ Time available for consultation _____
Family constellation (by age)_____
Family atmosphere _____
Specific description of learning difficulty or behavioral difficulty:
Is the problem focused primarily on one of the following 5 areas? Please circle.
These areas are listed only to suggest classifications. Obviously many problems
will overlap.
1. Intellectual deficiency
2. Learning problems, educational adjustment, questions regarding placement
3. Emotional problem, personality maladjustment, social adjustment
4. Discipline
5. Delinquent tendencies
Please describe the problem briefly. Anecdotal observations would be particularly
appropriate. The anecdotes should include the child's behavior, your response or
reaction, and the response to corrective efforts (antecedent event, behavior,
consequence).
Tentative ideas regarding reasons for the behavior:_____
Child's assets, strengths: _____
Corrective actions utilized to this point: _____
Procedures which work with this child: _____
Mutually acceptable recommendations: _____

Figure 8–1 Consultant Referral Form. From *Counseling: Facilitating Human Potential and Change Processes,* (p. 179), by D. Dinkmeyer and J. Carlson, 1973, Columbus, OH: Merrill.

of the relationship. Returning to Mrs. Hartz and Keela, if Mrs. Hartz were to respond to the counselor's request for an anecdote with, "Today Keela just didn't listen to me; she was so stubborn," her answer would be insufficient. The counselor helps the teacher reconstruct a situation to make specific behavioral evidence available: The counselor might stimulate the anecdote by asking, "Can you remember the last time this happened? If a security camera reached the scene, what would it see and hear?"

> For the past two weeks, I haven't been getting any cooperation from Keela at math time. Today when she doodled and daydreamed, I felt angry. I told her to get back to work, but she said "I need help from Jessica, that's why I'm talking to her." I tell her to be quiet, and she will just for a while. But then she starts up again. I have to keep her quiet so the class can get its work done.

Exploring Beliefs

At this point, the counselor should ask Mrs. Hartz for a tentative hypothesis, or guess, as to the purpose of Keela's behavior. This allows the teacher to share some of her beliefs about child behavior—her frame of reference. From our example, we already have a clue that Mrs. Hartz believes she must act "for the best interests of the class." Neither agreeing nor disagreeing with the teacher's ideas, the counselor accepts the teacher's point of view. Now counselor and teacher can begin to list the child's assets and strengths.

This tactic may seem strange to the teacher, who probably believes it is irrelevant or useless to dwell on the assets, when the problem is the concern. But by focusing on Keela's adequacies, the counselor can help the teacher build successful interactions with Keela. What has worked in the past? What has not worked? This procedure, included in the referral form in Figure 8–1 allows Mrs. Hartz to become aware of her own effectiveness. It allows teacher and counselor to move immediately from the specific problem to possible resources for solving the problem.

Tuning in to Feelings

After the counselor has obtained specific behavioral incidents, the next step is to help the teacher identify her feelings about the problem situation. The process moves into the teacher's affective domain. The child's misbehavior stimulates feelings in teachers. Recognizing and identifying unpleasant feelings may be challenging. Some teachers believe it is important not to admit that a student can "get to me." Allowing the teacher to share feelings, is helpful and an important part of the consultation process.

Finding Alternatives

Counselor and teacher may now make a tentative hypothesis about Keela's misbehavior. The student may be seeking attention, because she stops misbehaving as soon as the teacher pays special attention to her. Or the student might be seeking power, because Mrs. Hartz expresses anger about Keela.

The teacher then explores alternatives to her own behavior. She may, for example, decide to ignore Keela. She may have her do at home the work she didn't do in class. By seeking alternatives and creating consequences, the teacher finds her own behavior becoming more functional.

RECOMMENDATIONS FOR CHANGES IN THE CLASSROOM

Counselors do not suggest specific changes for a specific anecdote. The Adlerian view is that specific solutions come from applying principles. Specific answers come from broader concepts.

Encouragement is a significant concept in these classroom challenges. When teachers want students to stop certain behaviors, they should ignore those behaviors and fill the void by encouraging and reinforcing more acceptable behaviors. The relationship between student and teacher is a result of how the teacher chooses to influence the student.

Logical consequences are another useful concept. Consequences are a related, reasonable natural outcome of the misbehavior, while punishment is often arbitrary and unrelated to the behavior. Punishment tends to obscure the intended message, whereas consequences allow the student to experience the results of his choice of behavior. It removes the teacher as a potential focus of anger and resentment and allows the student to learn from choices.

The teacher learns what behaviors unintentionally reinforce, rather than decrease, misbehavior. A student who seeks attention and stops misbehaving when reminded has received negative attention. Power struggles may result when the teacher is determined to prove to the student that the teacher is in control of the classroom. Students who believe they are incapable of achieving may be relieved of reasonable expectations if the teacher agrees nothing can be done.

WORKING WITH TEACHERS IN GROUPS
Rationale

The Adlerian approach stresses the social significance and consequences of behavior. Counselors can provide opportunities for teachers to interact in a therapeutic climate—in groups, rather than in one-to-one consultation. It is an often overlooked opportunity.

Working with teachers in groups can be the counselor's most important contribution to the school staff. Group work makes efficient use of time, allows education as well as problem solving to occur, and removes one of the biggest barriers to an effective teacher/counselor relationship. Counselors are no longer the experts who "don't know what the classroom is really like," but become members of a group of peers with whom they can share their feelings as well as their skills.

The rationale for the group setting is that most problems for teachers originate in the group setting of the classroom. By working with teachers in a group, the counselor can see exactly how the teacher's lifestyle functions in the group setting, whether dominating, accepting, passive, or demanding. The group allows each teacher to function as an integral part of a group. This process gives participants insight into the group dynamics that operate in their classroom every day. The counselor's leadership skills shape the group experience so that each member benefits.

A number of unique therapeutic forces occur only in the group setting. The group can provide an atmosphere of acceptance, so that teachers receive empathy from their peers. In sharing their experiences, teachers learn that their problems are not unique and that there is a universal quality to classroom challenges. The group is a place where teachers can vent frustrations and express concerns and ideas. The group also provides the counselor and the individual teacher with a wealth of resources: the other teachers in the group. Each member of the group can become a supportive and therapeutic agent for the other members of the group.

Organization of the Group

Counselors can create a process and procedures to introduce the concept of group meetings to the staff. Their goal is to make the staff aware of the purpose and function of the group. Often inaccurate beliefs about groups include: This is a remedial group for inadequate teachers; this will take away from useful planning time; the administration does not support the groups.

A counselor might demonstrate during a faculty meeting what a teacher group will be like. This can be done by illustrating common classroom behavior challenges and their purpose. This gives the staff an opportunity to become aware of the value of the group.

A teacher group might meet weekly for a half-hour. Teachers make a commitment to stay with that group for at least four to six sessions. Groups can be part of faculty meetings if the principal agrees to devote the time to training and support. Counselors should not let imaginary barriers of time and space discourage their efforts to start a teacher group.

The group begins by establishing rules. No one should be allowed to join the group after it has started. New groups can be formed when interest arises. This allows the group to be closed; it avoids repeating basic theory groundwork. A physically comfortable and private area should be provided for the group. The group can sit in a circle so that each member can see all of the others and no member is "at the head of the table," especially the counselor.

It is important that the group be heterogeneous. It should be composed of experienced as well as inexperienced teachers, so that teachers can share a diversity of classroom experiences and training. On the other hand, the group should be composed of teachers from about the same grade level. Great discrepancy in the age level of the students the group discusses can become a major handicap.

Group size can be limited so that each member has an opportunity to share in each session; about five teachers plus the counselor is recommended. Membership in a group is always voluntary. The counselor might have brief interviews before the first meeting. Teachers qualify for participation by two criteria: (1) having a concern they wish to share with the group and (2) wanting to help others with their concerns.

Content

The first meeting of the group can be structured to allow all members to share something about themselves and listen to the others. The leader might take this opportunity to point out similarities in the concerns or ideas among the members. Therapeutic forces can be used immediately to generate cohesion and commitment. The leader must exercise control of the group and offer direction by providing the necessary psychological foundations as well as therapeutic forces. Introducing the Adlerian concepts of behavior promotes the group's problem-solving skills by providing a common basis for approach to problems.

Anecdote sharing is then the cornerstone technique for presenting situations to the group. The format for anecdotes is the same as that in individual consultation. A specific incident, not a general concern, is shared. After the teacher identifies the feelings during the incident, tentative hypotheses about the student's goal can be formulated. Each group member recognizes common elements in their classrooms—purposive misbehavior, discouragement, and practical alternatives to ineffective methods.

Several strategies can make the group more effective. A challenge for the leader is to see that all members of the group have an opportunity to be the focus. For the typical group, this means that one teacher will hold center stage for no more than 10 to 15 minutes each session and that no fewer than two or three teachers will actively present their challenges or problems at each meeting. As the group learns their method of sharing, diagnosing, and explaining incidents, the leader becomes a facilitator of the process.

The Teacher Group in Action

The following excerpt from the third session of a typical teacher group composed of second and third grade teachers shows the structure and movement in the group.

Counselor:	*Okay, who'd like to begin this week? Do you have comments on how things went the past week?*
Carla:	*That idea of ignoring Lisa's attention-getting behavior seems to be working! She doesn't go to the pencil sharpener much anymore. However, she isn't always interested in doing good, on-task behaviors.*
Craig:	*Was this the student who didn't do anything unless she got some attention?*
Carla:	*Yes, we said it was attention-getting misbehavior and that I should ignore the problem behaviors and pay attention to good things she was doing. It's not easy to find some though!*
Betty:	*Maybe you'll have to dig deep to encourage some of the positive things Lisa does. I had a student like this, and he wasn't too interested in cooperating until we talked about how he could be noticed in positive ways.*
Counselor:	*So, there were things he did which you couldn't control—in which he pursued power?*
Betty:	*Yeah, I got really angry about it.*
Michael:	*Then it seems that it was a power struggle rather than just attention-getting behavior.*
Betty:	*Ricky still likes to do certain things. As a matter of fact, today we had a hard time figuring out where his homework was.*
Counselor:	*It seems that your situation has improved, Carla. Can we move over to Betty for a few minutes?*
Betty:	*I'm interested in whether Ricky's goal is power or attention: I'm not too sure I see all the differences between the two.*
Counselor:	*Well, could you tell us about the homework incident?*

Betty: *As we were beginning social studies today, Ricky complained loudly that he couldn't find his homework. I held up the entire class—and looked for Ricky's homework.*

Michael: *It sounds as if you were pretty annoyed by this.*

Betty: *Yes, he knew we were waiting for him.*

Craig: *He really had you cornered!*

Betty: *Yes, I was pretty angry, because I felt like it was a game, and I lost—not my temper, but the power struggle.*

Counselor: *What would be the alternative to Betty's dealings with Ricky?*

Carla: *It would be to withdraw from the power struggle. But how do you avoid dealing with him when he needs the homework on his desk?*

Betty: *And this isn't the only time I get challenged by Ricky to see who's in control.*

Counselor: *Okay, but let's return to the incident. How would you withdraw from the situation?*

Betty: *Let him deal with his problem?*

Craig: *Can you leave a student alone with his problem? Do we help the most by doing "nothing"?*

Michael: *It's still his problem, and I think that probably he won't keep it up if there isn't any attention or prestige in holding up the class.*

Betty: *I can see the need to withdraw, but I'm not sure it's helping him.*

Craig: *I think it would be worth trying just to find out...*

Betty: *If this homework hassle does come up again, I'll do exactly that and see what happens. I have a feeling that it will come up again.*

Counselor: *He really got to you?*

Betty: *Yes. Sometimes I do get into power struggles with the kids, but I feel pretty responsible about the classroom atmosphere, and disruptions are my responsibility.*

Craig: *The kids know it. They can tell what bugs us, and some really work to almost be "the best at being the worst."*

This teacher group understands the purposive nature of behavior. It presents a format for identifying emotions, and relates them to the goals of misbehavior. Betty felt annoyed, even angry, at Ricky's homework. By sharing the anecdote with the group, Betty has made it possible for the others to help her identify Ricky's probable goal of power. The alternative is to withdraw from any "power contest." Betty has made a commitment to use an alternative response—to let Ricky be the owner of his own homework. The final exchange between Craig and Betty demonstrates and acknowledges the purposiveness of behavior and the lifestyles that promote certain behaviors.

The counselor monitors the group's progress during and after each session. As a session progresses, the leader must make certain that each member of the group becomes a "sharer" as well as a spectator. The leader recognizes and counteracts inherent tendencies to be withdrawn and shy, or verbal and dominating. Members are encouraged to contribute and are appreciated for the value of their contributions. When a problem is presented, or an opinion or idea is needed, counselors turn to a group member, instead of responding themselves.

The leader also refocuses discussions that wander from the group's purpose. The group is highly specific and focused. To change the focus of the group, the counselor must be willing to confront and redirect a topic. Effective teacher groups encourage members, nonverbally and verbally, to contribute their feelings and ideas and express their concerns. The leader directs the group without becoming the focus.

Teacher groups can be a positive catalyst for change within each school. Each school building reflects the priorities of the district, administration, and teachers. To facilitate learning and change, the teacher group is an efficient and effective process for dealing with student behaviors.

SUMMARY

This chapter covers the broad spectrum of opportunities to reach children and adolescents. Unifying our approach is the principle of systematic training, and understanding and influencing the systems (whether family or school) in which children, adolescents, and students thrive.

REFERENCES

Dinkmeyer, D., & Carlson, J. (1973). *Counseling: Facilitating human potential and change processes*. Columbus, OH: Merrill.

Dinkmeyer, D.C., & Dinkmeyer, D.C. Jr. (1980). *Developing understanding of self and others (DUSO)*. Circle Pines, MN: American Guidance Service.

CHAPTER 9

Counseling and Psychotherapy with the Elderly

"Not much is done for old people in our culture. . . . Many persons seem to be changed when they are older, and this is mainly due to the fact that they feel futile and useless. They try to prove their worth and value again in the same way as adolescents do. They interfere and want to show in many ways that they are not old and will not be overlooked, or else they become disappointed and depressed" (Adler, 1956, p. 443).

Besides this statement, Adler wrote relatively little about the elderly. Contemporary Adlerians also have written little about aging compared with what has been published on issues of childhood, adolescence, and adulthood. But one should not conclude that Individual Psychology has little relevance to the problems of aging. On the contrary, in his review of nine representative theories of personality and psychotherapy, Brinks (1979) concluded that the Adlerian approach was the most comprehensive theory in explaining the biopsychosocial issues of aging. The purpose of this chapter is to identify some of the challenges involved in the treatment of the elderly and to offer several applications of the theory of Individual Psychology in their treatment. First, let us look at some of the challenges involved in the treatment of the elderly.

THE CHALLENGE OF COUNSELING THE ELDERLY

Today, 11% of the total U.S. population, more than 20 million people, are older than 65. Projections are that this figure will rise to between 17% and 20% by 2030. Estimates are while 85% of these individuals have a chronic medical illness and 20% to 30% suffer from a psychiatric disorder, few elderly use health services, particularly mental health services. Only 1% are in private and public psychiatric hospitals, 2% are in long-term care facilities, and only 2% to 4% receive mental health outpatient services. The majority of this care is for organic brain disorders like Alzheimer's disease. The reasons for this underuse of services involve both the lack of services and the "gerontophobia" of mental health providers. It is not simply a financial issue (Larsen, Whanger, & Busse, 1983).

A major challenge for professionals working with the elderly is their attitudes about the aged. *Gerontophobia* refers to the professional's pessimistic outlook about achieving therapeutic successes with people older than 65. Professionals who believe that only a YAVIS patient—**Y**oung; **A**ttractive in terms of having similar values as the therapist; **V**erbal, **I**ntelligent, and **S**uccessful—is treatable will likely be disappointed with the elderly patient. Further, the professional is likely to expect less progress, to assume responsibility for things the individual is indeed capable of, and approach the relationship with an attitude of sympathy rather than empathy. Besides a different attitude—that is a more realistic attitude—toward the elderly, a somewhat different set of skills is needed to be a geriatric counselor or psychotherapist.

Social Interest, Community Feeling, and the Elderly

Adler's central concept is *gemeinschaftsgefühl,* which literally means "community feeling," but for a number of reasons is usually translated as "social interest" in English. Ansbacher (1992) notes that although *community feeling* and *social interest* are used synonymously by many, they are different concepts. Adler described community feeling as a sense of harmony and connectedness with the universe, and a form of self-transcendence. Social interest is also a form of self-transcendence which connotes a more proactive stance of cooperation, contribution, and generativity. Ansbacher (1992) notes that the concept of community feeling is more germane in that the elderly become less physically capable of the activity that social interest requires. It is rather the spiritual transcendence of community feeling that is required of the elderly person. In short, community feeling means "to identify with the mysterious phenomenon of life that existed before and will continue long after one dies, to accept cheerfully the inevitably of death and make the best of what is still left for one" (p. 408).

THERAPEUTIC ISSUES UNIQUE TO THE ELDERLY: THE LIFE TASKS

For Adler, the life tasks of work, love, and friendship embraced all human desires and activities. He believed that all human suffering originated from difficulties that complicated the tasks, whereas happiness and balanced personality were the result of successfully meeting the tasks of life with an attitude of social interest. Meeting the tasks of life is different for the elderly individual compared with the child or the young adult. Whereas attending school or working at the job or at home are the usual ways of meeting the task of work, how does the elderly person contribute to the welfare of others? How does one meet the tasks of love when one's spouse has died? What about the task of friendship when one is bedridden or wheelchair bound? Physical decline, loss of sensory function resulting in social isolation, chronic degenerative disease, economic deprivation, the loss of friends and spouse, and retirement are some of the factors that lead to widespread feelings of inferiority among the elderly. Thus old age is an especially difficult period of life because factors that engender inferiority feelings and loss of self-adequacy are on the rise while means of compensating for these feelings by the former means one used to meet the life tasks are decreasing (Shulman & Sperry, 1992).

A basic challenge for the counselor is to undercut inferiority feelings by helping the person find different means of meeting the tasks of life. This means cultivating independent behavior and facilitating mental, emotional and physical development, and whatever else develops rather than shrinks social interest. According to Keller and Hughston (1981), early reports on physical decline and decreased capacity in the elderly have been overstated, while recent evidence increasingly suggest that many elderly have the ability to further develop their potential in many physical, mental, and emotional areas. This research evidence indicates that even when some declines are noted in certain body systems, there are usually accommodative mechanisms that permit varying degrees of adaptation.

With advancing age the cardiovascular and respiratory system do show lowered efficiency, but are capable of continued development and exercise endurance. Many of the declines in the auditory, visual, and endocrine systems also can be accommodated. Physiological changes do occur in the sexual system but these in no way preclude sexual functioning. Finally, the only normal changes in cognitive functioning are decreases in speed and abstract reasoning, whereas memory loss and concentration difficulties are abnormal. Thus even amid physical decline there is potential for development in the physical as well as the emotional realms. Continued development depends on a growing sense of belonging and self-respect, and on the desire and opportunities for elderly individuals to maintain a sense of independence as long as possible. Finally, it means accepting the inevitability of death calmly and cheerfully (Ansbacher, 1992).

Counseling and Consulting with the Elderly

The most common mental health problems of the elderly involve problems of daily living—that is, problems involving only one life task that do not generalize to the other life tasks. In whatever capacity the professional encounters the elderly person— as caseworker, psychologist, nurse, physician, paraprofessional or administrator—an effective counseling or consulting intervention may take place in a formal one-to-one setting or in a group. Most often it will occur informally, usually in the context of some ongoing daily activity that would not normally be associated with "counseling." Most often these counseling interventions will involve encouragement, information, or goal disclosure. At other times more specialized techniques may be needed or a specific consultation must be sought.

Throughout this book the counseling and consulting process has been described in three phases: (1) relationship, (2) assessment, and (3) reorientation. Following are some guidelines and suggestions in each of the three phases that we have found helpful in counseling and consulting with the elderly.

Relationship

1. *Attitude*. The professional's attitude should be one of respect at all times. This is shown verbally by use of the person's surname, unless invited by the person to do otherwise, and nonverbally, by an unhurried and interested manner, and showing empathy with feelings, beliefs, and attitudes.

2. *Voice*. Emphasis should be on speaking slowly, distinctly, and louder if there is any indication of hearing loss.

3. *Touch*. Touch whether through handshake, hug, or pat on the shoulder communicates caring and concern. In our culture the usual social distance or "personal space" is about 3 feet between people. However, most elderly are comfortable with a smaller space and often prefer that others sit or stand much closer than that.

4. *Time*. Keep intervals short, especially if the person is easily fatigued. Several short sessions are better than one longer session.

5. *Focus*. Be supportive and issue-oriented, especially at the first encounter. Encourage the person to express themselves about general issues such as grief, loneliness, helplessness, and guilt.

Assessment

1. Always assess the individual's behavior in terms of the four goals or levels of unproductive behavior and their styles of coping. When possible, and as time permits, perform a brief lifestyle assessment. Family constellation material is especially valuable in understanding the person's functioning in group settings.

The Four Goals of Misbehavior (Dreikurs, 1953) has proved to be a valuable tool for assessing and intervening with child–adult relationship issues. Dreikurs describes a method for understanding children's misbehavior in terms of the goals of attention-getting, power, revenge, and inadequacy or psychological disability. Shulman and Berman (1988) have developed a schema that is loosely based on the four goals, but focused on aging parent–adult child relationship patterns. They designate these four patterns: (1) status equality, (2) status quo, (3) status conflict, and (4) status reversal. Keller and Hughston (1981) provide a detailed description of the four goals—which they term the "four levels of unproductive behavior"—and specific intervention strategies tailored to the elderly. Their approach more closely follows Dreikurs' schema. Because these four goals or levels have been described earlier in this text, we will not repeat that discussion but rather offer two case examples involving the application of these goals in understanding the behavior of the elderly.

> Florence J. is a 78-year-old widow who regularly congregates in the vicinity of the reception desk at the senior day care center. She will eagerly engage seniors, visitors, and staff in conversation. Increasingly annoyed but not wanting to hurt her feelings, the clerical staff had refrained from telling her that her interruptions diminish their job performance. In frustration they asked the center's psychological consultant for help. Concluding that the goal of Mrs. J.'s unproductive behavior was probably attention-getting, the consultant had four suggestions. First, that Mrs. J.'s distracting talk must be consistently ignored. Second, that her positive, socially useful behavior be vigorously reinforced. Third, she should be involved in group activities that can help satisfy her need for belonging and involvement. Finally, the clerical staff must apprise other staff of the plan and the need for consistency in implementing it, particularly regarding the first two points. Over the course of the first week in which the plan was implemented the staff noted that Mrs. J. spent less time in the reception area and more time participating in the activity groups. At the same time the clerical staff experienced less stress, were more productive, and felt they were more effective in dealing with seniors like Mrs. J.

> Arthur S. is a 69-year-old single male residing in an intermediate care nursing home for the past 12 months. During this time he has gradually withdrawn from nearly all activities. In the past three weeks he has taken meals only if they were served in his private room. He had not ventured into the dayroom or hall in the past 10 days. The only time he showed any positive reaction to patients or staff was when a female nursing assistant offered him some candy bars on Halloween. Staff tried repeatedly to engage him in conversation or activity, without success. Neither coercion nor threats seemed to work. Eventually, no one would ask or expect anything of him, believing it was hopeless to try. No medical condition could account for his behavior. The program's consultant was called in to help the staff evaluate the situation and set up a treatment plan. Because the likely goal of his unproductive behavior was judged to be disability, the consultant did not expect that Mr. S. would readily respond to encouragement and democratic-oriented initiatives that would ordinarily be effective with the other goals. The nursing assistant to whom Mr. S. had been most responsive was available and willing to work intensively with Mr. S. She was trained in behavioral shaping methods. The goal was to progressively reinforce Mr. S.'s active and socially useful behaviors, beginning with minimal nonverbal responses to others, to verbal responses, to initiating small conversations, to eating one meal per day in the dining area, to eating all three meals there, and then to involvement in other activity programs. After he began responding to the reinforcement program, democratically oriented strategies were begun. Concurrently, encouragement and support from other staff members and residents were used to further increase his personal and social skills.

2. Assess the individual's major risk factors in terms of the life tasks, particularly loss of spouse, friends, job, status, physical health, and independence. Other risk factors are social isolation—extent and availability of social support system such as friends, relatives, church and civic contacts; poverty; sensory deprivation—such as failing hearing and vision, which increases the individual's likelihood of misperceiving situations and others' intentions; and fears—particularly about death, inaccessibility to medical care and bank accounts, and similar issues.

3. Be aware of the individual's physical condition, and the degree to which the individual is able to be responsible for normal activities of daily living (ADLs). Be familiar with the effects and side effects of any medications the person may be taking. The side effects of many drugs prescribed for the elderly noticeably affect mood and cognitive functioning. A common response of a number of medications used with the elderly are depressive-like symptoms, decrease in immediate and short-term memory, and insomnia. Although medical and nursing personnel have primary responsibility for medical matters, all staff need to consider the effect physical condition and drugs have on a person's behavior and feelings.

Reorientation

1. Be available to the clients and their families if you are functioning in the counseling role, or to the staff if you are in the consultant's role. Be reachable by phone. If the counseling or consultation is a one-shot, informal event, make it known that you will be available for formal follow up if desired.

2. Always encourage social interest. Help the individual identify the possible ways the life tasks in question could be met. Emphasize the individuals' strengths and potential for development that exists at this stage of their life. Help them identify things they can still do for themselves and for others, and encourage them to keep doing them. Challenge them to do things that they haven't believed are possible or did not want to do, but of which they are physically capable.

3. Encourage self-esteem. This can be facilitated in many ways, but the technique of reminiscence and life review are particularly valuable with the elderly. Clients are helped to review the events of their life and see it as complete. This review reminds them that life is a series of crises and struggles as well as accomplishments, and that they have persevered and triumphed. To the extent that the counselor aids them in framing their past in this way, it can serve as a powerful motivation for elderly clients to try or to persevere in coping with the demands of the present.

4. The generic technique of encouragement is unquestionably the most important with the elderly. Encouragement is the primary antidote for inferiority feelings. When people encourage—that is, share their courage and the belief that the other person is important and worthwhile—elderly individuals are empowered in their quest to reconsider and relinquish feelings of inferiority in favor of feelings and behaviors more consistent with social interest.

5. Involve the family as fully as possible. It is usually necessary to teach them appropriate skills for dealing with their elderly relatives as well as for their own personal coping. With few exceptions, family members need help in adjusting their expectation for the functioning of the elderly person. Often family expectations are unrealistically low, such that their efforts to help actually result in decreasing adaptation, self-responsibility, and independence in their elderly relative. Standard counseling techniques are useful in helping the family to deal with the anger, frustration, and resentment related to caring for the elderly.

6. Develop a good working knowledge of available community resources and policies, especially regarding legal and financial issues involving the elderly.

Specific Techniques

1. *Reminiscence exercises.* The reminiscence technique involves the calling to mind of a experience or facts from the past to reconstruct and find added meaning in the past and subsequently in the present. This exercise can be done individually but is particularly valuable when used as a structured group activity. The technique usually involves a minimal amount of written response to stimulus items—"How old were you when you first saw a TV? When you first had a radio? Name the first person you dated"—which is followed by a group discussion. These exercises have been shown to stimulate cognitive processes; reduce depressive mood; stimulate common bonds, experiences and beliefs among group members; and stimulate a person's interest and motivate them to engage in activities in which they previously were uninvolved. Keller and Hughston (1981) provide some excellent materials for reminiscence exercises.

2. *Contracting.* Behavioral contracts are particularly suitable for dealing with the goals of power and revenge in the elderly. Contracts can promote desirable behavior while extinguishing undesirable patterns. The consequences for the desirable behavior are defined, clearly specified, and then agreed on by both counselor and the elderly individual. It is extremely important to specify the particular undesirable behavior as well as the expected desirable behavior. For example, it is too vague to say, "She is uncooperative. . . . Work at cooperating with others." Rather, state specific examples of undesirable behavior, such as, "He refuses to carry out morning household duties," "She is discourteous to other nursing home residents," "He makes critical remarks to group members." Examples of desirable behaviors might be, "She will remove all dirty dishes from the breakfast table seven days a week," or "He will make at least three encouraging remarks a day to other residents for the next five days."

3. *Group Assembly.* This group method is a variation of Dreikurs' Family Council concept for use in nursing homes and in the long-term care facilities for the elderly. The assembly involves regular meetings of residents on a particular unit or wing of a facility to foster personal independence and social interest within a democratic environment. The assembly makes a number of assumptions: All residents are to be treated equally and be extended mutual respect; nursing home policy directly relating to patient care is the business of all residents; and problems in the unit can be best solved when all residents work on them. If at all possible, the assembly is chaired by a resident who keeps order and allows everyone an opportunity to speak. Staff may need to organize the first meetings, but experience has shown that residents are able to take responsibility for the assembly to the extent that staff refrain from active involvement. The Group Assembly can revitalize the depressing atmosphere of most dependence-oriented nursing homes (Keller & Hughston, 1981).

4. *Couples Conference.* Like the Group Assembly, the Couples Conference can structure respect and self-dignity for spouses who live in their own homes. Keller and Hughston (1981) have found that the conference is a structure of support that ensures that each elderly spouse has equal access to the marriage rule-making

and goal-setting process. The counselor helps both spouses develop skills such as active listening, I–messages, and basic conflict resolution skills so the couple can meet weekly, and also discuss mutual concerns in their relationship on their own. Dinkmeyer and Carlson (1984) offer a further description of the Couples Conference.

Geriatric Psychotherapy

If counseling primarily addresses problems in daily living, involving only one life task, psychotherapy with the elderly can focus on both and address more global dysfunction. Research indicates that the most prevalent mental health problems of the elderly involve organic brain syndromes (OBS)—particularly dementias such as Alzheimer's disease—alcoholism, major depression, anxiety states, hypochondria, and paranoid disorders (Larson, Whanger, & Busse, 1983) Many of these types of dysfunction involve organic factors. Until recently, if any form of psychotherapy was available to the elderly it was primarily individual therapy, and it seldom was available to individuals with chronic, progressive OBS. Many traditionally trained therapists still believe that chronic OBS is an absolute contraindication for psychotherapy. However, Adlerian-oriented therapists like Brinks (1979) and Ionedes (1992) have found that a combination of individual and group psychotherapy can actually slow the progression of chronic OBS.

Dr. Lillian J. Martin, a pioneer in geriatric psychotherapy, developed the Martin Method in the 1930s. Her approach was brief—lasting only about five sessions—problem-focused, and centered on a comprehensive assessment of the individual's strengths. Positive affirmations were used as a form of thought stopping and self-control, and homework assignments involving daily activities and future goals were expected (Karpf, 1982). Needless to say, her method was largely ignored by the medical and psychological professions, in favor of psychoanalytically oriented approaches.

In the past, group, family, and behavioral approaches have been developed as stepchildren of individual approaches. A strong case can be made for therapeutic approaches that are problem-centered rather than those that are primarily insight or feeling-centered. Brinks (1979) believes that the mechanism for therapeutic efficacy lies in training the patient to think and act nonpathologically. He has found that the primary reason for the success of geriatric psychotherapy is that a long life constitutes valuable experience in effective coping, and that brief, problem-centered therapy provides the individual the additional training they need to cope with the problems of aging.

Brief, problem-focused psychotherapy can be provided in individual, group, family, and milieu contexts.

Individual and Group Therapy   The same guidelines that were given earlier for individual counseling also apply to psychotherapy, except that a formal but brief lifestyle assessment and life review is usually done. Most geriatric psychotherapy occurs in outpatient settings rather than in long-term inpatient care settings. The re-orientation phase may extend for five or more sessions and often may involve concurrent family or group sessions. Usually the focus is problem-oriented, with insight as a secondary goal.

The following case illustrates some features of both individual and group therapy.

> Jeanine G. is a 69-year-old who recently was widowed after 48 years of marriage. She has been living alone for the past 4 months and has become progressively depressed. She noted feelings of depression and rejection and avoidance of her regular friends. Spontaneous crying, weight and appetite loss, and early-morning awakening began around the first anniversary of her husband's death. Her family physician believed she was suffering from a delayed grief reaction and placed her on a low dose of antidepressant which soon resolved all symptoms except the feelings of rejection, isolation, and dysphoria.

> She was referred to a geropsychologist who began a brief course of Adlerian psychotherapy. The therapist's assessment indicated that Mrs. G. was ineffectively functioning in all three life tasks and that her lifestyle and coping strategies were of a person who needs to be liked and feels required to please others at all times. In individual sessions Mrs. G. learned that her rejection feelings—anger and hurt that her husband died and left her alone—were similar to those she experienced at other times in her life. This included the time her father and grandfather died in the same car accident when she was a child, and resulted in her need to be overly concerned with others' opinions of her and her need to please them. She was encouraged to meet daily with a friend outside her home and plan an activity that she really wanted, rather than simply acquiescing to her friend's plans. She agreed to this but found it difficult initially.

> Concurrent with her weekly individual sessions she was integrated into an ongoing therapy group of seven other elderly widows. She found that others experienced similar feelings of rejection and depression when their spouses died, and was encouraged and challenged by them to socialize with her friends and to assert herself when with them. Three months after beginning psychotherapy, Mrs. G. noted several positive changes in her life.

Milieu and Family Therapy   Milieu approaches for the elderly have recently been implemented in long-term care (LTC) facilities such as extended care, intermediate care, and skilled nursing facilities. Often a sizeable number of the residents of such facilities have Alzheimer's disease or other OBS conditions. In the past, only custodial care was extended to these individuals. Brinks (1979) describes in detail how the milieu approach has been successfully implemented in several facilities. Research shows that custodial care tends to reinforce a pampered patient role that often results in exaggerated disability, and that many patients who enter LTCs for purely physical reasons develop mental problems (Brinks, 1979). On the other hand, an effective milieu program trains patients to care for themselves and others, instead of how to be cared for by others. These kinds of Adlerian-oriented milieu programs emphasize patient activities: exercise programs, work therapy projects, arts and crafts, and reminiscence groups; behavior modification in many areas including incontinence—a problem for one-third of all patients in LTCs—and patient governance, including democratically based councils or assemblies. Family therapy involving the elderly often is a common feature of most day care programs for the elderly. It is particularly useful in connection with milieu programs, especially in dealing with the guilt, anger, and frustration that family members have about their elderly relatives.

The following case illustrates some of the features of milieu and family therapy.

> Joseph Z. is 70 years old, married, and recently entered a nursing home with a well-regarded milieu program. Since his retirement three years ago as service manager for a local car dealership, Mr. Z.'s family noted a progressive memory loss, which was subsequently diagnosed as Alzheimer's disease. He had been known as a strong-willed family man who demanded respect from friends and coworkers. Recently, he would get lost while taking walks in the neighborhood he has lived in for the past 35 years. This along with stubbornness, incontinence, and combativeness lead to his admission into the nursing facility.
>
> Within a few weeks, Mr. Z. was able to be integrated into many ongoing social, exercise, and work-group activities in the milieu program. Encouragement, contracting, and behavior modification techniques counteracted his incontinence, stubbornness, and combativeness with more socially useful and independent behaviors.
>
> In spite of the progression of his memory loss, Mr. Z. was able to participate in some of the reminiscence and group assembly sessions. Five family sessions were convened by the program's counselor to deal with Mr. Z. and the eldest son's guilt about "dumping" Mr. Z. in the nursing facility because they felt powerless in caring for him at home. The family's underlying anger and resentment about his dictatorial manner throughout the years, the more recent combativeness, and other losses of control such as his incontinence, were therapeutically addressed.

Concluding Comments

The quote of Adler that opened this chapter was penned nearly 50 years ago, yet it is remarkably cogent today. Although more is being done for the elderly now than in the past, much more is needed. Research confirms Adler's observation that inferiority feelings are widespread among the elderly, primarily because they can no longer meet the tasks of life as they were previously able. But to the extent that concerned and knowledgeable professionals and others can encourage and enable the elderly to find different ways of meeting the tasks of life, the elderly can remain productive rather than resorting to such unproductive behaviors as attention-getting, power, revenge, or the various kinds of disablement that remain all too common in our society.

RECOMMENDED READINGS

Following is a list of annotated resources that those working with the elderly have found helpful. Highlighted are three seminal books with an Adlerian approach to working with older adults. Also noted is a special issue of *Individual Psychology* focused on psychotherapy with the elderly.

Keller, J., & Hughston, G. (1981). *Counseling the elderly: A systems approach*. New York: Harper and Row.

This book has an acknowledged Adlerian orientation and focuses on the problems of daily living in the elderly. It specifically excludes issues or psychosis or OBS. Much of the therapeutic orientation is focused on the four goals or levels of unproductive behavior. Excellent materials for conducting reminiscence exercises are provided in an appendix.

Brinks, T. L. (1979). *Geriatric psychotherapy*. New York: Human Sciences Press.

This author acknowledges the Adlerian approach as the most viable psychological system for treating the elderly. He emphasizes psychotherapeutic interventions with the more seriously dysfunctional elderly, including those with OBS and various psychotic processes. His chapters on treating the elderly in LTCs reflect the author's years of experience as a master therapist.

Shulman, B., & Berman, R. (1988). *How to survive your aging parents*. New York: Hawthorne.

The authors address the many psychosocial concerns of adult children in caregiver roles with their aging parents. They suggest that aging parent–adult child relationships follow one of four patterns depending on the status the aging parent retains and the role the adult child plays. These four patterns are modifications of Dreikurs' four goals of misbehavior.

Sperry, L. (Ed.). (1992). Special issue: The process of aging and working with older adults. *Individual Psychology, 48*(4), 385–461.

Nine articles make up this special issue. Highlighted are descriptions of Adlerian psychotherapeutic interventions with Alzheimer's disease and depression, two common disorders of older adults present in to clinical settings. Ansbacher's article on community feeling as it relates to the elderly is probably the most important contribution to the Adlerian literature in the last 25 years.

Busse, E., & Blazer, D. (Eds.). (1980). *The handbook of geriatric psychiatry*. New York: Van Nostrand Reinhold.

Probably the authoritative handbook in the field to date. This exhaustive reference for professionals covers every conceivable mental health concern of the elderly.

Mace, N., & Rabins, R. (1981). *The 36 hour day*. Baltimore: Johns Hopkins University Press.

A comforting, encouraging, and useful resource for family members who wish to learn more about Alzheimer's disease and related disorders. This well-written book has become required reading for many professional courses and seminars on treating individuals with dementia.

Brinks, T. L. (Ed.). (All issues). *Clinical Gerontology*, a quarterly journal.

One of the few professional journals focusing on psychotherapeutic issues dealing with the elderly. Consistently theoretically sound and practically significant articles for counselors and therapists working in all settings involving the elderly.

REFERENCES

Adler, A. (1956). The Individual Psychology of Alfred Adler. In H. Ansbacher & R. Ansbacher (Eds.), New York: Harper and Row.

Ansbacher, H. (1992). Alfred Adler's concept of community feeling and of social interest and the relevance of community feeling for old age. *Individual Psychology, 48*(4), 402–412.

Brinks, T. (1979). *Geriatric psychotherapy*. New York: Human Sciences Press.

Dinkmeyer, D., & Carlson, J. (1984). *Time for a better marriage*. Circle Pines, MN: American Guidance Service.

Dreikurs, R. (1953). *Fundamentals of Adlerian psychology*. Chicago: Alfred Adler Institute.

Ionedes, N. (1992). A therapy program for Alzheimer's disease: An Adlerian orientation. *Individual Psychology, 48*(4), 413–418.

Karpf, R. (1982). Individual psychotherapy with the elderly. In A. Horton (Ed.), *Mental health interventions for the aging*. New York: Prager Publisher.

Keller, J., & Hughston, G. (1981). *Counseling the elderly: A systems approach*. New York: Harper and Row.

Larsen, D., Whanger, A., & Busse, E. (1983). Geriatrics. In B. Wolman (Ed.), *The therapist's handbook,* 2nd ed. New York: Van Nostrand Reinhold.

Shulman, B., & Berman, R. (1988). *How to survive your aging parents*. New York: Hawthorne.

Shulman, B., & Sperry, L. (1992). Consultation with adult children of aging parents. *Individual Psychology, 48*(4), 427–431.

CHAPTER 10

Health Counseling

T here have been a number of changes in the delivery of health-care services in the past few years, and it is anticipated that there will be many more. These changes involve both the service provided and the providers of the service. Research has shown that health counseling can increase a patients' understanding of and compliance with their treatment plan, as well as satisfaction with the service and the provider, it appears counseling is part of the solution to present health-care crisis (Strecher, 1982; Sperry, 1986; Sperry, Carlson, & Lewis, 1993).

Until recently, members of the health-care community had little interest or training in this area. Thus psychologists and other mental health professionals who are trained in counseling and behavior change skills are being actively recruited into the health-care community. In 1979 about 39% of doctoral-level applied psychologists were employed in health-care settings, and it was estimated that some 60% were by 1990. Not surprisingly, one of the fastest growing divisions of the American Psychological Association is the Division of Health Psychology. It has been suggested that changes in the marketplace and in reimbursement patterns will alter the traditional image of the mental health professional as a psychotherapist. DeLeon (1985) suggests that psychologists at the nation's largest health maintenance organizations

(HMO) view and project themselves as behavioral medicine specialists first and psychotherapists second. Recently the American Psychological Association has endorsed DeLeon's proposal.

The need for professionals trained in health counseling skills will continue to increase. With some additional training, professionals already trained in personal counseling and psychotherapy can be prepared to practice health-care counseling. This chapter will overview the skills and knowledge base of health-care counseling from an Adlerian perspective and suggest some of the major theoretical and professional issues unique to this field.

ISSUES IN HEALTH COUNSELING

Health counseling has two categories: (1) health restoration and (2) health maintenance/health promotion counseling. In health restoration counseling, the counselor intervenes to restore some measure of functional capacity in either an acute or chronic situation. Here is an example of an acute care intervention:

> An elderly female was brought into the emergency room in the late afternoon having dislocated her shoulder in a doorway. Several attempts to reduce the dislocation by manipulating the joint were unsuccessful and it appeared that surgery would be necessary. The liaison psychologist was called and, noting that the woman was deeply apprehensive and tense despite the pain medication and muscle relaxant given her, was able to calm and relax her with guided imagery and the conscious suggestion that she was so relaxed that her shoulder would gently slide into place. The orthopedic surgeon was subsequently able to easily reduce the dislocation.

With a chronic ailment, health restoration counseling would resemble the kind of intervention a rehabilitation counselor might use with a brain injured young male recovering from a motorcycle accident.

Health maintenance and health promotion counseling, on the other hand, focuses on maintaining or improving the current level of functioning. This usually takes the form of reducing risks of heart disease, stroke, or cancer. For example, health-care counseling might be indicated for the middle-level manager who has been passed over for promotion because of obesity and has been unsuccessful with several attempts at weight reduction and management. It could be indicated when previous attempts to manage stress, stop smoking, or to stay on an exercise program have been unsuccessful. It could also be indicated in situations where a hypertensive individual has difficulty complying with needed blood pressure medication thus compounding other risks that individual has for a stroke.

For the purpose of this chapter, we will limit our discussion to the second type of health counseling, variously called health promotion counseling, lifestyle change counseling or behavioral medicine counseling (Sperry, 1984). To avoid confusion, the term *lifestyle* retains its traditional Adlerian denotation as the individual's unique life plan or personality structure, while *lifestyle* will refer to an individuals' personal health habits such as diet, exercise, use of drugs and other substances, strategies for managing stress, and so on. Current health counseling literature prefers the use of *patient* rather than *client* and this convention will be followed in this chapter.

Health counseling and personal counseling or psychotherapy represent different ways of working with patients and clients (Sperry, 1987). Compared with psychotherapy, health counseling involves a more action-oriented and participative relationship between a patient with a need to reduce health risks or change lifestyle patterns, and a skilled clinician who can facilitate the individual's acquisition and maintenance of these health changes. The duration of treatment is usually brief, often no more than 6 to 10 sessions of 30 minutes each after an initial evaluation session of 60 to 90 minutes. Treatment is more oriented to prevention and is based on changing health beliefs and behaviors primarily through information and instruction, as well as behavior modification, skill training, and cognitive restructuring (Sperry, Carlson, & Lewis, 1993). Insight is a secondary consideration.

Health counseling has five key factors: (1) negotiation, (2) tailoring, (3) compliance, (4) relapse prevention, and (5) multimodal intervention strategies (Sperry, 1986). The reason that most efforts at health maintenance and promotion fail is the patient's lack of recognition of these key factors. No matter how excellent the lifestyle change program, it will likely fail if the patient perceives it as primarily the counselor's program. Extended discussion is usually needed to negotiate an agreement between the patient and counselor's expectations and involvement in a change program, and the specific ways the program is tailored to the needs of the individual and the demands of the individual's environment. Once planned and implemented, considerable effort must be accorded the patient's compliance or adherence to the program. Close supervision, training in self-management skills, and appropriate feedback is needed if the patient is to continue new patterns of behavior.

Relapse prevention also must be an intentional part of the change program (Sperry, 1985). Counselors must prepare patients for occasional slips—for example, the first cigarette for the individual on a smoking cessation program. Patients learn to apply some "brakes" so that the slip does not escalate into a full-blown relapse.

Finally, unlike most other kinds of counseling, an underlying assumption of health counseling is that multimodal intervention strategies are usually necessary to reverse deeply ingrained cognitive and behavioral patterns. Thus, cognitive, behavioral, and environmental change efforts must be combined to break habits as well as effect physiological and biochemical changes. This kind of multimodal approach usually implies that collaboration with other members of the health-care team will be necessary (Lewis, Sperry, & Carlson, 1993).

AN ADLERIAN APPROACH TO HEALTH COUNSELING

The professional involved in counseling for health maintenance/promotion will find a great deal of theoretical and practical wisdom in the Adlerian approach to counseling and psychotherapy. Conceptually, Adlerians had been writing about holistic medicine for 50 years before the term became fashionable. Unlike the reductionism of modern medicine and health care, Adler spoke of the indivisibility of the person and the need to treat the whole person. He explained that bodily functions:

> . . . speak a language which is usually more expensive and discloses the individual's opinion more clearly than words are able to do. . . . The emotions and their physical expression tell us how the mind is acting and reacting in a situation which it interprets as favorable or unfavorable. (Adler, 1956)

Rudolf Dreikurs (1977) further developed Adlerian thinking on holistic medicine and psychotherapy.

Adlerians view somatic symptoms holistically as manifestations of lifestyle convictions that are inwardly experienced and simultaneously outwardly expressed. Symptoms or conditions like smoking, obesity, hypertension, or chronic stress find their outward or organic expression through one or more of the following: a constitutional predisposition—organ inferiority, which makes it available to the person; social modeling by a family member: "Everyone in my family smokes"; symbolic values to the patient: obesity as a compensation or the loss of a love. The organic expression also may be chosen because it is fashionable. For example, bulimia is common today whereas hysterical paralysis is passé (Griffith, 1984).

Practically, the Adlerian notions of cooperation, lifestyle assessment, and treating the whole person complement the health counseling factors of negotiation, tailoring, compliance, relapse prevention, and multimodal interventions. Adlerians constantly stress the development of a participative therapeutic relationship based on cooperation and social equality. This focus on a participative relationship embodies the notion of negotiation which invariably fosters compliance or adherence to the treatment plan. Searching for the uniqueness of the individual's lifestyle convictions is a key to tailoring a treatment plan. Another distinguishing feature of Adlerian therapy is the wide range of techniques, often used in combination to effect change. On the other hand, relapse prevention is a concept that seems less well developed in Adlerian practice.

In an Adlerian approach to health counseling, health beliefs are a central feature. Health beliefs are the convictions that inform and affect a person's health and illness behaviors. As such, health beliefs are intimately related to one's lifestyle conviction. Just as there is a self-view or image component to the lifestyle, there is a body image component. Knowing an individual's body image will reveal much about that individual's susceptibility or immunity to stress and disease processes, as well as their likelihood to minimize or be oversensitive to a stressor.

Health beliefs are also reflected in one's world view. They suggest the value that illness or a health condition has for them, especially with regard to convictions about entitlement, superiority/martyrdom, and control/manipulation. Similarly, the individual's life goal and strategies reflect these health beliefs. These beliefs can be assessed in a number of ways. A method of assessing them through early recollections will be described later in the chapter.

Three phases of the counseling and psychotherapy process have been described throughout this book. We will describe the means of developing the relationship and engaging the patient, conducting the assessment, and reorienting and consolidating the lifestyle change process.

Relationship

The relationship between the counselor and the patient is developed in a fashion similar to that in personal counseling or psychotherapy. There are, however, some important differences involving timing and intentionality. In psychotherapy the task of developing the relationship can be leisurely accomplished over the course of the first three or four sessions, but due to the brief and focused nature of health counseling, achieving cooperation and a negotiated treatment agreement is the primary task of the first session. The first session is scheduled for 60 to 90 minutes and is not important of all sessions. During this time the counselor must come to understand the patient's reasons and the degree of motivation for wanting the particular lifestyle change. If the change is sought primarily to appease a spouse or the family physician, this needs to be dealt with at the outset, and if little or no intrinsic motivation can be elicited, the probabilities of limited success needs to be confronted and openly discussed (Sperry, 1994). A consideration of continuing or stopping treatment should be made.

Next, the "three questions" are asked of the patient. The first involves a functional assessment: "How does your (obesity; stress; high blood pressure) interfere with your daily life?" or "How would your life be different if you did not have _____?" This general question is followed by specific questions about the life tasks of work, love, and friendship. The extent of distress accompanying impaired functioning is often related to the patients' receptivity to change. The counselor must be alert to the payoff or gain that this dysfunction may provide patients and interfere with their change efforts.

The second question involves patients' personal explanations for the symptom or condition: "What do you believe is the reason for your (obesity; stress; high blood pressure)?" The answer to this and follow-up questions will begin to suggest the lifestyle—health beliefs as well as the extent of the factual accuracy that patients have of their condition and prognosis. This will be one determinant of the amount of information and education the counselor will need to provide at a later time.

The third set of questions help elicit patients' expectations for treatment in terms of their own and the counselor's involvement of time and effort, expected outcome and satisfaction: "What specifically were you hoping to accomplish?" "In what time?" "What sort of involvement do you expect of yourself?" "What do you expect of me?" Next, the counselor will do well to evaluate patients' previous efforts to make lifestyle changes. This is then followed by eliciting specific information about the number of attempts, the length of time, the extent of success, the outside help, and the reasons for quitting or noncompliance are important factors in patients' expectations for success or failure.

Based on an understanding of this background information, particularly patients' expectations for treatment and outcome, counselors can propose what they consider realistic expectations for a change program with broad timelines, level of involvement, and expected outcomes and discusses these in relation to the patients' expectations. The discussion that follows constitutes the negotiation process such that a mutually agreed on contract for change emerges. Often this agreement takes written form and is couched in performance-based language. Here is an example of the first phase:

> Jean S. is a 28-year-old, single middle manager at the national headquarters of a large insurance company. She was referred by her physician to a psychologist for help with a weight reduction program. The physician was concerned not only with her obesity but also a family history of early death from heart disease. In the first session the psychologist elicited the following information: Ms. S. came not only because of her doctor's referral but also because she was passed over for promotion twice in the past nine months presumably because of her weight and because she has felt herself losing all control over her cravings for certain foods recently. She lives with her mother and stepfather amid considerable family discord. Her father, who was morbidly obese, died at the age of 40 of a massive heart attack, and her life has not been the same since his death.
>
> Her responses to the three questions are noteworthy. First of all, she is able to function adequately at home and on the job but notes she has less energy for hobbies and social activities in the past two months. She attributes this to stress but admits she is a little depressed about being passed over for promotion when she believes she was clearly the first choice were it not for her appearance—75 pounds over her ideal weight. Thus, her life task functioning is somewhat impaired but not grossly. Secondly, she believes her overweight is due to family gland problems noting that all her older siblings and her parents were also overweight. She is also fearful that she too will die of a heart attack or stroke at an early age, and says, "It's just a matter of time." Third, she believes that the best treatment for her is a liquid protein diet which can result in rapid weight loss, but which her doctor has refused to prescribe because of the cardiac risks. She has instead placed her on a 1,200-calorie protein-sparing diet and an aerobic exercise program. She has heard that hypnosis has worked for some of her friends and was hoping the psychologist would try it with her. It was learned that Ms. S. had been on several "miracle" weight loss diets losing up to 20 pounds in 2 weeks but gaining it all back in a few days. She said she was "addicted" to chocolate and whenever she was overstressed, particularly with family matters, she would go to her room and binge on chocolate.
>
> The psychologist empathetically reflected Ms. S.'s concerns about losing control and her fear of death, and proposed what he thought would be an appropriate treatment plan: Rapid weight reduction of 40 pounds could be expected over 15 weeks on the doctor's diet plan, some kind of aerobics program and low demands at first—probably short walks—increasing in intensity every week, along with a behavioral approach to modify eating patterns and some cognitive restructuring to modify lifestyle—health belief convictions associated with loss of control and body image. He further suggested a family session to clarify issues at home and help establish a support system for her weight loss program. After considerable discussion Ms. S. agreed that exercise was really needed but was not willing to walk or jog because of joint problems. Both agreed that a group exercise program would be appropriate. She admitted that her reason for wanting hypnosis was "because it seemed like a quick fix," but that it probably would not be too helpful for that very reason. She was reluctant to have her family involved in her treatment, thinking that they had no effect on her, but she was willing to invite her family to one of the next biweekly sessions and possibly to one of the four monthly follow-up sessions after she had lost the target weight. She had no reservations about the behavioral or cognitive restructuring approaches. By the end of their first session a mutually negotiated treatment plan emerged which was put into writing and signed both by Ms. S. and the psychologist.

Assessment

The assessment phase in Adlerian health counseling tends to be more focused and briefer than in personal psychotherapy. It attempts to understand the person's present health beliefs and behaviors in terms of personal and contextual factors. The basic feature of the personal factors assessment involves an abbreviated examination of the Lifestyle if time does not permit a complete Lifestyle Assessment. An abbreviated Lifestyle would cover only those early recollections directly related to matters of health and illness. Other personal factors to be assessed are health beliefs and behaviors, past and current gain or payoffs for the current health condition or symptoms, and the extent and accuracy of the individual's knowledge about his condition. The earliest recollection should be sought and then it is helpful to elucidate the person's health beliefs through special recollections. This is done by asking the person to recall singular experiences when they were ill or that involved other family members or relatives who were ill. Often responses will provide valuable insights into the person's body image and Lifestyle convictions, particularly about entitlement, superiority—martyrdom, and control.

In terms of contextual factors it would be helpful to do a brief family constellation with a focus on family values related to health and illness behaviors, and to know about the health and illness behaviors of other family members or relatives that could have served as social models for the patient. It is essential that the counselor assess the patient's cultural health status, which according to Allen (1981) consists of the "silent" attitudes and norms of one's family, social and ethnic groups, and community that influences and reinforces certain health behaviors and not others. Allen indicated that we all are influenced by cultural norm indicators for exercise, smoking, stress, weight control, nutrition, alcohol and alcohol abuse, safety and mental health, and had developed several paper and pencil inventories to elucidate these cultural norms. Let's return to our case example:

> Ms. S.'s first health-related early recollection at age 6 involved a big argument between her parents about the amount of cake and snacks she had devoured at her birthday party. Her father was embarrassed while her mother defended Jean's overweight "as normal for a girl her age." As Jean began to cry, complaining of a stomach ache, her mother called the family doctor asking him to make an emergency house call. After the doctor assured the family that everything would be all right, the mother kissed Jean and whispered that she could eat the rest of the birthday cake and snacks whenever she wanted. Ms. S. remembers feeling fearful and helpless while her parents were quarreling. A second recollection at age 9 involved a shopping trip with her mother. Jean had picked out two dresses to try on only to find that she couldn't get into them because they were three sizes too small. Her mother laughed and said, "Don't feel bad, I'll take you to lunch." Ms. S. remembers looking at herself in the fitting room mirror wearing the small dresses and saying sadly, "I thought it would fit," while her mother laughed.
>
> Based on Ms. S.'s early recollections and other indicators of health beliefs, family values, and beliefs about health and illness, illness models, and cultural norms, the psychologist developed this formulation: Ms. S. views her inner self as small and inadequate within a big powerful body which commands the attention of others. She sees the world as demanding and dangerous, especially for the assertive, but less so for those who are ill or obese. Therefore her goal is to appear big and strong but to avoid conflict at all cost. Overeating serves as an illusion of safety for her and focuses attention away from family

problems, especially parental disputes. Because she failed to develop many proactive life skills, she is likely to feel out of control with job and family demands; thus, overeating symbolizes the control issue. Her payoffs for being ill and obese as a child involved special parental attention that diverted attention from the bitter fights between her parents, and being allowed to stay home from school because of "illness" when tests came up and occasionally on gym class days.

Not surprisingly, early life health behavior history showed that she modeled the illness–obesity behavior of her natural father. Currently, her mother appears to be a good source of support for a weight management program because, as in Ms. S.'s past weight-loss efforts, she was willing to prepare the special foods the diet required. Ms. S. has a girlfriend in the office who would probably be willing to serve as a support function during lunch and break times. Finally, Ms. S.'s responses to a paper-and-pencil inventory showed that she subscribes to a number of cultural norms which appear to reinforce her lifestyle convictions: "Being a few pounds overweight is perfectly natural"; "It's expected that if you lose weight through dieting you will gain it right back"; "Everybody loves a fat person"; "It's natural to eat when one is lonely or has hurt feelings"; "Sweets are a special reward for good behavior and therefore are more 'rewarding' than more nutritious foods"; and "It's natural to be overweight if you belong to certain ethnic groups" (Allen, 1981, p. 113).

Reorientation

Intervention can occur on two main levels: the individual level and the family level. At the individual level, encouragement is the basic nonspecific intervention. Specific interventions involve information and instruction; cognitive restructuring; and behavior modification, including setting behavioral goals, monitoring and pattern identification, stimulus control, reinforcement, and relapse prevention training. Some of these techniques are described in detail in Chapter 6 on counseling and psychotherapy techniques. Because relapse prevention is a relatively new approach, we will provide a brief overview and refer the interested reader to Marlatt and Gordon (1984) for a detailed discussion. Relapse prevention consists of teaching the patient both behavioral skills and cognitive strategies so that the individual can avoid high-risk situations and overly high expectations that could likely result in relapse or to apply the brakes so that once a slip occurs it does not escalate into a full-blown relapse. The individual is also helped to increase their ability to cope with cravings as well as anxiety and other determinants of relapse. "Relapse drills," in which the individual is able to practice these learned skills are an important aspect of relapse prevention.

Intervention at the family level has the express purpose of increasing compliance and minimizing relapse. Drop-out rates from lifestyle change programs are as high as 80% when no health counseling is provided (Lewis, Sperry, & Carlson, 1993). Enlisting the aid of social support systems like the family, co-workers, or friends is a critical task for both patient and counselor.

Not surprisingly, the more uninvolved and the more dysfunctional the family or the marital partner, the more the counselor can anticipate problems in implementing any change program. To the extent that family members can be incorporated in the change program the more likely that the program will be successful. For example, Brownell (1984) reports that when obese patients' spouses attended weight-loss sessions in which the spouses were encouraged to modify their own eating habits along with their spouse, weight loss and maintenance was greater than for the control group studies. Brownell also found that an unwilling spouse can and often does sabotage the patient's treatment program. Dishman, Sallis, and Orenstein (1985) reviewed the research on compliance with exercise programs and concluded that the spouses attitudes toward the change program are probably more important than the patients'. If family members can be directly involved in individual or group sessions, they should be encouraged or even required to participate. If this is not possible, the family's indirect support should be enlisted. Doherty and Baird (1983) describe family compliance counseling as one way of enlisting this support.

Family compliance counseling involves the following processes: After the change program has been negotiated, the patient is asked to come to the next session with his family. The counselor begins the session by providing information about the health condition to all family members and answers whatever content questions they may have. This is done to develop a common mindset and set the stage for a family commitment to the change program. The counselor then asks for the family's reaction to the patient's health problem and about the proposed change program. Next, the counselor helps the family make a contract for compliance to the change program. She does this by asking the patient if he would like help from the family. Assuming the response is affirmative, the counselor asks the patient what kind of help he would like, and so on until a family contract emerges. At this point the counselor might provide specific health promotional literature to family members, which could clarify and increase their involvement in the program. Finally, a follow-up session is scheduled to evaluate the patient's progress and the family's support contract (Sperry, 1995). Let's return to our case example.

> Although a contract for change was negotiated and the assessment suggested specific change strategies, a multimodal and collaborative intervention plan evolved. At the behavioral level, Ms. S. was instructed in behavior modification methods for changing her eating behavior. Skill training in assertiveness was begun. At the cognitive level, the psychologist worked with Ms. S. to challenge and restructure some of her lifestyle convictions—health beliefs in a more socially useful direction. He reframed Ms. S.'s occasional relapses as slips rather than failures. At the social support level, a family session resulted in Ms. S.'s mother agreeing to prepare meals consistent with her prescribed 1,200-calorie meal plan, and her mother was agreeable to adopting the plan for at least the first 15 weeks. Ms. S. enlisted the support of her girlfriend at work, and also joined a support group run by the psychologist for other business people who were involved in similar change programs. She joined a beginner's aerobic dance class at a local YWCA since she did not think she could motivate herself to exercise alone. At the physiological level, Jean continued to be monitored medically by her physician, and both the psychologist and the physician conferred with each other over the course of the eight months Ms. S. was formally involved with health counseling. After the seven biweekly sessions, four follow-up monthly sessions were planned, as well as a 12-month follow-up meeting. At the end of the eighth month, Jean has succeeded in reducing and maintaining within 5 pounds of her ideal weight.

This case illustrates health counseling in a private practice setting. Health counseling in a public clinic is illustrated in the following case.

Jim N. is a 42-year-old married salesman who had undergone a triple bypass operation nine weeks before being referred to the hospital's cardiac rehabilitation program counselor. Mr. N. was placed on a standard postsurgical exercise program in the hospital and did well enough to be discharged to the outpatient program after three weeks. But after adhering to the outpatient program for one week, Mr. N.'s attendance started to decline and he began to doubt that he would ever return to his job. Before the surgery, Mr. N. described himself as a hard-working, hard-drinking, charter member of the salespersons' million dollar club. He had been under considerable pressure to close his company's largest account at the time he experienced the crushing chest pain that led to his emergency surgery. Now he was unsure of his ability to even drive his car to the regional sales office, much less perform as a top salesman.

In response to the three questions, he mentioned his fear of having another heart attack and dying while jogging or riding his exercycle. With some embarrassment he recounted his fear of resuming sexual relations with his wife for the same reason. Thus he was unwilling to continue any exercise that could not be monitored closely as in the hospital program.

His family history shows that as the oldest child he assumed much of the responsibility for supporting his family. His alcoholic father was injured in World War I and could provide only a meager disability check each month. Mr. N. worked at a series of part-time jobs all the time he was in school to help meet the expenses of a family of seven. He was seldom ill, but when he was, his mother doted on him. He expects that he may never fully recover and has been considering the possibility of an early pension. But he does not think he has reached that point. His earliest health-related recollection was of developing a mild case of pneumonia at age 9. That rainy spring he had been working at an outdoor shoeshine stand for six to seven hours a day after school and about 12 hours a day on weekends for three weeks before succumbing to pneumonia. He recalls lying in bed feeling weak and pained every time he breathed while his mother told him how courageous and hardworking he was and his inebriated father shouted from anther room that Mr. N. was a quitter and would never amount to anything. Mr. N. believed he had failed and vowed he would never fail or become sick again. This and another two recollections showed that Mr. N. viewed himself as having little self-worth and the world as a big testing place that expected tremendous accomplishments from him. His goal was to prove himself through his job and even through sexual relations. His body image was that of a finely tuned sprinter who could successfully compete in short events but not endure the longer ones.

Both his wife and his boss were willing and able to provide all the social support he needed to comply with the treatment program. Mr. N. and the counselor were able to negotiate a contract aimed at returning him to at least his previous level of physical functioning, with the possibility of him returning to work. With the collaboration of his physician and the program's exercise physiologist, the counselor worked with Mr. N. on some behavioral and environmental restructuring. At the same time he worked with Mr. N. on challenging and restructuring some of his health beliefs. He met with Mr. N. and his wife to discuss his health conditions and concerns about the risks associated with lovemaking and returning to work. The more Mr. N. came to understand the basis of fears of disability or death from a second heart attack, the more willing he was to comply with the carefully laid out exercise and nutrition prescription worked out with his physician and the exercise physiologist. Within six weeks Mr. N. was able to return to work with a more realistic understanding of his needs and abilities. A phone check 12 months later found him promoted to regional sales manager and reporting a more satisfying marriage.

Both of these case examples suggest some of the ways in which health counselors function. In the first instance, the psychologist provided a full range of services in the private practice setting over a period of several months. In the second instance, the rehab counselor functioned in a more limited and focused role, and for a shorter period of time.

THE PRACTICE OF HEALTH COUNSELING

To be effective in the practice of health counseling the counselor or psychotherapist must be conversant with medical and health-care terminology as well as with the biopsychosocial view of health and illness. The terms of *behavioral medicine* and *health psychology* refer to the study of health and illness behavior from a behavioral science perspective. The interested reader is referred to handbooks by Stone, Cohen, and Adler (1980), Davidson and Davidson (1980), and Millon, Green, and Meagher (1982) for a readable introduction and overview of this newly emerging field. Graduate level courses and postgraduate CEU programs are now commonplace, as are pre- and postdoctoral internships and fellowships in health psychology and behavioral medicine.

Lewis, Sperry, and Carlson (1993) focus on health counseling strategies and tactics directed to traditionally trained counselors and psychotherapists who wish to extend their knowledge and skill base to health-related concerns. The book provides practical and effective methods of assessment and treatment—individual, group, couples, and family—to weight control, smoking cessation, drug and alcohol abuse, exercise, sleep problems, sexual problems, chronic pain, and other chronic medical problems.

Counselors and psychotherapists who have little familiarity with the referral process and working relationships with other health-care personnel, particularly physicians, may be in for some surprises. For better or worse, there is a certain protocol and pecking order in the health-care community. The counselor or psychotherapist who is flexible yet assertive can expect to be accepted and esteemed by other health-care workers after a brief "proving" period. There are various ways in which health counseling can be practiced. Currently, the kind of health counseling we have described in this chapter is being done by counselors or psychologists who are salaried by a behavioral medicine or wellness program in a hospital, clinic, or HMO. Our second case example typifies this application. A small but growing number of psychologists are involved in the private practice of health counseling, as exemplified in the first case example. The reader is referred to a special issue of the *Family Therapy Networker* (1984, January) for some first-person accounts of health counselor–physician collaborative relationships in different practice arrangements.

When a counselor undertakes the practice of health counseling certain medical–legal issues emerge. It is beyond the scope of this chapter to discuss these issues, however, we will mention one of the most important, which deals with the matter of diagnosis and treatment. Many states restrict the use of the terms *diagnosis* and *treatment* of health conditions in verbal and written language to those licensed to practice medicine, dentistry, and podiatry, while other states extend this usage to licensed psychologists. By and large, other health-care workers are intimately involved in the diagnostic and treatment process but they must exercise care in the specific use of these terms in verbal and written communication with the patient, medical records, and so on. Prudent judgment in this area shields the counselor from the increasing number of malpractice suits and claims of practicing medicine without a license.

REFERENCES

Adler, A. (1956). The Individual Psychology of Alfred Adler. In H. Ansbacher & R. Ansbacher (Eds.), New York: Harper and Row.

Allen, R. (1981). *Lifeagain*. New York: Appleton-Century-Crofts.

Brownell, K. (1984). The psychology and physiology of obesity: Implications for screening and treatment. *Journal of American Dietetics Association, 84*(4), 406–414.

Davidson, P., & Davidson, S. (1980). *Behavioral medicine: Changing health lifestyle*. New York: Brunner/Mazel Publishers.

DeLeon, P., Uyeda, M., & Welch, B. (1985). Psychology and HMOs: New partnership or new adversary? *American Psychologist, 40*(10), 1122–1124.

Dishman, J., Sallis, J., & Orenstein, D. (1985). Relationship between exercise and other health behaviors. *Public Health Reports, 100*(2), 158–171.

Doherty, W., & Baird, M. (1983). *Family therapy and family medicine*. New York: Guilford Press.

Dreikurs, R. (1977). Holistic medicine and the function of neurosis. *Journal of Individual Psychology, 13*(2), 171–192.

Griffith, J. (1984). Adler's organ jargon. *Individual Psychology, 40*(4), 437–444.

Lewis, J., Sperry, L., & Carlson, J. (1993). *Health counseling*. Pacific Grove: Brooks/Cole.

Marlatt, G., & Gordon, J. (Eds.). (1984). *Relapse prevention*. New York: Guilford Press.

Millon, T., Green, C., & Meagher, R. (Eds.). (1982). *Handbook of clinical health psychology*. New York: Plenum Press.

Sperry, L. (1984). Health promotion and wellness medicine in the workplace: Programs, promises, and problems. *Individual Psychology, 40*(4), 384–400.

Sperry, L. (1985). Treatment noncompliance and cooperation: Implication for psychotherapeutic, medical and lifestyle change approaches. *Individual Psychology, 41*(2), 228–236.

Sperry, L. (1986). The ingredients of effective health counseling: Health beliefs, compliance and relapse prevention. *Individual Psychology, 42*(2), 279–287.

Sperry, L. (1987). ERIC: A cognitive map for guiding brief therapy and health care counseling. *Individual Psychology, 43*(2), 237–241.

Sperry, L. (1994). Helping people control their weight: Research and practice. In J. Lewis (Ed.), *Addictions: Concepts and strategies for treatment* (pp. 83–98). Gaithersburg, MD: Aspen.

Sperry, L. (1995). *Psychopharmacology and psychotherapy*. New York: Brunner/Mazel.

Sperry, L., Carlson, J., & Lewis, J. (1993). Health counseling strategies and interventions. *Journal of Mental Health Counseling, 15*(1), 15–25.

Stone, G., Cohen, F., & Adler, N. (Eds.). (1980). *Health psychology: A handbook*. San Francisco: Jossey-Bass Publishers.

Strecher, V. (1982). Improving physician–patient interactions: A review. *Patient Counseling and Health Education, 4*(3), 129–136.

CHAPTER 11

Group Counseling and Therapy

The holistic, social, purposive, and decision-making nature of human behavior makes groups an effective resource for influencing attitudes and behavior. Group counseling and group psychotherapy are an interpersonal process led by a professional trained in group procedures. Group counseling usually focuses on exploring typical developmental problems—for example, getting along with peers, or meeting the challenges of life tasks. Group therapy is more concerned with the correction of mistaken assumptions about lifestyle. In this chapter, we will use the terms *group* and *therapeutic group* to refer to both group counseling and group therapy.

HISTORY

Group therapy has an interesting history. Although Dreikurs (1952) indicated that the origins of formal group therapy can be traced back to Franz Anton Mesmer's hypnotic sessions in Paris two centuries ago, group psychotherapy as we know it is basically a product of the 20th century. J. H. Pratt, a Boston internist, is credited with being the first to apply group psychotherapy. In the early 1900s, he used an educational group approach to treat tuberculosis patients.

The early period of group psychotherapy may be dated from 1900 to 1930. During this time the major steps toward a systematic use of the group method—then called *collective counseling*—were made in Europe. Dreikurs (1952) reports the early efforts of collective therapy by Wetterstrand with hypnosis, Schubert with stammerers, Hirschfeld with sexual disturbances, Stransky with neurotic patients, and Metzl (1937) with alcoholics. In Russia, Rosenstein, Guilarowsky, and Ozertovsky (Ozertovsky, 1927) used the group method. In Denmark, Joergeson used action methods with psychotics (Dreikurs & Corsini, 1960).

Some question exists concerning the relationship between collective counseling and our current forms of group therapy. It is clear that the early efforts never reached a degree of organization comparable to group therapy as we know it today, and that the psychiatrists who used the group method worked independently of one another. With the advent of totalitarianism in both Germany and Russia, these psychiatrists were forced to abandon their practices, including group methods.

In 1928, Dreikurs published "The Development of Mental Hygiene in Vienna." In this historically important paper, he described in detail—possibly for the first time anywhere—the dynamic differences between individual and group therapy, which he called "collective therapy."

In his child guidance clinics, Alfred Adler was probably the first psychiatrist to use the group method systematically (Adler, 1931) and formally started group therapy about 1910 (Moreno, 1953). Adler used techniques completely unrelated to the concepts and practices of individual therapy. He later developed a theoretical framework, *sociometry,* for the group approach (Dreikurs & Corsini, 1960). In 1931, Moreno coined the term *group psychotherapy,* which became the formal name of the new method.

The literature of group psychotherapy and group counseling developed slowly. From 1900 to 1929, only 31 papers on group psychotherapy were published in this country. The literature has expanded greatly in recent times. Articles can be found in *Small Group Behavior* (Beverly Hills, Calif.: Sage Publications), *International Journal of Group Psychotherapy* (New York: International Universities Press), *Group Organization Studies* (La Jolla, Calif.: University Associates), and *Together* (Washington, DC: Association for Specialists in Group Work (ASGW), American Counseling Association). Interest in group work in the United States has included a conference specifically devoted to group work. Sponsored by ASGW, this biannual conference draws hundreds of educators, counselors and therapists.

THE NATURE OF THE GROUP PROCESS

The group process focuses on the beliefs, feelings, and behavior of the members of the group. Attitudes, values, and purpose are considered. The interpersonal relationships that develop within the group make it possible for the members to become aware of their mistaken and self-defeating beliefs and actions and to feel encouraged to change them. Assets and efforts are also identified.

Requirements for membership are unique. People don't belong because of their status; they belong because they have problems and are ready to acknowledge and work on them. The focus is on helping members establish personal goals and, by challenging their perceptions, enabling them to cope more effectively with the tasks of life.

Group Interaction

Human beings are involved in continuous social interaction. Inevitably, each faces the dilemma between serving their own interests and those of the groups to which they belong. It is within the group interaction that one can observe how an individual decides to belong, or move away from, the group. In simple yet accurate terms, some believe, "I belong only if I can please," while others believe, "I belong only if they give me my way."

It is the Adlerian belief that one's social interest and, eventually, self-interest can often be best served through involvement in the give and take of cooperative endeavor with the group. This type of involvement creates a communal feeling and enhances the feeling of belonging. We are social beings who live in and are influenced by the social system and behave in such a way as to attain the approval of others. Our basic striving is to belong and to be accepted and valued. The methods we use to search for significance and recognition indicate how we decide to belong.

Psychological problems result from disturbed interpersonal relationships, reduced courage, and insufficient social interest. Yalom (1970) studied 20 successful group-therapy patients to determine the critical incident, or most helpful single event, for the members of the group. He found that, almost invariably, the incident involved a group member and not the therapist. Yalom lists the components of the corrective emotional experience in group therapy:

1. A strong expression of emotion which is interpersonally directed and which represents a risk taking on the part of the patient

2. A group supportive enough to permit this risk taking

3. Reality testing, which allows the patient to examine the incident with the aid of consensual validation from others

4. A recognition of the inappropriateness of certain interpersonal feelings and behavior or of the inappropriateness of certain avoided interpersonal behaviors

5. The ultimate facilitation of the individual's ability to interact with others more deeply and honestly. (Yalom, 1970, p. 23)

The therapeutic group will invariably move toward becoming a social microcosm of the members' experiences. All participants begin to interact in the group as they do in other real-life interpersonal relationships. Sometimes the members may seek the same position they held in their childhood family. Members also display in the group their faulty beliefs and ineffective approaches to the tasks of life. The participants' behavior reveals their lifestyle and assumptions about human relationships. The therapist, instead of hearing about how the members behave, observes and experiences the participants and their behavior, because each member's style of life emerges in the various transactions among the members.

Interpersonal Learning

Interpersonal learning facilitates change through the following process:

1. The group becomes a social microcosm, representing each member's social world.
2. Group members, through feedback and self-awareness, become aware of the purpose and consequences of their interpersonal behavior.

Through congruent and caring feedback, members' strengths and limitations are discussed. Unlike the typical social situation, in which an individual may not be able to communicate honestly, the group values openness and congruence—saying what one feels and means. Feedback permits members to learn from the transaction, because the message is not perceived as threatening and can therefore be accepted and internalized. This phenomenon occurs because feedback does not demand change, but rather the sharing of what one is experiencing and perceiving. Receivers of feedback are free to decide their own course of action.

3. For communication in the group to be effective, the transaction must be real and genuine. The participants must communicate their involvement and feelings about what they are experiencing, as well as the feelings others' communication provokes.
4. Change occurs as a result of awareness, involvement and commitment to make specific changes, the amount of belonging to the group the member feels and the resultant importance of being accepted and valued by the other members, and encouragement by members and by the group leader.
5. Through the process of trying on new behaviors and beliefs and learning that it is safe to change, the group member gains the courage to continue making positive movement.
6. The whole process can be described as setting a cycle in motion in which:
   a. perceptions and beliefs change.
   b. courage and belonging enable members to try on new behaviors.
   c. involvement and risk taking are rewarded by acceptance and belonging.
   d. fear of making a mistake is replaced by the courage to be imperfect, which reduces anxiety and insecurity.
   e. members become able to try additional change as their self-esteem and self-worth develop.

Progress in the Group

The measuring stick for progress is one's increased capacity to meet the tasks of life, to give and take, and to cooperate—what Adlerians call social interest. An individual's capacity to interact effectively with other members of the group is a measure of social growth, which is one of the goals of the group experience.

An effective group offers these opportunities to:

belong and be accepted

receive and give love and to have a therapeutic effect on others

see that one's problems are not unique but are experienced universally

develop one's identity and to try on new approaches to the various social tasks of life

THE SOCIAL CLIMATE OF THERAPEUTIC GROUPS

The therapeutic group provides a unique social climate and an atmosphere in which the individual's psychological movement can be observed and modified. The group setting creates opportunities to develop new perceptions of their member's approaches to the basic tasks of life.

Therapeutic groups are agents that promote values. A group accepts certain values and influences members of the group in terms of those values. The group therapy setting requires these conditions:

1. Members have their place regardless of deficits or assets. They are not judged in terms of any position or status they hold outside the group. They establish their own position inside the group and are accepted on that basis. The full worth of each member is taken for granted.

2. The members' capacity to reveal themselves honestly and openly is valued. Failing to reveal one's feelings, putting up a front, disguising hidden agendas, and covering up one's intentions—all accepted and even valued in certain other social situations—are challenged in the group. The group values congruence, the capacity to honestly reveal and share what one is experiencing.

3. Members learn not merely through verbal and cognitive understanding. They are expected to put their insights into action inside and outside the group. Insight is not valued unless it produces "outsights"—that is, some action or reality testing in the member's real worlds.

4. The leader models attentive listening, caring, congruence, confrontation, and interpretation to help participants acquire these interpersonal skills.

5. Members can express their true feelings without fear of permanently disrupting relationships. Interpersonal conflict between members is discussed and worked through, so members learn that conflict, when dealt with honestly, can produce improved relationships. The norms of the therapeutic group prescribe that participants continue to communicate despite negative feelings they may develop toward one another.

CONCEPTUAL FOUNDATIONS OF THERAPEUTIC GROUPS

The Adlerian approach to therapeutic groups recognizes certain conceptual foundations of the nature of behavior:

1. *All behavior has social meaning.* Each transaction between and among members of the group has social direction and social intention. Members are encouraged to understand the meaning of the transaction in terms of that direction and intention.

2. *Behavior can best be understood in terms of holistic patterns.* In the early stage of the group, participants are encouraged to become aware of their patterns. This process reveals the lifestyle, which includes characteristic patterns of responding and behaving. The Adlerian group is organized so as to reveal the lifestyle of each member. Participants learn to understand one another in terms of each person's unique style of living. They facilitate one another's development in various ways, by becoming aware of the faulty or mistaken assumptions that keep them from developing effective approaches to the tasks of life, and through willingness to process feedback about what they are experiencing.

3. *Behavior in the group is goal directed and purposive.* Members become aware of their own purposes and intentions and seek to understand the other members' behavior in terms of the purpose of the behavior. Participants learn to confront one another not only with the expressed beliefs, attitudes, and values, but also with the purpose of overall psychological movement. The psychological movement always clearly reveals directions and intentions.

4. Members are encouraged to become aware of their own motives and methods for finding a place all in groups' situations. Group transactions help reveal how members seek to find their place.

5. The group has specific hopes for each member's positive psychological development. The individual's capacity to belong to the group, to make a commitment, to engage in the give and take of life, and to expand his social interest are criteria for this development.

6. Members are understood in terms of how they see themselves and their situation—in terms of their subjective perception. They are actively encouraged to help one another understand how their perceptions influence their feelings and behavior.

These basic concepts about human behavior provide guidelines and structure for the social climate of the group. As members increase their social interest, feel belonging, and make a commitment to others, their emerging social interest becomes a major factor in their psychological growth.

THERAPEUTIC FORCES OF THE GROUP SETTING

The therapeutic forces that develop in a group setting stimulate changes in members' behavior. Leaders must be aware of the potential mechanisms that operate in the group and their effect on participants. Also, the leader must know how to facilitate the potential therapeutic effect of such mechanisms. The leader is responsible for stimulating a climate that will promote growth, self-understanding, and commitment to change. Group mechanisms do not occur automatically. *The leader deliberately creates situations in which the mechanisms are likely to operate.* When these processes do occur spontaneously, they must be recognized and encouraged. The mechanisms are catalysts for individual as well as group development.

Acceptance

Acceptance refers to the respect and empathy each one in the group receives. When acceptance has developed, group members identify with one another and have a strong communal feeling. The belief that "this is where I belong, and I can trust the members of the group to be concerned, caring, and honest" is indicative of acceptance. Feelings of acceptance and belonging are an essential part of the group's development. Acceptance is fostered as the leader not only models empathy but, when necessary, intervenes to help participants learn how to be more empathetic with one another. Each member of the group has a need to belong, and the therapeutic group provides the unique opportunity to find one's place and be accepted without having to undergo instant change.

Altruism

People have a desire to be of direct service and assistance to others. The group provides a situation that values this altruism. To stimulate altruism in the group, the leader models and demonstrates it and encourages any attempt of the members to express altruistic feelings. The group is organized so as to include opportunities to stimulate altruism.

Transference

Transference refers to the strong emotional attachment that members of the group develop as a result of their intensive experience with one another. Transference may originally be directed to the leader but eventually is manifested toward members of the group and even toward the group as a whole. Transference can involve both positive and negative feelings. Transference and the identification the members feel for one another form the glue that holds the group together. Unless this kind of transference develops, the group doesn't have enough feelings, positive and negative, to make the group a therapeutic experience.

Spectator Therapy

Spectator therapy permits group members to achieve some understanding of their own concerns by hearing the concerns of others. If a member of the group has a problem and another member brings up a similar problem, the first person has an opportunity to recognize that the situation is not unique. The behavior of the other member can act as a mirror in which one learns about self. It is important for the group leader to recognize that members can and do benefit from ongoing interaction even when they don't participate verbally. Through spectator therapy, participants observe others, learn more effective interpersonal skills, and benefit from the transactions that occur in the group.

Universalization

Universalization is the recognition that one's problems are not unique. The more group members universalize, the more they become aware that others share the same problems and the less they feel lonely and alienated from the rest of humanity. Recognizing the commonality of problems makes it easier to communicate their own problems. The leader intentionally stimulates universalization by creating a conducive climate and by asking, "Have any of you experienced that or felt that way?" Universalization is the process of identifying similarities in thoughts, feelings, and actions.

Feedback

Feedback refers to the learning process the group members undergo by sharing their reactions to one another. The purpose of feedback is to enable us to develop insight about our interpersonal relationships. Feedback allows us to explore our feelings, values, and attitudes, and reevaluate our faulty assumptions or mistaken perceptions. Authentic feedback requires the group members to be truly concerned and to care about one another. It also requires that participants recognize the feedback as an honest sharing of impressions that does not necessitate a change of behavior. Feedback becomes a strong source for creating psychological movement. If members truly feel part of the group and if they value peer evaluation, feedback can be a strong motivational force for change.

Ventilation

The group setting provides an opportunity for its members to express emotions they may have inhibited or repressed. Through ventilation, participants learn to expose and explore their inner feelings, both positive and negative, and to recognize that some concerns are exaggerated. By verbalizing strong feelings, members develop new insights that enable them to make therapeutic changes.

Reality Testing

In the group setting, participants can test certain concepts and work through relationships. This gives them the opportunity to see their behavior more accurately as it is experienced by others. For example, if a woman has problems relating to men, she can experiment in the group with new methods of relating to men. Thus she doesn't have to wait until she is outside the group to get some real-life experience in dealing with her new insights. The group provides an opportunity to practice new perceptions in a setting that is accepting, nonthreatening, and at the same time, provides open and honest feedback.

Interaction

The interactions that take place within the group make visible the goals and purposes of each member. We say "make visible" because leader and peers don't have to depend on what the individual says, but instead can observe the actual behavior. Words may deceive, but behavior seldom lies in its direction and intent. An individual may protest that he* intends to help or cooperate, but unless he does it, his words are inaccurate. Group interaction moves the participants beyond words into action.

GROUP COHESIVENESS

In the previous chapters, we have stressed the importance of the relationship in individual therapy. Cohesiveness in group therapy is the "relationship" in individual therapy. Cohesiveness refers to the positive pull or attraction that members of the group feel for one another. It refers to the forces that enable members to experience a feeling of belonging, solidarity, and a common bond. This cohesiveness creates conditions whereby individuals feel not only understood, accepted, and valued, but also free both to reveal themselves and to accept feedback from group members. A cohesive group is one in which members have a high level of mutual understanding and acceptance. Cohesiveness helps supply the feeling of belonging that is essential to all the other therapeutic forces.

The significance of cohesiveness is best understood when we recognize that many persons who come to a group for assistance have problems in establishing and maintaining a sense of personal worth and self-esteem, and in experiencing what it means to be an equal member of an equalitarian group. The group, because of its unique social climate, develops cohesiveness and provides an excellent corrective experience for these specific problems.

THE ROLE OF THE GROUP LEADER

The leader is responsible for forming, establishing, and keeping the group going. In the early stages, the leader is the only person with whom all the members in the group are familiar. Members expect the leader to assume responsibility for the group's growth.

Group leaders must be sensitive to the forces that make the group a therapeutic experience. They are facilitators who both create and encourage situations in which participants provide emotional support, universalization, feedback, and

---

*In this chapter, use of the gender pronouns "he" and "she" are for illustrative purposes only and do not connote a gender predisposition to that specific example.

opportunities to try on new behavior. These processes promote learning, personal growth, and cohesiveness.

Leaders must participate actively in the development of norms that facilitate growth and interpersonal learning. They intentionally establish a structure for the group and indicate guidelines for behavior, such as congruence, open interaction, involvement, nonjudgmental acceptance, confrontation, and commitment. Much of our social behavior is characterized by facades, surface interactions, inhibited expression of feelings, and other modes that are destructive to the development of a productive group. It is crucial to understand that the norms that govern the group don't come about automatically as a result of forming a group. Their development requires deliberate effort on the part of the leader.

Therapists or counselors must recognize that, as group leaders, they must provide a model as well as technical expertise. This stimulates movement. In the formative stages of a group, leaders may need to use exercises that create productive interaction. They may explicitly point out interactions that don't implement therapeutic goals and reinforce and encourage any attempts of members to effectively use the group's therapeutic forces. Some leaders like to believe that productive groups emerge without their guidance and even consider the kind of intervention we have discussed as manipulation.

Spontaneity is an important factor in effective group work. In some texts, this is referred to as the "here and now." It enables leaders to pick up on what is happening and turn the interaction into a growth-promoting experience. Leaders must use all their creativity and spontaneity, because both accelerate the progress of the group and provide a valuable model for the participants.

Group Leadership Competencies

Group leaders must be able to function in a continuously flowing process with all members, no matter how different their beliefs, feelings, and intentions. They must be able to create an atmosphere in which members can achieve their goals and learn to help one another grow.

Leaders pay attention not only to the content of members' messages but to the method, setting, and timing of messages. How are the feelings conveyed—with considerable involvement or apathetically? Does the message indicate the person is trying to focus the interaction on himself or that he wants to stay with the here-and-now transaction? Leaders are always aware of the purpose of members' communication, and, when appropriate, confront participants with their beliefs, feelings, and intentions.

Thus while leadership requires people who are open, honest, accepting, spontaneous, understanding, and congruent, these personality traits alone are not enough. Leaders also must be trained and skilled in these techniques and tactics:

structuring the group and communicating its purpose

using interaction exercises

universalizing

dealing with the here-and-now interaction

linking

blocking

encouraging and focusing on assets and positive feedback

facilitating participation by confronting nonverbal clues

facilitating I-messages

paraphrasing and clarifying to stimulate reality testing

offering feedback

formulating tentative hypotheses

setting tasks and getting commitment

capping and summarizing

To make the meaning of these competencies and skills clearer, we will describe each of them and explain the rationale for using it in the group setting.

Structuring the Group and Communicating Its Purpose

Definition   Structuring the group and communicating its purpose are essential for effective therapeutic groups. Defining goals and setting limits give the group a purpose and direct its activity. For example, the leader may indicate that each person in the group is there to work on a specific concern, that they will all be sharing the concern, and that they will help one another. More specifically, the leader may structure by indicating that members are to speak directly to the other members about their feelings and use I-messages, which express what one is experiencing but does not mandate change in others. Structuring may also encourage members to focus on the here and now—that is, on the dialogue within the group, in contrast to a discussion of events that happened outside the group.

Rationale   By structuring the group, the leader helps members focus their discussions on matters that are meaningful and purposeful. Structuring enables the leader and the group to set limits and to focus on tasks. Structuring is a demanding job, because the leader must be continually aware of what is happening and determine whether it is within the structure, goals, and purposes of the group. Once members are ready to stay within the structure, more productive group work is accomplished.

The following dialogues contrast ineffective and effective use of structuring.

Ineffective Use

David:	*I can never be on time. This makes my girlfriend really mad.*
Joan:	*David, tell us about your girlfriend.*
Frank:	*What kind of women do you consider attractive, David?*

Leader: *We are concerned about how you get along with women.*

If the group agreed and structured itself not to discuss personal problems unless the counselee volunteered such information, this dialogue is beyond the structure. Furthermore, David's personal goal is solving the problem he has in being punctual. Therefore, the above comments violate group structure. The leader should have interrupted the interaction to indicate a violation of contract.

Effective Use

Lynn: *Well, why are we here?*

Ramon: *Yes, silence makes me nervous (looking at the leader).*

Leader: *You have all met with me individually, but let's review our goals. Our purpose is to share our concerns and to help one another.*

Using Interaction Exercises

Definition   To begin a group, the leader chooses to initiate specific group behaviors to create experiences for the members. Programming is in contrast with permitting the interaction to be spontaneous and following whatever course of interaction happens to occur. Programs, or exercises, are usually aimed at specific goals. They are structured experiences that can be used to get people acquainted, build cohesiveness, help members understand certain phenomena by experiencing them, increase feedback, and create awareness of various group dynamics and processes.

Programs or exercises that are generally productive include the following:

Get-acquainted activity, in which people learn one another's names and some information about various members' interests

Strength recognition, in which members are asked to recognize, acknowledge, and state their own strengths

Multiple-strength perception, in which the group members present their perceptions of one another's strengths

Paraphrasing, in which a member can talk only after paraphrasing what the preceding person in the conversation has said

Learning to link, in which members are asked to show how previous statements by different people are similar or different

Having members present their position in the family constellation and indicate how they are most like or different from their siblings

Having members indicate their number one priority and have the group give feedback on the priorities they have observed

Rationale Although some leaders may be philosophically opposed to opening exercises, it is important to understand the rationale and timing of these activities. They are usually most effective early in group life, because they tend to improve communication, increase cohesiveness, and reduce anxiety when new members and inexperienced leaders are uncertain about what is expected. Some object that planned activities may provoke anxiety. The unstructured beginning of an open-ended group can itself generate considerable anxiety. Leaders who understand the use of exercises are familiar with a variety of structured experiences, and know how to use them appropriately can facilitate group movement. The purpose of exercises is to promote members' growth and communication within the group. The following dialogue shows an ineffective use of this competency.

Ineffective Use

Anne:	*Well, what should we do?*
Laura:	*I don't know what is expected of us.*
Anne:	*It seems so pointless without a topic.*
Leader:	*Now I'm going to show you how to become more involved with one another. Here is an experience. . . .*

The leader waited until the group was in a state of confusion and instead of working through it, proposes a solution. The leader should sense when there is a lack of understanding of purpose and a lack of skills and provide them in a more timely manner.

Universalizing

Definition Universalization is the process by which group leaders make group members aware that others share their concerns. The leader elicits responses that make it clear that there are elements of similarity in members' thoughts, feelings, or actions. The leader asks questions such as, "Has anyone ever felt that way?" In other instances, the leader shows how certain ideas and feelings are related. This requires listening for common themes and making members aware of those themes so they see that they have similar problems. By easing or, at times, even removing the feeling of isolation, universalization permits participants to realize they all share similar human concerns.

Rationale Universalization is basic to group cohesion. For cohesion to take place, group members must have positive feelings about one another and see one another as equals. By helping members see similarities in one another, the leader increases the group's cohesion. The leader encourages the sharing of concerns, because sharing creates a bond among group members and promotes growth. Awareness of the commonality of problems also provides reassurance and gives participants the courage to learn ways of becoming more effective.

The following dialogues contrast ineffective and effective use of this competency.

Ineffective Use

George: *I take after my father—the bad side of him. When he asks for juice and someone brings him water, he gets really mad. I'm like that. If I don't get my way, I feel mad.*

David: *Yeah, when my sister gets to hog the TV every Friday night, I get angry and pick a fight with her. She always gets what she wants.*

Leader: *Why do you think she gets what she wants?*

The leader could have pointed out the similarity of George and David's problems. By asking the reason for someone else's behavior, the leader is taking the group out of the here and now and is missing an opportunity to show George and David that their feelings are similar.

Effective Use

Marianne: *It's hard to say what I feel when I'm angry. I can't let myself get angry, it seems.*

Leader: *Has anyone else ever had difficulty expressing feelings?*

Dealing with the Here-and-Now Interaction

Definition   This competency refers to the ability to deal with what is happening now, as it is experienced by the entire group as well as by the individual members. It means moving away from the past or plans for the future to awareness of the current moment. To be concrete, specific, and in touch with one's sensitivities now; is the here-and-now. Refer only to those past events that are affecting one in the present moment; to be conscious of what is happening in this session rather than in the last—all this is part of the here-and-now focus in group work.

Rationale   Here-and-now interaction, as opposed to there-and-then interaction, is essential to the spontaneity, growth, and effectiveness of the group process. Dealing at length with distant concerns is like cutting off the group's oxygen supply. It is present worries and concerns, not past ones, that are the appropriate focus of the group. Lingering excessively on past feelings, without reference to the present, is a distraction that affects the growth of the group. Behavior is not caused by something that occurred in the past; behavior has a current purpose. If the group fails to deal with the here and now, it forfeits the opportunity to work through problems and resolve them.

The following dialogues contrast ineffective and effective use of the competency.

Ineffective Use

Tom: *I've never been very confident of myself. When I was a little kid, I used to hide behind the furniture when my mother had company.*

Leader:	*Has this pattern continued?*
Tom:	*Well, when I was in high school, I took as many baby-sitting jobs as I could on weekends so I could avoid going to dances and parties.*
Leader:	*Avoiding people made you feel secure.*
Laura:	*Gee, I used to feel the same way. . . .*

The group leader has failed to recognize what was happening. By not shifting the conversation to Tom's current feelings, the group misses an opportunity.

Effective Use

| Tom: | *I'm not very sure of myself, and I don't know how to talk about myself.* |
| Leader: | *You are not sure what is expected of you here.* |

Linking

Definition   Linking requires the leader to point out to group members the similarities and differences in what members are saying. Linking necessitates awareness of similarities in content and feelings. The leader can also link an individual's verbal and nonverbal messages.

Rationale   Linking allows the leader to show group members that their problems, although stated in different terms, are basically similar. This applies to feelings too; members are made aware of the relationship between their feelings and those of others, even if verbalized differently. The assumption is that linking promotes interaction. At the beginning, group interaction is often minimal and superficial. The interaction produced through linking promotes cohesion. Members' perception of these linkages and realization that their problems and feelings are shared promote greater understanding of human behavior and willingness to contribute to the group. Members are more willing and free to interact because they perceive that the others are interested in understanding one another.

The following dialogues contrast ineffective and effective use of the competency.

Ineffective Use

| Ramon: | *Mom and Dad always call my friends' homes when I'm a minute late getting home. All of the guys rib me about it the next day and call me "Mama's little boy."* |
| Tony: | *When I get home from school and just begin to relax, both my parents come at me and demand to see what I have for homework. If I don't have any—wow! The war starts! Sometimes they even call the teacher to check my story.* |

Leader: *Have you ever thought of having your teacher sign a no-homework slip for you?*

The leader has offered a possible alternative to Tony and left Ramon hanging alone. This limits interaction in the group. Ramon probably feels that he was not heard and must wonder what this group has to offer. He will probably be less willing and able to contribute the next time. The leader could link the feelings of anger from both men at not being trusted. This would have made them both aware of the similarity of their situations and feelings and enabled them to contribute more appropriately to the present situation.

Effective Use

Sally: *I like to go to the show on Sunday afternoon. Every time I suggest it to my friends, they want to do something else, so I just go along with them.*

Marianne: *When we break up into small groups in class to do a project, I get a good idea, but, before I have a chance to say it, someone else talks about his idea first. Most of the time, I just let mine go, and follow theirs.*

Leader: *I hear both of you saying that you get mad at yourselves when you let your ideas drop and just do what the group wants to do. How do you feel about that?*

Here the leader links both people's feelings and problems, thus helping Sally and Marianne realize that they are not alone.

Confronting

Definition   Effective confrontations require sensitivity and purpose. The leader enables members to become aware of discrepancies between their behavior and their intentions. The disclosure focuses on the purpose of the behavior. Disclosure may be expressed through tentative hypotheses—"Could it be?" or "I have an idea that perhaps. . . ."—and deals explicitly with the discrepancy between what one says and what one does, or between the behavior and its purpose.

Rationale   The goal of confrontation is not catharsis or challenge. Confrontation is aimed at making individuals aware of their effect on others, and how their beliefs and behaviors may be inconsistent. It helps group members to view their behavior more clearly and to become more congruent and sharing.

Confrontation should be offered with empathy. By caring and being congruent and authentic, the confronter offers a gift of great value.

If leaders operate with empathy and mutual respect, confrontation facilitates individual and group movement to new levels. Leaders who confront take a risk by sharing with the new members how others perceive them.

It can also be helpful to make participants aware of how they may be subtly provoking other members of the group. This confrontation is based on the hypothesis that each person's behavior in the group can be seen in light of psychological movement in relation to other group members. This movement reveals the member's intentions.

After the purpose of the behavior is ascertained, the group, with the member's consent, responds to the member's behavior by complying in an exaggerated way with the member's mistaken demands. For example, if one wants to be special, extensive time in the session is spent treating the person as very special. In other words, the group acts out the type of world the member wants. Thus the member's purpose is exposed and, through the group's focus on the mistaken demands, the behavior tends to be inhibited. This procedure is similar to paradoxical intention since it exaggerates the behavior and thereby makes it less satisfying. Adler called this technique "prescribing the symptom."

The following dialogues contrast ineffective and effective use of confrontation.

Ineffective Use

Wayne:	*I have had lots of problems in Mrs. Kasey's class. She picks on me.*
Joan:	*Yeah, she really is on you. I try to cooperate, but I won't let her treat me that way.*
Leader:	*Tell me what you do.*

Effective Use

Wayne:	*I have had lots of problems in Mrs. Kasey's class. She picks on me.*
Joan:	*Yeah, she really is on you. I try to cooperate, but I won't let her treat me that way.*
Leader:	*Could it be you want to show Mrs. Kasey that you can't be controlled?*

The leader takes the dialogue to another level by focusing on the purpose of Joan's resistance, but does so tentatively to permit Joan to consider the purpose of her behavior.

Blocking

Definition   Blocking is intervening in communication that is destructive to the group as a whole or to individual members. Because the leader's goal is the progress of the group, the leader blocks communication that hinders progress. For example, one of the participants may try to manipulate the leader into expressing her feelings toward other members, because the member fears a direct confrontation and wants the leader to do his work for him.

Rationale   Through the blocking technique, the leader encourages members to express inner feelings. Members are pressed to come out in the open with a clear statement of "where they are," manifesting openly their beliefs and feelings. The blocking technique must be handled gently so that it doesn't come across as rejection.

Blocking takes several forms. Leaders can block questions and make members come out with a clear-cut comment on their feelings and beliefs. Blocking can also help members focus on the here and now of group life instead of the there and then. This kind of blocking directs attention to current interpersonal experiences and feelings. Continuing certain types of honest confrontation produces growth. Blocking can also be used to stop the invasion of someone's privacy by someone else who is trying to guess that person's thoughts.

Blocking is like a traffic signal. Handled improperly, it causes a traffic jam; handled correctly, it results in smooth-flowing traffic. The true test of whether blocking is effective is when it helps the group fulfill its purposes. Blocking prevents being sidetracked by insignificant and harmful tactics.

The following dialogues contrast ineffective and effective use of blocking.

Ineffective Use

Lisa: *I don't like the way John always sits with his arms folded.*

Lynn: *Yeah, that bugs me too!*

Leader: *He's just not a part of the group.*

The leader has failed to have Lisa direct her remarks to John. Lisa wanted the leader to say something to John that she didn't dare say herself, because she feared the confrontation.

Effective Use

Frank (to the leader):   *I wish you would say something to Carol. She doesn't contribute anything to the group.*

Anne: *We all think you should say something to her.*

Leader: *You would like me to speak for you? But I think it would be more helpful for Carol if you spoke directly to her.*

Frank: *Carol, how do you feel about my difficulties with my mother?*

Carol: *To me, it seems as though you. . . .*

The leader effectively blocks the group's attempted gossiping. The comments are redirected to the member concerned. Her feelings are brought into the open, and a constructive suggestion is made.

Encouraging and Focusing on Assets and Positive Feedback

Definition   The leader is aware of the powerful effect of making assets and positive feelings explicit. Positive feedback from peers has considerable influence on our attitudes and self-esteem. The leader finds opportunities to focus on assets and to supply positive feedback. This encourages group members to do the same by offering encouragement to one another.

Rationale Individuals are often concerned about a place in the group and are generally much more open to suggestions and pressure from peers than from the leader. The leader can help the group encourage participants' development. As the group sees and accentuates the positive, social interest is stimulated and members grow by their opportunities to interact positively. As genuine encouragement is fostered and practiced, the group becomes more integrated and cohesive.

The following dialogues contrast ineffective and effective use of encouragement and positive feedback.

Ineffective Use

Tom:	*I don't seem to be able to get acquainted with girls easily.*
Laurie:	*Yes, you do seem very shy.*
Tom:	*I guess that's it; I'm just shy.*
Leader:	*Let's talk about your shyness.*

Here the leader falls into the trap of discussing an assumed deficit.

Effective Use

Tom:	*I don't seem to be able to get acquainted with girls easily.*
Laurie:	*Yes, you do seem very shy.*
Tom:	*I guess that's it; I'm just shy.*
Leader:	*I've noticed that you seem relaxed when you talk with the boys in our group.*

The leader is attempting to use Tom's strengths and transfer them to the area in which he doesn't function as well.

Facilitating Participation by Confronting Nonverbal Clues

Definition Group leaders are concerned about having contact with the whole person—the individual's thoughts, feelings, purposes, and actions. To understand the language of behavior, the leader begins by noting whether an individual's basic organic, emotional, and safety needs are being met. The group member's set of assumptions about self and others is constantly confirmed and occasionally rejected through reality testing in the group. The leader helps group members become aware of the language of nonverbal behavior and of which nonverbal behaviors open or close communication channels.

Rationale   By helping members become aware of nonverbal behaviors that open or close communication channels, the group leader adds another dimension to group communication. Members become aware of their own messages and learn to read the others' messages. They also learn to point out and deal with incongruencies in themselves and others.

The following dialogues contrast ineffective and effective use of the competency.

Ineffective Use

Gary (at the first meeting of the group, seats himself slightly but significantly outside the circle, away from the group)

Leader: *I often feel that, when people hang back there, they really don't want to be in the group. Gary, is there somebody here you don't like?*

The leader's comment is a direct attack on Gary's position. It could have been made more general by saying, "Let's all move in more closely."

Effective Use

Lisa (intellectualizes about herself and dominates the group with her reflections and recollections)

Wayne (begins to twist and stretch in his chair)

Leader: *You seem restless, Wayne. What's going on with you?*

The leader is commenting only on Wayne's actions. It is up to Wayne, if he wants to and if he can, to make a connection between his own and Lisa's actions.

Facilitating I-Messages

Definition   The I-message is a message clearly directed to someone concerning the sender's feelings and attitudes. The group leader's task is to facilitate the exchange of I-messages by modeling, providing examples, and intervening when indirect messages (you-messages) are being sent. The task also involves intervening when individuals ask questions instead of state their own feelings. The leader asks such a member to make a statement instead of asking the question—for example, instead of asking "Why are you doing that?" stating "I feel bothered when you do that."

Rationale   The I-message, as opposed to the you-message, is much less apt to provoke resistance and rebellion. When people send I-messages, their awareness increases. They are responsible only for themselves and identify their feelings. Senders of honest I-messages risk revealing themselves to others as they really are. It takes courage and inner security for a person to do so. I-messages state only what one's feelings are and do not demand change in the other person because of the statement.

A direct I-message in the group process eliminates the need for a third member to interpret and send the message to the member it was intended for. When members learn to deal directly with each other, more feedback and honest communication develop. When members are not communicating with each other or are using dysfunctional communication, the group becomes ineffective.

The following dialogues contrast ineffective and effective use of the competency.

Ineffective Use

Diego:	*Darnel keeps saying he can't help laughing at me, and I'm tired of it.*
Leader:	*You'd like to punch him in the nose.*

The leader's comment is ineffective because it picks up Diego's feeling instead of suggesting that Diego address his anger directly to Darnel.

Effective Use

Diego:	*Darnel keeps saying he can't help laughing at me, and I'm tired of it.*
Leader:	*Diego, can you speak directly to Darnel and tell him how you feel about it?*

Encouraging members to face each other concerning their feelings is much more effective. It helps participants face up to their feelings and get them out into the open so they can deal with them. As a consequence, group members are able to explore insights directly and not feel as though they are dealing with someone who is not in the group.

Paraphrasing and Clarifying to Stimulate Reality Testing

Definition   In paraphrasing, leaders selectively focus on content and feedback—on the essence of what has been said. They mirror the thoughts to make sure they have heard them accurately, then encourage members to clarify their assumptions, values, attitudes, and behavior through interaction in the group. The group provides a unique setting for going beyond the verbal and trying on behavior to study its appropriateness and effect.

Rationale   Paraphrasing helps members find out whether they are being understood. Through reality testing, members try on certain behaviors, learn from them, and evaluate their effects. The group can then help them "see themselves in action."

The following dialogues contrast ineffective and effective use of the competency.

Ineffective Use

Laurie:	*I've been having lots of problems with my mother.*
Anne:	*I'm getting tired of your always bringing up your mother in the group.*

Leader: *Each person has a right to discuss what he wants. Let's be patient.*

The leader fails to hear Anne's message.

Effective Use

Laurie: *I've been having lots of problems with my mother.*

Anne: *I'm getting tired of your always bringing up your mother in this group.*

Leader: *You are pretty angry that Laurie always talks about her mother. Could you tell us what you experience when that happens?*

The leader helps Anne to be heard and to clarify what she believes and feels.

Offering Feedback

Definition   The term *feedback* relates to the process whereby we learn how others perceive us, so we can modify our behavior accordingly. In everyday life, opportunities to obtain accurate feedback are quite limited. The group provides the psychological safety that makes it possible for people to give and receive true and valuable feedback.

Rationale   Feedback serves two functions: (1) It provides information about the effects of one's behavior on others, and (2) it provides positive or negative reinforcement. When feedback is related to specific responses, it is most helpful. Feedback about each response is better than information about overall progress, and precise information at the time of a response is better than general advice about a sequence of responses. Feedback in the group is most effective when it stems from here-and-now observations and when it follows the event as closely as possible.

In the process of feedback, individuals learn how they appear to others. The overly friendly type finds that others in the group resent her exaggerated friendliness; the man who weighs his words carefully and speaks with heavy precision discovers for the first time that others regard him as stuffy; a woman who shows a somewhat excessive desire to help others is told in no uncertain terms that some group members don't want her as their mother. Feedback can be upsetting, but as long as information is offered in a caring context, it can be highly constructive.

The following dialogues contrast ineffective and effective use of the competency.

Ineffective Use

Nikki: *I somehow feel that it's so easy for me to put myself inside another person, and I guess I feel that. . . .*

Leader: *Why is it so easy for you?*

Nikki: *Probably, I'm just sensitive.*

Leader: *You're really lucky to be like that. How about you, Sam?*

In this example, the leader doesn't give feedback about how Nikki's comments strike him but simply accepts and reassures.

Effective Use

Deke:	*What I meant by being careful is that, if I'm not careful about how I say something, it's twisted on me.*
Leader:	*I have the impression we can tell when you're being careful.*
Deke:	*I guess so, but it's my way. That's when I get into arguments.*
Leader:	*Is it possible that being honest is very hard for you?*

Formulating Tentative Hypotheses

Definition   Tentative hypotheses are the hypotheses the group leader makes about the purpose of a member's behavior in the group. Hypotheses help the group consider the purpose of behavior and become aware of the here and now by investigating what is happening in the moment. The previous example with Deke illustrated a tentative hypothesis in the feedback statement.

Rationale   The leader offers a tentative hypothesis of behavior in an attempt to help individuals develop insight into their behavior by understanding its purpose. Because the group is itself a social setting, it affords members a situation in which they can observe the purpose and consequences of their social behavior. Although tentative hypotheses are directed at one person, they are valuable for the entire group, because there is often considerable similarity in people's mistaken perceptions and self-defeating patterns. Feedback from peers in the group may make the hypothesis more valid and provide additional insights.

Tentative hypotheses are most effective when they are offered at the appropriate time, when the members are ready for them, and in the right way. The leader's attitude during a disclosure is crucial.

Disclosure is concerned not with the causes of the behavior but with its purpose. The leader avoids stating conclusions about the behavior, which may be discouraging, but makes the person aware of what the purpose of the behavior may be. These revelations may evoke an immediate recognition reflex. The disclosure is made in a friendly atmosphere of mutual respect; the leader asks the individual if he would like to know why he behaves in a certain way and offers the hypothesis tentatively, in terms such as, "I wonder . . . ," "Could it be . . . ," "I have the impression . . . ," and so forth.

The following dialogues contrast ineffective and effective use of tentative hypotheses.

Ineffective Use

Wayne:	*If the subject we're discussing in the group doesn't interest me, I sometimes yawn out loud.*

Leader: *You're obviously trying to draw attention to yourself and keep us busy with you.*

The leader has offered a hypothesis bluntly, telling Wayne what his goals are rather than hypothesizing about what his goals may be. Confronted with this attitude on the part of the leader, Wayne is likely to become defensive and deny the possibility that this is the true purpose of his behavior. He may also resent the leader for making such an "accusation."

Effective Use

Wayne: *If the subject we're discussing in the group doesn't interest me, I sometimes yawn out loud.*

Leader: *Is it possible that you yawn in an exaggerated way to keep us busy with you?*

Here the leader has offered the same hypothesis but in a much less assertive and abrasive manner. Wayne can consider the possibility that the leader's hypothesis reflects his real intention, without feeling trapped. And he can accept the leader's insight as a helpful suggestion rather than as an accusation.

Setting Tasks and Getting Commitment

Definition   Leaders set tasks by helping members verbalize the job or task they have set for themselves in the group. The members clearly state what they hope to accomplish through their interaction with the other members of the group in one session (or as is more often the case, in the entire series of sessions). The more specific the statement of the task, the easier it will be to accomplish it. The group leader promotes specificity by first hearing what the individual is attempting to say and then encouraging him to verbalize his ideas and commit to doing the job. Encouragement may come in the form of helping him see the value of accomplishing the task. The member makes specific contracts and is expected to report back on his progress at the next meeting.

Once the task has been specified, the leader should try to help the member say exactly how he thinks he can best accomplish the task. Here, too, specificity is important. The essential factor is for the individual to make some kind of commitment to the task he has taken upon himself.

Rationale   Task setting and commitment are important to the group process because little would be accomplished without them. It is important that the leader help all members become aware of some area they need to work on in the group. It is equally important that all members make some kind of definite commitment to follow through with the job or task they have set for themselves. Task setting and commitments usually occur early in the group, but they may be redefined as new perceptions and situations arise.

The following dialogues contrast ineffective and effective use of the competency.

Ineffective Use

Neresa:	*I'm not sure what the purpose of this group is. I know I'm not perfect, but I don't know what the group can do for me.*
Leader:	*Well, there must be something! With that attitude, nothing will be accomplished.*
Neresa:	*I already did say what I feel. I don't know what the group can do for me.*
Leader:	*You can't really mean that.*

The leader is trying too hard to get Neresa to react. This kind of tactic doesn't work, because Neresa feels distant from the leader.

Effective Use

Neresa:	*I'm not sure what the purpose of this group is. I know I'm not perfect, but I don't know what the group can do for me.*
Leader:	*I think we all share some of these feelings. The purpose of the group is to help us understand ourselves and relate more effectively with others. Is there something in that area you'd like to discuss?*
Neresa:	*Well, I feel uneasy in large groups of people. Perhaps we could talk about that.*
Leader:	*Would you want to discuss with the group this uncomfortable feeling?*
Neresa:	*Yes, I think I would.*
Leader:	*Can you tell us how you feel in large groups and how you would like to change?*
Neresa:	*Well, I just can't get my thoughts out, and I'd like to feel more free and relaxed.*

Here the leader does not try to force anything, but rather tries to get Neresa to decide on a task for the group. The leader doesn't give Neresa a task but lets her find one and then guides Neresa to explore the situation.

Capping and Summarizing

Capping. Capping takes place near the end of a session, when leaders help the group shift from the emotional aspect of interactions and focus instead on its cognitive dimensions. Leaders do this by responding to content rather than to feelings, by looking at ideas instead of picking up on feelings. When an emotional point is raised, the leader uses capping techniques to change the subject to something less intense. The subject can be changed back to a topic previously discussed or to a new and less loaded topic. In using capping techniques, the leader must make sure that no member is left in a state of crisis. Participants should not leave the session feeling they cannot cope with their feelings. At the end of the session, the leader may want to "go around" and give each member an opportunity to make a final comment.

Summarizing.   Summarizing is a way of looking at the themes that are coming through in the session. This can be done by the leader, by the members of the group, or collectively. It may occur during the session when the leader wants to pull together what has been happening and look at the meaning of the interaction. It can be stimulated by questions such as, "What's happening now?" or "Where are we?" In other instances, the leader will choose to cap and summarize to the group what she has been experiencing and what she believes is the emotional level of the group. The leader may choose to identify where various members of the group seem to be on certain issues. This can also be accomplished by asking members to indicate what they have learned and how they feel about what they are experiencing.

Rationale   Capping allows time for all members to get themselves together and back in touch with reality. Summarizing closes the session on a note of positive planning, lends a cognitive element to the interaction, and enables the group to tie structure and purpose to what has really been happening. Summarizing also provides all members with access to one another's perceptions and can generate new data for the group. Finally, it provides the leader with an accurate reading of what members of the group are experiencing.

The following dialogues contrast ineffective and effective use of the competency.

Ineffective Use

Diego: *I'm really uptight.*

Leader: *Well, it's about time to close, so let's leave that for next time.*

Effective Use

Darnel: *I'm not really sure whether we have solved our problem or not.*

Leader: *What do you think you've learned so far?*

The leader caps the discussion and requests a response to what has been learned to this point. This provides an opportunity to assess what development has occurred for Darnel so far.

GROUP METHODS

Adlerians place great emphasis on the social meaning of behavior. Recognizing that most problems are social and interpersonal, they believe in the necessity of understanding behavior in its social context. This approach, common to all Adlerian therapists and counselors, still allows some differences in group procedures.

LIFESTYLE GROUPS

Adlerian groups often employ the lifestyle to develop self-awareness and understanding. Usually, members of these groups present enough information about themselves to compile a mini-lifestyle, which covers the individual's relationship with parents, rating and trait comparison with siblings, and some early recollections. The leader provides a brief summary of the individual's mistaken perceptions, assets, and goals. In some groups, members indicate how successful they are in the various tasks of life.

The members' lifestyles and the way each participant copes with the life tasks are all "grist for the mill," because they enable group members to understand the perceptions, beliefs, goals, and values of the other members. The equalitarian nature of the group relationship is emphasized as the members get to know one another, participate in the diagnosis, and learn to guess or formulate tentative hypotheses about the purpose of each person's psychological movement.

Robert Powers uses an educational approach to group therapy. All participants actually keep some notes regarding the lifestyles in the group. The fact that leader and members of the group have access to the same information about lifestyle and interaction makes it possible for members and leader to treat one another as equals sharing in a learning experience.

This is Frank Walton's (1975) guide, based on Power's format:

PART I: A GUIDE FOR PRESENTING YOURSELF TO THE SEMINAR

A. You have ten minutes, uninterrupted, in which to tell us who you are.

B. Stay, as much as possible, in the present tense. Later on you will have an opportunity to tell us about your childhood.

C. Life challenges each of us, and each person is now approaching its challenges in a way unique to himself. Tell us about your responses to these challenges:

   1. What kind of friends have you made? What kind of friend are you? How do you get along with strangers in chance meetings? How do people treat you generally? How do you feel about other people, most of the time?

   2. What kind of work do you do? What kind of worker are you? Do you enjoy what you are doing? Do those with whom or for whom you work appreciate your contributions?

   3. Whom do you love? What kinds of problems have you had over loving and being loved? Do sex, closeness, and intimacy have a comfortable place in your life or not? What does masculinity mean to you? What does femininity mean to you? How do you measure up to whatever you expect of yourself as a man or a woman?

PART II: A GUIDE FOR SHARING IN RESPONSES

A. Someone has just spent ten minutes presenting himself. How did you receive what he presented?

B. Did you recognize things in yourself that he mentioned about himself? Was it easy to understand him or difficult? Did he sound strange or familiar?

C. How do you feel toward him? Did your feelings toward him change as a result of his presenting himself as he did? How?

D. Do you feel invited to act any particular way toward him? Did you welcome that invitation or resent it? What would you like to do for this person? What would you like to do with this person? What would you like to do to this person?

PART III: A GUIDE FOR DRAWING YOUR FAMILY CONSTELLATION

A. In childhood each of us learned how to define the place he had amongst others. Help the members of the seminar to see the kind of place you had as a pre-adolescent child in your family.

B. How many children were there in your family, and where did you fit in amongst them? How were you different from the others, and how were you like them? Which of the others was most nearly like you, and which was most different? What were you "good at"? What was hard for you?

C. What was father like? Who was his favorite? What did he expect from you? How did you feel about his expectations?

D. What was mother like? Who was her favorite? What did she expect from you? How did you feel about her expectations?

E. How did your parents get along with each other? What were their differences/arguments/fights about? To which parent did you feel closer? Why?

F. Were grandparents or other relatives important to you? How?

G. Did anything change at adolescence? How? What did puberty, physical development, and dating mean to you?

    1. For boys: What did "being a man" mean to you? Did you think you would have been happier, luckier, better off if you had been born a girl?

    2. For girls: What did "being a woman" mean to you? Did you think you would have been happier, luckier, better off if you had been born a boy?

PART IV: A GUIDE FOR DISCUSSING A FAMILY CONSTELLATION

A. Can you share any feelings about yourself in your family with the person who just told you about his childhood?

B. Can you understand this person better? How?

C. Can you see something in the way he presented himself initially which didn't make sense to you at the time?

D. What more do you want to know about this person?

E. Can you see a relationship between the role he played as a child, in his family and among other children, and the way in which he has tried to find a place in this seminar?

Parts I and II are repeated for each member of the group before the group moves on to Parts III and IV, which are also repeated for each member of the group. A fifth and sixth part can be added at the option of the leader. Part V would consist of obtaining two or three early memories, while Part VI would be devoted to the interpretation of the memories by the leader and participants. These additional segments are limited to 10 minutes each in the fashion of Parts I through IV.

A group may terminate at the conclusion of Part IV or Part VI, or it may continue to meet periodically to help group members work at relating the increased awareness of the purposes and patterns of their behavior to the challenges of social living.[1]

ACTION THERAPY

Action therapy is a group procedure developed by Walter O'Connell (1972, 1975). The format is similar to psychodrama, but the spontaneous release of emotions is not an end in itself but a move toward honesty with self and others. People are understood as decision-making beings who seek to enhance their self-esteem; their mistaken perceptions and faulty methods are highlighted in the group process. The hidden purposes of behavior are revealed, and the individual is encouraged to develop more socially responsible motivations and purposes.

Although the techniques of Jacob Moreno, the originator of psychodrama, helped generate action therapy, O'Connell indicates that his own system is Adlerian because of the following elements:

1. Man is not viewed as a mechanistic system powered by a closed source of energy. Feedback and resultant fluctuations in self-esteem better fit our worldview (Frankl, 1963; Mowrer, 1963) and seem capable of explaining our behavior, a necessary segment of the total treatment field (Oliver & Landfield, 1962).
2. We have worked ourselves free of intrapsychic overemphasis with its accentuation of infantile and pathological determinism in favor of behavioral responses amenable to change in the here-and-now.
3. The preference is for a diagnosis that attends to self-esteem, compensatory fantasy and extent of humanistic identification abstracted from behavior over time and changing external conditions.
4. Treatment is a process for correction of mistakes and stupidities instead of eliminating impersonal disease processes, and is carried out in a group setting which highlights the creative hypothetico-deductive lifestyle of the individual (e.g., experiences lead to cognitions which are self-reinforced and call forth strong expectations and demands toward others). (O'Connell, 1975, p. 63)

---

[1]Note: From "Group Workshop with Adolescents," by F. Walton, 1975, *The Individual Psychologist, 12*(1), 26–28. Reprinted by permission of *The Individual Psychologist*.

Basic Concepts and Tactics

This is O'Connell's description of the basic principles and tactics of action therapy:

1. *Guardian principle.* Every member of the group should have a "guardian," who shows understanding and acceptance and treats the person with dignity.
2. *Responsibility.* The goal is to educate each person to be responsible for his or her own behavior. Although feelings of anxiety and guilt are uncomfortable, the use of illness as an explanation for goal-directed behaviors is discouraged.
3. *Outsight.* If self-esteem is low, acceptance and belonging must be increased. This is accomplished by getting outsight into the motives and feelings of others.
4. *Awareness.* This is the concept of the Internalized Sentences and Negative Nonsense. Action Therapy avoids pointing to the past, instead highlighting the individual's immediate, automatic reactions to internalized sentences.
5. *Self-disclosure.* The leader's stimulus value as a positive-identification model is emphasized. The members will more often do as the leader does than as the leader says. (O'Connell, 1975, pp. 64–66)

Techniques

Our experience has taught us the recurrent utility of the mirror, double, role-reversal, aside, and dialogue techniques. In our experience, reluctant patients have always become involved in acting on their problems when a staff member temporarily enacts their kinetic and verbal reactions through the mirror play. The patient is generally quite astounded that someone seems to know him so well (without retaliating) and is willing to expend time and effort toward one who basically feels so unworthy. The double technique also provides for staff participation, with the protagonist standing behind the patient while verbalizing feelings and "automatic" reactions (e.g., "I feel that I'll be punished for whatever I think or say. I'll try to wriggle my way out by saying something strange. I don't dare try anything more. . . .") Role reversal has remained an excellent vehicle for introducing people to their unfruitful arbitrary demands on others, then launching the discussion and practice of attending to the needs of others as a means of cementing friendship bonds. In the aside technique, real feelings and hidden manipulatory games (Watzlawick, 1964) are verbalized, although the patient or staff protagonist might be behaving in a defensive, self-defeating style. Rather than aim an interpretation toward an uneasy avoiding patient and thereby compounding his lack of self-disclosure, staff or patients may debate the particular patient's motives and goals among themselves. Such an interchange (dialogue) is usually tempered with such overt themes as, "We know you've learned this in the past, but you can change if you want to and think it's possible. If you think we're wrong, tell us" (O'Connell, 1975, p. 67).

As O'Connell indicates, "Action therapy is a form of group therapy which is focused on what the patient can do for others, rather than on the patient as such" (O'Connell, 1975, p. 36).

Action therapy includes "lecturettes" on Adlerian theory, which explain in common language the participants' mistaken concepts and self-defeating beliefs and how these errors in living can be overcome. The need for self-esteem (significance or worth) and social interest are emphasized. The liabilities of low self-esteem are illustrated through examples of members' misbehavior, such as oversensitiveness, feelings of worthlessness, and unwillingness to risk imperfection. The courage to be imperfect is discussed, as well as the consequence of a lack of self-esteem-restricted social interest, which creates distance and either overdependence or active or passive competitiveness and aggressiveness.

A part of the lecturette is concerned with topics which help the director to get the group going, avoiding abstractions and past histories. One such topic is the specific error of lowering self-esteem and narrowing social interest in this present encounter. "We all do this. Why? And how? Why are you doing it right now?" Another topic is anxiety, feeling "certain" that something catastrophic is going to happen to one, beyond one's control. "What do you fear will happen? Tell the group in a fit of openness and honesty. Is it a fear of loneliness, of humiliation, of others detecting imperfections?" Still another topic is knowing another, i.e., understanding how he lowers his self-esteem and social interest in terms of outer and inner (cognitive) movements; knowing his hidden anxieties; understanding the nature of his habitual relationships (hyperdependent, cooperative, or competitive); lastly, knowing how he wants to be confirmed, as "what," and by what types of reinforcements, e.g., as the best speaker, by constant nodding and smiling of others. Ideally, all members know this information about all other members and are willing to share themselves, and confirm others. This builds authentic "community," and each member is able to mirror or double for every other. (O'Connell, 1975, pp. 38–39)

In action therapy, the members of the group, one at a time, volunteer to be the protagonist and contribute their concerns and challenges of living to the group. The protagonist's low self-esteem and negative nonsense are explored.

While working with the protagonist the director inquires from other members for similarities and understanding. "Why don't you understand Joe?" "What information do you need? What movements does he have to make before you understand him?" "What do you tell yourself about Joe to keep distance from him?" "What have you said or done to Joe to help him tell himself that he is (or you are) inferior as a person?"

The director might ask if others have had similar problems. "Let's see the hands of those who have had sex problems" (two hands, up, ten arms motionless). "I see we have two guys with guts and ten liars (laughter). I've had sex problems too. What do you think of that?"

The director can play upon competition itself to precipitate insight into the goals of competition on the useless side and develop group cohesion. One statement might be, "The group's task is to find the most depressed guys. Who is the sickest?"

The director can capitalize upon competitive power struggles to stimulate sharing and practice of openness. When Harry, a sullen violently passive alcoholic, steadfastly refused to play the son who infuriated Harry and led him to his drinking behavior, a bet was made with Joe. Joe, also on the stage because the director called for the group to select people with the "best tempers," was told by the director, "I'll bet you two bits you can't get Harry to play his son." Almost immediately the director lost his quarter and the group had a hearty laugh over their power to "defeat" authority. But authority in this case was not defeated since it also laughed and was pleased at the creativity of the group in demonstrating power struggles and provoking movement.

Guessing at another's constricting cognitions highlights the other's "creativity" (albeit of an unexpected negative kind) and focuses on the possibility of his making alternative choices. Guessing in itself is stressed because it is encouraging to realize that no one of us has absolute certainty and guessing is what we are all doing. Guessing at another's creativity also helps to show him a developmental route to the sense of humor through experiencing the tragicomic paradox, e.g., knocking oneself down while crying for help. The humor of unloving the self while demanding pampering from others, the humor of being the best or most perfect self-devaluator, can also be brought out through mirroring and doubling in action therapy (O'Connell, 1975, pp. 39–40).

Emphasis may be placed on the paradox of having participants strive harder to accomplish their "symptoms." The lesson is "either stop your negative nonsense, or immediately increase it and learn to enjoy your misery more fully" (O'Connell, 1975, p. 41).

> The leader or director moves to develop peer support, acceptance, and especially encouragement, stressing that self-esteem comes from positive reinforcement of self and others, from courage, and from social interest.

ENCOURAGEMENT LABS

O'Connell is also the founder of the encouragement labs, which developed because his concept of humanistic identification "conceives of man as having both a relatively stable inner core (lifestyle or existential–humanistic attitudes) and an innate potential for social intercourse (the need for power, seen as the ability to stimulate or resist interpersonal change)" (O'Connell, 1975, p. 52).

The goal of the encouragement labs is to teach participants, through lecturettes and experiences, that they are not passive victims of their environments. "The principal lab premise is that social interest does not emerge full-blown in the absence of psychological complaints (symptoms), but needs to be explicitly taught, especially in a competitive society like ours where there are no institutionalized efforts to teach the movements and responsibilities of love" (O'Connell, 1975, p. 53).

Encouragement includes in its progressive repertoire of social skills the art of courage: giving and asking for feedback about peoples' reactions to one's behaviors and guessing at the goals of misbehavior (self- and others). Encouragement in its most advanced state includes recognizing the importance of being open and self-disclosing and not provoking and reinforcing feelings of insignificance or feelings of significance in narrow, noncontributory social roles. Encouragement labs point toward knowledge and practice of the humorous attitude, for there is no more encouraging or growth-precipitating person than one with a humorous attitude. Contrary to popular practice, encouragement is definitely not pampering. . . . In these examples, students behaved as if they had no right to give feedback, or if they did it would be ignored or retaliated against: so they made themselves discouraged. Encouragement is not such destructive pampering as telling a person what he wants to hear about how wonderful he is, completely ignoring his motivated mistakes. Encouragement is a process of getting the message across, loudly and clearly, that one is responsible for constricting or expanding his feelings of self-esteem and belonging (O'Connell, 1975, pp. 53–54).

The encouragement lab includes lecturettes and exercises aimed at developing encouragement skills. The members of the group are taught to produce natural highs by increasing their self-esteem and social interest. Techniques include presenting opportunities to encourage various kinds of constricted individuals and using success bombardment (finding something good). Participants learn even to congratulate creatively arranged rejection and other forms of negative nonsense and misbehavior. They learn to give encouraging feedback instead of reinforcing negative nonsense and negative behaviors.

These are some of the essential elements for practicing the encouragement process in dyads:

1. Attend through eye contact and attentive listening.
2. Paraphrase your partner's message and feelings.
3. Identify similarities between yourself and your partner, since acceptance encourages belonging.
4. Share yourself through authentic self-disclosure of your feelings.
5. Give each other feedback, sharing the impressions that have been developed.
6. Find something good about everyone in the group—even how creatively someone arranges for reinforcement of her behavior.
7. Tell how your partner has encouraged you.
8. Make guesses as to how you have helped the group.

Becoming a Positive, Encouraging Person

This workshop was developed from *The Encouragement Book: Becoming a Positive Person* (Dinkmeyer & Losoncy, 1980). The workshop is designed to develop self-confidence, the ability to encourage oneself, and skills for encouraging others. The workshop combines minilectures, exercises and experiences, discussion groups, opportunities for feedback, and practice in various facets of the encouragement process. The workshop leader sets forth the psychological basis of encouragement, which exists in Adlerian psychology, with specific examples. Participants learn the process of self-affirmation and self-encouragement.

Encouragement is treated as part of the process of stress management. Participants learn about progressive relaxation, imagery, and combating their unhealthy beliefs. They learn the process of developing a positive relationship with themselves. They learn to recognize their accomplishments and to differentiate between self-esteem and ego-esteem. The focus is on developing courageous, congruent behavior.

The concept of a "natural high," as originated by Dr. Walter O'Connell, is presented. Participants learn the three steps of (1) overcoming constrictions, (2) encouraging, and (3) transcending or spirituality.

A section on humor teaches participants how to see things in perspective. The humor process teaches that we can respond to anything positively and successfully.

Encouragement skills are taught specifically and didactically, including the following:

communication that involves listening and empathy

focusing on strengths, assets, and resources

perceptual alternatives

focusing on efforts and contributions

identifying and combating discouraging fictional beliefs

the power of expectation

The encouragement circle is taught as a method for solving problems in a variety of settings. The workshop also includes an opportunity to apply this encouragement process to parenting, marriage, social relationships, and professions or occupation as well as to oneself.

SOCIAL THERAPY

Toni and Theo Schoenaker originated social therapy at the Rudolf Dreikurs Institute for Social Equality in Zuntersback, Germany. The process is called social therapy because all human beings are understood as social beings and all problems as social problems.

People are accepted in the group with all their strengths and weaknesses. The basic assumption is that neurotic disturbances and personality problems are not illnesses but exaggerations of problems we all hold in common. Change comes by making progress toward courage, affirmation of self, and social interest.

Social therapy groups are composed of participants who meet seven hours a day for five days. Members are encouraged to familiarize themselves with the principles of Adlerian psychology before joining a group.

Like all Adlerian groups, social therapy groups function in an atmosphere of equality. Efforts are made to foster feelings of belonging and acceptance on the part of group members, and there is emphasis on the positive use of constructive feedback to promote self-confidence and change. As the Schoenakers (1976) state, "In Social Therapy one expands usual behavior in a positive direction and dares to act on suggestions for behavioral change. We hope that self-confidence will be strengthened, that social interest and courage will increase" (p. 16).

Belonging and acceptance are created by emphasizing participants' mutual respect and responsibility for self and others. Disparagement and attack, as well as useless feedback, are therefore avoided. The goal is to experience equality and humanness instead of competition and rivalry. A basic rule is that nobody talks about the group members outside the group sessions. Social therapy exercises are organized and guided so that all members are aware that they are not there to fulfill others' expectations.

Exercises include relaxation to become aware of the body and its functions, respiration and movement exercises to help members regulate their respiration rhythm so that it matches the rhythm of the group, and sound exercises to learn how to express oneself.

Each participant creates her own emotions and seeks to belong according to her lifestyle. Mistaken ideas of belonging, such as "getter," "driver," "controller," "pleaser," and "morally superior," are discussed. Behavior is seen and discussed as useful and useless and as active and passive.

The ultimate goal is to help members believe they are good as they are and reduce their drive for self-elevation. In a meditative atmosphere, a member comes to state "I am I, and I accept myself as I am," "You are you, and I accept you as you are," and "You are you, and you are not here to live up to my expectations."

All participants come to understand aspects of their lifestyle. Because of the unity of the personality, the overall psychological movement in the group helps each member understand his own behavior. As Adler stated, "An individual's every slightest action, every behavior symptom is characteristic of the whole individual, and, like a stone from the mosaic, it indicates the style of the whole. From the way a person talks, moves, reacts to certain events, the traits and characteristics of his lifestyle can be more or less easily recognized" (Schoenaker & Schoenaker, 1976, p. 46).

To promote understanding of the lifestyle, the group leader may suggest that the group move around in the room without speaking, taking interest in one another. As the participants move about, the leader may ask questions, in the first person, such as:

Am I interested in the other person or am I occupied with the question What does the other think of me?

Do I seek contacts or do I just wait?

Do I go where the most contacts can be made, or do I move where I can only meet a few people?

Am I friendly for fear of not being accepted?

Am I afraid not to meet enough people and to leave one out?

Am I so active in contacting because I want to control the situation? (Schoenaker & Schoenaker, 1976, p. 40)

After the activity, discussion focuses on what one has learned from it.

Helping each other, participants try to determine their number one priorities, the methods they use to maintain the priority, and the price they pay for it (see Table 11–1). "Try on a behavior"—criticize while looking someone directly in the face, ask a person of the opposite sex out to lunch, or experiment with any other thing one finds difficult to do. The focus is thus not merely on insight but on outsight and action as well. Role playing, psychodrama, self-observation, relaxation, movement, and expression exercises all help the individual understand his mistaken beliefs and faulty approaches to the challenges of living and to see alternative, more effective beliefs and approaches.

TABLE 11–1	*Number One Priorities*		
Number One Priority	How the Other May Feel	The Price You Pay for Your Priority	What You Want to Avoid With Your Priority
Comfort	irritated or annoyed	reduced productivity	stress
Pleasing	accepting	stunted growth	rejection
Control	challenged	social distance and/or reduced spontaneity	unexpected humiliation
Superiority	inadequate	overburdened	meaninglessness

Note: From *Adlerian Social Therapy,* a monograph by T. Schoenaker and T. Schoenaker, St. Paul, MN: Green Bough Publications. Copyright 1976 by Green Bough Publications. Reprinted with permission.

TELEOANALYSIS: UNDERSTANDING SELF, OTHERS, AND THE PURPOSES OF BEHAVIOR

The teleoanalytic workshop, developed by Don Dinkmeyer, is designed to help participants become aware of their beliefs, values, goals, and style of life and to move toward more effective relationships with others by shifting from self-awareness (insight) to activated social interest (outsight).

The workshop is based on these Adlerian premises:

1. People are social, decision-making beings, whose actions have a purpose. All behavior has social meaning.
2. The members' lifestyles are expressed in their transactions with the group.
3. People's behavior is best understood by a holistic approach, which recognizes that psychological movement reveals the lifestyle and unitary striving toward a goal. To understand the person or a specific behavior, one should seek to understand the purpose.
4. Social interest and courage are criteria for mental health.
5. Individuals are understood in terms of their perceptions, or phenomenological field. The subjective factors of biased interpretations and perceptions influence people's decisions.

The workshop is didactic (it includes lecturettes to provide information) and experiential (it engages the participants in experiences that bring into play their feelings, beliefs, and values).

Topics might include the following:

self-esteem, self-image, self-acceptance

social interest

purpose and finalistic causality, goal striving, fictional goals

search for significance, power (active and passive)

understanding lifestyle: family atmosphere, family constellation and psychological position, methods of training, early recollections, creative capacity to decide and private logic

priorities and the triangle

life tasks and challenges

discouragement, failure to function, courage to be imperfect

encouragement and courage

unity of personality, holism, pattern

social equality: horizontal versus vertical communication

understanding and deciding feelings

commonly observed lifestyles: driver, controller, getter, self-elevator, righter, pleaser, morally superior, aginner, victim, martyr, excitement seeker

mistaken ideas about self: I am special, entitled, something only if first, must be perfect

self-acceptance, self-encouragement, being a winner

Exercises and experiences are carried out so as to develop feelings of belonging in the participants, through improved communication first in dyads, then in groups of four, then eight, and so on. Through this process, all the members become more visible, more transparent, and more congruent to one another. The exercises involve presenting oneself to the group in terms of one's strengths, priorities, self-esteem, family atmosphere, family constellation, and assets.

REFERENCES

Adler, A. (1931). *Guiding the child*. New York: Greenberg.

Dinkmeyer, D., & Losoncy, L. (1980). *The encouragement book: Becoming a positive person*. Upper Saddle River, NJ: Prentice Hall.

Dreikurs, R. (1952). Group psychotherapy: General review. *Proceedings of the First International Congress of Psychiatry*, Paris, 1950. Paris: Hermann.

Frankl, J. (1963). *Man's search for meaning*. New York: Washington Square Press.

Metzl, J. (1937). Die arbeitsmethoden der trinkerfuersorgestelle brigittenau. *Int. Zeits. gegen den Alcohol, 35*.

Moreno, J. L. (1953). *Who shall survive?* New York: Beacon House.

Moreno, Z. T. (1959). A survey of psychodramatic techniques. *Group Psychotherapy, 12*, 5–14.

Mowrer, O. (1963). *The new group therapy*. New York: Van Nostrand.

Papanek, H. (1958). *Change of ethical values in group psychotherapy. International Journal of Group Psychology, 18*, 114–124.

O'Connell, W. E. (1972). Adlerian action therapy techniques. *Journal of Individual Psychology, 28,* 184–191.

O'Connell, W. E. (1975). *Action therapy and Adlerian theory.* Chicago: Alfred Adler Institute.

Oliver, W., & Landfield, A. (1962). Reflexibility: An unfaced issue in psychology. *Journal of Individual Psychology, 18,* 114–124.

Ozertovsky, D. S. (1927). *Zhurn. Neuropath. i. Psichiat.* (20) 587.

Schoenaker, T., & Schoenaker, T. (1976). *Adlerian social therapy.* St. Paul, MN: Green Bough Publications (monograph).

Walton, F. (1975). Group workshop with adolescents. *The Individual Psychologist, 12*(1), 26–28.

Watzlawick, P. (1964). *An anthology of human communication.* Palo Alto, CA: Science & Behavior Books.

Yalom, I. D. (1970). *The theory and practice of group psychotherapy.* New York: Basic Books.

CHAPTER 12

Brief Therapy and Managed Care

L ong-term psychotherapy had long been synonymous with psychotherapeutic treatment, while brief therapy was considered an ancillary treatment with
very limited indications. Today, however, brief therapy has come to be considered a separate discipline as well as the treatment of choice for most clients.
The literature on brief therapy is growing at an exponential rate. More than
100 books and 1,000 journal articles have been published in English in the past
25 years, most in the past five years. Ironically, psychotherapy training today has
come to mean training in brief therapy. A number of reasons account for the current emphasis on brief therapy. First, research indicates that most clients expect
therapy to be brief with problem resolution in a relatively few number of sessions
(Garfield, 1986). Second, brief therapy methods have about the same success rates
as longer term therapies (Bloom, 1992; Perry, 1987, Hoyt, 1995). Brief therapy
methods are effective not only with acute and less severe concerns but also with
more chronic concerns, provided there is a focal issue and reasonable treatment
goals. Finally, third-party payers, insurance companies, and HMOs are beginning
to recognize the benefits of brief therapy and many limit payment to brief, time-
limited outpatient treatment.

MANAGED CARE AND BRIEF THERAPY

Managed-care plans such as Preferred Provider Organizations (PPOs), Individual Provider Associations (IPAs), Employee Assistance Programs (EAPs), Health Maintenance Organizations (HMOs) currently provide mental health coverage to about 180 million Americans. These plans, which regulate the costs, location, and use of services are having a tremendous impact on the clinical practice of counseling and psychotherapy. Recent evidence that brief therapy can also result in significant reductions in medical care use and costs has further increased the appeal of brief therapy to the managed-care establishment. Much has been published on brief psychotherapy in HMO settings.

Needless to say, there is widespread interest in and need for effective brief therapy: Not only HMOs, but insurance companies, public and private clinics and counseling services, as well as consumers desire and often financially require brief therapy for psychological problems as well as psychiatric conditions. Accountability, quality care, and value are their major concerns.

Efforts to deal with the matter of accountability and quality of care have given rise to considerable research efforts to study the efficiency and economy of brief therapy. How effective are six sessions of brief therapy? How many sessions are required to treat panic attacks, depression, or narcissistic personality disorder? Which therapists are most effective with certain clients with specific symptomatic presentations? Policy makers are increasingly studying these questions as managed-care payers are beset with uncertainties about psychotherapeutic treatment. Researchers have recently reported that the majority of clients with acute anxiety and depression symptoms will show clinical improvement in between one and nine sessions, while those with chronic conditions like panic disorders require seven to 27 sessions. Those with severe personality disorder may require up to 104 sessions (Kopta, Howard, Lowry, & Beutler, 1994). Similarly, research data is beginning to clarify the question of differential therapist effectiveness, i.e., which therapist is more likely to be effective with certain types of clients with specific psychological presentations (Peck, 1994).

CHAPTER OVERVIEW

It is probably no exaggeration to suggest that *psychotherapy* and *psychological treatment* will soon be synonymous with brief therapy. Increasingly, long-term therapy is being regarded as an ancillary treatment with limited indications and minimal reimbursement. Thus it behooves students and practitioners of counseling and psychotherapy to master the theory and skills of brief therapy.

In view of the growing importance of brief therapy, this chapter describes and illustrates the practice of brief therapy, and surveys the four major orientations to brief therapy: Psychodynamic, Cognitive–Behavioral, Systemic, and Experiential and then compares and contrasts them with each other and with Adlerian psychotherapy, which is considered the original form of brief therapy.

Long-Term Psychotherapy, Brief Therapy, and Planned Short-Term Psychotherapy

Usually *psychotherapy* is described as a therapeutic transaction continuing for a few months (brief therapy), or for a few years (long-term therapy). But therapeutic treatment can even be completed in a single session (Bloom, 1981; Talmon, 1990). Assuming they are the right words spoken at the right time and in the right way, the client is quite likely to profit from this transaction. In other words, the vehicle for psychotherapeutic change can span the time continuum from long-term therapy at one end to single-session encounters at the other end, with formal brief therapy in between. Some suggest that *planned short-term psychotherapy* is a more accurate term than *brief therapy*. They argue that planned short-term therapy is short term by decision, not by default, and should be distinguished from "unplanned" short-term therapy, i.e., services that are brief because treatment is terminated unilaterally by the client (Bloom, 1992).

Yet, embedded in the hallowed tradition of psychotherapy is the belief that a direct relationship exists between the length of treatment and patient improvement: the longer the course of therapy, the greater the improvement (Fiester & Rudestan, 1975). Unfortunately, neither clinical experience nor research has supported this assumption. Rather, experience indicates that when therapists respond to any encounters with patients—even unscheduled ones such as telephone calls or curbside consults—as potential therapeutic transactions, the outcome is likely to be therapeutic. Research consistently indicates that briefer modes of therapy are as effective or even more effective than longer term therapies (Perry, 1987).

Agreeing on goals is important. Clinicians often have different expectations about treatment outcomes than their patients. Whereas the majority of patients are usually seeking symptom relief from psychotherapy, the majority of clinicians usually expect to accomplish more extensive treatment outcomes (Beutler & Crago, 1987). Despite therapists' intent, the majority of psychotherapeutic treatments are short (Garfield, 1986). Phillips (1985) reports that the average length of psychotherapy—regardless of problem presentation, settings, or method—is only four sessions, with the median number of sessions being one. In other words, only 50% of patients deemed by the therapist as appropriate for long-term or even brief therapy return after the first session. Therapists typically respond to unplanned patient termination of treatment with a sense of personal failure and rejection. They may question their own therapeutic competence or attribute negative qualities to the patient such as "unmotivated" or "resistant."

A number of value differences have been observed between clinicians who are oriented to long-term therapy and those who are oriented to brief therapy. Budman and Gurman (1983, 1988) characterize the values of the clinician preferring long-term therapy as basically oriented to cure and basic character change, believing that psychological change is impossible in daily life without exposure to the "timeless" quality of formal psychotherapy. They also assume that psychotherapy is benign and useful without any untoward effects. Not surprisingly, these clinicians view therapy as the most important part of the patient's life, and "unconsciously recognize the fiscal convenience of maintaining long-term patients."

In contrast, clinicians receptive to the formal practice of brief therapy are portrayed as being more pragmatic about treatment goals such as symptom relief and increased coping instead of "cure" or basic character reconstruction. This is based on the premise that psychological change is inevitable across the span of one's life, and that therapy should focus on patient strengths and resources. These therapists believe that small changes that are initiated during the course of therapy will continue and generalize further after the formal course of therapy. Therefore, the formal part of therapy can and should be time limited because of the belief that it is more important to be in the world than in therapy. Psychotherapy is viewed as a potent change agent that can have harmful or iatrogenic effects if not properly used. Other researchers would add that the brief therapist is often more active in the treatment process than the long-term therapist (Koss & Butcher, 1986).

Among brief therapists are a group of clinicians who are also comfortable practicing very brief therapy. In addition to the ones already noted, these clinicians tend to share three other beliefs. First is the conviction that even a single session or encounter can be therapeutic. Research on patient attrition (Phillips, 1985) confirms the viability of this belief in planned single-session therapy (Bloom, 1981; Talmon, 1990). Thus, this clinician consciously approaches a therapeutic encounter as if it were the only session and communicates the expectation that change can and will occur both during and after the encounter. This applies not only to traditional psychotherapy issues (Powers & Griffith, 1989) but also to health-related issues (Carlson, 1989). Second, the clinician believes that effective brief treatment can take place not only in the traditional settings with scheduled appointments but also in nontraditional settings with unscheduled sessions or encounters, in a variety of treatment formats. Besides private and public practice settings, very brief therapy encounters can occur on hospital rounds (O'Connell & Stubblefield, 1989), at social events, corridors, and even on the telephone. Besides the usual one-to-one format, brief therapeutic interventions can occur in didactic demonstrations (Shulman 1989a), groups (Starr & Weisz, 1989), with couples (Pew, 1989), family (Croake & Myers, 1989), as well as in supervisory formats (Ireton & Peterson, 1989). Finally, effective brief therapy can occur in a number of time frames besides the 50-minute hour. The duration of the encounter may range from 5 minutes to marathon length.

The next section of this chapter overviews a number of formal brief therapy systems and approaches that attempt, to varying degrees, to accommodate client need and style.

The Psychodynamic Orientation to Brief Therapy

A few constructs distinguish the psychodynamic from other approaches to brief therapy. The most prominent is the interpretation of unconscious wishes, fears, and defenses. The purpose of a dynamic interpretation in brief therapy is to clarify and resolve a narrowly focused intrapsychic conflict, while the goal is to provide symptom relief. Most of the approaches also attempt to produce character change in the area of the focal conflict.

The general indications for brief psychodynamic therapy include several diagnostic categories, provided that the patient's presenting problem can be conceptualized as a focal intrapsychic conflict. Sifneos (1984) selects patients with oedipal conflicts. Mann (1973) and Mann & Goldman (1982) limit treatment to patients with conflicts over separation—individuation. However, Malan (1980), Davanloo (1980), and Bellak and Siegel (1983) only demand that the issue be focal.

Each particular psychodynamic approach indicates specific contraindications for treatment. Sifneos's are the most stringent, while Bellak's are the least. In general, patients with chronic alcoholism or other addictions, grossly destructive acting-out behaviors, severe personality disorders, serious suicide attempts, or psychotic conditions are excluded from treatment. Bellak will, however, attempt treatment with both psychotic and suicidal patients. Other contraindications would be patients with problems that are too diffuse or multifocal, patients who have been nonresponsive to other treatment modalities, and people who desire or need more extensive character change.

Of all the brief therapy approaches, the psychodynamic approaches have the most stringent patient selection factors. With the exception of Bellak's approach, only certain YAVIS patients are acceptable: Young, Attractive in terms of value similarity to the therapists; Verbal and able to communicate thoughts, feelings, and fantasies; Intelligent and psychologically minded; and Successful socially and occupationally. In addition to possessing high ego-strength, patients must be motivated to change and not merely want symptom relief. Patients must also have had one significant interpersonal relationship during early childhood; be able to experience, tolerate, and discuss painful affects; and be able to internalize interpretations dealing with the focal conflict. Finally, the patient must be willing to work with the therapist on the focal issue and be able to relate quickly and freely with the therapist. If the patient does not meet these criteria, another form of brief therapy or a long-term dynamic approach would be suggested.

Sifneos's Short-Term Anxiety Provoking Psychotherapy (STAPP)   Patient selection is the cornerstone of this approach because of its anxiety-provoking nature. Unlike supportive psychotherapy approaches, which tend to be anxiety-suppressing, Sifneos (1979, 1984) selects only patients with a history of intact object-relations. Such a patient will have had at least one meaningful and positive relationship in childhood and so can be expected to develop a mature relationship with the therapist and withstand the anxiety produced by the STAPP method. This criterion tends to exclude borderline, narcissistic, and other severe personality disorders. Sifneos also requires that a patient specify a focal issue that is oedipal in origin. He believes that failure in other brief dynamic therapies is due to attempts to work with patients with pre-oedipal conflicts. Typically the pre-oedipal patient complains of reactive depression following the loss of a loved one and then regresses when termination issues are broached. This leads to a treatment impasse and often to treatment failure.

During the pre-treatment evaluation, Sifneos looks for patients with symptoms of anxiety, phobias, depression, conversion reactions, mild obsessive–compulsive features, and mild personality disorders involving interpersonal issues. The patient must be able to specify a single focal conflict and be able to tolerate anxiety by post-poning work on other issues. Furthermore, the patient must show curiosity, a willingness to make reasonable sacrifices, and have realistic expectations of treatment results. During the evaluation session the patient and therapist collaborate to develop a list of written treatment objectives. These are then evaluated over the course of the treatment and at long-term follow-up. Sifneos estimates that only about 20% of outpatients are appropriate for this approach (Sifneos, 1978).

During the initial phase of therapy, the therapist must be able to establish the kind of rapport with the patient that will ensure a therapeutic alliance. The therapist must take an active role and be comfortable and competent using anxiety-provoking confrontations to clarify issues regarding the patient's early life circumstances as well as current conflicts. At all costs, the therapist avoids issues that would promote moderate regression. Instead STAPP confrontations are used to directly attack the patient's defenses.

The usual length of treatment is 3 to 4 months. Sessions of 45 minutes are scheduled weekly, usually for 12 to 15 sessions, and never more than 20 sessions. When there is tangible evidence of change, termination is considered.

Mann's Time-Limited Psychotherapy   Mann (1973) and Mann and Goldman (1982) views the variable of time as a specific factor in therapy as well as an element in its curative effect. Mann believes that the patient's basic problem is overdependency. The aim of therapy is to increase the patient's ability to separate from the sustaining figure by overcoming separation anxiety and developing more positive, less ambivalent, internal representations of important figures. This is accomplished by a corrective emotional experience, that is, through the therapist's role as an emphatic helper who supports the patient's negative as well as positive feelings. Termination plays a central role in Mann's time-limited approach. The patient always knows the end date of treatment and this specification in the treatment contract with the patient allows the treatment to have a clear beginning, middle, and end.

The selection of a *central issue* for therapy is critical. The central issue becomes the vehicle through which the patient engages in treatment and on which successful outcome depends. The central issue is formulated in terms of time, affect, and an image of the self. It is a "paradigm of the transference" expected to emerge in treatment. Mann emphasizes that the central issue is always different from the complaints that brought the patient to therapy. This issue represents the patient's "present and chronically endured pain." Therapy attempts to resolve this and the patient's negative self-image.

Besides the general selection criteria for the brief dynamic therapies, Mann disqualifies patients who have had difficulty engaging and disengaging rapidly from previous treatments. He also excludes patients with strong dependency needs, depressive patients who are not able to form a therapeutic alliance quickly, and patients with psychosomatic disorders who tolerate loss poorly. Schizophrenia, bipolar disorders, and severe borderline, and narcissistic personality disorders are not treated using this method. The patient must currently have a satisfactory stable relationship and occupational status.

The time-limited therapist employs some of the same analytic techniques as Sifneos but emphasizes empathetic responding. Transference is interpreted from within the identified central issue/conflict. Confronting separation and termination issues are critical to the success of this approach. In the opening sessions the therapist makes few comments, accepts the positive transference of the patient, and observes defense mechanisms, coping styles, and genetic roots of the central issue. During the middle four sessions, the patient experiences the frustration that all of the wished-for changes may not occur. Resistance and negative transference is likely to appear in these sessions. In the closing sessions, concerns about termination in the face of unresolved problems in other areas of life are noted. The resolution of both the central issue and the unfolding of an attachment–separation process with the therapist occur through the development and interpretation of the transference.

Klerman's Interpersonal Psychotherapy   Klerman, Weissmann, Rounsaville, and Chevron (1984) have developed a unique form of brief intervention for depressive disorders. Their approach is one of the first of the so-called manual-based psychotherapies. It has been studied extensively in a number of national psychotherapy research projects, and has been the major psychotherapeutic intervention used in combination with drug therapy. Because depression is one of the most common presenting problems of outpatients, a brief description of this approach is included here. Interpersonal Psychotherapy (IPT) consists of 12 to 26 weekly sessions that focus on current interpersonal problems in outpatients with unipolar, nonpsychotic depressions. Klerman's IPT is derived from the interpersonal school of psychiatry and approaches assessment and treatment from the viewpoint of social support systems and attachments. Therapeutic strategies and techniques involve reassurance, feeling identification, improving interpersonal communications, and perception testing. The goal of treatment is increased interpersonal relating, rather than personality reconstruction.

In the initial sessions a detailed symptom history is taken via a structured interview. These symptoms are reviewed with the patient, and psychoeducation about the natural course of clinical depression is provided. A second part of the assessment involves the specification of the interpersonal problem areas. Klerman indicates that there are four areas of interpersonal problems in depression: (1) grief reactions, (2) interpersonal disputes, (3) role transitions, and (4) interpersonal deficits. The assessment should isolate one or more of these problem areas as the focus of treatment.

The middle sessions are directed toward resolving the problem area(s). Although specific techniques are used for each particular problem area, some general strategies apply to all four areas. These are feeling identification; identifying past models for relationships; and guiding and empowering the patient in decision making and problem solving. The focus is on current dilemmas, not past interpersonal concerns. Although much of IP is based on psychodynamic theory, there is an absence of concern for intrapsychic and cognitive processes.

As stated previously, this approach has a very limited indication, which is nonpsychotic, non-bipolar depression. No specific contraindications are reported

beyond the general patient selection factors noted for the problem-solving orientation. Clinical research has demonstrated the advantage of this approach in symptom
reduction and improved personal and social functioning during recovery from depression (Klerman et al., 1984).

The Cognitive–Behavioral Orientation to Brief Therapy

The cognitive–behavioral orientation is composed of a number of separate behavioral and cognitive therapy approaches, and some approaches which combine both
elements. The variety of techniques include eliciting and testing automatic thoughts,
as well as exposure, role-playing, modeling, cognitive restructuring, social skills
training, relapse prevention, and reinforcement. Brief cognitive behavioral therapy,
can be accomplished in an individual format, as well as in groups, and marital family formats.

The usual indications for this orientation are the various anxiety and depressive
disorders. Standard behavior therapies have been particularly effective with panic,
agoraphobia, simple and social phobias, obsessive–compulsive disorders, generalized and performance anxiety, primary sexual dysfunction, and deficits in social
skills. In fact, behavior therapy has been judged to be the treatment of choice
for simple phobias and primary sexual dysfunction (Beutler & Crago, 1987). The
cognitive–behavioral orientation is often used as part of a comprehensive treatment
plan for eating disorders and chronic pain syndromes.

Contraindications are few in number compared with the psychodynamic approaches. Basically, the behavioral–cognitive approaches are contraindicated where
the chronicity of the patient's concerns are beyond the reach of any limited treatment.
Usually this includes chronic schizophrenia, severe personality disorders, and other
chronic psychotic or nonpsychotic conditions without a specific focus or treatable
target symptom, such as uncontrollable acting out or somatoform conditions. Obviously, lack of motivation for change or willingness to cooperate with the treatment
plan within and outside of sessions would be a contraindication. Similarly, when the
goals of treatment are broad and ambitious—such as character reconstruction—the
cognitive–behavioral, as well as other brief treatments, would be contraindicated.

Patient selection factors are rather limited. The patient must be willing to attend
sessions and to cooperate with the therapist's suggestions and treatment interventions. It also must be assumed that the patient is motivated to make change. Although
psychological-mindedness is not required for the behavioral approaches, it is helpful for the cognitive approaches.

Beck's Cognitive Therapy   Cognitive therapy views pathology as a consequence of
dysfunctional patterns of thoughts. Specific cognitions, schemata, and logical errors
account for the onset and persistence of symptoms. Cognitions are the thoughts and
images that are immediately brought to mind when an individual is faced with a situation. The initial phase of therapy involves teaching patients to recognize and challenge their dysfunctional cognitions and replace them with more functional cognitions. In so doing, symptoms—usually dysphoria or anxiety—that resulted from

these faulty cognitions are reduced. The later stages of treatment focus on the identification and modification of schemata and logical errors. Schemata are the silent assumptions based on the individual's early experience that determine the content of cognitions. They form the basis for evaluating, categorizing, and distorting experiences. Logical errors, by contrast, are the consequences, not the cause, of dysfunctional thinking. They include incorrect conclusions or inferences such as selective attention, personalization, overgeneralization, and magnification.

Through empathy and in a spirit of cooperation that Beck (1976) calls "collaborative empiricism," the therapist helps the patient recognize these dysfunctional patterns, challenge them, and develop more adaptive patterns of thinking and behaving. Besides cognitive disputation and restructuring, Beck also employs various techniques like role-playing, reinforcement, and behavioral techniques including homework assignments. Medication is sometimes used as an adjunct.

Anxiety disorders and nonpsychotic unipolar depression, such as dysthymia are the two major indications for this approach. Recently, Beck has elaborated this method for paranoid and substance abuse disorders, and even for major depressive episodes, especially those secondary to physical disorders. The approach is less likely to be successful in patients with chronic schizophrenia, severe personality disorders, and those with severe cognitive defects, such as in organic mental disorders.

Patient selection factors favor individuals who are capable of quickly forming a therapeutic relationship and who have some capacity for self-reflection and psychological-mindedness. Unlike the dynamic approaches, intact object relations are not required.

Usually treatment for mild to moderate depression is twice weekly for up to 15 sessions. If symptom relief has not occurred by the seventh session, antidepressants are indicated. Follow-up sessions may be scheduled on a monthly or twice-monthly basis for 6 to 12 months to consolidate gains and prevent relapse. Scores on the Beck Depression Inventory (BDI) are regularly monitored over the course of treatment. On the other hand, cognitive therapy of anxiety disorders is likely to be scheduled on a once-weekly therapy of anxiety disorders is likely to be scheduled on a once-weekly basis for 12–20 sessions.

Although Rational-Emotive Behavior Therapy (REBT) developed by Albert Ellis shares a number of commonalities with Beck's approach, Beck and Greenberg (1979) note two differences between the two systems. First, Beck differs with Ellis on the assessment of dysfunctional cognitions. Ellis views a patient's irrational beliefs in universal terms while Beck believes that problem-causing ideas are idiosyncratic and must be detected on an individual basis. Second, Beck's technique in disputing functional beliefs is much less confrontive than Ellis's.

Weiss and Jacobson's Brief Behavioral Marital Therapy

This form of brief therapy is based on the assumption that problem behaviors represent a form of maladaptation but also may have adaptive qualities. This approach attempts to make changes in four target areas: (1) responses, (2) competencies, (3) skills, and (4) concepts. Responses refer to behavior that one or both partners exhibit that appear to be destructive to the relationship. Skills refer to specific proficiencies that can enhance a relationship, such as active listening, or positive reinforcing statements. Competencies are generic skills such as the ability to be supportive and understanding in relating to the partner, and the ability to problem solve and thus achieve mutually shared objectives. Finally, contexts refer to specific areas of the couple's interaction such as child care or communication processes.

The goal of brief behavioral marital therapy is to assist the couple in exercising better control over their context-specific behavior, their patterns of mutual reinforcement, their problem solving skills, and their ability to recognize patterns to their own behavioral histories. This form of treatment involves a therapeutic contract or master plan linking specific techniques to accomplish specific treatment objectives. Treatment usually lasts eight to 10 sessions and involves a variety of traditional behavioral intervention techniques such as reinforcement and social skills training to role playing and to prescribing directive tasks. The therapist's role is to guide the treatment process by emphasizing overt behavior change, compliance with directives, and ensuring relapse prevention (Weiss & Jacobson, 1981).

The Systems Orientation

The systems approaches are the most variable, eclectic, and versatile of the four orientations to brief therapy. The dominant characteristic of this orientation is the focus on defining and resolving a specific presenting problem usually as it relates to the family or relational system. The goals of treatment are symptom relief, reintegration, and more effective coping. Character change is not considered a treatment goal. A variety of techniques and strategies are used including (1) clarifying the situation, (2) exploring the implications of alternative decisions, (3) advice, (4) paradox, (5) role-playing, (6) environmental manipulation, and (7) mobilizing social networks. Insight and interpretation of unconscious processes are not particularly consistent with this orientation.

When compared with the brief dynamic and cognitive–behavioral orientations, this approach has the widest of indications for treatment. Essentially the patient must be sufficiently distressed or dysfunctional in response to a precipitating event to require a clinical intervention. Usually treatment is sought for acute concerns about self, job, or marital/family issues. Occasionally, the problem is superimposed on a long-standing but stable disorder which does not become the focus of treatment.

The contraindications and patient selection factors for the systems orientation are essentially the same as those for the cognitive–behavioral orientation.

The MRI Brief Therapy Approach   This approach has been articulated and popularized by Weakland, Fisch, Watzlawick, and Bodin (1974), and Fisch, Weakland, and Segal (1982) of the Brief Therapy Project at the Mental Research Institute (MRI) in Palo Alto, California. Problems and problem-maintaining solutions are two of their key concepts. With the exception of organic deficits, problems are viewed as essentially behavioral in nature, and as shaped and maintained by interactions in significant ongoing relationships. There is no need to postulate unconscious mechanisms;

it is sufficient to focus on the vicious circles of problem behavior and the inappropriate solutions that perpetuate it in the present. When a patient presents with some persistence of unproductive behavior, the goal of treatment is simply to interdict to create a more useful solution.

Treatment centers on three pieces of clinical information that are elicited in the crucial initial interview. First, the presenting problem is clearly articulated. Patients are asked what brings them to treatment now and what it is they wish to change. Second, problem-maintaining solutions used by the patient, and often significant others, are elicited. Third, the therapist formulates with the patient the anticipated therapy goal in explicit, clear, and specific behavior terms. Patients are encouraged to "think small" and move away from unrealistic goals. MRI therapists believe that setting the goal of treatment states the nature of the therapy and implicitly produces a problem-solving context. Within the initial session the therapist establishes a 10-session contract, which creates an expectation for rapid behavior change.

This approach uses specific strategies and interventions to interdict the patient's misguided solutions. These methods are designed to replace the attempted solution with an opposite or incompatible behavior. Two of the most potent techniques are reframing and paradoxical directives, such as symptom prescription. At the conclusion of each session, patients are generally given a directive or homework assignment. This frequently involves the continuation or exaggeration of the symptomatic behavior that brought them to therapy.

Weakland et al. (1974) list several indications for this approach. They range from learning disabilities and eating disorders to schizophrenia, sexual dysfunction, and somatoform disorders. Apparently there are no specific contraindications. Treatment is limited to 10 sessions, and Weakland reports that his brief therapy has been successful in achieving limited but significant goals in relation to the patient's main complaint in about 75% of cases (Fisch et al., 1982).

Brief Family Therapy and Solution-Focused Therapy

In the early 1980s de Shazer and colleagues at the Brief Family Therapy Center in Milwaukee, Wisconsin described a form of family therapy that was novel and deceptively simple. He defined brief family therapy as an effort to help individuals change their "frames," that is, their viewpoints or customs that create difficulty within the family. This form of treatment is intended to change or "reframe" the way in which family customs develop so that the meaning of the same specific situation is modified and perceived and reacted to differently. This form of therapy is conducted by a team wherein one team member interacts with the family while the others observe through a one-way mirror and then during the consulting break offer the therapist advice.

A further iteration of de Shazer clinical and theoretical work has been the development of what he has called "solution focused family therapy" (de Shazer, 1988). This approach is illustrated in the basic question asked of families during the first session: "Suppose that one night while you were asleep, there was a miracle and this problem was solved. How would you know? What would be different"? This is the "miracle question" (1988, p. 5.) The basic premise of solution-focused therapy is therapists should focus as much attention on solutions as they do on problems. For often all solutions involve a family member doing something different, and the purpose of therapy is to assist family members to do something different.

Rather than spending an inordinate amount of time in the initial sessions describing the problem that led the individual or family to seek help, the solution-focused therapist explores the exceptions to the problems, i.e., the times and circumstances in which the problem does not occur. These exceptions can be identified by asking the individual or family to observe and report at the next session what happens when what they would like to happen, does happen. When clients report on this task they often report having done something different or having had something different happen. This phenomenon is the basis for solution-focused therapy.

This approach is applicable to a wide range of personal and family problems ranging from depression and eating disorders to parent–child disagreements. Treatment tends to be relatively short, ranging from 1 to 10 sessions, and averaging about 6 sessions. The basic goal of treatment is symptom relief and problem resolution. Treatment strategies include attending to exceptions to the stated problem, asking the "miracle question," and emphasizing solution focus rather than problem focus. Reframing is the basic treatment technique. This treatment approach does not necessitate a team of consultants behind a one-way mirror, as with its brief family therapy precursor. Also, it does not require that the entire family be present. In fact solution-focused treatment can also be used in an individual therapy format.

EXPERIENTIAL ORIENTATION TO BRIEF THERAPY

Budman Brief Interpersonal–Developmental–Experiential Therapy

Budman (Budman & Gurman, 1988) has developed an experiential approach to brief therapy that focuses on three domains: (1) the interpersonal, (2) the developmental, and (3) the existential (I–D–E). For Budman, *existential* refers to factors such as the meaning and values of one's life, including confronting the issues of one's death. Budman's approach is not a symptom-oriented, nor an intrapsychic, nor an interpersonal approach. Rather it is an amalgam based on currently evolving principles of individual, group couple and family theory and therapy as well as existential theories of interpersonal relationship and models of human potential. This I–D–E focus provides the therapist a frame of reference for conceptualizing the answer to the central question of brief therapy: "Why now?" According to Budman a client seeks therapy because of interpersonal, developmental and existential changes that are occurring within and around the individual. The answer to the "why now?" question helps the therapist establish a focus for treatment that clarifies where the push for change originates. Budman notes that the five most common foci for therapy are (1) losses; (2) developmental dysynchronies; (3) interpersonal conflicts; (4) symptomatic presentations, such as depression, insomnia, or panic; and (5) severe personality disorders.

Accordingly, Budman and Gurman (1988) have articulated some treatment guidelines for each of these five therapeutic foci. Treatment formats such as individual, couple or family, and groups are strategically employed to accomplish specific treatment goals for each focus. They note that when active alcohol or other substance abuse is noted, this problem must be addressed prior to or concurrently with the development of any other focal areas. It may be necessary to delay or refuse treatment to a client who is currently abusing alcohol or other substances.

Budman and Gurman provide a unique framework for conceptualizing short term psychotherapy that makes flexible use of individual, group, couples, and family therapy strategies that can be used with a broad range of patient presentations. This approach was developed by Budman at the Harvard Community Health Plan, a large HMO serving the New England area. Thus its origins are different from the other approaches describes in this chapter. Another way this approach is different is that it does not assume that treatment should be continuous for a given number of sessions. Instead Budman would permit treatment be discontinuous with regularly weekly sessions scheduled in the beginning and then reducing sessions to biweekly, monthly, or even bimonthly if warranted by the developmental focus of treatment. Furthermore, Budman (Budman & Gurman, 1988) would argue that some clients are not reasonable candidates for brief therapy unless there is an appropriate patient–therapist match or a match with a specific treatment modality. If the presentation is a certain psychotic process or severe personality disorder, a longer term, discontinuous mode of treatment might be more appropriate.

The Adlerian Approach to Brief Therapy

Originally conceived by Alfred Adler (1956, 1964), the Adlerian or Individual Psychology approach has been further developed by others such as Rudolf Dreikurs, Kurt Adler, Bernard Shulman, and Harold Mosak. Adler usually saw patients for 20 or fewer sessions (Adler, 1956, 1964), a tradition followed by a number of contemporary Adlerian clinicians (Kern, Yeakle, & Sperry, 1989; Shlien, Mosak, & Dreikurs, 1962). Ansbacher (1972) concludes that Adler's approach was the first brief therapy approach. Surprisingly, few outside Adlerian circles are aware of this legacy.

Kurt Adler (1972) correctly noted that even though the Adlerian approach is probably the first of the brief therapies, it is not primarily a brief nor a long-term psychotherapy method, but rather an approach that can accommodate patient needs and style. At its best, the Adlerian approach is tailored to the patient's needs, expectations, and individual differences. If a formal course of brief therapy is both indicated and negotiated, then a brief course of treatment will follow. Similarly, if long-term therapy is indicated by the clinician's judgment and desired by the patient, then long-term therapy proceeds. Or, if all that is possible or deemed necessary is a brief therapeutic intervention, then that occurs.

The decision on the time course for a particular case depends on a number of both patient and therapist factors. One such factor involves life tasks. A rule of thumb among Adlerian therapists is that briefer treatment is indicated when dysfunction is focused on only one of the life tasks, while longer treatment is indicated when two or more life tasks are involved. Shulman (1989b) also notes that individuals with better-developed social interest can be helped in a shorter time frame than those with developed social interest. Similarly, those with more optimistic expectations are more amenable to help. Furthermore, a good match between client and therapist facilitates therapy. On the other hand stressful life situations can complicate and lengthen treatment, while certain types of private logic are more challenging, specifically, when transference issues are involved. Finally, resistance from any cause tends to increase the length of therapy.

The Adlerian approach views the person as an open system striving for fulfillment. This striving is determined by the interaction between innate perceptions and early life experiences. As a result of this interaction, a unified perceptual system or master plan emerges which Adler called *the lifestyle,* the unity of the personality. Although stress may be implicated in maladaptive behavior, dysfunctional behavior is the result of faults in the master plan. According to Shulman (1984), the person with a skewed lifestyle is more vulnerable to insecurity; disturbed human relationships; discouragement; inferiority feelings, e.g., low self-esteem; and fear of facing the tasks of life—love, work, and friendship.

The goal of Adlerian therapy is to increase the patient's level of social interest or relatedness and ability to function more effectively. Often this occurs with changes in mistaken lifestyle convictions, but insight is not the necessary nor sufficient condition for change. The therapist has three tasks in the course of treatment which correspond to the three phases of Adlerian psychotherapy: (1) relationship, (2) assessment, and (3) reorientation. Unlike longer-term psychotherapy in which these three phases may be quite separate (e.g., assessment of lifestyle may occur over two to four sessions, followed by several sessions of reorientation), in brief therapy these three phases may occur in a single session. First, to establish a collaborative, therapeutic relationship; second, to assess and understand the person's perceptual system and lifestyle convictions; third, to reveal the mistaken convictions to the patient in such a way that fourth, they become subject to self-correction and facilitate change (Shulman, 1984).

Assessment includes the patient's level of adaptive functioning—which is based on the patient's response to the life tasks, and the lifestyle—which is inferred from family constellation data and early childhood recollections. This information can be collected formally and systematically in one or more intake sessions, or can be elicited in a short time in the first therapy session, as is usually the case in a brief treatment format. In the early phase of treatment the focus is on developing some degree of awareness, whether it be goal or priority recognition or insight into mistaken lifestyle convictions related to the particular focus of brief therapy. The later phase of treatment involves experimentation with alternative modes of behavior. Here the therapist works to encourage, guide, support, and serve as a model for the patient's efforts to function more effectively and courageously. The flexibility of this approach allows for many combinations of techniques from the cognitive, behavioral, analytic, existential, and client-centered approaches. Kurt Adler (1972) suggested a number of techniques that shorten the time frame of therapy. Among them are (1) refraining, (2) acting "as if," (3) humor, (4) rechanneling, and (5) symptom prescription. Shulman (1972) has described 11 other techniques.

What about single-session Adlerian therapy? Several descriptions of this format have been reported (Powers & Griffith, 1989; Shulman, 1989a; Adler, 1989). Common to any Adlerian single-session treatment—whether in a formal scheduled session, in a demonstration interview, or in a brief consultation—is the following: The therapist begins by asking the reason the individual is seeking help at this time, the "why now?" question. From this answer the therapist begins to explore the current situation, asks a few questions about the past and quickly connects the present to the past by finding the thread of continuity. The Adlerian therapist searches for a line of movement that seems identical both in the early recollections and in present. The problem is then redefined or reframed as a misperception and the therapist may use exaggeration, paradox, or an unexpected statement to capture the individual's attention and suggest alternative ways of thinking and acting. For example the therapist may say, "Nothing can change unless you stop believing you are worthless," and then prescribe a paradoxical injunction such as telling the next five people the individual meets that he is a worthless bum. Using gentle confrontation to expose the private logic behind their behavior, self-created obstacles, unrealistic expectations, or interpersonal maneuvers, the therapist reflects how these lines of movement were learned during the early years and continue into the present (Shulman, 1989b). To complete this change many clients will need encouragement, and continued efforts to disconfirm their private logic and confirm their self-esteem. This may occur in self-therapy, support groups, or additional sessions with the therapist.

The Adlerian approach shares similar indications, contraindications, and selection factors with the cognitive-behavioral, the experiential and the systemic approaches, as well as with some of the psychodynamic approaches. It lends itself to use in community mental health settings, schools, corrections systems, and medical settings, as well as in the private practice of psychotherapy.

Comparative Analysis of Nine Brief Therapy Approaches

A number of commonalities as well as differences exist among these nine approaches. In this next section, we will compare and contrast the eight contemporary approaches with the Adlerian approach. These approaches are summarized in Table 12–1.

There are some striking differences among the approaches for indications and contraindications. Generally, the psychodynamic approaches have the narrowest range of diagnostic categories that are considered treatable. This is the case not only for Sifneos (1979) and Mann (1973) but also for the well-publicized approaches of Malan (1980) and Davanloo (1980). IPT and Cognitive Therapy also have limited indications, as they were initially developed as tailored treatments for depression. In the past few years, Beck (Alford & Beck, 1998) has adapted his approach to several indications, and Klerman and Weissman (1993) have extended IPT to anxiety and substance disorders. The solution-focused, Budman's experiential, and the MRI approaches share with the Adlerian approach a much wider range of applicability.

In terms of patient selection factors, a pattern similar to indications and contraindications is noted. The psychoanalytic approaches have the most stringent

TABLE 12–1 *Comparison of Nine Brief Therapy Approaches*

Approach	Indication/ Contraindication	Selection Factors	Number of Sessions
STAPP/Sifneous	limited to neurotic disorders; excludes severe personality disorders	most stringent; YAVIS with focal oedipal issue	12–15
Time-Limited/ Mann	limited to neurotic disorders; excludes severe personality disorders	very stringent; YAVIS with separation issue	10
IPT/Klerman	primarily depressive disorders	less stringent	12–26
Cognitive/Beck	utilized for anxiety, depressive, substance abuse, and paranoid disorders	less stringent; some self-reflective capacity	variable
Brief Behavioral Marital Therapy/ Weiss & Jacobson	limited to couples relational problems	less stringent	8–10
MRI/Weakland	wider range	less stringent	10
Solution-Focused/ de Shazer	wide range	least stringent	1–10
Experiential/ Budman	very wide range	least stringent	variable depending on pt. need/availability of tx match
Adlerian	wider range	less stringent	1–20

Approach	Treatment Outcome Goal(s)	Treatment Strategy/Plan	Therapeutic Techniques
STAPP/Sifneos	symptom relief; issue resolution; focal character change	establish therapeutic alliance; assess oedipal conflict/issue; confront issue	transference and resistance interpretation; defense analysis; anxiety-provoking confrontations
Time-Limited Mann	symptom relief; issue resolution; focal character change	establish therapeutic alliance; assess central issue; confront separation/termination issues & fears; facilitate termination	transference & resistance interpretation; defense analysis; empathetic responding
Solution-Focused/ de Shazer	symptom relief; problem resolution	focus on exceptions to problem; miracle question; emphasizing solutions over problem	reframing

TABLE 12–1 *Continued*

Approach	Treatment Outcome Goal(s)	Treatment Strategy/Plan	Therapeutic Techniques
Cognitive/ Beck	symptom relief; functional cognitions & schemata	establish collaborative relationship; assess cognitions, schemas, logical errors; modify dysfunctions	cognitive disputation & restructuring; various behavioral methods; role-playing; intersession tasks
Brief Behavioral Marital Therapy/ Weiss & Jacobson	symptom relief; improved relational functioning	establish collaborating working relationship & treatment contract; careful pretreatment assessment of maladaptive responses, skills, competencies, contexts; replace maladaptive patterns with more adaptive patterns	mutual reinforcement schedules; social skills training; directive tasks, role-playing
IPT/Klerman	symptom relief, resolution of grief, interpersonal disputes, role transition, or interpersonal deficits	assess symptoms, course and problem area(s); resolve problem area(s)	reassurance, feeling identification; communication training; decision-making training, adjunct: drugs
MRI/Weakland	symptom relief; problem resolution system changes	develop mutual treatment contract; assess problem & problem maintenance solutions; interdict problem maintenance solutions	advice, alternative exploration, reframing, paradox, intersession directives/tasks
Experiential/ Budman	symptom relief; resolution of loss; IP conflict; developmental dyschrony, or character change	establish collaborative relationship; assess therapeutic foci; determine best treatment match; patient–therapist; patient intervention, and duration (continuous or discontinuous)	various modalities (individual, group, family, couple; and appropriate intervention strategies from cognitive dynamics, behavior, experiential, systemic approaches)
Alderian	symptom relief; increased social interest & coping with life tasks	establish collaborative relationship; assess relevant lifestyle data; awareness/insight; experimentation with alternative behaviors	various: analytic, cognitive, client-centered, behavioral, paradoxical, etc. methods

criteria. Bellak, again, is the exception. Many have observed that the psychoanalytic method favors the well-to-do, worried-well, or YAVIS patient (Ellenberger, 1970). This seems to be borne out with the selection criteria of Sifneos (1979), Mann (1973), Malan (1980), and Davanloo (1980). Like the Adlerian approach, solution-focused, experiential, MRI, Cognitive, and IPT approaches are considered appropriate for a majority of the patient population.

All the approaches endorse symptom reduction or relief as a general treatment goal. Beyond this, each approach has a specific outcome goal which is consistent with its basic premise. While Sifneos (1979) and Mann (1973) indicate that circumscribed character change occurs as a result of successful treatment, most classical analysts doubt character change is possible outside of long-term therapy (Bibring, 1954; Perry, 1987). Although the various other approaches do not speak of character change, but rather of sustained changes in behavior—thoughts, images, feelings, and actions—for all practical purposes these changes appear to be the equivalent of focal character change. The Adlerian therapist would view change in lifestyle convictions and manifest behavior as synonymous with character change.

Similarly, a comparison of therapeutic strategies reveals basic correspondence among all eight approaches. Whether *termed therapeutic alliance, treatment contract,* or *collaborative relationship,* all approaches agree on the importance of quickly and intentionally engaging the patient in the treatment process. However, there appear to be differences in the nature of the relationship. At one end of the continuum are the Adlerian and cognitive approaches which suggest an equalitarian stance, while at the other end of the continuum are the psychoanalytic and MRI approaches, with a more authoritative and therapist-oriented stance. The other approaches appear to be somewhere between these two end points. Assessment and reorientation phase are shared by all approaches. Obviously what is assessed, how problems or issues are worked through, and how changes are extrapolated outside therapy differ for each approach. The psychoanalytic and the Adlerian approaches are the only ones to formally recognize psychodynamics and insight.

It is in comparing treatment techniques formally specified for each approach that many differences appear. Sifneos (1979) and Mann's (1973) approaches report a rather parochial focus, that is, only psychoanalytic techniques and methods are reported. For the most part, the other approaches report a more eclectic stance, freely using techniques from other approaches. Researchers observing effective psychoanalytic therapists have noted that these therapists do use a variety of nonpsychoanalytic techniques in their practice, including behavioral, cognitive, and problem-solving techniques (Weiner, 1986). Budman's Experiential and the Adlerian approaches are the most eclectic and pragmatic in terms of choice of techniques, with the Adlerian therapist open to the use of psychoanalytic techniques.

Summary

In essence, a comparison of the above approaches suggests that, to one degree or another, these formal brief therapy approaches are responsive to the need and demand for time-limited psychotherapeutic treatment. With the possible exception of the Adlerian approach (Sperry, 1987), none of the approaches has articulated a formal strategy for brief therapeutic interventions.

There is considerable commonality among these brief approaches. In fact, there may be more similarity among the brief therapies in general, than among longer-term psychotherapy approaches. Yet, there are some notable differences. Specifically, it can be concluded that the psychoanalytic approaches are generally the most restrictive regarding patient selection and diagnostic indications for treatment, and specify the narrowest range of intervention methods and techniques. Yet, they share a similar treatment strategy and outcome goals with the other approaches. Although the cognitive and interpersonal approaches were originally developed specifically for treating depressive disorders, and thus have limited treatment indications, they are remarkably similar to the nonpsychoanalytic approaches in most respects. Finally, the Adlerian approach is quite similar to all the nonpsychoanalytic approaches, yet it shares with the psychoanalytic approaches an appreciation of the influence of early experiences on current functioning and use of insight as a treatment strategy.

■ A CASE EXAMPLE OF BRIEF ADLERIAN THERAPY

Jackie L. was a 24-year-old, single, white female when I was asked to see her by a colleague who was working in psychotherapy with Ms. L.'s cousin. The cousin reportedly had a history of early sexual abuse, which had recently manifested itself in selective dissociative symptoms such as short-term memory loss, depersonalization, and emotional numbing. The cousin had recently talked with Ms. L. and suggested that Ms. L.'s own memory lapses might represent dissociation, and even dissociative identity disorder, which was previous called multiple personality disorder. Ms. L. became increasingly alarmed at this suggestion and sought out psychological evaluation for herself. HMO permitted up to six evaluation and treatment sessions with provision for up to 20 additional sessions within a calendar year if they were warranted and approved.

Session 1

At our first meeting, my goal was to begin an assessment of Ms. L.'s current and past levels of functioning, her strengths, her personality or lifestyle, her capacity to develop a therapeutic relationship, her readiness for treatment and, of course, her presenting concern: memory lapses and anxiety that the lapses might represent a serious dissociative disorder.

Ms. L. reported that she had recently graduated from college with an accounting major and immediately took a job with a high-tech biomedical firm as an associate in their accounting department. And although she indicated that "memory problems" were constant throughout her life, they had worsened in the past two months. She also reports she engages in considerable fantasy and daydreaming, particularly when authority figures, like her boss, have given her a task with deadline. Her fantasies are largely about men and sex. She indicated a single incident of fondling by her older brother when she was 10 years old about which she was frightened and confused and reportedly had only recalled when Ms. L.'s cousin recounted her own experience of sexual taunting by Ms. L.'s brother. However, Ms. L. remembered instances of "memory lapse" that occurred much earlier in her life and these instances usually involved her mother and father.

I also learned that Ms. L. had considerable difficulty establishing and maintaining intimate relationships with eligible men over the past five years. Before that she indicated that she seldom dated even though she was quite attractive, interesting, and available. The four men she had became intensely attracted to turned out to be "womanizers" who would flaunt the other women they were involved with in front of Ms. L. Her response was to become "insanely jealous" of these women, and "promise to do anything" to hold onto these men. In addition she reported compulsive nail biting, and trichotillomania (compulsive hair pulling), which left her with a small bald spot that she effectively camouflaged by changing her hair style. Nail biting was also listed as problematic. Occasional binge drinking was also reported.

Ms. L. indicates she had never been involved in counseling or psychotherapy before this session. Her medical history and health behaviors appear to be noncontributory, except for occasional binge drinking. Her family consists of both parents who are alive and well and still residing in the home where Ms. L. was reared. Ms. L. is the youngest of five siblings, and the only female. Her mother is described as emotionally distant, demanding, and as having been "unconcerned" with Ms. L.'s feminine needs. Ms. L. seldom wore dresses, used makeup, or adopted "feminine manners" until she started college. The mother had a "breakdown" when Ms. L. left home for college, presumably a depressive episode. Father is described as caring and concerned but made little effort to shield Ms. L. from her mother's demands. He apparently was grieved over his wife's expectation that Ms. L. "dress and act like a boy" but did not voice his concern at least publically. The four brothers were described as "jocks" who were extremely competitive. Ms. L. describes herself as a "tomboy" in grade school, but was "boy-crazy with hormones" throughout high school.

An investigation of her current life situation shows that she has a stable network of female friends, difficulty relating to her parents, an unsatisfying and distressing relationship with her current boyfriend and a confusing and distressing relationship with her female boss. She had received high evaluations for her job performance from her subordinates and from her superior's boss, but not from her immediate superior. On the Dissociative Disorders Interview Schedule, a structured interview for assessing dissociative disorder Ms. L.'s "memory lapse" did not appear to represent a dissociative disorder. The rest of the mental status exam was unremarkable, meaning that she was oriented to person, place, and time, that there was no obvious cognitive or perceptual deficits noted, and that she denied suicidal and homicidal ideation. Based on these findings, Ms. L. met the DSM-IV criteria for Anxiety Disorder NOS, or AXIS I, and histrionic, passive aggressive, and self-defeating traits on AXIS II.

Although quite anxious at the beginning of the session, she was easily calmed and showed other indications that she could and probably would be able to form an effective collaborative therapeutic relationship. Because she had been successful in meeting personal goals she had set for herself, i.e., losing 15 pounds and maintaining the weight loss for 3 years, and giving up smoking 4 years ago, it seemed she had sufficient capacity and readiness for change in therapy. A contract for five sessions was agreed on and subsequently authorized by her HMO. The focus of the sessions was to be reduction of both anxiety and memory loss. Accordingly, five weekly sessions were scheduled. Ms. L. was asked to complete the Lifestyle Interview Guide which would be discussed in the session.

Session 2

At the beginning of a second meeting, Ms. L. mentioned she had not binged during the weekend nor consumed any alcohol since our last session. Furthermore, she reported that she had refrained from hair pulling when she was anxious, even though she was quite anxious at work after meeting with her boss. It seemed that drinking and hair pulling served as anxiety reducers for her. This disclosure was interesting because I had not suggested she reduce or stop either behavior. And it confirmed my prediction that she was indeed ready and motivated for therapeutic change. During this session her response on the Lifestyle Interview Guide and early family constellation recollections were discussed (see appendix at the end of this case study for this data). Following this a tentative lifestyle formulation was presented. Ms. L.'s feedback on the formulation was sought. She was initially surprised at the psychological meaning of her memory loss but agreed that the formulation, particularly the lifestyle convictions, were accurate. Specific treatment objectives were negotiated. The work of the remaining three sessions was to explore the ways that memory lapses served to safeguard Ms. L. from expressing her anger and subsequent anxiety at her parents, especially her mother, as well as her female boss. An additional objective was to experiment with more effective ways of dealing with her anxiety and anger.

Sessions 3 to 6

The discussion of memory lapses as a safeguard proved painful but freeing for Ms. L. She shared her feelings of hopelessness and rejection regarding her painful relationship with her mother and current and past boyfriends and her inability to emancipate from painful abusive relationships. By the fifth session it became clear that systemic issues involving authority and power at home and in the workplace were very deeply intertwined with Ms. L.'s personal dynamics and that additional sessions would be needed. Even though Ms. L. was relieved she did not have a dissociative disorder and had experienced some symptomatic relief (e.g., reductions in anxiety and binge drinking, and no further hair pulling), it was agreed to seek authorization for additional sessions. The request was made and the utilization reviewer authorized up to 20 additional sessions, with a review after the 10th additional session. The treatment focus would now be primarily on job functioning and career development, and secondarily on her enmeshed relationship with her mother and the abusive nature of her relationships with male friends and lovers. Framing therapy around work-related issues has been found to reduce therapeutic regression and complex transferences, while requiring fewer session when more global interpersonal and intrapersonal issues are the focus (Lowman, 1993).

Sessions 7 to 11

These sessions focused largely on examining Ms. L.'s relationship with her female boss. Ms. L. viewed her as essentially incompetent at the newly created position she was promoted to six months before Ms. L. was hired. Because the position was new and her boss's superior was frequently traveling for the company, this woman had little oversight or accountability. She refused to meet regularly with Ms. L. to review Ms. L.'s performance. Instead, she would delegate much of her run work to Ms. L. and provided only vague feedback to her: "Don't worry about things, I'll let you know when you screw up." There were some rather obvious similarities between this woman and Ms. L.'s mother which were discussed in detail. With both women, Ms. L. was nonassertive and essentially backed away from any conflict. Because she could not directly express her concern or anger, Ms. L. used indecision, under-achievement, and "memory lapses." As a result Ms. L. was frustrated, dissatisfied, and anxious, which she dealt with by drinking, hair pulling, and becoming increasingly attracted to and jealous over the abusive men she dated. Assertive communication training accompanied this insight work, as did cognitive restructuring.

Sessions 12 to 15

In the twelfth session Ms. L. reported that despite her increasing assertiveness with her boss, she was unwilling to continue "in such a sick relationship with that woman." As a result she resigned from her job with the plan to start work on an MBA and find a part-time position in a broader management area than accounting. She also indicated she would no longer allow her boyfriend to continue his emotional abusiveness through his infidelity. She would require that the relationship be exclusive or she would leave. In the 14th session she would report that she had ended her current relationship, and would now look for men who could be nurturing, caring, and respecting.

In the thirteenth session she felt more confident that she could control her anger and anxiety without drinking. Career issues dominated the next two sessions. She had planned to be a literature major and become a teacher, probably at the college level, but had been "talked out of it by my family." In her second semester of un-dergraduate studies, although her advisor considered her to be the most capable student in the accounting program, Ms. L. did not apply herself and underachieved, completing her degree with a C+ average. She now believed she could make her own decisions about how she would spend her life.

Session 16

This session reviewed the progress of the previous 10 sessions. This review showed no new memory lapses, with short-term memory intact. She had not pulled out any more hair, and had recently started dating a fellow student who was so far quite loving, respectful, and supportive. She did note increased discord with her mother as Ms. L. became more assertive. As a result Ms. L. had stopped her daily telephone calls home. Although she was proud of herself, it was painful and anxiety provoking. The utilization reviewer approved up to 10 additional sessions.

Sessions 17 to 19

These sessions focused largely on reorienting Ms. L.'s self-view and world-view specifically as they related to job and career. The themes of talent and competence in ERs 1 and 5 were used to modify and restructure her view of self and others. Ms. L. was able to accept that winning the birthday game and rescuing the family dog from drowning (see appendix at the end of this case study) were neither flukes nor occasions to deny her talent and capability. She was also able to accept that choosing to recognize and develop her strengths and interests were not only possible but necessary for her to grow and individuate from her family. Doing so would not have disastrous consequences for her parents. She had feared that becoming successful would dishonor and somehow annihilate her mother. Furthermore, she discovered, being successful would not emasculate her father or brothers.

Sessions 20 to 23

In the 20th session Ms. L. reported that she was doing well in her MBA courses, particularly in organizational behavior. Her professor was impressed with her ability and had urged her to consider taking a doctorate in this area, for the purpose of teaching at the university level. She indicated that she had finally come to terms with her work situation in the past week. She quit her job. Her plans were to pursue a job and career track that was of her own choice and based on her needs and strengths rather than on family expectations. Interpersonally, she began choosing more non-abusive friends and intimates, and individuated from her family—particularly her brother—to a considerable degree. Her presenting symptoms of memory loss, hair pulling, nail biting, and occasional binge drinking were significantly reduced or eliminated. Although additional sessions could be helpful in working through and reorienting the clients interpersonal relationship with family members and further mode function of lifestyle convictions, the client has considerable facility with the therapeutic process and can become her own therapist. Her HMO has authorized one more session, however, the client is comfortable contacting me by phone at 4- and 12-month intervals for a brief follow up.

Ms. L. did in fact follow up by phone at the 4th and 12th month and indicated that her symptoms remained in regression and that she and Chris, her boyfriend, were considering marriage. Family relationships were cordial, yet Ms. L. still maintained a healthy distance, suggesting that individuation had occurred. Although after a lot of inner turmoil she had to make a career decision based on her needs and strengths rather than on family expectations. In the 22nd session she reported finding a part time job that was not only challenging and well paying but involved working for an older male who was not only respectful but also encouraging and supportive of her career plans. By now she had dated the same man for nearly six weeks, and was finding it rewarding but somewhat frightening to share deeply of her dreams and fears with another person. Her boyfriend, Chris quite easily shared his feelings, a significant change from previous boyfriends. Further reorientation using the ER themes of talent and competence was the focus of these sessions.

Session 24

This was the last of our planned formal sessions at this point; therapeutic progress was reviewed and plans for follow up were discussed. Here is what my progress note for this session stated: "This is last of 24 planned sessions. While the original referral was to evaluate and treat a dissociative disorder, an atypical anxiety disorder was diagnosed and individual psychotherapeutic treatment involving systemic, psychodynamic, and cognitive–behavioral strategies was employed. The client collaborated fully and effectively in the treatment process and several positive changes were noted. While she occasionally drank, she denied bingeing or intoxication."

Eighteen Months Later: Premarital Counseling

About 18 months after our last formal session, Ms. L. called to say that she and Chris were engaged to marry in four months and requested some premarital counseling. "I don't want to repeat my parents experience," she said. Subsequently, three conjoint sessions were scheduled. In addition to meeting with Chris and Ms. L. to assess several relational dimensions and their lifestyle convictions, these sessions provided an opportunity to evaluate the effect of our previous 24 therapy sessions. I had both Chris and Ms. L. complete the Lifestyle Interview Guide as well as several relational system inventories (Gottman, 1994) I was able to compare her early recollections with those reported years earlier. These ERs and an evaluation of positive changes are provided in the appendix to this case study. In short, Ms. L. had maintained all the gains from the formal therapy, and furthermore, these changes were reflected in her second set of ERs.

Resources on Brief Adlerian Therapy

A number of clinically useful resources can be found in Adlerian Psychology on brief therapy. Two special issues in Adlerian brief therapy are recommendations. The first appeared in the *Journal of Individual Psychology* in 1972, volume 28. It consists of 11 papers that were presented at the Brief Therapy conference sponsored Chicago Medical School in honor of Rudolf Dreikurs. The second was a double issue of *Individual Psychology* for 1989, volume 45. Here some 45 articles on a wide variety of applications of Adlerian brief therapy to adults, children, the elderly, couples, families, and medical patients in various treatment contexts are described and illustrated.

Appendix

Family Constellation Data

Kurt (38). Fourteen years older than Ms. L. Described as opinionated with a temper: a man's man and chauvinist. Teased Ms. L. the most; "He wanted me to do things against my will." He was the most rebellious, the most critical of others, the strongest, and had the most temper tantrums. Kurt was most like mother. Currently owns an insurance agency, has three children and is married to a "very unassertive wife."

Kevin (34). Ten years older than Ms. L., and considered the sibling who teased her the least. Ms. L. liked him the most. Described as the most successful of her brothers; currently the vice president of marketing for a major financial corporation. Married with two boys. He was the most popular, the best-looking, the most charming, and the best athlete. He was also father's favorite. He took care of Jackie and protected her from others.

Jay (30). Six years older than Ms. L. and considered by her to be the most intelligent, getting the best grades, the most selfish, the tallest, and the most masculine, but also the most temperamental. Currently, he is an accountant and single.

Jaime (28). Four years older than Ms. L., and considered by her to be the hardest worker, having the highest moral standards, and being the most considerate, sensitive, conforming, and helpful. Also described as the best-looking and most feminine. He fought the most with Ms. L. and was mother's favorite. Father was the "hardest" on Jaime in terms of expectations of academic achievement and good behavior.

Jackie (24). She described herself as a child as the most idealistic, pleasing, athletic, and having the most friends. She believed she got her way the most and was spoiled by her father (as his favorite), and was more like him than the other sibs. She rated herself as having the poorest grades in school. She was told she had the highest I.Q. in the family and her mother constantly compared her with Jay, who had the highest grades. Nevertheless, Jackie believes she was most like Jay, particularly in that they had the same strained relationship with mother, and the same level and pattern of peer acceptance. She saw herself as most different from Jaime, particularly with regard to the way they related so differently to the parents. Currently, she describes herself as indecisive, evasive, weak, nonproductive, reactive, and conformist. She has higher expectations of others than she has for herself, and believes, "I get away with a lot of things because no one calls my bluff."

Father (58). Described by Jackie as smart and competitive in his business and some dealings with men, but dominated by his wife. Had a great sense of humor, and was warm and compassionate. Owned his own insurance business before retiring recently because of poor health.

Mother (59). Described by Jackie as intelligent but scatterbrained. She was ambitious but never had a career except housewife. Instead she had extremely high expectations for the material success and well being of her children. Unhappy most of the time, emotionally distant, nonfeminine. That is, she dressed in unisex fashion, seldom wore a dress and rarely used makeup. While she could be sensitive toward others, Ms. L. believed her mother was basically intrusive and manipulative, betraying confidences and distorting what others would say to her advantage.

Family Atmosphere and Values

Competitive, teasing and boisterous, machismo atmosphere wherein soft feelings and affection were not to be expressed but drinking was encouraged. Family values involved achievement and striving for material success, and conventionality. Individual expression and individuation were frowned on and disobedience and rebellion were not permitted. However, emotional abuse was common. Modeled by the parents, this behavior was regularly engaged in by the older siblings, which occasionally led to physical abusiveness, and reportedly to sexual abuse in two occasions involving Ms. L. and her cousin.

Relationship Between Parents

Described as argumentative and fighting; "never affectionate, and always talking of divorce".

Jackie's Relationship with Parents

Quite strained in the early years until Jackie left home to attend college out of state. Much better in the past three years, especially since Jackie lives in her own apartment. Yet she feels obligated to call them at least once a day "to check in".

Early Recollections

1. *Age 7:* Recalls playing the game of states at her birthday party. She remembered the most states and won the prize. The prize was a dumb practical gift, a comb, picked out by her mother. Mother looked expressionless when Jackie won the prize. Ms. L. mostly vividly recalls looking around at her girlfriends and seeing their discomfort at losing and the lack of recognition from her mother. She felt glad she had won but didn't want to be rejected by others. She hated the thought that she could be better and brighter than others, yet she got very excited at winning. Ms. L. concluded: I shouldn't show others I'm smart, because they won't like me and will think I'm selfish.

2. *Age 6:* At their summer cottage, Jaime got mad at her and held her head underwater for a while, Ms. L. struggled momentarily and then stopped. Then Jaime pulled her head up as she coughed out a lot of water. He said: "Come on, knock it off; it's no big deal." The most vivid aspect was being held underwater, and giving up, thinking, "It's no use; I'm near the end." She felt completely helpless, but also peaceful that the struggle was over.

3. *Age 3:* Mother was bathing me and washing my hair. She rinsed it with a green cup. She didn't like it because some soap got in her eyes. The most vivid aspect of the recollection is the soapy water being poured over her head. Thought it was strange that soapy water was being used to rinse her hair and that mother seemed so mechanical and uncaring. Felt uncomfortable and a lack of closeness with mother.

4. *Age 5:* While on summer vacation at the family cabin, Jackie was put to bed on the second floor. Everyone else was downstairs having fun playing a card game. They—brothers and parents—were laughing and joking. Ms. L. listened to it all, and kept hoping her brothers would soon have to go to sleep too. She most vividly recalls waiting and listening. She felt alone and afraid but thought she'd be secure and happy as soon as the others came up to bed.

5. *Age 11:* Playing tennis in driveway and hitting a ball over the garage into the family's swimming pool. Her dog, Frisky, ran after the ball and fell under the

pool cover and nearly drowned. Jackie began looking for the ball, not having any idea the dog was in the pool. Following her intuition she decided to see if the ball had gone into the pool. As she approached the pool she heard scratching noises coming from under the pool cover and finding Frisky there she pulled him out. Later she started to cry only to have her father say, "Why are you upset over something [dog's death from drowning] that didn't happen?" She vividly recalled Frisky struggling under the pool cover, and felt "total panic" when she rescued the dog. She thought it was a fluke that she had checked the swimming pool area, and concluded that following her intuition could be scary and that she really couldn't be smart, competent, and helpful to others.

Formulation

Ms. L. grew up in a family system that was notable for its high expectations of achievement, obedience, competitiveness, feeling avoidance and emphasis on "masculine prerogatives." While the family appeared quite proper and conventional there were family secrets that were too shameful to be discussed and boundaries that were occasionally breached without parental response. These included the alleged sexual impropriety between Kurt and Ms. L. and Kurt and Ms. L.'s cousin. Ms. L. found her place in the family by trying to be "one of the boys," but not outshine them even though she was quite talented. Ms. L. viewed herself as talented but not competent because she was "just a girl." She viewed life as unfair, overly demanding, and intrusive. It was a place where males get all the breaks and rewards. Therefore, her goal became to appear to comply with the expectations and demands of authority figures, but never try too hard. Her strategies for accomplishing this goal are indecision, conflict avoidance, underachievement, self-defeating behavior, particularly in intimate relationships, and "memory lapses." Memory loss and underachievement in her job permit Ms. L. to "forget" about her anger at the expectations demands of authority figures as well as her fear that she is basically incompetent to handle the life tasks of work and love.

Changes in Early Recollections

Eighteen months after the 24-session treatment was completed, Ms. L. returned for three sessions with her fiancé seeking premarital counseling. She again completed the Lifestyle Interview Guide which included the following early recollections.

1. *Age 7:* At my 7th birthday party where a game was played that involved listing the names of the states, I remembered more than anyone else, and so I won the prize. I was a little embarrassed that I won, so I tried not to smile and make my friends sad, but I was happy I did so well.
2. *Age 5:* I was upstairs in bed at our summer cottage while everyone else was downstairs playing a game. I felt a little lonely but knew my brothers would soon be sent up to bed, too.
3. *Age 8:* It was winter and I was making snowflakes to put on the Christmas tree. I felt really happy and creative and cozy.

4. *Age 6:* I was with my dad fishing off the pier in front of our summer cottage. I
    was really excited and happy to be with him. I caught a fish, and it was just a
    wondrous experience.

Clearly, there have been changes in these recollections. There are two new ERs—
Nos. 3 and 4—than were given earlier. Both show Ms. L. to be productive and creative and happy working by herself, and alongside an authority figure, her father. The
first three recollections are repeated but they are qualitatively different. Ms. L. is much
more comfortable with her intellectual talents while showing appropriate empathy
and concern for her peers in ER No. 1. Also, the nonresponsive but ever-vigilant
mother that appeared in the first recounting of this experience is not present. In ER
No. 2, the fear and feeling of rejection do not appear as prominent themes as they
did in the earlier recounting. She likes males and appreciates that they can enhance
her sense of comfort, but the compulsive longing for abusive males and fear of rejection by them does not seem present. All in all, these four recollections reflect Ms.
L. at a much higher level of functioning, personal integration, and life satisfaction.

Essentially, over the course of therapy Ms. L.'s self-view had shifted to, "I'm pretty
competent and I feel confident showing it, at least to some degree." Similarly, her
world-view had shifted to, "Life can be unpredictable, and others can have expectations for me, but sometimes the unpredictable can be pleasant, and meeting my own
expectations is energizing and allows me to express my creativity and other strengths."

REFERENCES

Adler, A. (1956). *The individual psychology of Alfred Adler.* In H. Ansbacher & R. Ansbacher
    (Eds.), New York: Basic Books.
Adler, A. (1964). *Superiority and social interest.* In H. Ansbacher & R. Ansbacher (Eds.),
    Evanston, IL: Northwestern University Press.
Adler, K. (1972). Techniques that shorten psychotherapy. *Journal of Individual Psychology,
    28,* 155–168.
Adler, K. (1989). Techniques that shorten psychotherapy. *Individual Psychology, 45,* 62–74.
Alford, B., & Beck, A. (1998). *The integrative power of cognitive therapy.* New York:
    Guilford.
Ansbacher, H. (1972). Adlerian psychology: The tradition of brief psychotherapy. *Journal of
    Individual Psychology, 28,* 137–151.
Beck, A. (1976). *Cognitive therapy of emotional disorders.* New York: International
    Universities Press.
Beck, A., & Greenberg, R. (1979). Brief cognitive therapies. *Psychiatric Clinics of North
    America, 2*(1), 23–37.
Bellak, L., & Siegel, H. (1983). *Handbook of intensive brief and emergency psychotherapy.*
    Larchmont, NY: C.P.S.
Beutler, L., & Crago, M. (1987). Strategies and techniques of prescriptive psychotherapeutic
    intervention. In R. Hales & A. Frances (Eds.), *Psychiatric updates: The American
    psychiatric association annual review.* Washington, DC: American Psychiatric Press,
    pp. 378–397.

Bibring, E. (1954). Psychoanalysis and the dynamic psychotherapies. *Journal of the American Psychoanalytic Association, 12,* 745–770.

Bloom, B. (1981). Focused single-session therapy: Initial developments and evaluation. In S. Budman (Ed.), *Forms of brief therapy.* New York: Guilford Press, pp. 167–216.

Bloom, B. (1992). *Planned short-term psychotherapy: A clinical handbook.* Boston: Allyn & Bacon.

Budman, S., & Gurman, A. (1983). The practice of brief therapy. *Professional Psychology, 14*(3), 272–292.

Budman, S., & Gurman, A. (1988). *Theory and practice of brief therapy.* New York: Guilford Press.

Carlson J. (1989). Brief therapy for health promotion. *Individual Psychology, 45,* 220–229.

Croake, J., & Myers, K. (1989). Brief family therapy with childhood medical problems. *Individual Psychology, 45,* 159–177.

Davanloo, H. (Ed.). (1980). *Short-term dynamic psychotherapy.* New York: Jason Aronson.

de Shazer, S. (1988). *Clues: Investigating solutions in brief therapy.* New York: Norton.

Ellenberger, H. (1970). *The discovery of the unconscious: The history and evolution of dynamic psychiatry.* New York: Basic Books.

Fiester, A., & Rudestan, K. (1975). A multivariate analysis of the early treatment dropout process. *Journal of Consulting and Clinical Psychology, 43,* 528–535.

Fisch, R., Weakland, J., & Segal, L. (1982). *The tactics of change: Doing therapy briefly.* San Francisco: Jossey-Bass.

Garfield, S. (1986). Research on client variables in psychotherapy. In S. Garfield & A. Bergin (Eds.), *Handbook of psychotherapy and behavior change.* New York: John Wiley & Sons, pp. 191–232.

Gottman, J. (1994). *Why marriages succeed or fail.* New York: Simon & Shuster.

Hoyt, M. (1995). *Brief therapy and managed care: Readings for contemporary practice.* San Francisco: Jossey-Bass.

Ireton, H., & Peterson, T. (1989). Brief developmental counseling with family physicians. *Individual Psychology, 45,* 201–211.

Kern, R., Yeakle, R., & Sperry, L. (1989). Survey of contemporary Adlerian clinical practices and therapy issues. *Individual Psychology, 45,* 38–47.

Klerman, G., Weissman, M. (Ed.). (1993). *New applications of interpersonal psychotherapy.* Washington, DC: American Psychiatric Press.

Klerman, G., & Weissman, M. (Eds.). (1993). *New applications of interpersonal psychotherapy.* Washington, DC: American Psychiatric Press.

Kopta, S., Howard, K., Lowry, J., & Beutler, L. (1994). Patterns of symptomatic recovery in psychotherapy, *Journal of Consulting and Clinical Psychology, 62*(5), 1009–1016.

Koss, M., & Butcher, J. (1986). Research in brief therapy. In S. Garfield & A. Bergin (Eds.), *Handbook of psychotherapy and behavior change.* New York: John Wiley & Sons, pp. 664–700.

Lowman, R. (1993). *Counseling and psychotherapy of work dysfunctions.* Washington, DC: American Psychological Association.

Malan, D. (1980). *Toward the validation of dynamic psychotherapy.* New York: Plenum.

Mann, J. (1973). *Time-limited psychotherapy.* Cambridge: Harvard University Press.

Mann, J., & Goldman, R. (1982). A *casebook in time-limited psychotherapy.* New York: McGraw Hill.

O'Connell, W., & Stubblefield, S. (1989). The training of the encouraging therapist and the thirty-minute psychiatric interview. *Individual Psychology, 45,* 126–142.

Peck, R. (1994). Measuring behavioral treatment: Interview with Peter Brill, M.D. *Behavioral Health Management, 14*(4), 21–25.

Perry, S. (1987). The choice of duration and frequency for outpatient psychotherapy. In R. Hales & A. Frances (Eds.), *Psychiatric update: The American psychiatric association annual review.* Washington, DC: American Psychiatric Press, pp. 226–248.

Pew, M. (1989). Brief marriage therapy. *Individual Psychology, 45,* 191–200.

Phillips, E. (1985). *Psychotherapy revised: New frontiers in research and practice.* Hillsdale, NJ: Lawrence Erlbaum Associates.

Powers, R., & Griffith, J. (1989). Single-session psychotherapy involving two therapists. *Individual Psychology, 45,* 99–125.

Shlien, J., Mosak, H., & Dreikurs, R. (1962). Effects of time limits: A comparison of two psychotherapies. *Journal of Counseling Psychology, 9,* 31–34.

Shulman, B. (1972). Confrontation techniques. *Journal of Individual Psychology, 28,* 177–183.

Shulman, B. (1984). Adlerian psychotherapy. In R. Corsini (Ed.), *Encyclopedia of psychology.* New York: John Wiley & Sons.

Shulman, B. (1989a). Single-session psychotherapy: A didactic demonstration. *Individual Psychology, 45,* 82–98.

Shulman, B. (1989b). Some remarks on brief psychotherapy. *Individual Psychology, 45,* 34–37.

Sifneos, P. (1978). Techniques of short-term anxiety provoking therapy. In H. Davanloo (Ed.), *Basic principles and techniques in short-term dynamic psychotherapy.* New York: Spectrum, pp. 433–453.

Sifneos, P. (1979). *Short-term dynamic psychotherapy: Evaluation and technique.* New York: Plenum.

Sifneos, P. (1984). The current status of individual short-term dynamic psychotherapy and its future. *American Journal of Psychiatry, 37,* 472–483.

Sperry, L. (1987). ERIC: A cognitive map for guiding brief therapy and health care counseling. *Individual Psychology, 43*(2), 237–241.

Sperry, L. (1989). Contemporary approaches to brief psychotherapy: A comparative analysis. *Individual Psychology, 45,* 3–25.

Starr, A., & Weisz, H. (1989). Psychodramatic techniques in the brief treatment of inpatient groups. *Individual Psychology, 45,* 142–147.

Talmon, M. (1990). *Single-session therapy.* San Francisco: Jossey-Bass.

Weakland, J., Fisch, R., Watzlawick, P., & Bodin, A. (1974). Brief therapy: Focused problem resolution. *Family Process, 13,* 141–168.

Weiner, M. (1986). *Practical psychotherapy.* New York: Brunner/Mazel.

Weiss, R., & Jacobson, N. (1981). Behavioral marital therapy as brief therapy. In S. Budman (Ed.), *Forms of brief therapy.* New York: Guilford Press, pp. 387–414.

CHAPTER 13

Family Therapy

T oday's family is more diverse and complex than ever. Leaf through almost any magazine and you'll find stories about the American family. Many of the stories depict its tragic demise. Television delivers the same message. Family violence, cohabiting singles, drugs, divorce, remarriage, single parents, and latchkey kids are all said to be symptomatic of today's "dysfunctional family." There is no question that the family today is different from the traditional nuclear family of the 1950s, where the husband was the sole breadwinner and the wife was the homemaker and stay-at-home mother of two children.

Today, the traditional nuclear family comprises less than 10% of living arrangements. The most prevalent family type is the child-free or post-childbearing family (23%). This is followed by single, widowed, or divorced people (21%); single-parent families (16%); dual-breadwinner families (20%), and stepfamilies (15%) (Glick, Clarkin, & Kessler, 1987). Social scientists describe the family as evolving from the traditional to the modern and, recently, to the postmodern family all within a period of 40 years. The changing roles of women and men, the increasing reliance of the family on two or more paychecks, called the "work-centered family" (Sperry

& Carlson, 1993)—and the increased longevity of Americans so that up to five generations might be alive at one time (Carlson & Sperry, 1993).

Therapeutic issues are considerably different for single-parent families and stepfamilies than for single breadwinner/nuclear families. Those practicing family therapy today will need an integrative and systemic perspective of the family and a broad range of diagnostic and intervention strategies. Fortunately, the Adlerian approach to family therapy provides such perspectives and strategies.

Dinkmeyer and Sherman (1989) establish the Adlerian approach as a systems theory that examines the patterns of interactional relationships within the family system and among its subsystems. The context of the family, both historically and in interaction with its culture and community, is carefully considered. Functioning in love, friendship, work, relationship to the community, and the self-esteem of person and family are all critical factors in human behavior. Each family member's place—called the family constellation—and the boundaries among individual family members are assessed. Behavior and symptoms are regarded as purposive and organized within the family system. These and many other elements of general systems theories, and of structural and strategic family therapy approaches are relevant to the Adlerian approach to families.

ADLERIAN FAMILY THERAPY AND ADLERIAN FAMILY COUNSELING

The terms *family therapy* and *family counseling* are sometimes used interchangeably. Actually, there is considerable difference between the two, and it is useful to make this distinction. This chapter will describe Adlerian *family therapy* in detail and briefly mention Adlerian *family counseling*.

In the 1920s Adler began the practice of public demonstration. He counseled school children and adolescents together with their parents and siblings in front of audiences of teachers, mental health workers, and other interested parents. Adler's intention was to train teachers and counselors in interviewing methods. He also found that both participants and observers learned much about themselves and the dynamics of their interactions within the family through these sessions. Today we would call such these benefits "spectator therapy". Thus, Adlerian family counseling came into being, and continues today with minor refinements from that practiced in the early years.

The goal of Adlerian family counseling is to facilitate the improvement of adult/child and parent/child relationships. The counselor's role is to help parents develop new attitudes toward their children through understanding family, and learning how to relate more effectively. Children are helped to more fully understand the purposes or goals of their behavior. A family is usually seen for two or more public interviews. The first interview begins with only the parents. During this time the counseling elicits information on the family constellation, the presenting problem, and a description of a typical day in the life of the family. Then the counselor interviews the child or children after the parents have left the room.

The counselor briefly interviews the child or children to recognize and disclose the goals of their behavior and misbehavior. All this information is combined to diagnose the children's goals, assess the parents' methods of discipline, understand the family constellation, and develop a plan of action. Then the parents rejoin the children, and the counselor offers an explanation of the dynamics of the child's behavior and provides specific recommendations and suggestions. The counselor then asks the interviewed parents and audience for their opinions, and a group discussion ensues.

At the follow-up interview, usually the parents share what they learned in the first interview and what they did to deal with the family problems. Further discussion ensues with the counselor offering further explanations, advice, and encouragement. The audience also provides support, encouragement, and feedback on how they handled similar issues and concerns. Many families are able to follow the recommendations and make significant changes in the form of family counseling, which is also referred to as Family Education Center counseling (Lowe, 1982). In cases where parents are not able to implement recommendations, referral to family therapy may be necessary. This public demonstration model can also be used for a more conventional, or private, family counseling session.

In contrast to Adlerian family counseling, which has a decidedly educational emphasis, Adlerian family therapy has a more therapeutic emphasis. Families or couples are seen together in private, with the therapeutic focus on changing the family system and individual functioning within the new system. In contrast, family counseling provides new coping strategies within the existing family structure and system (Sherman & Dinkmeyer, 1987).

INTEGRATIVE CONCEPTS IN FAMILY THERAPY

Today, the number of systems of family therapy is increasing. It is beyond the scope of the chapter to review these systems. The interested reader is referred to Gurman and Kniskern (1981, 1991) for an extensive description of the major approaches. Instead, this section will describe three overarching concepts inclusive of these major systems and note these three concepts are integrally represented in only one family therapy system: Adlerian family therapy.

All couples and family relationships can be characterized in terms of three concepts that essentially combine and integrate concepts and principles of most family therapy systems. These three concepts are (1) boundaries or inclusion, (2) power or control, and (3) intimacy (Doherty & Colangelo, 1984; Doherty, Colangelo, Green, & Hoffman, 1985; Fish & Fish, 1986).

Boundary issues center on family membership and structure. Membership in the sense of who is involved in the family system and to what degree. Structure in terms of the extent to which family members are part of but at the same time apart from the couple subsystem or family unit. Boundary issues also refer to interpersonal boundaries, specifically the degree of intrusiveness that will be accepted in the relationship. For a married couple, that might mean commitments to jobs, extended family, friends, and other outside interests. For children, boundaries usually center on the sense of belonging to the family, while also having a sense of being recognized as an individual.

In terms of family therapy, the structural approach (developed by Minuchin, 1974) and the contextual approach (advocated by Boszormenyi-Nagy & Spark, 1973) emphasize the inclusion or boundary dimension of family functioning. Such therapeutic efforts are primarily directed at assessing and intervening in the boundary and role patterns to modulate the extent of enmeshment and distancing within the nuclear family—particularly the boundaries involving the marital/parental subsystem and sibling subsystems—as well as intergeneralization boundaries (Doherty & Colangelo, 1984).

Power issues include responsibility, control, discipline, decision making, and role negotiation. Family interactions continually involve overt as well as covert attempts to influence decisions and behavior. Control or power issues are typically tied to issues of money, reward, and privileges. They also manifest themselves in more subtle ways, such as escalation of conflict or one-upmanship in efforts to manipulate another family member's behavior. Couple interaction also involves struggle for control of the relationship in various ways. The basic dynamic in marital conflict involves who tells whom what to do under certain circumstances. Both couple and family interactions range from positive to negative, emotionally, and from chaotic democratic to autocratic. Thus, power becomes a meta-rule for all decisions about boundaries as well as intimacy. It determines which member or partner will pursue and which will distance, and how this is accomplished.

In terms of family therapy schools, the strategic approach (advocated by Haley, 1976), the interactional approach developed by the MRK Group (Watzlawick, 1984), and the behavioral system (such as described by Jacobson & Margolin, 1979) emphasize this power and control dimension of family functioning. These therapeutic approaches focus on changing the family's rule system for mutual regulation. This can be accomplished by returning the parent's authority with regard to a troubled adolescent, or teaching a feuding couple communication and problem-solving skills, or indirectly, such as with a paradoxical prescription to neutralize a specific power struggle between siblings (Doherty & Colangelo, 1984).

Intimacy issues in families are evident in areas such as self-disclosure, friendship, caring, and appreciation of individual uniqueness. Intimacy involves negotiating emotional as well as physical distance between partners or among family members. In either instance, the goal is to balance a sense of autonomy with feelings of belonging. When issues of affection in a family become a source of difficulty, they can be manifest in various ways ranging from complaints such as, "You don't understand my feelings," "I'm being taken for granted," or "The romance has gone out of the relationship."

Family therapy is discussed in the works of Ackerman (1966) and Framo (1992); Family Systems Theory (developed by Bowen, 1978), the Symbolic–Experiential (described by Whitaker & Bumberry, 1988); and the Humanistic/Communications (advocated by Satir, 1967) emphasize the intimacy dimension in couples and families. These approaches place a premium on optimal family functioning and self-differentiation.

Resolving issue of boundaries and control are viewed as prerequisites to helping partners or family members relate in a healthy, intimate fashion (Doherty & Colangelo, 1984).

Because these concepts of boundaries, power, and intimacy are broad and inclusive they can be quite useful in assessing and formulating treatment issues with all types of families: traditional, blended, single-parent. As we noted in Chapter 2, Adlerian Psychotherapy is an integrative approach, and thus includes most other psychotherapy schools and systems. This is particularly evident with Adlerian family therapy. In Sherman and Dinkmeyer's (1987) masterful comparative analysis of the major schools of family therapy on 30 basic concepts as well as 36 basic intervention strategies, the Adlerian approach was found to be more inclusive and compatible than any other major system of family therapy. The overarching concepts of boundary, power, and intimacy are clearly represented in Adlerian family therapy. The remainder of this chapter describes the unique contributions of Adlerian family therapy.

GOALS OF ADLERIAN FAMILY THERAPY

When one or more members of the family are having problems, the whole family unit is affected.

> A couple with two sons, ages 10 and 14, are experiencing severe marital problems. The mother has developed profound depression with marked suicidal tendencies necessitating hospitalization. Before she is ready for discharge, the father, too, requires hospitalization for his severe psychosomatic disorders. When the entire family is seen together, it becomes apparent that these disruptions have been and still are a major source of concern for the children. The 10-year-old boy is worried that his parents will get divorced. The 14-year-old boy is keeping his feelings to himself; he has become more and more socially withdrawn and shows a tendency toward obesity.

In its most traditional form, family therapy is based on the assumption that chronic family conflict involves, in one way or another, all the members of a family and is responsible for the problems of one or more individuals within the family group. Therefore, family therapy should include all members of a family. Because of the holistic Adlerian approach, the object of treatment is a particular group of people who are currently forming an indivisible unity, a unique whole called "the family."

Although family therapy may result in changes in the personal lifestyles of various family members, such change is not the primary goal. Adlerian family therapy is aimed at teaching a group of people how to better deal with one another and how to live together as social equals. This aim is accomplished by sharing with the family group the principles of democratic conflict resolution, by reorienting the family members away from destructive modes of communication, and, most importantly, by teaching all members of the family to be agents of encouragement. A major goal of family therapy is to increase the self-esteem and feelings of worth of family members while stimulating their social interest (Dinkmeyer & Dinkmeyer, 1981).

The overall goal of family therapy is for therapists to work themselves out of a job by teaching families to communicate accurately, honestly, and openly, with all members speaking for themselves about their own ideas and feelings. This overall goal is the outcome of several specific goals. One is to teach family members to resolve their own conflicts by relying on the principles of (1) manifesting mutual respect, (2) pinpointing the issues, (3) reaching new agreements, and (4) participating responsibly in decision making.

As we have said, it is important for parents to learn to recognize the mistaken goal of their children's misbehavior. The process of learning is not easy, however, and may be more efficiently carried out in a family education center or in a parent study group. Another goal of family therapy is to help members learn to be responsible for their own behavior and to become cooperative and contributing parts of the family group. For a family to operate democratically, parents often have to make major adjustments in their roles. Sometimes the adjustment cannot be made in family sessions but require individual sessions, group therapy for one or both parents, or marital therapy. Therapists should not assume that all problems can best be handled by dealing with the whole family as a group.

Family therapy is used when the degree of conflict or the duration of the problems is such that more intense work is necessary than could be done, for example, in the family education center. However, family therapy can be enhanced if the members attend a family education center at the same time, or if the parents participate in a parent study group. Family therapy is also enhanced when the parents read material that can help them carry out their tasks more successfully. Some materials are: *Raising a Responsible Child,* by Dinkmeyer and McKay (1998); *Systematic Training for Effective Parenting,* by Dinkmeyer, McKay, and Dinkmeyer (1998); and the classic *Children: The Challenge,* by Dreikurs and Soltz (1964).

THE PROCESS OF ADLERIAN FAMILY THERAPY

Adlerian family therapists emphasize psychological movement and its meaning. When a person's actions seem confusing, it is actually consistent with the person's goals; the person might not be aware of the goal; nevertheless, "trust only movement" is a guiding, useful principle.

Once family therapy has been agreed on as the treatment of choice, initial sessions should, if possible, include all members of the family. After the entire family has been seen together, a decision may be reached to exclude certain members—for example, the very young.

Families often ask whether sessions can take place in the family home. While certain kinds of information can be obtained only with a "house call," therapists are generally in a strategically better position working on their own turf. The ideal location for family therapy is a room large enough to seat all members—preferably in equal-size chairs—in a circle, without distractions.

Family members often ask early in the course of therapy about prognosis, a question that usually also refers to the probable duration of therapy. We believe that giving a prognosis is mischief. If we give a favorable prognosis, some family members might feel constrained to prove us wrong. If we give a bad prognosis, the prognosis is often interpreted to mean we don't think we can help. And if we don't think we can help, we probably can't. As to duration, we usually ask the family to agree to meet four to six times and then re-evaluate the situation at the end of that period.

> A woman was quite doubtful whether she wanted to stay married to her husband, because she felt she was always being manipulated by him. From time to time he showed some temporary improvement, but his wife didn't think she could trust his long-range commitment to their marriage. The husband acknowledged that she was right as far as the past was concerned. He seemed to realize that he was likely to lose her and the children if he didn't change his ways. He wanted to do something about it.

Family therapy was recommended, and the couple reached an agreement to put off a decision about their marriage until they had been in therapy. This agreement provided an important sense of stability for the children, who might otherwise have felt a great deal of concern as to whether their parents were going to stay married. This concern might have prevented them from becoming as deeply involved in family therapy.

Sessions of less than 1 1/2 hours are generally not as effective; sessions that last beyond 2 or 2 1/2 hours invite disruption on the part of family members and fatigue on the part of therapists. Family therapy sessions should take place weekly to give family members time to process what has gone on during the session and to carry out the specific recommendations they have received from the therapists. At least in the early stages, meeting with the family less often than every other week is apt to disturb the continuity of therapy and make each session almost a separate experience.

STAGES OF FAMILY THERAPY

The process of therapy involves three major steps: (1) establishing the relationship, (2) understanding the family, and (3) reorienting and reeducating. These steps are not distinct, but overlap. For example, it is effective to establish the relationship by showing the family they are being understood, by empathizing, or by commenting on psychological movement. Reeducation is also continuous and not restricted to the last phase.

Stage 1: Establishing the Relationship

The initial interview establishes the nature of the relationship and what family members can expect. The goal of the relationship is to develop mutual respect between the therapist and the family and between members of the family. This is accomplished by the therapist modeling respect and caring for the family. It recognizes that the identified client may not be the real client. Instead, the family system and the way in which it discourages its members becomes the focus of treatment. Equally important is the establishment of goals and the alignment of goals between therapist and family and among members of the family.

The therapist deals with family members to get some ideas about their priorities, attitudes, and beliefs. It is important from the start to make some kind of contact or connection with each member of the family. This therapeutic alliance with each individual positively influences the family system. The therapist talks with members directly, asking them to tell a little bit about their perception of the problem, and comes to understand their meanings, feelings, and beliefs. Even though young children may not understand the purpose for being there, it is important to respect them and to get some idea about how they can see relationships. In this initial phase, the therapist seeks answers to certain questions, even though they are usually not presented as formally as the following list:

What is hurting or painful in the family as a whole?

What does each person want to happen in the family relationship?

What does each family member see as the main challenge or issue the family faces?

Are family members aware that the purpose of this session is to focus on change, and not just to complain?

What does it feel like for each person to live in this family?

Identify the family atmosphere. Is it autocratic, democratic, or permissive?

At this point the therapist also identifies family constellation information. It is important to identify the position of the father and mother in their families of origin and how they perceive their positions. It is interesting to note whether family members often have conflict with children who are in the same position that they were in as children. For example, if the father was an oldest child, is he having problems with the oldest child in this family?

Through this process the therapist begins to identify the roles various members play in the family. Do the family members have restricted roles or do they function in a variety of tasks? Have boundaries been set up? How confined do they feel to their roles?

Adlerian family therapy observes and notes certain family faults and weaknesses. Even more important, however, is the diagnosis and identification of the family's assets. From the first contact, the therapist seeks to determine: What are the general assets of the family as a unit? What are the assets of each family member? How can these assets blend into the family system? (Sherman & Dinkmeyer, 1987).

Stage 2: Understanding the Family: Assessment

The objective is to understand the family dynamics, the pattern of transactions and their purpose. The therapist is interested in identifying family goals and the transactions that result from the goal and beliefs. The therapist must also investigate priorities and how they influence certain characteristic patterns. As we have said, Adlerians investigate the private logic and goals by a procedure called the *tentative hypothesis*. The therapist suggests hunches to an individual or the family as a whole, framing them tentatively: "Could it be . . . ?" or "Is it possible . . . ?" and alluding to the goal and pattern of behavior.

In the diagnostic procedure it is important to understand who is seeking change. More important, are they willing to change? What type of change do they desire for the family or individuals in the family and in themselves? It is always important to analyze and identify who resists change and to clarify the purpose of the resistance. Determine what reward the person gets for the resistance.

Family system data, including constellation and the psychological position of each member, are basic to understanding the family. The family therapist uses this information to understand how family position, chronologically and psychologically, influences transactions among members of the family.

Stage 3: Reeducation and Reorientation

To investigate the family system, the therapist could state, "Families operate by rules, many of which they are unaware of. What rules do you think your family operates by?"

Investigation is made of the family atmosphere and how each member of the family perceives that atmosphere by asking, "How are decisions made in the family—cooperatively or by certain people?" "Who has the power or control?" "How do they use it?"

The family constellation and psychological position of the siblings as well as ordinal position or birth order is considered. While the parents influence the behavior and self-esteem of the children, the siblings have an important effect on each other's development and personality. As the therapist observes the interaction and gets the perception of who is considered brightest, most cooperative, rebellious, sociable, or most responsible, the effect of family constellation on personality is understood.

This stage focuses on changing the beliefs, goals, and structures that influence the behavior and transactions among family members. Both the individual's purpose and the purpose of the process among people is confronted. Efforts to modify family structure, such as realigning boundaries and the balance of power are achieved with traditional structural and strategic family interventions (Minuchin, 1974; Minuchin & Fishman, 1981; Haley, 1976). This situation can be obtained by having family members talk directly with each other. Family members are asked to speak for themselves. The family is asked to select tasks that will help implement change. This could involve family meetings, communication exercises, and practicing encouragement.

Encouragement is considered the most important technique for promoting change. Most interpersonal problems are the result of discouragement. Encouragement is the process of building individuals' self-esteem, enabling them to cooperate with other members of the family. The encouraging family therapist plays a significant role during the diagnostic phase of therapy. Instead of focusing only on the pathology, liabilities, and weaknesses, the therapist is equally interested in strengths, assets, and resources. The therapist becomes a talent scout who identifies assets that will enable family members to deal more effectively with the challenges of living. Therapists learn to look for and affirm positive movement or involvement. They try to see the positive side in anything that first appears to be negative (Dinkmeyer & Dinkmeyer, 1983).

TECHNIQUES IN ADLERIAN FAMILY THERAPY

Adlerian family therapy focuses on understanding and influencing psychological movement. The therapist is concerned not only with what is said but also with what people do and with their nonverbal communications. Transactions among people help us understand their goals, priorities, and beliefs.

There is intensive work with the methods the family uses to communicate with each other. A therapist is likely to note that ineffective communication seems to be from superior to inferior positions. Families are encouraged to focus their communication on the positive. The therapist makes some simple communication rules:

1. All members speak for themselves.
2. Speak directly to each other, not through the therapist or another person in the family.
3. Listen and be empathetic to other member's feelings and beliefs.
4. Do not look for someone to blame.

The therapist must remember to focus on real issues, not symptoms. The therapist observes transactions and interactions to determine the purpose of what is being communicated and how these patterns and beliefs influence the family's behavior. The real issue may have to do with some of the priorities we discussed earlier, such as control, superiority, getting even, or displaying power.

The therapist must also be encouraging. Family therapy is encouraging when it includes these characteristics:

1. All members now feel they are listened to.
2. Members of the family are intentionally empathetic and understanding.
3. The focus is on strengths, assets, and resources of a relationship.
4. Perceptual alternatives are developed, first by the therapist and then by members of the group. Members learn that there are positive ways to look at any negative situation.

The therapist applies other techniques of Adlerian counseling to a family as with other therapeutic groups.

Confrontation of the Private Logic and Beliefs

The private logic includes goals, ideas, and attitudes. Confrontation is the procedure by which the therapist, sensitively and perceptively, makes family members aware of the discrepancies between their behavior and their intentions, their feelings and the feelings they reveal, and between their insights and their actions. Confrontation thus stimulates therapeutic movement by mirroring to the family their mistaken goals.

Paradoxical Intention

Paradoxical intention or antisuggestion persuades one to produce the symptom one is complaining about. The symptom is actually prescribed and the family member is encouraged to become even more "symptomatic." The paradox helps to reframe the system, and helps change the entire meaning a family gives to a situation.

Role Reversal

Family members often do not understand how others perceive their behavior. In role reversal we ask family members to act as if they were the other family member. We then ask for a clear and honest expression of how the person believes the other family member perceives their relationship. The second person then has an opportunity to react, indicating which parts of the role reversal were accurate and inaccurate.

Resistance and Goal Alignment

Resistance in family therapy usually presents itself as a lack of common goals between therapist and family. Aligning goals so that all are moving toward the same purpose is basic to bringing about change. Family therapy becomes complicated if Mother is concerned about the children's academic achievement, Father pushes athletics, and the son or daughter is mainly interested in social life. From these confused purposes the therapist helps the family find areas of compromise so they can live together more cooperatively.

Setting Tasks and Getting Commitment

The therapist works with the family to establish certain tasks and commitments to specific changes that the family and individual members indicate they desire. Setting the task occurs in the first session, when all members are asked to state their goals and what they would like to see change. The more specific the tasks, the more readily they can be accomplished. Family members make specific contracts and are expected to share their progress at the next meeting.

Summarizing

Summarizing is a way to get at family members' perceptions and look at the theme of the session. The therapist may decide to have family members summarize what they have learned at the end of each session; the therapist also summarizes and clarifies commitments and tasks.

Resistance

Resistance is a difference between the goals of the family and those set forth by the therapist or differences among the goals of different members or groups within the family. Resistance must be dealt with immediately.

One of the most effective ways to overcome resistance and get things moving again is to add another ingredient to the therapeutic process. This ingredient can be an additional therapist or other family members who are not locked into the nuclear family system or into the new system that has developed in therapy (which includes the therapists).

If there is disagreement concerning goals and if the addition of new elements to the therapeutic process doesn't help, termination of therapy may be contemplated and discussed. Termination must always be an option, therefore the therapist must avoid becoming so identified with the counseling process that termination becomes a personal issue.

The Role of Absent Members

With some family systems—for example, blended families (a family in which each partner brings children from a previous marriage into the new marriage)—there are often absent members who, although never physically incorporated into the family therapy sessions, cannot be ignored as significant influences.

> A woman lost her husband through death and married a widower. With her children and his children under the same roof, a complicated family system developed. He studiously avoided talking about his first wife, while she, even after several years, felt herself a stranger in another woman's home. If this family had undergone therapy, the man's first wife would have been discussed, because of her continuing influence on the various members of the family.

> In another family, one child with extremely severe behavior problems required institutionalization. The father maintained close contact with his son. The mother, instead, feared the boy and was unwilling to discuss the possibility of his return into the family. The other children were pulled first in one direction and then in another, showing how deeply this absent member was still affecting the everyday life of the family.

In family therapy, we usually think of two generations, parents and children; however, in some instances, three or even four generations have been successfully incorporated into family therapy.

> In one family, the paternal grandfather had been living with his son and daughter-in-law from the day of their marriage. The wife resented every moment of his presence, which she considered a heavy burden. According to her husband, she consistently lined up the children against their grandfather. Successful therapy for this family obviously would have required consideration of the role of the grandfather.

MULTIPLE THERAPY

Probably in no other form of therapy is the concept of multiple therapy (therapy conducted by more than one therapist) so important as in family therapy. If the family is any larger than the parents and one child, it is virtually impossible for a single therapist to be both an active participant and an acute observer of all the verbal and nonverbal communication in the family.

Ideally, co-therapists should represent both sexes, but that is a point of limited importance. What is truly important is whether the co-therapists impress the family as people who communicate well and who show mutual respect. This does not mean it is inappropriate for co-therapists to disagree. Occasional disagreement provides opportunities to demonstrate to the family that people can disagree without disastrous consequences and can resolve their disagreements peacefully and cooperatively.

For the most part, it is desirable for co-therapists to discuss various issues of the therapeutic process in the presence of the family, allowing family members to take advantage of and learn from the therapist's discussions. As with any other form of group therapy, it is important for the therapists not to begin the session with any preconceptions of what should happen.

Many families "elect" a member as the scapegoat, or symptom bearer, for the family's troubles. A child is often identified as "the problem," allowing the other family members to avoid looking at themselves and facing the part they play in their problems.

> Raichon, 16 years old, had been a problem to her parents "from the day she was born." Now she was failing school, experimenting with drugs, and associating with unsuitable companions. She was indignant that her mother wouldn't permit her to go to another city and visit her 19-year-old boyfriend, who was in prison. Her younger sister, Vanessa was sweetness and light and goodness in every way. Father and Mother insisted that theirs was the best marriage ever. During family therapy sessions, all members converged on Raichon, repeatedly implying in one way or another that the family would be just fine if it weren't for her bad behavior. Vanessa was seemingly genuinely concerned about her sister but, at the same time, judgmental. The therapists were unable to get the parents and sister "off Raichon's case," because these members, totally unwilling to look at the role they played in the family problems, insisted on scapegoating Raichon.
>
> After hospitalization and several more family sessions, Raichon disappeared and no one heard from her again. If the therapists had known in advance of the seriousness of Raichon's situation and the unwillingness of the family to stop scapegoating her, they might have arranged for Raichon to be placed in a foster or group home.

Another reason for scapegoating (or any other kind of fault-finding or standing in judgment) is the common need to avoid the here and now. By recounting in detail the "facts" of the past, including all the injustices each has suffered, family members avoid dealing with themselves and one another in the present. Other families avoid the present by being future-oriented. In still other families, some members have become highly skilled at minding the business of other members while neglecting their own problems. Here is an example:

> At the first family therapy session, Mother began by saying that Joan, 13, was not going to talk. Joan actually sat behind her vivacious little sister, Karen. When Joan was asked a question, Karen answered for her. When Karen talked about herself and described how she felt, her father listened with obvious impatience, bouncing up and down in his chair,

until he could give an edited version of what Karen had said, explaining how Karen really felt and why she felt that way. Then, when Father expressed his disapproval of Mother's behavior, she interrupted him halfway through. His wife insisted that she knew what had really happened and that he wasn't speaking for himself but, rather, was repeating his mother's comments about her daughter-in-law. At home, the story was the same—each person interfered constantly with the others and injected herself into the other's business. There was constant criticism, bickering, and marked defensiveness on the part of all the family members.

When therapists are faced with a family like this one, they have to be firm, insisting that all members speak for themselves. Another situation often encountered in family therapy is the attempt by one or more family members to lead the discussion away from those present and talk instead of family members who are absent. Also, as we mentioned earlier, family members are often adept at taking sides, and will try to involve the therapist in the family feud. Many children in troubled families have become highly skilled at the divide-and-conquer process with their own parents and will try this technique with therapists, too.

It is essential that the therapists recognize and avoid the pitfall of pity. Feeling sorry for someone is a discouraging and demeaning way to treat another human being.

> Aaron, 5 years old and the smallest in his kindergarten class, had not had a good year. His teacher recommended that he repeat kindergarten. In a family therapy session, it became apparent that Mother felt terribly sorry for Aaron, believing that his whole future would be blighted by his current failure in school. In pursuing this subject further, the therapist discovered that Mother too, had been held back in school, that she had found this a source of constant discouragement, and that she was now taking Aaron's "failure" as a personal failure. When she learned to stop feeling sorry for Aaron, she discovered a perceptual alternative for the school's recommendation.

Psychoeducational Interventions

Psychoeducational interventions are perhaps more important in family therapy than they are in individual therapy. Skill deficits can limit a family's progress in therapy or can incapacitate family members in communicating their basic needs. Adlerian therapists have developed and used a variety of skill training methods in such areas as parenting, conflict resolution, communication, and problem-solving skills. Family Education Centers have been organized by Adlerians for more than 60 years. In these centers, which usually meet regularly in public places like schools and community centers, volunteer families are interviewed and counseled in front of an audience which participates in the counseling process.

REFERENCES

Ackerman, N. (1966). *Treating the troubled family*. New York: Basic Books.
Boszormenyi-Nagy, I., & Spark, G. (1973). *Invisible loyalties: Reciprocity in intergenerational family therapy*. New York: Harper & Row.

Bowen, M. (1978). *Family therapy in clinical practice*. New York: Aronson.

Carlson, J., & Sperry, L. (1993). The future of families: New challenges for couples and family therapy. *Family Counseling and Therapy, 1*(1), 144.

Dinkmeyer, D., & Dinkmeyer, D. Jr. (1981). Adlerian family therapy. *The American Journal of Family Therapy, 9*(1), 45–52.

Dinkmeyer, D., & Dinkmeyer, J. (1983). Adlerian family therapy. *Individual Psychology, 39*(2), 116–124.

Dinkmeyer, D., & Sherman, F. (1989). Brief Adlerian family therapy, *Individual Psychology, 45*(1), 148–158.

Dinkmeyer, D., & McKay, G. (1998). *Raising a responsible child*. New York: Simon & Schuster.

Dinkmeyer, D. C., & McKay, G. D., and Dinkmeyer, D. C. Jr. (1998). *Systematic training for effective parenting*. Circle Pines, MN: American Guidance Service.

Doherty, W. J., & Colangelo, N. (1984). The family FIRO model: A modest proposal for organizing family treatment. *Journal of Marital and Family Therapy, 10*(1), 19–29.

Doherty, W. J., Colangelo, N., Green, A. M., & Hoffman, G. (1985). Emphases of the major family therapy models: A family FIRO analysis. *Journal of Marital and Family Therapy, 11*(3), 299–303.

Dreikurs, R., & Soltz, V. (1964). *Children: The challenge*. New York: Hawthorn.

Fish, R., & Fish, L. S. (1986). Quid pro quo revisited: The basics of marital therapy. *American Journal of Orthopsychiatry, 56*(3), 371–384.

Framo, J. (1992). *Explorations in marital and family therapy: Selected papers of James L. Framo*. New York: Springer.

Glick, I., Clarkin, J., Kessler, D. (1987). *Marital and family therapy* (2nd ed.). New York: Grune & Stratton.

Gurman, A. J., & Kniskern, D. P. (Ed.). (1981). *Handbook of family therapy*. New York: Brunner/Mazel.

Gurman, A. J., & Kniskern, D. P. (Ed.). (1991). *Handbook of family therapy*, vol. 2. New York: Brunner/Mazel.

Haley, J. (1976). *Problem-solving therapy*. San Francisco: Jossey-Bass.

Jacobson, N., & Margolin, G. (1979). Marital therapy: *Strategies based on social learning and behavior exchange principles*. New York: Brunner/Mazel.

Lowe, R. (1982). Adlerian/Dreikursian family counseling in A. Horne & M. Ohlsen (Eds.), *Family counseling and therapy*. Itasca, IL: Peacock Publishers.

Minuchin, S. (1974). *Families and family therapy*. Cambridge, MA: Harvard University Press.

Minuchin, S., & Fishman, H. (1981). *Family therapy techniques*. Cambridge, MA: Harvard University Press.

Satir, V. (1967). *Conjoint family therapy* (rev. ed.). Palo Alto, CA: Science and Behavior Books.

Sherman, R., & Dinkmeyer, D. (1987). *Systems of family therapy: An Adlerian integration*. New York: Brunner/Mazel.

Sperry, L. (1985). Family processes in health promotion: Applications to weight management. *Individual Psychology, 41*(4), 544–551.

Sperry, L. (1986). Contemporary approaches to family therapy : A comparative and meta-analysis. *Individual Psychology, 42*(4), 591–601.

Sperry, L. (1992). Tailoring treatment with couples and families. *Topics in Family Psychology and Counseling, 1*(3), 1–6.

Sperry, L., & Carlson, J. (1993). The work–family connection: What clinicians need to know. *The Family Journal, 1*(1), 12–16.

Sperry, L., Carlson, J., & Lewis, J. (in press). *Family therapy: Insuring treatment efficacy.* Pacific Grove, CA: Brooks/Cole.

Watzlawick, P. (1984). *The invented reality.* New York: Norton.

Whitaker, C., & Bumberry, W. (1988). *Dancing with the family: A symbolic–experiential approach.* New York: Brunner/Mazel.

CHAPTER 14

Marital and Couples Therapy

The designation *couples therapy* is gradually replacing *marital therapy*. Couples therapy is more inclusive, and many couples who are not married present for conjoint psychotherapeutic treatment of their relationship. For the purposes of this chapter, references to "marriage" designates the intimate relationship between two partners who may or may not be legally married.

The changing roles of men and women and the concomitant reduction of sex-role expectations are the source of special kinds of problems that many couples face today. Alfred Adler (1978) predicted this phenomenon in his book *Cooperation Between the Sexes*, originally published more than a half century ago.

The shift toward equality between marriage partners began in the United States during the Great Depression, when high unemployment among men often made it necessary for the woman to become the breadwinner, or second wage earner, in the family. The shift became even more pronounced during World War II. Thousands of women moved into the labor force and discovered that they no longer had to be second-class citizens controlled by their husbands. Just as husbands lost control over their wives, parents lost control over their children. Authoritarianism gave way to increasingly equalitarian relationships between parents and children. The old ways of relating in a marriage and in a family were fading. Couples were forced to try to live together in a relationship of equality for which they had neither background nor training. Their family of origin experiences were not a role model.

In the 1960s and 1970s, the changing nature of the marital relationship was influenced first by the civil rights movement and then by the women's movement. In the late 1980s, economic changes forced the majority of couples to become dual-paycheck couples, meaning that both partners were employed. When both working partners are professionals the designation *dual-career couple* is used. Dual-paycheck and dual-career couples have unique needs and problems and psychotherapy and couples therapy must be tailored accordingly (Sperry, 1992, 1993; Criswell, Carlson, & Sperry, 1993).

These changes in relationship expectations continue. The problems they generate for the married couple and their relationship are still unresolved. Change is a potential source of conflict in any relationship. Partners change but rarely in tandem. Consequently, problems of differential growth in partners can greatly strain the relationship. By rejecting their subservient role of the past, women have also rejected the concept that their own growth and development as people—rather than only as wives—are not valid or are of secondary importance compared with the success of the marriage. Many men still don't know how to function in a relationship other than as the "superior male." They are baffled at their wives' demands for an equalitarian relationship, self-actualization, and sexual satisfaction.

THE INTIMATE RELATIONSHIP AS A SYSTEM

People are indivisible, decision-making beings whose actions and movements have a purpose. The pattern of interaction between partners evolves into a system. This relational system reflects the individual goals, beliefs, and priorities of each partner as well as the goals, priorities, beliefs, and conflict resolution style of the couple. When the partners' goals are aligned, and their conflict style is effective their relational system functions smoothly. When goals and beliefs conflict and are not resolved, the system produces dysfunctional behavior. Not surprisingly, couples therapy requires the therapist to understand both the individual partners and the relationship system.

Gottman (1994) has studied more than 2,000 couples and concludes that a lasting and satisfying intimate relationship depends primarily on the couple's ability to resolve the conflicts that are inevitable in any relationship. His research on couples systems reveals three styles of conflict resolution or problem solving: (1) validating, (2) volatile, and (3) conflict-avoiding.

Validating couples compromise, work out problems calmly, and accept differences. Volatile couples have intense disputes, and may be defensive and critical. But they seem to enjoy their intensity, which is followed by renewal, and conflict strengthens their sense of individuality. Conflict-avoiding couples merely leave their disagreements alone, minimize them, and use solitary activities to handle or relieve tensions. Gottman points out that, far from being inevitably pathological compared with the validating type (which therapists find more ideal), the volatile and conflict-avoiding types also can lead to stable adjustments.

More significant to effective functioning of the couple system is the ratio of positive feeling and interaction versus negative. Using a variety of measures—laughter, touching, facial expression, physiological measures, and frequency of fights—Gottman (1994) found that a ratio of 5 or more positive interactions to 1 negative predicts marital stability; less than that tends to predict divorce. In fact, this ratio can predict with 94% accuracy which relationships succeed and which fail in divorce.

Gottman (1994) identified the "Four Horsemen," the warning signs that the marriage is failing and the couple is becoming increasingly preoccupied by negativity:

1. *Criticism.* This means attack through personalizing, blame, and character attack. While expressing differences is healthy, blame and attack—listing multiple complaints which are never resolved, accusations of infidelity, overgeneralizations, "always" and "never" statements—are destructive.
2. *Contempt.* This involves perception of the partner as devalued, as well as the desire to hurt, demean, and insult the partner. "Why did I ever marry YOU!" and "You're Stupid!" are examples of contempt. The romance of the marriage is buried and forgotten; the feeling of closeness and the capacity to compliment are lost in a flurry of sneering, eye-rolling, and name-calling.
3. *Defensiveness.* This involves feeling hurt and victimized and deflecting blows by refusing any responsibility for change. It means making excuses for actions rather than trying to modify them, attributing generalized negative beliefs and attitudes to the partner, fighting fire with fire (answering complaints with more complaints), or winning through intimidation. Defensiveness leads to intense, escalating conflict.
4. *Stonewalling.* This means cutting off communication with the partner. Any communication might be cold disapproval, which increases distress.

Once any of these horsemen arrive and predominate the relationship, negative cognitions create a system which is often destined to fail.

COUPLES THERAPY

The process of Adlerian couples therapy involves three stages: (1) establishing a therapeutic relationship, (2) understanding the couple, and (3) reorienting and re-educating (Carlson & Dinkmeyer, 1987). Following the format of other chapters, couples therapy treatment process is described in the following three subsections. Major emphasis is placed on the third stage.

Attraction and Priorities: Choice of Partners

The number one priority is a more recent development in Adlerian couples therapy (Sperry, 1978). A partner's number one priority often becomes particularly clear at a time of stress or conflict. These priorities readily reflect aspects of the couples relationship system. The therapist's recognition and disclosure of the couple's priorities is one of the most effective ways of demonstrating to the couple that they are understood, and lays the foundation for an effective therapeutic relationship.

Phyllis:	*Steve tries to control me constantly through criticism.*
Therapist:	*Could it also be that, with your number one priority of superiority and your emphasis on justice and fairness, you compound the problem by criticizing him for his criticalness?*
Phyllis:	*I think it's possible . . .*
Therapist:	*Would both of you agree to refrain from criticizing each other for one week and, instead, say one encouraging thing to each other every day?*
Steve:	*I'm willing to do that. But how do I know that what I say is encouraging?*
Therapist:	*There are no guarantees, but encouragement means giving honest recognition for whatever you appreciate about your wife. Naturally, if she doesn't believe that about herself, she may not find it encouraging. How about trying it right now? What do you appreciate about Phyllis?*
Steve:	*She is very bright and has a good sense of humor.*
Therapist:	*And what do you appreciate about Steve, Phyllis?*
Phyllis:	*He is honest and reliable.*

It appears that people may choose intimate partners on the basis of their own number one priorities; that is, people choose partners with whom they can be themselves and pursue their number one priority. For example, a male whose number one priority is control is likely to choose a female who, he believes, will permit him to exert his leadership and organizational ability. If her number one priority is superiority, she may have chosen him because, at some level of awareness, she believed she could be better than him.

Problems in intimate relationships develop when the individual moves toward the "only if" absurdity (an extreme form of the number one priority), such as, "Only if I am comfortable, do I really belong." The more an individual moves toward the "only if" absurdity, the higher the price. As each learn about their own and their partner's number one priorities, they become aware of some of their partner's vulnerabilities. One of the tasks of the therapist is to teach each partner to be an effective agent of encouragement, instead of attacking vulnerabilities.

Intimate couples seldom have the same number one priority. The most common pairings are control/superiority and comfort/pleasing. If the therapist is skilled at pinpointing the number one priorities early in the initial interview, insight into the lifestyle of the partners, will help the clients feel understood and facilitate an effective therapeutic alliance.

What is the process of attraction and mate selection? Potential partners go through a complex, interpersonal dance of which they have little conscious awareness. Attraction can be thought of on two levels (1) similarities: "birds of a feather flock together" and (2) complements: "Opposites attract" (Sperry, 1978; Sperry & Carlson, 1991). Beyond the obvious similarities of interests, hobbies, religious affiliations, people are attracted at a deeper, unconscious level. At this level of attraction, opposite lifestyles attract because they complement one another; filling the "gaps" or wants and needs.

In other words, interpersonal attractions are not based on common sense but on private logic. The partner to whom we are attracted offers us "an opportunity to realize our personal patterns, who responds to our outlook and conception of life, who permits us to continue or to revive plans which we have carried since childhood. We even play a very important part in evoking and stimulating in the other precisely the behavior which we expect and need" (Dreikurs, 1946, pp. 68–69).

Thus it should not be surprising that couples who have lived together for some time discover that the very attributes that attracted them in the first place may later create dissonance. A quiet man who was attracted to a gregarious woman may complain later that "she never wants to leave the party." A passive woman who was attracted to an aggressive man may later complain that he wants to make all the decisions.

For example, an aggressive, determined person may want a spouse who is willing to be led and supportive, just as a passive, submissive person may seek a mate on whose strength one can rely. Or the person with a need to please others and to be accepted may choose someone who demands, often in a selfish way, admiration and submission. Because these deeper personality needs and patterns lead to strong attraction, how is it that two people who are strongly attracted to each other come to a point that they can no longer tolerate each other? Dreikurs (1946; 1968) was one of the first to observe that qualities that initially attracted two people to each other were basically the same factors causing discord and divorce.

Dreikurs notes that any human quality or trait can be perceived in a positive or a negative way. A person can be considered either kind or weak, another strong or domineering, depending on how one looks at that person. He suggests that we do not like a person for their virtues or dislike them for their faults. When we like another, we emphasize their positive points, and when we reject him, we emphasize the weaknesses. Emphasizing the individual's weakness or negative trait provides us with an excuse for having to communicate, to negotiate, and to resolve conflicts.

Stage 1: Establishing a Therapeutic Relationship

Establishing an effective therapeutic relationship involves developing a trusting relationship and a working contract. A therapeutic relationship between therapist and couple does not exist until there is sufficient trust among all parties, and a mutual agreement or contract to work together toward specific goals.

Let's first look at establishing a trusting relationship. For people who have never had a trusting relationship with anyone, establishing such a relationship may take considerable time. In some cases, it is easier for one partner to become involved in the counseling relationship than for the other. But, in general, establishing a relationship is easiest when the therapist can demonstrate to both partners an understanding of their problems. To do this, the Adlerian therapist uses a number of shortcuts, or tactics, that permit the partners to see that some aspects of their personalities or some characteristics of their relationship make sense to that individual.

One of the most reliable methods is to pinpoint each partner's number one priority. When a wife with a priority of pleasing becomes aware of that priority, she also realizes the price she pays for it—self-neglect, reduced personal growth, and a grossly exaggerated significance of rejection. She sees, often for the first time, that she takes her husband's rather innocuous behavior as personal rejection, and she understands why. If the husband's number one priority is control, he may, for the first time, understand how he brings about distance from others. This new awareness and the concomitant feelings of being understood and accepted make an effective therapeutic relationship much more likely, as we see in these two cases:

Therapist:	*I can't entirely explain it, but I find myself feeling somewhat annoyed with you, Malcolm.*
Malcolm:	*Is it something I'm doing?*
Therapist:	*No, not really doing. I think it has something to do with your number one priority. I'd guess that your priority is comfort. If that is so, the more you strive for comfort, the less productive you're likely to become. The price people pay for a number one priority of comfort is reduced productivity. I suppose my feeling annoyed has to do with my Puritan work ethic.*
Malcolm:	*You're possibly right. I set goals for myself, but I never seem to accomplish as much as I want to.*
Therapist (to wife):	*Do you find it difficult to pin Malcolm down—to get him to deal with issues?*
Diana:	*I do, How can you tell?*
Therapist:	*Many people with a number one priority of comfort behave like artful dodgers. The worst thing for them is to feel trapped. I think Malcolm has become very competent at avoiding conflict with you, which is a way of avoiding stress for himself.*
Diana:	*Well, I certainly appreciate that someone else understands what a big problem that is for me.*

Here is a good example of the counselor identifying practices to help establish the therapeutic alliance.

Therapist:	*I think that your number one priority is pleasing.*

Deb: *You're probably right. If I'm not pretty sure that what I'm about to do will be accepted. I'm likely to pull back.*

Therapist: *And, if Bob fails to give you approval, that's a personal rejection.*

In addition to establishing a relationship of trust, it is also necessary to develop a working contract with the couple. Only when both are present can it be said that a therapeutic relationship has been established. Establishing a working contract requires, first of all, a clear indication on the part of the therapist that there is hope for the relationship. It is the Adlerian position that, as long as people are alive, they have a potential for growth. It is also the Adlerian position that any couple can, if their relationship is one of mutual respect and cooperation, work out their difficulties, regardless of how complicated and profound their problems are (Dinkmeyer and Dinkmeyer, 1982).

After asking both partners to explain briefly why they are seeking counseling, we ask early in the interview whether they want to stay married. If the answer is yes, we propose personal lifestyle formulations before we look at the problems in the relationship. If one or both partners are doubtful, we might propose that they postpone any decision until we have completed the lifestyle formulation.

Even if both parties say they don't want to stay together; we still offer to formulate their lifestyles. If they agree, the partners may learn something from the dissolution of their relationship that will reduce the likelihood of their repeating the process with another partner. If one partner wants to maintain the relationship and the other does not, we again suggest lifestyle formulation, asking the partner who wants out of the relationship to hold off on any action until we have completed it. Sometimes, of course, a couple comes in for therapy as a final gesture to show that they have done everything they can do, but in fact have already made up their minds to end the relationship.

We prefer to establish a definite contract that has an end point as well as a clearly defined initial arrangement. The arrangement usually entails four to six hours of therapy—enough time to complete formulation of the lifestyle for each partner. At the end of that period, it is appropriate to renegotiate the contract. Sometimes the partners feel that, for the moment, that's as far as they want to go. In other instances, the partners would like to spend some time working on their relationship alone and then return for more therapy. Others, after completing the lifestyle formulation, want to continue working on the relationship in therapy. If at the end of the lifestyle formulation, it becomes clear that one partner needs ongoing individual therapy, an agreement is reached to resume the couples therapy later with both parties.

In couples therapy, we must always face the issue of limited versus ideal goals. This is another way of saying that therapists and clients must try to answer the question, "How much therapy is enough?" For one individual, a relatively minor change in attitude about one aspect of life may be sufficient; for one couple, a recommitment to working at the relationship and greater tolerance of each other may be all that is needed. The therapist can often see that, ideally, a couple would benefit from extensive therapy, including basic reorientation of the lifestyles, but ultimately the couple must decide for themselves what their therapy goals will be. Resistance develops when there is a lack of alignment between the goals of the couple and those of the therapist or between the goals of the two partners.

Whenever resistance is detected, it is important to halt the therapeutic process until a new set of goals that is acceptable to all parties can be negotiated. Sometimes negotiation leads to the agreement that goal alignment is not possible and that termination is indicated. No matter what the outcome, the process is essentially to work toward consensus. By "consensus" we mean not that everybody agree 100%, but that they commit to a particular decision, preferably for a limited period of time. This may even be referred to as an "experiment." Thus a married couple may decide to suspend any major decisions and work on their relationship for two months, with the intent of reevaluating and renegotiating the agreement at the end of that time. If the therapist feels comfortable working within such parameters, a consensus is reached, even though the therapist might like to see the couple commit themselves for a longer period of time.

The marital inventory was developed to provide a systematic approach to couples therapy (Dinkmeyer & Dinkmeyer, 1983). It is used in conjunction with the brief Lifestyle Scale (Kern, 1997).

One of the values of the marital inventory is that it communicates a serious purpose to the diagnostic phase and to the entire relationship. The inventory helps the therapist align goals with the couple and determine what they want to see happen. The inventory helps the therapist distinguish among complaints, symptoms, and real issues by identifying the purpose of the symptoms and clarifying individual priorities.

The inventory emphasizes being positive, searching for assets and strengths, and being encouraging. The theme is, "What is right about the relationship?" and "Where are the resources for improving the relationship?" We do not emphasize diagnosing pathology but believe that identifying strengths, assets, and resources is essential for improving the relationship system.

The inventory helps identify the patterns in the relationship, such as who strives to be in control, who wants to get even, who is the peacemaker and compromiser, and who is interested in growth and change. The inventory thus assesses the lifestyle of the marriage or the system. We believe that marital happiness is achieved insofar as each partner has good self-esteem, a willingness to cooperate, to give and take, and a sense of humor.

Stage 2: Understanding the Couple

This stage involves a careful assessment of five dimensions of the couple and their relational system. These dimensions and their associated factors are detailed and described in Figure 14–1.

Situation/Severity refers to the symptoms and the severity of stressors the couple faces, along with demographic factors and the couple's level of functioning. One marker of couple functioning is the level of their marital discord.

System refers to the couple's history; developmental stage; systems factors of boundary, power, and intimacy (Fish & Fish, 1986); adequacy of asynchronism. As described by Sekaran and Hall (1989), *synchronism* is a condition in which an indi-

---

Situation/Severity
  1. Presenting complaint and problem(s)
  2. Demographics: ages, job and career status, sociocultural and financial status
  3. Level of relational conflict functioning
System
  4. History of relationship and developmental stage; genogram
  5. Synchronism/asychronism
  6. Boundaries, power, intimacy
  7. Support network
Skills
  8. Self-management skills
  9. Relational skills
Style/Status
  10. Lifestyle assessment of partners
  11. Individual functioning: health and psychological status
  12. Couple formulation of problem(s)
Suitability for Treatment
  13. Expectation for treatment
  14. Readiness or motivation for treatment

Figure 14–1   Dimensions and Factors of Four Marital/Couples Assessment

vidual or couple's experience is on schedule in relationship to some timetable of development, while *asynchronism* is being off schedule. These timetables are defined by the family, the couple, and the work organization. For instance, couples who marry late and have children late are usually considered out of sync with social norms. This is called *family asynchronism*. When an individual is not promoted to a managerial level by the age of 40, that individual is considered behind schedule and may never subsequently receive such a promotion. This is called *organizational asynchronism*. Among dual-career couples, the more types and levels of asynchronism, the more stress the couple is likely to experience.

Skills refers to the level of self-management and relational skills that the spouses possess and use within their relationship. For example, a spouse may effectively use assertiveness on the job, but for some reason does not within the couple's relationship. Or a spouse may not have acquired a skill needed inside or outside the relationship. Self-management skills include assertiveness, problem solving, money management, time management, and stress reduction. Essential relational skills for couples include communication, negotiation, and conflict resolution.

Style/Status refers to the spousal subsystem dimension. This includes physical and psychological health as well as the personality or character style of each spouse. *Lifestyle* refers to the enduring pattern of perceiving, responding, and thinking about the relationship, life, and oneself. Assessment of both partners' lifestyles is a core feature of Adlerian couples therapy.

Suitability for Treatment refers to the couple's explanation or formulation of their problems, as well as their expectations, readiness, and motivation for treatment.

Three criteria for assessing a couple's readiness for therapy are (1) willingness, (2) ability, and (3) confidence in engaging in therapeutic tasks.

The purpose of assessing both partners' lifestyles is to determine their mistaken or dysfunctional beliefs and convictions about themselves and life; their strengths and assets; and the goals they set for themselves. Lifestyle assessments are conducted in the presence of both partners whenever possible. Recreation of a style of living (Adler, 1958) is based on a fairly specific method of data collection. (Appendix A shows lifestyle forms.) The family constellation is diagrammed, including brief descriptions of each member of the family or origin, with particular attention to all the parental figures who were influential in the formative years, as well as deceased siblings and other children who, although perhaps unrelated, were extremely close to the person. When this inquiry is carried out in the presence of the partner, each may learn for the first time some significant elements of the partner's childhood. The nonparticipating partner is asked to withhold comments at this stage, because we are trying to get into the subjective world of the person whose lifestyle is being formulated and the partner cannot contribute to our understanding if he or she wasn't there. It is important that the therapist pay attention to the person whose lifestyle is being formulated and not be unduly influenced by whatever the other partner says.

The formulation of the lifestyle is meant to provide us with an understanding of the individual's subjectivity; therefore, there are no "right" answers. We are merely looking for overall patterns and trying to get some idea of this individual's place in the family. Brief inquiries are made into physical, sexual, and social development, and educational and occupational experience. Here, too, the partner often learns significant new things about the spouse which had perhaps never been discussed before.

In the area of sexual development, for example, a partner may learn "secrets" that can be very upsetting.

Domita:	*I want you to know that we were up all night after our last session.*
Paulo:	*Yes, it was a very difficult time, and I don't know whether we have everything worked out yet.*
Therapy:	*What came up that was so disturbing? The information about Paulo's early sex life?*
Domita :	*That's it. I was so sure that I had married an inexperienced man—a man who was, well, pure. And then, to find that he had had all that sexual experience in the service. . . .*
Paulo:	*It wasn't that much. Only a few brief relationships. I never saw any reason to mention it.*

It is similarly useful to assess each partner's attitude toward oneself and the spouse in terms of the various life-tasks. For this purpose, Adler's three life tasks of love, friendship, and work have been broken down into subdivisions: worker, friend, lover, spouse, relating to the other sex, getting along with oneself, searching for meaning, relating to members of the same sex, parent, and player. This person is presented with a scale of 1 to 5 (5 being the highest rating) and asked to rate herself, for example, as a worker. The question we ask is, "How responsibly are you attending to the task of work at this point in your life?" After the individual answers this question and predicts how her partner will rate her, the partner is asked to give his rating using the same procedure. This is a way to bring the other partner back into the process, after he has been involved only passively for some time. "Taking the temperature of the marriage" often pinpoints trouble areas or areas that need to be explored more fully. The therapist gets some idea of how well the partners know themselves and each other and has a base line to refer to later to evaluate the success of the treatment.

Next, early childhood recollections and dreams are elicited and recorded verbatim. Both reveal subjective themes and melodies in a person's self-view and show how one finds one's place in life. Both partners are also asked to recall a song, a fairy tale, a nursery rhyme, a poem, a character from the Bible, a biblical story, a television show, a radio show, or a movie that made a special impression on them when they were children and to describe what impressed them about each item. These selected, subjective impressions are useful to the treatment process.

Stage 3: Reorientation and Reeducation

This stage involves providing feedback to the couple as well as implementing the plan and process for therapeutic change. Providing feedback includes disclosing the therapist's formulations of the source of the couple's distress and conflict as related to their lifestyles and skill deficits as well as their strengths and potential for change. Adlerians talk about the change process in terms of reorientation to a more effective relational style, especially involving conflict resolution; and problem solving, which is focused on cooperation and social interest.

The therapist may begin the feedback process by summarizing data about the couple's relational systems, severity of presentation, skills, lifestyles, and suitability for treatment. Adlerian psychotherapists tend to emphasize lifestyle interpretation. After listing the primary themes that have emerged (the individual convictions and guidelines about self, the world, conclusions and ethical conviction's) both partners and the therapist collaborate in listing the strengths of the person whose lifestyle is being formulated.

When the formulations are completed, each partner can receive a copy. At the session following the summary, each partner may be asked to read their summaries aloud. The therapist pays particular attention to word slips and to what the reader emphasizes and omits.

Meshing the Lifestyles

"Meshing the lifestyle" refers to the process of learning about the relationship as the lifestyles of both partners become known. "We fell in love," people often say when asked why they decided to get married. The acknowledgement that one chooses the direction of one's love in accordance with one's fundamental purposes makes it possible to accept that one also decides whether or not to fall in love. Similarly, "we are not in love" is often given as a reason for separation or divorce.

As we look at the two lifestyles together, we always find some areas of agreement. For example, both partners have as part of their personality styles what Adler called the "masculine protest"—a tendency to think that this is a man's world and that men have a better deal, are more important, have more power, and perhaps are more dangerous than women. Another couple may agree that life must be exciting and dramatic. We may also find sharp differences in how the partners view life and in what expectations they have of other people. If people were psychologically identical twins, they wouldn't get married in the first place. Ultimately, the goal of marriage therapy is for the couple to increase tolerance for individual differences within the relationship.

Often the process of comparing lifestyles and pointing out the differences clarifies for the first time why the partners see life so differently. The differences can add great richness to the relationship, or they can be a source of conflict.

> Ruth and Jim consulted a therapist primarily because of Ruth's paranoid psychosis. She was constantly plagued with delusions and hallucinations. For example, she got "special messages" on television and billboards, and she believed that the husband was plotting to kill her and their children. The therapist referred her to a psychiatrist who prescribed antipsychotic medication. Then the therapist began to work with both partners conjointly. It became clear that Jim was a computer-type person who depended on logic and careful analysis before making a decision or showing feelings. Whenever he and Ruth got into a discussion and he had the upper hand because of his "logic," Ruth would switch into her psychotic mode, becoming more unreachable. As the therapist and both partners came to understand this process, the therapist could actually point it out as it was happening during the counseling session. The therapist was also able to make the spouses understand that Ruth's sensitive, thematic, and carefree approach to life was what had appealed to Jim in the first place and that Jim's careful, analytic, and well-planned approach to life had been a great source of security for Ruth. But in time, his analytic approach to life had become a problem, especially as it was related to intimate conflicts. Successful therapy centered on helping each partner appreciate the other, including the way the other experienced life, and to understand how both approaches added value to the relationship.

Ongoing use of lifestyle material is an integral part of Adlerian couples therapy. The couple chooses to continue to work together after formulation of the lifestyle. Each recurrent question in the relationship is examined in light of the personal lifestyle of each partner. The therapist needs to have a summary of each lifestyle at all times as a reference. From time to time the therapist can ask, "Now that you understand you own lifestyle, how do you explain to yourself why you do what you do? And now that you understand your spouse's lifestyle, how do you explain to yourself why he behaves as he does?"

Many of the partner's questions and observations are just different ways of asking, "Why can't he (or she) be more like me?" Discussion and understanding of the lifestyle helps to answer that question and shows rather precisely the ways the partner is not like the other and is not likely to become like the other. Furthermore, it helps back up the therapist's repeated admonitions that one cannot control another person—something that people often attempt, in one way or another, in marriage. The lifestyle is neither good nor bad; it just is. A wide range of possibilities exists within a given lifestyle, but a goal in couples therapy is to help both partners accept themselves as they are at the moment and become more accepting of each other.

Reorientation of the lifestyle can be considered a necessity, a luxury, or anything in between. In most cases, it is not necessary for either partner to make basic lifestyle changes, because most lifestyles are broad enough to allow a variety of behavioral possibilities. For example, a person with a "very" lifestyle tends to see things in extremes: something is either all black or all white; a job is either done perfectly or not well at all. People with such a personality tend to think in superlatives; hence the term *very*. She is not merely a good cook; she is a very, very good cook. He is not merely a good provider, he is a very, very good provider. If someone has a relatively broad lifestyle, counseling may be limited to helping that person become aware of the choices that are available within, say, the "very" lifestyle.

Certain aspects of the lifestyle may be so limiting, however, that the therapist or the partner concludes that therapy should be aimed at changing the lifestyle. An example illustrates this point, but note that this is not, strictly speaking, an example of couples therapy, but rather of premarital counseling, because the woman's goal is to find out whether she can adjust her attitude toward men enough to find a mate.

> Keesha had an unfaltering hatred of men. She had grown up in a male-dominated family with four boys and only one girl (Keesha). When she grew up, she ended up working in a predominantly male office. The result was that Keesha had devoted her life to outdoing men, both as a child and as an adult, and had never felt anything but prejudice and dislike toward men.
>
> When she began treatment, the first hurdle was to develop a trusting relationship with the male co-therapist. Because she was being interviewed in a marriage-education center, on many occasions men in the audience had a chance to show her that they empathized with her and that men can be sensitive, tender, and gentle. Therefore, she was forced to reconsider her basic premise that "all men are bastards."
>
> Eventually, she had readjusted her bias enough to enter a relationship with a man. But, consistent with her lifestyle, she chose a man who was likely to fulfill her negative expectations—which he did. However, at this point she was able to resume therapy, reevaluate what had happened, and see rather clearly what had brought her to choose a man who would be most likely to let her down.

If one person elects to work at changing lifestyle, this goal may be pursued in individual, group, or couples therapy. However, therapists must not "force" one partner to change or collude with one partner to change the other. It is much more important for both partners to learn to accept themselves and their spouse as they are at the moment. Whether or not to strive toward basic changes in the lifestyle ultimately become a matter of choice for the individual. If each partner learns to understand and accept the other with all the strengths and weaknesses, lifestyle changes may not be so important.

Intervention in couples therapy can then focus on a variety of goals—changes of behavior, change of feelings, change of environment, or change of attitudes, which is basically aimed at changing the lifestyle. None of these is exclusive of or unrelated to the others. Some people can make rather marked changes in behavior without a particular change in insight. Some people can learn to deal with their emotions by understanding the purpose of the emotion—that is, by understanding the goal they are pursuing. If and when they decide to change their goal, the emotions take care of themselves. Naturally no one can consciously change feelings; it is much more important to get to the point where one can say "I'm a pretty good person, and, if I feel that way I feel, I must have some reason for it."

Mini-Lifestyles

A mini-lifestyle involves a brief overview of the family constellation and atmosphere and the interpretation of two or three early recollections. This elucidates a few of the basic themes but is in no way a complete lifestyle formulation. Because managed-care directives or clinic policies may limit the number of sessions an individual or couple may have, the mini-lifestyle format may prove necessary. Here is an example of the use of mini-lifestyles.

> Sara and Mike are a young couple who work in the same accounting firm. She is one of only a few females on staff. From her comments, it is pretty clear that she has a difficult relationship with her fellow employees because of her lack of acceptance of male behavior. She is critical, for example, of their constant discussion of sports. Mike, as a fellow employee, is not spared her criticism. Because most of her colleagues are men, Sara wonders whether there might be something in her lifestyle that would cast light on their current situation.
>
> A brief diagram of Sara's family constellation shows that her Gegenspieler, (i.e., the child often closest in the constellation, against whom the person plays in the childhood drama), was her older brother and that she revered her father. From one of her early recollections it appears that she was stunned at the sudden revelation of a flaw in a man's character. Another early recollection clearly shows that she was very impressed with how good and important men must be. With the help of the therapist, Sara began to understand how these conflicting views of men presented problems in her daily work. The mini-lifestyle also helps Mike, who, until now, has not been able to understand her job-related concerns.

Resolving Conflict in Intimate Relationships

Because Individual Psychology is an interpersonal psychology, all conflicts are seen as interpersonal. Adlerian therapists see problems that develop in a marriage as problems in the relationship. As we have said, many marital difficulties result from the spouses' attempts to experience an equalitarian relationship, without having the necessary background to enable them to treat each other (and others) as equals. Most human relationships are characterized by some degree of superiority and inferiority. Adler, as early as 1931, saw the fallacy of this position and pointed out that equality is the only standard for a successful marriage. Whenever one partner tries to elevate herself or himself above the other, the relationship becomes shaky and temporary, because the partner in the inferior position will always attempt to reverse the situation.

Relational conflict such as fighting not only does not solve the problem, but lays the groundwork for additional conflict. Only with courage and self-confidence can people face the challenge of cooperation. Dreikurs (1946) said that two misconceptions exist with regard to human cooperation: "One is the belief that resentment can lead to improvement. . . . The husband will gladly adjust himself to his wife's desires if he feels fully accepted by her. But he may drive in the opposite direction if he senses her resentment and rejection" (pp. 103–104). Another misconception about cooperation is expressed in the statement, "When interests clash, nothing can be done except to fight or yield."

The Adlerian marriage therapist deals with marital problems using Dreikurs' four principles of conflict resolution:

- showing mutual respect,
- pinpointing the issue,
- reaching a new agreement, and
- participating in decision making.

Every marriage conflict involves violation of one or more of these principles.

Showing mutual respect is neither fighting nor giving in; it is neither overpowering nor capitulating. Mutual respect acknowledges that the resolution of conflict rests with understanding and respecting each other's point of view, not with winning or losing.

Pinpointing the issue takes into consideration the fact that behind most marital complaints lies a social issue. For example, a couple may complain about sex, in-laws, work, money, or children. Behind the complaint will be some threat to personal status, prestige, or superiority, and some concern with who is winning or who is going to decide or who is right. The partners are specifically taught the technique of pinpointing the issue so they can learn to resolve conflicts on their own, without requiring the help of professionals.

Resolution of conflict is based on the understanding that partners fight because they have "agreed" to fight. Therefore, to resolve conflict, a new agreement must be reached. Reaching a new agreement ultimately comes down to each party's stating, "I'm willing to do this with no strings attached." It is best to make the new agreement for a limited time; at the end of that time, the partners should re-evaluate to determine whether the new agreement works.

Intimate partners must participate in decisions that affect them both. Participation is not limited to the decision-making process, but includes assuming responsibility for the decision. Violation of this principle reflects lack of respect for one's partner and is bound to be resented.

A husband came home and announced rather emphatically and enthusiastically that he had made arrangements for them to spend a weekend at a resort motel and has also made reservations for dinner at a fine restaurant. He was quite surprised and disappointed when his wife didn't show the enthusiasm he had expected. What he didn't realize was that, by acting without consulting her, he had shown little respect for her and violated the principle of participation in decision making.

Detailed information on conflict resolution in intimate relationships and can be found in *Time for A Better Marriage* (Dinkmeyer & Carlson, 1984b).

MULTIPLE THERAPY

Multiple therapy is therapy conducted by more than one therapist. The advantage of this approach is more evident in couples and family therapy than in other therapeutic modalities. One therapist can work effectively with a couple, but two therapists add many dimensions to the therapy process, particularly if they represent both sexes. The ideal situation probably exists when the therapists themselves are married to each other, so that the two couples can sit together in "fourway" or "four track therapy" (Pew & Pew, 1972). When the therapist is a male, the female partner may feel besieged by two males and is often helped when a female therapist is part of the process.

Ben:	*I think that Meg and I should meet each week and have an evaluation—particularly of how we are using our time.*
Meg (in tears):	*That's not what I'm talking about at all.*
Male co-therapist:	*I think Ben's idea has merit. It might be incorporated in a family-council meeting.*
Female co-therapist:	*What Meg is looking for is some appreciation. I suspect that the term evaluation sounds like she's going to be graded.*
Meg:	*That's just it. And, if I don't pass, Ben will have one more way to control me.*

However, women do not always identify with female therapists, nor men with male therapists. Frequently, the male therapist finds that he can understand the woman's point of view better, and vice versa. If the therapists are married to each other, their credibility with the couple is considerably higher, particularly if they are able to be open about the rough spots they have handled in their own relationship. While we emphasize married co-therapists, we recognize this is the exception and not the rule in co-therapy. Any co-therapy arrangement offers distinct advantages in couples therapy.

Female co-therapist:	*I get so mad at Larry I could bite him. But when I have a chance to be heard for a whole half hour in a marriage conference, I often find that I calm down considerably.*
Male co-therapist:	*But you still always want some kind of resolution.*

Female co-therapist: *Yes, that's true, and you seem to be able to function better when things are left hanging.*

Clients together: *That's just the way it is with us.*

Whenever couples therapy is faltering, the addition of another therapist to the on-going therapeutic process or simply for consultation can be helpful. Co-therapy and multiple therapy can be excellent methods for training and therapist, and it is quite possible to have three or more therapists working with a couple at one time.

Most couples are pleased to have more than one therapist. They often believe they are getting their money's worth, so to speak, and that the more therapists that are involved, the more points of view are introduced into the therapy process. When a new therapist joins the process, the "temperature of the marriage" is often taken again to provide the new therapist some idea of the quality of the relationship and of the current trouble spots, compared with those that existed at the beginning of counseling. Sometimes this re-evaluation opens up new directions in the therapy process.

> A couple had initially both rated themselves "3" as lovers (on a scale of 1 to 10). There was no discrepancy between the partners' ratings. When the process was repeated a few months later, both partners had gained considerably in their self-esteem and were much more assertive about what they wanted in their relationship. At this time, they still rated themselves "3" as lovers. Because they were rating themselves so much better in other areas, they were now able to bring up and deal with the problems they were experiencing in the area of sexuality. Therefore, the counseling focused for several sessions on the issue of sexuality. The spouses were asked to read an appropriate bibliotherapeutic book or booklet and to underline with pencils of different colors, the things that impressed them. By doing so, both partners discovered there were areas of sexuality they didn't know much about. They were also advised to attend a weekend sexual-awareness reassessment session. During this session, they saw multimedia presentations and participated in numerous group discussions. Finally, they were recommended various techniques and asked to pay special attention to those that emphasized the importance of giving pleasure to the other partner.
>
> With their increased sophistication, it became clear that the issue behind their conflict in the area of sexuality was often one of control. The partners were asked to conduct an experiment. During the first week, the wife was to make all the decisions concerning expressions of affection, tenderness, and sexuality. The following week, the husband was to be in charge. The partners agreed to the experiment and also to cooperate with each other to the best of their ability. She learned to be assertive and that it was okay to be the initiator. He learned that he didn't require immediate gratification every time he felt sexually aroused. Both partners learned to greatly enhance their own and the other's pleasure. As a result, they learned to deal more effectively not only with sexuality but also with parenthood, and their relationship with their teen-age children improved considerably.

TECHNICAL QUESTIONS

Separation

Many couples keep the threat of separation dangling between them. In that case, we occasionally recommend that they separate. We do so when we suspect that a separation will help the couple realize how much they love and miss each other. We also recommend separation when the fighting between counseling sessions is so extreme that the partners don't seem to have time or energy for any kind of conflict resolution or problem solving. Generally, however, separation is not frequently recommended. When it occurs, it is much more likely to have been decided on by the couple than to have been recommended by the therapists.

Individual and Family Therapy

Individual therapy is sometimes indicated as part of the couples therapy process; however, individual problems that are essentially unrelated to the intimate relationship must be kept separate from those that are related to it. Even though one partner may seem to need more intensive individual work, it is important to stay away from the view that she is "the problem" in the relationship. Problems that might better be dealt with individually rather than jointly include unresolved grief over the loss of a parent, difficulty in relating to persons of the same sex, problems in discovering and mobilizing one's own strengths (which may require vocational or academic counseling), psychosomatic complaints, and problems related to chronic medical conditions.

In family therapy, it often becomes apparent that the problems of the family are essentially problems between the partners and that the entire family will not run smoothly until both partners have worked out their difference. At that point, the family therapist often recommends couples therapy, which sometimes can be done concurrently with family therapy sessions. At other times, family therapy is temporarily discontinued until couples therapy has been completed.

The Absent Partner

Sometimes a person comes in alone, complaining about the relationship and protesting vigorously that the partner will not join in couples therapy. Our strategy in such cases is to ask immediately for permission to get in touch with the reluctant partner. It can be by telephone, right at that moment. It has been our experience that the other partner often agrees to therapy and frequently is very cooperative.

Absent partners are often different from the description. We know, of course, that we are hearing a biased account and that, if the partner we are interviewing is angry and intolerant, we will hear mostly about the partner's bad points. This is often accompanied by blindness to one's own defects. It is most important to win the cooperation of a reluctant partner, to point out that one can only speak for self. Speaking to only one partner about a intimate relationship is like seeing two actors on the stage but hearing only one of them deliver lines.

> A man was referred by his family physician. His complaint was premature ejaculation. He claimed that his problem was medical and that his wife had nothing to do with it. He also repeatedly refused to let us get in touch with his wife. A lifestyle formulation was completed, and, as a trusting relationship was established, we were finally able, with his permission, to get in touch with his wife and invite her to join us.

When she came in (willingly), she told, to her partner's surprise, quite a different story. He had never mentioned, for example, that he had left home several times, threatening to end the relationship. Also, it became obvious in the course of the session that he didn't know the depth of her affection and her commitment to their relationship. Her lifestyle was completed in his presence. Couples therapy was initiated. Special attention was paid to the symptom of premature ejaculation, which we viewed as a problem that originated from their relationship and that, therefore, had to be solved through the partners' joint efforts. After a relatively short period of counseling, the couple had resolved their differences enough to want to keep working at their relationship.

Children

When children are involved in the relational conflict, the situation becomes much more complex. It is crucial that the therapist influence and inform the partners about the devastating effects of parental conflict on children.

A couple who had been in a conflict situation for many years also disagreed on how to deal with their troublesome "hyperactive" child. The child was eventually removed from the home and put in residential treatment. In her deep discouragement, the mother reached the conclusion that she couldn't tolerate the child in the household again. The father did not accept the separation from his son but never tried to work out the conflict.

By the time the couple sought couples therapy, the child's treatment was seriously handicapped by the fact that, because he couldn't return to his home, long-range planning was almost impossible. After the husband announced that his son was ready to come home and the wife refused to accept the child back, the husband decided that he would move out and take care of his son. This led to a most serious marital crisis, which culminated in divorce.

Children, of course, know when there is disagreement between their parents, and there is no point in trying to hide it from them. The children can be told simply that their parents are having some difficulties and that they are working on them. Beyond that, it is usually not advisable to draw the children into the marriage therapy process. Occasionally, with adolescent or adult children, we have found it helpful to include the young people in some of the sessions, if the children are deeply enmeshed in their parents' relationship. If a couple is planning divorce, we remind them that they will continue to be the parents of their children. We also try to help them see that there is an advantage to dissolving the marriage peacefully and cooperatively, thus maintaining some type of friendly relationship, if for no other reason than to make it easier for the children to deal with the disruption of the family.

Often, when a couple begins to think about the children and the effects of parental conflict on their growth and development, they can be led to more cooperation and less battling. As the partners begin to realize how selfish they are and to what extreme they are concentrating on what each is getting out of the relationship to the exclusion of anyone else's interest and well-being, they can be led toward a state of higher social interest and more courage. On the other hand, we never recommend that couples stay together "for the good of the children." If a relationship is built on pretense, the children typically sense it and suffer from it. A destructive parental relationship is not a decent model for children if they are expected to know later in life what a good, intimate relationship is like.

Other Parties

In our experience, it is unusual for a marriage relationship to survive the prolonged existence of another party in the life of one or both spouses. People today try in so many different ways to overcome loneliness and achieve intimacy that long-lasting monogamous marriage has almost become only one possibility in the large list of alternate lifestyles. We believe that, ultimately, monogamy will again be seen as the most viable form of a lasting relationship between a man and a woman. We also think that people will choose a monogamous relationship not because of pressure from church, family, or state, but because of the advantages of the relationship for both parties.

Individuals must choose their own definition of *monogamy* and agree on that definition with their partners. A monogamous relationship might mean, for example, a long-term, deep commitment on the part of both parties, yet still allow significant relationships with members of the opposite sex, from time to time, for both partners. Our couples therapy experience, however, has taught us that infidelity is usually a symptom, not a cause, of the degeneration of the marriage relationship. Frequently, an affair is revealed to the partner in an effort to get the partner off dead center. We say "revealed," but there are seldom any secrets in an intimate relationship; the other partner usually knows at some level of awareness about the affair.

Frequency and Length of Therapy

The frequency of therapy sessions is often dictated by factors that are extraneous to the therapy process itself, such as financial considerations and available time. The optimal frequency seems to be once a week. This gives the couple enough time to work on things between sessions yet maintains the intensity of the counseling experience. After six to eight weekly sessions, most couples can be seen less frequently. Returning at monthly intervals for checkups is a useful interval.

The length of each session in marriage therapy can be the same as in individual counseling, commonly the 50-minute hour. In cases of four-track therapy, we have experimented with two-hour sessions with very good results. Because it is often difficult to get the therapists and the couple together, it helps to have a longer block of time. With a two-hour block of time, we are able to get into the relationship more deeply and still have enough time to bring about resolution. We have also experimented with more intensive kinds of therapy—for example, meeting with couples six or eight hours a day for three consecutive days. Although some of these couples had profound and complex problems, the process has been brought to completion by the end of the third day.

As we have said, marriage therapy can be combined with individual or group therapy. Generally, if one partner is receiving individual therapy, the marital relationship should not be part of that therapy process, and the therapist should insist on dealing with relationship problems only when both partners are present. When one partner seems to need a group experience, certain hazards should be kept in mind, such as the likelihood of the partner's differential growth and the possibility that the other partner may feel left out and worry about what is going on in the group. When these kind of problems are present, participation in a couples group may be a better solution.

Marital History

In our experience, a complete marital history is seldom necessary. We obtain sufficient information by discussing the current situation and by completing the personal lifestyle assessments. When we are puzzled and do not understand the dynamics of the relationship, however, it may be important to go back and ask the couple to describe in considerable detail their courtship, the early days of their marriage, and the various phases of their marriage relationship.

We look for recurring patterns and often see that the very things that attracted the partners to each other in the first place are those that, in their current fights, are brought up most often and objected to most strongly.

> Josh appreciated Stephanie's sociability and witty conversation, but now, when they fight, he claims that she talks too much. Stephanie appreciated Josh's strong, quiet, and logical manner, but now, when they fight, she complains that he wants to make all the decisions.

Sexual Problems

The sex act represents the ultimate test of a couple's willingness to cooperate and contribute to each other's welfare. Therefore, it is not surprising that most sexual problems turn out to be relationship problems. We seldom find it useful to accept the couple's diagnosis that they have a sexual problem, thus dealing only with the symptom. Many couples report that, as their relationship improves, their sexual life improves also. If a couple has ever had a good sexual relationship, chances are they can have it again; if a couple has never had a good sexual relationship, it is more likely that we are dealing with a sexual problem per se.

A complete sexual history is sometimes indicated to help clarify a confusing situation. In this case, the partners are asked to describe their early experiences with sex, both before and after they met, and provide a fairly detailed history of their sex lives up to the present. An important process—but one that can be conducted only by therapists who are comfortable with their own sexuality—is to have the couple describe their lovemaking in great detail, from the beginning to the end of the experience. This often makes it possible for the therapist to identify the trouble spots and for the couple to learn a great deal about themselves and each other. We strongly recommend that such histories be obtained with both partners present, although sometimes one partner is unwilling to discuss certain aspects or portions of past sexual history in the presence of the other. Naturally, we must be sensitive to such situations, and hear the person out in private, although we tend to recommend that partners be as open with each other in this area as they can possibly be.

Sexual problems can have a physical basis. We routinely refer a couple for a medical evaluation when there is any indication that the sexual dysfunction has an organic basis, or may be related to a medication taken by one of the partners.

Divorce and Divorce Mediation

Before or during the course of couples therapy, both partners may choose not to continue the relationship, and divorce becomes a serious consideration. Often, the therapist who has been involved with the couple during the period leading up to their decision to divorce is excluded from the divorce proceedings, particularly when attorneys are engaged by the couple. Because the legal process is basically adversarial, it is not surprising that old conflicts and unfinished business in the couple's relationship is exacerbated. Divorce mediation is an alternative to this adversarial process (Huber, 1983). Techniques for couples therapy are extensively presented in Sperry (1993) and Sperry and Carlson (1990, 1991).

ADDITIONAL STRATEGIES IN COUPLES THERAPY

The Marriage Conference

The marriage conference is one of the most satisfactory ways of dealing with intense conflict situations. This technique was first described by Corsini (1967).

The partners are asked to make a series of appointments to meet with each other for an hour at a time, in a place where they are unlikely to be interrupted. The appointments should be at least two or three days apart. With couples who are experiencing significant conflict, we usually recommend at least three appointments. The marriage conference is a self-help process that couples can carry out in their own time and at their own convenience. It is quite normal for couples who are using the marriage conference for the first time to report disappointment with the experience, unless they follow the directions carefully. Innovating is not advised until the couple have had some experience with the technique.

At the time of the first appointment and as a result of a previous agreement, one partner has the floor for the first half hour while the other partner listens silently and refrains from interrupting, making faces, or in any other way interfering with what the other says. We generally recommend that partners avoid television, radio, note taking, smoking, eating, drinking, or any other distraction. During one's half hour, one is free to say whatever one chooses and also has the option to remain silent. It is one's half hour to use as one chooses. At the end of exactly half an hour, the process is reversed, and the first partner becomes the listener. At the end of the second half hour, the conference is over. As a result of a previous agreement, the partners do not discuss until the next marriage conference any controversial items that came up during the conference. Noncontroversial items or any other subject can, of course, be discussed between conferences. At the time of the second conference, the process is repeated, except that the partners reverse the order in which they speak and listen (Dinkmeyer & Carlson, 1984b).

> Julie and James are extremely busy professionals with complicated schedules. Devoting 15 minutes a week to a marriage conference, which they refer to as "board meeting," has probably saved them from divorce. They sit down every Sunday and work out the schedule for the week, transportation, who's going to do what work, financial matters, and so forth—in other words, all the regular business of living together and operating a household.

Psychoeducational Interventions

Psychoeducational interventions for couples is often associated with specific programs such as Marriage Encounter, or Time for a Better Marriage (Dinkmeyer & Carlson, 1984b). Accordingly, such psychoeducational efforts are thought by many to be useful only with "normal" couples rather than "clinical" couples (i.e., those with a level of distress and relational conflict that qualify for referral to couples therapy or individual psychotherapy). Actually, considerable data suggest that certain psychoeducational interventions may be even more effective with severely troubled couples than with nonclinical or "normal" couples (Ross, Baker, & Guerney, 1985; Giblin, Sprenkle, & Sheehan, 1985). Carlson and Sperry (1990) have made the case that psychoeducational strategies are not only useful adjuncts to couples therapy but also are indispensable for couples who have considerable skill deficits in empathy, assertive communication, or problem solving. Others believe that psychoeducational methods should actually be the primary mode of treatment with some couples (Anderson, Reiss, & Hogarty, 1986).

The Adlerian approach to couples therapy is quite receptive to the incorporation of psychoeducational interventions in the course of therapy (Carlson & Dinkmeyer, 1987; Pew & Pew, 1972; Carlson & Sperry, 1993). Adlerians have developed a number of psychoeducational strategies ranging from the Marriage Conference (Corsini, 1967) also called marriage meetings (Carlson, Sperry, & Dinkmeyer, 1992); Training in Marriage Enrichment (TIME) (Dinkmeyer & Carlson, 1984b); to Marriage Education Centers.

Psychodrama

Psychodrama refers to a group of techniques in which the client acts out various situations to gain insight into a better understanding of the situation. For example:

> Kelsey, age 24 and married, thinks she is in love with another man. She reports great torment in trying to decide what to do. We ask her to sit half on one chair and half on another. We talk with her about how it feels to be sitting on two chairs, and we ask her to predict how long she will be able to remain in that position. We also ask whether she has

some idea about which "chair" she is leaning toward. Then we ask Kelsey, "Do you think the chances that in one year you'll still be living with Jon are larger or smaller than 50%?" She says, "It's still 50/50." Had she said that the chances were greater than 50%, we would have told her that, on the basis of her own admission (at least at this moment), she really had decided to stay with Jon. We would also have pointed out that the main issue then was how big a production she was going to make out of her decision.

In another psychodramatic technique, the partners change chairs, playing each other's role and experiencing each other. Additional psychodramatic techniques, useful in couples therapy are: auxiliary egos, doubling, and mirroring.

Couples Group Therapy

Adlerians have adapted the group process to marriage therapy. A group of five or six married couples is seen for two hours a week, usually for a limited period of time, perhaps 10 weeks. Couples benefit from the group by identifying with and getting ideas from peers. They discover that they are not alone and that their problems are not unique. Ideally, the couples will also have private sessions, including formulation of their lifestyles. Couple group therapy may take place in conjunction with attendance at a marriage-education center.

Homework

We regularly prescribe homework. The partners agree to commit themselves to doing the prescribed activity. The kinds of homework are limited only by the imagination of the counselors and of the audience (when the counseling takes place in a center). For a couple who hasn't been away from their children for many months and resents the situation, the assignment may be to hire a baby-sitter and spend an afternoon and perhaps overnight away from the child. For a couple who complains about sex but whose underlying problem seems to be one of control, the homework may require each spouse to take full responsibility and make all decisions in the area of sex and affection for alternate weeks.

Paradoxical Intention

One of the most powerful techniques in couples therapy is the paradoxical intention. The partners are asked to go home and do whatever they have been doing all along, but to do it on schedule. For example, a couple who has been fighting all the time may be urged to carry on a 10-minute fight each evening, using the same procedures they have always followed—but being sure to do it every night and for 10 minutes.

Many couples can't believe that such a recommendation will do them any good. They have come for help and are being told to go home and do exactly what they had been doing before. But if they are serious about improving their relationship, they usually do the homework. The paradoxical intention is always put in the form of an experiment: "See what you can learn." Whether the couple follows the recommendation, they learn that they can choose when to fight and when not to fight. Frequently, couples have a great deal of difficulty carrying out the recommendation without laughing, and the absurdity of their fight becomes apparent to them.

> A couple reported that they had problems because of the husband's premature ejaculation. We asked them to have intercourse twice a day and without foreplay. We emphasized that the husband was supposed to ejaculate as quickly as possible. The reason for our recommendation was that a symptom cannot be maintained unless one fights against it. Under the right circumstances, the symptom of premature ejaculation often disappears. In fact, it is not unusual for a couple to report the opposite experience—that is, the man had difficulty ejaculating or even reaching orgasm.

Reframing

An important therapeutic tactic is reframing or redefinition. If Doug keeps referring to Allie as stubborn, we reframe the characteristics as persistence and identify in considerable detail all the advantages Allie brings to the marriage because of her persistence.

At all times, and not just when we employ this technique, we try to help partners communicate clearly, using the right words, being specific and direct, and avoiding anything that can confuse the message.

REFERENCES

Adler, A. (1958). *What life should mean to you*. New York: Capricorn.

Adler, A. (1978). *Cooperation between the sexes: Writings on women and men, love and marriage, and sexuality*. Edited and translated by H. Ansbacher and R Ansbacher. New York: Norton.

Anderson, C., Reiss, D., & Hogarty, G. (1986). *Schizophrenia and the family: A practitioner's guide to psychoeducation and management*. New York: Guilford Press.

Carlson, J., & Dinkmeyer, D. (1987). Adlerian marriage therapy. *American Journal of Family Therapy, 15*(4), 326–332.

Carlson, J., & Sperry, L. (1990). Psychoeducational strategies in marital therapy. *Innovations in Clinical Practice, 9,* 389–404.

Carlson, J., Sperry, L., & Dinkmeyer, D. (1992). Marriage maintenance: How to stay healthy. *Topics in Family Psychology and Counseling, 1*(1), 84–90.

Carlson, J., & Sperry, L. (1993). Extending treatment results in couples therapy. *Individual Psychology, 49,* 3–4, 450–455.

Corsini, R. J. (1967). Let's invent a first-aid kit for marriage problems. *Consultant,* 40.

Criswell, F., Carlson, J., & Sperry, L. (1993). Adlerian marital strategies with middle income couples facing financial stress. *American Journal of Family Therapy, 21*(4), 324–332.

Dinkmeyer, D., & Dinkmeyer, J. (1982). Adlerian marriage therapy. *Individual Psychology, 38*(2), 115–122.

Dinkmeyer, D., & Dinkmeyer, J. (1983). *Marital inventory*. Coral Springs, FL: CMTI Press.

Dinkmeyer, D., & Carlson, J. (1984b). *Time for a better marriage*. Circle Pines, MN: American Guidance Service.

Dreikurs, R. (1946). *The challenge of marriage*. New York: Hawthorn.

Dreikurs, R. (1968). Determinants of changing attitudes of marital partners toward each other. In S. Rosenbaum & I. Aler (Eds.), *The marriage relationship: Psychoanalytic perspective*. New York: Basic Books.

Fish, R., & Fish, L. (1986). Quid pro quo revisited: The basis of marital therapy. *American Journal of Orthopsychiatry, 56,* 317–324.

Giblin, P., Sprenkle, D., & Sheehan, R. (1985). Enrichment outcome research: A meta-analysis of premarital, marital and family interventions. *Journal of Marital and Family Therapy, 11,* 257–271.

Gottman, J. (1994). *Why marriages succeed or fail*. New York: Simon & Shuster.

Huber, C. (1983). Divorce mediation: An opportunity for Adlerian counselors, *Individual Psychology, 39*(2), 125–132.

Kern, R. (1997). *Lifestyle scale*. Coral Springs, FL: CMTI Press.

Pew, M., & Pew, W. (1972). Adlerian marriage counseling. *Journal of Individual Psychology, 28*(2), 192–202.

Ross, E., Baker, S., & Guerney, B. (1985). Effectiveness of relationship enhancement therapy versus therapist: Preferred therapy. *American Journal of Marital and Family Therapy, 15,* 11–21.

Sekaran, & Hall, D. (1989). Asynchronism in dual career and family linkages. In M. Arthur, D. Hall, & B. Lawrence (Eds.). *Handbook of career theory* (pp. 159–180). Cambridge: Cambridge University Press.

Sperry, L. (1978). *The together experience: Getting, growing and staying together in marriage*. San Diego: Beta Books.

Sperry, L. (1992). Tailoring treatment with couples and families: Resistances, prospects and perspectives. *Topics in Family Psychology and Counseling, 1*(3), 1–6.

Sperry, L. (1993). Tailoring treatment with dual-career couples. *American Journal of Family Therapy, 21*(1), 51–59.

Sperry, L., & Carlson, J. (1990). Enhancing brief marital therapy with psychoeducational interventions. *Journal of Couples Therapy, 1*(1), 57–70.

Sperry, L., & Carlson, J. (1991). *Marital therapy: Integrating theory and technique*. Denver: Love Publishing.

Guide for Initial Interviews and Assessments

GUIDE FOR INITIAL INTERVIEW
ESTABLISHING THE LIFESTYLE

Name _____ Date _____

1. Reason for coming:
2. History of this concern:
3. Current life tasks (how things are going in these areas); rate from 1 to 5 (a rating of 5 means that things are going very well; a rating of 1, that they are very dissatisfying):

   Occupation _____
   Friendship _____
   Opposite sex _____
   Self _____
   Meaning _____
   Leisure _____
   Parenting _____

4. Father's age _____   Mother's age _____
   Occupation _____   Occupation _____
   Personality: Personality:
   Ambitions for children: Ambitions for children:
   Relationship to children: Relationship to children:
   Ways you are similar/different   Ways you are similar/different from
      from father: mother:

5. Nature of parents' relationship:

6. Other family information (e.g., divorce, remarriage):

7. Additional parental figures:

8. Description of siblings; list siblings from oldest to youngest:

   Which is most different from you? _____ How?
   Which is most like you? _____ How?
   What kind of child were you?
   Were there unusual talents, achievements, or ambitions?
   Any sickness or accidents?
   Childhood fears?

9. Physical and sexual development:

10. Social development:

11. School and work experience:

12. Sibling ratings; list highest and lowest sibling for each attribute. If you are at neither extreme, indicate your position in relationship to siblings:

Intelligence	Critical to self
Grades and general standards of achievement	Charming; trying to please
	Sociable; friendships
Hardest worker; industrious	Withdrawn
Responsible	Sense of humor
Methodical; neat	Demanded and got own way
Athletic	Temper and stubbornness
Appearance	Sensitive; easily hurt
Mischievous	Idealistic
Rebellious: openly, covertly	Materialistic
Conforming	Most spoiled
Standards of right/wrong; morals	Most punished
Critical of others	

13. Early recollections. How far back can you remember? (Obtain recollections of *specific incidents,* as detailed as possible, including the client's reaction at the time.)

14. Choose the number one priority that best fits you; the next closest fit, through the fourth (least fitting) priority

Number One Priority	How the Other May Feel	The Price You Pay for Your Priority	What You Want to Avoid with Your Priority
Comfort	irritated or annoyed	reduced productivity	stress
Pleasing	accepting	stunted growth	rejection
Control	challenged	social distance and/or reduced spontaneity	unexpected humiliation
Superiority	inadequate	overburden or overresponsiblity	meaninglessness

15. Summary:
    Mistaken self-defeating perceptions:
    Assets:

LIFESTYLE ASSESSMENT EXAMPLE*

Instructions

You will be presented lifestyle information segment by segment. After each portion is presented to you, you are to react to the statements on the answer sheet according to the directions provided below.

This exercise will enable you to compare your evaluation of collected information regarding lifestyle to experts in the field. As you accumulate more information, you may change your judgment regarding some of the statements you have made. That is expected to happen and is very common. *Base each judgment on all the information available up to that particular point.* Do not look ahead, but you are encouraged to look back to the previous information if it is helpful to you to do so.

How To Mark the Answer Sheet

  I. First decide if the statement should be marked

    A. true

    B. false

    C. no basis for judging either way

  II. Then decide how certain you are of your answer and select, by circling

    1 for statements you are *very* sure of

    2 for statements you are *reasonably* sure of

    3 for statements you are *somewhat* sure of but which could easily be marked otherwise.

Examples

	True	False	No Evidence
1. Alice is a power-oriented person	1 2 3	1 ②3	1 2 3
2. Alice is a person who is a getter in life.	①2 3	1 2 3	1 2 3

In #1 the respondent felt the statement was false and was moderately sure of his belief.

In #2 the respondent felt the statement was true and was very sure of his answer.

---

*Reprinted by permission of Dr. Thomas Edgar.

INFORMATION FROM THE INITIAL INTERVIEW

Appearance

Jane is attractive and neat. She is a tall woman. Her clothing is expensive and stylish.

Occupation

Assistant to the director of a national television series. Her salary is good according to her report.

Marital status

Single. No steady or serious relationship with a man at the present time. She has never been married, although she has been engaged to marry three times in the past five years.

Present stated problem

Jane expressed a feeling of general boredom with life. Specifically, Jane feels her work is not satisfying and that her work is not appreciated by her boss. Her social life is unsatisfactory. She would like a permanent, long-term relationship with a male, but none have appeared who even come close to being the person she is seeking for such a relationship. Jane cries easily as she discusses her unhappiness with life in general. She does not feel accepted by her co-workers.

THE LIFESTYLE INVENTORY

Name _____ Jane X _____

Date _____

1. Bill $+4\frac{1}{2}$	2. Jane 30

Very good to her.
Took care of her.
Bought her things.
Got along well. Kind.
Not scholarly. Athletic.
Lots of boyfriends.
Tall and skinny.

Always had lots of girlfriends.
Cute. Happy. Outgoing.
Lessons—singing and dancing.
Never shy.
Good in school; teachers
  liked her
Not good in sports.
No boyfriends.

Sibling ratings

Most different from respondent:

How? He's much more interested and quiet. More conservative. Not as good a student as she is.

Most like respondent:

How? Same sense of humor. Same tastes, e.g., music (except for wife). Always very close.

Groupings (age, sex, etc.):

Which played together? Yes—he teased her a lot and drove her crazy.

Which fought each other?
He'd hit her once in a while—a punching bag.

Sickness, surgery, or accident? No.

Unusual talents or achievements?

Respondent's childhood fears? The dark. Little people lived under her bed but wouldn't bother her.

Respondent's childhood ambitions?
Theater—a star.

Most	Most
Intelligence – equal	Cheerful
Grades – Jane	Sociable – Jane
Industrious – Jane	Sense of humor – equal
Standards of achievement – Jane	Considerate – equal
Athletic – Bill	Bossy – Jane
Daring – Bill	Demanded way – Jane
Looks – Bill	Got way – Bill
Feminine	Temper – equal
Masculine	Fighter – both

Obedient – Jane
Made mischief – Bill
Openly rebellious – Bill
Covertly rebellious – neither
Punished – never punished
Standards of right-wrong – Bill
Critical of others – Jane
Critical of self – Jane
Easy-going – both
Charm – Jane
Excitement seeker – neither

Chip on shoulder – neither
Sulked – neither
Stubborn – neither
Shy – neither
Sensitive and easily hurt – Jane
Idealistic – Jane
Materialistic – neither
Methodical, neat – neither
Responsible – Bill
Withdrawn – neither
Spoiled – neither
Overprotected – Jane

Parental information

Father, Oliver, Age 54 Occupation: owns store

Never hit me. Always even-tempered. Made me laugh. Got along well with him. Loves to sing and dance—interested in opera and things she likes, too. Generous. Anything he could do for family. Never admits he's wrong. Narrow-minded about certain things. Somewhat protective of her. Worried.

Favorite? Nobody. Why?
Ambitions for children? Bill—loose standards for him but college expected; for me, none.
Relationship to children? very close.
Sibling most like father? Bill in business.
In what ways? Jane: home personality.

Mother, May, Age 49 Occupation: housewife

Always got along well. Loved her and felt close to her. Temper on her. Wake up Sunday morning in rotten mood and then apologize. She was around and would let them have it. Couldn't stand for being fresh or pouting, but could have what they wanted. Got a kick out of raising a daughter. Very sensitive; not much confidence in self. Nice person; good-hearted. Got feelings hurt easily.

Favorite? Nobody. Why? Wanted a daughter, if anybody.
Ambitions for children? College.
Relationship to children? Do things for me. Be giving.
Sibling most like mother? Both.
In what ways? Get feelings hurt easily. Very sensitive.

Nature of Parents' Relationship

Very good marriage; but Mother feels inferior and Father feels confident. Similar interests. Always together. A few fights over stupid little things. Father makes major decisions. She raised kids. Father controls the money.

Physical Development

13 at menses; school and Mother prepared her. Getting dressed to go out and called Mother "God damn it; why now?" Took it lightly. Father went and got Kotex from drugstore, and she went out. It was just a thing that happened. It was time. It was a nuisance at the moment and always has been. No difficulties. 13 at first bra (didn't need it). Doesn't remember getting first time. Feels like she could lose 5 lbs. now.

School Information

B.A. in radio and T.V. from State University. Always a good student except in math and science. Partied and still got good grades. Good in writing and reading.

Social Information

Always had lots of friends. With one friend, Beth, friends in grammar school through high school. Very close. Best of friends, but always competitive. Real cute and never trusted her with men/boys. Jane always felt Beth was doing things better than she did them. Very selfish, spoiled, and self-centered.

Sexual Information

Dated one boyfriend in high school. Necking and petting (but not really into it). Intercourse first time at 21 years. Went with one boy in college who didn't turn her on (Peter), then did it at 21 (2 years later). Not good. Terrible. But John did turn her on, and she had a good time. Six or seven men since then, but Eric the most and the best.

Other Family Information

Additional Parental Figures

Early Recollections

1. Age 2 yrs.   Crapping in my pants in the crib. Didn't say anything. Mother took care of "it." Father was annoyed when it happened. At night. I know it was wrong.

2. Age 3–4 yrs.   I was fat. On the beach. Had on just bottoms. Playing in the sand. I think Mother was there. I was in my own little world. Felt good.

3. Age 3–4 yrs.   During the day. Don't remember what I did. But Mother spanked me. It had something to do with Bill. I thought she was the meanest person in the world for hitting me like that. Mother said "Wait until Father gets home." I know he wouldn't do anything. Mad at Mother.

4. Age 6 yrs.   Bill tied me to a tree in the park. Another little boy was there. They thought it was funny. I was scared and thought they were going to leave me there the rest of my life. They left, and I screamed "Bill, Bill." They came back a few minutes later, untied me, and let me go. I didn't think it was funny and was mad at brother for making me look foolish in front of *my* peer, *my* boyfriend. Big brother acted like the "big shot." I was scared and then mad.

5. Age 5 yrs.   Fighting with two girls at recess. Just one at first, and then the other decided to help. One held my arms back, and I bit the stomach of the girl in front of me. She deserved it. Girl had mark on stomach for years. I felt bad afterwards.

6. Age 6 yrs.   First grade. Teacher would send two people to thank another class for play given. Teacher asked for relatives to raise their hands. I raised mine and teacher said "Do you have a relative?" (She knew the family.) I said "Yes, a sister you couldn't know about. Her name is Emma." Teacher said "O.K." and let me go. I got nervous that I couldn't carry it off and realized it didn't make sense. Later, I was embarrassed and didn't feel right. I didn't feel guilty. Knew I wouldn't do it anymore. "That's what you get for lying. It doesn't make sense."

7. Age 7 yrs.   Being on top of slide in playground. Afraid to go down and afraid to climb back down. 5th-grade patrol boys calling me down. Scared to death. Afraid to move either way. Finally slid down and felt relieved that I was off the slide and could go down. Embarrassed at all the attention.

8. Age 9–10 yrs. Girlfriend Jane and I crawled under barbed wire at concert. Went on empty stage and sang and danced and had wonderful time. Scared we'd get caught. Feeling real good. Imagining orchestra and audience.

	True	False	No Evidence
1. Jane may provoke others to abuse her so she can feel morally superior.	1 2 3	1 2 3	1 2 3
2. She finds others to be unfair.	1 2 3	1 2 3	1 2 3
3. Jane, psychologically, is an only child.	1 2 3	1 2 3	1 2 3
4. Jane often feels victimized by life.	1 2 3	1 2 3	1 2 3
5. It is better for Jane to be on the edge of the action, not in the middle of it.	1 2 3	1 2 3	1 2 3
6. Jane, as a child, was actively engaged in competition with her brother.	1 2 3	1 2 3	1 2 3
7. She feels that, while she is not perfect, others are worse.	1 2 3	1 2 3	1 2 3
8. Jane expects others to exercise control over her.			
9. Jane will tend to criticize other people a lot.	1 2 3	1 2 3	1 2 3
10. Jane is likely to become depressed often by the circumstances of life.	1 2 3	1 2 3	1 2 3
11. Jane questions her own femininity and would prefer being a male, given the choice.	1 2 3	1 2 3	1 2 3
12. One of Jane's mistaken ideas in life is: women are inferior to men.	1 2 3	1 2 3	1 2 3
13. Jane's family valued getting along with others.	1 2 3	1 2 3	1 2 3
14. Jane will tend to become frightened and/or furious when others try to control her.	1 2 3	1 2 3	1 2 3
15. Jane learned from her family that what she merely *wants* she needs.	1 2 3	1 2 3	1 2 3
16. Jane's parents modeled a sharing cooperative relationship.	1 2 3	1 2 3	1 2 3
17. People who try to prevent Jane from doing what she wants are liable to get hurt.	1 2 3	1 2 3	1 2 3
18. Jane was given responsibilities in her family.	1 2 3	1 2 3	1 2 3
19. Jane has a great deal of confidence in herself.	1 2 3	1 2 3	1 2 3
20. The family valued making the best of any bad situation.	1 2 3	1 2 3	1 2 3
21. Jane tries hard to find her way in life through conformity.	1 2 3	1 2 3	1 2 3
22. Jane's brother dominated her, much like her father.	1 2 3	1 2 3	1 2 3
23. Jane finds it difficult to work cooperatively with others.	1 2 3	1 2 3	1 2 3
24. Jane, when she finds herself in a difficult situation, will often be unable to act in *any* way.	1 2 3	1 2 3	1 2 3
25. Relationships are a matter of who is on top.	1 2 3	1 2 3	1 2 3

Nine Adlerian raters, all experienced in counseling and psychotherapy, were asked to complete the preceding Lifestyle Assessment questionnaire. The responses are listed below. On the left are the responses based on information up to and including the family constellation. On the right are the responses based on all the information available in the Lifestyle Assessment, including early recollections. The modal responses to each question are listed to give the readers using this questionnaire some standard to evaluate their own responses. (T = True; F = False; NE = No evaluation)

Question No.	Mode	Question No.	Mode
1	T2	1	T1
2	T2, T3	2	T1
3	F1	3	F1
4	T2	4	T1
5	F2	5	T2
6	T2	6	T1
7	T2	7	T1
8	T2	8	T2
9	T1	9	T1
10	T2	10	T2
11	T3	11	T3
12	T1, T2	12	T2
13	T1	13	T1
14	T2	14	T2
15	T3	15	T3
16	F2	16	F2
17	T3, F2, F3	17	T1
18	F2	18	F1
19	F1	19	F1
20	NE2, F1	20	F2
21	T2	21	T2
22	T2	22	T1, T2
23	T2	23	T1
24	T1	24	T1
25	T2	25	T2

THE LIFE-STYLE INVENTORY

Harold H. Mosak, Ph.D.   Name _____

Bernard H. Shulman, M.D.   Date _____

Copyright © 1971, by H. H. Mosak & B. H. Shulman

List siblings in chronological order

Sibling Ratings

Most different from respondent:	How?
Most like respondent:	How?
Groupings (age, sex, etc.)	Which fought each other?
Which played together?	Unusual talents or achievements?
Sickness, surgery or accident?	Respondent's childhood
Respondent's childhood fears?	ambitions?

Most to Least	Most to Least
Intelligence	Cheerful
Grades	Sociable
Industrious	Sense of humor
Standards of achievement	Considerate
Athletic	Bossy
Daring	Demanded way
Looks	Got way
Feminine	Temper
Masculine	Fighter
Obedient	Chip on shoulder
Made mischief	Sulked
Openly rebellious	Stubborn
Covertly rebellious	Shy
Punished	Sensitive and easily hurt
Standards of right-wrong	Idealistic
Critical of others	Materialistic
Critical of self	Methodical—Neat
Easy going	Responsible
Charm	Withdrawn
Pleasing	Excitement seeker

Physical Development

School Information

Social Information

Sexual Information

Parental Information

Father	Age	Occupation	Favorite? Why? Ambitions for children? Relationship to children? Sibling most like father? In what ways?
Mother	Age	Occupation	Favorite? Why? Ambitions for children? Relationship to children? Sibling most like mother? In what ways?

Nature of Parents' Relationship

Other Family Information

Additional Parental Figures

Early Recollections

Summary of Family Constellation

Summary of Early Recollections

Mistaken or Self-Defeating Apperceptions

Assets

CHILDREN'S LIFESTYLE GUIDE (CLSG)*

1. Family constellation

Name	Age	Education
_____	_____	_____
_____	_____	_____
_____	_____	_____
_____	_____	_____

   Who is most different from you? Why?

   Who is most like you? Why?

   Tell about your life before you went to school:

2. Functioning at life tasks

   If choice go to school/stay home, what would you do? Why?

   What do you like about school? Why?

   What do you dislike about school? Why?

   What is your favorite subject? Why? Least favorite? Why?

   What would you like to be when you grow up? Why?

   Who is your best friend? At school?

   Are you a leader or follower?

   What do you usually do when you are with your friends?

   When you play a game, are you usually picked first/last/middle?

   Family atmosphere

   What kind of person is father?

   What kind of person is mother?

   How do mother/father get along?

   Which child acts most like father?

   Which child acts most like mother?

   When you misbehave, who disciplines you? Why?

   What do you like to do best with mother or father? Why?

   What do you like to do least with mother or father? Why?

   What do your parents expect of you at home? In school? At play? In special activities?

   What jobs do you have at home?

---

*Adapted with permission from Dinkmeyer, D., and Dinkmeyer, D. Jr., (1977) Concise counseling assessment: The children's lifestyle guide. *Elementary School Guidance and Counseling* (12) 117–124.

Rating

List highest & lowest sibling for each attribute (including yourself):

Intelligent

Hardest worker

Best grades school

Conforming, obedient

Rebellious

Helps around house

Tries to please

Wants their way

Most punished

Critical

Considerate

Shares

Selfish

Responsible

Sensitive, feelings easily hurt

Temper

Bossiest

Materialistic

Friends (most)

Most spoiled

High standards of achievement; wants to be best

Athletic

Strongest

Prettiest

Cares about other's feelings

3. Early recollections

4. Three wishes

   If you were going to pretend to be an animal, which would you choose? Why?

   Which animal would you not want to be? Why?

   What is your favorite fairy tale or story? Why?

5. Summary:

   Mistaken self-defeating perceptions:

   Assets:

Adlerian Counseling and Psychotherapy Competencies

ADLERIAN COUNSELING AND PSYCHOTHERAPY COMPETENCIES

	Unsatisfactory	Good	Exceptional Ability
1. Can present the Adlerian theoretical foundations underlying the therapeutic process	_____	_____	_____
2. Can explain the psychopathology of the neuroses and psychoses as set forth by Adlerian psychology—that is, purpose of symptoms, interrelationship of the neuroses, and so forth	_____	_____	_____
3. Can describe and demonstrate the Adlerian counseling relationship	_____	_____	_____
4. Can deal with the disturbances and defenses that interfere with the relationship, such as externalization, rebellion, inadequacy, and projection	_____	_____	_____
5. Can explore the current situation and the way in which the person approaches the challenges of living and the life tasks	_____	_____	_____
6. Can use the number one priority as a clinical method to investigate one facet of the lifestyle	_____	_____	_____
7. Can identify and interpret the essential lifestyle information—that is, family constellation and family atmosphere	_____	_____	_____
8. Can interpret and utilize early recollections in formulating the lifestyle	_____	_____	_____
9. Can identify here-and-now psychological movement and interpret it to the client	_____	_____	_____
10. Can understand the commonly observed lifestyles, such as "getter," "driver," and "controller"	_____	_____	_____
11. Is able to attend to the client's verbal and nonverbal behavior	_____	_____	_____
12. Is able to align counselor/counselee goals	_____	_____	_____
13. Can empathically understand and reflect feelings while understanding the purpose of the feelings being shared	_____	_____	_____
14. Can paraphase and allude to a goal or purpose	_____	_____	_____
15. Can confront clients with their subjective views, mistaken beliefs, private goals, or destructive behaviors	_____	_____	_____

The Lifestyle Scale

T he Lifestyle Scale is a 35-item paper-and-pencil inventory developed by Kern (1982, 1997). It is continuously being refined via validity studies and item-reliability analysis. In addition to its use with couples, it can be employed with individual clients, management personnel, or work teams. It was developed for the purpose of attaining lifestyle information on priorities that might be helpful in understanding one's relationship with a partner, career decisions, managerial and conflict management styles, or how one responds to stressful situations. (For information on the Kern Scale, contact CMTI Press at 800-584-1733.)

The scale assesses factors such as control, perfectionism, pleasing, self-esteem, and expectations, which can be further organized into three factors of control, conforming, and discouraged. Completing the Lifestyle Scale usually generates immediate interest and conversation by the couple or client. In addition, it helps the individual to feel understood and more likely to take suggestions from the therapist/counselor.

Interpretation of the inventory, regardless of setting, takes the form of how each scale relates to the predominant lifestyle theme or factor. Some simple rules of thumb for interpretation are the following:

1. Look at all scale scores and determine both the predominant theme (the high score on the factor) and the other complementary factors in the scale that help the individual deal with particular life situations or intimate relationships. For example, if all scale scores are at the mean with no high score it may indicate the client controlled the scale just as she wishes to control the partner or life situations in general.

2. If there are two high scale scores, one might investigate how they complement each other; for example, a high control score with a high perfectionistic score may indicate a person who controls situations, people, and life's problems by being cautious, intellectual, and fearing to make mistakes. On the other hand, if the perfectionistic scale and pleasing scale are high, the individual may be more interested in pleasing his spouse to avoid making mistakes.

3. If the two factors of "self-esteem" and "expectations" are higher than the other scales, there is a high probability that the individual has low social interest, low self-esteem, and is a likely candidate for assistance from the therapist.

4. A high expectations scale, coupled with pleasing or controlling, may indicate an individual who is having a crisis in a particular life task area but is not necessarily extremely discouraged.

5. Finally, the scale is also helpful in gaining information on what types of characteristics a client dislikes in others as well as situations that may be most distressing to her. For example, a low quantitative score on control may indicate an individual who resents or dislikes being involved with individuals or a partner who exhibits controlling characteristics.

FACTOR PROFILES

Control Scale

The active controlling scale indicates an individual who attempts to deal with life's problems by being logical and rational, controlling his emotions, and actively leading others. Others may perceive the individual as bossy, opinionated, unwilling to listen, and more prone to confrontation than cooperation. Relationships with others may be a contest of winning and losing. Assets of this theme are the individual's ability to confront and solve problems rationally and to meet conflict situations head on. Other assets include the ability to lead, organize, and follow through with assigned tasks.

The passive dimension of this scale may be characterized by the individual who appears cool and calm and gives the appearance of having most situations under control. This person is quiet, shows few emotions, either positively or negatively, and seems to be difficult to "get to know."

Perfectionistic Scale

This factor seems to indicate individuals who wish to control others or conform with others' demands. One who scores high on this factor may portray characteristics of conscientiousness, thoughtfulness, sensitivity, and caution, or the perfectionism may be a strategy for gaining control of situations or others. Scoring high on this factor may indicate an individual who likes to complete tasks individually, is conscientious, extremely sensitive to making mistakes, and somewhat obsessive and conservative in responses to life tasks.

Conforming Scale (Pleasing)

The conforming factor may be active or passive. It may have the ingredients of perfectionism and at other times pleasing. If it is active conforming, the individual's goal will be to seek approval from others, and to serve as a peacemaker or diplomat in interpersonal situations. The individual will be sensitive to others' needs and avoid confrontation and conflict situations. He will generally demonstrate caring characteristics and most likely appear to possess high levels of social interest.

The passive conformer "goes with the flow." This person follows directions, is quiet, and on the surface appears somewhat shy. Passive conformers are usually excellent listeners who have difficulty getting their needs met because it is difficult for them to use "I" statements such as, "I want . . . , I need . . . , I prefer . . ."

The active or passive conforming factor represented by this scale suggests someone who is sensitive, a good listener, shy, apologetic, and who may experience difficulties in the areas of confrontation, conflict resolution, and getting needs met.

Self-Esteem Scale

The individual who scores high on this factor and the martyr factor may show feelings of low self-esteem, discouragement, and low energy levels. Symptoms take the form of being unable to control life situations related to career, relationships, or peers. Other behaviors include oversensitivity to others' feelings, difficulties in problem solving, and interest in avoiding problems or stressful situations. This individual usually exhibits passive behaviors until stress or conflict surfaces, then exhibits unpredictable behavior.

Expectations Scale

If not coupled with a high score on the self-esteem scale, this factor may indicate an individual whose expectations of self and others are so high that she continually sets up problem situations at work, with others, or with loved ones that are characterized by criticism, frustration, and feelings of unfairness and falling short of personal expectations. Other behavioral characteristics may include criticism of self and others, overbearing expectations, and high levels of frustration in one or more of the life tasks of career, social relationships, or intimacy. The term *overachiever* may best characterize this individual.

USE WITH COUPLES

The Lifestyle Scale is useful as a quick screening instrument in couples therapy. Identifying the varied lifestyle factors or themes can immediately provide insight into potential problems in the relationship. In the early stages, couples may be confused as to what makes a complementary relationship. Therefore, if the therapist can, for example, identify one partner as a controller and the other as a pleaser early in the therapy process, the counselor can begin to investigate how this combination enhances the couple's relationship as well as how it can create problems. If one partner appears to be a controller and the other a pleaser on the surface, this would seem to be a complementary relationship; however, further investigation may uncover that this individual's controlling theme has a strong need to control by being perfect. If this is true, it may be hopeless to try to please this individual. Thus the partner who is bent on pleasing may end up extremely discouraged.

If the therapist can help the couple to identify how these characteristics initially attracted them, the couple may be able to redirect their efforts toward recognizing that these lifestyle themes can also inhibit problem solving and complementary interactions. The controller may not need to change as much as to redirect controlling tendencies in a more complementary way toward the other partner. The pleaser may also come to realize that seeking constant approval may need to be re-evaluated and redirected in some other way.

At this point, the therapist has many choices. During one session she might assign an exercise in role reversal or communication techniques. Whatever the suggestion or intervention, understanding the couple's lifestyle via the Lifestyle Scale provides opportunities to improve problem solving.

BASIS-A INVENTORY

Kern has expanded his work into lifestyle themes with a more extensive inventory. The BASIS-A (Basic Adlerian Scales for Interpersonal Success—Adult Form) inventory (Kern, Wheeler, and Curlette, 1993) has been the subject of research and validity studies. While there are more items in the BASIS-A, it can be completed in less than fifteen minutes. The authors highly recommend this inventory. For more information, contact TRT Associates, 65 Eagle Ridge Drive, Highlands, NC 28741 or call (704) 526-9561.

Author Index

Subject Index